Ashok Vajpeyi is a Hindi poet and lover of arts, apart from being a noted cultural and arts administrator, and a former civil servant. He was Chairman, Lalit Kala Akademi, from 2008 to 2011. He is a recipient of the Sahitya Akademi Award (1994), Dayawati Kavi Shekhar Samman (1994) and Kabir Samman (2006). He has also been decorated by the President of the Republic of Poland with the outstanding national award The Officer's Cross of Merit of the Republic of Poland (2004), and by the French government as Officier de L'Ordre des Arts et des Lettres (2005). His publications include poetry collections *Kahin Nahin Vahin, Bahuri Akela, Ibarat Se Giri Matrayein, Kahin Koi Darwaza* (Hindi) and *A Name for Every Leaf* (English). His critical works include *Philhal, Samay Se Bahar, Kavita Ke Teen Darwaze* (Hindi) and *Raza: A Life in Art* (English).

INDIA DISSENTS

3,000 Years of Difference, Doubt and Argument

Edited and with an Introduction by
Ashok Vajpeyi

SPEAKING
TIGER

SPEAKING TIGER PUBLISHING PVT. LTD
4381/4 Ansari Road, Daryaganj,
New Delhi–110002, India

First published by Speaking Tiger in paperback 2017
Anthology copyright © Speaking Tiger 2017
Introduction copyright © Ashok Vajpeyi 2017

ISBN: 978-93-86338-08-2
eISBN: 978-93-86338-07-5

10 9 8 7 6 5 4 3 2 1

Typeset in Arno Pro by Jojy Philip
Printed at

CONTENTS

DISSENT AND DEMOCRACY

INTRODUCTION

India and the Plurality of Dissent

Bow to him who is the word
both occult and manifest,
his glory revealed by the power
of the independent mind.

—From *Subhashitavali*, an anthology of Sanskrit verse
compiled in the fifteenth century by Vallabhadeva
(translated by A.N.D. Haksar)

It can be reasonably argued that in India, from the beginning of its civilizational enterprise, nothing has remained singular for long; in fact, nothing has been, in a sense, *allowed* to be singular for long. Whether God or religion, philosophy or metaphysics, language or custom, cuisine or costume, every realm is marked by plurality. It is not accidental that in many Western languages the word India is plural—'Indes', meaning 'Indias'.

It is impossible, therefore, to talk about *the* Indian tradition: there are multiple traditions, all authentically and robustly Indian. Even within a single major religion, Hinduism, there are four Vedas, millions of gods, eighteen Upanishads, six schools of classical philosophy, two epics (and numerous versions of both), four purusharthas or goals of life. It can be easily claimed that India as a country—and, equally, as a civilization—is an unending celebration of human plurality. This is how it has survived through millennia.

Central to the plural tradition, or sensibility, is the notion that there are many ways of looking at and living in the world. Plurality accommodates differences; and differences, in their turn, embody and enact dissent. When the Vedic seer ordains, 'Aano Bhadrah Kratvo Yantu Vishwatah' (Let noble thoughts come to us from all directions), what is being sanctified is the idea that there are many different ideas and truths spread all over the world and they are all welcome. Another Vedic saying, 'Vasudhaiva Kutumbakam' (The world is one family), embraces all humanity, and therefore every idea, emotion, lifestyle that exists. Such openness and acceptance, or, at the very least, accommodation, is the core of the Vedic cosmic vision. Through the millennia, many dilutions and distortions may have occurred in real life and practice, as would inevitably happen everywhere, but Indian tradition and civilization never lost this remarkable, largely inclusive vision.

Dr Amartya Sen has pointed out in his book *The Argumentative Indian* that the 'Nasadiya Sukta', the Hymn of Creation, a major verse in the *Rig Veda*, ends with radical doubt:

> Who really knows? Who will here proclaim it? Whence was it produced?
>
> Whence is this creation? The gods came afterwards, with the creation of this universe. Who then knows whence it has risen?
>
> Whence this creation has risen—perhaps it formed itself, or perhaps it did not—the one who looks down on it, in the highest heaven, only he knows—or perhaps he does not know.

This is evidently the beginning of Indian skepticism. Nothing, not even the creation of the universe, or the supremacy and omniscience of God, is taken for granted. It may be noted that the hymn is also clear that the gods came *after* creation—they are, in that sense, no different from fish or trees or human beings. Into a major sukta of perhaps the oldest and one of the most important texts of Hinduism, then, the Vedic seers inserted a deeply metaphysical note of dissent.

A similar note was struck by a rishi named Kauntya, who declared that if what had been said in the Vedas could not be communicated in any other language or in any other way, the Vedas must be meaningless. This was pure blasphemy since the Vedas were held to be inviolable, 'apourusheya'. But Yaska, an ancient grammarian and commentator on the Vedas, includes this view in *Nirukta*, his compilation of Vedic interpretations which became one of the central texts of Sanskrit scholarship.

In these and other passages from the earliest texts of Hinduism, there is ample evidence that the Indian traditions *begin* with enquiry, doubt and challenge—the hallmarks of plurality.

These traditions continued and grew with the other major religions that arose in India—Buddhism, Jainism and, later, Sikhism. Their founders, Buddha, Mahavir and Nanak, dissented from the ritualistic and caste rigidities of orthodox Hinduism to discover new paths of spirituality, metaphysics, social organization and liberation. Here was religious plurality being created through religious dissent. Buddhism and Jainism were particularly radical faiths; they were not posited on the notion and existence of God, and they rejected completely the scriptures of Hinduism and many of its foundational concepts like the eternal soul and the four goals of life. The rejection was forceful, fearless and rooted in intellectual inquiry and debate.

Buddha, the great challenger, was later included as one of the ten avatars of God—Dashavatar—in classical Hinduism, along with Rama and Krishna. Here, too, was proof of India's irrepressible plurality and genius for accommodation!

~

There was also a strong and multi-layered tradition of disagreement and debate in the fields of thought, conduct, knowledge and morality in pre-modern India. Two aspects are easily noticeable. First, no one could propose a new concept or insight or theory without first faithfully summarizing the existing body of reflection on it. This was 'poorvapaksha', and only then could there be 'uttarpaksha'—the thinker or debater proposing that which he or she claimed to be different or new, delineating it in meticulous detail. This was the standard intellectual practice.

Secondly, any new or different idea, theory or insight had to be publicly debated and accepted before being given a place in the scheme of things. The institution of shastrarth—philosophical contests—was well entrenched and there are many examples of this. The most celebrated instance is of the great thinker Shankaracharya having to engage in a shastrarth with Mandana Mishra and his wife Ubhaya Bharati over several days. There are many examples of such discussions and debates between Shaivites and Vaishnavites, Hindus and Buddhists, Buddhists and Jains; between different schools of philosophical and ethical thought; between agnostics and believers. The interrogative and dialogical ethos also finds place in literature, and the epic *Mahabharata* is full of such dialogues and debates. It is apt of Dr Amartya Sen to have called us 'argumentative' Indians: these age-old conventions of dissent, dialogue, debate and disagreement are ample evidence that India created a civilization which was marked by curiosity and quest, by questions and doubts, by accommodation and acceptance of contrary viewpoints.

It cannot be denied that India had a very restrictive, indefensible caste system and many elements of a feudal structure. But simultaneously it also had a republic of the imagination in which ideas and wisdom had a democratic remit. Almost everything, including God, gods, spiritual ideas and practices, metaphysical and philosophical concepts, notions of morality and political structures, has been brought into the realm of debate and interrogation. When in 1950 we declared ourselves a democracy it was, in many ways, a culmination of some age-old ideas of the democratic spirit.

Whether in traditions of creative expression or in the repertoire of intellectual articulation, in India dissent from faith or from the State has always not only been acknowledged but has also been allowed to grow. The vital condition of plurality has often been strengthened and expanded through dissent. For instance, when the tyranny of classical Sanskrit was questioned and subverted, the many modern Indian languages we speak today came into being. The vernacular did not demolish the classical, or even aspire to occupy the hallowed space of the classical; instead, it became a dissenting parallel. Every modern Indian language embodies and sustains a world-view that deviates from the classical world-view of Sanskrit. The presence of nearly a thousand versions of the *Ramayana* in India, ranging from Santhali and other tribal versions to retellings from the Jain point of view, is evidence that the dominant narrative and the world-view it enacted and expressed was creatively challenged and transformed. A Kannada *Ramayana* or a Hindi *Ramcharitmanas* deviate quite substantially from the original in Sanskrit by Valmiki, and *all* of them had validity.

It is also interesting to note that Buddhism and Jainism, born as religious and radical dissent, also got divided into different sects over time. The Mahayana and Hinayana sects in Buddhism and the Shwetamber and Digamber sects in Jainism can, arguably, be seen as dissent within an overriding structure of faith.

In Sanskrit drama, a lot of which has been preoccupied with the ironies of life and fate and the celebration of gods and regal heroes, there was, too, the irrepressible vidushak, the fool, the court jester, who not only provided comic relief but also sarcastic comments on kings, gods, fate and so on. He spared no one and his utterances were never censored or objected to. This tradition seems to have continued in more earthy and robust ways in folk theatre across the country. In many of these popular forms, watched night after night by thousands of faithful viewers, sometimes it is the narrator who assumes the role of the vidushak, just as he or she also enacts the hero or other heroic or divine characters.

The easy morality of the pious was also challenged—or ignored altogether. In the twelfth century, Jayadeva composed *Geeta Govind*, a bold erotic poem which depicts in vivid detail the love and lovemaking of Radha and Krishna. Apart from occupying a central place in the classical dance form Odissi, this masterpiece of the Bhakti movement is still sung daily in temples across India, from Kerala in the south to Manipur in the north-east.

The Bhakti period, beginning in the sixth century, saw a great and golden flowering of poetry and many other arts. While making God or gods accessible to all, without the negotiating instruments of priesthood, mosque, temple or holy books, this poetry democratized religions and spirituality. Most of the poets belonged to the lower classes (for instance, Kabir, a weaver; Madara Chennaiah and Ravidas, both cobblers; Soyarabai, a Mahar; Namdev, a tailor) and their poetry liberated devotion and poetic expression from the stranglehold of the Brahminical class. This poetry, widespread and popular till today, has been the most eloquent and passionate articulation of dissent, subversion and interrogation.

It may be recalled that during the freedom struggle, important political leaders recalled the work of Bhakti and Sufi poets to evoke a spirit of freedom and forge a unity of purpose amongst the masses. This was done most crucially and effectively by Mahatma Gandhi. In the prayer meetings of the Mahatma in Sewagram and elsewhere, the devotional poetry of all the major religions of India and the rest of the world was sung. These prayer meetings became a unique forum of political dissent vis-à-vis the colonial power. We may also recall that the Mahatma was shot dead while going to a prayer meeting by a Hindu religious fanatic a few months after Independence: a blinkered, exclusivist vision had announced itself through murder almost at the very moment of the birth of free India.

As we come to modern, independent India, there is no doubt that while many towering figures played a role in shaping it, the central figure was Mahatma Gandhi. In many ways, he epitomized radical dissent in the twentieth century. He articulated and practised the concepts of civil disobedience, satyagraha and non-cooperation. While all over the world empires have been demolished through armed revolution and wars, Gandhi, dissenting from them all, took to truth and non-violence. A deeply religious man, he also maintained that all religions were true but that all of them were also imperfect, thereby suggesting that they needed to learn from each other. He went to the extent of proclaiming that if it was proved that the Vedas supported untouchability in India, a form of racial and caste apartheid, he would reject the Vedas.

The fact that it was at Gandhi's behest that the brilliant iconoclast B.R. Ambedkar, who often opposed him bitterly, was included by Nehru in his cabinet and assigned the job of drafting the Constitution of India is yet another instance of the Mahatma's respect for dissenting voices.

~

In 1950 India chose to become a democratic republic and adopted a Constitution that guarantees every citizen, among other freedoms, the freedoms of life, faith and expression. This was entirely in keeping with the millennia-long Indian tradition of creativity, reflection and fearless articulation. The Constitution also prescribed that any infringement of these basic freedoms by the State or anybody else would be legally actionable and an independent judiciary would be charged with the task of protecting them. However, it has not been easy to ensure these freedoms, which are also organically related to the right to dissent. Unfortunately, the conduct of the State, our political parties and other institutions has been often hypocritical, even cynical. While they zealously guard their own right to protest, they all resent and endeavour to suppress dissent and interrogation among others, especially individuals.

In recent years these paradoxes have assumed violent and murderous dimensions. It began with the assassination of the Mahatma himself. Since then, self-styled 'armies' of upper-caste landlords have slaughtered the dispossessed who have dared to ask for what is rightfully theirs. The Naxalites have killed innocent civilians who did not follow or support their violent means. And in many parts of the country—Kashmir, West Bengal, Assam, Manipur, Bastar, to name a few—the State, insurgents and communally furious groups have taken to annihilating those who oppose them.

Democracy's one glaring failure in India has been that it gives the elected representatives of the people unbridled power and sanction to crush or curtail the people's right to question, differ and disagree with the government and official narratives. The Emergency, imposed by Indira Gandhi's regime in the mid-1970s, was the first clear evidence of the danger that democracy reduced to mere numbers in Parliament could pose to liberty and human rights. The judiciary, which should have acted to check the excesses of a government that had turned dictatorial, also failed in its duty.

Forty years after that dark period in Independent India's history, the spirit of democracy is being undermined and subverted again. A political party—the Hindu majoritarian Bharatiya Janata Party (BJP)—that was elected with less than 32 per cent of the total votes polled, has been in power since the summer of 2014. In just over three years in office, it has either directly suppressed dissent, especially on the university campus, by terming it anti-national, or has kept quiet when Dalits and minorities have been attacked, often brutally, by social outfits affiliated to it. There are open attempts to punish dissent by raising the bogey of beef-eating, religious conversion, 'love jihad', national security or 'hurt sentiments'.

All these actions are throwing India into social turmoil. If you disagree with or question the government, you are branded an enemy of the country. The distinction between the State and the nation is being blurred. A large majority of Indians—almost 68 per cent—did not vote for the BJP in the 2014 national elections. But that has not prevented the party from arrogating to itself the right to decide what Indian society should be, what we can hear, see, eat, wear, speak, read or think. The Narendra Modi regime appears to have convinced itself that it has the democratic right to crush all dissent, disagreement and opposition, even independent thought.

A lot of this is sought to be justified on the grounds that Indian traditions are being wrongly interpreted, and that there's an urgent need to correct such distortions and prevent a civilizational collapse. In providing such a corrective, bypassing the rule of law is unavoidable, and violence is acceptable, even necessary. Also central to this enterprise is propaganda and distortion of history. A massive cultural amnesia is being spread through biased, unpardonably partisan cultural events, education and media. Majority Hindu communities are told repeatedly that they have been wronged, discriminated against and unjustly treated. Selective facts and figures and downright lies are being brazenly propagated by right-wing groups that have appropriated the right to speak for all Hindus, and the current Indian State is either complicit or provides tacit support to these divisive forces by its silence and inaction.

When three courageous intellectuals, namely, Narendra Dabholkar, Govind Pansare and M.M. Kalburgi, were killed for no ostensible reason except for the fact that they were rationalists and creative dissenters who questioned religious tradition, it brought the simmering intolerance against rationality, knowledge, reason and creativity into the open. The governments at the Centre and in the states reacted to these murders with callous disregard, and investigations into the killings were delayed for several months. Some of us writers, nearly fifty from various Indian languages, spontaneously decided to protest by returning our Sahitya Akademi awards and other state honours. A statement we issued in November 2015 summarized the situation and our concerns:

> We are deeply disturbed at the growing trends of violence, intolerance, and undermining of the age-long plurality of faith, belief, values, viewpoints, etc.; the almost daily assault on amity and mutual trust. We believe that at this juncture of our democratic existence and growth, there is, unfortunately, increasing evidence of the emergence of an ethos of bans and disruptions, physical assault on and suppression of dissent and difference. We strongly hold that Indian tradition, Indian democratic polity and indeed its complex social structure have been sustained and nourished by an innate and deeply rooted sense of multiplicity, mutual respect and trust amongst communities and values of cooperation, social amity and harmony. We are witnessing a socio-political climate in which minorities, whether of faith, belief, opinion or ideas, are feeling threatened. We see that voices of dissent and difference are being increasingly subjected to unethical attacks, character assassination, mudslinging, etc. We also watch that some of the most important national institutions of culture and education are being meddled with, their stature and vision being systematically diluted and devalued. We are forced to conclude that the liberal space, both of thought and action, is fast shrinking. As members of the creative and reflective community of India we have decided to raise our voice in protest and in resistance.
>
> We urge the people of India, our fellow-citizens, who are primarily and ultimately responsible for strengthening and sustaining both Indian democracy and Indian tradition, to pay heed and act in unison to ensure that the divisive forces do not succeed and that both democracy and tradition continue to deepen and nurture our plurality. We call upon the political parties, the Central Government and the State Governments that they actively discourage such trends [and refrain from] supporting or encouraging by deed or in action, by words or silence, institutions and groups which are undermining the cardinal republican values and which are working to spread an

atmosphere of hatred, revenge, violence without fear of the law and in utter disregard of the constitutional spirit of India. We wish to remind them that they draw their legitimacy from the Constitution and, therefore, it is incumbent upon them not to bypass or subvert the basic principles and vision of the Indian Constitution. We wish to request our MPs that they should fully and responsibly use their right of free speech in the Parliament in public interest.

We appeal to our fellow writers, artists, intellectuals, academics, scientists and all thinking people across the country to be alive and alert to the threats and dangers that our pluralistic culture, creative and intellectual courage, dissent and difference are facing and offer the divisive forces moral, creative and intellectual resistance at all levels. We must not allow misinterpretations and vested misreading of our culture, our traditions, our religions and forms of spirituality, [and] of our intellectual, ethical and spiritual underpinnings, to go unchallenged and uncontested.

This protest was immediately joined by over 400 artists and art critics, more than 100 historians, social scientists and intellectuals and nearly 500 scientists and technocrats. The President of India, the then Governor of the Reserve Bank of India and a few prominent industrialists and film personalities also warned against growing intolerance. The protest had international resonance as well, and the International PEN passed a resolution condemning violence against the creative and reflective community in India. Even the then President of the USA, Barack Obama, at the end of his Indian visit pointed to the growing religious intolerance in India.

Indian literature in the last seven decades or so, since Independence, has been written, historically for the first time, in a democracy. Equally remarkable, though hardly noticed by political parties or modern sociology, is the fact that this literature has been largely anti-establishment. It has been, both eloquently and subtly, adversarial towards controlling regimes and narratives. It has questioned the country's political setup and ideological muddle and the established norms of morality. It has lamented or raged against the continuing and growing injustices and inequities in our society. It has protested the tyranny of the market and big business, the shrinking conscience of the elite and middle classes, the imposing zeal of the global, the disappearance of the local and the displacement of the community by the market.

In a manner of speaking, some of the values that informed the freedom struggle, including constant questioning of the State, continue in post-Independence Indian literature. These values are also alive, and often centre stage, in the visual arts, theatre and other forms of creative expression. The nation-wide spread of these values must also be seen as an unbroken continuum of the vital, irrepressible millennia-old Indian tradition of difference, doubt, disagreement and resistance. Dabholkar, Pansare and Kalburgi, to name just three creative minds, spoke as Kabir or Akka Mahadevi did centuries earlier, or the anonymous sage-poets who composed the 'Nasadiya Sukta' of the *Rig Veda*. It is a comment on where we are as a society today that unlike the Rig Vedic poets, unlike Akka and Kabir, the three rationalists were killed for expressing themselves.

Despite the challenges and dangers that artists and thinkers have faced in recent times, Indian literature continues to celebrate and nurture plurality, dissent and difference, and remains open to new ideas and insights from all over the world. Three distinct movements can be mentioned in this context: Marxism, feminism and the Dalit movement. Each of these has been born in dissent from the dominant literary and cultural establishments and has brought within the geography of creative expression new experiences, new perceptions, new anxieties, new aesthetic strategies, thus enriching the spirit of plurality and democracy.

When Bheeshma, the sagacious elder in the *Mahabharata*, lying on a bed of arrows, close to death, was asked about raj dharma, or royal duty, he said that it was the duty of the king to respect the wise men who lived in his domain, not engage foolish and greedy persons in running the affairs of the state, and protect his subjects from all kinds of fears. In Tulsi's *Ramcharitmanas*, an epic which in north India enjoys the status of a scripture, Rama, after being coronated as the King of Ayodhya, beseeches the citizens to intercede without any fear if they ever feel that he is acting unethically. In the winter of 2015 and later, some of us tried to remind the powers that be of these wise insights contained in our glorious literary tradition. They responded by orchestrating a campaign against us, indulging in character assassination and accusing us of 'manufactured politics'.

Commenting on the climate of intolerance, the *Economic and Political Weekly* wrote recently, 'While Dabholkar, Pansare and M.M. Kalburgi's murders (as well as the harassment meted out to others like them) are deplorable, what is even more despicable is the silence of large sections of the population and the continuing support of political interests to their tormentors. This lack of response is a clear indication that citizens feel they are not safe if they speak out against entrenched religious vested interests and that the State will not take their complaints seriously. A society that cannot tolerate dissenting views or keeps quiet in the face of a violent reaction to such views is staring at a cultural and intellectual abyss.'

Anticipating the difficult time that is upon us today, the great Hindi poet and literary and cultural commentator Gajanan Madhav Muktibodh wrote nearly half a century ago:

> Litterateurs and poets
> thinkers and artists and dancers
> are all indifferent:
> It is all a rumour,
> they think.
> They are all parasites
> of the bloodsucking classes.
> They are all impotent
> and self-indulgent.
> They are all
> Superficial, unaware of the way
> the oppressors run riot—
> a fire here
> a firing there.

But we can derive satisfaction and confidence from the fact that there are, in fact, writers, artists, intellectuals, teachers, students, and many nameless brave men and women who have refused to be silent. They have protested and continue to raise their voices against oppression, demagoguery and bigotry. They have stood by the glorious and unbroken tradition of plurality and dissent in India. This collection brings together some the best recorded examples of this tradition, in written and spoken words, over three millennia. It is by no means exhaustive. Readers will find many words here that they recognize, and many words that they have heard or read that aren't here. Perhaps the latter will find their rightful place within the covers of this volume in future editions. May this volume grow; may the spirit and tradition of dissent in India grow ever larger.

Hopefully, many of us will continue the good fight—the fight, through creative and intellectual means, for the values of freedom, justice and equality enshrined both in our tradition and our Constitution. We owe it to the Indian heritage that we profess to be so proud of.

ASHOK VAJPEYI

DISSENT IN HISTORY

Nasadiya Sukta
(The Hymn of Creation)

from the *Rig Veda*

A canonical text of Hinduism, the Rig Veda *is also, perhaps, the world's oldest religious text still in use. It is believed to have been composed between 1500 and 1200 BCE and comprises 1028 hymns and 10,600 verses organized into ten mandalas or books. The Nasadiya Sukta is the 129th hymn in the 10th Mandala. Especially considering when this hymn was composed and where it was preserved for posterity, it is one of the most remarkable articulations of radical doubt in human society.*

> There was no non-existent then, nor existent;
> There was no in-between and no heaven beyond.
> What stirred? Was there fathomless water or deep abyss?
>
> There was neither death nor deathlessness then;
> There was no night, and no sign of day.
> The One breathed without air; there was nothing else.
>
> There was darkness covered in darkness then;
> A formless, unseen ocean was everywhere.
> In the emptiness, the One emerged from the power of heat.
>
> Then was desire born, and of it the first seed of thought.
> The sages who looked within their hearts with wisdom,
> They knew that in the non-existent was the existent.
>
> They stretched their cord cross-wise and saw:
> There is something above and something below;
> There is the great seminal above and the vast fertile below.
>
> But who really knows? Who can tell where all arose?
> For the gods themselves came after Creation.
> Who then shall proclaim how Creation happened?

Then He, who created all that is, or did not,
Who looks upon everything from the highest heaven,
He alone knows. Or maybe He too does not.

Translated by Sharad Raghav

THE AJIVIKAS AND THE CHARAVAKS

The Ajivika, founded around fifth century BCE by Makkhali Gosala, was a heterodox school of Indian philosophy that rejected ritualistic Vedic society. It believed primarily in Niyati, that is determinism and fate. According to it, there was no free will or cause-and-effect determining a person's destiny.

The Charavak, was a school of materialism in Indian philosophy that flourished around sixth century BCE, rejected the authority of the Vedas, belief in Karma and Moksha and all forms of received knowledge, in favour of knowledge gained through lived experience. The Charavaks were among the earliest voices of revolt and protest in Indian philosophy.

Makkhali Gosala

Makkhali Gosala (c. 484 BCE) was a contemporary of Mahavir and Gautam Buddha. He was a disciple of Mahavir for six years before separating from him due to their difference in beliefs. He believed that everything was preordained and no amount of 'good' or 'bad' deeds, or penance would help anyone escape their fate.

There is no deed performed either by oneself or by others [that can affect one's future births], no human action, no strength, no courage, no human endurance or human prowess [that can affect one's destiny in this life]. All beings... are without power, strength or virtue... There is no question of bringing unripe Karma to fruition, nor of exhausting Karma already ripened, by virtuous conduct, by vows, by penance or by chastity. That cannot be done. Samsara is measured as with a bushel, with its joys and sorrows and its appointed end. It can neither be lessened or increased, nor is there any excess or deficiency of it. Just as a ball of thread will, when thrown, unwind to its fullest length, so fool and wise alike will take their course, and make an end of sorrow.

Brihaspati Sutra

The Brihaspati Sutra, *composed around 600 BCE, is the foundational text of the Charavak school of Indian philosophy.*

> There is no heaven, no final liberation, nor any soul in another world,
> Nor do the actions of the four castes, orders or priesthoods produce any real effect.
> The Agnihotra, the three Vedas, the ascetic's three staves, and smearing one's self with ashes,
> Were made by Nature as the livelihood of those destitute of knowledge and manliness.
> If a beast slain in the Jyotishtoma rite will itself go to heaven,
> Why then does not the sacrifice forthwith offer his own father?
> If the Sraddha produces gratification to beings who are dead,
> Then here, too, in the case of travellers when they start, it is needless to give provisions for the journey.
> If beings in heaven are gratified by of our offering the Sraddha here,
> Then why not give the food down below to those who are standing on the housetop?
> While life remains let a man live happily, let him feed on ghee even though he runs in debt;
> When once the body becomes ashes, how can it ever return again?
> If he who departs from the body goes to another world,
> How is it that he comes not back again, restless for love of his kindred?
> Hence it is only as a means of livelihood that Brahmans have established here
> All these ceremonies for the dead—there is no fruit anywhere.
> The three authors of the Vedas were buffoons, knaves, and demons.
> All the well-known formulae of the pandits, jarphari, turphari, and
> And all the obscene rites for the queen commanded in the Aswamedha,
> These were invented by buffoons, and so all the various kinds of presents to the priests,
> While the eating of flesh was similarly commanded by night-prowling demons.

Ajita Kesakambali

Ajita Kesakambali (sixth or fifth century BCE) is the earliest documented materialist in India, and a contemporary of Gautam Buddha.

There is no [merit in] almsgiving, sacrifice or offering, no result or ripening of good or evil deeds. There is no passing from this world to the next… There is no afterlife… Man is formed of the four elements; when he dies earth returns to the aggregate of earth, water to water, fire to fire, and air to air, while the senses vanish into space. Four men with the bier take up the corpse; they gossip [about the dead man] as far as the burning ground, where his bones turn the colour of dove's wings, and his sacrifices end in ashes. They are fools who preach almsgiving, and those who maintain the existence of immaterial categories speak vain and lying nonsense. When the body dies both fool and wise alike are cut off and perish. They do not survive after death.

BUDDHISM

Buddhism, as a faith and a philosophy, developed from the teachings of Gautam Buddha sometime between the mid-sixth and mid-fourth centuries BCE. It spread from India to Central and Southeast Asia and continues to have a wide following all over the world. The main goal in Buddhism is to attain enlightenment by following the eight-fold path prescribed by the Buddha—right views, right aspirations, right speech, right conduct, right livelihood, right effort, right mindfulness and right meditational attainment. Buddhism, like Ajivika philosophy and Jainism, was opposed to orthodox Vedic rituals and practices.

Gautam Buddha

Gautam Buddha (c. 567–484 BCE), the enlightened one, was born as Siddhartha into a royal family and renounced worldly life at the age of twenty-nine.

> By birth is not one outcast,
> By birth is not one a Brahmin,

By deeds is one outcast,
By deeds is one a Brahmin.

~

Every man loves liberty and freedom.
Do not interfere with another's freedom.

~

Monks, when the great rivers Ganga, Yamuna, Achiravati, Sarabhu and Mahi empty into the ocean, they no longer retain their names, but become one great body of water. In like manner the four castes, be they Kshatriya, Brahmin, Vaishya, or Shudra, when accepted into the Order, all leave their castes and lose their names. They become Samana Sakya, without exception.

~

A man doesn't become a Brahmana by his plaited hair, by his family or by birth; in whom there is truth and righteousness, he is blessed, he is a Brahmana.

~

In whom there is no sympathy for living beings, know him as an outcast.

Visuddhi Magga

A treatise on the Theravada Buddhist doctrine composed by Buddhaghosa in approximately 430 CE in Sri Lanka.

No God, no Brahma can be found,
No matter of this wheel of life,
Just bare phenomena roll
Dependent on conditions all.

Assalayana Sutta (From *Majjhima Nikaya*)

The 'Assalayana Sutta' is a Buddhist scripture composed between the fourth and third centuries BCE. In this episode from the scripture, a young sixteen-year-old Brahmin, Assalayana, is urged by a group of Brahmins to argue with the Buddha regarding the superior and 'pure' nature of the Brahmins.

...The Brahman student Assalayana went with a large group of Brahmans to the Blessed One and, on arrival, exchanged courteous greetings with him. After an exchange of friendly greetings and courtesies, he sat to one side. As he was sitting there he said to the Blessed One: 'Master Gotama, the Brahmans say, "Brahmans are the superior caste; any other caste is inferior. Only Brahmans are the fair caste; any other caste is dark. Only Brahmans are pure, not non-Brahmans. Only Brahmans are the sons and offspring of Brahma: born of his mouth, born of Brahma, created by Brahma, heirs of Brahma." What does Master Gotama have to say with regard to that?'

'But, Assalayana, the brahmans' brahman-women are plainly seen having their periods, becoming pregnant, giving birth, and nursing [their children]. And yet the Brahmans, being born through the birth canal, say, "Brahmans are the superior caste; any other caste is inferior. Only Brahmans are the fair caste; any other caste is dark. Only Brahmans are pure, not non-Brahmans. Only Brahmans are the sons and offspring of Brahma: born of his mouth, born of Brahma, created by Brahma, heirs of Brahma".

...'What do you think, Assalayana? Is it only a noble warrior who—taking life, stealing, engaging in sexual misconduct, telling lies, speaking divisively, speaking harshly, engaging in idle chatter, greedy, bearing thoughts of ill will, and holding wrong views—on the break-up of the body, after death, reappears in the plane of deprivation, the bad destination, the lower realms, in hell, and not a Brahman? Is it only a merchant...? Is it only a worker who—taking life, stealing, engaging in sexual misconduct, telling lies, speaking divisively, speaking harshly, engaging in idle chatter, greedy, bearing thoughts of ill will, and holding wrong views—on the break-up of the body, after death, reappears in the plane of deprivation, the bad destination, the lower realms, in hell, and not a Brahman?'

'No, Master Gotama. Even a noble warrior... Even a Brahman... Even a merchant... Even a worker... [Members of] all four castes—if they take life, steal, engage in sexual misconduct, tell lies, speak divisively, speak harshly, engage in idle chatter, are greedy, bear thoughts of ill will, and hold wrong views—on the break-up of the body, after death, reappear in the plane of deprivation, the bad destination, the lower realms, in hell.'

'So what strength is there, Assalayana, what assurance, when the Brahmans say, "Brahmans are the superior caste...the sons and offspring of Brahma: born of his mouth, born of Brahma, created by Brahma, heirs of Brahma"?'

...'Even though Master Gotama says that, still the Brahmans think, "Brahmans are the superior caste...".'

'What do you think, Assalayana? Is it only a Brahman who is capable of developing in any direction a heart of good will—free from animosity, free from ill will—and not a noble warrior, not a merchant, not a worker?'

'No, Master Gotama. Even a noble warrior... Even a Brahman... Even a merchant... Even a worker... [Members of] all four castes are capable of developing in any direction a heart of good will—free from animosity, free from ill will.'

'So what strength is there, Assalayana, what assurance, when the Brahmans say, "Brahmans are the superior caste..."?'

'Even though Master Gotama says that, still the Brahmans think, "Brahmans are the superior caste...".'

'What do you think, Assalayana? Is it only a Brahman who is capable of taking a loofah and bath powder, going to a river, and scrubbing off dust and dirt, and not a noble warrior, not a merchant, not a worker?'

'No, Master Gotama. Even a noble warrior... Even a Brahman... Even a merchant... Even a worker... [Members of] all four castes are capable of taking a loofah and bath powder, going to a river, and scrubbing off dust and dirt.'

'So what strength is there, Assalayana, what assurance, when the brahmans say, "Brahmans are the superior caste... Only Brahmans are pure, not non-Brahmans....."?'

'Even though Master Gotama says that, still the Brahmans think, "Brahmans are the superior caste...".'

'What do you think, Assalayana? There is the case where a consecrated noble warrior king might call together one hundred men of different births [and say to them], "Come, masters. Those of you there born from a noble warrior clan, from a Brahman clan, or from a royal clan: taking an upper fire-stick of saala wood, salala wood, sandalwood, or padumaka wood, produce fire and make heat appear. And come, masters. Those of you there born from an outcast clan, a trapper clan, a wicker workers' clan, a cartwrights' clan, or a scavengers' clan: taking an upper fire-stick from a dog's drinking trough, from a pig's trough, from a dustbin, or of castor-oil wood, produce fire and make heat appear." What do you think, Assalayana? Would the fire made by those born from a noble warrior clan, a Brahman clan, or a royal clan—who had produced fire and made heat appear by taking an upper fire-stick of saala wood, salala wood, sandalwood, or padumaka wood—be the only one with flame, colour, and radiance, able to do whatever a fire might be needed to do? And would the fire made by those born from an outcast clan, a trapper clan, a wicker workers' clan, a cartwrights' clan, or a scavengers' clan—who had produced fire and made heat appear by taking an upper fire-stick from a dog's drinking trough, from a pig's trough, from a dustbin, or of castor-oil wood—be without flame, colour, and radiance, unable to do what a fire might be needed to do?'

'No, Master Gotama. The fire made by those born from a noble warrior clan, a Brahman clan, or a royal clan...would have flame, colour, and radiance, able to do whatever a fire might be needed to do. And the fire made by those born from an outcast clan, a trapper clan, a wicker workers' clan, a cartwrights' clan, or a scavengers' clan...would have flame, colour, and radiance, able to do whatever a fire might be needed to do. For all fire has flame, colour, and radiance, and is able to do whatever a fire might be needed to do.'

'So what strength is there, Assalayana, what assurance, when the Brahmans say, "Brahmans are the superior caste..."?'

'Even though Master Gotama says that, still the Brahmans think, "Brahmans are the superior caste..."'

'What do you think, Assalayana? There is the case where a noble warrior youth might cohabit with a Brahman maiden, and from their cohabitation a son would be born. Would the son born from the noble warrior youth and Brahman maiden be like the father and like the mother? Should it be called a noble warrior and a Brahman?'

'Yes, Master Gotama...'

'What do you think, Assalayana? There is the case where a Brahman youth might cohabit with a noble warrior maiden, and from their cohabitation a son would be born. Would the son born from the Brahman youth and noble warrior maiden be like the father and like the mother? Should it be called a noble warrior and a Brahman?'

'Yes, Master Gotama...'

'What do you think, Assalayana? There is the case where a mare might mate with a donkey, and from their mating a foal would be born. Would the foal born from the mare and the donkey be like the father and like the mother? Should it be called a horse and a donkey?'

'Master Gotama, from the mixed breeding it would be a mule. Here I see that it [the mixed breeding] makes a difference, but there [in the other two cases] I don't see that it makes a difference.'

'What do you think, Assalayana? There is the case where there might be two Brahman-student brothers, born of the same mother: one learned and initiated, the other not learned and uninitiated. Which of the two would the Brahmans serve first at a funeral feast, a milk-rice offering, a sacrifice, or a feast for guests?'

'The Brahman student who was learned and initiated, Master Gotama... For what great fruit would there be for what is given to one who is not learned and uninitiated?'

'What do you think, Assalayana? There is the case where there might be two Brahman-student brothers, born of the same mother: one learned and initiated [but] unvirtuous and of evil character, the other not learned and uninitiated, [but] virtuous and of fine character. Which of the two would the Brahmans serve first at a funeral feast, a milk-rice offering, a sacrifice, or a feast for guests?'

'The Brahman student who was not learned and uninitiated, [but] virtuous and of fine character, Master Gotama... For what great fruit would there be for what is given to one who is unvirtuous and of evil character?'

'First, Assalayana, you went by birth. Then, having gone by birth, you went by mantras. Then, having gone by mantras, putting them both aside, you have come around to the purity of the four castes that I prescribe.'

When this was said, the Brahman student Assalayana sat silent, abashed, his shoulders drooping, his head down, brooding, at a loss for words.

Translated by Thanissaro Bhiku

Terigatha

Terigatha or Verses of the Elder Nuns is a collection of poems by Buddhist nuns from around 600 BCE and one of the oldest scriptures composed by women. In this important text, the nuns not only recorded their lives but also addressed questions regarding gender equality and the role of women in society.

Punnika and the Brahman

—Punnika

[*Punnika:*]
I'm a water-carrier, cold,
always going down to the water
from fear of my mistresses' beatings,

harrassed by their anger and words.
But you, Brahman,
    what do you fear
that you're always going down to the water
with shivering limbs, feeling great cold?
[*The Brahman:*]
Punnika, surely you know.
You're asking one doing skillful kamma
and warding off evil.
Whoever, young or old, does evil kamma
is, through water ablution,
from evil kamma set free.

[*Punnika:*]
Who taught you this
   —the ignorant to the ignorant—
'One, through water ablution,
is from evil kamma set free?'
In that case, they'd all go to heaven:
    all the frogs, turtles,
    serpents, crocodiles,
    and anything else that lives in the water.
Sheep-butchers, pork-butchers,
fishermen, trappers,
thieves, executioners,
and any other evil doers,
would, through water ablution,
be from evil kamma set free.

If these rivers could carry off
the evil kamma you've done in the past,
they'd carry off your merit as well,
and then you'd be
    completely left out.
Whatever it is that you fear,
that you're always going down to the water,
    don't do it.
Don't let the cold hurt your skin.'

[*The Brahman:*]
I've been following the miserable path, good lady,
and now you've brought me
    back to the noble.
I give you this robe for water-ablution.

Translated by Thanissaro Bhikkhu

~

Mutta

So freed! So thoroughly freed am I!
From three crooked things set free:
from mortar, pestle,
and crooked old husband.
Having uprooted the craving
that leads to becoming,
I'm set free from aging and death.

Translated by Thanissaro Bhikkhu

Dharmakirti

Dharmakirti was a Buddhist philosopher and logician from the sixth or seventh century. He rejected all scriptures and encouraged reasoning and logical thinking because he believed that perception and inference are the only two sources of knowledge.

Believing that the Vedas are perfect and holy,
Believing in a Creator of the universe,
Bathing in holy waters to gain merit,
Having pride about one's caste,
Performing penance to absolve sins:
These are five symptoms of having lost one's sanity.

~

Nobody goes ahead of me
None follows me
But the way is not trampled by fresh feet altogether
So why say that I am alone?
Let them know

That this was the way
Frequented earlier
Now it may be deserted
I have plainly chosen to energize
the other path
which is different but has a potency.

Translated by Radhavallabh Tripathi

JAINISM

Jainism is one of the earlier Indian traditions rooted in the Śramanic ethics of austerity and asceticism, as well as non-violence and respect towards all living beings. By emphasizing asceticism and divesting themselves of all worldly desire, Jain teachers and scholars challenged the hierarchies of social order, theological systems and scriptural beliefs in various contexts and forms.

Rishabhdev

Rishabhdev or Rishabhanatha is the first Tirthankara of the present cycle of time in Jainism.

O King, what for is a man walking on this earth has to be a king?
(Like any other man) he also has two feet, two ankles on them
Topped by two shanks and two knees
two thighs, one middle, one chest, one neck and two shoulders.
Calling yourself the king of the land of Sindhus
Completely blinded by conceit
Rooted firmly in your ego
You ride on this palanquin
Which carries the name of the king of Sauviras
With its wooden plank being carried on my shoulder
Picking up these poor people for drudgery
who are suffering and need to be pitied
You are completely devoid of compassion
You boast of being the protector of the people,

But you stand exposed
In the assembly of the knowledgeable ones!

Translated by Radhavallabh Tripathi

Yogindu

Yogindu was a Jain philosopher and mystic from the sixth century. He composed Paramatmaprakasa—*a treatise on Jaina mysticism and the path to liberation.*

'I am a Brahman,' 'I am a Vaishya,' 'I am a Kshatriya'; or 'I am a Shudra,' etc.; also 'I am a man,' 'I am a woman'; or 'I am a eunuch'; all these and other like thoughts belong to a *Mithya Drishti* [false believer]. (81–82)

'I am young,' 'I am old,' 'I am beautiful,' 'I am brave'; 'I am a Pandit' (a learned man); 'I am *Uttama*' [high]; 'I am *Digambara*' [naked saint]; 'I am *Bodh Guru*' [Buddhist saint]; or 'I am a *Svetambara Sadhu*' [Jain saint weaving white clothes]—those who possess such like thoughts should be considered as *Mithya Drishtis*. (82)

~

Those saints who give up sensual pleasures deserve encomiums; one who is bald, deserves no credit for having his head shaved. (105)

Mahapurana

The Mahapurana *is a Jain text composed by Acharya Jinasena and his disciple Gunabhadra in the ninth century.*

> The belief in a creator is foolish and must be rejected.
> If god created the universe, where was he himself before creation?
> If it is said he was transcendent then, existing of himself, where is
> he now?
> How can an immaterial god create this material world?...
> If god is perfect, how could the will to create have arisen in him?
> And if he is not perfect, he could no more create the universe than
> a potter could.
> If he is formless, complete in himself and contains all that is,
> How could he have created?
> For such a soul would have no desire to create anything.
> If it is said that he created to no purpose, on a whim, then god is
> pointless.

If he created the world as a sport, it was as the sport of stupid child
  that leads to trouble.
If he created the world out of love for living things, why did he not
  make it wholly blissful?
If god were transcendent, he would not create...
Uncreated, without beginning and without end, the world just is,
It endures under the compulsion of its own nature.

Somaprabha

Somaprabha composed the Kumarapalapratibodha, *a text which contains
the basic teachings of Jainism, sometime in the eleventh century. The following
is an extract from the text in which Somaprabha declares work for the self as
being superior to service of any king.*

If you spend only five days in the service of a king you bring sin upon
yourself
  And you must go, O Soul, to the dark gulf of hell, with its inevitable,
intolerable, innumerable woes.
  So give up the king's service; though it seems as sweet as honey—it
brings scorn and disillusion, it is basically wretched.
  Work, O Soul, for righteousness, and put aside your lethargy,
  Lest in hell you find not a few unpleasantnesses.

Somadeva

Somadeva was a Digambara teacher from the tenth century. He wrote the
Upasakadyayana, *the text central to Jain teaching which lays down the rules
and norms to be followed by the lay followers of Jainism.*

Of what use is a barren cow, which gives no milk? Of what use is the
king's grace if he does not fulfil the hopes of his people? For an ungrateful
king there is no help in trouble. His court is like a hole full of snakes,
which no one will enter.

Hemachandra

*Hemachandra, a Svetambara teacher and influential Jain scholar and
polymath from the twelfth century, composed the* Yogashastra—*an important
treatise on religion, morality, yogic practices and Jain principles.*

The Gods who are tainted with the passions of attachment and hostility and hence have women and weapons along with strings of beads, who favour some and disfavour others, are not the gods to be worshipped by those who are desirous of emancipation.

Can the gods, who themselves are unsteady and disturbed by drama, boisterous laughter and music, ever lead their followers to the tranquil path of moksha? (29-30)

~

There can never be a speech/word without the speaker. Even if we believe for the sake of argument that there could be such a text possible, there still remains the doubt about the validity of such a text because it is always the integrity of the speaker that determines the validity of a speech. (31)

~

If himsa (violence) is not totally given up, sense control, inner-discipline, service to God and Guru, charities, study, and penance are all fruitless. (40)

~

In what hell will those atheists who commit heinous crimes and brutal acts and who openly preach himsa in their scriptures be born? Poor Charvaka is definitely better as he preaches himsa, no doubt, but openly. But Jaimini is no better than Charvaka as he is a monster in the guise of an ascetic who preaches that himsa is enjoined in the Vedas. Those merciless persons, who kill the animals under the pretext of offering oblation to the gods for the sake of sacrifice are condemned to most terrifying existence.

Leaving aside a religion which is for universal good and is rooted in quietude, noble character, and compassion, the dull-witted proclaim that injury to living beings also is a bonafide religion. (41-42)

~

The himsa which is committed, in order to please the forefathers, as laid down in the Smritis (the Brahmanic scriptures) by the dull-witted people, paves the way for existence in a birth in the lower regions.

To please the dead, who have already taken rebirth in other categories of existence, by acts of himsa is not possible at all. It is the considered opinion of Acharya Hemachandra that himsa committed with a desire to please the dead ones becomes the cause of evil existence after death for the doer and one who has it done for the other. Both are ignorant about the real meaning and significance of the scriptural injunctions.

One who protects living beings, protects one's self—just as one gives, one receives.

It is a matter of great grief that the gods, who wield such weapons as bow and arrow, mace, disc, sword, trident, and shakti, are worshipped as if they are true gods. (44)

Translated by A.S. Gopani

Uttaradhayayanasutra

The Uttaradhayayanasutra *is one of the four core texts of the Jain canon. It is a work in thirty-six chapters, each a sermon on aspects of Jain doctrine and discipline, interspersed with lively narratives from folk literature. It is believed by orthodox Jains to contain the actual words of Mahavira, the founder of Jainism.*

One does not become a śramaṇa by the tonsure, nor a Brahmaṇa by the sacred syllable, nor a muni by living in the woods, nor a tāpasa by wearing clothes of kuśa grass and bark.

One becomes a śramaṇa by equanimity, a Brahmaṇa by celibacy, a muni by knowledge, and a tāpasa by penance.

By one's actions one becomes a Brahmaṇa, by one's actions one becomes a kśatriya, by one's actions one becomes a vaiśya or by one's actions one becomes a śūdra. (79)

SUBHASHITAS

The Subhashita is a form of Sanskrit and Prakrit poetry which was popular in ancient and medieval India. These short poems carry an inherent moral and ethical message. They address issues of politics, religion, kingship and love, amongst others, by deftly presenting them in the guise of praise. Often sarcastic, they can be considered as guides to developing a richer consciousness. The following verses have been selected and translated by Radhavallabh Tripathi specially for this volume.

Bhartrihari

Although his exact year of birth is still debated, Bhartrihari is widely believed to have been a Sanskrit poet from the fifth century. Shatakatraya, a collection of Sanskrit poetry, is widely attributed to him. His verses on ethics, morality and renunciation are examples of a mind that questioned social mores.

Do not waste effort, good man, in pursuit of too many virtues...
Renunciation of worldly bonds is just vain talk of wordy savants.

~

Honest and lying; full of wrath and the sweetest speaker;
Savage and gentle; frantic after wealth and liberal;
A great squanderer and a greater hoarder still;
The king's finesse has many faces—like a whore.

~

If you are the king
We are also superior in intellect,
which we nurtured serving our teachers.
You are known for your riches,
Our fame is spread far and wide by poets
O glorious one! There is not much difference
between you and us.
But if you turn away from us
we also are absolutely free from any longing.

Translated by Radhavallabh Tripathi

Sohnoka

Sohnoka was an eleventh-century Bengali poet who wrote in Sanskrit, and not much is known of him except for the two verses attributed to him. Through his verses, he subtly reproached the king for not paying enough attention to his subjects. The following is a verse from Saduktikarnamrita.

The terrace is shattered and foundations shrivelled
The walls are falling down and boundaries are decaying

The serpents crawl inside this house, the rats wander freely
And the frogs play hide and seek.
Wheezing sounds arise when the bats toss their wings
O king, the jewel of the Saina dynasty!
Our house is just as
the house of your enemy ought to have been!

Translated by Radhavallabh Tripathi

Kshemendra

Kshemendra was an eleventh-century Kashmiri poet writing in Sanskrit. In his poems, he commented on the avaricious nature of kings, the rampant corruption and the exploitation of the poor. Following are some verses from Sevyasevakopadesha.

They did not lose the jewel of self-respect
in the pretence of making efforts at serving [a king].
Their heads remained untouched
by the dust on the streets.
They really have earned real victory,
They are to be saluted for good.

~

What is to be done with kings
even if at all they are somehow available
after taking pains
they are all surrounded by the caucus of rogues.
We already have the real Kings of the earth—
the mountains!
Even the sages are sheltered under them.

~

Take refuge in that holy forest
Where real servants have made a permanent retreat
Where there is daily clinching of the hurry
For a nonsense prostration
Where the face is not blurred by the mud of the streets
Where there is not tussle with the security personnel on the gates
Where the cruel kings

fierce with their arrogance
are not there!

Translated by Radhavallabh Tripathi

Bilhana

Bilhana was an eleventh-century Kashmiri poet. According to legend, he left Kashmir after the discovery of his secret affair with the king's daughter and subsequent imprisonment. He was later appointed as the chief poet in the court of King Vikramaditya VI of Kalyana, in whose honour he wrote Vikramankadevacharita.

Let the King of Kuntala confiscate everything I possess
But then my store house of learning remains alive inside me
Intact and unbroken;
You petty people! Don't rejoice.
Very soon the rich will frequent my house,
riding on the back of elephants
swinging their long ears with sport.

Translated by Radhavallabh Tripathi

Kalhana

Kalhana was a twelfth-century Kashmiri poet credited with composing Rajtarangini, a history of Kashmir and its kings. In this epic, he didn't limit himself to merely glorifying the kings but censured them for not devoting enough time to their subjects and leading the empire to a state of ruin.

Fie upon the state for which
sons and fathers
kill each other.
They suspect each other
and have sleepless nights.
Kings are apprehensive of their own sons,
wives, friends and servants.
We simply do not know
who will enjoy their confidence.

~

Kings waste their riches
on buying women whose eyes are like the eyes of deer
and who are unattainable.
They waste their riches on buying the hissings of horses,
vulgar talks of the touts.
They waste their time in pleasing the ladies,
in the discussions of the breeds of horses,
in the flattery of the servants,
or in discussion of hunting.

Women prevail upon them during nights.
The ministers assert themselves during the day.
What a make believe
that still the kings wield authority here!

Translated by Radhavallabh Tripathi

Anonymous Sanskrit Poet in *Subhashitavali*

The Subhashitavali, *compiled by Vallabhdeva of Kashmir around the fifteenth century, is a collection of satirical and comic verses.*

Salute the gods? But even they
cannot escape relentless fate.
Salute that fate? But even it
bears fruit to deeds proportionate.
Then, if fruit depends on deeds,
are gods and fate of any avail?
Salutations to deeds on which
even fate cannot prevail.

Translated by A.N.D. Haksar

THE VIRASHAIVAS

Vachana poetry in Kannada reached its peak in the twelfth century through the Sharana movement. This movement challenged caste hierarchies, the

vanity of wealth and the evils of social divisions. It also gave birth to the
Virashaiva movement, which was devoted to the heroic Shiva. The poets of
these movements wrote intense, passionate verses that liberated language from
the artificial conventions of courtly writing, thereby making their poems more
accessible to the common person and promoting an egalitarian society.

Chennaiah

Chennaiah, an eleventh-century cobbler saint-poet, is regarded as the first
poet of the Vachana tradition. It is said that the great saint-poet Basavanna
considered him his guru. He was the first person to reject the caste system and
encourage an egalitarian approach in the Vachana movement.

> Semen, blood, marrow, flesh,
> Hunger, thirst, grief, sensuality
> These are one and the same.
> Only the trade of men are different
> For the spirit that sees
> Appearances are the same.
> No matter what one's caste
> Thanks to realization
> One becomes absorbed in primal truth
> And a kinsman of defilement and limitation
> Through forgetfulness
> Realizing both
> I have never forgotten them.
> Do not be enslaved
> By the hand-awl, blade or peg
> But realize
> Ramarama, your own true self, the joy of joys!

Translated by H.S. Shivaprakash

Basavanna

Basavanna (c. 1150 CE), born into a Shaivite Brahmin family in Bagewadi,
Karnataka, was a leading figure of the Virashaiva movement and an advocate
of equality across gender, caste and religion. His poems not only question the
bigoted and hypocritical customs of the society he lived in but are also deeply
personal and self-critical.

Earth is one and the same
For pariah street
And Shiva temple;
Water is one and the same
For washing shit
And ritual cleaning;
All castes are one
For a man with self-knowledge
Salvation's fruit is one and the same
For all six systems;
Truth is one,
O master Kudalasangama
For the one who knows you.

Translated by H.S. Shivaprakash

~

God, O God, mark my prayer:
I shall call all devotees of Shiva equal,
from the Brahmana at one end
to the lowest-born man at the other end;
I shall call all unbelievers equal,
from the Brahmana at one end
to the untouchable at the other end;
this is what my heart believes!
In saying this—should I have any doubt—
be it so small as a sesamum bud—
O master Kudalasangama,
chop off my nose so that the teeth stick out!

Translated by Armando Menezes and S.M. Angadi

Akka Mahadevi

Akka Mahadevi (c. 1150 CE), a contemporary of Basavanna and Allama Prabhu, was a wandering mystic poet. One of the greatest Virashaiva poets, she rebelled in more ways than one. She walked out of her marriage with a local king, renounced worldly life, declared herself to be betrothed to Lord Chennamallikarjuna (Shiva) and also shed her clothes in the process, covering herself with just her long hair. Her powerful verses reflect her deep love for the lord and utter disregard for social conventions.

I have Maya for mother-in-law;
the world for father-in-law;
three brothers-in-law, like tigers;

and the husband's thoughts
are full of laughing women;
no god, this man.

And I cannot cross the sister-in-law.

But I will
give this wench the slip
and go cuckold my husband with Hara, my Lord.

My mind is my maid:
by her kindness, I join
my Lord
my utterly beautiful Lord
from the mountain-peaks,
my lord white as jasmine,
and I will make Him
my good husband.

~

People,
male and female,
blush when a cloth covering their shame
comes loose.

When the lord of lives
lives drowned without a face
in the world, how can you be modest?

When all the world is the eye of the lord,
onlooking everywhere, what can you
cover and conceal?

Translated by A.K. Ramanujan

~

Those who have become equal by love,
should they need background or pretensions?
Those who have gone mad,

do they know shame or restraint?
Those who are loved by the lovely Lord of the Jasmines,
could they have loyalty to the world?
Inside my husband, outside my lover,
I cannot handle them both!
Everyday life and supreme quest,
I cannot handle them both!
O Lovely Lord of the Jasmines,
a pear and an apple
cannot be held in one hand.

~

You can confiscate the riches in the land,
but can you confiscate the riches of the body?
You can rip off all clothing and ornaments from the body,
but can you rip off the bliss that covers and veils me?
O fool, what is the need of clothing and ornaments
for the shameless woman
who is clad in the light of the divine Lovely Lord of the Jasmines?

~

A pot of shit, a can of piss,
a frame of bones, the stench of pus—
this body, burn it! Do not get ruined
by pressing the body,
you fool who doesn't know
the Lovely Lord of the Jasmines!

Translated by Armando Menezes and S.M. Angadi

Allama Prabhu

Born in Balligave in Karnataka, Allama Prabhu (c. 1150 CE) was a mystic-saint poet and the head of the Anubhava Mantapa established by the Sharana movement. Through his deceptively simple but profound vachanas, he sharply attacked the prevailing customs and practices in society and did not spare the Sharanas either. He urged people to look inwards rather than outwards for spiritual fulfilment.

I saw
The fragrance fleeing
When the bee came,
What a wonder!
I saw
Intellect fleeing
When the heart came.
I saw
The temple fleeing
When God came,
O Gogeshwara!

~

If I am not god,
Are you god?
If you are god,
Why do you not take care of me?
When thirsty, I offer myself a pitcher of water
When hungry, I give myself a morsel of rice
Look!
I am god, O Gogeshwara!

Translated by H.S. Shivaprakash

~

Gold is temptation, they say,
and woman is temptation, they say,
and land is temptation, they say.
But gold is not temptation,
and woman is not temptation,
and land is not temptation.
See, Lord of the Caves,
the real temptation
is the desire in one's own mind.

Translated by Armando Menezes and S.M. Angadi

Adaiah

Adaiah was a twelfth-century vachana poet who hailed from Sowrashtra and settled down in Puligere (Lakshmeshwara).

Four Vedas are similes:
So are sixteen Shastras
Eighteen Puranas
Twenty-eight sacred Agamas
Thirty-two Upanishads
Seven million great mantras.
Similes, all just similes
Countless words, scriptures,
Systems of logic and grammar—
Similes
Many many mantras, tantras
The mastery of yantras or black magic
Similes.
Hearing the unheard
Attaining the unattainable
Penetrating the impenetrable—
Similes, always.
Unable to stop similes
Unable to transcend the web of similes
Unable to free themselves
From the thick paste of similes and non-similes
Unable to prevent the contamination of feelings
Thought forming or not,
Unable to see the truth
Of Sowrashtra Someshwara
These simile-bound people
Make similes with similes
Come into being through similes.

Translated by H.S. Shivaprakash

Kalavve

Born in the twelfth century, Kalavve is the first woman Dalit poet. She spoke fiercely against the double standards espoused by the upper castes and men of religion.

They say—
All those are high born

Who eat sheep, fowl and tiny fish,
They say—
All those are low born
Who eat the cow that rains on Shiva
Sacred milk sanctified five times.
What the Brahmins had eaten adorned the grass
And a dog licked it up and went away.
What the cobblers had eaten adorned the grass—
Now Brahmin's ornament.
In other words
Bags are made of cow's hide
For ghee and for water.
Senseless Brahmins who drink
Ghee and water from such leather bags
Thinking it sacred
They can't escape
Utmost perdition.
The master of Uriligapeddi
Doesn't approve of such men.

Translated by H.S. Shivaprakash

~

In thirty-two lakhs of years in Kritayuga they (Brahmins) killed
    elepahnts for homa
In sixteen lakhs of years in Tretayuga they killed buffaloes for
    homa
In eight lakhs of Dvapara yuga they offered to the fire horses
In the four lakhs of the Kaliyuga they now offer goats
Brahmins have killed so many although as every Shiva bhakta
    knows
'Anonraniyan mahatomahiyan' God is smaller than the smallest,
    larger than the largest
Therefore one who offers salutations to Brahmins will be born as
    a pig for eighty-four lakhs of years!

Translated by Vijaya Ramaswamy

Molige Mahadevi

Molige Mahadevi belonged to the Sharana movement that believed work is worship.

> Sir, why all this chatter
> About being established
> In union with Shiva?
> This is no play of eternal truths
> This stunt you indulge in
> Who has given you permission?
> Who are you going to tell this to?
> Tell me
> Who do you think you are?
> Be aware of that feeling
> Know yourself,
> O beloved of my lord
> Mallikarjuna, of two-fold purity.

Translated by H.S. Shivaprakash

Kadire Remmavve

Kadire Remmavve belonged to the spinner caste. She is said to have left her husband and taken up spinning for her livelihood. In her poems we see a rejection of patriarchy and contempt for dominant notions of purity and beauty.

> All husbands (men) are
> destroyers of enemy forces
> My husband crushes
> the petals of my mind
> Other husbands are hunters of elephants
> My husband is the hunter of my mind.

~

> All wives wash and give to their husbands
> I do not give my husband, he does not need
> All husbands have seeds.
> All husbands are up above
> My husband below, I'm above him!

Translated by Vijaya Ramaswamy

Goggave

Goggave was a Virashaiva woman saint who came to Kalyana from Kerala in the twelfth century.

When breasts and braid are coming,
they say: a woman;
When moustache and loincloth are coming,
they say: a man;
But the knowledge of these two—
is that female or male,
O Lord of Nothingness?

Translated by Armando Menezes and S.M. Angadi

Urilingadeva

Urilingadeva was one of the Virashaiva poets. In his verses, he assumed the female persona to express his intense spiritual love and devotion towards Shiva.

In my great rapture
Of making love with my darling
I can't tell myself from the world.
While making love with my love
I can't tell myself from my darling
After making love with Urilingadeva
The god of the burning member
I can't tell whether it is me, him
Or something else.

Translated by H.S. Shivaprakash

Dhoolaiah

Dhoolaiah was a poet of the Vachana tradition, and as a cobbler belonged to the lowest rung of the caste hierarchy. Like many other Sharana poets, he equated his work with worship and asserted the dignity of his profession through his poems.

Everyone pierces the hide of cattle
With awareness.
Everyone pierces the hide of cattle

In forgetfulness.
But I pierce the hide
Of dead cattle.
I cut away the hide
And the truthful ones put sandals on
I expect them to show me
Emptiness
Take your paths, all of you
Mine is the path
Of the master of lust, dust and smoke.
That is enough for me.

~

Like a lightning creeper
Like a roar in the sky
Like a bubble
Like the riches of coral
That appears in a dream—
The attitude unattached to these,
That of your own self,
The anarchist, uncommitted
Without faith
Freed of the defiling touch of the mean
Attached to none, nothing,
The master of lust, dust and smoke.

Translated by H.S. Shivaprakash

Sarvajna

Sarvajna was a sixteenth-century Vachana poet and philosopher. Although born into a Shaivaite Brahmin family, he was critical of the orthodox Brahmanical rituals and practices.

The whole world is born
In the impurity of menstruation
Why should a Brahmin fly away from the woman in her period?
Must he not know the secret
Of his own birth?
Sarvajna

~

If a Brahmin wearing a triple thread
Could rise to Heaven,
Why not then a shepherd swain
Wearing a blanket of countless threads
Go too?
Sarvajna

Translated by Basavaraj Naikar

CLASSICAL TAMIL POETS

Classical Tamil poetry, primarily Sangam Literature, is unique because, while most other literature was focused on religion, it was uninhibitedly about love, heroism and politics. Over time, religious matters took over and the Alvar saints composed poems about their relationship with god; some like Andal called god their lover while others angrily questioned god. Eventually, poets from both upper and lower castes also expressed strong dissent against orthodox rituals and patriarchy.

Purananuru

Composed between the seventh and fifth centuries BCE, Purananuru is one of the eight books that make up Tamil Sangam literature. A treatise on kingship, it includes commentaries on the violent nature of war and the attitude of kings and clansmen who engage in it.

Nettimaiyar: on King Peruvaluti

Your bards are wearing lotuses of gold
and the poets
are getting ready to ride
fancy chariots
drawn by elephants
with florid brow-shields:
    is this right,
    O lord rich in victories,

this ruthless taking
   of other men's lands

while being very sweet to proteges?

Translated by A.K. Ramanujan

Kovur Kilar: to Netunkilli and Nalankilli

To warring clansmen
Your enemy is not the kind who wears
the white leaf of the tall palmyra

nor the kind who wears garlands
from the black-branched neem trees.

Your chaplets are made of laburnum,
your enemies are made of laburnum too.

When one of you loses
the family loses,
and it is not possible
for both to win.

Your ways show no sense of family:
they will serve only to thrill
alien kings
        whose chariots are bannered,
        like your own.

Translated by A.K. Ramanujan

Sundarar

Sundarar was a Tamil Shaiva poet from the eighth or ninth century. His poems appear in the seventh volume of Tirumarai, *a twelve-volume anthology of Tamil Shaiva poets. Although most of his poems are in praise of Shiva, he also chided the god for ignoring his devotees.*

I don't call to him as my mother. I don't call to him as my father.
I thought it would be enough to call him my Lord—
But he pretends I don't exist, doesn't show an ounce of mercy.
If that lord who dwells in Paccilacciramam, surrounded by pools

Filled with geese, postpones the mercies for his devotees—
Can't we find some other god?

Translated by David Shulman

Manikkavachakar

Manikkavachakar was a ninth-century Tamil poet who wrote Tiruvasakam,
*a book of Shaiva hymns. In his poems, he treats Shiva as his friend and doesn't
hesitate to threaten and abuse him if he abandons a faithful devotee.*

I shall call you madman—
madman draped in elephant skin,
poison-throated madman,
madman sporting
midst the fires
of the burning ground,
madman clad in tiger skin.
Madman who enslaved
even me!

Translated by Vidya Dehejia

Andal

*Andal, a ninth-century mystic, was the only woman among the twelve Alvar
or Vaishnava saint-poets. She believed she was betrothed to Vishnu and
refused to marry. In her explicit, passionate verses, she addresses the god as
her intended groom and expresses her love.*

Smell they of camphor
or lotus blossom new?
Do they taste sweet
his lips of coral hue?
O tell me
white conch from the vast deep sea
I ask longingly
I need to know
How do they taste?
How smell the lips of Madhavan who broke the tusk?

~

My swelling breasts I dedicated
to the Lord who holds
the sea-fragrant conch—
If there is but a whisper
of me to a mortal,
I shall not live, O Manmatha—
Would you permit a roving jackal
to sniff and make its own
the sacrificial foods
that brahmins offer
to celestial gods?

~

In vain I wait for a sight of my dark Lord
he knows not the sorrow of women
I look for soft words
but you pour acid into my open wound—
Bring me the yellow silk
the Lord wraps around his waist
fan me with it
cool the burning of my heart.

Like soft earth trampled by black bull
broken and crushed am I
by him who stole the hearts
of the maidens of Ayarpadi—
What now can bring me solace?
Only the nectar of the Lord's mouth
the Lord who is himself
the nectar that never cloys
bring me that nectar
let me taste it
it will wipe away my pain.

I pine and languish
but he cares not whether I live or die—
If I see that thief of Govardhana
that looting robber, that plunderer
I shall pluck out by their roots
these breasts that have known no gain

I shall take them
and fling them at his chest
putting out the hell-fire
which burns within me.

Translated by Vidya Dehejia

Sivavakkiyar

Sivavakkiyar was a tenth-century Shaiva poet. He rebelled against the Brahminical order and resolutely opposed the caste system. As a result, he was left out of canonical literature and very little information about him is available now.

Oh! You build huge houses and protect it with tall doors
but poor you, you are unable to protect
yourself being taken by yeman (God of Death).
What would happen to the luxury of having
herds, wealth, family and palaces
when yemen calls on you?
Will herds of cow and goats, elephants,
armory, crores of wealth back you
when you resist yemen?

~

In mother's womb, baby grows when thumai (menstrual blood) ends. This is common to all castes. Even the Brahmins who recite Veda are born out of thumai. You did not mind when you were born with thumai, then how can this be an obstacle in accessing God? To realize the Supreme Being, one should realize the fact that humans are born from thumai. Oh, Fools! You take bath to ward off theettu (impurity). You recite Veda after taking dips in water like a tortoise. Can you not understand that the body is a creation of thumai? Men and women, lower caste and upper caste—all were the same when they were in the form of thumai.

Translated by Vijaya Ramaswamy

Uttiranallur Nangai

Uttiranallur Nangai was a fifteenth-century woman who belonged to the untouchable caste but learned the Vedas from a Brahmin, and also married him. She composed Paichalur Padigam *as a response to the elders of the village who came to punish her for her dual transgression.*

> Brahmins of the village gather
> build a wall.
> Dip in the river
> And pour ghee on fire:
> Like frogs in the rain
> croak the four Vedas.
> Do they gain deliverance
> O elders of paichalur?

> ~

> Neem and sandalwood
> smell distinct when they burn.
> But the smell of the burning Brahmin
> you cannot tell.
> Does fire smell different
> when unwashed Pulaya burns?
> The stuff that burns
> and the flames that burn,
> how do they differ
> O elders of Paichalur?

Translated by Vijaya Ramaswamy

TULSIDAS

Tulsidas was a sixteenth-century poet-saint, reformer and philosopher renowned for his devotion to Lord Rama. He composed several works in Sanksrit and Awadhi and is best known as the author of the Ramcharitmanas, *a retelling of the Sanskrit Ramayana in the vernacular Awadhi.*

> Call me swindler, call me saint,
> Call me Rajput, or call me Julaha,
> I've no son to offer anyone's daughter,

Nor spoil anyone's caste by proximity.
Tulsidas is a famous disciple of Ram,
Let people say what suits their taste.
I will beg for food, sleep at the mosque,
Not a cent from others, nor two cents to give.

Translated by Manash Firaq Bhattacharjee

LAL DED

Lal Ded was a fourteenth-century mystic poet from Kashmir. Married at the tender age of twelve, she decided to renounce her family at twenty-six and became the disciple of a Shaiva saint. After completing her discipleship, she became a wandering mendicant, and started writing poetry. Her poetry oscillates between the vulnerability of doubt and the assurance of insight, reflecting her questing yet resolute nature.

Don't torture this body with thirst and hunger,
Give it a hand when it stumbles and falls.
To hell with all your vows and prayers:
Just help others through life, there's no truer worship.

~

Up, woman! Go make your offering.
Take wine, meat and a cake fit for the gods.
If you know the password to the Supreme Palace,
you can reach wisdom by breaking the rules.

~

Some, who have closed their eyes, are wide awake.
Some, who look at the world, are fast asleep.
Some who bathe in sacred pools remain dirty.
Some are at home in the world but keep their hands clean.

~

Master, leave these palm leaves and birch barks
To parrots who recite the name of God in a cage.
Good luck, I say, to those who think they've read the scriptures.
The greatest scripture is the one that's playing in my head.

Translated by Ranjit Hoskote

THE VARKARI POETS

The Varkari movement, which began in the thirteenth century in Maharashtra and northern Karnataka, was a revolt against the existing socio-political and religious order and an extension of the Bhakti movement. Its message was of universal humanism and it negated class and gender distinctions in devotion. The most striking feature of this movement is the use of everyday folk language by its poets. Their poems directly attack the prevailing social order and express pure bliss in discovering their 'own' god.

Namdev

Namdev, born in the thirteenth century, was one of the earliest Varkari poets. Born to a low-caste family, he was an ardent devotee of Lord Vitthal. Although most of his abhangas are about his unshakeable love and faith, he also spoke of the insignificance of caste in the spiritual world. This is said to have won him a wide following among all those who were conventionally excluded by religious men.

Seeking the truth, I went to the scholars of the Vedas
And found them full of 'You shall' and 'You shall not'.
They had neither knowledge nor peace,
Their minds bloated to distress with the mighty 'I'.

Janabai

Janabai was a Marathi bhakti poet of the thirteenth century. Born into a Shudra family, she worked as a maidservant at the saint-poet Namdev's parents' house and considered Namdev to be her guru. She was an ardent devotee of Lord Vitthal and, although unlettered, she composed exquisite verses in his praise, often expressing her desire to own him.

I have let my veil drop to my shoulders.
Bare-headed, I shall walk through the market.
In my hands the cymbals, on my shoulder the veena
Let who will try and stop me now.
Come wish me well, anoint my wrists with oil.
Jani says: I have become your whore, Keshava.
I have come now to wreck your home.

Translated by Jerry Pinto and Neela Bhagwat

Soyarabai

Soyarabai was a fourteenth-century Marathi saint-poet of the Varkari movement. Born into the untouchable Mahar caste, she severely criticized orthodoxy, particularly the caste system, through her abhangas.

You say some bodies are untouchable.
Tell me what you say of the soul.
You say defilement is born in the body.
If menstrual blood makes me impure,
Tell me who was not born of that blood.
This blood of mine fertilizes the world.
Tell me who was not sprung from this source.
Soyara says: this impurity is the cornerstone of your world.
That's why I praise only Panduranga,
Who lives in every body, pure, impure.

Translated by Jerry Pinto and Neela Bhagwat

Tukaram

Born in the seventeenth century, Tukaram is an illustrious poet of the Varkari tradition. He chose to write in colloquial Marathi in praise of Lord Vishnu, thereby challenging the monopoly of the Brahmins. Many of his poems address Vishnu with immediacy and directness, while others excoriate ritualistic and caste practices.

For the servant of God there is no caste, no varna, so say the Vedic
    sages...
He who becomes enraged at the touch of a Mahar is no Brahmin.
There is no penance for him even by giving his life.

There is the taint of untouchability in him who will not touch a
   Chandal.
Tuka says: A man becomes what he is continually thinking of.

Translated by Mahatma Gandhi

CHARPATNATH

*Charpatnath was a poet writing during the end of the thirteenth century
and the beginning of the fourteenth century. He was a member of the Nath
Siddha sect—a prominent sect in northern India whose followers renounced
worldly life and practiced hath yoga and tantric rituals. Charpatnath not
only dissented against the mainstream Brahminical order, but also within the
Nath Siddha sect, as he found the rituals practiced by its followers insincere
and didn't agree with their lifestyles.*

Some wear ochre robes,
Some are robe-less.
Some mark the forehead; wear sacred thread,
Dangle long matted-hair.
Some are Faqirs; Some are Munis,
Some split-eared Kanaphatas.
When the deathly storm shall blow,
Will blow away the external robes!
Those who do not understand the Reverse Flow,
Charpat ridicules them as Clowns with stomachs.

~

Draping torn-patched garment,
Holding a begging bowl,
Wooden clogs on feet
Face smeared red
Greedy eating! Thirsty drinking!
Yet an austere practitioner?
Charpat asks: Why bring bad name to ascetics.

~

Feet over one stone,
The other stone is revered?
Says Charpat, the world is strange!
Why is this stone a STONE,
Why that stone a GOD?

Translated by Mahesh Sharma

KABIR

Kabir was a fifteenth-century Indian mystic poet and saint who, through his poems, emphasized the direct relationship of the individual with the divine. He was critical of the dogmatic strains in both Hinduism and Islam and impatient with orthodoxy. Through his poems, which have been recited for centuries, he preached compassion for all human beings and detachment from worldly affairs.

Saints, I see the world is mad.
If I tell the truth they rush to beat me,
If I lie they trust me.
I've seen the pious Hindus, rule-followers,
early-morning bath takers—
killing souls; they worship rocks.
They know nothing.
I've seen plenty of Muslim teacher, holy men reading their holy
    books,
and teaching their pupils techniques.
They know just as much.
And posturing yogis, hypocrites,
hearts crammed with pride,
praying to brass, to stones, reeling
with pride in their pilgrimage,
fixing their caps and their prayer-beads,
painting their brow-marks and arm-marks,
braying their hymns and their couplets,
reeling. They never heard of soul.

The Hindu says Ram is the Beloved,
the Turk says Rahim.
Then they kill each other.
No one knows the secret.
They buzz their mantras from house to house, puffed with pride.
The pupils drown along with their gurus.
In the end they're sorry.
Kabir says, listen saints:
They're all deluded!
Whatever I say, nobody gets it.
It's too simple.

~

Saints I've seen both ways.
Hindus and Muslims don't want discipline, they want tasty food.
The Hindu keeps the eleventh-day fast, eating chestnuts and milk.
He curbs his grain but not his brain, and breaks his fast with meat.
The Turk prays daily, fasts once a year, and crows 'God!, God!'
    like a cock.
What heaven is reserved for people who kill chickens in the dark?
    Instead of kindness and compassion, they've cast out all desire.
One kills with a chop, one lets the blood drop, in both houses
    burns the same fire.
Turks and Hindus have one way, the guru's made it clear.
Don't say Ram, don't say Khuda, so says Kabir.

Translated by Linda Hess and Sukhdev Singh

~

If God be within the mosque, then to whom does this world
    belong?
If Ram be within the image which you find upon your pilgrimage,
then who is there to know what happens without?
Hari is in the East, Allah is in the West.
Look within your heart, for there you will find both Karim and
    Ram;
All the men and women of the world are His living forms.
Kabir is the child of Allah and of Ram: He is my Guru, He is my Pir.

Translated by Rabindranath Tagore

THE SIKH GURUS

Guru Nanak

Guru Nanak (1469–1539), the founder of Sikhism, lived at a time when orthodoxy, ritualism and the rigid caste system of Hinduism were at their peak and Islam, too, was hostage to narrow-minded and politically motivated classes. Nanak challenged these practices by emphasizing the idea of One God and the importance of love, equality and compassion.

> Religion lies not in the yogi's patched garment,
> Nor in his staff,
> Nor in covering the body with ashes.
> Religion lies not in wearing large rings
> From split ears
> Nor in shaving the head nor in the blowing of
> the conch
> To live pure amid temptations of the world
> Is to understand religion.

Translated by Navtej Sarna

~

> Which was the moment
> which was the hour
> which was the moon
> which was the day
> which was the season
> which was the month
> when the universe was created?
> The pundit knows not the moment
> even if it is written in the Puranas;
> nor does the qazi know
> even if he recites and copies the Quran;
> yogis know not that time of night or day,
> nor the season nor the month.
> When He created the universe—
> only the Primal One knows.
> What phrase can we have for Him? What praise?

What description? What knowledge of Him?
Says Nanak, there are many who claim they know,
each wiser and louder than the other;
but great is the Lord, great is His name;
all that happens is by his will.
Says Nanak, they who claim they know
never shall they reach the other shore.

Translated by Reema Anand

~

If sandal-paste is rubbed on an ass, he will still roll in the dust.
Nanak, the robes we spin from falsehood are false; mere rags.
Reciting His name is superior to the cries of the muezzin and
    the yogi.

~

O pundit, you are a priest only in body.
Make your mind the ceremonial dhoti,
Knowledge of God your sacred thread,
Meditation the scared grass in your fingers;
Let the words you speak be the names of God.
Then, by the grace of the guru, you will be one with Him....

The scared thread has no meaning;
Seek the Divine within your soul.
The tilak and ceremonial dhoti are useless;
Seek His name and nothing else....

Make Love your prasad and offering
And banish all fear and superstition.
With the watchman alert, no thieves break in:
Wake up; understand that God is One.

Translated by Gurbachan Singh

~

The Qazi tells untruth and eats filth
The Brahmin kills and takes a holy bath

The blind yogi knows not the true way
All three make for mankind's ruin.

Translated by Navtej Sarna

~

A verse that illustrates Nanak's belief that wearing a thread—a Brahminical symbol—doesn't elevate the status of a man but his thoughts and actions do.

From the cotton of Compassion, spin the thread of Contentment,
Give knots of Continence and twists of Truth;
This is the sacred thread for the soul—
If thou hast one such, O Brahman, then put it on me.
It will not snap, nor soil; nor will it be burnt or lost
Blessed is the man, O Nanak, who wears such a thread around
his neck.

Translated by Navtej Sarna

Guru Arjun Dev

Guru Arjun Dev (1563–1606) was the fifth Sikh guru and the first martyr of the Sikh faith. Like the previous gurus, he did not believe in either Hinduism or Islam and propagated the idea of One God. He was captured and executed by Jahangir, the Mughal emperor at the time.

Not for me the Hindu's fast or the Muslim's Ramzan;
I abide by Him alone, for He alone is my refuge.
I don't bathe in holy rivers, and I don't go to Mecca;
To me, Gosain, the Creator, and Allah are one.

I don't pray to idols, and I don't say the namaz;
I serve and bow to the One and no other.
I worship at the feet of the Formless Lord within;
For we are neither Hindu nor Musalman.

Translated by Gurbachan Singh

Guru Gobind Singh

Guru Gobind Singh (1666–1708) was the tenth and last of the living Sikh gurus. He was made Guru after his father, Guru Tegh Bahadur, was executed by the Mughal emperor Aurangzeb. Guru Gobind Singh fought and led the Sikhs on many wars against the emperor's increasing tyranny and active hostility to the Sikhs. He composed the Zafarnama or 'Epistle of Victory' in 1705. Written in Persian, its 111 stanzas indict Aurangzeb and his commanders and expose their spiritual and moral bankruptcy.

Some worship stones, bear them on their heads,
Some wear phalluses around their necks.
Some see their God in the south,
Some bow their heads to the west,
Some pray to idols, some to the dead:
All the world is bound in false ritual;
None grasps the secret of the True One.

Translated by Gurbachan Singh

From the *Zafarnama*

13
I have no faith at all
In the oath that you swear,
That the God who is One
Your witness does bear.

14
Not a jot of trust
Do I now have in you,
Whose generals and ministers
Are all liars, untrue.

15
Such oaths on the Quran
Whosoever does believe,
Will be wretched at the end,
Destroyed, beyond reprieve.

16
The one touched by Huma's[1] shadow
And taken under its wing
Is beyond harm from clever crows,
Their designs mean nothing.

17
As one protected by the lion
Is set free from all fear,
He cannot then be harmed
By goats, sheep and deer.

18
In your false oath on the Quran
Had I not believed,
My brave army wouldn't be crippled,
Nor in such manner deceived.

19
Forty brave but hungry men
How are they expected to defend
When countless enemy hordes
Upon them suddenly descend?
20
All of a sudden they descended,
Giving the lie to their words,
Brandishing their guns,
Raining arrows, waving swords.

21
Then left with no choice
I joined battle with your hordes,
Came with much deliberation
Amidst the arrows and swords.

22
When all has been tried, yet
Justice is not in sight,
It is then right to pick up the sword,
It is then right to fight.

23
Why should I then believe
In oaths on the Holy Word?
If I had not been deceived,
Would I go down this road? ...

45
Unaware was I that this perjurer
Worshipped no God but gold,
His faith he had flung aside,
His rotten soul he had sold.[2]

46
There is no belief in religion,
And faith is discarded,
The Lord is ignored,
The Prophet disregarded.

47
Those who are firm of faith
And true believers of God,
Break not their promises thus
But stay firm to their word.

48
There can be no trust in a man who
Swears on the Quran and One God,
But values not the holy oath
And is false to his given word.

49
And now even a hundred times
If on the Quran were he to swear,
His word I would never believe,
For his promises I do not care....

66
You sit on a mighty throne,
You are king of all you survey,
But strange is your justice,
Strange the virtues you display.

67
Strange are your ways of faith,
Strange the justice you claim,
Shame upon such a rule,
A hundred times, shame!

68

Your decrees and commands
Are strange, very strange indeed,
For words shorn of truth
Only to grievous harm lead.

69

Do not in such heartless manner
Put innocents to the sword,
Else this too shall be your fate
At the hands of the Lord.

Translated by Navtej Sarna

Notes

1. Huma is the mythological and legendary bird whose touch or shadow is said to be auspicious.
2. Some commentators believe, contrary to traditional interpretation, that the promise-breaker in this and some other verses is not Aurangzeb but the local Mughal commander.

MEERABAI

Meerabai, a sixteenth-century Bhakti poet, was born into a Rajput family. She was a devotee of Lord Krishna, and when married to Bhoja Raj, a prince, she refused to accept him as her husband as she believed she was betrothed to Krishna. According to legend, she was treated poorly by her mother-in-law and a young male relative also tried to poison her, but this did not deter Meera. She defied patriarchy and social conventions to join her fellow Bhaktas, and wander through the streets while singing verses of despair and ecstatic union with Krishna. She is one of the few Bhakti poets who continues to enjoy immense pan-Indian popularity.

I dance
wearing
ankle-bells

people say
I'm mad
mother-in-law says
the ruin of our clan

Rana
sent me poison
I drank it
and laughed

offered
body and soul
for one look
at you

Girdhar
my master
now let me come
to you

Translated by Rahul Soni

~

My friend, I've bought up Govind.
Did you say it was done in hiding?
I took him beating my drum.

Did you say he came expensive?
I tell you, I weighed all upon the scales

and then I gave my body, my life, and things like that.

Let me, says Meera, see you.

You said so a life ago.

Translated by Shama Futehally

THE SUFIS

Sufi Islam, as it evolved in India and the rest of South Asia, was influenced by the rituals and pantheism of Hinduism. It shared many elements with the Bhakti movement, and Sufi pirs, or saints, had followers from all the different faiths of South Asia, much as they do today. While some Sufi schools were very orthodox, most were inclusive, and many pirs and poets were non-conformists and dissenters. They rejected dogmatic, exclusivist and divisive traditions, often openly challenging and defying the clergy and even kings and emperors. Some paid for their dissent with their lives.

Amir Khusro

Poet, musician and scholar, Amir Khusro is believed to have been born in 1252 or 1253 in what is now Uttar Pradesh. He composed some of India's greatest poems and songs, in Persian and Hindavi. Though very much a man of the world, and patronized by the rulers of the Delhi Sultanate, his true loyalty was to the great Sufi saint Nizamuddin Auliya. Influenced by Nizamuddin, Khusro wrote some bold, passionate poetry that went against orthodox faith and tradition.

> I'm a kafir. A pagan,
> I worship Love; I have no need of Islam.
> Kafirs wear the thread of their faith,
> I have no need of that, either.

> I'm drunk on the nectar of His Love.
> He sings in my blood:
> Each vein a thread of my faith.

Translated by R.J. Yadav

Sarmad

Sarmad (1590–1661) was a Persian poet, mystic and saint, who made India his home. He initially came to the subcontinent as a trader but when he reached Sindh, he fell in love with a young Hindu boy. Eventually, he abandoned his wealth, stopped clipping his nails and cutting his hair, and started wandering around the streets as a naked faqir. The Mughal prince Dara Shikoh was a follower of Sarmad. However, when Aurangzeb took over the empire, he beheaded Sarmad on charges of blasphemy.

If I am a devotee, my object is the Friend,
What have I to do with the rosary and the sacerdotal thread!
This woollen garment wherein lie a hundred evils
Never shall I put on my shoulder: it is disgusting to me.

~

Our everyday avocation is villainy and wickedness.
Our flatterers and vessels have been filled with sins.
Creation is laughing and life is wailing
At our prayers, genuflections and fastings.

~

Not only are these temples and sanctuaries His house
This earth and this sky are entirely His abode.
The whole world is mad about His fictions.
He is truly mad who is mad about Him.

~

His tyrannous passion, ho! is Satan:
Always visible, yet hidden.
Thou art thyself the Devil, why are thou ill-disposed to the Devil?
Before thy thoughts, he is bewildered.

~

Sarmad! If He is true to his word, He Himself will come:
If His coming is permissible, He Himself will come.
Why shouldst thou wander aimlessly after Him?
Sit down: if He be the Khud-a[1]; He Himself will come.

~

Although a hundred friends have turned mine enemies,
Owing to the friendship of the one, my mind has become
    contented.
I have accepted Unity and been freed from multiplicity
At last I became of Him and He of me.

~

He who gave thee the sovereignty of the world,
Gave me all the causes of anxiety.

He covered with a garment those with whom He found fault.
To the faultless He gave the robe of nudity.[2]

~

O King of Kings. I am not a hermit like thee, I am not nude,
I am frenzied, I am distracted, but I am not depressed,
I am an idolater, I am an infidel, I am not of the people of the faith,
I go towards the mosque, but I am not a Mussulman.

~

Sarmad! thou shouldst shorten thy murmurings.
Thou shouldst adopt one course out of these two courses—
Either, thou shouldst give thy body for the pleasure of the Friend;
Or, thou shouldst sacrifice thy life in His way.

~

Sarmad! speak not of the Kaaba and of the temple.
In the valley of doubt do not wander like the strayed wayfarer.
Go and learn from Satan[3] how to worship.
Accept one qebla and do not bow before every stranger.

~

Say, who is in the world that has not committed a sin?
He who has sinned not: say, how could he live?
I do evil thou requitest with evil,
Then say, what is the difference between me and thee?

~

Sarmad! thou hast done strange injury to the religion,
Thou hast bartered thy faith for one with an intoxicating eye.
With supplication and belief—thy entire wealth—
Thou didst go and squander on an idol-worshipper.[4]

Translated by Mesrovb Jacob Seth

Notes

1. 'Khuda' is here used in a double sense. 'Khuda' is the Persian word God and 'Khud-a' means a self-comer.
2. Sarmad's clothes' philosophy or 'Sartor resartus' is beautifully expressed in this quatrain.

3. According to Mohammedan tradition, the Devil fell for refusing to pay homage to Adam at the command of God.
4. In this beautiful quatrain, Sarmad apparently refers to his prosperous and happy days at Thatta, his love for the Hindu lad Abhai Chand, his neglect of his flourishing business as a merchant and his renunciation of the exoteric religion of Islam, being a faithful follower of the esoteric doctrine of the Safis.

Dara Shikoh

The Mughal prince Dara Shikoh (1615–1659) was a firm believer in the harmonious coexistence of religions and faiths, and a discerning patron of the arts. He was a follower of Sarmad and Lahore's Qadri Sufi saint, Hazrat Mian Mir. He was killed by his younger brother, Aurangzeb, in a bitter struggle for the throne after the death of their father, Emperor Shah Jahan.

> Paradise is there where no mulla exists—
> where the noise of his discussions and debate is not heard.
> May the world become free from the noise of the mullah,
> And none should pay any heed to his decrees!
> In the city where a mullah resides,
> no wise man ever stays.

Sultan Bahu

Sultan Bahu (c. 1630) was a popular Sufi saint of Punjab who founded the Sarwari Qadiri order. The order has no strict rules of dress or practice, which reflects Bahu's own vision of faith—an essential openness, an emphasis on a personal connection with the divine and favouring universality rather than strict doctrine. Bahu is credited with having written over forty books on Sufi mysticism in Punjabi and Persian.

> You've read the words of Allah, you're a master of the Quran
> But there's a veil before your eyes; wise man, you lust for gold.
> Those countless books you read, reread will only feed your ego
> None but the love-mad fakir will slay this thief who sits within.

> ~

> If ablution and bathing in holy waters
> took one to God, fish and frogs would find Him.
> If shaving the head and clipping hair

took one to God, goats and sheep would find Him.
If staying awake all night and waiting
took one to God, bats and owls would find Him.
If staying chaste and being celibate
took one to God, castrated bulls would find Him.

Bahu, only they become one with God
Whose hearts and thoughts are noble.

~

The portals of religion are impossibly high,
They won't lead to the narrow path to God.
Steal quietly past the mullahs and pundits,
They trip and trouble His faithful lovers.

Bahu, come, let us go some place
Where there is none but He.

Translated by Neelum Gill

Bulleh Shah

*One of Punjab's and India's greatest mystic poets, Bulleh Shah (1680–1758)
belonged to the Qadriyya Shattari order of Sufism. His humanism, integrity
and fearlessness, together with his extraordinary ability to express complex
mystical ideas simply, made him extremely popular in his lifetime, and he
remains one of the most widely quoted and sung poets of the subcontinent.*

There is no God in the mosque,
There is no God in the Ka'aba,
There is no God in the Book,
There is no God in prayer.

~

Tear down the mosque
And tear down the temple
And shatter what will be broken.

But do not ever break a heart—
for *that* is where God lives.

~

I've understood now; I know. So what's all the fuss
About Ram, Rahim and Maula?

~

Bulla, the preacher and torch-bearer say that they light the way.
Oh, but look how they stumble and sway in the dark themselves!

~

Money pleases the mighty qazi and death the learned mullah,
The lover seeks only [the unheard] music and his faith is ever strong.

~

Thugs live in the temple and killers in the mosque;
Fakirs are found at His threshold; this is our belief.

~

Bulla, build a fire with your bones, cook a meal
Of meat, drink wine;
Break down the door, storm in, burgle
The house of the Thief of Thieves.

~

The ever-new spring of Love:
When I read the book of Love
I feared the mosque and took another path
I asked around and entered a temple
But a thousand drums were beating.

The ever-new spring of Love:
I'm tired of reading the Vedas and the Quran
My forehead's worn thin kneeling and prostrating
There's no God on the ghats, nor in Mecca
Whoever finds Him is the emperor of light.

The ever-new spring of Love:
Set fire to the prayer mat, melt the water pot
Put away the prayer beads, throw away the staff
Listen to the lovers who proclaim aloud:
'Forget halal, eat the dead!'

Translated by Neelum Gill

Shah Latif

Shah Abdul Latif (1689–1752) is regarded as one of the greatest poets of the Sindhi language. A Sufi mystic and scholar, he is often compared to Rumi. His Urs—death anniversary celebration—still brings together many thousands of Hindu, Muslim and Sikh devotees at his dargah in Bhit Shah, Sindh, in what is now Pakistan.

Mullahs, shrine-keepers and pimps
They're all of the same ilk
They've sucked Allah dry
Like marrow from the bone

Don't call them 'mullahs'
They're hunters who sell
Sacred verses like pig's meat
They're a disgrace, says Latif

Don't call them 'mullahs'
God made them into donkeys
They beg and thieve to fill their bellies
Long after they're dead
God will still be angry
Don't call them 'mullahs'
They're blind as bats
Leave them to their debates
They read, but grasp nothing.

Translated by Shabnam Virmani and Vipul Rikhi

CLASSICAL TELUGU POETS

Although classical Telugu poetry is a part of the mainstream Indian dance and music tradition, it also carries some traces of dissent. These poems, resonant of the Bhakti tradition, are directed towards god—sometimes berating him for neglecting his devotees and at others, imagining him as a lover. Unfortunately, these unapologetically passionate, often erotic, verses were supressed when moralistic Victorian sensibility took root in Indian artistic practice.

Annamacharya

Annamacharya was a Telugu saint-poet of the fifteenth century. He settled in the Tirupati region and his padams are addressed to Venkateswara, Lord of the Hill. He composed poems on his relationship with and feelings for the god, as well as on the god's intimate life. In the love poems, he assumed the persona of the goddess Alamelu, Venkateswara's consort.

He's worn out. Bring him to me.
I'm the specialist in that disease.

Too many eyes have pierced him.
I may have to use love-charms, extra-strength.
His muscles are sore from battling breasts.
I'll massage him with a warm embrace.

I'm the specialist.

He must be exhausted from so much loving.
I'll touch him with the herb that revives.
His sensitive parts have melted down.
I'll bring them to life
with charms of shyness.

I'm the specialist.

Those artless women—how exciting can they be?
I have the right drug.
He's the handsome god on the hill,
and I'm Alamelumanga.
He's with me now. I can cure him.

I'm the specialist.

~

When I'm done being angry,
then I'll make love.
Right now, you should be glad
I'm listening.

When you flash that big smile,
I smile back. It doesn't mean I'm not angry.
You keep looking at me,
so I look too. It isn't right
to ignore the boss.

Right now you should be glad.

You say something, and I answer.
That doesn't make it a conversation.
You can call me to bed, I don't make a fuss.
But unless I want it myself,
it doesn't count as love.

Right now you should be glad.

You hug me, I hug you back.
You can see I'm still burning.
I can't help it, god on the hill,
I'm engulfed in your passion.

Right now you should be glad.

~

We get a lot out of you.
You don't have that skill.
God, your servants are better than you.

We grab you with a show of devotion.
We stick you in our mind.
For a little basil on your feet,
we've got freedom wholesale.
Your servants are very clever.

You don't have that skill.

Giving back what you've created,
we suck up all your goodness.
We've figured it out.
We bow once and twice, and put the burden
on you.

You don't have that skill.

We bring water from the pond, sprinkle a little on you,
and get whatever we ask.
God on the hill, with tricks like these,
we always come out on top.

You don't have that skill.

Translated by V. Narayana Rao and David Shulman

Kshetrayya

Kshetrayya, a seventeenth-century Telugu poet, composed padams which were to be performed by a female courtesan. Here, the courtesan's lover or patron is addressed as Muvva Gopala (Lord Krishna), and the intimacy of feeling and knowledge between the two is explicitly sensual.

A Woman to Her Reluctant Lover

Because I'm a good woman, I forgave you this time.
Would any other woman have let you off?

You follow me around like a servant,
you say humble things,
yet when I ask you to come home, you don't.
Why do you hurt me like this?

Now I've got you all alone.
If I hold you prisoner in this house,
who is there to release you?

Because I'm a good woman

You hold my hand, you say nice things.
But when I ask you to get into bed,
you say, 'I've taken a vow,' and do nothing.

Now I've caught you.
If I tie you down to my bed,
who is there to release you?

Because I'm a good woman

Only for a bet in a game you enter my bedroom.
When I call you, 'My handsome,

my Muvva Goapala!' why this indifference, dear parrot
in the hand of the Love of God?

If I choose to make love to you now,
Who is there to stop me?

Because I'm a good woman

A Married Woman to Her Lover

Go find a root or something.
I have no girlfriends here I can trust.

When I swore at you, you didn't listen.
You said all my curses were blessings.
You grabbed me, you bastard,
and had me by force.
I've now missed my period,
and my husband is out of town.

Go find a root or something.

I've set myself up for blame.
What's the use of blaming you?
I've even lost my taste for food.
What can I do now?
Go to the midwives and get me a drug
before the women begin to talk.

Go find a root or something.

As if he fell from the ceiling
my husband is suddenly home.
He made love to me last night.
Now I fear no scandal.
All my wishes, Muvva Gopala,
have reached their end,
so, in your image,
I'll bear you a son.

Go find a root or something.

Translated by A.K. Ramanujan, V. Narayana Rao and
David Shulman

Vemana

Vemana (c. 1652) was a Telugu poet and philosopher whose poems were celebrated for their simple language and use of native idioms. His poems typically question moral and religious beliefs.

> Will the application of white ashes do away with the smell of a
>   wine pot?
> Will a cord over your neck make you twice-born?
> What are you the better for smearing your body with ashes?
> Your thoughts should set on God alone; for the rest,
> an ass can wallow in dirt as well as you.

> The books that are called the Vedas are like courtesans,
> deluding men, and wholly unfathomable; but the hidden
> knowledge of God is like an honourable wife.
> O ye asses! Why do you make balls of food and give them to
> the crow to be an ancestor of yours?

> He that fasts shall become (in his next birth) a village pig;
> he that embraces poverty shall become a beggar; and he
> that bows to a stone shall become a lifeless image.

Translated by C.P. Brown

VANCHANATHA'S *MAHISASATAKAM*

The Mahisasatakam (roughly translated as 'Hundred Verses on a Buffalo') was composed by Vanchanatha, an eighteenth-century poet from Tanjore who wrote in Sanskrit. It is a poem of protest in which the farmer complains to his buffalo about the unjust ways of the rulers and landlords, giving us a rare glimpse into the rural and agricultural community of India of that time.

The king is a fool. The ministers are even greater fools. The wicked, the traitors of the country and the lowly who are up to snatch away everything, are deceiving both of them. Therefore, O buffalo, do not put any hope in this country of Chola beyond agriculture. At least I am left with a small piece of cloth to hide my private parts, you do not have even that!

~

Competing with each other to grab more of grains and money, the pseudo courageous niggardly persons have joined with the hope of seizing the country under their power. Having got the king's men under their control by bribes, they are forcibly snatching everything from the people. Let these wicked die.

~

O lord of buffalo, I have served you for long by acts (performed regularly) in order, such as feeding through grass-bundles, by bathing you in waters, by rubbing your body etc. Now I make this much request to the god Yama—who makes you his vehicle—that please make this Subedar, an enemy of mine, reach your premises quickly.

~

O buffalo! Why do you have to suffer so much by tilling and tilling this earth? Go and live happily with the councillors of today in the royal court. Don't entertain this silly thought that you neither have knowledge nor skills; because these councillors are utter fools in comparison to you, and you are master of speech amidst them.

~

My ears had overflowed by hearing the cruel words of wicked kings with their ever increasing corrupt power and ego. I had fallen out of the pittance of their petty grace. Then you made your bellowing sound which was elixir to my ears. O buffalo, it is good luck that you are still toiling in the fields, making effort for agriculture.

~

Their hearts roped and dragged by hope, the people in vain stand in the royal yards that are like traps, and belong to the kings who just appear horrible with all their foolishness and contempt. Pity that they would not approach our king—the buffalo, who is so soothing, who fulfils all the desires and protects us by all the fruits of this earth.

Translated by Radhavallabh Tripathi

THE BAULS

The Bauls are a religious sect of wandering mystic-poets from West Bengal and Bangladesh, with a distinct musical tradition. They are believed to have evolved in opposition to the hegemony of Hindu orthodoxy and Islamic clergy. Their philosophy, which they spread through their music, is an amalgamation of different schools of thought, such as Tantra, Vaishnavism, Buddhism and Sufism, transcending religion and rigid customs.

Madan

Madan was a Baul poet of the sixteenth or seventeenth century. His songs are fine examples of Baul philosophy, which rejects rituals and religious practices in favour of pure love and devotion as a pathway to god.

Thy path, O Lord, is hidden by mosque and temple:
I hear thine own call, but the guru stops the way.
What gives peace to my mind, sets the world ablaze,—
The cult of the One dies in the conflict of the many.
The door to it is closed by many a lock, of Koran, Puran and the
    rosary.
Even the way of renunciation is full of tribulation: Wherefore
    weeps Madan in despair.

Translated by Rabindranath Tagore

Lalon Fakir

Lalon Fakir (1774–1890) is one of the most celebrated figures in the Baul tradition. His poems—repudiating narrow creedal affiliations, religious and communal intolerances and hierarchies of class and caste—have influenced modern writers ranging from Rabindranth Tagore to Kazi Nazrul Islam and Allen Ginsberg.

Everyone wonders, 'What's Lalon's faith?'
Lalon says, 'I've never "seen" the face
of Faith with these eyes of mine!'

Circumcision marks a Muslim man,
what then marks a Muslim woman?

A Brahmin I recognize by the Holy thread;
how do I recognize a Brahmin woman?
Everyone wonders, 'What's Lalon's faith?'

Some wear a garland and some the tasbi,
that's what marks the Faiths apart.
But what marks them apart when
one is born or at the time of death?
Everyone wonders, 'What's Lalon faith?'

The whole world talks about Faith,
everyone displaying their pride!
Lalon says, 'My Faith has capsized
in this Market of Desire....'
Everyone wonders, 'What's Lalon's faith?'

Translated by Sudipto Chatterjee

~

There goes, there goes, my caste,
What a strange factory is this!
No one's prepared for truth-work,
All I see everywhere is tana na na

What caste were you when born?
What caste did you adopt here?
What caste will you be at death?
Think of it and tell me, will you?

Brahmin, Chandal, Chamar, Muchi,
All are purified by the same water,
Taste doesn't come from caution,
Yama won't spare any one of you

Eating from a whore in secret—
What harm does it cause faith?
Lalon says, what really is caste?
This delusion hasn't disappeared

Translated by Manash Firaq Bhattacharjee

CLASSICAL URDU POETS

Urdu poetry has a long history of dissent, often nuanced and sometimes expressed in complex, sophisticated metaphor. This is especially true of the ghazal form, which draws upon Sufi philosophy and imagery—mystically intoned love, intense longing, intoxication, wilderness, and the concept of 'fana'—annihilation of the self. Among the classical Urdu poets, Mir, Sauda and Ghalib produced some memorable verse that challenged, or disregarded, the conventions and dogmas of their age.

Sauda Mohammad Rafi

Sauda (1712–1781) was one of the early greats of Urdu poetry. Considered a master of the qasida, or the ode, he was also a brilliant satirist.

> Preacher, take that turban off your head before you sit for namaz;
> You might leave your head on the floor when you rise from prayer!

~

> Holy-man, I'll show you such errors of your faith;
> Too much religion has addled your brain.

~

> What have I to do with belief or unbelief, it's simple:
> I amuse myself watching the circus of mosque and temple.

~

> The preacher thought he saw an idol here last evening;
> Now he stalks the lane with a lamp all night, looking for Islam.

Mir Taqi Mir

Mir (1722–1810), whose popularity and reputation among lovers of Urdu poetry is second only to Ghalib's, is often referred to as Khuda-e-Sukhan (God of Poetry). Romantic, passionate and outspoken in his poetry, as in his life, he wrote against the notions of propriety and piety that were dominant in his time.

> You ask Mir for his faith and religion, but what can he tell you?
> He wears a tilak, he sits in a temple; he gave up Islam long ago.

~

What Ka'aba, what prayer, what Mecca, what pilgrim-dress?
We salute them from afar; our entire world is the beloved's lane.

~

The preacher who stands naked in the mosque, he was in the
    tavern last night;
Cloak and robe, collar and cap—the good man gifted them all
    away last night.

~

The mosque to you, to me the tavern
Hey preacher, to each his fate and fortune.

~

Far from the beloved, in the Ka'aba I thought I'd die!
Friends, I've fled the house of God and returned to life.

~

The tavern was ruined in the shadow of the mosque
Now the wine-bearer's gaze has taken revenge.

~

Mir, stay well away from the mighty of this age
Their riches have made beggars of us all.

~

The head that wears the crown with such pride today,
Tomorrow, right here, it will be wreathed in cries of mourning.

Mirza Asadullah Khan Ghalib

*Mirza Ghalib (1797–1869) is widely regarded as one of the greatest poets
of India and of the Urdu language. Like Mir, whom he admired, Ghalib was
opinionated, irreverent and an iconoclast. He openly criticized and ridiculed
orthodoxy, ritualism and moralizing, his favourite targets being mullahs and
self-righteous maulvis.*

Whenever I open my mouth you snap: And who are *you*?
Is it your culture that I must not speak, only listen to you?

~

You give us Heaven in exchange for the unholy life of the world;
I'm afraid this is wine without intoxication, it leaves me cold.

~

For the meddling angels who wait to ambush me with questions
    in the afterlife
I shall flavour my breath with stale wine; it is they who'll beg for
    mercy, not I.

~

The tavern and the preacher, never shall the twain meet! And yet
Was it not the good preacher I saw slink in as I staggered out?

~

A tavern, a gambling den beside every mosque—this is what we
    need.
Men of compassion as close to us as brow to eye—this is what we
    need.

~

There is no strength in the noose of the sacred thread or the rosary;
The pundit and the mullah will be tested today, it should be fun
    to see.

~

Not there today, but there before they were exiled, all:
These idols have a connection with the Ka'aba after all.

And why have we assumed everyone will get the same reply?
Come, let us also seek the Word, let us climb Mount Sinai.

~

Ghalib knows well the truth of Paradise, you see.
But it's a beautiful illusion, so he shall let it be.

~

Listen, God, why not stir a little hell into Paradise?
Why not a different garden for us to take a stroll?

~

Faith holds me back, but I'm drawn to unbelief;
The Ka'aba's now behind me, the Temple lies ahead.

All translations by T.P. Dhar

RAMMOHAN ROY AGAINST SATI

Raja Ram Mohan Roy (1772–1833), also known as Rammohan Roy, founded the Brahmo Sabha movement in 1828, which led to the Brahmo Samaj, an influential Bengali socio-religious reform movement. He is best known for his efforts to abolish the practice of Sati. The following is an extract from his response to an advocate of Sati, who insisted it ensures that women do not bring disgrace to their families by pursuing and enjoying worldly pleasures after the deaths of their husbands.

The reason you have now assigned for burning widows alive is indeed your true motive, as we are all aware; but the faults which you have imputed to women are not planted in their constitution by nature; it would be, therefore, grossly criminal to condemn that sex to death merely as a precaution. By ascribing to them all sorts of improper conduct, you have indeed successfully persuaded the Hindu community to look down upon them as contemptible and mischievous creatures, whence they have been subjected to constant miseries. I have, therefore, to offer a few remarks on this head.

Women are in general inferior to men in bodily strength and energy; consequently the male part of the community, taking advantage of their corporeal weakness, have denied to them those excellent merits that they are entitled to by nature, and afterwards they are apt to say that women are naturally incapable of acquiring those merits. But if we give the subject consideration, we may easily ascertain whether or not your accusation against them is consistent with justice. As to their inferiority in point of understanding, when did you ever afford them a fair opportunity of exhibiting their natural capacity? How then can you accuse them of want of understanding? If, after instruction in knowledge and wisdom, a person cannot comprehend or retain what has been taught him, we may consider him as deficient; but as you keep women generally void of education and acquirements, you cannot, therefore, in justice pronounce on their inferiority. On the contrary, Lilavati, Bhanumati, the wife of the prince of Karnat, and that of Kalidasa, are celebrated for their thorough knowledge of all the *Sastras*: moreover in the *Brihadaranyaka Upanishad* of the *Yajur Veda* it is clearly stated that Yajnavalkya imparted divine knowledge of the most difficult nature to his wife Maitreyi, who was able to follow and completely attain it!

Secondly. You charge them with want of resolution, at which I feel exceedingly surprised: for we constantly perceive, in a country where the name of death makes the male shudder, that the female, from her firmness of mind, offers to burn with the corpse of her deceased husband; and yet you accuse those women of deficiency in point of resolution.

Thirdly. With regard to their trustworthiness, let us look minutely into the conduct of both sexes, and we may be enable to ascertain which of them is the most frequently guilty of betraying friends. If we enumerate such women in each village or town as have been deceived by men, and such men as have been betrayed by women, I presume that the number of deceived women would be found ten times greater than that of betrayed men. Men are, in general, able to read and write, and manage public affairs, by which means they easily promulgate such faults as women occasionally commit, but never consider as criminal the misconduct of men towards women. One fault they have, it must acknowledged; which is, by considering others equally void of duplicity as themselves, to give their confidence too readily, from which they suffer such misery, even so far that some of them are misled to suffer themselves to be burnt to death.

In the fourth place, with respect to their subjection to vile passions, this may be judged of by the custom of marriage as to the respective sexes; for one man may marry two or three, sometimes even ten wives and upwards; while a woman, who marries but one husband, desires at his death to follow him, forsaking all worldly enjoyments, or to remain leading the austere life of an ascetic.

Fifthly. The accusation of the want of virtuous knowledge is an injustice. Observe what pain, what slighting, what contempt and what afflictions their virtue enables them to support! How many Kulin Brahmans are there who marry ten or fifteen wives for the sake of money, that never see the greater number of them after the day of marriage, and visit others only three or four times in the course of their life. Still amongst those women, most, even without seeing or receiving any support from their husbands, living dependent on their fathers or brothers, and suffering much distress, continue to preserve their virtue; and when Brahmans, or those of other tribes, bring their wives to live with them, what misery do the women not suffer? At marriage the wife is recognized as half of her husband, but in after-conduct they are treated worse than inferior animals. For the woman is employed to do the work of a slave in the house, such as, in her turn, to clean the place very early in the morning, whether cold or wet, to scour the dishes, to wash the floor, to cook night and day, to prepare and serve food for her husband, father, mother-in-law, sisters-in-law, brothers-in-law and friends and connections! (for amongst Hindus more than in other tribes relations long reside together, and on this account quarrels are more common amongst brothers respecting their worldly affairs.) If in the the preparation or serving up of the victuals they commit the smallest fault, what insult do they not receive from their husband, their mother-in-law and younger brothers of their husband? After all the male part of the family have satisfied themselves, the women content themselves with what may be left, whether sufficient in quantity or not. Where Brahmans or Kayasthas are not wealthy, their women are obliged to attend to their cows, and to prepare the cowdung for firing. In the afternoon they fetch water from the river or tank, and at night perform the office of menial servants in making the beds. In case of any fault or omission in the performance of those labours they receive injurious treatment. Should the husband acquire wealth, he indulges in criminal amours to her perfect knowledge and almost under her eyes, and does not see her perhaps once a month. As long as the husband is poor, she suffers every kind of trouble, and when he becomes rich, she is altogether heart-broken. All this pain and affliction their virtue alone enables them to support. Where a husband takes two or three wives to live with him, they are subjected to mental miseries and constant quarrels. Even this distressed situation they virtually endure. Sometimes it happens that the husband, from a preference for one of his wives, behaves cruelly to another. Amongst the lower classes, and those even of the better class who have not associated with good company, the wife, on the slightest fault, or even on bare suspicion of her misconduct, is chastised as a thief. Respect to virtue and their reputation generally makes them forgive even this treatment. If unable to bear such cruel usage, a wife leaves her husband's house to live separately from him, then the influence of the husband with the magisterial authority is generally sufficient to place her again in his hands; when, in revenge for her quitting him, he seizes every pretext to death. There are facts occurring every day, and not to be denied. What I lament is, that, seeing the women thus dependent, and exposed to every misery, you feel for them no compassion, that might exempt them from being tied down and burnt to death.

JYOTIRAO PHULE

Jyotirao Govindrao Phule (1827–1890), also known as Mahatma Jyotiba Phule, was an activist, social reformer and writer from Maharashtra. His work extended to many fields including eradication of untouchability and the caste system, women's emancipation and the reform of Hindu family life. In September 1873, Phule, along with his followers, formed the Satyashodhak Samaj (Society of Seekers of Truth) to attain equal rights for peasants and people from lower castes. He and his wife, Savitribai Phule, were pioneers of women's education in India, and they opened the first school for girls in India in August 1848. The following is an extract from the preface to Gulamgiri *(Slavery) published in 1873.*

Preface to *Slavery*

[The Brahmins] originally settled on the banks of the Ganges whence they gradually spread over the whole of India. In order, however, to keep a better hold on the people they devised that weird system of mythology, the ordination of caste, and the code of cruel and inhuman laws, to which we can find no parallel amongst other nations. They founded a system of priest-craft so galling in its tendency and operation, the like of which we can hardly find anywhere since the times of the Druids. The institution of Caste, which has been the main object of their laws, had no existence among them originally. That it was an after-creation of their deep cunning is evident from their own writings. The highest rights, the highest privileges and gifts, and everything that would make the life of a Brahmin easy, smooth going and happy, everything that would conserve or flatter their self-pride, were specially inculcated, and enjoined, whereas the Sudras and Atisudras were regarded with supreme hatred and contempt, and the commonest rights of humanity were denied [to] them. Their touch, nay, even their shadow, is deemed a pollution. They are considered as mere chattels, and their life of no more value than that of meanest reptile; for it is enjoined that if a Brahmin 'kill a cat or an ichneumon, the bird Chasha, or a frog or a dog, a lizard, an owl, a crow or a Sudra' he is absolved of his sin by performing the 'chaandryan prayaschit', a fasting penance, perhaps for a few hours or a day and requiring not much labour or trouble. While for a Sudra to kill a Brahmin is considered the most heinous offence he could commit, and the forfeiture of his life is the only punishment his crime is considered to merit. Happily for our Sudra brethren of the present day our enlightened British Rulers have not recognized these preposterous, inhuman and unjust penal enactments of the Brahmin legislators. They no doubt regard them more as ridiculous fooleries than as equitable laws. Indeed, no man possessing even a grain of common sense would regard them as otherwise. Any one, who feels disposed to look a little more into the laws and ordinances as embodied in the *Manava Dharma Shastra* and other works of the same class, would undoubtedly be impressed with the deep cunning underlying them all.

...Anyone who will consider well the whole history of Brahmin domination in India, and the thraldom under which it has retained the people even up to the present day, will agree with us in thinking that no language could be too harsh by which to characterize the selfish heartlessness and the consummate cunning of the Brahmin tyranny by which India has been so long governed. How far the Brahmins have succeeded in their endeavours to enslave the minds of the Sudras and Atisudras, those of them who have come to know the true state of matters know well to their cost. For generations past they have borne these chains of slavery and bondage. Innumerable Bhat writers, with the same objects as those of Manu and others of his class, added from time to time to the existing mass of legends, the idle phantasies of their own brains and palmed them off upon the ignorant masses as Divine inspiration, or as the acts of the Deity himself. The most immoral, inhuman, unjust actions and deeds have been attributed to that Being who is our Creator, Governor and Protector, and who is all Holiness himself. These blasphemous writings, the products of the distempered brains of these interlopers, were received as gospel truths, for to doubt them was considered as the most unpardonable of sins. This system of slavery, to which the Brahmins reduced the lower classes is in no respect inferior to that which obtained a few years ago in America. In the days of rigid Brahmin dominancy, so lately as that of the time of the Peshwa, my Sudra brethren had even greater hardships and oppression practiced upon them than what even the slaves in America had to suffer. To this system of selfish superstition and bigotry, we are to attribute the stagnation and all the evils under which India has been groaning for many centuries past.

...Under the guise of religion the Brahmin has his finger in everything, big or small, which the Sudra undertakes. Go to his house, to his field or to the court to which business may invite him, the Brahmin is there under some specious pretext or other, trying to squeeze out of him as much as his cunning and wily brain can manage. The Brahmin despoils the Sudra not only in his capacity of a priest, but does so in a variety of other ways. Having by his superior education and cunning monopolized all the higher places of emolument, the ingenuity of his ways is past finding out as the reader will find on an attentive perusal of this book. In the most insignificant village as in the largest town, the Brahmin is the all in all; the be-all and the end-all of the Ryot. He is the master, the ruler. The Patil of a village, the headman, is in fact a nonentity. The Kulkarni, the hereditary Brahmin village accountant, the notorious quarrel-monger, moulds the Patil according to his wishes. He is the temporal and spiritual adviser of the ryots, the Soucar in his necessities and the general referee in all matters. In most instances he plans active mischief by advising opposite parties differently, so that he may feather his own nest well. If we go up higher, to the Court of Mamlutdar, we find the same thing. The first anxiety of Mamlutdar is to get round him, if not his own relatives, his castemen to fill the various offices under him. These actively foment quarrels and are the media of all corrupt practices prevailing generally about these Courts. If a Sudra or Atisudra repairs to his Court; the treatment which he receives is akin to what the meanest reptile gets. Instead of his case receiving a patient and careful hearing, a choice lot of abuse is showered on his devoted head, and his prayer is set aside on some pretext or other. Whereas if one of his own castemen were to repair to the Court on the self-same business, he is received with all courtesy and there is hardly any time lost in getting the matter right. If we go up still higher to the Collector's and Revenue Commissioner's Courts and to the other Department of the Public Services, the Engineering, Educational, etc. the same system is carried out on a smaller or greater scale. The higher European officers generally view men and things through Brahmin spectacles, and hence the deplorable ignorance they often exhibit in forming a correct estimate of them.

...The Brahmin of the present time finds to some extent, like Othello, that his occupation is gone. But knowing full well this state of affairs, is the Brahmin inclined to make atonement for his past selfishness? Perhaps, it would have been useless to repine over what has been suffered and what has passed away, had the present state been all that is desirable. We know perfectly well that the Brahmin will not descend from his self-raised high pedestal and meet his Kunbee and low caste brethren on an equal footing without a struggle. Even the educated Brahmin who knows his exact position and how he has come by it, will not condescend to acknowledge the errors of his forefathers and willingly forego the long cherished false notions of his own superiority. At present not one has the moral courage to do what only duty demands, and as long as this continues, the sect distrusting and degrading another sect, the condition of the Sudras will remain unaltered, and India will never advance in greatness or prosperity.

Perhaps a part of the blame in bringing matters to this crisis may be justly laid to the credit of the Government. Whatever may have been their motives in providing ampler funds and greater facilities for higher education and neglecting that of the masses, it will be acknowledged by all that in justice to the latter this is not as it should be. It is an admitted fact that the greater portions of the revenues of the Indian Empire are derived from the Ryot's labour—from the sweat of his brow. The higher and richer classes contribute little or nothing to the State exchequer. A well-informed English writer states that:

> Our income is derived, not from surplus profits, but from capital, not from luxuries but from the poorest necessaries. It is the products of sin and tears.

That Government should expend profusely a large portion of revenue thus raised, on the education of the higher classes, for it is these only who take advantage of it, is anything but just or equitable. Their object in patronizing this virtual high-class education appears to be to prepare scholars, 'Who, it is thought, would in time vend learning without money and without price.' 'If we can inspire,' say they, 'the love of knowledge in the minds of the superior classes, the result will be a higher standard of morals in the cases of the individuals, a large amount of affection for the British Government, and an unconquerable desire to spread among their own countrymen the intellectual blessings which they have received.'

Regarding these objects of Government the writer, above alluded to, states that:

We have never heard of philosophy more benevolent and more utopian. It is proposed by men who witness the wondrous changes brought about in the Western world, purely by the agency of popular knowledge, to redress the defects of the two hundred million of India, by giving superior education to the superior classes and to them only. [...] We ask the friends of Indian Universities to favour us with a single example of the truth of their theory from the instance which have already fallen within the scope of their experience. They have educated many children of wealthy men, and have been the means of advancing very materially the worldly prospects of some of their pupils. But what contribution have these made to the great work of regenerating their fellowmen? How have they begun to act upon the masses? Have any of them formed classes at their own homes or elsewhere, for the instruction of their less fortunate or less wise countrymen? Or have they kept their knowledge to themselves, as a personal gift, not to be soiled by contact with the ignorant vulgar? Have they in any way shown themselves anxious to advance the general interests and repay philanthropy with patriotism? Upon what ground is it asserted that the best way to advance the moral and intellectual welfare of the people is to raise the standard of instruction among the higher classes? A glorious argument this for aristocracy, were it only tenable. To show the growth of the national happiness, it would only be necessary to refer to the number of pupils at the colleges and the lists of academic degrees. Each wrangler would be accounted a national benefactor, and the existence of Deans and Proctors would be associated, like the game laws and the ten-pound franchise, with the best interests of the Constitution.

Perhaps the most glaring tendency of the Government system of high-class education has been the virtual monopoly of all the higher offices under them by the Brahmins. If the welfare of the Ryot is at heart, if it is the duty of Government to check a host of abuses, it behoves them to narrow this monopoly, day by day, so as to allow a sprinkling of the other castes to get into the public service. Perhaps some might be inclined to say that it is not feasible in the present state of education. Our only reply is that if Government look a little less after higher education and more towards the education of the masses, the former being able to take care of itself, there would be no difficulty in training up a body of men every way qualified and perhaps far better in morals and manners.

My object in writing the present volume is not only to tell my Sudra brethren how they have been duped by the Brahmins, but also to open the eyes of Government to the pernicious system of high-class education which has hitherto been so persistently followed and which statemen like Sir George Campbell, the present Lieutenant Governor of Bengal, with broad and universal sympathies, are finding to be highly mischievous and pernicious to the interests of Government. I sincerely hope that Government will ere long see the error of their ways, trust less to writers or men who look through high-class spectacles and take the glory into their own hands of emancipating my Sudra brethren from the trammels of bondage which the Brahmins have woven round them like the coils of a serpent. It is no less the duty of such of my Sudra brethren as have received any education to place before Government the true state of their fellowmen and endeavour to the best of their power to emancipate themselves from Brahmin thraldom. Let there be schools for the Sudras in every village, but away with all Brahmin school-masters! The Sudras are the life and sinews of the country, and it is to them alone and [not] to the Brahmins that the Government must ever look to tide them over their difficulties, financial as well as political. If the hearts and minds of the Sudras are made happy and contented the British Government need have no fear for their loyalty in the future.

Jyotirao Phule
1 June 1873

SAVITRIBAI PHULE

Savitribai Jyotirao Phule (1831–1897) was an important member of the Social Reform movement in Maharashtra. Along with her husband, Jyotirao Phule, she worked to improve the condition of women in society and campaigned against discrimination based on caste and gender. Kavya Phule, a collection of her poems, was published posthumously in 1934. The following poems from Kavya Phule *have been selected and translated by* **Shanta Gokhale** *specially for this volume.*

Says Manu

Plough pushers and tillers of the land,
are brainless, says Manu.

Oh Brahmins, do not till the soil,
Manusmruti tells you.

Shudras are paying in this birth
for sins of their past lives.

A cunning, inhuman morality
thus man from man divides.

Arise and Learn

Arise brothers, lowest of low shudras
wake up, arise.
Rise and throw off the shackles
put by custom upon us.
Brothers, arise and learn.

Manu-loving Peshwas are dead and gone,
the English are here.
The ban on learning that Manu decreed
forever has disappeared.
With English knowledge-givers
we have a chance to learn.
A chance that was denied to us
for hundreds of years.

We will educate our children
and teach ourselves as well.
We will acquire knowledge
of religion and righteousness.
Let the thirst for books and learning
dance in our every vein.
Let each one struggle and forever erase
our low-caste stain.

In the kingdom of King Bali
let learning enter our soul.
Let our triumph echo around

like the roll of a temple drum.
And may the brahmin's evil eye
not fall upon our goal.

Let this be the clarion call
that drives us to arise
And break the chains of tradition
with education, our prize.

PANDITA RAMABAI SARASWATI

Pandita Ramabai (1858–1922) was a social reformer, a champion of women's emancipation, and a pioneer in education. She was one of the few women of her generation who were able to support themselves through their writings. A relentless critic of orthodox Hindu tradition and patriarchy amongst the higher castes, she converted to Christianity in 1883. The following is an excerpt from The High-Caste Woman *(1888) in which she highlighted the ways in which women were oppressed in Hindu caste society.*

Woman's Place in Religion and Society

Those who diligently and impartially read Sanskrit literature in the original, cannot fail to recognize the law-giver Manu as one of those hundreds who have done their best to make woman a hateful being in the world's eye. To employ her in housekeeping and kindred occupations is thought to be the only means of keeping her out of mischief, the blessed enjoyment of literary culture being denied her. She is forbidden to read the sacred scriptures, she has no right to pronounce a single syllable out of them. To appease her uncultivated, low kind of desire by giving her ornaments to adorn her person, and by giving her dainty food together with an occasional bow which costs nothing, are the highest honours to which a Hindu woman is entitled. She, the loving mother of the nation, the devoted wife, the tender sister and affectionate daughter is never fit for independence, and is 'as impure as falsehood itself.' She is never to be trusted; matters of importance are never to be committed to her.

I can say honestly and truthfully, that I have never read any sacred book in Sanskrit literature without meeting this kind of hateful sentiment about women. True, they contain here and there a kind word about them, but such words seem to me a heartless mockery, after having charged them, as a class, with crime and evil deeds.

...Virtues such as truthfulness, forbearance, fortitude, purity of heart and uprightness, are common to men and women, but religion, as the word is commonly understood, has two distinct natures in the Hindu law; the masculine and the feminine. The masculine religion has its own peculiar duties, privileges and honours. The feminine religion also has its peculiarities.

The sum and substance of the latter may be given in a few words: To look upon her husband as a god, to hope for salvation only through him, to be obedient to him in all things, never to covet independence, never to do anything but that which is approved by law and custom.

Marital Rights

'He only is a perfect man who consists of three persons united, his wife, himself and his offspring; thus says the Veda, and learned Brahmanas propound this maxim likewise, "The husband is declared to be one with the wife."'

—Manu, ix, 45

The wife is declared to be the 'marital property' of her husband, and is classed with 'cows, mares, female camels, slave-girls, buffalo-cows, she-goats and ewes.' (See *Manu* ix, 48–51)

The wife is punishable for treating her husband with aversion.

...But no such provision is made for the woman; on the contrary, she must remain with and revere her husband as a god, even though he be 'destitute of virtue, and seek pleasure elsewhere, or be devoid of good qualities, addicted to evil passion, fond of spirituous liquors or diseased,' and what not!

How much impartial justice is shown in the treatment of womankind by Hindu law, can be fairly understood after reading the above quotations. In olden times these laws were enforced by the community; a husband had absolute power over his wife; she could do nothing but submit to his will without uttering a word of protest. Now, under the so-called Christian British rule, the woman is in no better condition than of old. True, the husband cannot as in the golden age, take her wherever she may be found, and drag her to his house, but his absolute power over her person has not suffered in the least. He is now bound to bring suit against her in the courts of justice to claim his 'marital property,' if she be unwilling to submit to him by any other means.

A near relative of mine had been given, in her childhood, in marriage to a boy whose parents agreed to let him stay and be educated with her in her own home. No sooner however, had the marriage ceremony been concluded than they forgot their agreement; the boy was taken to the home of his parents where he remained to grow up to be a worthless dunce, while his wife through the kindness and advanced views of her father, developed into a bright young woman and well accomplished.

Thirteen years later, the young man came to claim his wife, but the parents had no heart to send their darling daughter with a beggar who possessed neither the power nor the sense to make an honest living, and was unable to support and protect his wife. The wife too, had no wish to go with him since he was a stranger to her; under the circumstances she could neither love nor respect him. A number of orthodox people in the community who saw no reason why a wife should not follow her husband even though he be a worthless man, collected funds to enable him to sue her and her parents in the British Court of Justice. The case was examined with due ceremony and the verdict was given in the man's favour, according to Hindu law.[1] The wife was doomed to go with him. Fortunately she was soon released from this sorrowful world by cholera. Whatever may be said of the epidemics that yearly assail our country, they are not unwelcome among the unfortunate women who are thus persecuted by social, religious and state laws. Many women put an end to their earthly sufferings by committing suicide. Suits at law between husband and wife are remarkable for their rarity in the British Courts in India, owing to the ever submissive conduct of women who suffer silently, knowing that the gods and justice always favour the men.

The case of Rakhmabai, that has lately profoundly agitated Hindu society, is only one of thousands of the same class. The remarkable thing about her is that she is a well-educated lady, who was brought up under the loving care of her father, and had learned from him how to defend herself against the assaults of social and religious bigotries. But as soon as her father died the man who claimed to be her husband, brought suit against her in the court of Bombay. The young woman bravely defended herself, declining to go to live with the man on the ground that the marriage that was concluded without her consent could not be legally considered as such. Mr Justice Pinhey, who tried the case in the first instance, had a sufficient sense of justice to refuse to force the lady to live with her husband against her will. Upon hearing this decision, the conservative party all over India rose as one man and girded their loins to denounce the helpless woman and her handful of friends. They encouraged the alleged husband to stand his ground firmly, threatening the British government with public displeasure if it failed to keep its agreement to force the woman to go to live with the husband according to Hindu law. Large sums were collected for the benefit of this man, Dadajee, to enable him to appeal against the decision to the full bench, whereupon, to the horror of all right-thinking people, the chief-justice sent back the case to the lower court for re-trial on its merits, as judged by the Hindu laws. The painful termination of this trial, I have in a letter written by my dear friend Rakhmabai herself, bearing date March 18th, 1887, Bombay. I quote from her letter:

> The learned and civilized judges of the full bench are determined to enforce, in this enlightened age, the inhuman laws enacted in barbaric times, four thousand years ago. They have not only commanded me to go to live with the man, but also have obliged me to pay the costs of the dispute. Just think of this extraordinary decision! Are we not living under the impartial British government, which boasts of giving equal justice to all, and are we not ruled by the Queen-Empress Victoria, herself a woman? My dear friend, I shall have been cast into the State prison when this letter reaches you; this is because I do not, and cannot obey the order of Mr Justice Farran.
>
> There is no hope for women in India, whether they be under Hindu rule or British rule; some are of the opinion that my case, so cruelly decided, may bring about a better condition for woman by turning public opinion in her favour, but I fear it will be otherwise. The hard-hearted mothers-in-law will now be greatly strengthened, and will induce their sons, who have for some reason or other, been slow to enforce the conjugal rights to sue their wives in the British Courts, since they are now fully assured that under no circumstances can the British government act adversely to the Hindu law.

Taught by the experience of the past, we are not at all surprised at this decision of the Bombay court. Our only wonder is that a defenceless woman like Rakhmabai dared to raise her voice in the face of the powerful Hindu law, the mighty British government, the one hundred and twenty-nine million men and the three hundred and thirty million gods of the Hindus, all these having conspired together to crush her into nothingness. We cannot blame the English government for not defending a helpless woman; it is only fulfilling its agreement made with the male population of India. How very true are the words of the Saviour, 'Ye cannot serve God and Mammon.' Should England serve God by protecting a helpless woman against the powers and principalities of ancient institutions, Mammon would surely be displeased, and British profit and rule in India might be endangered thereby. Let us wish it success, no matter if that success be achieved at the sacrifice of the rights and the comfort of over one hundred million women.

Meanwhile, we shall patiently await the advent of the kingdom of righteousness, wherein the weak, the lowly and the helpless shall be made happy because the great Judge Himself 'shall wipe away all tears from their eyes.'

Note

1. In all cases except those directly connected with life and death, the British Government is bound according to the treaties concluded with the inhabitants of India, not to interfere with their social and religious customs and laws; judicial decisions are given accordingly.

TARABAI SHINDE

Tarabai Shinde (1850–1910) was a feminist activist who protested against patriarchy and caste discrimination in nineteenth-century India. She is known for her essay, Stri Purush Tulana (A Comparison between Women and Men), *originally published in Marathi in 1882. The essay is a critique of upper-caste patriarchy, and is often considered the first modern Indian feminist text. It was very controversial for its time as it identified the Hindu religious scriptures themselves as a source of women's oppression. The following is an extract from it.*

This incredible world was created by God and it was certainly also God who created both Men and Women. So how can anyone say that only women and their bodies are responsible for all the wickedness and vices that exist? My desire was to make this absolutely clear and I have, therefore, written this little book to uphold and defend the honour of the women of this country whom I consider as my sisters. Let me make it clear that I am not discussing any specific castes or genealogies. My aim is to make a comparison only between women and men.

~

Nowadays newspapers are full of reports about the wicked things that poor powerless women supposedly do. Why doesn't someone step forward and put an end to these disastrous allegations?

Just note how the custom of widows not being allowed to remarry has become widespread like a pernicious malady all over the country among all castes. The anguish and suffering of these widows is unimaginable, not to speak of the disastrous effects of this custom. Stridharma does not lie in making an individual a prisoner in her own home and controlling her. Actually, what a woman does with her eyes and thoughts can make her just as guilty. So what happens when all the joyous signs of a woman's married state are snatched away from her, if her hair is shaved off and the vermillion from her forehead is obliterated? Women will continue to have the same hearts and emotions and will also continue to harbour the same thoughts of good and evil. It is possible to strip and expose the outside in its nakedness, but is it really possible to do this to the inside? We have to ask ourselves what stridharma actually means. Does it mean always obeying orders from your husband and doing everything he wants? He can hit you and abuse you, go to whores, squander his money on drinking and gambling and then yell that he has no money, steal, commit manslaughter, betray and slander others and blackmail them for bribes. He has license to do all these things but when he comes home, his wife, because of stridharma, has to overlook everything and tell herself that he is only a mischief-maker, just like our little baby Krishna, who stole the milkmaids' curds and milk and blamed Chandravalli for it. After that she has to smile at him and offer him her devotion and do his bidding as if he was nothing less than a Paramatma.

Is it possible to have faith in the idea of stridharma once an effort is made to think about what is good and evil? Isn't it likely that these ideas would change immediately? When a man runs off with another man's wife it is not against the rule of pavitrata. He in fact would find a thousand reasons for flouting the rule. But you are obliged to worship your husband because for you he is supposed to be God incarnate. We all know the story of Savitri, which is supposed to be the gold standard of pavitrata. In this day and age is there any woman who would try to follow such an example to the letter? That fable tells us that a wife should smile at her husband when he kicks her and sweetly tell him: 'My lord, you will hurt your foot if you do that.' Then she should waste no time in caressing and massaging his foot. She is not to shed a tear if he raises his fist at her or even if he beats her with a stick. Hers is to smile and say, 'My lord, your palms must be stinging, please allow me to rub them with butter.' And run to the market to fetch some if she finds there is no butter in the house, or get it from the neighbour's.

~

Nowadays who really follows each and every tenet of the shastras or expects others to? If a husband is supposed to be a god-like personage to his wife then shouldn't he be obliged to behave like one? And if a wife is really supposed to worship her husband like a loyal devotee, then isn't it only fair that a husband should reciprocate with kindly concern and share his wife's happiness and suffering like a true god would?

BALGANGADHAR TILAK

Balgangadhar Tilak (1856–1920) was one of the first leaders of the Indian independence movement and was known as 'The Father of the Indian Unrest'. He published two newspapers, Kesari *and* The Mahratta, *in which he bitterly criticized the British government. In 1908, he was imprisoned in Mandalay for six years on charges of seditious writing. In 1916, he and Annie Besant founded the Home Rule League. The following speech was delivered by Tilak at Nashik in 1917, on the first anniversary of the formation of the Home Rule League.*

Swaraj Is My Birth Right

I am young in spirit though old in body. I do not wish to lose this privilege of youth. Whatever I am going to speak today is eternally young. The body might grow old, decrepit and it might perish, but the soul is immortal. Similarly, if there might be an apparent lull in our home rule activities, the freedom of the spirit behind it is eternal and indestructible, and it will secure liberty for us. Freedom is my birthright. So long as it is awake within me, I am not old. No weapon can cut this spirit, no fire can burn it, no water can wet it, no wind can dry it. We ask for home rule and we must get it. The science which ends in home rule is the science of politics and not the one which ends in slavery. The science of politics is the 'veda' of the country. You have a soul and I only want to awaken it. I want to tear off the blind that has been let down by ignorant, conniving and selfish people. The science of politics consists of two parts. The first is divine and the second is demonic. The slavery of a nation constitutes the latter. There cannot be a moral justification for the demonic part of the science of politics. A nation which might justify this, is guilty of sin in the sight of God. Some people do and some do not have the courage to declare what is harmful for them. Political and religious teaching consists in giving the knowledge of this principle.

Religious and political teachings are not separate, though they appear to be so on account of foreign rule. All philosophies are included in the science of politics.

Who does not know the meaning of home rule? Who does not want it? Would you like it if I enter your house and take possession of your kitchen? I must have the right to manage the affairs in my own house. We are told we are not fit for home rule. A century has passed and the British Rule has not made us fit for home rule; now we will make our own efforts and make ourselves fit for it. To offer irrelevant excuses, to hold out any temptations and to make other offers will be putting a stigma on English policy. England is trying to protect the small state of Belgium with India's help; how can it then say that we should not have home rule? Those who find fault with us are avaricious people. But there are people who find fault even with the all-merciful God. We must work hard to save the soul of our nation without caring for anything. The good of our country consists in guarding this birthright. The Congress has passed this home rule resolution.

In practical politics some futile objections are raised to oppose our desire for swaraj. Illiteracy of the bulk of our people is one of such objections; but to my mind it ought not to be allowed to stand in our way. It would be sufficient for us even if the illiterate in our country have only a vague conception of swaraj, just as it all goes well with them if they simply have a hazy idea about God. Those who can efficiently manage their own affairs may be illiterate; but they are not idiots. They are as intelligent as any other educated man and if they could understand their immediate concerns they would not find any difficulty in grasping the principle of swaraj. If illiteracy is not a disqualification in civil law there is no reason why it should not be so in nature's law also. Even the illiterate are our brethren: they have the same rights and are actuated by the same aspirations. It is, therefore, our bounden duty to awaken the masses. Circumstances have changed, and are favourable. The voice has gone forth 'Now or Never'. Rectitude and constitutional agitation is alone what is expected of you. Turn not back, and confidently leave the ultimate issue to the benevolence of the Almighty.

RABINDRANATH TAGORE

Rabindranath Tagore (1861–1941) was a writer, poet, artist, musician and cultural reformer. In 1916, he went to USA to deliver lectures on the concept of nationalism. In his essay 'The Nation,' he explains the idea of a nation as a 'cult' that encourages mob mentality and negates individuality and creativity. He believed that a nation is a mere socio-political construct and denounced the idea of patriotism. The following is an extract from 'Nationalism in India,' written in 1917.

Nationalism in India

Our real problem in India is not political. It is social. This is a condition not only prevailing in India, but among all nations. I do not believe in an exclusive political interest. Politics in the West have dominated Western ideals, and we in India are trying to imitate you. We have to remember that in Europe, where peoples had their racial unity from the beginning, and where natural resources were insufficient for the inhabitants, the civilization has naturally taken the character of political and commercial aggressiveness. For on the one hand they had no internal complications, and on the other [hand] they had to deal with neighbours who were strong and rapacious. To have perfect combination among themselves and a watchful attitude of animosity against others was taken as the solution of their problems. In former days they organized and plundered, in the present age the same spirit continues—and they organize and exploit the whole world.

But from the earliest beginnings of history, India has had her own problem constantly before her—it is the race problem. Each nation must be conscious of its mission and we, in India, must realize that we cut a poor figure when we are trying to be political, simply because we have not yet been finally able to accomplish what was set before us by our providence.

... India has never had a real sense of nationalism. Even though from childhood I had been taught that the idolatry of Nation is almost better than reverence for God and humanity, I believe I have outgrown that teaching, and it is my conviction that my countrymen will gain truly their India by fighting against that education which teaches them that a country is greater than the ideals of humanity.

... I am not against one nation in particular, but against the general idea of all nations. What is the Nation?

It is the aspect of a whole people as an organized power. This organization incessantly keeps up the insistence of the population on becoming strong and efficient. But this strenuous effort after strength and efficiency drains man's energy from his higher nature where he is self-sacrificing and creative. For thereby man's power of sacrifice is diverted from his ultimate object, which is moral, to the maintenance of this organization, which is mechanical. Yet in this he feels all the satisfaction of moral exaltation and therefore becomes supremely dangerous to humanity. He feels relieved of the urging of his conscience when he can transfer his responsibility to this machine which is the creation of his intellect and not of his complete moral personality. By this device the people which loves freedom perpetuates slavery in a large portion of the world with the comfortable feeling of pride of having done its duty; men who are naturally just can be cruelly unjust both in their act and their thought, accompanied by a feeling that they are helping the world in receiving its deserts; men who are honest can blindly go on robbing others of their human rights for self-aggrandizement, all the while abusing the deprived for not deserving better treatment. We have seen in our everyday life even small organizations of business and profession produce callousness of feeling in men who are not naturally bad, and we can well imagine what a moral havoc it is causing in a world where whole peoples are furiously organizing themselves for gaining wealth and power.

Nationalism is a great menace. It is the particular thing which for years has been at the bottom of India's troubles. And inasmuch as we have been ruled and dominated by a nation that is strictly political in its attitude, we have tried to develop within ourselves, despite our inheritance from the past, a belief in our eventual political destiny.

There are different parties in India, with different ideals. Some are struggling for political independence. Others think that the time has not arrived for that, and yet believe that India should have the rights that the English colonies have. They wish to gain autonomy as far as possible.

In the beginning of our history of political agitation in India there was not that conflict between parties which there is to-day. In that time there was a party known as the Indian Congress; it had no real programme. They had a few grievances for redress by the authorities. They wanted larger representation in the Council House, and more freedom in the Municipal government. They wanted scraps of things, but they had no constructive ideal. Therefore I was lacking in enthusiasm for their methods. It was my conviction that what India most needed was constructive work coming from within herself. In this work we must take all risks and go on doing our duties which by right are ours, though in the teeth of persecution; winning moral victory at every step, by our failure, and suffering. We must show those who are over us that we have the strength of moral power in ourselves, the power to suffer for truth. Where we have nothing to show, we only have to beg. It would be mischievous if the gifts we wish for were granted to us *right* now, and I have told my countrymen, time and time again, to combine for the work of creating opportunities to give vent to our spirit of self-sacrifice, and not for the purpose of begging.

The party, however, lost power because the people soon came to realize how futile was the half policy adopted by them. The party split, and there arrived the Extremists, who advocated independence of action, and discarded the begging method—the easiest method of relieving one's mind from his responsibility towards his country. Their ideals were based on Western history. They had no sympathy with the special problems of India. They did not recognize the patent fact that there were causes in our social organization which made the Indian incapable of coping with the alien. What would we do if, for any reason, England was driven away? We should simply be victims for other nations. The same social weaknesses would prevail. The thing we, in India, have to think of is this—to remove those social customs and ideals which have generated a want of self-respect and a complete dependence on those above us—a state of affairs which has been brought about entirely by the domination in India of the caste system, and the blind and lazy habit of relying upon the authority of traditions that are incongruous anachronisms in the present age.

... India has all along been trying experiments in evolving a social unity within which all the different peoples could be held together, yet fully enjoying the freedom of maintaining their own differences. The tie has been as loose as possible, yet as close as the circumstances permitted. This has produced something like a United States of a social federation, whose common name is Hinduism.

India had felt that diversity of races there must be and should be whatever may be its drawback, and you can never coerce nature into your narrow limits of convenience without paying one day very dearly for it. In this India was right; but what she failed to realize was that in human beings differences are not like the physical barriers of mountains, fixed forever—they are fluid with life's flow, they are changing their courses and their shapes and volume.

Therefore in her caste regulations India recognized differences, but not the mutability which is the law of life. In trying to avoid collisions she set up boundaries of immovable walls, thus giving to her numerous races the negative benefit of peace and order but not the positive opportunity of expansion and movement. She accepted nature where it produces diversity, but ignored it where it uses that diversity for its world-game of infinite permutations and combinations. She treated life in all truth where it is manifold, but insulted it where it is ever moving. Therefore Life departed from her social system and in its place she is worshipping with all ceremony the magnificent cage of countless compartments that she has manufactured.

The same thing happened where she tried to ward off the collisions of trade interests. She associated different trades and professions with different castes. It had the effect of allaying for good the interminable jealousy and hatred of competition—the competition which breeds cruelty and makes the atmosphere thick with lies and deception. In this also India laid all her emphasis upon the law of heredity, ignoring the law of mutation, and thus gradually reduced arts into crafts and genius into skill.

...The general opinion of the majority of the present-day nationalists in India is that we have come to a final completeness in our social and spiritual ideals, the task of the constructive work of society having been done several thousand years before we were born, and that now we are free to employ all our activities in the political direction. We never dream of blaming our social inadequacy as the origin of our present helplessness, for we have accepted as the creed of our nationalism that this social system has been perfected for all time to come by our ancestors who had the superhuman vision of all eternity, and supernatural power for making infinite provision for future ages. Therefore for all our miseries and shortcomings we hold responsible the historical surprises that burst upon us from outside. This is the reason why we think that our one task is to build a political miracle of freedom upon the quicksand of social slavery. In fact we want to dam up the true course of our own historical stream and only borrow power from the sources of other peoples' history.

Those of us in India who have come under the delusion that mere political freedom will make us free have accepted their lessons from the West as the gospel truth and lost their faith in humanity. We must remember whatever weakness we cherish in our society will become the source of danger in politics. The same inertia which leads us to our idolatry of dead forms in social institutions will create in our politics prison houses with immovable walls. The narrowness of sympathy which makes it possible for us to impose upon a considerable portion of humanity the galling yoke of inferiority will assert itself in our politics in creating tyranny of injustice.

When our nationalists talk about ideals, they forget that the basis of nationalism is wanting. The very people who are upholding these ideals are themselves the most conservative in their social practice. Nationalists say, for example, look at Switzerland, where, in spite of race differences, the peoples have solidified into a nation. Yet, remember that in Switzerland the races can mingle, they can intermarry, because they are of the same blood. In India there is no common birthright. And when we talk of Western Nationality we forget that the nations there do not have that physical repulsion, one for the other, that we have between different castes. Have we an instance in the whole world where a people who are not allowed to mingle their blood shed their blood for one another except by coercion or for mercenary purposes? And can we ever hope that these moral barriers against our race amalgamation will not stand in the way of our political unity?

Then again we must give full recognition to this fact that our social restrictions are still tyrannical, so much so as to make men cowards. If a man tells me he has heterodox ideas, but that he cannot follow them because he would be socially ostracized, I excuse him for having to live a life of untruth, in order to live at all. The social habit of mind which impels us to make the life of our fellow-beings a burden to them where they differ from us even in such a thing as their choice of food is sure to persist in our political organization and result in creating engines of coercion to crush every rational difference which is the sign of life. And tyranny will only add to the inevitable lies and hypocrisy in our political life. Is the mere name of freedom so valuable that we should be willing to sacrifice for its sake our moral freedom?

The intemperance of our habits does not immediately show its effects when we are in the vigour of our youth. But it gradually consumes that vigour, and when the period of decline sets in then we have to settle accounts and pay off our debts, which leads us to insolvency. In the West you are still able to carry your head high though your humanity is suffering every moment from its dipsomania of organizing power. India also in the heyday of her youth could carry in her vital organs the dead weight of her social organizations stiffened to rigid perfection, but it has been fatal to her, and has produced a gradual paralysis of her living nature. And this is the reason why the educated community of India has become insensible of her social needs. They are taking the very immobility of our social structures as the sign of their perfection—and because the healthy feeling of pain is dead in the limbs of our social organism they delude themselves into thinking that it needs no ministration. Therefore they think that all their energies need their only scope in the political field. It is like a man whose legs have become shrivelled and useless, trying to delude himself that these limbs have grown still because they have attained their ultimate salvation, and all that is wrong about him is the shortness of his sticks...

Letter from Rabindranath Tagore to Lord Chelmsford, Viceroy of India

On 13 April 1919 a group of non-violent protestors had gathered in Jallianwala Bagh in Amritsar, Punjab. Without any warning, the British Army, on the orders of Colonel Reginald Dyer, opened fire on this gathering. Hundreds were killed and thousands gravely injured. In protest, Rabindranath Tagore returned the Knighthood conferred upon him by the British Empire.

Calcutta
31 May 1919

Your Excellency,

The enormity of the measures taken by the Government in the Punjab for quelling some local disturbances has, with a rude shock, revealed to our minds the helplessness of our position as British subjects in India. The disproportionate severity of the punishments inflicted upon the unfortunate people and the methods of carrying them out, we are convinced, are without parallel in the history of civilized governments, barring some conspicuous exceptions, recent and remote. Considering that such treatment has been meted out to a population, disarmed and resourceless, by a power which has the most terribly efficient organization for destruction of human lives, we must strongly assert that it can claim no political expediency, far less moral justification. The accounts of the insults and sufferings by our brothers in Punjab have trickled through the gagged silence, reaching every corner of India, and the universal agony of indignation roused in the hearts of our people has been ignored by our rulers—possibly congratulating themselves for what they imagine as salutary lessons. This callousness has been praised by most of the Anglo-Indian papers, which have in some cases gone to the brutal length of making fun of our sufferings, without receiving the least check from the same authority—relentlessly careful in smothering every cry of pain and expression of judgement from the organs representing the sufferers. Knowing that our appeals have been in vain and that the passion of vengeance is blinding the nobler vision of statesmanship in our Government, which could so easily afford to be magnanimous as befitting its physical strength and moral tradition, the very least that I can do for my country is to take all consequences upon myself in giving voice to the protest of the millions of my countrymen, surprised into a dumb anguish of terror. The time has come when badges of honour make our shame glaring in the incongruous context of humiliation, and I for my part wish to stand, shorn of all special distinctions, by the side of those of my countrymen, who, for their so-called insignificance, are liable to suffer degradation not fit for human beings.

These are the reasons which have painfully compelled me to ask Your Excellency, with due deference and regret, to relieve me of my title of Knighthood, which I had the honour to accept from His Majesty the

King at the hands of your predecessor, for whose nobleness of heart I still entertain great admiration.

Yours faithfully,
Rabindranath Tagore

HASRAT MOHANI

Maulana Fazal-ul-Hasan (1875–1951), popularly known as Hasrat Mohani, was a freedom-fighter, a fearless journalist and a renowned Urdu poet. A fierce advocate of Bal Gangadhar Tilak's radical thoughts, he was the first to demand complete freedom and was one of the first Indians to be imprisoned by the British authorities for his subversive political activities. He coined the term 'Inquilab Zindabad' in 1921.

The following are selections from his couplets concerned with themes of love beauty and freedom.

> The flight of fancy was sin for him,
> How distant is the dry ascetic from poetic sensibility.

~

> The capitalists are a-tremble with fear,
> As the strength of the mazdoor is apparent to the world now!

~

> If this is the gift of Love, I wonder Hasrat,
> What difference will be left between the Brahmin and the Sheikh.

~

> Worshipping thy Beauty is no sin, Hasrat,
> Let the moralist criticize to his heart's content.

~

> Free is thought, free the soul,
> Why then confine oneself in a body, Hasrat?

~

As your anger rises at my 'sin' of loving you,
So does my desire for martyrdom grow stronger in me.

Translated by Khadija Azeem

~

Mohani first proposed the idea of non-cooperation and boycott of English goods in 1919, but it was opposed by Gandhi then. Eventually in September 1920, a resolution for total non-cooperation with the British government was passed. In 1921, when the Civil Disobedience Movement took a violent turn, Gandhi went on a fast unto death. Mohani, unhappy with Gandhi's insistence on non-violence, placed a resolution for complete independence from British rule in the general body meetings of the National Congress, Khilafat Committee and the Muslim League, which had gathered to find a solution and persuade Gandhi to discontinue his fast. However, the resolution was rejected at all these meetings. The following is an excerpt from the fiery presidential address he delivered at the Muslim League session:

They [National Congress] should either avoid to claim non-cooperation as their belief, or they must free the same from the bonds of violence and non-violence, both. It is not within our power to keep the non-cooperation peaceful, because it can remain so only if and when the British Sarkar restrains from the use of chains and shackles; but when it takes to guns and gallows, well, then it is just not possible for the non-cooperation movement to remain peaceful. Having thoroughly discussed the question amongst themselves the Hindus and Muslims should jointly request Mahatma Gandhi to declare self-government, so that in the days to come the English are not left with any possibility to deceive the Indian people, nor are we left to be deceived. Having declared the self-government as the final goal, the Congress and the League would be left with just the task of protecting Swaraj. Dear Indians the most suitable date to declare self-government is 1 January 1922, because, thus our promise to achieve Swaraj will also be fulfilled within a year of that.

MAHATMA GANDHI

Mohandas Karamchand Gandhi (1869–1948), also known as Mahatma Gandhi and Bapu, was the principal political and spiritual leader of India's independence struggle. After training as a barrister, he spent twenty years in South Africa where he fought for the rights of the Indians settled there and developed the concept of satyagraha. Upon returning to India, he spearheaded the independence movement by employing the ideas of satyagraha, non-cooperation and civil disobedience against the British government.

Statement at Court, 1922

After the suspension of the Non-cooperation Movement, the British government came down heavily on agitators. Mahatma Gandhi, editor, and Shri Shankarlal Ghelabhai Banker, printer and publisher, of Young India, were charged with sedition and arrested on 10 March 1922. Following is the statement Gandhi delivered on 18 March 1922 at his trial. It is considered to be the most scathing indictment of British rule in India.

I owe it perhaps to the Indian public and to the public in England, to placate which this prosecution is mainly taken up, that I should explain why from a staunch loyalist and cooperator, I have become an uncompromising disaffectionist and non-cooperator. To the court too I should say why I plead guilty to the charge of promoting disaffection towards the Government established by law in India.

My public life began in 1893 in South Africa in troubled weather. My first contact with British authority in that country was not of a happy character. I discovered that as a man and an Indian, I had no rights. More correctly I discovered that I had no rights as a man because I was an Indian.

But I was not baffled. I thought that this treatment of Indians was an excrescence upon a system that was intrinsically and mainly good. I gave the Government my voluntary and hearty co-operation, criticizing it freely where I felt it was faulty but never wishing its destruction.

Consequently when the existence of the Empire was threatened in 1899 by the Boer challenge, I offered my services to it, raised a volunteer ambulance corps and served at several actions that took place for the relief of Ladysmith. Similarly in 1906, at the time of the Zulu 'revolt', I raised a stretcher-bearer party and served till the end of the 'rebellion'. On both the occasions I received medals and was even mentioned in dispatches. For my work in South Africa I was given by Lord Hardinge a Kaiser-i-Hind gold medal. When the war broke out in 1914 between England and Germany, I raised a volunteer ambulance corps in London, consisting of the then resident Indians in London, chiefly students. Its work was acknowledged by the authorities to be valuable. Lastly, in India when a special appeal was made at the War Conference in Delhi in 1918 by Lord Chelmsford for recruits, I struggled at the cost of my health to raise a corps in Kheda, and the response was being made when the hostilities ceased and orders were received that no more recruits were wanted. In all these efforts at service, I was actuated by the belief that it was possible by such services to gain a status of full equality in the Empire for my countrymen.

The first shock came in the shape of the Rowlatt Act—a law designed to rob the people of all real freedom. I felt called upon to lead an intensive agitation against it. Then followed the Punjab horrors beginning with the massacre at Jallianwala Bagh and culminating in crawling orders, public flogging and other indescribable humiliations. I discovered too that the plighted word of the Prime Minister to the Mussalmans of India regarding the integrity of Turkey and the holy places of Islam was not likely to be fulfilled. But in spite of the forebodings and the grave warnings of friends, at the Amritsar Congress in 1919, I fought for co-operation and working of the Montague–Chelmsford reforms, hoping that the Prime Minister would redeem his promise to the Indian Mussalmans, that the Punjab wound would be healed, and that the reforms, inadequate and unsatisfactory though they were, marked a new era of hope in the life of India.

But all that hope was shattered. The Khilafat promise was not to be redeemed. The Punjab crime was whitewashed and most culprits went not only unpunished but remained in service, and some continued to draw pensions from the Indian revenue and in some cases were even rewarded. I saw too that not only did the reforms not mark a change of heart, but they were only a method of further draining India of her wealth and of prolonging her servitude. I came reluctantly to the conclusion that the British connection had made India more helpless than she ever was before, politically and economically. A disarmed India has no power of resistance against any aggressor if she wanted to engage in an armed conflict with him. So much is this the case that some of our best men consider that India must take generations, before she can achieve Dominion Status. She has become so poor that she has little power of resisting famines. Before the British advent, India spun and wove in her millions of cottages, just the supplement she needed for adding to her meagre agricultural resources. This cottage industry, so vital for India's existence, has been ruined by incredibly heartless and inhuman processes as described by English witnesses. Little do town-dwellers know how the semi-starved masses of India are slowly sinking to lifelessness. Little do they know that their miserable comfort represents the brokerage they get for the work they do for the foreign exploiter, that the profits and the brokerage are sucked from the masses. Little do they realize that the Government established by law in British India is carried on for this exploitation of the masses. No sophistry, no jugglery in figures, can explain away the evidence that the skeletons in many villages present to the naked eye. I have no doubt whatsoever that both England and the town-dweller of India will have to answer, if there is a God above, for this crime against humanity, which is perhaps unequalled in history. The law itself in this country has been used to serve the foreign exploiter. My unbiased examination of the Punjab Martial Law cases has led me to believe that at least 95 per cent of convictions were wholly bad. My experience of political cases in India leads me to the conclusion, in nine out of every ten, the condemned men were totally innocent. Their crime consisted in the love of their country. In ninety-nine cases out of hundred, justice has been denied to Indians as against Europeans in the courts of India. This is not an exaggerated picture. It is the experience of almost every Indian who has had anything to do with such cases. In my opinion, the administration of the law is thus prostituted, consciously or unconsciously, for the benefit of the exploiter.

The greater misfortune is that the Englishmen and their Indian associates in the administration of the country do not know that they are engaged in the crime I have attempted to describe. I am satisfied that many Englishmen and Indian officials honestly believe that they are administering one of the best systems devised in the world, and that India is making steady, though, slow progress. They do not know that a subtle but effective system of terrorism and an organized display of force on the one hand, and the deprivation of all powers of retaliation or self-defence on the other, has emasculated the people and induced in them the habit of simulation. This awful habit has added to the ignorance and the self-deception of the administrators. Section 124 A, under which I am happily charged, is perhaps the prince among the political sections of the Indian Penal Code designed to suppress the liberty of the citizen. Affection cannot be manufactured or regulated by law. If one has no affection for a person or system, one should be free to give the fullest expression to his disaffection, so long as he does not contemplate, promote or incite to violence. But the section under which Mr Banker and I are charged is one under which mere promotion of disaffection is a crime. I have studied some of the cases tried under it; I know that some of the most loved of India's patriots have been convicted under it. I consider it a privilege, therefore, to be charged under that section. I have endeavoured to give in their briefest outline the reasons for my disaffection. I have no personal ill-will against any single administrator, much less can I have any disaffection towards the King's person. But I hold it to be a virtue to be disaffected towards a Government which in its totality has done more harm to India than any previous system. India is less manly under the British rule than she ever was before. Holding such a belief, I consider it to be a sin to have affection for the system. And it has been a precious privilege for me to be able to write what I have in the various articles tendered in evidence against me.

In fact, I believe that I have rendered a service to India and England by showing in non-cooperation the way out of the unnatural state in which both are living. In my opinion, non-cooperation with evil is as much a duty as is cooperation with good. But in the past, non-cooperation has been deliberately expressed in violence to the evil-doer. I am endeavouring to show to my countrymen that violent non-cooperation only multiplies evil, and that as evil can only be sustained by violence, withdrawal of support of evil requires complete abstention from violence. Non-violence implies voluntary submission to the penalty for non-cooperation with evil. I am here, therefore, to invite and submit cheerfully to the highest penalty that can be inflicted upon me for what in law is deliberate crime, and what appears to me to be the highest duty of a citizen. The only course open to you, the Judge and the assessors, is either to resign your posts and thus dissociate yourselves from evil, if you feel that the law you are called upon to administer is an evil, and that in reality I am innocent, or to inflict on me the severest penalty, if you believe that the system and the law you are assisting to administer are good for the people of this country, and that my activity is, therefore, injurious to the public weal.

Quit India Resolution, 1942

Gandhi's clarion call delivered to Britain to leave India—after the failure of the Cripps Mission to secure Indian support for the British war effort in World War II. This resolution marked the launch of the Civil Disobedience Movement which continued for two years.

Whereas the British War Cabinet proposals by Sir Stafford Cripps have shown up British imperialism in its nakedness as never before, the All-India Congress Committee has come to the following conclusions:

- The committee is of the opinion that Britain is incapable of defending India. It is natural that whatever she does is for her own defence. There is the eternal conflict between Indian and British interest. It follows that their notions of defence would also differ.
- The British Government has no trust in India's political parties. The Indian Army has been maintained up till now mainly to hold India in subjugation. It has been completely segregated from the general population, who can in no sense regard it as their own. This policy of mistrust still continues, and is the reason why national defence is not entrusted to India's elected representatives.
- Japan's quarrel is not with India. She is warring against the British Empire. India's participation in the war has not been with the consent of the representatives of the Indian people. It was purely a British act. If India were freed, her first step would probably be to negotiate with Japan.
- The Congress is of the opinion that if the British withdrew from India, India would be able to defend herself in the event of the Japanese, or any aggressor, attacking India.
- The committee is, therefore, of the opinion that the British should withdraw from India. The plea that they should remain in India for the protection of the Indian princes is wholly untenable. It is an additional proof of their determination to maintain their hold over India. The princes need have no fear from an unarmed India.
- The question of majority and minority is the creation of the British Government, and would disappear on their withdrawal.

For all these reasons, the committee appeals to Britain, for the sake of her own safety, for the sake of India's safety and for the cause of world peace, to let go her hold on India, even if she does not give up all her Asiatic and African possessions.

This committee desires to assure the Japanese Government and people that India bears no enmity, either toward Japan or toward any other nation. India only desires freedom from all alien domination. But in this fight for freedom the committee is of the opinion that India, while welcoming universal sympathy, does not stand in need of foreign military aid.

India will attain her freedom through her non-violent strength, and will retain it likewise. Therefore, the committee hopes that Japan will not have any designs on India. But if Japan attacks India, and Britain makes no response to its appeal, the committee will expect all those who look to the Congress for guidance to offer complete non-violent non-cooperation to the Japanese forces, and not to render any assistance to them. It is no part of the duty of those who are attacked to render any assistance to the attacker. It is their duty to offer complete non-cooperation.

It is not difficult to understand the simple principle of non-violent non-cooperation:

First, we may not bend the knee to an aggressor, or obey any of his orders.

Second, we may not look to him for any favours nor fall to his bribes, but we may not bear him any malice nor wish him ill.

Third, if he wishes to take possession of our fields we will refuse to give them up, even if we have to die in an effort to resist him.

Fourth, if he is attacked by disease, or is dying of thirst and seeks our aid, we may not refuse it.

Fifth, in such places where British and Japanese forces are fighting, our non-cooperation will be fruitless and unnecessary.

At present, our non-cooperation with the British Government is limited. Were we to offer them complete non-cooperation when they are actually fighting, it would be tantamount to bringing our country deliberately into Japanese hands. Therefore, not to put any obstacle in the way of the British forces will often be the only way of demonstrating our non-cooperation with the Japanese.

Neither may we assist the British in any active manner. If we can judge from their recent attitude, the British Government do not need any help from us beyond our non-interference. They desire our help only as slaves.

It is not necessary for the committee to make a clear declaration in regard to a scorched-earth policy. If, in spite of our non-violence, any part of the country falls into Japanese hands, we may not destroy our crops or water supply, etc., if only because it will be our endeavour to regain them.

The destruction of war material is another matter, and may, under certain circumstances, be a military necessity. But it can never be the Congress policy to destroy what belongs, or is of use, to the masses.

Whilst non-cooperation against the Japanese forces will necessarily be limited to a comparatively small number, and must succeed if it is complete and genuine, true building up of swaraj [self-government] consists in the millions of India wholeheartedly working for a constructive program. Without it, the whole nation cannot rise from its age-long torpor.

Whether the British remain or not, it is our duty always to wipe out our unemployment, to bridge the gulf between the rich and the poor, to banish communal strife, to exorcise the demon of untouchability, to reform the Dacoits [armed bandits] and save the people from them. If scores of people do not take a living interest in this nation-building work, freedom must remain a dream and unattainable by either non-violence or violence.

Kazi Nazrul Islam

Kazi Nazrul Islam (1899–1976), popularly known as the rebel poet, was a leading freedom fighter. His revolutionary poems and essays were regularly proscribed by the British authorities, leading to his arrest on charges of sedition on 23 November 1922.

Those Iron Gates of Prison

Destroy those iron gates of prison,
Demolish the blood-stained stony altars
Of chain worshipping!
O youthful Israfil,
Blow your horn of universal cataclysm!
Let the flag of destruction
Rise amidst the rubble of prison walls
Of the East!
Play the music of the festival of Shiva!
Who's the master? Who's the king?

Who is it that gives punishment
Having snatched away the truth of freedom?
Ha! Ha! Ha! It's a laugh—
God is to be hanged?
Rumour-monger—
Who gives this nasty lesson?
O you forgetful mad guys—
Shake—shake the prisons
With your forceful cataclysmic pulls!
Send the call of Ali the bravest,
Play your war-drums—
Call the Death
Unto the Life!
There, the norwester is dancing—
Would you mind to pass the days doing nothing?
Let's see
You shake up the foundation
Of that terrible prison.
Kick, break the locks!
All those prisons—
Set them on fire,
Burn them down, uproot them forever!

Translated by Sajed Kamal

Communistic

I do sing of equality
In which dissolve
All the barriers and estrangements,
In which have been united
Hindus, Buddhists, Muslims, Christians.
I do sing of equality.

Who are you?—A Parsee? A Jain? A Jew?
A Santhal, a Bheel or a Garo?
A Confucian? A disciple of Charvak?
Go on—tell me what else!
Whosoever you are, my friend,
Whatever holy books or scriptures

You swallowed up or carry on your shoulder
Or stuff your brains with—the Quran, the Puranas,
the Vedas, the Bible, the Tripitaka, the Zend-Avesta,
the Grantha Sahib—why do you waste your labour?
Why inject all this into your brain?
Why all this—like petty bargaining in a shop
When the roads are adorned with blossoming flowers?
Open your heart—within you lie
All the scriptures,
All the wisdom of all ages.
Within you lie all the religions,
All the prophets—your heart
Is the universal temple
Of all the deities.
Why do you search for God in vain
Within the skeletons of dead scriptures
When he smilingly resides in the privacy
Of your immortal heart?
I'm not lying to you, my friend.
Before this heart
All the crowns and royalties surrender.
This heart is Neelachal, Kashi, Mathura,
Brindaban, Buddha-Gaya, Jerusalem, Madina, Ka'aba.
This heart is the Masjid, the temple, the church.
This is where Jesus and Moses found the truth.
In this battlefield
The young flute player sang the divine Geeta.
In this pasture
The shepherds became prophets.
In this meditation chamber
Shakya Muni heard the call of the suffering humanity
And decried his throne.
In this voice
The Darling of Arabia heard his call,
From here he sang the Quran's message of equality.
What I've heard, my friend, is not a lie:
There's no Ka'aba
Greater than this heart!

Translated by Sajed Kamal

Deposition of a Political Prisoner

Nazrul wrote 'Rajbandir Jabanbandi' (Deposition of a Political Prisoner) while awaiting trial in Presidency Jail, Calcutta. He delivered the speech in the court of Chief Presidency Magistrate Swinho on 16 January 1923. Nazrul was sentenced to one year of hard labour.

The charge against me: I'm a rebel against the Crown. Therefore, I'm now a prisoner, convicted by a royal court. On one side is the Royal Crown, on the other, the flame of the Comet. One is a king, with a sceptre in his hand; the other is the Truth, with the sceptre of Justice. On the side of the king are state-paid government employees. On my side is the King of all kings, the Judge of all judges, the eternal Truth—the awakened God.

No one has appointed my Judge. In the eye of this Judge Supreme, kings and subjects, rich and poor, happy and sad—all are equal. On His throne are placed side by side the Royal Crown and the beggar's monochord. His law is Justice, Religion. That law is not created by any human conqueror for a particular conquered people. That law is created by the global humanity from its realization of the Truth. It belongs to the universal Truth. It's the law of the Supreme God. On the side of the king is a molecular piece of the creation; on my side, the primordial, infinite, indivisible Creator.

What is behind the king is insignificant; behind me is Shiva. The goal of the one on the side of the king is selfish, monetary reward; the goal of the one on my side is the Truth, the reward of Bliss.

The message of the king is like bubbles; mine—the boundless ocean. I'm a poet, sent by God to speak the unspoken Truth, to give form to the formless creation. God speaks through the voice of the poet. The message is the revelation of the Truth, the message of God. The message may be judged seditious in a state-court, but in the court of Justice, that message is not against Justice, not against Truth. That message may be punishable in a state-court, but in the light of Religion, at the door of Justice, it is innocent, untainted, untarnished, inextinguishable as the Truth itself.

The Truth reveals itself. No angry look or royal punishment can suppress it. I'm the lyre of that timeless self-revelation—the lyre in which the message of eternal Truth has been resounded. I'm the lyre in the hands of God. A lyre may break, but who can break God? There's Truth, there's God—there's always been and always will be. One who is obstructing the message of Truth today, trying to silence it, he too is but a minuscule, insignificantly powerful, part of God's creation. It is due to God's gesture, God's presence, God's will that he is here today, and may not be here tomorrow. There's no limit to a human being's foolish pride; he wants to imprison, to punish his own creator! But one day, that pride will definitely drown in tears.

Anyway, as I was saying, I'm an instrument for revealing the Truth. Maybe some cruel power may be able to imprison that instrument, may even be able to destroy it; but the One who plays the instrument, in that lyre who plays the message of Shiva, who can imprison Him? I'm mortal! But my God is immortal, I'll die, the king will die—because many rebels like me have died, as have many kings who have brought such charges. But never—for no reason—it's been possible to suppress the Truth, to kill His message. That's how He is revealing Himself today and will do so through eternity. This proscribed message of mine will once again be expressed through other voices. The music of my flute will not die simply because my flute has been confiscated—I can play the music through another flute I can get or create. The music is not in my flute—it's in my heart; and the flute—in my creative skill of constructing it. Therefore, neither the flute nor the music is to be blamed. Rather, I'm the one to be blamed—I, the player of the flute. Likewise, for the message which has flowed out of my voice, I'm not responsible. It's not my fault, nor my lyre's; rather, it's His fault—who, through my voice, plays His lyre. Therefore, it isn't me who is the rebel against the state. The real rebel against the state is that Musician of lyre, God Himself. There's no royal power or a second god who can punish Him. No police force or prison has yet been created who can punish Him. The state-employed translator, in the state-language, has merely translated the language of that message, but not its life-spirit. The translation merely expresses the rebellion against the state, because the purpose of that translation is to please the king. My writing expresses the Truth, Power and life-spirit. My purpose is to worship God; on behalf of the oppressed, distressed global humanity, I'm the shower of Truth, tears of God. I have not rebelled against a mere king, I have rebelled against injustice.

I know and I have seen—I'm not alone standing convicted in this court today. Standing behind me is the beauteous Truth, God Himself. Throughout ages He stands quietly behind His soldiers of Truth turned political prisoners. A state-employed judge cannot be a judge of the Truth. Through farcical trials like this when Jesus was crucified, Gandhi was imprisoned, that day too, God quietly stood behind them. The judge could not see Him. Between him and God stood the emperor. In fear of the emperor, his conscience, his two eyes were blinded. Otherwise, he would have trembled in fear and awe in his seat, turned blue, along with his seat of the judge, burn to ashes.

The judge knows that what I've said and written is not unjust in the eyes of God, not a lie in the court of Justice. But he will probably punish me, because he is not on the side of the Truth; he is on the side of the king. He is not on the side of Justice, he is on the side of law. He is not free, he's a servant of the king. Yet, I ask—whose courtroom is it? The king's or of Religion? This judge—is he accountable to the king, or to his conscience, to the Truth, to God? Who rewards this judge? The king or God? Wealth or self-satisfaction?

… Today, India is subjugated. Its people are slaves. This is the absolute truth. In this kingdom, to call a slave a slave, injustice an injustice, is sedition. This cannot be the rule of Justice. This forcible twisting of a truth into a lie, injustice into justice, night into day—can the Truth go on tolerating this? Can such rule last forever? It's been possible this long, maybe because the Truth was oblivious. But today the Truth is awakened—any awakened soul with eyes can see that for sure. Am I a rebel because I voiced the distressed cry of the Truth stricken by this unjust rule? Is it only my own crying? Or, is it the united, loud voice of the entire oppressed Heaven and Earth? I know the cataclysmic roar of my voice is not mine alone—it's the cry of the suffering of the entire world. This cry cannot be silenced simply by intimidating me, even killing me. Suddenly, in someone else's voice, this lost message will be heard thunderously!

Instead of India being subjugated, if England was subjugated by India and if the defenceless, oppressed people of England, like the people of India, would be anxious to liberate their own motherland, and, if at that time, I was the judge and, like me, this judge, charged with sedition, was to be tried by me, then, what this judge at that time from his defendant's dock would have said, I too am saying the same thing in the same way.

I'm highly self-confident. What I've understood to be unjust, oppression, a lie—I've called it just that—without trying to please anyone or to receive praise or favour. I have not merely rebelled against the injustices of the king, but my Truth-sword has also attacked and rebelled against the society, race, nation. For this, in and outside my home, I've been subjected to too much ridicule, humiliation, reproach, attacks. But

I've not let anything intimidate me into debasing my Truth, my God; out of greed I did not sell off my self-realization; I did not shorten my austerely attained self-satisfaction—because I'm dear to God; a lyre of Truth. I'm a poet, my soul is one with the soul of the truth-seeing saint. I've been born with an unexplainable, boundless sense of fulfilment. This is not my arrogance, but a simple and honest acknowledgement of the truth of self-realization and self-confidence. I cannot accept a lie out of blind faith, greed, fear of the king or the public. I cannot accept tyranny.

Periyar E.V. Ramasamy

Periyar E.V. Ramasamy (1879–1973), the founder of the Dravid Kazhagam and the Self-Respect Movement, was one of the greatest leaders from south India. A staunch atheist, he advocated principles of rationalism, women's empowerment, self-respect and abolition of caste. Although he had once been a member of the Congress party, he became a bitter critic of Gandhi and the Brahminism entrenched in the Congress party. The following are selections from his writings in which he forcefully puts forth these views.

Duties of a Revolutionary

It would have been more appropriate if you could have chosen as your president one who is a firm believer in social reform. I am fast losing my faith in social reform as an agency for the regeneration of our country. The advancement of the country can only be through social revolution born of invincible courage and undaunted boldness. I have arrived at this conclusion after long and patient deliberations. I beg to tell you that I am endeavouring to serve the country by destroying the useless and harmful undergrowth that is threatening its very life. Society, in my humble opinion, has degenerated to an extent which it is impossible to remedy by social reform. The much talked of social reform of the present day is one of the crafty weapons of the educated and the wealthy classes who are competing with one another in an attempt to gain popularity and influence over the people. Such methods of social reform are not intended to confer any benefit on those [for] whose welfare they are apparently intended. These methods are adopted to serve the selfish interest of those so-called reformers themselves. But those whose lot requires to be bettered always believe in the genuineness of these reformers. And the result of it all is that day by day, their condition is growing worse, they are degenerating into a state from which they cannot be reformed and uplifted easily. The chief reason for this is the fact that those set of people whose attitude of mind towards society brought about the degeneration of certain classes which need reformation at present, those class of people to whose selfish activities much of the unsettled condition of our society is due—it is these men who are now working and benefiting by their work in the department of social amelioration.

The most important of the evils that stare us in our face is that which is responsible for the division of the people into superiors and inferiors in society on the basis of birth. These evils have come to exist in our country on account of the fact that they have been established in the name of religion, God and heaven. The anxiety to reform society and purge it of its evils was in the minds of men long ago. It might be said that Buddha, Ramanuja and Thiruvalluvar were the foremost in their age to attempt something in this direction. But it cannot be said that in these directions there has been the least progress which redounded to the benefit of society from the efforts made from that time onwards till now. It is impossible for our people to effect anything by social reform, because the sentiments of religion and the veneration of God have been so inextricably connected with these superstitious ideas and beliefs. But this state of things is advantageous to some sets of people, and that is the reason, I think, for the failure of the efforts to improve the condition of the people.

It is not an easy task to enunciate more wise theories or do more strenuous work than was done by Buddha, Kapilar, Thiruvalluvar, Ramanuja and others. That is the reason why the opponents of social reform have strong belief in their obstructive propaganda. The feelings towards religion and the attitude towards God have been built on the foundations of ignorant belief and blind faith. Worshipping God out of blind belief, man has come to accept and live according to many of the purblind conceptions of religion.

To say that ignorant belief and blind faith should be destroyed is national service destined for the benefit of humanity. People have for a very long time been carrying on this propaganda with caution, patience, love, sympathy, good words and persuasive arguments. What has been the result of their attempts? How long we are going to be experimenting like this? We find that such propaganda is done by people who are anxious to ingratiate themselves into the good books of the opponents of social reform and gain popularity and prestige as reformers. It is also due to a lack of courage to push onward on the part of the reformers. Some people might quote the opinions of Swami Vivekananda, Gandhiji and others to disprove my contentions. I frankly accept that my opinions are opposed to theirs. Some people say, 'Do not destroy the old symbolisms, the ancient pictures and the hoary traditions and culture.' Such things which these people want to foster are responsible for the degeneration of our country and demoralization of our people, and this we must impress on the mind of every reasonable man by our propaganda work. Otherwise, a state of things will come into existence from which it will be well nigh impossible to obtain liberation and salvation.

For instance, Ramanuja with a view to reform society and at the same time preserve the old symbols, caught hold of many of those who were called 'Pariahs' and put the 'namam' on their foreheads and invested them with the sacred thread so as to bring about equality in society. The old symbols were no doubt preserved, but did the people get equality! Were the followers imbued with the feelings of fraternity?

Let us take the temples of the land. Instead of being a symbolical abode of the supreme being, they have degenerated into dens of all kinds of iniquity and hotbeds of vice. Even in the case of ancient culture, the art and the paintings, it will be clear that they also stand in the way of social reform. What benefit have the Vedas and the Puranas conferred on mankind? What have the people gained by reading the *Bharatham*, the *Ramayanam, Siva Puranam, Vishnu Puranam, Thiruvilayadal Puranam* et hoc genus omne? Consider whether you do not find in these books doctrines which go against the principles of human conduct and human character, and do you think that some of the worst books and worst set of people could be guilty of graver wrongs and more serious crimes than some of those mentioned in these books? Also seriously consider the fact whether these old books do not stand in the way of social reform. Do not the social reactionaries quote from these texts and these scriptures and cite authorities to support their position? It is said that there are some passages in these books which support the standpoint of the reformers. In my opinion, this is empty talk to deceive gullible people. I feel that so long as the people want to hang to these scriptures, so long will be they be unable to achieve success in their efforts to reform society. I have not come here to speak about God, I think the less we speak about Him, the better it will be for us.

So far as religion is concerned, there is no paucity of propaganda and publicity. Every man believes that it is only through his religion that salvation could be reached. Why should there be so much competition between religions? When we deeply consider all this, it would be clear that religion is an absurdity. But if it is considered that religion is an institution brought into existence so as to define certain rules and draft certain regulations for the better functioning of society, then it may be entitled to some consideration. But then religion should change according to the needs and requirements of the times, but if the word of God or preachings of the Son of God or the doctrines of the messenger of the Almighty are as sacred and sacrosanct as God himself then the paramount duty of social reformers is to abolish and destroy those religions. The principle of social reform is the principle of adoption to the changing conditions of the times. And so the social reformer should not flinch in destroying at once the things which would not change accordingly as the changed conditions of the world require.

The next thing that the social reformers should devote their attention to is that of the relationship between man and woman. In our society women are being treated worse than untouchables. Women are considered to be slaves of men. If such a system has been made by God, the first thing that we should do is to destroy that God. It is a great pity that so many things should be foisted upon the devoted head of poor God. Especially in our country, the position of our womenfolk is the worst that could be thought of. Chastity is considered to be the foremost duty of women. The gods that men worship have been symbolized as having their wives on their hands, tongue or shoulders.

But the people have not learnt chivalry from their Gods and do not treat their women with decency. As a result of the slavery of women, children are bred up as slaves and the whole country is enslaved. If we are to be free, we must free our women who must be allowed the same liberty and the same privileges as our men. Women must depend upon themselves for their emancipation from their slavery and should boldly come forward and break their bonds. Turkey, Afghanistan and China are standing examples of women achieving their freedom.

I would next draw your attention to the most inhuman institution of widowhood by which our sisters are subjected to untold hardships. We fail to understand why the ancients created this institution. It could not be because there was surplus womanhood in our country in those days. For our Gods had not less than two wives each, and our kings married a thousand, a ten thousand, and a sixty thousand wives at a time! Probably our forefathers intended the institution of widowhood in order to make provision for the need of the Sanyasis and the guests to whom hospitality had to be extended as a religious duty. Whatever be the reason, this institution has done incalculable harm to the womanhood of the country, and deserves to be abolished without a moment's delay. In this connection, I would appeal to the widows themselves to take courage in both their hands and work out their own salvation. They should not be deterred by the shame and obloquy that society may heap upon them, and should come forward to choose husbands and publish their choice before the world. An exhibition of courage in this matter, even by a few widows, would serve as an object lesson for the others, and would pave the way for the coming generations. I would also appeal to those women who are not widows to lend a helping hand to their suffering sisters who are unfortunate enough to be widowed. The wives should help the widows to secure husbands for the latter and lend a hand at the purification of society and creation of a healthy moral atmosphere for their husbands and their children.

Distinctions of caste were created in our society at a time when the strong man oppressed the weak. The continuance of these distinctions is evidence of the fact that we have not advanced from the stage of barbarism. No reasons have so far been urged to prove the superiority of one man to another by the right of his birth alone. Morality and intellect are not the outcome of one's birth. The division of caste by birth has been condemned by almost all the reformers and the concomitant evils of caste system have been condemned for many years. All has been in vain. I strongly believe that this monstrosity cannot be wiped off by means of preachings to the masses. The only way to get rid of the scourge is by legislation and communal representation in the services. This may seem paradoxical to you. I shall explain my position. If communal representation is granted, there will be no chance for the privileged classes to ride roughshod over the oppressed. Politicians object to the idea of communal representation in services urging that it would disunite the people. When we express our wish to gather the conflicting elements of society into a harmonious whole there is the rub. The religionists raise their hue and cry. If we attempt to remove the obstacles of religion from our path by means of legislation, the so called religious teachers and Acharyas raise their vehement protestations. If we heed to the voice of religion and desist from amalgamating the communities but keep them separate there is enough justification for communal representation.

Now to the curse of untouchability. Our country has the monopoly for see-me-not-isms and touch-me-not-isms. A country where there is a class of people who are not entitled to walk in public streets, who are not allowed to worship God in their own temples, who are prevented from using the common wells and tanks—such a country may as well be destroyed by an earthquake, burnt out by a volcano, or submerged by the ocean. If God is all merciful, He should have obliterated our country long ago. Is it not shameful on the part of such a country to aspire for Swaraj, Dominion Status or complete Independence? Politicians may say that untouchability will go if we get Swaraj. To them I say not merely Swaraj but Dharma Raj, Rama Raj, Harichandra Raj and the Raj of the very Gods—these were responsible for originating and organizing this blot on humanity. If these Governments come to life once again, I fear the position of this class would become unredeemable. I appeal to the reformers both social and political to carry on the mission of removing the sin of untouchability and clean our society of the dirt that has accumulated for centuries.

Another important thing that needs mention is education. True education is that which imparts knowledge on human nature. Thiruvalluvar says, 'however educated one may be, if one does not adjust himself to the world current, he is worse than an illiterate.' The education that is now obtained in schools and colleges is useful to produce slaves, who are helping the foreign domination. It is sheer nonsense that devotion to God, devotion to religion and devotion to king should be taught in schools. If they deserve any devotion at all let them earn it by displaying their intrinsic merit. My ardent wish is that no education be imparted to the communities from which the intelligentsia of the land have sprung up. I like to see the existing schools and colleges closed at least for a period of fifteen years and the ladies and the illiterate communities imparted the true education referred above. This is the first duty of any good Government and all sincere reformers.

(Excerpts from the articles from Revolt, *5 and 12 December 1928)*

On the Nationalism of the Congress Brahmins

For thousands of years India's wealth has been undermined by the 'in-comers' in the name of religion, god, festivals, caste, ceremonies and rituals, etc. As a result, people have been plunged into the mire of ignorance and illiteracy. In recent years likewise, in the political arena, a section of the people are squandering our wealth, acting as spies for foreigners, and playing havoc with the country in the name of Nationalism, Swaraj, Independence, etc. People are not able to recognize this sort of sham, for in our country, however educated a man is, his reasoning is curbed by religion and his power of discrimination is arrested by it. His power of discretion ceases to function in respect of politics. Just as a set of people seek their selfish ends in the name of religion, there are also those who call themselves educated that have similar interests in politics. This conclave of people has enshrouded humanity in ignorance, which has ultimately brought the country to a calamitous state. For forty to fifty years, this sham of politics wrought countless wrongs upon our country and kept the masses under its thumb, never allowing them to raise their heads. The selfishness of the educated class and the misguided blind beliefs of the uneducated people, arising out of their ignorance, keep us away from the search for truth and justice.

Let us examine the present condition of politics in our country. Today there are two sets of people that are making a din, viz., the Congressmen and the Independents. What are their qualifications? Let us examine their 'deeds' and 'sacrifices' in the name of politics. On the Congress platform, they declare that the 'Satanic' British Government should be swept away. People also applaud them. But their sons, brothers and relations will be earning 500, 1000, 2000 or 3000 rupees a month as munsiffs and judges under the same Government. Their heroic declarations only serve to strengthen the positions of their relations in the various professions and yet they will be masquerading [as opponents], in the name of the country.

The Secretary of the Congress, Mr Rangasami Iyengar will roar, 'we must obstruct the Government from functioning and beard the lion in its own den.' But his brother crawls into the den of Government, bows low to the Britisher, licks his feet and holds high the banner of the bureaucracy. Mr S. Srinivasa Iyengar, the Independent-wallah asks others to do away with the British connection, but every morning he unconsciously finds himself at the feet of the judges addressing the representatives of the 'Satanic' government as 'Your Lordship, Your Honour' etc. and coolly pockets a few thousands. His creed of Independence will also help him in securing fresh appointments for his kith and kin.

And there are other political magnates who are said to be intoxicated with too much of patriotism. Messrs Srinivasa Sastri, T. Rangachari, Mani

Iyer, V. Krishnasami Iyer, C.P. Ramasami Aiyar, C. Vijayaraghavachari are names to be conjured with. And surely their sons, nephews, brothers, brothers-in-law and other relations are reaping the fruits of these 'patriotic' brains. Those that are unfit for Government services and those that are retired from service have come out as patriots, but their sons, and relations are in the service of the 'Satanic' Government.

After the advent of the Congress, i.e., thirty to forty years back, the Brahmins have managed to enter into almost all branches of Government services. This is proof that the national organization, the Congress, has done nothing but to obtain 97 per cent of the appointments for the Brahmins who are but 3 per cent of the entire population.

Year after year resolutions are passed in the Congress demanding provincial autonomy and reforms in the machinery of Government. But the number of new appointments is going up in geometrical progression, leading to increase in taxation. The Government are forced to throw loaves and fishes of office to these patriots, and if they refuse to do this, there is a big agitation brought about in the name of the illiterate masses. By providing appointments for such agitators and their kith and kin the Government finds itself on a bed of roses day by day. That is why the Government also is helping the Congress. The Britishers are here to earn and to enjoy. And there are the Congressmen to secure comforts and conveniences for the Britishers.

A number of political parties have sprung up within the Congress itself, like Independence, Swarajya, Liberal, Home Rule, etc. Each of them sing the same chorus of 'amelioration of the distressed.' Create new appointments, new committees, new delegations to foreign countries and the like. The ultimate result is a heavy taxation on the people and the consequent impoverishment of the nation. For example, today we find thrice the number of officers in each of the departments of Government as that before the advent of the Congress. Has the population increased thrice after the Congress?

They ask people not to learn English since it is a foreign tongue. But they educate their children in English schools with the help of their earnings got from us by such fraudulent methods as festivals, ceremonials and other rites. And today we find the Brahmins who were fed in chatrams, employed as proprietors, and those who studied under municipal lanterns, occupying all places in Government services. And this is done again in the name of Nationalism.

Before the advent of the Congress, i.e. before the Government bribed the monopolist community with appointments, the revenue of our country was about twenty-five to thirty crore rupees. As a result of the work of the Congress for these forty years or more, 140 to 150 crores are being collected from us in the shape of taxes. The aggrieved party is not the Independence-wallahs who were once beggars (for that is the verdict of history) but we the agriculturists, traders and labourers. And the result is there is an increasing flow in the emigration of labourers to foreign countries. Yet there is a masquerade of Nationalism in the land.

But when we press for communal representation, there is the cry from the so-called Nationalists that it is an obstacle to national progress, and we are labelled as 'unpatriotic'. Then, there is no longer the usual pressure for fresh appointments. We are styled as 'Brahmin-haters' and the Nationalists use this weapon as one of their election tactics when they come to the people with their fire-eating promises. This is again done in the name of patriotism.

(Excerpts from the article in Revolt, *29 March 1929)*

On Gandhi and His Nationalism

No sooner had Congress decided to abandon its principles for the sake of a spurious 'unity', than the Mahatma disengaged himself from politics, and like a hooded Shankaracharya, retired to a corner. And then began all those rituals one witnesses in a religious cult; just as how devotees throng the premises of a mutt, now several 'shastris' visit the Gandhi mutt, sit at his feet, sing his praise and thereby enhance their prestige. The reason why Gandhian Constructive principles have lost all value is because in the name of a fraudulent unity they were abandoned and in their place a Gandhi mutt was established. Since madness is characteristic of all mahatmas, our own is no exception to this general rule. Perhaps he still hopes he may alter the situation; but no man or institution or nation which compromises on its principles has been known to prosper.

(Excerpt from the article in Kudi Arasu, *12 June 1927)*

Though the public believes that Mahatma Gandhi wishes to abolish untouchability and reform religion and society, the Mahatma's utterances and thought reveal that he holds exactly the opposite view on this matter.... Though he claims openly that untouchability should be abolished, he interprets his own words in such a manner as will enable the persistence of untouchability... [Thus] if we are to follow

the Mahatma's untouchability creed, we will slip into the very abyss of
that untouchability we are attempting to abolish. We have been patient
and tight-lipped but today in the interests of abolition and self-respect
we are, sadly, forced to confront and oppose the Mahatma... [His]
frequent utterances, that varnashrama dharma exists in our social life
and it is based on our birth, are akin to those routinely mouthed by
the Brahmins. Recently, while addressing a public meeting at Mysore,
he claimed that varnashrama dharma has a place in the Hindu society
and that it is essential for our society. He has also said that each varna
has been enjoined with a duty proper to it, and that the varna becomes
superior to the extent it discharges its duties, the Brahmin, too, achieving
the high position only when he carries out the duty assigned to him.
The Brahmins, too, make their claim of their birth-based superiority
on the basis of such arguments as are advanced by the Mahatma...
Untouchability is practiced only through the varnashrama dharma and if
the latter is absent, there is no way the principle of untouchability could
spread. Varnashrama dharma is the body and the untouchability is the
soul. If the body of varnashrama dharma did not exist, untouchability
which constitutes the very life of this body would not be alive today...

What the Thuvar Brahmin Sammelan [the All India Brahmin
Conference held at Thuvar near Thanjavur in Tamil Nadu in 1927] has
unanimously endorsed in a resolution is nothing but what the Mahatma
says... The Sammelan invokes the same scriptural authority which the
Mahatma also quotes in order to claim that at present the Kshatriya and
Vaishya varnas have become extinct and what now obtains are only two
varnas, viz. the Brahmin and the Shudra. We would like to ask what are
the duties assigned by the Mahatma to those two varnas that have become
extinct now. How can one who accepts the birth-based varnashrama
dharma and the separate duties that it speaks of deny untouchability? If
we look for an authority for varnashrama dharma other than the one the
Brahmins invoke, we are not able to find anything, even until today...
The Mahatma has said in his Mysore address that a Brahmin's dharma
was to render public service and has drawn on the scriptures to uphold
his claims. The same scriptures say that a Shudra's dharma was to render
service to the Brahmin. The logical conclusion one can draw from the
Mahatma's observations is that if the Brahmin could attain the superior
status by rendering public service, by the same token, the Shudra could
attain his superior status only by rendering service to the Brahmin. So,
we are at a loss to understand how the Mahatma could consider the

Shudra to be co-eval with the Brahmin... He has also said that there is no question of superiority or inferiority amongst these four varnas and there would be co-evality so long as each one carries out its duty assigned to it. By that same token, we would like to then ask, in that case why there should be separate dharma for each of these varnas and what is wrong in the members of one varna doing the duties of the other. But the Mahatma has not uttered a single word to clarify this. ... If we go by the logic of the Mahatma, he should by birth be either a Shudra or a Vaishya. If so, does he have the right to render public service, which is the dharma assigned to the Brahmin. Is it not meaningless to ask others to pursue the varnashrama dharma which he himself is not able to practice?

(Excerpt from the article in Kudi Arasu, *7 August 1927)*

Gandhi considers only the northern merchants and the southern Brahmins to be human. He keeps company with them and considers their problems to be universal problems. His plans will always keep their concerns in mind and not those of the poor and the depressed classes. As far as the latter are concerned, Gandhi entreats them to take to spinning and assures them that he considers the practice of untouchability a sin. But even with respect to these matters, interpretations vary and are contingent on what the mill owners and the Brahmins say.

(Excerpt from the article in Kudi Arasu, *26 July 1931)*

His [Gandhi's] religious guise, god-related talk, his constant references to truth, non-violence, Satyagraha, cleansing of the heart, the power of the spirit, sacrifice and penance on the one hand, and the propaganda of his disciples and others—Nationalists and journalists—who in the name of politics and the nation consider him a rishi, a sage, Christ, the Prophet, a Mahatma...and a veritable avatar of Vishnu on the other, along with the opportunistic use of Gandhi's name by the rich and the educated...have together made Gandhi a political dictator.

(Excerpt from the article in Kudi Arasu, *23 July 1933)*

Translated by V. Geetha and S.V. Rajadurai

On Hinduism

... Religion not only creates the high and low discrimination in our social life, but also establishes high and low discrimination in our economy.

Think it over! Has not religion created a separate class of people who are hardworking and a separate class of people who enjoy without any hard work? ...

No Casteism among Birds or Animals

Birds, animals, worms, which are considered to be devoid of rationalism do not create castes, differences as high and low, in their species. But man considered to be a rational being is suffering from all these because of religion.

Amongst dogs you don't have a Brahmin dog and pariah dog. Among donkeys and monkeys we do not find. But amongst men you have. Why? Is it not because of our religion? How many years old is Hinduism? What good has it done to society so far? The low caste existed even in the days of Rama who was considered as an incarnation of god. In the days of King Harichander there existed a pariah in the burial ground. Selling away one's wife too was prevalent. To this day these evils are seen in our society. How are we to say that Hindu religion helped the people to progress?

See, what foolish notions are taught to the people by religion. The dead bodies are burnt to ashes and the ashes are immersed in water. But they are believed to be alive. The descendants of the dead hand over rice, dholl, vegetables, footwear, etc. to a Brahmin to be safely and surely passed over to the dead.

How are we to believe that a man has an iota of sense or rationalism in doing all these? Why should you give things only to Brahmins? Why should you fall at his feet? Why should you wash his feet and drink the water? If this is Hindu doctrine and philosophy, such a religion must go. Take the other rituals. Christening, house warming, marriage, puberty or anything, all are for Brahmin's gain. Do people of other religions and countries behave like this? We do not respect our knowledge nor are we ashamed of our actions. Are we merely a mass of flesh and bones? Why should anybody get angry when I say all these to make you think over? Who is responsible for our degradation? Is it religion or government?

One God of Christians, Muslims

In the scientifically advanced world, we are talking of gods and their great deeds. This is nothing but barbarous. Because our enemies find no reasonable charges against us, they are calling us atheists, with a bad motive and to create mischief.

So far as god is concerned we find the Christians and Muslims somewhat reformed from the olden days of barbarians. They say that there can be only one god. They say that it is beyond human comprehension. They say that god does good to those who are good and punishes those who are bad. They say that god has no name or shape. They talk of good qualities. We need not worry about their god. Wise people accept their gods because they feel that their god would serve the purpose of creating a better society. What about Hindus and their thousands of gods created by Brahmins? Why should Hindus worship so many gods? How did they come? See what all are made as gods! From cow, horse, bullock, monkey, bandicoot, stone, birds, metals, paper, all are deemed as gods. When I was in Kasi, I saw two dogs being worshipped. Moreover gods have wives, concubines, and prostitutes. These gods are believed to eat, sleep and reproduce. They also have marriages and funerals.

Let them attribute anything to these gods. Kidnapping girls, gods enjoying with prostitutes are celebrated as festivals. Crores of rupees are wasted for these. The precious time of the people is wasted. Think over, whether all these are things to be done in the twentieth century.

Idiotic Marriages, Expenses, Offerings

Should we not feel ashamed of all these? Is it just or right to call us atheists? If there are gods, should they be like this? Will any intelligent man accept this? Does god require all these things we do, as pooja, offerings, marriages, etc.? Does any god approve all these? Seeing these gods as mere toys, we perform marriage thrice a year to them, why that? If gods really need wives, should we not find out what happened to the wives married last year? Were they divorced? Were they segregated? Have they deserted their husbands and ran away or have all died? Should we not think of all these? Why celebrate marriages every year for gods? Why music, show, pomp and expenses? Do you know who eats the feast at marriages? How many festivals every year and at various places? What have we gained by all these? So far as our education is concerned 95 per cent people are illiterate. In the world, our India is a very poor country. Should we not think why we should squander money in the name of god?

How many times do we perform poojas and place offerings to god in a day? How many measures of rice, dholl and other articles are placed before god? People have no education, no work, no meal. Please consider how many crores of rupees are wasted year after year for celebrating

Ekadasi, Arudra, Thai Poosam, Karthigai, and for visiting temples at Tirupati, Thiruchendur and Rameswaram.

If we consider what pains are taken for these expenses, none could assert that gods have done good to our people in any manner. If the huge amount spent this way is diverted to other fields, we can run the government without taxes. If we create new industries and educational institutions we can solve the problems of illiteracy and unemployment. There will be no exploitation by foreign countries. Just to make a particular section of people (Brahmins) remain lazy and yet lead their lives well, why all others should bestow their hard-earned money foolishly for all these?

How senselessly are we behaving in the name of god and devotion? How ugly do we seem when we carry the kavadai (a bent pole with metal vessels at both ends) on our shoulders! Wearing saffron colour cloth people roll in the streets! People shave their head, smear mud and ashes on the body! People prick themselves with small arrows into their tongue and other parts of the body. People bathe in dirty water. All these in the name of god and devotion!

Moreover, milk, ghee, curd, honey, fruit, juices are being poured on the stone idols. They flow into gutters. All eatables are wasted. Are we to see this as mere fun? Do all these gods need gold jewels worth crores? Are costly silk garments needed? Why tall towers and big compound walls? Why gold and silver 'vimanas'? Are they not public property? Does religious duty mean that we should waste money on idols and thus help the lazy Brahmins to loot our money, enabling their people to become Indian Administrative Service (IAS) officers, judges, state diwans, etc.? If all these are for god's blessings, should there be such gods? Think it over.

Do the Muslims follow this sort of worship of god? Do the Christians? Will the rationalist Indian accept all these?

PURNA SWARAJ: THE DEMAND FOR FULL INDEPENDENCE (BY THE INDIAN NATIONAL CONGRESS)

Even though there was gathering outrage in the years leading up to 1930 against British colonial rule for its many failures—lack of political reform, curtailing of basic rights, pernicious draining of the Indian economy, outright neglect of the Indian population, and state violence—there weren't many political parties which embraced the idea of completely severing ties with the British Empire. 'Purna Swaraj', officially promulgated by the Indian National Congress on 26 January 1930, was the first step towards achieving full independence.

We believe that it is the inalienable right of the Indian people, as of any other people, to have freedom and to enjoy the fruits of their toil and have the necessities of life, so that they may have full opportunities of growth. We believe also that if any government deprives a people of these rights and oppresses them the people have a further right to alter it or to abolish it. The British Government in India has not only deprived the Indian people of their freedom but has based itself on the exploitation of the masses, and has ruined India economically, politically, culturally, and spiritually. We believe, therefore, that India must sever the British connection and attain *Purna Swaraj*, or complete independence.

India has been ruined economically. The revenue derived from our people is out of all proportion to our income. Our average income is seven pice per day, and of the heavy taxes we pay, 20 per cent are raised from the land revenue derived from the peasantry and 3 per cent from the salt tax, which falls most heavily on the poor.

Village industries, such as hand-spinning, have been destroyed, leaving the peasantry idle for at least four months in the year, and dulling their intellect for want of handicrafts, and nothing has been substituted, as in other countries, for the crafts thus destroyed.

Customs and currency have been so manipulated as to heap further burdens on the peasantry. British manufactured goods constitute the bulk of our imports. Customs duties betray clear partiality for British manufactures, and revenue from them is used not to lessen the burden on the masses but for sustaining a highly extravagant administration. Still more arbitrary has been the manipulation of the exchange ration, which has resulted in millions being drained away from the country.

Politically, India's status has never been so reduced as under the British regime. No reforms have given real political power to the people. The tallest of us have to bend before foreign authority. The rights of free expression of opinion and free association have been denied to us, and many of our countrymen are compelled to live in exile abroad and cannot return to their homes. All administrative talent is killed, and the masses have to be satisfied with petty village offices and clerkships.

Culturally, the system of education has torn us from our moorings, and our training has made us hug the very chains that bind us.

Spiritually, compulsory disarmament has made us unmanly, and the presence of an alien army of occupation, employed with deadly effect to crush in us the spirit of resistance, has made us think that we cannot look after ourselves or put up a defense against foreign aggression, or even defend our homes and families from attacks of thieves, robbers, and miscreants.

We hold it to be a crime against man and God to submit any longer to a rule that has caused this fourfold disaster to our country. We recognize, however, that the most effective way of gaining our freedom is through nonviolence. We will therefore prepare ourselves by withdrawing, so far as we can, all voluntary association from the British Government, and will prepare for civil disobedience, including non-payment of taxes. We are convinced that if we can but withdraw our voluntary held and stop payment of taxes without doing violence, even under provocation, the end of this inhuman rule is assured. We therefore hereby solemnly resolve to carry out the Congress instructions issued from time to time for the purpose of establishing *Purna Swaraj*.

BHAGAT SINGH

Bhagat Singh (1907–1931) was an Indian socialist and is considered to be one of the most influential revolutionaries of the Indian independence movement. He was imprisoned and subsequently hanged on 23 March 1931 for his role in the John Saunders murder case. The following essay was written by twenty-three-year-old Bhagat Singh in response to a prison inmate's efforts to convince him of the existence of God.

Why I Am an Atheist

It is a matter of debate whether my lack of belief in the existence of an Omnipresent, Omniscient God is due to my arrogant pride and vanity. It never occurred to me that sometime in the future I would be involved in polemics of this kind. As a result of some discussions with my friends, (if my claim to friendship is not uncalled for) I have realized that after having known me for a little time only, some of them have reached a kind of hasty conclusion about me, that my atheism is my foolishness and that it is the outcome of my vanity. Even then it is a serious problem. I do not boast of being above these human follies. I am, after all, a human being and nothing more.

…I totally reject the existence of an Omnipresent, all powerful, all knowing God…. By the end of 1926, I was convinced that the belief in an Almighty, Supreme Being who created, guided and controlled the universe had no sound foundations.

…We find differences in Oriental and Occidental philosophies. There are differences even amongst various schools of thoughts in each hemisphere. In Asian religions, the Muslim religion is completely incompatible with the Hindu faith. In India itself, Buddhism and Jainism are sometimes quite separate from Brahmanism. Then in Brahmanism itself, we find two conflicting sects: Aarya Samaj and Snatan Dheram. Charvak is yet another independent thinker of the past ages. He challenged the Authority of God. All these faiths differ on many fundamental questions, but each of them claims to be the only true religion. This is the root of the evil. Instead of developing the ideas and experiments of ancient thinkers, thus providing ourselves with the ideological weapon for the future struggle,—lethargic, idle, fanatical as we are—we cling to orthodox religion and in this way reduce human awakening to a stagnant pool.

It is necessary for every person who stands for progress to criticize every tenet of old beliefs. Item by item he has to challenge the efficacy of old faith. He has to analyze and understand all the details. If after rigorous reasoning, one is led to believe in any theory of philosophy, his faith is appreciated. His reasoning may be mistaken and even fallacious. But there is chance that he will be corrected because Reason is the guiding principle of his life. But belief, I should say blind belief, is disastrous. It deprives a man of his understanding power and makes him reactionary.

...I ask: Was the creation of man intended to derive this kind of pleasure?

Open your eyes and see millions of people dying of hunger in slums and huts dirtier than the grim dungeons of prisons; just see the labourers patiently or say apathetically while the rich vampires suck their blood; bring to mind the wastage of human energy that will make a man with a little common sense shiver in horror. Just observe rich nations throwing their surplus produce into the sea instead of distributing it among the needy and deprived. There are palaces of kings built upon the foundations laid with human bones. Let them see all this and say 'All is well in God's Kingdom.' Why so? This is my question. You are silent. All right. I proceed to my next point.

You, the Hindus, would say: Whosoever undergoes sufferings in this life, must have been a sinner in his previous birth. It is tantamount to saying that those who are oppressors now were Godly people then, in their previous births. For this reason alone they hold power in their hands. Let me say it plainly that your ancestors were shrewd people. They were always in search of petty hoaxes to play upon people and snatch from them the power of Reason.

...The so-called theory of 'Puranas' (transmigration) is nothing but a fairy tale. I do not have any intention to bring this unutterable trash under discussion. Do you really know the most cursed sin in this world is to be poor? Yes, poverty is a sin; it is a punishment! Cursed be the theoretician, jurist or legislator who proposes such measures as push man into the quagmire of more heinous sins. Did it not occur to your All Knowing God or he could learn the truth only after millions had undergone untold sufferings and hardships? What, according to your theory, is the fate of a person who, by no sin of his own, has been born into a family of low-caste people? He is poor so he cannot go to a school. It is his fate to be shunned and hated by those who are born into a high caste. His ignorance, his poverty, and the contempt he receives from others will harden his heart towards society. Supposing that he commits a sin, who shall bear the consequences? God, or he, or the learned people of that society? What is your view about those punishments inflicted on the people who were deliberately kept ignorant by selfish and proud Brahmans? If by chance these poor creatures heard a few words of your sacred books, Vedas, these Brahmans poured melted lead into their ears.

If they committed any sin, who was to be held responsible? Who was to bear the brunt? My dear friends, these theories have been coined by the privileged classes. They try to justify the power they have usurped and the riches they have robbed with the help of such theories.

... Society must fight against this belief in God as it fought against idol worship and other narrow conceptions of religion. In this way man will try to stand on his feet. Being realistic, he will have to throw his faith aside and face all adversaries with courage and valour. That is exactly my state of mind. My friends, it is not my vanity; it is my mode of thinking that has made me an atheist. I don't think that by strengthening my belief in God and by offering prayers to Him every day, (this I consider to be the most degraded act on the part of man) I can bring improvement in my situation, nor can I further deteriorate it. I have read of many atheists facing all troubles boldly, so I am trying to stand like a man with the head high and erect to the last; even on the gallows.

Converted from the original Gurmukhi (Punjabi) to Urdu/Persian script by Maqsood Saqib; translated from the Urdu to English by Hasan

---

M.N. ROY

Manabendra Nath Roy, (1887–1954), revolutionary and thinker, founded the first Communist Parties in the world outside Russia, i.e. the Mexican Communist Party in 1919 and the Indian Communist Party in October 1920. He had worked with Lenin, Stalin and Trotsky for many years as an important member of the executive of Communist International till his break with Stalin in 1927. He returned to India in 1930 and was imprisoned for almost six years (1930–36) under Section 121-A of the Indian Penal Code, 'conspiring to deprive the King Emperor of his sovereignty in India'. He was one of the staunchest critics of Gandhian methods, mainly of the mixing of politics and religion. Later, he developed the philosophy of 'Radical Humanism' which he thought was an improvement on Marxism. The following essay was written when Roy was jailed in Bareilly and had heard the news that after the suspension of the Civil Disobedience movement, Congress had decided to revive the Swaraj Party and participate in the forthcoming assembly election.

Whither Congress? A Manifesto

I

The decision of the Delhi Conference to revive the Swaraj party indicates a definite turn of the Congress politics towards the Right. A great majority of the Congress leaders were present at the Conference. The decision, therefore, reflects the tendency of the leadership as a whole. The Mahatma has conferred his blessing upon the decision, sooner than the most optimist expected.[1] This action of the Mahatma renders meaningless the attitude of the few leaders who still stick to the bankrupt policy of Civil Disobedience.

Once again a momentous change in the Congress politics is made without consulting the membership. Once again leaders have committed the Congress to a policy utterly disregarding the sentiment of the rank and file. Let alone the masses of the members and adherents; even the minor leaders of the movement have been deprived of the right of participating in the making of such a fateful and fatal decision. The leaders of a democratic movement have no regard for the very elementary principles. Nor is it a question of academic principle. Experience has shown that whenever leaders made momentous changes in the Congress politics without consulting or disregarding the spirit of the masses, the new policy proved to be as futile as the old. ... Bitter experience should no longer allow blind faith in the supreme wisdom of the leaders. The leaders must guide the movement according to the spirit of the masses. Otherwise, they are bound to mislead or betray. Once again, the Congress is going to be misled and betrayed. Should it be allowed?

The Poona Conference was much more representative than the conclave in Delhi. Through a large number of local leaders present there, the Poona Conference, to some extent, reflected the mood of the masses. It is true that those demanding a change of policy did not present a definite Left-wing programme; but the general tendency of the local leaders was a move to the Left—for the adoption of a more effective form of militant action. When the demand for a change came from the masses, the Mahatma obstinately opposed it. But today he graciously endorses a turn to the Right decided by the leaders in an informal conference with no authority to make such a fundamental decision. The inference is clear. The Mahatma would not permit the Congress to abandon the bankrupt tactics of Civil Disobedience with the object of adopting a more effective form of militant mass action; but a turn to the Right—to neoconstitutionalism—he readily sanctions on the flimsy pretext that he does so without changing his views about the usefulness of the legislatures under present conditions, and his faith in Civil Disobedience. Despite the sophistry with which the Mahatma justifies his action, the fundamental fact is that the leaders are resolved to follow a line of policy which represents repudiation of the creed, programme, and objective striving of the Congress.

...The resurrected Swaraj Party, that is to say, the Congress as represented by the present leaders, will reject the White Paper scheme.[2] This is an empty gesture. For, according to the decision of the Delhi Conference, the new policy of the Congress will be to stand by the 'National Demand' presented by the Mahatma at the Second Round Table Conference. What was that demand? That 'national' demand itself represented a repudiation of the 'Independence Resolution' of the Congress by its sole representative.

If the programme of independence is to be seriously taken, it means that the Congress is committed to a revolutionary anti-imperialist struggle. The programme indirectly calls for separation from the British Empire and the Indian people can never argue out of the chains of colonial slavery. Nevertheless, the Mahatma, as the sole accredited representative of the Congress to the Second R.T.C., declared that India was willing to accept 'equal partnership in the Empire'. And according to him, slavery would become partnership provided that the new constitution included some control over the finance and military—a demand, if conceded, would mean a concession not to the Indian masses but to the upper classes. But the Mahatma was careful to make it understood that he was not giving an ultimatum; that he was ready to negotiate on the condition on which he would have the Congress accept 'equal partnership'. Thus, it is pure fiction that the Mahatma went to London, laid down his condition (of Independence and nothing but Independence) and came back, when his term was not accepted forthwith, to continue the 'war'. The Second R.T.C. was not broken up by the Mahatma's intransigence. He came back empty-handed, owing to his woeful ineptitude as a politician. By his readiness to compromise, he encouraged the British Government to doubt the strength of the movement he represented. He was sent back home to bring the Congress round to his view—to give up the programme of Independence in favour of 'equal partnership'. But the arrogant autocrat who had, in the meantime, occupied the viceregal throne, wanted to force the Congress into a struggle just at the moment its forces were all put to sleep with the silly song of 'victory'. The second Civil Disobedience campaign was launched not because the Mahatma came back to renew the 'war' (he came to work for peace), but for the sake of his vanity—because the Viceroy would not give him an interview.

To go back to the 'National Demand' as presented by the Mahatma at the Second R.T.C., is to repudiate the programme of Independence and to commit the Congress to 'equal partnership' within the British Empire. The new policy inaugurated at the Delhi Conference and sanctioned by the Mahatma, proposes this backsliding. It is a betrayal. One should not mince words in this fateful moment.

In view of this palpable implication of the new policy, the rejection of the White Paper scheme is an empty gesture, made to drive a bargain at the last moment. If the rejection of the White Paper was a rejection on the principle, then the demand for 'equal partnership' must also go. For, those who reject on principle the White Paper or any alternative scheme of constitution framed by a similar body, must challenge the self-arrogated prerogative of the British Parliament to dictate the political destiny of India. The goal of 'equal partnership' is not compatible with such a challenge. The fact that the leaders would commit the Congress to the ideal of 'equal partnership' proves that their rejection of the White Paper is not rejection on principle. It does not represent a challenge to the authority of the British Parliament. It does not imply the demand for the right of self-determination. It is merely a protest against certain details of the scheme. The attitude of the Congress towards the White Paper thus ceases to be any different from that of the Liberal Federation or of those even more to the Right. Let some of the details be improved, and the Congress leaders would agree to work the constitution, for what it is worth, and it would not be difficult to persuade the Mahatma to welcome the new constitution as containing the 'Substance of Independence', and the Mahatma, in his turn, would know how to cajole the Congress to follow him blindly. No matter how far the leaders would go eventually, the accomplished fact is that they have repudiated the creed of Independence.

It is not the first time that the ideal of Independence has been set aside. It was done at the Karachi Congress through the instrument of the Delhi Pact. At that time, the movement was prevented from grasping the implication of the policy followed by the leaders through the adoption of the 'economic programme'. While the leaders were conspiring to take the Congress away from the path of national democratic revolution, they were held as Apostles of Socialism. It is silly, indeed sheer hypocrisy, to talk about Socialism when you are ready to compromise with imperialism. A successful anti-imperialist struggle— triumphant national democratic revolution—is the *sine qua non* for the realization of Socialism. No socialist—no conscious member of the working class—of course, took the 'economic programme' seriously. They looked upon it as an instrument of deception. The Left-wing of the Congress, however, was greatly enthused. In that groundless enthusiasm, the reformist deviation on the vital issue of the anti-imperialist struggle was not noticed.

Presently the 'economic programme' became a dead letter. Now, the Delhi Conference has given it an unceremonious burial. It has curtly rejected the proposal for the adoption of an economic programme. There is, however, no politics without economics. Every political policy is determined by some economic interest. Every political party is formed to defend or advance the economic interest of this or that class. The resurrected Swaraj Party will have its economic programme. Its founders have declined to accept an economic programme reflecting the interests of the masses. Why? Because such a programme—even the colourless one adopted at Karachi—would deprive it of the support of the upper classes, whose votes it wishes to catch.

The economic programme of the Swaraj Party is an old familiar story. It was the programme of Indian capitalism. Worse still: it included the defence of parasitic landlordism. C.R. Das's cry 'Swaraj for the 90 per cent' had alarmed the upper classes. So, it was made clear that the party would fight for the interests of capitalism, and the landlords were praised as pillars of society, which should be zealously guarded against any possible blow. In the Legislature the party fought valiantly for Indian capitalism and totally disregarded the elementary welfare of the workers. It did absolutely nothing for the peasants. At least in one province, namely Bengal, it threw out a Government Bill for tenancy reform, which placed some restriction on the right of the landlords to rack-rent the peasantry. In Punjab, it defeated a private member's Bill which proposed control of usury in defence of the peasant. There can be [no] doubt about the economic programme of the revived Swaraj Party. Its economic programme is totally antagonistic to the 'economic programme' of Karachi. The rejection of the latter is, therefore, a corollary to the new policy adopted by the Congress leaders.

The refusal to adopt a programme of economic betterment of the masses is a cynical betrayal of the cherished ideal of the Congress. Shall this go unchallenged?

...The Congress stands on a crossing of ways. The alternatives before it have been very aptly indicated recently by Sardar Sardul Singh as relapse into liberalism or armed insurrection. The decision of the Delhi conference and its endorsement by the Mahatma leave no room for any doubt about the road the leaders want to take. They have chosen the safe road of a relapse into liberalism. But it is a blind alley for the oppressed masses.

The road to the liberation of the masses lies through the revolution. The antagonism between the present leaders of the Congress and the masses of the nationalist movement is irreconcilable. The leaders must betray the masses unless these can strike out their own way under a new revolutionary leadership. A great betrayal is in preparation. Let us frustrate it. Let us liberate the movement for national freedom from the leaders who refuse to lead it on the road to victory. Let us transform the Congress into the organ of a mighty mass movement against foreign imperialism and national reaction.

II

There is no use in entertaining the illusion that the Delhi decision does not affect the Congress which will continue to be faithful to its creed and programme. Such illusions will be dangerous.... The Delhi decision, in course of time, will inevitably become the policy of the Congress unless the Congress adopts an alternative policy in opposition to it. The policy of 'no-change'—of sticking to a form a struggle which has failed—will mean tacit acceptance of the new policy. This was the case in the last no-change vs pro-change controversy.

...The relapse of the Congress to neo-constitutionalism promises to be quicker this time thanks to the accommodating attitude of the Mahatma. Only political initiative on the part of the rank and file can avert that catastrophe.

To secure the Mahatma's sanction for their repudiation of his bankrupt policy, not in favour of a more effective policy of revolutionary mass action, but of the policy of relapse into neo-constitutionalism; the Right-wing leaders pledge lip loyalty to the gods of the Mahatma. The Delhi decision, while repudiating it in practice, does not so much as mention the Civil Disobedience movement. Further, the 'Constructive programme', advocated by the Mahatma at the Poona

Conference, in opposition to the demand for the calling off of the Civil Disobedience campaign, remains in force—formally. The main items of the 'Constructive programme' are removal of untouchability or uplift of the Depressed Classes, Khadi, Swadeshi, prohibition of alcoholic drinks, cottage industries, agricultural improvement, and labour organizations. These are all old familiar gods—with clay feet. Years of experience have demonstrated that to worship at their shrines is a dreary cult. The new 'programme' is but an elaboration of the famous 'constructive programme' of Bardoli, which owing to its impracticability, signally failed to enthuse the nationalist masses, disorganized and demoralized by the sudden and entirely unwarranted retreat.[3] The economic items of the programme are positively reactionary or, at the best, represent the demand for some petty reform. In short, it is not a political programme. It cannot serve the purpose of a lever for developing the political activity of the masses. It is not the programme of a militant mass action. It is the cult of political passivity.

...The Congress will not be able to avoid this inglorious journey to a compromise with Imperialism, on terms dictated by the latter, unless it definitely stands on the only other alternative road—the way of revolutionary mass action leading up to armed insurrection. The Gandhian ideology of the Congress has not permitted it to move in this direction, and has, therefore, brought it to the gate of neo-constitutionalism. Should the Congress not enter the realm of futility, the house of shame, it must disown the ideology which has brought it to the very gate of that realm. The adhesion to the Gandhian ideology must deliver the Congress to the right-wing policy, must force it to betray its ideal, repudiate its programme and disown its cherished profession regarding the welfare of the masses.

The search for a ground between the two extremes will end in political passivity. The Congress must either fight Imperialism or surrender. There is no middle course. Those who propose to steer the Congress in an imaginary middle course simply deceive their followers. The middle course is the diehard adherence to a naive political cult which has miserably failed and which cannot be revived, plus the 'constructive programme', which is a programme of political inactivity. If the movement could be steered in this course of political passivity, the field would be free for the right wing. Thus, the middle-roaders are actually allies of the right wing. Those who are really opposed to the change as inaugurated by the Delhi Conference must not allow themselves to be deceived by the lure of the imaginary golden mean. The right-wing policy of compromise and capitulation can be combated only by a revolutionary left-wing programme of militant mass action.

The present leadership of the Congress must be overthrown. There must appear a courageous new revolutionary leadership to take command. Definite crystallization of the left wing is hindered by the lingering faith in Civil Disobedience. The disapproval of the projected reversal to neo-constitutionalism is generally expressed through obstinate adherence to the tactics of Civil Disobedience which is looked upon as the direct action of the masses. Those who still persist in not admitting that in the last Civil Disobedience campaign the Congress has been defeated, are incorrigible. They are the middle-roaders—the tacit allies of the right wing. But there are others who admit the defeat, but would not agree that thereby the efficacy of the Civil Disobedience has been disproved. They hope to save the Congress through another Civil Disobedience campaign in the future. This hope is based upon the failure to grasp the pernicious implication of the Gandhian ideology which is inseparable from the political policy of the Civil Disobedience.

Direct action of the masses is more efficacious than any other form of action to enforce their demands because it is but the prelude to the application of force—to armed uprising. Precisely for this reason, the demands of a movement, based upon direct action of the masses, are often conceded, at least partially, before the point of clash is reached.... Direct action of the masses implies a threat to subvert the established order by force. In other words, direct action of the masses is a form of applying force in defence of the interest of the oppressed, and it implies that force will be applied in more effective forms if the established order does not give in to popular pressure.

This being the case, the fact of the policy of Civil Disobedience being hitched on to the cult of non-violence deprives it of the potentiality of direct mass action. When a mass movement is preached by its own ideology against applying its latent force (which alone makes it what it is) into practice, even in the case of extreme necessity, it becomes a monstrous futility. Why should the Government fear a movement which is morally bound not to go beyond a limit, and would not retaliate under any circumstances? In the beginning, the Government was not sure that Gandhian ideology could be such a decisive check upon a great mass movement. Therefore, it showed signs of nervousness. But presently it discovered the Achilles' heel, and launched upon a policy of ruthless repression, confident of success. It has come out easily victorious. It has won not so much owing to its own strength, as thanks to the weakness of the movement.

The Civil Disobedience campaign has failed under the burden of its own contradiction. It will fail again and again, unless it is freed from the cult of non-violence. But as soon as the Congress will throw off the paralysing ballast of Gandhian ideology, it will find innumerable channels of mass activity open before it. It will not be necessary to make a politico-religious faith out of one single form of political activity, the efficacy of which is doubtful even under the most favourable circumstances. For, its appeal being purely emotional, it is mostly confined to the urban lower middle-class; it cannot capture and hold for any length of time the workers and peasant masses, who are engrossed by the more practical issues of daily life. Indeed, its Gandhian ideology, particularly the cult of non-violence, compels the Congress to stake its entire fortune on the dark horse of Civil Disobedience. The very conception Civil Disobedience excludes the notion of aggressive struggle. Its ambition is not to fight and conquer. Its ideal is to suffer. The entire conception is saturated with a defeatist spirit—it is the conception of slave mentality.

As a matter of fact, Civil Disobedience, foregoing automatic development into a genuinely militant mass movement, is bound either to degenerate into neo-constitutionalism or to be demoralized and disintegrate after a defeat. Both these tendencies are today clearly discernible in the Congress; and, unfortunately, they are the predominating tendencies.

The Delhi decision is a logical outcome of the Congress politics conceived under the sinister shadow of the Gandhian ideology. It is no accident that it has received the benediction of the Mahatma just for the asking. On the other hand, the political stultification of the orthodox no-changer, the depressing perspective of the imaginary middle course, with its attendant demoralization and disintegration—this is also a consequence of the Gandhian politics.

To survive the crisis, the Congress must be reborn. A new chapter of its history, entirely different from the old, must be opened, just as was done in 1920 with the inauguration of the non-cooperation movement. The Congress must become the organ of a new form of struggle, with a new programme, under a new leadership, inspired by a consciously revolutionary ideology.[4]

III

A programme of action, calculated to stimulate the greatest possible political activity of the masses, under the limitations of the present situation, and a plan for reinforcing the Congress organizationally, have been proposed in a recent 'Address to the Rank and File of the Congress'. Not only in the address but as early as a year ago, we advocated suspension of the Civil Disobedience and recommended the adoption of measures for developing new forms of mass action. We demanded that an ineffective weapon should be discarded in favour of the more efficacious. We agitated for a change in the policy towards the Left— its radicalization. We raised the banner of left-wing revolt. We sounded the call for a struggle for the leadership of the Congress. We pointed out the danger from the Right. We proposed that the left wing must go swiftly to the offensive. We provided a platform for the left wing. But, unfortunately, the majority of the left-wing leaders were too slow to act.

They still remained under the spell of Gandhian ideology. Their political radicalism was rendered inoperative by their ideological preoccupations. Their better judgment was overcome by the emotional factor of faith in the wisdom of the great leaders.

...The immediate task is to foment mass activity. The leaders can do whatever they like, simply because the rank and file of the movement have been deprived of their activity and opinion. The liquidation of the local Congress committees was an immensely greater blow for the movement than the cumulative effect of all the repressive measures of the Government.[5] The reconstruction of these organs of mass activity is the first condition for the revival of the movement and revitalization of the Congress. The new leadership of the Congress must grow out of the activity of those organs. They can be revived by the agitation in support of the proposed programme. The question of illegality is a technical matter. A meeting of the A.I.C.C. was not called on the ground that it had been declared illegal. This, however, did not prevent the right-wing leaders to have innumerable conferences, and finally work out a new policy, to be imposed upon the Congress before long. Why can't the left wing act in the same way? Informal meetings of local leaders can be always held, and mass movement on specific demands can be inaugurated and developed by Congressmen, acting through ad hoc committees. The determining factor is the will to act and a definite programme of action. The rank and file are eager for action. Any noticeable apathy or pessimism has been created by the obvious futility of the forms of struggle hitherto practised. It is quite natural that the average human being should lose the enthusiasm for going to jail over and over again, for nothing. But the dynamic factor of mass discontent is there. It is steadily becoming broad and deep in consequence of the rapid deterioration of the economic condition of the lower middle class as well as the workers and peasants. Provided a suitable channel of expression, the popular discontent will swiftly transform into a powerful mass movement with a great political significance. The function of a new programme is to indicate the various ways and means for the canalization of mass energy towards a definite goal.

The proposed programme of action having been endorsed by local leaders in informal conferences, similar conferences should be held on provincial scale. Finally, the new programme should be brought before the A.I.C.C. The demand for the meeting of the A.I.C.C. backed by such a widespread rank and file movement will be irresistible.

...The issues will, thus, be joined at last. The meeting of the A.I.C.C. will be the scene for the fateful struggle for the leadership of the Congress. The future of the Congress will be determined by the outcome of that struggle. With determination, courage, and above all ideological clarity, the left wing, crystallized definitely out of the rank and file activity, is sure to win.

The crystallization of a left-wing leadership, and its victory over the right wing as well as the orthodox Gandhian middle-roaders, are historically determined, being conditions for the further development of the struggle for freedom. The objective conditions for the national democratic revolution are maturing rapidly. The vast bulk of the population is sinking into the lowest depth of poverty and destitution. The conditions of their life are becoming unbearable. Colonial exploitation, aggravated by the world crisis of capitalism, renders any reform impossible. The coveted ideal of bourgeois nationalism, an ideal shared by the right wing of the Congress, the ideal of a capitalist development of India, is a utopia under given conditions. The measures demanded by the Indian capitalists, and partially conceded by imperialism (protective tariff for example), instead of helping the capitalist development of India, positively harm it. The expansion of the internal market is the basic condition for the growth of capitalist production. Colonial exploitation places a limit to the purchasing power of the Indian masses. The present trade depression has reduced that limited capacity by half. Protective tariffs will further aggravate the situation.

So, there is absolutely no prospect for the least amelioration of the economic conditions of the Indian masses, including the lower middle classes. They must choose between pauperization, moral as well as physical degeneration, or revolution. If India is not to follow ancient Egypt, Babylon, etc. to extinction, she must break her chains of slavery—foreign exploitation, and its ally as well as protégé, native reaction.

Revolution implies application of force for the liberation of the oppressed and exploited. The road to freedom from the degrading and demoralizing effects of colonial exploitation lies through an organized revolutionary struggle of the masses, which must eventually develop into the final stage of armed insurrection. The masses, however, cannot be drawn into a revolutionary political movement except through the struggle for enforcing their immediate economic demands. It is only in the course of this struggle that the political consciousness of the masses is awakened, and progressively stimulated into an irresistible will to power. The spirit of the Congress should be not that of sacrifice and suffering. It must be that of fight and conquest. The masses will become alive to the basic necessity for the conquest of political power only in consequence of the experience gained in the fight for the realization of smaller ideals, so vital for their daily life. Revolutionary politics must have a basis of economic realities.

Unless the Congress decidedly rejects the Gandhian ideology, and boldly stands on the road to the conquest of power and finds suitable ways and means for mobilizing the revolutionary energy of the masses in an unflagging struggle for the purpose, it will, under the influence of the right wing, degenerate into neo-constitutionalism, into the shameful policy of compromise with imperialism. That would mean its disintegration as a mass movement. That would mean a great setback to our struggle for freedom. That would mean a temporary check upon the development of the national democratic revolution, so essentially necessary for the progress and prosperity, indeed, for the very physical existence of the Indian people.

Should the rank and file or the leaders of the Congress permit the liquidation of the mass movement for the salvage of a bunch of reactionary notions, and in favour of futile reformist politics? Should the freedom of the Indian people be sacrificed for the cult of non-violence? Should the personal prestige of the Mahatma and his faithful followers be allowed to stand in the way of rank-and-file action? Should the Congress remain bound hand and foot by the prejudice of Civil Disobedience, and the blind faith in its false prophet, even after the prophet has himself thrown away his political cult all but in name? Should the interest and welfare of the masses be betrayed in the name of pragmatic policies of the Swarajists?

These are the questions that challenge the Congress today. The answer must be given not in words, but in deeds. It must take the convincing form of the rise of a new leadership with [a] left-wing programme of revolutionary mass action. It must be given, clearly and unequivocally, the clarion call of a renewed struggle for freedom with the realistic and electrifying slogans: Land to the peasants; Bread to the workers, manual as well as mental. Concretely, these slogans will take different forms in different localities. But essentially, they summarize the immediate economic demands of the 90 per cent of the Indian people. By placing itself at the head of this new form of mass movement, will the Congress avoid the inglorious fate that threatens it today

Notes

1. Gandhi had prepared a draft statement on 2 April 1934, and circulated it among his close friends and followers. When, after the Delhi Conference, Dr Ansari, Dr B.C. Roy, and Bhulabhai Desai met him in a deputation at Patna, he revised and abridged the original draft, and then issued it in full support of the Delhi resolutions.
2. The White Paper, based on the discussions at the Round Table Conference and containing proposals for the reform of the Indian Constitution, was published in March 1933.
3. This refers to the suspension on 12 February 1922 of the earlier Civil Disobedience movement. On that day the Congress Working Committee meeting at Bardoli resolved that Congressmen should immediately stop all mass Satyagraha activities, and take to the Constructive Programme.
4. Attacking the suspension of the Civil Disobedience movement by Gandhi on 8 May 1933, Vithalbhai J. Patel and Subhas Chandra Bose issued a joint statement from Vienna which was broadcast by Reuter. According to this statement.

    Mr Gandhi as a political leader has failed. The time has, therefore, come for a radical reorganization of the Congress on a new principle with a new method, for which a new leader is essential. If the congress as a whole can undergo this transformation, it will be the best course. Failing that, a new party will have to be formed within the congress, composed of radical elements. [*The Indian Annual Register*, 1933, Vol. I].

However this joint attack from abroad had no more effect than Roy's critique from inside prison.

5. When Mass Civil disobedience was suspended, 'all who are able and willing were advised to offer individual Civil Disobedience. Under the orders of the acting President all Congress organizations and war councils ceased to function' (Sitaramayya, *History of the Indian National Congress*, p. 948) However, 'the previous leaders... did not carry out their pledges, except in a few cases. Those who were released from jails found themselves unable or unwilling to face another conviction. In the statement is issued by Gandhi on 7 April 1934, he advised all Congressmen to suspend Civil resistance for Swaraj. They should leave it to me alone. It should be resumed by others in my lifetime only under my direction' (ibid., p. 955). After this, in the words of the official *History of the Congress*, 'the Civil Disobedience movement was switched off and Council-entry programme was switched on (ibid., p.961). At its Bombay Session (26–8 October 1934) the Congress Constitution was changed, and Gandhi formally 'retired' from that organization.

B.R. AMBEDKAR

Dr Bhimrao Ramji Ambedkar (1891–1956) was one of the tallest leaders and thinkers of modern India, and the chief architect of the Indian Constitution. Born into the Mahar community, which was considered 'untouchable', he spent his entire life fighting against social discrimination. Annihilation of Caste *was a speech prepared by B.R. Ambedkar for the annual conference of the Jat-Pat-Todak Mandal of Lahore in 1936. When he wasn't allowed to deliver his speech, Ambedkar published it himself.*

Annihilation of Caste

Turn in any direction you like, Caste is the monster that crosses your path. You cannot have political reform, you cannot have economic reform, unless you kill this monster.

~

There is no doubt in my opinion, that unless you change your social order you can achieve little by way of progress. You cannot mobilize the community either for defence or for offence. You cannot build anything on the foundations of caste. You cannot build up a nation, you cannot build up a morality. Anything that you will build on the foundations of caste will crack and will never be a whole.

The only question that remains to be considered is—How to bring about the reform of the Hindu social order? How to abolish caste? This is a question of supreme importance. There is a view that in the reform of caste, the first step to take is to abolish sub-castes. This view is based upon the supposition that there is a greater similarity in manners and status between sub-caste than there is between castes. I think this is an erroneous supposition. The Brahmins of Northern and Central India are socially of lower grade, as compared with the Brahmins of the Deccan and Southern India. The former are only cooks and water-carriers while the latter occupy a high social position. On the other hand, in Northern India, the Vaishyas and Kayasthas are intellectually and socially on a par with the Brahmins of the Deccan and Southern India. Again, in the matter of food there is no similarity between the Brahmins of the Deccan and Southern India, who are vegetarians and the Brahmins of Kashmir and Bengal who are non-vegetarians. On the other hand, the Brahmins of the Deccan and Southern India have more in common so far as food is concerned with such non-Brahmins as the Gujaratis, Marwaris, Banias and Jains. There is no doubt that from the standpoint of making the transition from one caste to another easy, the fusion of the Kayasthas of Northern India and the other non-Brahmins of Southern India with the non-Brahmins of the Deccan and the Dravidian country is more practicable than the fusion of the Brahmins of the South with the Brahmins of the North. But assuming that the fusion of sub-castes is possible, what guarantee is there that the abolition of sub-castes will necessarily lead to the abolition of castes? On the contrary, it may happen that the process may stop with the abolition of sub-castes. In that case, the abolition of sub-castes will only help to strengthen the Castes and make them more powerful and therefore more mischievous. This remedy is therefore neither practicable nor effective and may easily prove to be a wrong remedy. Another plan of action for the abolition of Caste is to begin with inter-caste dinners. This also, in my opinion, is an inadequate remedy. There are many Castes which allow inter-dining. But it is a common experience that inter-dining has not succeeded in killing the spirit of Caste and the consciousness of Caste. I am convinced that the real remedy is inter-marriage. Fusion of blood can alone create the feeling of being kith and kin and unless this feeling of kinship, of being kindred becomes paramount, the separatist feeling—the feeling of being aliens—created by Caste will not vanish. Among the Hindus inter-marriage must necessarily be a factor of greater force in social life than it need be in the life of the non-Hindus. Where society is already well-knit by other ties, marriage is an ordinary incident of life. But where society is cut asunder, marriage as a binding force becomes a matter of urgent necessity. *The real remedy for breaking Caste is inter-marriage. Nothing else will serve as the solvent of Caste.* Your Jat-Pat-Todak Mandal has adopted this line of attack.

It is a direct and frontal attack, and I congratulate you upon a collect diagnosis and more upon your having shown the courage to tell the Hindus what is really wrong with them. Political tyranny is nothing compared to social tyranny and a reformer, who defies society, is a much more courageous man than a politician, who defies Government. You are right in holding that Caste will cease to be an operative farce only when inter-dining and inter-marriage have become matters of common course. You have located the source of the disease. But is your prescription the right prescription for the disease? Ask yourselves this question: Why is it that a large majority of Hindus do not inter-dine and do not inter-marry? Why is it that your cause is not popular? There can be only one answer to this question and it is that inter-dining and inter-marriage are repugnant to the beliefs and dogmas which the Hindus regard as sacred. Caste is not a physical object like a wall of bricks or a line of barbed wire which prevents the Hindus from co-mingling and which has, therefore, to be pulled down. Caste is a notion, it is a state of the mind. The destruction of Caste does not therefore mean the destruction of a physical barrier. It means a *notional* change. Caste may be bad. Caste may lead to conduct so gross as to be called man's inhumanity to man. All the same, it must be recognized that the Hindus observe Caste not because they are inhuman or wrongheaded. They observe Caste because they are deeply religious. People are not wrong in observing Caste. In my view, what is wrong is their religion, which has inculcated this notion of Caste. If this is correct, then obviously the enemy, you must grapple with, is not the people who observe Caste, but the Shastras which teach them this religion of Caste. Criticizing and ridiculing people for not inter-dining or inter-marrying or occasionally holding inter-caste dinners and celebrating inter-caste marriages, is a futile method of achieving the desired end. The real remedy is to destroy the belief in the sanctity of the Shastras. How do you expect to succeed, if you allow the Shastras to continue to mould the beliefs and opinions of the people? Not to question the authority of the Shastras, to permit the people to believe in their sanctity and their sanctions and to blame them and to criticize them for their acts as being irrational and inhuman is an incongruous way of carrying on social reform. Reformers working for the removal of untouchability, including Mahatma Gandhi, do not seem to realize that the acts of the people are merely the results of their beliefs inculcated upon their minds by the Shastras and that people will not change their conduct until they cease to believe in the sanctity of the Shastras on which their conduct is founded. No wonder that such efforts have not produced any results. You also seem to be erring in the same way as the reformers working in the cause of removing untouchability. To agitate for and to organize inter-caste dinners and inter-caste marriages is like forced feeding brought about by artificial means. Make every man and woman free from the thraldom of the Shastras, cleanse their minds of the pernicious notions founded on the Shastras, and he or she will inter-dine and inter-marry, without your telling him or her to do so.

It is no use seeking refuge in quibbles. It is no use telling people that the Shastras do not say what they are believed to say, grammatically read or logically interpreted. What matters is how the Shastras have been understood by the people. You must take the stand that Buddha took. You must take the stand which Guru Nanak took. You must not only discard the Shastras, you must deny their authority, as did Buddha and Nanak. You must have courage to tell the Hindus, that what is wrong with them is their religion—the religion which has produced in them this notion of the sacredness of Caste. Will you show that courage?

~

What are your chances of success? Social reforms fall into different species. There is a species of reform, which does not relate to the religious notion of people but is purely secular in character. There is also a species of reform, which relates to the religious notions of people. Of such a species of reform, there are two varieties. In one, the reform accords with the principles of the religion and merely invites people, who have departed from it, to revert to them and to follow them. The second is a reform which not only touches the religious principles but is diametrically opposed to those principles and invites people to depart from and to discard their authority and to act contrary to those principles. Caste is the natural outcome of certain religious beliefs which have the sanction of the Shastras, which are believed to contain the command of divinely inspired sages who were endowed with a supernatural wisdom and whose commands, therefore, cannot be disobeyed without committing sin. The destruction of Caste is a reform which falls under the third category. To ask people to give up Caste is to ask them to go contrary to their fundamental religious notions. It is obvious that the first and second species of reform are easy. But the third is a stupendous task, well-nigh impossible. The Hindus hold to the sacredness of the social order. Caste has a divine basis. You must therefore destroy the sacredness and divinity with which Caste has become invested. In the last analysis, this means you must destroy the authority of the Shastras and the Vedas.

SUBHAS CHANDRA BOSE

Among the most prominent figures in the Indian imagination, Subhas Chandra Bose (1897–1945?), also known as 'Netaji' set up and commanded the Indian National Army (INA) in order to liberate India from British rule. In this well-argued, deeply respectful letter, prescient in many ways, Bose sets out his case: why he thinks the non-violent path chosen by Gandhi, and the Indian National Congress, will not work; and why, given world events, the military way to freedom is the only available means.

Message to Mahatma Gandhi, 6 July 1944

Mahatmaji,

Now that your health has somewhat improved and you are able to attend to public business to some extent, I am taking the liberty of addressing a few words to you with a view to acquainting you with the plans and the activities of patriotic Indians outside India. Before I would do so, I would like to inform you of the feelings of deep anxiety which Indians throughout the world had for several days, after your sudden release from custody on grounds of ill-health. After the sad demise of Srimati Kasturbaji in British custody, it was but natural for your countrymen to be alarmed over the state of your health. It has, however, pleased providence to restore you to comparative health, so that 388 millions of your countrymen may still have the benefit of your guidance and advice. I should next like to say something about the attitude of your countrymen outside India towards yourself. What I shall say in this connection is the bare truth and nothing but the truth. There are Indians outside India, as also at home, who are convinced that Indian Independence will be won only through the historic method of struggle. These men and women honestly feel that the British Government will never surrender to persuasion or moral pressure or non-violent resistance.

Nevertheless, for Indians outside India, differences in method are like domestic differences. Ever since you sponsored the Independence Resolution at the Lahore Congress in December 1929, all members of the Indian National Congress have had one common goal before them. For Indians outside India, you are the creator of the present awakening in our country. In all their propaganda before the world, they give you that position and the respect that is due to the position. For the world-public, we Indian nationalists are all one. Having but one goal, one desire and one endeavour in life. In all the countries free from British influence that I have visited since I left India in 1941, you are held in the highest esteem, as no other Indian political leader has been, during the last century. Each nation has its own internal politics and its own attitude towards political problems.

But that cannot affect a nation's appreciation of a man who served his people so well and has bravely fought a first-class modern power all his life. In fact, our worth and your achievements are appreciated a thousand times more in those countries that are opposed to the British Empire than in those countries that pretend to be the friends of freedom and democracy. The high esteem in which you are held by patriotic Indians outside India and by foreign friends of India's Freedom, was increased a hundred-fold when you bravely sponsored the Quit India Resolution in August 1942.

From my experience of the British Government while I was inside India, from the secret information that I have gathered about Britain's policy while outside India, and from what I have seen regarding Britain's aims and intentions throughout the world, I am honestly convinced that the British Government will never recognize India's demand for Independence. Britain's one effort today is to exploit India to the fullest degree, in her endeavour to win this war. During the course of this war, Britain has lost one part of her territory to her enemies and another part to her friends.

Even if the Allies could somehow win the war, it will be the United States of America [USA], and not Britain, that will be the top dog in future and it will mean that Britain will become a protégé of the USA. In such a situation, the British will try to make good their present losses by exploiting India more ruthlessly than ever before. In order to do that, plans have been already hatched in London for crushing the nationalist movement in India, once and for all. It is because I know of these plans from secret, but reliable sources, that I feel it my duty to bring it to your notice. It would be a fatal mistake on our part to make a distinction between the British Government and the British people.

No doubt there is a small group of idealists in Britain as in the USA who would like to see India free. These idealists who are treated by their own people as cranks, form a microscopic minority. So far as India is concerned, for all practical purposes, the British Government and the British people mean one and the same thing. Regarding the war aims of the USA. I may say that the ruling clique at Washington is now dreaming of world domination. This ruling clique and its intellectual exponents, talk openly of the American Century...

There is no Indian, whether at home or abroad, who would not be happy if India's freedom could be won through the method that you have advocated all your life and without shedding human blood. But things being what they are, I am convinced that if we do desire freedom we must be prepared to wade through blood.

If circumstances had made it possible for us to organize an armed struggle inside India, through our own efforts and restores, that would have been the best course for us. But Mahatmaji, you know Indian conditions perhaps better than anybody else. So far as I am concerned, after twenty years' experience of public service in India, I came to the conclusion that it was impossible to organize an armed resistance in the country without some help from outside—help from our countrymen abroad, as well as from some foreign power or powers. Prior to the outbreak of the present war, it was exceedingly difficult to get help from a foreign power, or even from Indians abroad. But the outbreak of the present war threw open the possibility of obtaining aid both political and military from the enemies of the British Empire. Before I could expect any help from them, however, I had first to find out what their attitude was towards India's demand for freedom.

British propagandists, for a number of years, had been telling the world that the Axis Powers were the enemies of freedom and therefore of India's freedom. Was that a fact? I asked myself. Consequently, I had to leave India in order to find out the truth myself and as to whether the Axis

Powers would be prepared to give us help and assistance in our fight for freedom. Before I finally made up my mind to leave home and homeland, I had to decide whether it was right for me to take help from abroad. I had previously studied the history of revolution all over the world in order to discover the method which had enabled other nations to obtain freedom. But I had not found a single instance in which an enslaved people had won freedom without foreign help of some sort. In 1940, I read my history once again, and once again I came to the conclusion that history did not furnish a single instance where freedom had been won without help of some sort from abroad. As for the moral question as to whether it was right to take help, I told myself that in public, as in private life, one could always take help as a loan and repay that loan later on. Moreover, if a powerful Empire, like the British Empire, could go round the world with the begging bowl, what objection could there be to an enslaved and disarmed people like ourselves taking as a loan from abroad. I can assure you, Mahatmaji, that before I finally decided to set out on a hazardous mission, I spent days, weeks and months in carefully considering the pros and cons of the case. After having served my people so long, to the best of my ability, I could have no desire to be a traitor, or to give anyone a justification for calling me a traitor.

It was the easiest thing for me to remain at home and go on working as I had worked so long. It was also an easy thing for me to remain in an Indian prison while the war lasted. Personally, I had nothing to lose by doing so. Thanks to the generosity and to the affection of my countrymen, I had obtained the highest honour which was possible for any public worker in India to achieve. I had also built up a party consisting of staunch and loyal colleagues who had implicit confidence in me. By going abroad on a perilous quest, I was risking not only my life and my whole future career, but also what was more, the future of my party. If I had the slightest hope that without action from abroad we could win freedom, I would never have left India during a crisis. If I had any hope that within our lifetime we would get another chance, another golden opportunity for winning freedom, as during the present war, I doubt if I would have set out from home. But I was convinced of two things: firstly, that such a golden opportunity would not come within another century, and secondly, that without action from abroad, we would not be able to win freedom, merely through our own efforts at home. That is why I resolved to take the plunge.

Providence has been kind to me, in spite of manifold difficulties; all my plans have succeeded so far. After I got out of India, my first endeavour was to organize my countrymen, wherever I happened to meet them. I am glad to say that everywhere I found them to be wide-awake and anxious to do everything possible for winning freedom for India. I then approached the governments that were at war with our enemy in order to find out what their attitude was towards India. I found out that contrary to what British propagandists had been telling us for a number of years the Axis powers were now, openly, the friends of India's freedom. I also discovered that they were prepared to give such help as we desired and as was within their own power.

I know the propaganda that our enemy has been carrying on against me. But I am sure that my countrymen, who know me so well, will never be taken in. One, who has stood for national self-respect and honour all his life and has suffered considerably in vindicating it, would be the last person in this world to give in to any other foreign power. Moreover, I have nothing to gain personally at the hands of a foreign power. Having received the highest honour possible for an Indian at the hands of my own countrymen, what is there for me to receive from a foreign power? Only that man can be a puppet, who has either no sense of honour and self-respect or desire to build up a position for him through the influence of others.

Not even my worst enemy can ever dare to say that I am capable of selling national honour and self-respect. And not even my worst enemy can dare to assert that I was nobody in my own country and that I needed foreign help to secure a position for myself. In leaving India, I had to risk everything that I had, including my life. But I had to take that risk, because only by doing so could I help the achievement of India's freedom.

There remains one question to answer with regard to the Axis Powers. Can it be possible that I have been deceived by them? I believe it will be universally admitted that the cleverest and the most cunning politicians are to be found among Britishers. One who has worked with and fought British politicians all his life, cannot be deceived by any other politicians in the world. If British politicians have failed to coax or coerce me, no other politician can succeed in doing so. And if the British Government, at whose hands I have suffered long imprisonment, persecution and physical assault, has been unable to demoralize me, no other power can hope to do so.

How much help we shall need from Japan till the last Britisher is expelled from the soil of India, will depend on the amount of co-operation that we shall receive from inside India. Japan herself does not desire to thrust her assistance upon us. Japan would be happy if the Indian people could liberate themselves through their own exertions. It is we who have asked for assistance from Japan after declaring war on Britain and America, because our enemy has been seeking help from other powers. However, I have every hope that the help we shall receive from our countrymen at home will be so great that we shall need minimum help from Japan.

Nobody would be more happy than ourselves, if, by any chance, our countrymen at home should succeed in liberating themselves through their own efforts or if, by any chance, the British Government accepts your Quit India Resolution and gives effect to it. We are, however, proceeding on the assumption that neither of the above is possible and that an armed struggle is inevitable.

Mahatmaji, there is one other matter to which I shall refer before I close and that is above the ultimate outcome of this war. I know very well the kind of propaganda that our enemies have been carrying on in order to create the impression that they are confident of victory. But I hope that my countrymen will not be duped thereby and will not think of compromising with Britain on the issue of independence under the mistaken notion that the Anglo-Americans will win this war.

Having travelled round the world under war-time conditions with my eyes open, having seen the internal weakness of the enemy on the Indo-Burma frontier and inside India, and having taken stock of our own strength and resources, I am absolutely confident of our final victory. I am not so foolish as to minimize, in the least, the strength of the enemy. I know that we have a long and hard struggle in front of us. I am aware that on the soil of India, Britain will fight bravely and fight hard in a desperate attempt to save her Empire. But I know also that, however long and hard the struggle may be, it can have but one outcome namely, our victory. India's last war of independence has begun. Troops of the Azad Hind Fauj are now fighting bravely on the soil of India and in spite of all difficulty and hardship they are pushing forward slowly but steadily. This armed struggle will go on, until the last Britisher is thrown out of India and until our tri-colour national flag proudly floats over the Viceroy's House in New Delhi.

Father of our Nation: In this holy war for India's liberation, we ask for your blessings and good wishes.

Jai Hind

ISMAT CHUGHTAI

*Ismat Chughtai (1915–91), one of the most powerful voices in Urdu literature
of the twentieth century, was known for her free and fearless explorations of
the themes of feminine sexuality and middle-class morality in her writing
and for the fierce determination with which she defended her right to express
herself. While she wrote prolifically, her best-known work is the short story
'Lihaaf' (Quilt) which explores the theme of homoeroticism and for which
she was brought before a judge on charges of obscenity—along with Sa'adat
Hasan Manto, who was being tried for the same charge for his story 'Bu'
(Odour). This essay is an account of the trial.*

An Excerpt from *Kaghazi Hai Pairahan* (The 'Lihaf' Trial)

I went to stay at Mr Aslam's house with Shahid Sahab. Hardly had we
exchanged greetings that he blew his top over the alleged obscenity in
my writings. I retaliated like a woman possessed. Shahid Sahab tried to
restrain me, but in vain.

'You've used such vulgar words in your *Gunaah Ki Ratein*! You've
even described the details of the sex act, just to titillate,' I said.

'My case is different. I'm a man.'

'Am I to blame for that?'

'What do you mean?' His face was flushed with anger.

'What I mean is—God has made you a man, I had no hand in it, and
HE has made me a woman, you had no hand in it. You have the freedom
to write whatever you want, you don't need my permission. Similarly, I
don't feel any need to seek your permission for writing the way I want to.'

'You're an educated girl from a decent Muslim family.'

'You're also educated. And from a decent Muslim family.'

'Do you want to compete with men?'

'Certainly not. I always endeavoured to obtain higher marks than the
boys in the class and often succeeded in that.'

I knew that I was being pig-headed as usual. Aslam Sahab's face was
red hot with anger. I was afraid he would hit me or his jugular vein would
burst. Shahid Sahab was aghast, almost in tears. I assumed a softer tone
and said humbly, 'Aslam Sahab, actually no one had told me that it was
a sin to write on the topic with which "Lihaf" is concerned. Nor had
I read in any book that such a…disease…such aberrations should not
be written about. Perhaps my mind is not an artist's brush like Abdur

Rahman Chagtai's but an ordinary camera that records reality as it is. The pen becomes helpless in my hand because my mind overwhelms it. Nothing can interfere with this traffic between the mind and the pen.'

'Wasn't any religious education imparted to you?'

'Aslam Sahab, I've read *Behishti Zevar*. Such explicit things are written there ...' I said innocently. Aslam Sahab looked upset. I continued, 'When I read it in my childhood I was shocked. Those things seemed vulgar to me. But when I read it again, after my B.A., I realized that they were not vulgar, they were important facts of life about which every sensible person should be aware. Well, people can brand the books prescribed in the course of Psychology and Medicine vulgar if they so want.'

... I had teased him enough. To make up for it I now began to praise his writings. I had read *Nargis* and *Gunaah ki Ratein* and began to praise them in superlative terms. Eventually he came round to the view that a deliberately stark style of narration made for both clarity and instruction. Then he began to enumerate the merits of all the books that he had written. Now he was in a genial mood.

'Tender an apology to the judge,' Aslam Sahab advised gently.

'Why? Our lawyer says that we'll win the case.'

'Nonsense! If you and Manto tender your apologies the case can be wound up in five minutes.'

'Many respectable people here have put pressure on the government to bring the suit against us.'

'Nonsense!' Aslam Sahab said but he could not look me in the eye.

'Do you mean the King of England or the people in the government have actually read the stories and thought about filing this suit?'

'Aslam Sahab, some writers, critics and people in high positions have drawn the attention of the government to the books as being detrimental to morality and urged to ban them,' said Shahid Sahab in a subdued tone.

'If morally detrimental writings are not banned, should we offer homage to them?' Aslam Sahab growled and Shahid Sahab cowered in embarrassment.

'Then we deserve punishment,' I said.

'Being pig-headed again.'

'No, Aslam Sahab, I really mean it. If I've committed a crime and innocent people have been lead astray, why should I escape punishment merely by tendering an apology? If I've committed the crime and if it's proved, then only punishment can bring peace to my conscience,' I said without any trace of sarcasm.

…We appeared before the court on the day of the hearing. The witnesses who had to prove that Manto's story 'Bu' and my story 'Lihaf' were obscene, were all present there. My lawyer instructed me not to open my mouth till the interrogation began. He would answer the queries as he thought fit.

'Bu' was taken up first.

'Is this story obscene?' Manto's lawyer asked.

'Yes,' answered the witness.

'Can you put your finger on a word which is obscene?'

Witness: 'The word "chest".'

Lawyer: 'My Lord, the word "chest" is not obscene.'

Witness: 'No. But here the writer means a woman's breasts.'

Manto was on his feet instantly and blurted out: 'A woman's chest must be called breasts and not groundnuts.'

The court reverberated with loud guffaws. Manto too began to laugh.

'If the accused shows frivolity a second time he will be turned out or punished for severe contempt of court.'

Manto's lawyer whispered into his ear and he understood the situation. The debate went on. The witness could find no other word except 'chest' and it could not be proved obscene.

'If the word "chest" is obscene, why not knee or elbow?' I asked Manto.

'Nonsense!' Manto growled.

…The court was crowded the next day. Several people had advised us to tender an apology. They were ready to pay the fine on our behalf. The excitement surrounding the lawsuits was waning. The witnesses who had wanted to prove 'Lihaf' obscene were thrown into confusion by my lawyer. They were not able to put their finger on any word in the story that would prove their point. After a good deal of reflection one of them said: 'This phrase… "collecting lovers" is obscene.'

'Which word is obscene: "collect" or "lover"?' the lawyer asked.

'Lover,' replied the witness a little hesitantly.

'My Lord, the word "lover" has been used by great poets most liberally. It is also used in naats, that is, poems written in praise of the Prophet. God-fearing people have accorded it a very high status.'

'But it is objectionable for girls to collect lovers,' said the witness.

'Why?'

'Because… because it is objectionable for good girls to do so.'

'And if the girls are not good, then it is not objectionable?'

'Mmm…no.'

'My client must have referred to the girls who were not good. Yes, madam, do you mean here bad girls collect lovers?'

'Yes.'

'Well, this may not be obscene. But it is reprehensible for an educated lady from a decent family to write about such things,' the witness thundered.

'Censure it as much as you want. But it does not come within the purview of law.'

The issue lost much of its steam.

'If you agree to apologize, we'll pay up the entire expense incurred by you ...,' someone I didn't know whispered into my ear.

'Should we apologize, Manto Sahab? We can buy a lot of goodies with the money we'll get,' I suggested to Manto.

'Nonsense!' Manto growled Manto and his peacock eyes bulged out again.

'I'm sorry. This madcap Manto doesn't agree.'

'But you ... why don't you ... ?'

'No. You don't know what a quarrelsome fellow he is! He'll make my life miserable in Bombay. I'd rather undergo the punishment than risk his wrath.

The judge called me into the anteroom attached to the court and said quite informally, 'I've read most of your stories. They aren't obscene. Neither is "Lihaf". But Manto's writings are littered with filth.'

'The world is also littered with filth,' I said in a feeble voice.

'Is it necessary to rake it up, then?'

'If it is raked up it becomes visible and people feel the need to clean it up.'

The judge laughed.

I was not terribly worried when the suit was filed, neither did I feel elated now that I had won it. Rather I felt sad at the thought that it might be a long while before I got a chance to visit Lahore again.

Translated by M. Asaduddin

On Radha and Krishan

The following is an excerpt from a letter Chughtai wrote to Ram Lal, a well-known Urdu writer whose views on the god Krishan caused a huge uproar in society.

Arre bhai, you caused much distress when you called Kanhaiyaji a womanizer. He alone was a god of some calibre. Certainly the most progressive and literary. I mean, having created the *Gita*, he was one of us, one of our tribe, wasn't he?

He was unique because he counted even women among human beings. In the world's different literatures, there is no comparable expression of a woman's love for a man, portrayed so freely and with such courage. No other tradition has drawn attention to the woman as a lover and man as the beloved. Even in French and English classics, the woman is the beloved. Usually only the prostitute has indulged in free love but her lover is characteristically depicted as vulgar and commercialized. But Krishanji has given romantic love the status of Bhakti, an act of devotion. Radha was a married woman who had an unbounded passion for Krishan and was turned into a figure worthy of worship. One cannot find another instance of such rebellious and reckless love. For the woman has been set on earth in the mould of the beloved, over whom the lover holds sway. If the respectable woman, resorting to subterfuge, dares to engage in illicit love, she either drowns or dies after taking poison. A married woman's husband is her god, but the wedded Radha belongs to Krishan and not to her husband. What was the name of Radha's husband, the one with name and status? I don't even know his name, but the whole world knows the name of her beloved.

And that is not all. If a man, who was not related to a woman, even dared to glance in the direction of the mother or sister of another man, he would have had his eyes plucked out. However, when Arjun falls in love and the father of his beloved rejects his suit, Krishan tells him, 'I will find a pretext to bring my sister to you and you can run away with her.' How many men born of women would have the courage to help a sister elope with her lover?

Krishan gave sexuality the status of the sacred. Then, as now, the coming together of a woman and man was surely prohibited. It acquired legitimacy only after much bargaining. The relationship was not based on the attachment between a man and a woman but depended on pecuniary interactions. Men could acquire flocks of women as material possessions, and the lives of widows, the living dead, could even be snuffed out on funeral pyres of their husbands. Krishanji did not purchase Radha with gold, nor did he stamp her with the mark of ownership. He drew her to him with the melody of his flute and no power on earth could restrain her. No other tradition, of any country or religion, provides similar examples of independence in a woman's actions although there are many instances of male autonomy.

Look at history, emperors, kings and nawabs maintained women in herds. Did they attract them with their won charm or did they purchase them? People forced these women into their keeping, receiving in return jagirs and titles. Here was a gamble, a game of cards, in which mothers, sisters and daughters were the trumps played. Why did Krishan regard sexual freedom as a component of religious conviction? Has anyone researched the social mores and prohibitions of the time? Were women regarded to be as lowly, helpless, and half-dead then, as they are now? Bought and sold like chattel? Ignited on a funeral pyre like unwanted rubbish that has accumulated in the home?

In what state could one expect to find the mental health of a society where relations between women and men had degenerated to this level? Could men have been sexually satisfied by women who were treated no better than the shoes on their feet? A surfeit of sumptuous feasting results in indigestion and worse, but can the appetite be satiated by devouring an object? One can die without food, but those who condemn the poor to remain hungry by forcibly taking away their rights, learn soon enough that, of all the cravings which their oppressive acts seek to satisfy, sexual indulgences take the highest toll. The communities of women maintained by the oppressors, bring with them the financial burden of their families, whose men have to be provided with women of their own, and so it goes on.

A major share of the nation's wealth is diverted towards supporting the ruler and his minions in luxury. This has been the history of imperialism and it continues today in the form of capitalism. The people die of hunger; only thieves and bandits prosper.

Krishanji overpowered the serpent Kalia and many other forms of evil. However, Kanhaiyaji ultimately faces defeat when he was transformed into an idol to be worshipped. Devotees sway to the rhythm of songs celebrating the union of Radha and Krishan, but if they were to learn that their own wives were clandestinely meeting with some Kanhaiya, neither the wife nor the lover could hope to be spared. They bow their heads before a Krishan of stone but have failed to grasp the wisdom of his words. They have forgotten that if the man is free while the woman is enslaved, their union can only be fraudulent.

Translated by Madhu Prasad and Sohail Hashmi

Sa'adat Hasan Manto

Sa'adat Hasan Manto (1912–1955) was an acclaimed Urdu writer—perhaps the biggest name in Urdu prose—whose works unflinchingly tackled some of society's most taboo and urgent topics. The following piece, most probably written before Independence and originally published as 'Hindustan Ko Leaderon Se Bachao', was his protest against politicians who he thought were bringing the nation to ruin.

Save India from Its Leaders

We've been hearing this for some time now—Save India from this, save it from that. The fact is that India needs to be saved from the people who say it should be saved.

They're experts in making up this sort of thing, there's no doubt. The last thing they are, however, is sincere.

After an evening of fiery speeches and righteous denunciation, when they return to their luxuriant bedrooms, their brains are empty of all thoughts of saving us.

They waste not a second on what actually ails India. Their concerns are personal, not national, and so occupied are they with this that there's actually no space for us.

These people, who can't even run their homes efficiently, and whose character is lowly, want to straighten out the country and lecture us on what is right.

It would be funny if it weren't so ridiculous.

These people—'leaders'—see religion and politics as some lame, crippled man. They peddle him around to beg for money. They shoulder his corpse and appeal to those who will believe anything said from high on up. They claim they are bringing the corpse back to life with their effort.

But the fact is that religion is what it used to be and will forever remain that. The principle of religion is intact, solid. It is unalterable, the sort of mountain that waves can never erode.

When these leaders shed tears and wail, 'Mazhab khatre mein hai' (Religion is in danger), it is all rubbish. Faith isn't the sort of thing that can come into danger in the first place. If anything is in danger, it's these leaders who want to be saved by claiming religion is in peril.

Save India from its leaders, who are poisoning our atmosphere. You may not know this but these leaders go around with scissors. With these they snip your pocket and take all your money. Their life is a long run—towards wealth. Every time they exhale, you can smell the odour of insincerity and greed.

At the head of enormous processions, weighed down by fat garlands, delivering unending speeches full of empty words, they make a path to power for themselves. A path to luxury. They raise and make huge sums of money for themselves as you have seen, but have they told you how unemployment will end? They scream 'religion' all the time but when did they last follow the teachings of their faith?

These fellows—who live in houses given to them, who live on the money they raise from others—how can they make us self-sufficient?

India doesn't need many leaders, each singing a different tune from the other, but those who sing together using the same words. We need only one, as wise as the Caliph Umar and as brave as Ataturk. Someone who will rein in the runaway horse of the State. Who will lead us manfully towards independence.

Remember—the greedy will never be able to lead us in the right way. Those dressed in silk have nothing to offer those who sleep on stones. Fling such people aside.

They are bed bugs who creep inside the crevices and emerge only to suck our blood. They should be forced out with the heat of our despise.

They rant against the rich for no reason other than that they want to be rich themselves. They are the worst sort of people imaginable. They are the thieves among thieves. Let them know what you think of them.

What's needed is for our young men, who may be clothed in tatters but are strong and broad-chested, to stand up and toss them aside from the pedestals they've occupied without our permission.

They have no right to claim empathy with us, the poor. And remember—there's no shame in poverty. Those who think there is are themselves shameful.

The man who fends for himself is the superior of the man who lives off the work of others. Be the man who fends for himself. Look coldly at what is in your best interest. Once we take our fate into our hands, these leaders will have nowhere to run.

Translated by Aakar Patel

KRISHAN CHANDER

Krishan Chander (1914–1977) was one of the pillars of the Progressive Writers' Association. Apart from being a novelist and short-story writer in Urdu, he was also a brilliant essayist. In his satirical essay 'Hindi Ka Naya Qayda' or 'New Primer for Hindi', he re-introduces the Hindi alphabet to his readers. Following is an extract from the essay in a recent translation which appeared in DailyO.in.

New Primer for Hindi

For Adolescents

Children, H for Hindu. A Hindu is one who considers a Muslim his enemy and doesn't do things that a Muslim does. That's why a Muslim eats meat while a Hindu eats vegetables. A Muslim shaves his head, a Hindu grooms a pony tail. A Muslim considers cow kosher and slaughters her while a Hindu treats cow as his mother and worships her. A Muslim considers pig non-kosher so the Hindu pickles it. A Muslim goes to the mosque, a Hindu goes to the temple. The Muslim offers a silent namaz and a Hindu blows a conch and beats cymbals to offer aarti. In spite of this the Hindu and the Muslim are brothers.

The Hindu holds Prithviraj Chauhan in esteem, while the Muslim honours Shahbuddin Ghouri. The Hindu worships Rana Sangha, while the Muslim writes paeans in Babar's glory. The Hindu believes Rana Pratap is greater than Akbar, while the Muslim places Akbar ahead of Rana Pratap. The Hindu's hero is Shivaji, while the Muslim's is Aurangzeb. In spite of this the Hindu and the Muslim are brothers.

Hindus do not let Muslims enter the neighbourhood they stay in; Hindus do not allow Muslims to step into the rooms where they eat; Hindus would not even let a Muslim shadow cast across the room where they sleep. All Hindus drink 'jal', and all Muslims 'paani'. Muslims divorce their wives while Hindus cultivate them for life. Muslims prefer to be buried after death while Hindus prefer cremation. In spite of this the Hindu and the Muslim are brothers.

The Hindu considers the Muslim untouchable, while for the Muslim the Hindu is a kafir. The Muslim does not believe in caste distinctions, while the Hindu places them at the centre of his belief system. The Hindu's sacred language is Sanskrit, while the Muslim's Arabic. The

Hindu believes that Tagore is the poet of the east, while for the Muslim it is Iqbal. The Hindu wants an undivided India, while the Muslim desires a Pakistan. In spite of this the Hindu and the Muslim are brothers.

If Hindus and Muslims are brothers then we might have to invent a new word for 'enemy'. But till that time you may take it that a Hindu is a Muslim's enemy, and they both are brothers. And both these brothers live in the same country about which it has been said, 'Saare jahaan se achha Hindustan hamaara' and 'Aey Aab-e-Rood-e-Ganga'. However, in this very country there are people who prefer to call themselves 'humans'—Children of God! But these very people are mistaken. They are not children of god, they are godless atheists. A pack of wolves! Children, wherever you spot these people, spit on their faces. Because Inspector Saheb's orders are so.

Hindus and Muslims are brothers and address each other as brothers-by-nation or 'desh-bhai'. When desh-bhais, overcome by exuberance and affection, play with each other, it results in 'riots'. 'Riots' is an exciting game and is often played in India because Hindus and Muslims live in large numbers in this country. Often riots begin with a pandit or a maulvi and end with Section 144. During this period rivers of blood flow in which Hindus and Muslims bathe with joy. Later, the Police brings matters under control, and preparations begin for the next set of riots. This game is super exciting. And because Hindus and Muslims have always been busy with it, they handed over the business of dispensing justice to the British for the longest time. That is the reason the British are called justice-loving, and Hindus and Muslims are called riot-loving people. And those who are not riot-loving are called progress-loving or progressives. But these fools are very few in the country. That's why call out aloud; H for Hindu.

Translated by Danish Hussain

DISSENT AND DEMOCRACY

The Constituent Assembly Debates

The Constituent Assembly, consisting of indirectly elected representatives, was formed to draft a Constitution for India (including the now-separate countries of Pakistan and Bangladesh). The Assembly met for the first time in New Delhi on 9 December 1946, and its last session was held on 24 January 1950.

Jaipal Singh Munda

Jaipal Singh Munda (1903–1970), popularly known as Marang Gomke, represented the Adivasis of India at the Constituent Assembly. During this time, he actively championed the rights of the scheduled tribes. Later, when Gandhians proposed that Prohibition be added to the list of Directive Principles, Jaipal Singh Munda made a strong case against it by arguing that it would be an encroachment on the religious freedom of the Adivasis.

On Representation of the Minorities

Mr Chairman, Sir, I rise to speak on behalf of millions of unknown hordes—yet very important—of unrecognized warriors of freedom, the original people of India who have variously been known as backward tribes, primitive tribes, criminal tribes and everything else, Sir, I am proud to be a Jungli, that is the name by which we are known in my part of the country. Living as we do in the jungles, we know what it means to support this Resolution. On behalf of more than thirty million of the Adibasis (cheers), I support it not merely because it may have been sponsored by a leader of the Indian National Congress. I support it because it is a resolution which gives expression to sentiments that throb in every heart in this country. I have no quarrel with the wording of this Resolution at all. As a jungli, as an Adibasi, I am not expected to understand the legal intricacies of the Resolution. But my common sense tells me, the common sense of my people tells me that every one of us should march in that road of freedom and fight together. Sir, if there is any group of Indian people that has been shabbily treated it is my people. They have been disgracefully treated, neglected for the last 6,000 years. The history of the Indus Valley civilization, a child of which I am, shows quite clearly that it is the newcomers—most of you here are intruders as far as I am concerned—who have driven away my people from the Indus Valley to the jungle fastness. This Resolution is not going to teach Adibasis democracy. You cannot teach democracy to the tribal people; you have to learn democratic ways from them. They are the most democratic people on earth. What my people require, Sir, is not adequate safeguards as Pandit Jawahar Lal Nehru has put it. They require protection from Ministers, that is position today. We do not ask for any special protection. We want to be treated like every other Indian.

There is the problem of Hindustan. There is position of Pakistan. There is the problem of Adibasis. If we all shout in different militant directions, feel in different ways, we shall end up in Kabarasthan. The whole history of my people is one of continuous exploitation and dispossession by the non-aboriginals of India punctuated by rebellions and disorder, and yet I take Pandit Jawahar Lal Nehru at his word. I take you all at your word that now we are going to start a new chapter, a new chapter of Independent India where there is equality of opportunity, where no one would be neglected. There is no question of caste in my society. We are all equal. Have we not been casually treated by the Cabinet Mission, more than thirty million people completely ignored? It is only a matter of political window-dressing that today we find six tribal members in this Constituent Assembly. How is it? What has the Indian National Congress done for our fair representation? Is there going to be any provision in the rules whereby it may be possible to bring in more Adibasis and by Adibasis I mean, Sir, not only men but women also? There are too many men in the Constituent Assembly. We want more women, more women of the type of Mrs Vijayalakshmi Pandit who has already won a victory in America by destroying this racialism. My people have been suffering for 6,000 years because of your racialism, racialism of the Hindus and everybody else. Sir, there is the Advisory Committee. My people, the Adibasis—they are also Indians—are deeply concerned about what is going to happen about the selection to the Advisory Committee. When I was first given a copy, of the Memorandum, as first submitted by the Cabinet Mission, in section 20 the language read as follows:

The Advisory Committee on the rights of citizens, minorities and tribal and excluded areas should contain full representation (mark 'should contain full representation') of the interests affected...

Now, when I read a reprint of that in Command Paper 6821, the same paragraph 20 seems to read differently. Here it reads:

The Advisory Committee on the rights of citizens, minorities and tribal and excluded areas will contain due representation.

I want to be quite clear on that point. I think there has been juggling of words going on to deceive us. I have heard of resolutions and speeches galore assuring Adibasis of a fair deal. If history had to teach me anything at all, I should distrust this Resolution, but I do not. Now we are on a new road. Now we have simply got to learn to trust each other. And I ask friends who are not present with us today that they should come in, they should trust us and we, in turn, must learn to trust them. We must create a new atmosphere of confidence among ourselves. I regret there has been too much talk in this House in terms of parties and minorities. Sir, I do not consider my people a minority. We have already heard on the floor of the House this morning that the Depressed Classes also consider themselves as Adibasis, the original inhabitants of this country. If you go on adding people like the exterior castes and others who are socially in no man's land, we are not a minority. In any case we have prescriptive rights that no one dare deny. I need say no more.

On Prohibition

We have heard such a lot of pious language about a democratic State, of a secular State, of our being voluntarily opposed to the establishment of the democracy in India. Here, Sir, I submit, by the back door we are trying to interfere with the religious rights of the most ancient people of this country. You may laugh. Excess in everything is wrong. If you eat too much rice, it is bad for you. There are so many other things that you take in excess. But, if you take anything in its right quantity, it is good for you. Drink certainly is one of the things taken in excess which does no one good, but, let us remember that we should not be hasty in putting into the Constitution anything which is going to work for more bitterness than there is already. During our discussions in the Advisory Committee, Maulana Abul Kalam Azad was pleased to put a direct question to me and it was this: 'Kya yah mazhabi chij hai?' Is it really a religious right? On that occasion, the Chairman of the Advisory Committee, the Honourable Sardar Patel gave me an opportunity to explain what the position was. Now, as far as the Adibasis are concerned, no religious function can be performed without the use of rice beer. The word here used—the phrase used is 'intoxicating drinks'. Sir, that is a very vague way of describing the thing, and, also 'injurious to health'. My friend Prof. Shibban Lal has tried to put forward the argument of economic efficiency. He thinks that if prohibition were installed in this country, the economic efficiency of the workers would be enhanced. I dare say it would be. But what I want to tell him is that it is not merely the industrial workers whom he has particularly in mind, that are affected. I would like to point out to him the position of the very poor people, the Adibasis, and, members who come from West Bengal and other places will bear me out in what I say about the Adibasis who are in such large numbers in West Bengal, southern Bihar, Orissa and other places. In West Bengal, for instance, it would be impossible for paddy to be transplanted if the Santhal does not get his rice beer. These ill-clad men, without even their barest wants satisfied, have to work knee-deep in water throughout the day, in drenching rain and in mud. What is it in the rice beer that keeps them alive? I wish the medical authorities in this country would carry out research in their laboratories to find out what it is that the rice beer contains, of which the Adibasis need so much and which keeps them against all manner of diseases.

Well, Sir, I am not opposing this amendment because I want drink to increase in this country. I am all for seeing to it, and, seeing vigorously to it, that the Adibasis do not injure themselves by this drink habit. But that is quite apart from the religious needs and religious privileges; we shall educate them to lead a life of temperance. I am all for that. But this amendment is a vicious one. It seeks to interfere with my religious right. Whether you put it in the Constitution or not, I am not prepared to give up my religious privileges. (Hear, hear.)

Begum Aizaz Rasul

Begum Aizaz Rasul (1908–2001) was the only Muslim woman representative in the Constituent Assembly. In the following speech, she warns against regressive panchayati raj and policies that would transfer the rights of individuals to the state machinery.

Much has been said about the fact that most of the provisions have been borrowed from the Constitutions of USA, England, Australia, Canada, Switzerland, etc. Sir, I for my part see nothing wrong in borrowing as long as the higher interests of the nation and the well-being and prosperity of the country are kept in mind. There is no doubt that the draft Constitution has been framed to fit in with the present administration. But this had to be so in the very nature of things. After all, we have all become used to a certain way of life of government and of administration. If the draft

Constitution had changed the whole structure of Government, there would have been chaos. India is a new recruit to the democratic form of Government. Its people have been used to centuries of autocratic rule and, therefore, to carry on more or less on the lines they have been accustomed for some time more, with changes here and there according to changed conditions, is the best thing possible. The important thing is that power is derived from the people and it is the people who will make or mar the destiny of India.

A lot of criticism has been made about Dr Ambedkar's remark regarding village polity. Sir, I entirely agree with him. Modern tendency is towards the right of the citizen as against any corporate body and village panchayats can be very autocratic.

Sir, coming to the Fundamental Rights, I find that what has been given with one hand has been taken away by the other. Fundamental Rights should be such that they should not be liable to reservations and to changes by Acts of legislature. It is essential that at least some of the civil liberties of the citizen should be preserved by the Constitution and it should not be easy for the legislature to take them away. Instead of this, we find the provision relating to these Rights full of provisos and exceptions. This means that what has been given today could easily be changed tomorrow by an Act of the legislature.

To my mind it is necessary that some sort of agency should be provided to see that the Fundamental Rights and the Directive Principles are being observed in all Provinces in the letter and in the spirit. Otherwise it may be that the absence of such an agency may give rise to the formation of communal organizations with the object of watching the interests of their respective communities. It should be the function of the agency I have suggested to bring to the notice of the Government the cases where the Fundamental Rights and the Directive Principles are not being followed properly. I hope this point of mine will be seriously considered by this august Assembly when we come to discuss the Draft Constitution clause by clause.

Purnima Banerji

Purnima Banerji (1911–1951), member of the constituent assembly, highlighted the need to discourage religious classes in schools, especially during a child's formative years. She proposed establishing state-aided schools where the focus would be on developing a broader outlook and respect for all religions rather than sectarian values.

Sir, I move: That in Clause 16 the following new paragraph be added as an explanation—

All religious education given in educational institutions receiving State-aid will be in the nature of the elementary philosophy of comparative religions calculated to broaden the pupils' mind rather than such as will foster sectarian exclusiveness.

The object of the clause, Sir, is as the Mover of the Report has suggested, to prevent the students attending these schools being forced to attend the religious classes, if they do not wish to do so. With that I am in perfect agreement. But I know there are a large number of institutions which are run on religious lines and which came into the field of education much before the State came in. There are in my Province 'Maktabs' and 'Pathasalas' which perform the function of imparting education to children of school-going age. But we have seen that the religious instructions given there are of such a nature that, instead of broadening the mind of the child, they mis-educate the mind and sometimes breed a certain type of fanaticism and religious bigotry as a result of receiving education in these 'Maktabs' and 'Pathasalas'. It is a controversial point as to whether we should give any aid to denominational schools at all. I do not wish to open that subject at all because there are experts appointed for this purpose and their report is awaited and I am sure after that the legislature will enter into that subject in fuller detail. My object in moving the amendment is that the education imparted in these institutions should be restricted or controlled by the Government without any fear of interfering with anybody's religion. The curriculum should be in the control of the Government and should be of such a nature that it broadens the mind rather than create an exclusiveness. When we were discussing the Minority Rights Report, we said that our aim should be to form a united nation and we have done away with separate electorate and agreed on fundamental rights and given each the right to follow his own religion. But I do believe that however secular a State you may wish to build up, unless one member of it appreciates the religion of another member of the State, it would be impossible for us to build up a united India. Therefore, without interfering with the religion of anybody, the State should be perfectly entitled to see that in the formative age of the child, when he is of the school-going age, the religious instruction is controlled and that the syllabus is of such a nature that the child will develop into a healthy citizen of India capable of appreciating each other's point of view. We may be united by political parties, but if we do not appreciate each other's religion, we shall find that instead of having really men of religion in our midst, we shall be breeding a type of exclusiveness which will be most harmful and on that type of mind, I am afraid, the future of the nation cannot be built up. With these few words, Sir, I move my amendment and I hope the House will agree with me and accept it.

O.V. ALAGESAN ON LINGUISTIC STATES

The matter of a separate Telugu state was at the centre of a 1952 Lok Sabha resolution addressing 'linguistic states'. O.V. Alagesan, a legislator from Chingleput (Madras Province) which was proposed to be given up to the new Andhra state, strongly criticized the split. Elaborating the extremes to which the notion of linguistic states could be stretched, he points out that this criterion of state formation would undermine the unity and solidarity of the polity. The speech was made on 12 July 1952.

The debate has gone on for more than six hours and at long last I am glad that one representing the Tamil area has been called to speak. It looked as if there are no representatives in this House from the Tamil area, more so from Madras. There was much bandying of words about the city of Madras. Several honourable Members spoke about the position that it should take under the future redistribution scheme. I was wondering what happened to representatives from the city of Madras in this House. There are several of them. The south of Madras is very ably represented by my honourable friend Mr T.T. Krishnamachari, who fortunately or unfortunately has got into the Treasury Benches and therefore his mouth is shut. But, that does not mean that nobody in this House knows his opinion about the city of Madras. Again, three-eighths of the city of Madras is represented equally ably by my honourable friends Mr Natesan and Shrimati Chandrasekhar. I hope they will be given an opportunity to speak their minds. They will be really voicing the opinion of the people of Madras in this matter, where they want to remain, and where they want to be tagged on. Up till now, the debate has assumed a tilted and unreal aspect, because the real representatives of the city of Madras in this House have not been called upon to give their opinion in this matter.

I shall first deal with the immediate background of this resolution and then take up some of the controversial points that have been raised by my friends from Andhra area. If I have counted rightly, so far five of them, including you, Sir, have, spoken, and several others from the Kerala area, and several others from the Karnataka area have also spoken. This demand for linguistic provinces is more emotional in content than either political or economic. People are deeply stirred over this question, and very much agitated and in the Andhra area people are going on fast. I do not know whether to call it satyagraha or otherwise and they demand linguistic province. It is a sort of glorification of the past. When the achievements of the people become memories of the past, it is language that holds up the mirror to those achievements and reminds them of those. When everything else decays and dies, language alone lives. It is because of this that language evokes the deepest emotions in the human heart. Take the Maharashtrian, for instance. He dreams of the valiant days of Shivaji and longs to relive them.

...He contemplates the great saint of Maharashtra and his sacred abhangs, and feels very much elevated. So also Andhra friends dream of the empire of the pre-Christian era, which has nothing in common with the Telugu except the name, Andhra.

...The Tamil poets have sung how Tamilian kings conquered north Indian chieftains and planted their flag on the Himalayas. They have very discreetly omitted all mention of the defeats that they suffered at the hands of others. The honourable Finance Minister, the clever man that he is, quoted a simple Kural from the book of Tiruvalluvar, ending his reply to the general discussion on the Budget and the whole of Tamil Nadu was aglow with pride that, here is a Finance Minister, who is himself a Maharashtrian, but has chosen to quote Kural. Even if he had set apart about ten crores to the Tamil area, he would not have evoked such a response, because the people would have still said, here is a Finance Minister who could have given much more, but he has given only this much.

That is the magic that language exercises over the minds of men. If the people and their representatives are agitated over it, I can perfectly understand that.

Just as my honourable friend Mr Nijalingappa said a few minutes ago, our friends opposite have not been slow to seize this question of high emotional value and they have come out as the champions of linguistic provinces. They are the foremost in demanding redistribution on linguistic bias. That is perfectly understandable. It would be very interesting to know from them how many languages and dialects they have recognized for the purpose of linguistic redistribution. There are certain languages in this country which do not have any script. Yet, my honourable friends opposite would give him the luxury of a separate State, because they would recognize even dialects. *We should improve them; we should develop them;* that is what they would say. There is another language called Tulu, which is spoken in a portion of South Kanara. Half of that district will go to Tulu and half to Konkani. If my friends opposite have their way, they will have the entire country cut up into all sort of little linguistic bits so that there may not be the requisite amount of unity and solidarity in the country. They would ask us to follow blazing example of the Fatherland and ask us to develop every little dialect because it serves their purpose eminently well. We now carry on our public affairs through the medium of language and that too a foreign language. Though the language is one we could voice different opinions. Yesterday, we saw how the honourable Home Minister had his opinion changed and introduced a major change in the Bill in deference to the wishes of the Opposition.

When our friends opposite have it all their own way, they would not have any diversity of opinion. They will enforce total conformity and uniformity. Having ensured that, they would allow any amount of diversity in language. What if there are 100 languages? They will all sing in the same chorus; they will sing the greatness of the State symbolized in its Head. So, it suits them very well to bring up this question at this moment and try to weaken this country. It will be very profitable to enquire how our friends who believe in ultra-centralism seemingly adopt a course which decentralizes power in the hands of various linguistic units. Therein lies the secret of their strategy. They adopt methods which are diametrically opposite to the ends they desire.

B.R. Ambedkar on the Constitution

Dr Bhimrao Ramji Ambedkar was the Chairman of the Constitution Drafting Committee and independent India's first law minister. On 2

September 1953, in the Rajya Sabha, while discussing the Andhra State Bill,
1953 and the role of a governor, he argued strongly in favour of amending the
Indian Constitution, especially if its provisions did not safeguard the rights of
minorities.

But in our country linguism [sic] is only another name for communalism.
What happens when you create a linguistic province is that you hand over
the strings of Administration to one single community which happens
to be the majority community and I can cite many provinces where
this is likely to happen. That community charged with a feeling of its
own sacred existence begins to practise the worst kind of communalism
which otherwise is called discrimination. Discrimination creates
injustice and injustice creates ill-feeling. If our linguism [sic] was not
charged with communalism our linguism [sic] would not be a danger to
us at all; but the fact is that it is. But it seems to me that in order to do
away with the community practising communalism being in office these
two remedies are worthwhile, namely, to give the power to the Governor
to override and, secondly, to appoint small committees who can make
representations either to the Ministry or to the Governor.

Now. Sir. We have inherited a tradition. People always keep on saying
to me: 'Oh, you are the maker of the Constitution.' My answer is I was a
hack. What I was asked to do, I did much against my will.

... But, Sir, we have inherited, on account of our hatred of the British,
certain ideas about democracy which, it seems to me, are not universally
accepted. We inherited the idea that the Governor must have no power
at all, that he must only be a rubber stamp. If a Minister, however
scoundrelly [sic] he may be, however corrupt he may be, if he puts up
a proposal before the Governor, he has to ditto it. That is the kind of
conception about democracy which we have developed in this country.

... Sir, therefore, my submission is this that no harm can be done
to democracy and to democratic Constitution if our Constitution was
amended and powers similar to those given to the Governor General
under Section 93 were given to the Governor. At any rate, that would
be some kind of a safeguard to certain small linguistic areas or linguistic
groups who find that the majority in the State are not doing justice to
them.

.... Sir, my friends tell me that I have made the Constitution. But I am
quite prepared to say that I shall be the first person to burn it out. I do not
want it. It does not suit anybody. But whatever that may be, if our people

want to carry on, they must not forget that there are majorities and there are minorities, and they simply cannot ignore the minorities by saying, 'Oh, no. To recognize you is to harm democracy.' I should say that the greatest harm will come by injuring the minorities.

SA'ADAT HASAN MANTO

Sa'adat Hasan Manto, the acclaimed Urdu poet and writer, was a fearless questioner of authority, best known for his stories about Partition. Although he initially absolutely refused to entertain the idea, Manto eventually moved to Lahore from Bombay after Partition. The following is the letter he wrote to Jawaharlal Nehru regarding the Kashmir issue.

Pundit Manto's First Letter to Pundit Nehru

Pundit-ji, assalamu alaikum!

This is the first letter I'm sending you. By the grace of God you're considered very handsome by the Americans. Well, my features are not exactly bad either. If I go to America, perhaps I'll be accorded the same status. But you're the Prime Minister of India, and I'm the famed story writer of Pakistan. Quite a deep gulf separating us! However, what is common between us is that we are both Kashmiris. You're a Nehru, I'm a Manto. To be a Kashmiri is to be handsome, and to be handsome...I don't know.

I have a long-cherished desire to meet you. (We might yet meet during our lifetime.) The older people from my side often meet those from yours. But so far I have not had any opportunity to meet you. What a great pity that I've not even seen you! Of course, I've once heard you on the radio.

As I said, I've long harboured this desire to meet you. Being Kashmiris, we're bound together. But now I wonder where the need is. One Kashmiri does run into another in bylanes or at crossroads.

You settled on the bank of a nahr (river) and came to be known as Nehru. I ponder how I became a Manto. You may have visited Kashmir a million times. I could just go up to Banihal. My Kashmiri friends who know the Kashmiri language tell me that Manto means 'munt', i.e., a measuring stone weighing one and a half ser! I'm sure you know Kashmiri. If you take the trouble to write a reply to this letter, do write to me about the origin of the word 'Manto'.

If I'm just one and a half ser, then there is no comparison between us. You're the whole stream while I'm just one and a half ser! How can I take you on? But we both are the kind of guns that—as the well-known proverb about the Kashmiris goes—'take a shot in the dark.' Please don't take it amiss. When I heard this so-called proverb, I felt terrible. But I mention it light-heartedly because it sounds interesting. Otherwise we both know that we Kashmiris have never accepted defeat in any field.

In politics I can mention your name with pride because you know well the art of contradicting yourself. To this very day, who could beat us Kashmiris in wrestling? Who can outshine us in poetry? But I was surprised to learn that you want to stop rivers from flowing through our land. Pundit-ji, you're only a Nehru. I regret that I'm just a measuring stone of one and a half ser. If I were a rock weighing thirty or forty thousand maunds, I would have thrown myself into the river so that you would have to spend some time consulting with your engineers about how to pull it out.

Pundit-ji, there's no doubt that you are a great personality. You are the Prime Minister of India. You are the ruler of the country that was formerly mine. You are everything. But pardon me if I say that you have never cared for this humble person.

I would like to tell you an interesting anecdote. Whenever my late father—who was, obviously, a Kashmiri—ran into a hato, he would bring him home, seat him in the vestibule and treat him to some Kashmiri salty tea and kulchas. Then he would tell the hato proudly, 'I'm also a kosher.' Pundit-ji, you're a kosher too. By God, if you want my life, it is yours for the asking. I know and believe that you've clung to Kashmir because, being a Kashmiri, you feel a sort of magnetic love for that land. Every Kashmiri, even if he has not seen Kashmir, should feel this way.

As I've already mentioned, I have been to Banihal only. I have seen places like Kud, Bataut and Kashtwar. I have seen their poverty alongside their beauty. If you have removed this poverty, then keep Kashmir to yourself. But I'm sure you cannot do it, despite being a Kashmiri, because you have no time.

Between us Pundit brothers, do this: call me back to India. First I'll help myself to shaljam shabdeg at your place and then take over the responsibility for Kashmiri affairs. The Bakshis and the rest of them deserve to be sacked right away. Cheats of the first order. For no reason you've given them such high status. Is that because this suits you? But why at all...? I know you are a politician, which I am not. But that does not mean I don't understand anything.

The country was partitioned. Radcliffe put Patel to do the dirty work. You've illegally occupied Junagarh, which a Kashmiri could do only under the influence of a Maratha. I mean Patel. (God forgive him!)

You are a litterateur in English. Over here, I write short stories in Urdu, a language which is being wiped out in your country. Pundit-ji, I often read your statements which indicate that you hold Urdu dear. I heard one of your speeches on the radio at the time the country was divided. Everyone admired your English. But when you broke into so-called Urdu, it seemed as though some rabid Hindu Mahasabha member had translated your English speech, which was obviously not to your liking. You were stumbling on every sentence. I cannot imagine how you agreed to read it aloud.

It was the time when Radcliffe had turned India into two slices of a single loaf of bread. It is regrettable that they have not been toasted yet. You're toasting it from that side, and we, from this side. But the flames in our braziers are coming from outside.

Pundit-ji, this is the season for babbogoshas. I've eaten lots of goshas, but I long to eat babbogoshas. What injustice that you've given Bakshi all the rights over them and he does not send me even a few as a gift! Well, let the gift go to hell, babbogoshas too... No, on second thought, let them be. Actually, I wanted to ask you: Why don't you read my books? If you've read them, I'm sorry to say that you've never appreciated them. However, it is more regrettable if you have not read them at all, because you are a writer yourself.

I have one more grievance against you. You're stopping water from flowing in our rivers, and taking a cue from you, the publishers in your capital are hurriedly publishing my books without my permission. Is this proper? I thought that no such unseemly act could be perpetrated under your regime. You can find out right away how many publishers in Delhi, Lucknow and Jallundhar have pirated my books.

Several suits have already been filed against me on charges of obscenity. But look at the injustice that in Delhi, right under your nose, a publisher brings out a collection of my stories and calls it *The Obscene Stories of Manto*. I wrote the book *Ganje Farishte*. An Indian publisher has published it as *Behind the Curtains*. Now tell me, what should I do?

I've written a new book. This letter addressed to you is the preface to it. If this book, too, is pirated, then by God I'll reach Delhi some day, catch you by the throat and will not let go… I'll cling to you in such a manner that you will remember it your whole life. Every morning you'll have to treat me to salty tea along with a kulcha. Shaljam shabdeg, in any case, will have to be there every week.

As soon as the book is out, I'll send you a copy. I hope you will acknowledge receipt and let me know your opinion of it.

You may smell the scent of burnt meat in this letter of mine. You know there was a poet in our Kashmir, Ghani by name, who was well known as 'Ghani Kashmiri.' A poet from Iran came to visit him. The doors of his house were open. He used to say, 'What's there in my house that I should keep the doors locked? Well, I keep the doors closed when I'm inside the house because I am its only asset.' The poet from Iran left his poetry notebook in the vacant house. One couplet in that notebook was incomplete. He had composed the second line but could not do the first one. The second line ran thus: 'The smell of kebab is wafting from your clothes.' When the Iranian poet returned and looked in his notebook, he found the first line written there: 'Has the hand of a blighted soul touched your fore-cloth?'

Pundit-ji, I am also a blighted soul. I've taken issue with you because I am dedicating this book to you.

Sa'adat Manto
27 August 1954

Translated from the Hindi version of the original Urdu
by M. Asaduddin

Mirza Changezi

Mirza Wajid Husain Yagana Changezi (1884–1956), a celebrated Urdu poet, was born in Patna and lived in Lucknow till his death.

Kafir

All besides you are infidels; in the end what does it say?
It makes lunatics of men, what kind of religion is this, I pray?

Translated by Khushwant Singh and Kamna Prasad

Firaq Gorakhpuri

Firaq Gorakhpuri (1896–1982), the pen name of Raghupati Sahay, was one of the most influential Urdu poets and critics of contemporary India.

Desire

We mortals will make our world the envy of paradise, come what
   may
Let those who have no faith in us go to their heaven, they don't
   have to stay

Faith

In the new world, our ancient past too will have a place
In our museums, our faiths and creeds will be given some space.

Drunkard

O holy man, if there is power in your prayer
Let me see you make the mosque's walls shake,
If not, come, take a swig or two of wine
And watch how the mosque quakes.

Translated by Khushwant Singh and Kamna Prasad

FEROZE GANDHI

Feroze Gandhi (1912–1960), a Congress worker and a member of the Indian Independence movement, was married to Indira Gandhi. As a member of parliament, he frequently highlighted the shortcomings of his own party and government. Most famously, he brought to light the Haridas Mundhra scandal and misapplication of funds by the government-controlled Life Insurance Corporation of India. This ultimately led to the resignation of the then finance minister, Tiruvellore Thattai Krishnamachari. The following is the speech he delivered in the Lok Sabha on 16 December 1957.

Mr Speaker, sir, a mutiny in my mind has compelled me to raise this debate. When things of such magnitude, as I shall describe to you later, occur, silence becomes a crime. Public expenditure shall be subject to severest public debate, is a healthy tradition, especially so in an era of growing public enterprise. There is nothing to be ashamed of if a public undertaking has made a mistake, if some people have made a mistake. We should confess it. Parliament must exercise vigilance and control over the biggest and most powerful financial institution it has created, the Life Insurance Corporation of India, whose misapplication of public funds we shall scrutinize today.

Much as I have tried to, I have failed to understand how the Life Insurance Corporation became a willing party to this questionable transaction with the mystery man of India's business underworld...

Mr Speaker, there is going to be some sharpshooting and hard hitting in the House today, because when I hit, I hit hard and expect to be hit harder. I am fully conscious that the other side is also equipped with plentiful supplies of TNT.

A friend of mine in this House, sir, mentioned to me that the finance minister's statement was well fortified. Let me see if I can breach the ramparts at the very first shot. It appears the Life Insurance Corporation has committed a breach of privilege of this House, causing to be placed on the table of the House a statement withholding important information. May I know why one important transaction with Shri Mundhra has been kept a secret from the House? In the absence of this vital information the statement of investments becomes worthless, not even worth the paper on which it is cyclostyled.

You, Mr Speaker, are the guardian of the rights of this House, and it is for you to decide this issue. On 29 November the finance minister stated in the House: 'The question is not one of favouring one particular individual or group, but seeing that the corporation benefits and the policy holders, ultimately, benefit by the investment made.'

I ask, was it in fulfilment of this policy that the corporation purchased by direct negotiation from an individual, Shri Mundhra, shares worth Rs 1,25,00,000 in his concern on 25 June 1957? In March, in April, in June, in July—July is the one which the statement has left out—in August, in September, for six months in this year and on nineteen different occasions the corporation purchased shares of the Mundhra Group for a sum of Rs 1,56,00,000. If this is not favouring and financing one particular individual or group, then what else is it?

The finance minister, in reply to another question on 29 November, stated: 'They', meaning the corporation, 'wanted to augment their shares'.

And, whenever the corporation wanted to augment its shares, one Mundhra was always there willing to oblige, so much so that on one occasion the Life Insurance Corporation transacted business on a day when both the Calcutta and Bombay Stock Exchanges were closed.

Look at the dates and then find out the day. To my own question: 'May I know whether it is a fact that a few months ago some shares were purchased at a higher price than the market price of those very shares on the particular day?' The finance minister gave an emphatic reply: 'I have been told that no such thing happened.'

What does the statement reveal? According to the quotations on the Calcutta Stock Exchange given by the minister himself on 24 June 1957, there is an overpayment of seventy-seven thousand rupees. According to the quotations on 25 June given by the hon'ble minister in the statement, there is an excess payment of about three lakh rupees. What are the results of these augmentations?

Such was the stability of these concerns, such was the soundness of the investment, so stable was the man with whom the corporation had struck nineteen deals, that within two months of their last augmentation, in September the government had to appoint administrators and directors in these concerns. This is not investment. This is a conspiracy to beguile the corporation of its funds.

From the finance minister's statement it would appear as if these investments were made through the open market. The truth is that this was a negotiated deal with Shri Mundhra himself. In the case of such bulk purchases, the market value dwindles into insignificance. Taking into consideration the fact that no lone investor would have touched most of these shares with a tadpole's tail, I am led much against my will, to the sad conclusion that this was a device to help Shri Mundhra who happened to be in financial difficulties at that time, as I shall prove later. The sacred savings of the insured were misused for this purpose and, if I may say so, almost gambled away.

I shall now scrutinize the shares purchases made on 25 June and, Mr Speaker, I shall confine myself to an analysis of the purchase of 25 June alone. The purchases totalled Rs 1,24,44,000. Obviously all the inspiration to augment their shares could not have burst forth suddenly on the 25th. Deep thought must have been given to this investment. Prevailing prices of these shares on the stock exchange must have been thoroughly scrutinized. Balance sheets must have been looked into. I am sorry, sir, I made a mistake. Some of these concerns have not published their balance sheets since 1955. I do not know what procedure the corporation adopted in the absence of balance sheets to arrive at a conclusion as to the value of the shares they were purchasing.

Let us have a look round the Calcutta Stock Exchange, armed with the same authority as that of the finance minister, the official report of the stock exchange. The 25th was a Tuesday, 24th was a Monday, 22nd and 23rd were Saturday and Sunday when the stock exchange was closed. Let us see how much less the corporation would have paid had they concluded the transactions, say, on the 21st. The answer is Rs 10,73,000. These very shares could have been purchased according to the market value on the 21st, and the quotations are, from the official report of the Calcutta Stock Exchange, for Rs 10,73,000 less. But let us move a little backward and see how much less would they have paid on the 20th. Again, according to the same source, the official report of the stock exchange it is Rs 9,42,000 less. On the 19th, Rs 11,52,000 less; on the 18th, Rs 13,47,000 less; on the 17th, that is Monday— Monday week—Rs 13,62,000. My figures do not seem to be creating much impression.

I am going to jump one week from the 17th to give you an idea of how much less the corporation would have paid had the purchase been made on 10 June at prices prevailing and quoted at the Calcutta Stock Exchange. The corporation could have purchased these very shares on the 10th for Rs 20,83,000 less than what was paid on the 25th June. I have made no calculations of prices before the 10th. My nerves gave way.

Occasionally you, Mr Speaker, are very helpful to members, and on the 29th... I think you understood what was in the minds of members when they were groping in the dark and asking questions. You clarified the position. You, Mr Speaker, said: 'The hon'ble member wants to know whether to push up the falling prices of the shares of this company, either the government or this corporation went to the aid by investment in shares.'

Mr Speaker, you let the cat out of the bag. It had never occurred to me. But I gave very serious thought to all that you said. This is exactly what happened. For purchases affected on the 23rd, the prices were artificially created by crude market manipulations on the 24th, when, all of a sudden, all these shares reached their peak. On Monday, the peak was reached. On Tuesday the purchases were made.

Let us see, as I shall prove to you and to the House, how it was worked up. What happened on the very next day, Tuesday? The peak had passed. The downward trend began and as on Friday, 13 December the corporation's investment has depreciated by about Rs 37 lakhs against the total investment of Rs 1,24,44,000.

This, it may be argued, is not a loss, because I have purchased shares and as long as I do not sell them there is no loss. Actually, it would be difficult to argue that way, because, the investment has depreciated and what would happen when the actuarial valuation takes place? An insurance actuary will take the market value of those shares; not what you have paid for them. Therefore, the insured will lose heavily. The actual amount by which the capital investment has depreciated will be much more, because the total investment is about Rs 1,56,00,000. I have only taken into account Rs 1,24,00,000 odd in the calculation of Rs 37 lakhs.

Now, how was the market manipulated? Let us take the case of one concern—Angelo Brothers. Mr Speaker, on 17 June the price of the share which Angelo Brothers quoted at the Calcutta Stock Exchange was Rs 16.87 lakhs. On the 18th, Rs 16.87. On the 19th, Rs 16.87. On the 20th, Rs 16.87; on the 21st, 16.87. On the 22nd and 23rd, Saturday and Sunday—the stock exchange was closed. What happens on the 24th? With the ringing in of the Angelus on the 24th, Angelo Brothers was booked by the Insurance Corporation for Rs 20.25 per share—Rs 3.38 more than the quotation of the previous five days. This is how the market was manipulated.

I shall give you another example—the Osier Lamp Manufacturing Company. It is a very interesting company. It was floated in 1947—ten years ago. Let us see how the shares moved from 10 June up to 24 June.

On 10 June, the price is 2.78 in the Calcutta Stock Exchange. On 17 June, the price is Rs 2.81. On 18 June, Rs 2.81; on 19 June, Rs 2.87; on 20 June, Rs 2.84; on the 21st, 2.84; Saturday and Sunday, 22nd and 23rd. Quotation on Monday, the 24th, Rs 4. What happens on the 25th? The prices collapsed. It goes down to 2.87. It has come to its original, and the Life Insurance Corporation paid Rs 4 per share. The total investment runs into several lakhs.

But what is the condition of this company in which we have invested the money—the Osier Lamp Manufacturing Company? The dividend on preference shares has not been paid since August 1949. Preference shares dividend has not been paid since August 1949. No dividend has been paid on ordinary shares for the last ten years, that is, ever since the company was floated. And the Life Insurance Corporation was looking all round for a healthy investment. This is the kind of concern that they put their money in.

Now, I come to the British India Corporation. The British India Corporation in which on one day, 25 June, they invested forty-two lakh rupees; paid a dividend of 1.25 per cent in 1954, nil in 1955 and 2 per cent for the year ending 1956.

This will work out at about 1.87 per cent on the corporation's investment. Forty-two lakh rupees were invested, and they were handed over to this corporation on a return of 1.87 per cent. This is what we have done with the monies of the insured.

The British India Corporation, once a tower of strength to the city of Kanpur, is in a state of collapse. One of its mills is either closed or there is notice of closure. It is in a state of collapse. The ruins are a testimony to its pristine glory.

The corporation has an Investment Board. May I know why the chairman did not consult the Investment Board before the investment of 25 June was made? Rs 1,24,00,000 is not a small amount. I doubt very much if the chairman has got the sole right to go about investing these huge sums of money in any manner he likes on his own authority, without the consent of the Investment Committee. Is it not a fact that the board was presented with a fait accompli and the members of the board took strong objection to the manner in which the corporation's funds had been frittered away? I would like the finance minister to tell me that I am wrong and I shall correct what I have stated.

On 29 November the finance minister stated that these shares were not spurious. What does 'spurious' mean? I do not know whether you have to rule it out again. That is the first word given here and you have once declared it unparliamentary. You can remove it from the record if you feel so later. 'Spurious' means, according to the *Chamber's Dictionary*—and the *Oxford Dictionary* agrees with it—'bastard, illegitimate, not genuine, false.' No one in this House said these shares were all these. Nobody had it in mind. I do not know how the finance minister said it; probably he used it in its general sense.

The point is this. Was the financial instability of these concerns known to the government and to the corporation? Was it known? Did they know that this money was going to be locked up in unstable financial concerns? It is here that I have an important clue contained in the report of the textile commissioner on the working of the British India Corporation and its subsidiaries and I shall read out the relevant portion from the report. I quote:

> The State Bank of India has recently demanded the mills to mortgage the fixed assets of the British India Corporation also as a security for the hypothecation loan. This is rather an unusual step and apparently this is due to the banker having lost confidence in the corporation.

The State Bank of India had lost confidence in the British India Corporation. The textile commissioner further states:

> In fact, in the directors' meeting held on 23-3-1957, it was reported by the Deputy Managing Director Mr Powell, that when he contacted the chairman and the managing director of the State Bank of India and also the chairman of the Reserve Bank of India in connection with the application to enhance the loan facilities from Rs 1.25 crores to Rs 1.50 crores—i.e. Rs 25 lakhs—for the Kanpur Sugar Works Limited, a company launched by a subsidiary of the B.I.C., the three senior officials of the State Bank had expressed their concern with the financial position of the corporation's group.

The three senior officials of the State Bank and the Reserve Bank were concerned about the financial position of the group, and what happened? Why did I say that I have a clue? The NIDC also refused a loan somewhere in the month of February or March. The State Bank of India and the Reserve Bank refused help in the month of March and in the month of March the Life Insurance Corporation started investing money in these companies. 23rd March is very significant, because the financial condition of the Mundhra group was becoming worse and worse. The State Bank and the Reserve Bank refused help because of the unsoundness of the concerned. But the Life Insurance Corporation was only too willing and rushed in. The textile commissioner's survey concluded on 10 June and the Life Insurance Corporation, a fortnight later, recklessly invested its funds in these very concerns.

I shall read out to the House an extract from the 1955 balance sheet of the British India Corporation Directors' report on the accounts: 'Mr Mundhra has taken a keen interest in the affairs of the Corporation and is lending every support to the directors and the management in their endeavours to ameliorate the condition.' Another paragraph begins: 'The results for the year are most disappointing.'

If the corporation, before it had invested its funds, had had a look at these balance sheets, had seen what the condition of the corporation was, they would never have touched it, as I said, with a tadpole's tail.

Now, let us see the seriousness of the entire transaction. Mr Speaker, where are the scrips of these shares? Did the corporation receive the share scrips before payment was made on 25 June? That is a very important point. Or, did they make payment without having the share scrips in their possession? I would like to have that clarified. Have they even today in their possession all the shares? I would like that to be clarified too, and if they have, have they got the genuine scrips?

There is nothing to laugh about. Have they got the genuine scrips? My information is that there are in the market originals, duplicates and also forged scrips of these very shares. The House would like to know which variety the corporation has got.

I hope I have established collusion between the Life Insurance Corporation of India and Shri Mundhra. I have, I hope, established a conspiracy in which public funds were wrongfully employed for financing the interests of an individual at the cost of the insured. To me this discussion is a measure of the strength of democracy. We do not hang people. We do not chop off their necks, but we can make their existence pretty difficult. If we cannot knock off their heads, what can we do? Let me see if I can secure by pressure of public debate that which I have failed to achieve by peaceful negotiation.

I demand that the government institute an inquiry into this questionable transaction. There is already a precedent for such action. When charges less serious than this were levelled against the Industrial Finance Corporation, the then finance minister, Mr Deshmukh, appointed a committee and the chairman of the committee was a member of the opposition. Let us hope that our finance minister will follow the example of his predecessor. Mr Speaker, this debate has been a very heavy strain on me both mentally and physically.

It has not been easy to collect all these facts and place them before the House in a concise way because the transactions go into lakhs and lakhs. An unfortunate thing has happened. But I don't think there is any reason to be ashamed of it. I am a champion of the public sector. I was one of the persons who championed life insurance nationalization. I am not ashamed to face an inquiry. I would like the public to know, I would like the government to know, and I would like the members of Parliament to know that in the public sector, if such a thing happens, we are prepared to face an inquiry and get to the bottom of it.

I hope that the finance minister will accept this suggestion of mine and appoint a committee in which this House shall be well-represented. But I would prefer a committee of this House. I am not much enamoured of the word judicial. I think we are quite capable; I think we can look after these inquiries. And I hope in the end that this small suggestion of mine will be acceptable.

J.B. KRIPALANI

J.B. Kripalani (1888–1982) was an inspiration and a guiding figure for generations of activists and dissenters, from the Non-Cooperation Movements of the 1920s to the Emergency in the 1970s. He was also one of the staunchest critics of Jawaharlal Nehru's policy on China. The following speech, delivered on 12 September 1959 in the Lok Sabha, was a significant attack on Nehru's failure in dealing with Chinese aggression and expansionism in Tibet and other areas along the border. It highlighted the moral failure in the Indian government's response to China's takeover of Tibet as a dereliction of the principles of justice and fair play.

It is a very serious matter we are discussing here today. You will not, therefore, mind if I make constant reference to my notes. I have been speaking upon this topic inside and outside the House since 1950. In connection with Tibet, in 1950, I said: 'Our government's attitude is understandable on the assumption that Tibet is a far-off country, and none of our business. But supposing what has happened in Tibet happens to Nepal, supposing the Chinese liberation forces come to Nepal, then, I am sure we will fight, whether we are ready or not.'

Again, in 1954, after signing of the Indo–Chinese agreement, I said that the destruction of a buffer state was an unfriendly act, and was dangerous for the security and safety for India. Many nations have gone to war on that issue. I am not saying this to remind the House that I said so. We have more serious business than that. Why did I say all these things? It was because I had taken note of the serious nature of the revolution that had taken place in China. Our Prime Minister while speaking in the Rajya Sabha said that 'the revolution was a major factor in history, and any appraisal of the situation neglecting the fact of the revolution would be utterly wrong; and many of the troubles in the international world were due to the fact that a deliberate attempt was made not to recognize the major events in human history'.

I entirely agree with the Prime Minister. I may submit that if some countries in the West have failed to recognize the significance of the Chinese Revolution, I am afraid we have done no better. This Revolution, by whatever name we may call it, has established in China a totalitarian government. Such a regime can only be a military regime. It is based upon power and force. Its appeal is to authority and not to reason. It does not believe in cooperation but strict obedience and regimentation. All education is turned into propaganda. Truth is subject to party loyalty. Such a regime is fanatical. It pays no regard to the purity of means. It is controlled either by a dictator or by a self-perpetuating junta of politicians. Whatever such a regime may do at home may not be the concern of neighbouring countries. But it is a concern of every peaceful neighbour to see what its international policy is.

The foreign policy of a totalitarian government cannot but be expansionist. It is natural. Power, if not increased, will fade away. Therefore, if we are really to take note of the tremendous revolution that has taken place in China, we must not forget its aggressive nature.

History has also proved that whatever effect a revolution may have in internal politics, it does not change the foreign policy of a nation. The French Revolution did not change the foreign policy of France initiated by Louis XIV. The Fascist revolution in Italy and Germany did not change the foreign policy of these countries. Bolshevik Russia follows the foreign policy of Peter the Great and the Czars of nibbling at its neighbours. We see today China is following the expansionist policy of its predecessor imperial regimes. There is nothing to wonder at that.

I submit that if some Western nations have overemphasized the totalitarian and militarist and expansionist character of the Chinese Revolution, we in India have minimized it. May I submit that if there is a choice in international affairs, it is better to overemphasize danger than to underemphasize it? If we do the latter, we shall be caught unaware and unprepared and our people will also be caught so.

So, we had the taste of this new totalitarian regime in China. Immediately after the Communists had established their rule on the mainland the old Imperial policy was followed in Tibet, a helpless and disarmed country. While the former imperial regimes in China were content and were satisfied with the exercise of suzerainty, the new regime wanted complete control of Tibet. They would have nothing less than that.

Again, we had other indications about the character of this regime. In October 1949, in reply to a telegram of congratulations from the Indian Communist Party on the success of the communists in China, Mr Mao Tse-tung sent the following telegram: 'I firmly believe that relying on the brave Communist Party of India and the unity of all patriots, India will not certainly remain long under the yoke of imperialism and its collaborators. Like China, India will one day merge in the socialist democratic family.'

It is family indeed, for there is one and the same family for communists all over the world, wherever they may be born. Further, in Chinese eyes, and unfortunately in the communists' eyes here, we were not free even in 1949, and our Government was a collaborator. Our Government was collaborating with Western imperialists. I suppose in the eyes of China and in the eyes of some of our own countrymen, we do not seem to have achieved freedom yet; liberation is yet to come, and, therefore, we see the march of Chinese armies on our borders; and they are liberation forces. The idea that we were stooges of Western imperialism was again made clear to us when instinctively, our Prime Minister protested against Chinese excursion in Tibet. He said, 'It was not quite clear from whom the Chinese were liberating Tibet.' History has given the answer. Every fanatical creed, whether it be religious or political, undertakes to make people free from themselves, and make them happy against their will. We are familiar with it. This apart, we got a prompt answer to our protest;

we were told that we had made our protest because we were stooges of Western imperial powers. In fact, the language was more vulgar. This vulgarity has continued all through the years. Our Prime Minister has politely called it the language of the cold war. Instead of resenting these insults, we merely submitted to them and recognized Chinese sovereignty over Tibet. This proved to the Chinese that we would submit to their bullying tactics. I am afraid we have been doing so throughout these years.

Some people have asked: What could India have done? Could it have gone to war on the issue of Tibet? It need not have. But while recognizing the de facto sovereignty of China on the mainland, India should have refused to recognize Chinese rule in Tibet. It would have put us morally in the right. We do not recognize the right of France over Algeria. Are we, therefore, at war with that country? Do we not have diplomatic and friendly relations with it? By submitting to the rape of Tibet, I am very sorry to say, the Prime Minister has repudiated what he has often said, that wherever there is injustice and tyranny, India shall not remain neutral; it will always stand for justice and fair play. It is but fair that I remind him of these words.

I want the House and the country to know and to mark that China in her internal and international advance is even more quick and thorough than Russia. Russia began its expansion only when its revolution was twenty-three years old, and even then when Europe was in the throes of the world war. China began its campaign as soon as its power was established on the mainland. I want the House to mark that difference between the two regimes.

I have talked of the totalitarian and military character of the new Chinese regime. This fact comes out more clearly more recently. In a statement of the Chinese Ambassador made to our Foreign Secretary as late as May this year, he says: 'China will not be so foolish as to antagonize the United States in the East and again to antagonize India in the West.'

This, Sir, reminds me of Hitler's theory of war on one front. But strangely enough, the Chinese have chosen not the eastern, but the western front... which they have done in spite of the fact that in the east, the territory they want to liberate is undoubtedly Chinese territory and the people are also Chinese people and not foreign people. Of course, they tried the eastern front a couple of years back when they attacked the off-shore islands under the sway of Chiang Kai-shek. It should not have been difficult for the Chinese to take possession of these islands.

They were not useful to the United States or to Chiang Kai-shek. But the USA resisted the attack on these islands which were not of much use to it. The late Mr Dulles made it plain that communists will move out of the mainland only at the expense of a third world war. For this, China with her population of 600 million was not prepared. They were not prepared for a war. Therefore, what remained for Communist China was an incursion in the west, on the Indian frontier. They think they are avoiding a second front as Hitler did. But who knows one day they may have no choice but to fight on both the fronts?

In 1954, we entered into a treaty with the Chinese Government. I am sorry to say that by that treaty, we recognized not only the suzerainty, but also the sovereignty, of China over Tibet. If we did that, it was very necessary to try and settle the borders with China. All along, we had common borders with Tibet. Now, these were turned into common borders with China. We are told there was some talk of borders at the time the treaty was signed, but nothing was decided. Later too, there was some talk about that in 1956 when the two Prime Ministers met here, but there was nothing in writing. We knew, or ought to have known, that between China and Burma, there are border disputes and they have not yet been decided, and the Chinese Government has not been able to carry out its own promises. This, I quote from the Prime Minister. In international dealings, treaties or other documents, it is dangerous to leave matters at the level of talk without any signed documents. It is best to have everything in writing. Even when there is a talk, the notes of the talk must be accepted by both parties and signed. This seems not to have been done, in spite of the fact that semantic difficulties were felt by both the parties, as we are told by the Prime Minister. Our Prime Minister is too shrewd a politician not to know that in international intercourse, words have today ceased to have ordinary dictionary meaning. Therefore, it was all the more necessary that everything should be in black and white. Even then, there are apprehensions of misinterpretation, but the field of misunderstanding is narrowed down. At least, the neutrals can see what is right and what is wrong in a document.

Some members in the Rajya Sabha said that the Chinese had become wild with us after the grant of asylum to the Dalai Lama and the Tibetan refugees. The Prime Minister seemed to endorse this view. It may be that their wrath has increased after these events. But in this, too, the Chinese are different from the Russians: the Chinese are more unreasonable.

The Hungarian refugees sought asylum in many European countries, but Russia has not on that account indulged in border aggression against those countries. However, the Chinese aggression began earlier. According to Dr Kunzru, aggression began in 1952. In 1954 we had Panchsheel—the five principles of peaceful co-existence. I need not discuss here these five principles except to say that all these principles are based upon the maintenance of the status quo, however cruel and iniquitous it may be.

The principles were enunciated in order to put a seal of approval on the sovereignty of China over Tibet. Therefore, on one occasion, I was constrained to say in this House that the Panchsheel was born in sin. In spite of the agreement and the Panchsheel, aggression on our borders began three months after the signing of the treaty, as pointed out in the White Paper. It has since been going on and it has been increasing. It would appear as if the Chinese were simply waiting for the signing of the treaty which recognized their sovereignty in Tibet. Every time they have indulged in the aggression, they have blamed us and drawn our attention to the Panchsheel. I am reminded of a Hindi proverb which I need not quote here. It has something to do with the Kotwal and the danda.

Our territories have been occupied, our people have been kidnapped, our guards have been fired at, taxes have been collected, roads have been built leading towards India; check and observation posts established along our borders and even, as the report says, trenches have been dug in many places along the frontier. In Ladakh a regular motor road has been built and it is said that an aerodrome has been established in our territory.

Sir, much as I dislike Chinese aggression on our borders, I am much more concerned with what our Government has done or proposes to do about it. After all, the Chinese, as I have said, are working in consonance with the genius of their regime and in pursuance of their international goal. But, whatever aggressions have been there so far I regret to say that the country has been kept in ignorance of this aggression for a long period, even though many notes, through the years, have passed between the two countries. The Parliament elicited this through questions in this and the other House. No information was even given voluntarily. Even then, it has been meagre, and often, the acts of aggression have been minimized—may I say almost excused. Sometimes, it would appear there has been special pleading for the Chinese.

Recently, Sir, when there was a question about the road built by

China in Ladakh, the House was told, if I remember aright and speaking subject to correction, that it was not a regular road but stones were kept to mark the passage. But, now, we know it is a motor road. No mention was made of the aerodrome built in our territory. We were told that the territory was mountainous—where nothing could grow, not even a blade of grass—and no people lived there.

There are places in Rajasthan today where all these conditions exist. May I know what the Government would do if some of those parts are invaded by Pakistan? Sir, then, another question arises. If these places are so uninhabitable for man and vegetable, then, why do the Chinese want to occupy them? It is a strange thing that they should earn the ill-will of India and occupy portions of territory that are of no use to them. Our people have a shrewd suspicion and it is this that these uninhabitable places are occupied to serve as springboards for future action. A springboard has not to be green or populated. Our people are not thinking in terms of a few miles of barren rock. They are thinking in terms of the honour of the country which has some meaning for them. Apart from that, they are thinking of something more and it is this that they are thinking about the safety and freedom of their country in the near future. Here then lies the trouble which people with their horse-sense are able to sense.

...While there are acts of aggression on our territory, while violent and angry notes are sent to us, on our side we are satisfying ourselves merely with sending back polite notes or protests. Also, all the time, what is more painful, our people are being encouraged to keep on repeating the mantram, 'Chini Hindi Bhai Bhai'. This, I am sure, makes our people, if not our leaders, look ridiculous before the world. Such conduct lowers our dignity of which we are reminded so often by our Prime Minister.

Sir, I also do not understand this over-politeness of ours. After all, in ordinary conversation, we regulate the pitch of our voice according to the hearing capacity of the listener. If he is hard of hearing, we raise our voice; if a man does not understand polite language, we may not abuse him, but we must speak in plain and unvarnished language. Nobody would be more polite and courteous than Gandhiji. But many times, he had to use hard and harsh words against British Imperialism. On one occasion, I remember he wrote an article in *Young India* with the caption 'Shaking the Mane of the British Lion'. It formed part of the prosecution which he had to face and for it he was awarded six months' imprisonment. (Some Hon. Members: Six Years.) Six years. Sir, we cannot be more polite than the Father of the Nation when dealing with aggression. It is natural for us to be anxious to avoid a major complication which may precipitate a war. A war between the two countries is bound to develop into a global war whether one likes it or not. But we cannot avoid war through appeasement. Appeasement is always at the expense of one's honour. It has also never saved peace. It did not save peace in Europe in 1939.

I would like to know what the government proposes to do under the present circumstances. I have read the Prime Minister's speech in the Rajya Sabha several times. I am afraid, I find no indication of this in the Prime Minister's speech. Is there any idea to throw back the Chinese out of the territories they have occupied? As their aggression is described by our communist friends as merely 'border incidents', so will our action in turning them back be a 'border incident'. When we have cleared our borders of aggression, we can, then, think in terms of negotiations, but always on the basis of McMahon line. The maintenance of the status quo can only be when aggression has been stopped and the territories occupied by the Chinese re-occupied by our people. Our Prime Minister has as a last resort proposed arbitration. It is not usual to submit the cases of national territories to arbitration. National territory belongs to the people of the country. (Hear, hear.) It cannot be the subject of arbitration. Apart from this, who can arbitrate in this case? What country except Russia will be acceptable to China? All other countries, whether they are capitalist or socialist, in the world are capitalist and as such imperialist! Even communist Yugoslavia, if it is not capitalist, is a stooge of capitalists and the imperialists, though it may call itself communist or Marxist. However, all this can come after our territory has been cleared of aggression.

During the course of his speech in the Rajya Sabha, our Prime Minister has, in answer to Dr Kunzru, said that there could be no change in our foreign policy and that it stands as firm as a rock though today even the Himalayas are shaking. I am afraid that, when the Prime Minister says this, he is thinking merely in terms of the basic principles of our policy. What are these principles? India stands for peace. India stands for disarmament. India stands for non-alignment with the power blocs. That is not all. There is a furthersome thing. India also stands for international justice and fair play. The Prime Minister himself has often said that in the case of injustice and tyranny, India will not remain neutral. I am afraid we have not acted upon this principle in the case of Tibet.

In this House talking about our foreign policy two years back, I have said that it is a mistake to suppose the foreign policy of a country consists merely in enunciating abstract and basic principles. It must also think in terms of appropriate strategy and tactics, through which these principles are to be given effect to. We have failed to embody our principles into appropriate strategy and tactics for effective action. It may be that in evolving these, we may have to modify our principles to some extent. There will always be a gulf between principles and practice, between the ideal and the actual. That cannot be avoided in this defective world. I submit for the consideration of the Prime Minister that we have failed in our foreign policy at the level of strategy and tactics. Herein some modification is surely necessary if we are to be effective.

Sir, in conclusion, I would beg of the Government to be firm. Their vacillation and the Prime Minister's varying statements confuse the public minds. A confused people cannot be ready for an emergency. Even in his Press interview yesterday, the Prime Minister talked of restraint. Restraint without action is meaningless. I can quite understand that there should be restraint in giving expression to the feelings when our people go and demonstrate against an Embassy. That is not desirable and I am one with the Prime Minister when he condemns these things. But how are the feelings of the people to get expression unless there is action behind what they want to be done? Talking of this restraint is just like talking of restraining a horse and tightening when the damn horse does not exist. I can assure the Prime Minister, if he needs any assurance that the country will be behind him to a man—and even to a woman—if he takes effective action against foreign aggression.

BABURAO BAGUL

Baburao Ramaji Bagul (1930–2008), radical thinker and one of the ideologues of the Dalit Panthers, was a pioneer in modern Marathi literature who inspired many later generations of Dalit writers and thinkers. His best-known work is Jevha Mi Jat Chorali *(When I Concealed My Caste), a book of stories which created a stir when it was first published for the stark way in which it depicted social exploitation.*

You Who Have Made the Mistake

Those who leave for foreign lands
embrace other tongues, dress in alien grab
and forget this country
—them I salute.
And those who don't forget
and don't change even after being beaten up for centuries
—such hypocrites I ask:
What will you say if someone asked you—
what is untouchability?
Is it eternal like God?
What's an untouchable like? What does he look like?
Does he look like the very image of leprosy?
Or like the prophet's enemy?
Does he look like a heretic, a sinner, a profligate, or an atheist?
Tell me,
What will your answer be?
Will you reply without hesitation:
'Untouchable—that's me?'
That's why I say—
You who have made the mistake of being born in this country
must now rectify it: either leave the country
or make war!

Translated by Vilas Sarang

BAPURAO JAGTAP

Bapurao Jagtap was an important Marathi Dalit poet. In this poem he articulates the agony and anger of the Dalits who have been continuously driven into the margins of Indian society.

This Country Is Broken

This country is broken into a thousand pieces
its cities, its religion, its castes,

its people, and even the minds of the people
—all are broken, fragmented.
In this country, each day burns
scorching each moment of our lives.
We bear it all, and stand solid as hills
in this our life
that we do not accept.
Brother, our screams are only an attempt
to write the chronicle of this country
—this naked country
with its heartless religion.
The people here rejoice in their black laws
and deny that we were ever born.
Let us got to some country, brother,
where, while you live, you will have
a roof above your head,
and where, when you die, there will at least be
a cemetery to receive you.

Translated by Vilas Sarang

RAGHUVIR SAHAY

Raghuvir Sahay (1929–1990) was a leading figure of post-Independence Hindi literature, deeply committed to the rights of the oppressed, and equally to the freedom of every individual, regardless of class or ideology. In his poetry, he could be effortlessly lyrical, and brilliantly satirical. His poem 'Adhinaayak' is a fine example of his satire, socialist spirit and impatience with bombast and grand rhetoric.

Adhinaayak

So who is this Lord of India's Destiny in our anthem
whose glories the everychild in torn pyjamas sings?

Who are they—the carriage-borne, attended
by turbaned whisk-bearers, lance-bearers, buglers,

and honoured with parasol, gun-salute, drum beat—
who command everyone to stand up and be anthemic?

Who descends from the velvet throne to pin badges
on naked skeletons that rattle in from east and west?

And just who exactly is this Jana-Gana-Mana-Adhinaayak,
This Emperor of our hearts and minds, whose praise
the frightened parrot every day, whether they want to or not?

Translated by Sharad Raghav

Kanu Sanyal

Kanu Sanyal (1932–2010) was one of the radical communists who later came to be known as Naxalites. Sanyal, along with Charu Mazumdar and others, was critical of the policies of the Communist Party of India and the Communist Party of India (Marxist). They began to organize themselves in the late 1960s and spearheaded a militant peasant uprising in 1967 in Naxalbari, a small village in northern West Bengal. On 1 May 1969, Sanyal declared the formation of the third communist party—Communist Party of India (Marxist-Leninist)—in a meeting at Shaheed Minar in Calcutta.

Declaration of the Formation of CPI (M-L)

Comrades and friends! I feel ashamed and embarrassed at the high regard that is shown to me. I am an ordinary cadre, a servant of the people, and my abilities are very limited.

The reason why Naxalbari stirred the whole of India and the whole world is that it was a correct application of Mao Tse-tung's thought in the concrete conditions of India. It was our respected leader Comrade Charu Mazumdar who pointed out the path along which Naxalbari developed; that is, it was under his leadership that the correct application of Mao Tse-tung's thought in the concrete conditions of our country was carried out for the first time and provided the basis on which the heroic peasants of Naxalbari rose in armed revolt against imperialism, feudalism, comprador capital and the old and new revisionists. This is how they advanced along the path blazed by the Chinese revolution and lighted the torch of Indian revolution, and thus proved in the concrete conditions of India that it is not men like Indira Gandhi, Morarji, Dange, Namboodiripad and Jyoti, but the people of India who are the really decisive force of history, it is the people who are the real heroes. So when people applaud me, I cannot but remember the faces of Comrades Tribeni kanu, Sobhan Ali, Appalaswamy Naidu, Rengim and Babulal Biswakarmakar, and realize how small I am compared to them!

... In the revolutionary situation which prevails in India today, class struggle has intensified to such a degree that the revisionists are finding it impossible to retain their deceptive mask, and yet, retain it they must. The revisionists and neo-revisionists, in their eagerness to serve their masters well have landed themselves in a fix, and do not know how to get out of it!

... In India there never has been such a party. The agents of imperialism, feudalism and comprador capital have hitherto prevented the Communist Party from adopting a correct line. The Indian people have repeatedly risen up in revolt and the Indian peasants have repeatedly carried on valiant armed struggles against imperialism and feudalism. But all this heroism and sacrifice ended in failure, not because imperialism and its running dog, the Congress government, could suppress the people with bullets and lathis; the reason for this failure lies in the fact that the old and new revisionist leading clique in the communist movement stabbed the people's movements in the back. From the very beginning, these revisionists, acting as faithful lackeys of imperialism, feudalism and comprador capital, compounded revisionism with native Gandhism and consistently and cynically betrayed the country and the Indian people in their frantic effort to keep the mass struggles securely confined within the limits of parliamentary democracy. This is why the cause for which the heroic workers of the Punnapra-Vayalar struggle of 1946–47 shed their blood has remained unfulfilled to this day; this is how the heroic struggle of Telangana peasants (1946–51) was smothered by these renegades. Whenever the party ranks revolted against these treacherous actions this revisionist leading clique repeatedly managed to fool the ranks by substituting a 'new' individual from among their own clique for the discredited one and then frantically resumed once more, through this new leadership, their old game of imprisoning the mass struggles within the musty dungeon of electioneering and parliamentary democracy. But how can a few flies ever shut out the blazing brightness of the sun? Similarly, it is not possible for a few traitorous renegades to stop the working of the inexorable laws of history. And so, we find that all the trickery and opposition of this traitorous leading clique of the communist movement could not prevent the victorious onward march of Chairman Mao Tse-tung's thought in India. Thus, the conditions for the emergence of a genuine communist party in India were created.

Of course, it has not been easy, nor smooth. When, in 1965, our respected leader, Comrade Charu Mazumdar rebelled against the neo-revisionist leading clique of Sundarayya, Ranadive, Namboodiripad, Promode, Jyoti and company and called upon the revolutionaries in the CPM to build peasants' armed struggle, he was subjected to the vilest slanders. People like Promode Babu, Harekrishna Babu raved that he was a mad man, a man who was mentally sick, and in open statements termed him a police agent and created a fascist atmosphere inside the party with a view to preventing comrades from knowing what Comrade Charu Mazumdar had written and from meeting Charu-da. But what has been the result? Were these lackeys of reaction able to smother the revolutionary clarion call of Marxism, Leninism, Mao Tse-tung's thought? No, they couldn't; on the contrary, the call given out by Comrade Charu Mazumdar created a stir throughout India. The analysis made by Comrade Charu Mazumdar inspired us, the revolutionaries of Darjeeling district. When we went among the peasant masses in the Terai region with a view to applying through concrete practice the great teaching of Chairman Mao: 'Learn warfare through warfare,' we saw how eagerly the peasant masses accepted our views and how an idea was transformed into a material force—and thus was created Naxalbari—the Chingkang Mountain of India! Having failed in their attempt to prevent the revolutionary application of Marxism-Leninism and seeing that the parliamentary path, which they had been so frantically peddling, was going completely bankrupt, the traitorous revisionist clique adopted the method of the notorious Congress reactionaries and madly tried to drown the Naxalbari struggle in blood. Cloaked as communists, this traitorous bunch of revisionists shot down ten peasant women. In their mad attempt to smother the ringing call of Mao Tse-tung's thought, they even drowned the thirteen-year-old son of a peasant in a well by tying a rope round his neck. But they failed all the same. Inspired by the success of the correct application of Mao Tse-tung's thought in India, the communist revolutionaries all over the country, led by our respected leader Comrade Charu Mazumdar formed the All India Co-ordination Committee of Communist Revolutionaries (AICCCR) and, thus, laid the basis for building a genuine communist party in India. It is under the leadership of the Co-ordination Committee that peasants' armed struggle has been organized in Srikakulam in Andhra, Lakhimpur Kheri in Uttar Pradesh, Mushahari in Bihar, Koraput in Orissa, that the communist revolutionaries of Assam, Maharashtra, Rajasthan, Madhya Pradesh, Mysore, Kerala, Punjab, Haryana, Tamil Nadu and Kashmir have rallied under the banner of revolution and boldly established throughout India the path of seizing power through armed struggle as opposed to the rotten and stinking parliamentary path peddled by the revisionists, and were able to present before the international communist movement the decision that in the post-Second World War period boycott of parliamentary elections has become a matter of strategy.

The task before the AICCCR was to lay the basis for building a genuine communist party. That task has been successfully completed.

With great pride and boundless joy I wish to announce today at this meeting that we have formed a genuine communist party—the Communist Party of India (Marxist-Leninist). ...I firmly believe that the great Indian people will warmly welcome this event, will realize the formation of this party as a historic step forward for the Indian revolution and will come forward to raise the struggle to a higher stage under the leadership of the party. On the other hand, I am also convinced that the announcement of the formation of the party will strike terrible fear in the hearts of all the enemies of the people—open or disguised.

...The all-conquering thought of Mao Tse-tung has already struck firm roots into the soil of India, people's revolutionary struggles are bursting forth everywhere—from Kashmir in the north to Kumarika [Cape Comorin] in the south, and from Assam in the east to Maharashtra in the west—and the sparks of Naxalbari are spreading far and wide. In such a situation we may justifiably hope that our cherished revolutionary dream will come true—the dream that India, our great motherland, will liberate herself by sending all the reactionaries to their graves. Shouldn't the revolutionaries dream? Yes, they must not lose sight of our achievements, must see the bright future... This is what is meant by dreaming revolutionary dreams. It is not enough for us to have such dreams ourselves, we must encourage the people also to dream of a bright future. How was it possible for our heroic comrades like Tribeni Kanu, Sobhan Ali, Babulal Biswakarmakar, Barka Majhi, Naidu and Rengim to raise the banner of revolution higher still by shedding their own blood and to sacrifice their lives displaying total unconcern for their own selves? This was possible only because they had dreams—revolutionary dreams, dreams of liberating India and the people from exploitation and oppression.

SANT RAM UDASI

Sant Ram Udasi (1939–1986) was one of the major poets who emerged in the 1960s from the Naxalite movement in Punjab. During the 1970s he wrote three collections of poetry, Lahu Bhije Bol, Saintan *and* Chounukrian. *The following poem has been selected and translated by* **Nirupama Dutt** *for this volume.*

A Plea to My Mother

Do not give birth to me in a village where dreams are forever
    shackled
Where the hot beads of my brother's sweat have no value
Where no tears accompany a couple as they ritually circle to take
    vows
Where the groom's tinsel-and-flower headgear gives off no sparks
Where dowry follows girls like a deadly infection
A village where, instead of being adorned with gold,
The ears hear only the wails of the wretched, the sick and the
    hungry
Do not give birth to me in a village where dreams are forever
    shackled
Where our rights are buried under boulders
Where intellect has long rusted beyond recognition
On the blood-stained wrist, seems to have cracked,
The forlorn glass bangle which met such an end
No one caresses the blossoms on the cotton plants
That seem to be weeping even at full bloom
Do not give birth to me in a village where dreams are forever
    shackled
In the fat moneylender's ledger, tied with a red ribbon,

The fire of what is rightfully ours lies long imprisoned
Where, kicked by heavy nailed boots in the street,
Our father's turban lies tattered and torn
Our livelihood is cursed says the sigh of a poor woman
Someone else is wrongfully taking our share of the moon
Do not give birth to me in a village where dreams are forever
   shackled

LAL SINGH DIL

*Lal Singh Dil (1943–2007), a popular revolutionary poet who emerged from
the Naxalite movement in Punjab in the 1970s, was born into the Ramdasia
Chamar caste. A consciousness of the divisions of caste, and the desire to break
free from its shackles, informs and permeates all of his writing. Lal Singh Dil
wrote three books of poetry,* Setluj Di Hawa (*Breeze from the Sutlej*), Bahut
Sarey Suraj (*Innumerable Suns*), Aj Billa Phir Aaya (*Billa Came Again
Today*) *and an autobiography,* Dastaan (*Story*). *The following poems have
been selected and translated by* **Nirupama Dutt** *for this volume.*

My Country

My country has another face
Another set of people
Where a settlement
Half-hungry
Half-asleep
Retires for the night
And counts the stars
To soothe aching limbs

Beyond my country
This is my country
These are my people
Whenever I want to sing a song
To this country of mine
I touch the strings of a sitar and

All the melodies from across the seas
Accompany me
Who will welcome them?
Who is filling these rivers,
These boundaries, with blood?
My country has another face
Another set of people

Words

Words have been uttered
long before us
and will be
long after we're gone

Chop off every tongue
if you can
but the words will still
have been uttered.

Paash

Avtar Singh Sandhu (1950–1988), 'Paash', was a revolutionary poet of the Naxalite movement in Punjabi literature in the 1970s and a popular political figure of the Left during this period. Paash was editor of the literary magazine Siarh *(The Plow Line) and his works include* Loh-katha *(Iron-Tale),* Uddian Bazan Magar *(Following the Flying Hawks),* Saadey Samiyaan Vich *(In Our Times) and* Khilre Hoye Varkey *(Scattered Pages). Paash was gunned down by Khalistani extremists in March 1988. The following poem has been selected and translated by* **Nirupama Dutt** *for this volume.*

Lines to Our Insecurity

If the security of the nation
Demands that to be without conscience is a pre-condition to life;
That any word bar 'yes' seems obscene;

That the mind should bow in reverence before injustice;
Then the security of the nation is a threat to us.

We had thought of the nation as home—pure,
with no place for gloom.
Where a person flows freely in the streets like patter of falling rain,
Sways in fields like ears of wheat,
and gives meaning to the immensity of the sky.
We had thought of the nation as tender as an embrace;
We had thought of the nation as heady as work;
We had thought of the nation as loyal as sacrifice.
But if the nation is a factory for our souls,
If it is a laboratory to transform us into fools,
Then it is a threat to us.

If the peace of the nation is such
That our identities are pulverized,
like rocks breaking off and rolling down mountains of debt;
That rising prices laugh, and spit in the faces
of our pitiful wages;
That to bathe in our own blood is our only pilgrimage,
Then we are in danger from this peace.

If the security of the nation demands
That every protest be extinguished in the name of peace;
That to die at the border is the only meaning of courage;
That art should blossom only at the despot's window;
That intellect should be put to use only by order,
and labour only remain a sweeper outside the citadel;
Then the security of the nation is a threat to us.

KUMAR VIKAL

Kumar Vikal (1935–1997) was a prominent Hindi poet from Punjab, and was extremely popular from the 1970s to the '90s. At a time when Punjab was rife with communal and ideological tensions, his poems highlighted the

need for a secular and humanitarian society. The following poem has been
*selected and translated by **Nirupama Dutt** for this volume.*

The Last Scream

Though I may be killed by a sword,
a trident, or a police bullet;
Before death I will certainly scream:
It is religion that teaches us to hate,
turns a human into a trident or a sword!

I will scream:
Religion is an opium-pill.
In these times it becomes, all at once,
a bullet fired from a gun.
It comes, ripping the wind apart,
to pierce the hearts of
children playing in a park,
rickshaw-pullers,
out-of-work labourers,
people queued up outside ration shops.

Religion is an elitist curse which hides itself
behind the veil of purity in every religious text.
And, ever seamlessly changing form,
permeates the common person's resolve
so that she does not change the world
and, muttering curses,
becomes one with the hell of existence.

BALRAJ SAHNI'S CONVOCATION ADDRESS AT
JAWAHARLAL NEHRU UNIVERSITY

Balraj Sahni (1913–1973) was a noted Indian film and stage actor. The
following are excerpts from the convocation address delivered by him at
Jawaharlal Nehru University in 1972. A powerful critique of the Indian

tendency to imitate the West without question, the speech is extremely relevant even today.

...I'd like to tell you about an incident which took place in my college days and which I have never been able to forget. It has left a permanent impression on my mind. I was going by bus from Rawalpindi to Kashmir with my family to enjoy the summer vacation. Halfway through we were halted because a big chunk of the road had been swept away by a landslide caused by rain the previous night. We joined the long queues of buses and cars on either side of the landslide. Impatiently we waited for the road to clear. It was a difficult job for the PWD and it took some days before they could cut a passage through. During all this time the passengers and the drivers of vehicles made a difficult situation even more difficult by their impatience and constant demonstration. Even the villagers nearby got fed up with the high-handed behaviour of the city-walas.

One morning the overseer declared the road open. The green flag was waved to the drivers. But we saw a strange sight. No driver was willing to be the first to cross. They just stood and stared at each other from either side. No doubt the road was a makeshift one and even dangerous. A mountain on one side, and a deep gorge and the river below. Both were forbidding. The overseer had made a careful inspection and had opened the road with a full sense of responsibility. But nobody was prepared to trust his judgment, although these very people had, till yesterday, accused him and his department of laziness and incompetence. Half an hour passed by in dumb silence. Nobody moved. Suddenly we saw a small green sports car approaching. An Englishman was driving it; sitting all by himself. He was a bit surprised to see so many parked vehicles and the crowd there. I was rather conspicuous, wearing my smart jacket and trousers. 'What's happened?' he asked me.

I told him the whole story. He laughed loudly, blew the horn and went straight ahead, crossing the dangerous portion without the least hesitation. And now the pendulum swung the other way. Everybody was so eager to cross that they got into each other's way and created a new-confusion for some time. The noise of hundreds of engines and hundreds of horns was unbearable.

That day I saw with my own eyes the difference in attitudes between a man brought up in a free country and a man brought up in an enslaved one. A free man has the power to think, decide and act for himself. But the slave loses that power. He always borrows his thinking from others, wavers in his decisions, and more often than not only takes the trodden path…

I told you about an Englishman. I think that in itself is symptomatic of the sense of inferiority that I felt at that time. I could have given you the example of Sardar Bhagat Singh who went to the gallows the same year. I could have given you the example of Mahatma Gandhi who always had the courage to decide for himself. I remember how my college professors and the wise respectable people of my home town shook their heads over the folly of Mahatma Gandhi, who thought he could defeat the most powerful empire on earth with his utopian principles of truth and non-violence. I think less than 1 per cent of the people of my city dreamt that they would see India free in their lifetime. But Mahatma Gandhi had faith in himself, in his country, and his people…

This year we are celebrating the twenty-fifth anniversary of our Independence. But can we honestly say that we have got rid of our slavish mentality—our inferiority complex?

Can we claim that at the personal, social, or institutional level, our thinking, our decisions, or even our actions are our own and not borrowed? Are we really free in the spiritual sense? Can we dare to think and act for ourselves, or do we merely pretend to do so—merely make a superficial show of independence?

I should like to draw your attention to the film industry to which I belong. I know a great many of our films are such that the very mention of them would raise a laugh among you. In the eyes of educated, intelligent people, Hindi films are nothing but a tamasha. Their stories are childish, unreal and illogical. But their worst fault, you will agree with me, is that their plots, their technique, their songs and dances betray blind, unimaginative and unabashed copying of films from the west. There have been Hindi films which have been copied in every detail from some foreign film. No wonder that you young people laugh at us, even though some of you may dream of becoming stars yourselves…

When I was a student like you, our teachers, both English and non-English, tried to convince us in diverse ways that the fine arts were a prerogative of white people. Great films, great drama, great acting, great painting, etc., were only possible in Europe and America. The Indian people, their language and culture, were as yet too crude and backward for real artistic expression. We used to feel bitter about this and we resented it outwardly, but inwardly we could not help accepting this judgment.

The picture has changed vastly since then. After Independence, India has made a tremendous recovery in every branch of the arts. In the field of film making, names like Satyajit Ray and Bimal Roy stand out as international personalities. Many of our artistes, cameramen and technicians compare with the best anywhere in the world. Before Independence, we hardly made ten or fifteen films worth the name. Today we are the biggest film-producing country in the world. Not only are our films immensely popular with the masses in our own country, but also in Pakistan, Afghanistan, Iran, the Eastern Republics of the Soviet Union, Egypt, and other Arab countries in the Far East and many African countries. We have broken the monopoly of Hollywood in this field.

Even from the aspect of social responsibility, our Indian films have not yet degenerated to the low level to which some of the western countries have descended. The film producer in India has not yet exploited sex and crime for the sake of profit to the extent that his American counterpart has been doing for years and years, thus creating a serious social problem for that country.

But all these assets are negated by our one overwhelming fault that we are imitators and copyists. This one fault makes us the laughing stock of intelligent people everywhere. We make films according to borrowed, outdated formulas. We do not have the courage to strike out on our own, to get to grips with the reality of our own country, to present it convincingly and according to our own genius.

I say this not only in relation to the usual Hindi or Tamil box office films. I make this complaint against our so-called progressive and experimental films also, whether they be in Bengali, Hindi or Malayalam. I do not lag behind anyone else in admiring the work of Satyajit Ray, Mrinal Sen, Sukhdev, Basu Bhattacharjee or Rajinder Singh Bedi. I know they are highly and deservingly respected; but even then I cannot help saying that the winds of fashion in Italy, France, Sweden, Poland or Czechoslovakia have an immediate effect on their work. They do break new ground, but only after someone else has broken it.

In the literary world, in which I have considerable interest, I see the same picture. Our novelists, story writers and poets are carried away with the greatest of ease by the currents of fashion in Europe, although

Europe, with the exception of the Soviet Union perhaps, is not yet even aware of Indian writing. For example, in my own province of the Punjab there is a wave of protest among young poets against the existing social order. Their poetry exhorts the people to rebel against it, to shatter it and build a better world free from corruption, injustice and exploitation. One cannot but endorse that spirit wholeheartedly, because, without question, the present social order needs changing.

The content of this poetry is most admirable, but the form is not indigenous. It is borrowed from the west. The west has discarded meter and rhyme, so our Punjabi poet must also discard it. He must also use involved and ultra-radical imagery. The result is that the sound and fury remains only on paper, confined to small, mutually admiring literary circles. The people, the workers and the peasants who are being exhorted to revolution, cannot make head or tail of this kind of poetry. It just leaves them cold and perplexed. I don't think I am wrong if I say that other Indian languages too are in the grip of 'new wave' poetry.

And what about the academic world? I invite you to look into the mirror. If you laugh at Hindi films, maybe you are tempted to laugh at yourselves.

This year my own province honoured me by nominating me to the senate of Guru Nanak University. When the invitation to attend the first meeting came, I happened to be in the Punjab, wandering around in some villages near Preet Nagar—the cultural centre founded by our great writer S. Gurbakhsh Singh. During the evening's gossip I told my villager friends that I was to go to Amritsar to attend this meeting and if anyone wanted a lift in my car he was welcome. At this one of the company said, 'Here among us you go about dressed in tehmat-kurta, peasant fashion; but tomorrow you will put on your suit and become Sahib Bahadur again.' 'Why,' I said laughingly, 'if you want I will go dressed just like this.' 'You will never dare,' another one said. 'Our sarpanch sahib here removes his tehmat and puts on a pyjama whenever he has to go to the city on official work. He has to do it, otherwise, he says, he is not respected. How can you go peasant-fashion to such a big university?' A jawan who had come home on leave for the rice sowing added, 'Our sarpanch is a coward. In cities even girls go about wearing lungis these days. Why should he not be respected?'

The gossip went on, and, as if to accept their challenge, I did make my appearance in the Senate meeting in tehmat-kurta. The sensation I created was beyond my expectation. The officer—perhaps, professor—

who was handing out the gowns in the vestibule could not recognize me at first. When he did he could not hide his amusement, 'Mr Sahni, with the tehmat you should have worn khosas, not shoes,' he said, while putting the gown over my shoulders. 'I shall be careful next time,' I said apologetically and moved on. But a moment later I asked myself, was it not bad manners for the professor to notice or comment on my dress? Why did I not point this out to him? I felt peeved over my slow-wittedness.

After the meeting we went over to meet the students. Their amusement was even greater and more eloquent. Many of them could not help laughing at the fact that I was wearing shoes with a tehmat. That they were wearing chappals with trousers seemed nothing extraordinary to them.

You must wonder why I am wasting your time narrating such trivial incidents. But look at it from the point of view of the Punjabi peasant. We are all full of admiration for his contribution to the green revolution. He is the backbone of our armed forces. How must he feel when his dress or his way of life is treated as a matter of amusement?

It is well known in the Punjab that as soon as a village lad receives college education he becomes indifferent to the village. He begins to consider himself superior and different, as if belonging to a separate world altogether. His one ambition is to somehow leave the village and run to a city. Is this not a slur on the academic world?

I agree that all places are not alike. I know perfectly well that no complex against the native dress exists in Tamil Nadu or Bengal. Anyone from a peasant to a professor can go about in a dhoti on any occasion. But I submit that the habit of borrowed and idealized thinking is present over there too. It is present everywhere, in some form or degree. Even twenty-five years after Independence we are blissfully carrying on with the same system of education which was designed by Macaulay and Co. to breed clerks and mental slaves. Slaves who would be incapable of thinking independently of their British masters; slaves who would admire everything about the masters, even while hating them; slaves who would consider it an honour to be standing by the side of the masters, to speak the language of the masters, to dress like the masters, to sing and dance like the masters; slaves, who would hate their own people and would be available to preach the gospel of hatred among their own people. Can we then be surprised if the large majority of students in universities are losing faith in this system of education?

....Ten years ago, if you asked a fashionable student in Delhi to wear a kurta with trousers he would have laughed at you. Today, by the grace of the hippies and the Hare-Rama-Hare-Krishna cult, not only has the kurta-trousers combination become legitimate, but even the word kurta has changed to guru-shirt. The sitar became a star instrument with us only after the Americans gave a big welcome to Ravi Shankar, just as fifty years ago Tagore became Gurudev all over India only after he received the Nobel Prize from Sweden.

Can you dare to ask a college student to shave his head, moustache and beard when the fashion is to put the barbers out of business? But if tomorrow, under the influence of Yoga, the students of Europe begin to shave their heads and faces, I can assure you that you will begin to see a crop of shaven skulls all over Connaught Circus the next day. Yoga has to get a certificate from Europe before it can influence the home of its birth.

I work in Hindi films, but it is an open secret that the songs and dialogues of these Hindi films are mostly written in Urdu. Eminent Urdu writers and poets—Krishan Chandar, Rajinder Singh Bedi, K.A. Abbas, Gulshan Nanda, Sahir Ludhianvi, Majrooh Sultanpuri and Kaifi Azmi are associated with this work.

Now, if a film written in Urdu can be called a Hindi film, it is logical to conclude that Hindi and Urdu are one and the same language. But no, our British masters declared them two separate languages in their time. Therefore, even twenty-five years after Independence, our government, our universities and our intellectuals insist on treating them as two separate and independent languages. Pakistan radio goes on ruining the beauty of this language by thrusting into it as many Persian and Arabic words as possible; and All India Radio knocks it out of all shape by pouring the entire Sanskrit dictionary into it. In this way they carry out the wish of the Master, to separate the inseparable. Can anything be more absurd than that? If the British told us that white was black, would we go on calling white black for ever and ever? My film colleague, Johnny Walker, remarked the other day, 'They should not announce "Ab Hindi mein samachar suniye" they should say, "Ab Samachar mein Hindi suniye".'

I have discussed this funny situation with many Hindi and Urdu writers—the so-called progressive as well as non-progressive. I have tried to convince them of the urgency to do some fresh thinking on the subject. But so far it has been like striking one's head against a stone wall. We film people call it the 'ignorance of the learned'. Are we wrong?

Lastly, I would like to tell you about a hunch I have...

Pandit Jawaharlal Nehru has admitted in his autobiography that our freedom movement, led by the Indian National Congress, was always dominated by the propertied classes—the capitalists and landlords. It was logical, therefore, that these very classes should hold the reins of power even after Independence. Today it is obvious to everyone that in the last twenty-five years the rich have been growing 'richer' and the poor have been growing poorer. Pandit Nehru wanted to change this state of affairs, but he couldn't. I don't blame him, because he had to face very heavy odds all along. Today our Prime Minister, Indira Gandhi, pledges herself to take the country towards the goal of socialism. How far she will be successful, I can't say. Politics is not my line. For our present purposes it is enough if you agree with me that in today's India the propertied classes dominate the government as well as society.

I think you will also agree that the British used the English language with remarkable success for strengthening their imperial hold on our country.

Now, which language in your opinion would their successors, the present rulers of India, choose to strengthen their own domination? Rashtrabhasha Hindi? By heavens, no. My hunch is that their interests too are served by English and English alone. But since they have to keep up a show of patriotism they make a lot of noise about Rashtrabhasha Hindi so that the mind of the public remains diverted.

Men of property may believe in a thousand different gods, but they worship only one—the God of profit. From the point of view of profit the advantages of retaining English to the capitalist class in this period of rapid industrialization and technological revolution are obvious. But the social advantages are even greater. From that point of view, English is a God-sent gift to our ruling classes.

Why? For the simple reason that the English language is beyond the reach of the toiling millions of our country. In olden times Sanskrit and Persian were beyond the reach of the toiling masses. That is why the rulers of those times had given them the status of state language. Through Sanskrit and Persian the masses were made to feel ignorant, inferior, uncivilized and unfit to rule themselves. Sanskrit and Persian helped to enslave their minds, and when the mind is enslaved bondage is eternal.

It suits our present ruling classes to preserve and maintain the social order that they have inherited from the British. They have a privileged position; but they cannot admit it openly. That is why a lot of hoo-haa is made about Hindi as the Rashtrabhasha. They know very well that this Sanskrit-laden, artificial language, deprived of all modern scientific and technical terms, is too weak and insipid to challenge the supremacy of English. It will always remain a showpiece, and what is more, a convenient tool to keep the masses fighting among themselves. We film people get a regular flow of fan mail from young people studying in schools and colleges. I get my share of it and these letters reveal quite clearly what a storehouse of torture the English language is to the vast majority of Indian students. How abysmally low the levels of teaching and learning have reached! That is why, I am told preferential treatment is being given to boys and girls who come from public schools i.e. schools to which only the children of privileged classes can go.

It is not necessary for me to comment on the efforts being made to strengthen English in every sphere of life, despite assurances to the contrary. They are all too obvious. It is admitted that English is too alien and hence too difficult to learn for the average Indian. And yet, it helps the capitalists and industrialists to consolidate their position on an all-India scale. That one consideration is more important than any other. According to them, whatever serves their interest automatically serves national interest too. They are hopeful that in the not too distant future the people themselves will endorse their stand that English should retain its present status for ever.

This was my hunch and I confided it one day to a friend of mine who is a labour leader. I told him that if we are serious about doing away with capitalism and bringing in socialism, we have to help the working class to consolidate itself on an all-India scale with the same energy as the capitalist class is doing. We have to help the working class achieve a leading role in society. And that can only be done by breaking the domination of English and replacing it with a people's language.

My friend listened to me carefully and largely agreed with me.

'You have analyzed the situation very well,' he said, 'but what is the remedy?'

'The remedy is to retain the English script and kick out the English language,' I replied.

'But how?'

'A rough and ready type of Hindustani is used by the working masses all over India. They make practical use of it by discarding all academic and grammatical flourishes. In this type of Hindustani, "Larka bhi jata hai" and "Larki bhi jata hai." There is an atmosphere of rare freedom in this patois and even the intellectuals indulge in it when they want to relax. And actually this is in the best tradition of Hindustani. This is how it was born, made progress and acquired currency all over India. In the old days it was contemptuously called Urdu—or the language of the camps or bazaars.

'Today in this bazaari Hindustani the word university becomes univrasti—a much better word than vishwa vidyalaya, lantern becomes laltain, the chassis of a car becomes chesi, spanner becomes pana, i.e. anything and everything is possible. The string with which the soldier cleans his rifle is called "pullthrough" in English. In Roman Hindustani it becomes fultroo—a beautiful word. "Barn door" is the term the Hollywood lights man uses for a particular type of two blade cover. The Bombay film worker has changed it to bandar, an excellent transformation. This Hindustani has untold and unlimited possibilities. It can absorb the international scientific and technological vocabulary with the greatest of ease. It can take words from every source and enrich itself. One has no need to run only to the Sanskrit dictionary.'

'But why the Roman script?' my friend asked.

'Because no one has any prejudice against it,' I said. 'It is the only script which has already gained all-India currency. In north, south, east and west, you can see shop signs and film posters in this script. We use this script for writing addresses on envelopes and post cards. The army has been using it for the last thirty years at least.'

My friend, the labour leader, kept silent for some time. Then he smiled indulgently and said, 'Comrade, Europe also experimented with Esperanto. A great intellectual like Bernard Shaw tried his best to popularize the Basic English. But all these schemes failed miserably, for the simple reason that languages cannot be evolved mechanically; they grow spontaneously.'

I was deeply shocked. I said, 'Comrade, Esperanto is just that Rashtrabhasha which the Hindi Pandits are manufacturing in their studies from the pages of some Sanskrit dictionary. I am talking of the language which is growing all round you, through the action of the people.'

But I couldn't convince him…

No country can progress unless it becomes conscious of its being—its mind and body. It has to learn to exercise its own muscles. It has to learn to find out and solve its own problems in its own way. But whichever way I turn I find that even after twenty-five years of Independence, we are like a bird which has been let out of its cage after a prolonged imprisonment—unable to know what to do with its freedom. It has wings, but is afraid to fly into the open air. It longs to remain within defined limits, as in the cage.

I am sure there must be some police officers in this country who in their hearts want to be regarded as friends rather than enemies of the public. They must be aware that in England the behaviour of the police towards the public is polite and helpful. But the tradition in which they have been trained is not the one which the British set for their own country but the one which they set for their colonies. So, the policeman is helpless. According to this colonial tradition, it is his duty to strike terror into anyone who enters his office, to be as obstructive and unhelpful as possible. This is the tradition which pervades every government office, from the chaparasi to the minister.

One of our young and enterprising producers made an experimental film and approached the Government for tax exemption. The minister concerned was being sworn into office the next day. He invited the producer to attend the ceremony, after which he would meet him and discuss the matter. The producer went, impressed by the informality with which the minister had treated him. As the minister was being sworn in, promising to serve the people truly, faithfully and honestly, his secretary started explaining to the young producer how much he would have to pay in black money to the minister and how much to the others if he wanted the tax exemption.

The producer got so shocked and angry that he wanted to put this scene in his next film. But his financiers had already suffered a loss with the first one. They told him categorically not to make an ass of himself. In any case, if he had insisted in making an ass of himself the censors would never have passed the film, because it is an unwritten law that no policeman or minister is corrupt in our country.

But there is something which strikes me as being even funnier. Those same people who scream against ministers every day cannot themselves hold a single function without some minister inaugurating it, or presiding over it, or being the chief guest. Sometimes the minister is the chief guest and a film star is the president, or else the film star is the chief guest and the minister is the president. Some big personality has to be there, because it is the age-old colonial tradition.

During the last war, I spent four years in England as a Hindustani announcer at the BBC. During those four years of extreme crisis I never even once set my eyes on a member of the British cabinet, including Prime Minister Churchill. But since Independence I have seen nothing else but ministers in India, all over the place.

When Gandhiji went to the Round Table Conference in 1930, he remarked to British journalists that the Indian people regarded the guns and bullets of their empire in the same way as their children regarded the crackers and phatakas on Diwali day. He could make that claim because he had driven the fear of the British out of Indian minds. He had taught them to ignore and boycott the British officers instead of kowtowing to them. Similarly, if we want socialism in our country we have firstly to drive out the fear of money, position and power from the minds of our people. Are we doing anything in that direction? In our society today who is respected most—the man with talent or the man with money? Who is admired most—the man with talent or the man with power? Can we ever hope to usher in socialism under such conditions? Before socialism can come we have to create an atmosphere in which possession of wealth and riches should invite disrespect rather than respect. We have to create an atmosphere in which the highest respect is given to labour whether it be physical or mental; to talent, to skill, to art and to inventiveness. This requires new thinking and the courage to discard old ways of thinking. Are we anywhere near this revolution of the mind?

JAYAPRAKASH NARAYAN

On 26 June 1975, President Fakhruddin Ali Ahmed declared a state of internal emergency under Article 352 of the Constitution of India. The presidential address proclaimed that 'the security of India is threatened by internal disturbance'. Between 26 June 1975 and 21 March 1977, when the Emergency was in force, Prime Minister Indira Gandhi's government assumed draconian powers and crushed all dissent. In the following days, civil liberties were suspended, media censored, and amendments that threatened to alter the basic character of the Constitution were made. Most of Gandhi's political opponents were imprisoned.

Jayaprakash Narayan (1902–79) was the face of the opposition to the Emergency, and one of the first leaders to be imprisoned after its declaration. In the following letter to Indira Gandhi, he expressed his surprise and disgust at her actions, and rebuked her for, above all, putting in danger the democratic core of India.

An Open Letter to Indira Gandhi

Dear Prime Minister,

I am appalled at press reports of your speeches and interviews. (The very fact that you have to say something every day to justify your action implies a guilty conscience). Having muzzled the press and every kind of public dissent, you continue with your distortions and untruth without fear of criticism or contradiction. If you think that in this way you will be able to justify yourself in the public eye and damn the Opposition to political perdition, you are sadly mistaken. If you doubt this, you may test it by revoking the Emergency, restoring to the people their fundamental rights, restoring the freedom of the press, releasing all those whom you have imprisoned or detained for no other crime than performing their patriotic duty. Nine years, Madam, is not a short period of time for the people, who are gifted with a sixth sense, to have found you out.

The burden of your song, as I have been able to discover, is that (a) there was a plan to paralyze the Government, (b) that one person had been trying to spread disaffection among the ranks of the civil and military forces. These seem to be your major notes. But there have been also minor notes. Every now and then you have been doling out your *obiter dicta*, such as the nation being more important than democracy and about the suitability of social democracy to India, and more in the same vein.

As I am the villain of the piece, let me put the record straight. This may be of no interest to you—for all your distortion and untruth are wilful and deliberate—but at least the truth would have been recorded. About the plan to paralyze the Government. There was no such plan and you know it. Let me state the facts.

Of all the states of India, it was in Bihar alone where there was a people's movement. But there, too, according to the Chief Minister's many statements, it had fizzled out long ago, if it had ever existed. But the truth is—and you should know if your ubiquitous Intelligence has served you right—that it was spreading and percolating deep down in the countryside. Until the time of my arrest, 'janata sarkars' were being formed from the village upwards to the block (ward) level. Later on, the process was to be taken up, hopefully, to the district and state level.

If you have cared to look into the programme of the janata sarkars, you would have found out that for the most part it was constructive, such as regulating the public distribution system, checking corruption at the lower levels of administration, implementing the land reform laws, settling disputes through the age-old custom of conciliation and arbitration, assuring a fair deal to Harijans, curbing such social evils as 'talak' and 'dahez' etc. There was nothing in all this that by any stretch of imagination could be called subversive. Only where the 'janata sarkars' were solidly organized were such programmes as non-payment of taxes taken up. At the peak of the movement in urban areas an attempt was made for some days, through dharna and picketing, to stop the working of Government offices. At Patna, whenever the Assembly opened, attempts were made to persuade the members to resign and to prevent them peacefully from going in. All these were calculated programmes of civil disobedience, and thousands of men and women were arrested all over the state.

If all this adds up to an attempt to paralyze the Bihar government, well, it was the same kind of attempt as was made during the freedom struggle through non-cooperation and satyagraha to paralyze the British government. But that was a government established by force, whereas the Bihar government and legislature are both constitutionally established bodies. What right has anyone to ask an elected government and elected legislature to go? This is one of your favourite questions. But it has been answered umpteen times by competent persons, including well-known constitutional lawyers. The answer is that in a democracy the people, too, have the right to ask for the resignation of an elected government if it has gone corrupt and has been misruling. And if there is a legislature that persists in supporting such a government it too must go so that the people might choose better representatives.

But in that case, how can it be determined what the people want? In the usual democratic manner. In the case of Bihar, the mammoth rallies and processions held in Patna, the thousands of constituency meetings held all over the State, the three-days' Bihar bandh, the memorable happenings of November 4, and the largest ever meeting held at the Gandhi maidan, on November 18, were a convincing measure of the people's will. And what had the Bihar government and Congress to show on their side? The miserable counter-offensive of November 16, which had been masterminded by Shri Barooah and on which, according to reliable reports, the fantastic sum of Rs 60 lakh rupees were spent. But if that was not conclusive enough proof, I had asked repeatedly for a plebiscite. But you were afraid to face the people.

While I am on the Bihar movement, let me mention another important point that would illumine the politics of such a type of movement. The students of Bihar did not start their movement just off the bat as it were. After formulating their demands at a conference they had met the Chief Minister and the Education Minister. They had had several meetings. But unfortunately the inept and corrupt Bihar Government did not take the students seriously. Then the latter gheraoed the Assembly. The sad events of that day precipitated the Bihar movement. Even then the students did not demand the resignation of the Ministry nor the dissolution of the Assembly. It was after several weeks during which firing, lathi charges and indiscriminate arrests took place that the Students' Action Committee felt compelled to put up that demand. It was at that point that the Rubicon was crossed.

Thus in Bihar, the Government was given a chance to settle the issues across the table. None of the demands of the students was unreasonable or non-negotiable. But the Bihar government preferred the method of struggle, i.e. unparalleled repression. It was the same in Uttar Pradesh. In either case, the Government rejected the path of negotiation, of trying to settle the issues across the table, and chose the path of strife. Had it been otherwise, there would have been no movement at all.

I have pondered over this riddle: Why did not those governments act wisely? The conclusion I have arrived at is that the main hurdle has been corruption. Somehow the governments have been unable to deal with corruption in their ranks, particularly at the top level—the ministerial level itself. The corruption has been the central point of the movement, particularly corruption in the government and the administration.

Be that as it may, except for Bihar there was no movement of its kind in any other state of India. In Uttar Pradesh, though satyagraha had started in April, it was far from becoming a people's movement. In some other states though, struggle committees had been formed, there seemed to be no possibility of a mass movement anywhere. And as the general election to the Lok Sabha was drawing near, the attention of the opposition parties was turned more towards the coming electoral struggle than to any struggle involving civil disobedience.

Thus, the plan of which you speak, the plan to paralyze the Government, is a figment of your imagination thought up to justify your totalitarian measures.

But suppose I grant you for a minute, for argument's sake, that there was such a plan, do you honestly believe that your erstwhile colleague, the former Deputy Prime Minister of India, and Chandrashekhar, a member of the Congress Working Committee, were also a party to it? Then why have they also been arrested and many others like them?

No, dear Prime Minister, there was no plan to paralyze the Government. If there was a plan, it was a simple, innocent and short-time plan to continue until the Supreme Court decided your appeal. It was this plan that was announced at the Ramlila grounds by Nanaji Deshmukh on June 25 and which was the subject matter of my speech that evening. The programme was for a selected number of persons to offer satyagraha before or near your residence in support of the demand that you should step down until the Supreme Court's judgement on your appeal. The programme was to continue for seven days in Delhi, after which it was to be taken up in the states. And, as I have said above, it was to last only until the judgement of the Supreme Court. I do not see what is subversive or dangerous about it. In a democracy the citizen has an inalienable right to civil disobedience when he finds that other channels of redress or reform have dried up. It goes without saying that the satyagrahi willingly invites and accepts his lawful punishment. This is the dimension added to democracy by Gandhi. What an irony that it should be obliterated in Gandhi's own India!

It should be noted—and it is a very important point—that even this programme of a satyagraha would not have occurred to the Opposition had you remained content with quietly clinging on to your office. But you did not do it. Through your henchmen you had rallies and demonstrations organized in front of your residence (begging you not to resign). You addressed these rallies and, justifying your stand, advanced spurious arguments and heaped calumny on the head of the Opposition. An effigy of the High Court Judge was burnt before your residence. Posters appeared in the city suggesting some kind of link between the Judge and the CIA. When such despicable happenings were taking place every day, the Opposition had no alternative but to counteract the mischief. And how did it decide to do it? Not by rowdyism but by orderly satyagraha, self-sacrifice.

It was this 'plan' and not any imaginary plan to paralyze the Government that has aroused your ire and cost the people their liberties and dealt a deathblow to their democracy.

And why was the freedom of the press being suppressed? Not because the Indian press was irresponsible, dishonest or anti-Government. In fact, nowhere under conditions of freedom is the press more responsible, reasonable and fair than it has been in India. The truth is that your anger against it was aroused because on the question of your resignation, after the High Court's judgement, some of the papers took a line that was highly unpalatable to you. And when on the morrow of the Supreme Court judgement all the metropolitan papers, including the wavering *The Times of India* came out with well-reasoned and forceful editorials advising you to quit, freedom of the press became too much for you to stomach. That cooked the goose of the Indian press, and you struck your deadly blow. It staggers one's imagination to think that so valuable a freedom as the freedom of the press, the very life-breath of democracy, can be snuffed out because of the personal pique of a Prime Minister.

You have accused the Opposition of trying to lower the prestige and position of the country's Prime Minister. But in reality, the boot is on the other leg. No one has done more to lower the position and prestige of that great office than yourself. Can you ever think of the Prime Minister of a democratic country who cannot even vote in his Parliament because he has been found guilty of corrupt electoral practices? The Supreme Court may reverse the High Court's judgement—most probably it will in this atmosphere of terror—but as long as that is not done your guilt and your deprivation of your right to vote remain.

As for the 'one person' who is supposed to have tried to sow dissatisfaction in the armed and police forces, he denies the charge. All that he has done is to make the men and officers of the forces conscious of their duties and responsibilities. Whatever he has said in that connection is within the law, the Constitution, the Army Act, and the Police Act.

So much for your major points, the plea to paralyze the Government and the attempt to sow dissatisfaction in the armed and police forces. Now a few of your minor points and *obiter dicta*.

You are reported to have said that democracy is not more important than the nation. Are you not presuming too much, Madam Prime

Minister? You are not the only one who cares for the nation. Among those whom you have detained or imprisoned there are many who have done as much for the nation as you. And every one of them is as good a patriot as yourself. So, please do not apply salt to our wounds by lecturing to us about the nation.

Moreover, it is a false choice that you have formulated. There is no choice between democracy and the nation. It was for the good of the nation that the people of India declared in the Constituent Assembly on November 26, 1949, that 'we, the people of India, having solemnly resolved to constitute into a Sovereign Democratic Republic...give to ourselves this Constitution.' This democratic Constitution cannot be changed into a totalitarian one by a mere ordinance or a law of Parliament. That can be done only by the people of India themselves in their new Constituent Assembly, especially elected for that special purpose. If Justice, Liberty, Equality and Fraternity have not been rendered to 'all its citizens' even after a quarter of century of signing of that Constitution, the fault is not that of the Constitution or of democracy but of the Congress party that has been in power in Delhi all these years. It is precisely because of that failure that there is so much unrest among the people and the youth. Repression is no remedy for that. On the other hand, it only compounds the failure.

I no doubt see that the papers are full these days of reports of new policies, new drives, show of new enthusiasm. Apparently you are trying to make up for lost time, that is to say, you are making a show of doing here and now what you failed to do in nine years. But your 20 points will go the same way as your 10 points did and the 'stray thoughts'. But I assure you this time the people will not be fooled. And I assure you of another thing too: a party of self-seekers and spineless opportunists and 'jee-huzurs' such as the Congress, alas, has become, can never do anything worthwhile. (Not all Congressmen are such. There are quite a few exceptions, such as those who have been deprived of their Party membership and some of them their freedom.) There will be a lot of propaganda and much ado on paper but on the ground level the situation will not change. The condition of the poor—and they are in great majority over the greater part of the country—has been worsening over the past years. It would be enough if the downward trend were arrested. But for that your whole approach to politics and economics will have to change.

I have written the above in utter frankness without mincing words. I have done so not out of anger or so as to get even with you in words.

No, that would be a show of impotence. Nor does it show any lack of appreciation for the care that is being taken of my health. I have done it only to place the naked truth before you, which you have been trying to cover up and distort.

Having performed this unpleasant duty, may I conclude with a few parting words of advice? You know I am an old man. My life's work is done. After Prabha's going I have nothing and no one to live for. My brother and my nephew have their family and my younger sister—the elder died years ago—has her sons and daughters. I have given all my life, after finishing education, to the country and asked for nothing in return. So, I shall be content to die a prisoner under your regime.

Would you listen to the advice of such a man? Please, do not destroy the foundations that the Father of the Nation, including your noble father, had laid down. There is nothing but strife and suffering along the path that you have taken. You inherited a great tradition, noble values and a working democracy. Do not leave behind a miserable wreck of all that. It would take a long time to put all that together again. For it would be put together again, I have no doubt. People who fought British imperialism and humbled it cannot accept indefinitely the indignity and shame of totalitarianism. The spirit of man can never be vanquished, no matter how deeply suppressed. In establishing your personal dictatorship, you have buried it deep. But it will rise from the grave. Even in Russia, it is slowly coming up.

You have talked of social democracy. What a beautiful image those words call to the mind. But you have seen in eastern and central Europe how ugly is the reality: Naked dictatorship and in the ultimate analysis Russian overlordship. Please, please do not push India towards that terrible fate.

And may I ask to what purpose all these draconian measures? In order to be able to carry out the 20 points? But who was preventing you from carrying out the 10 points? All the discontent, the protest, the satyagraha were due precisely to the fact that you were not doing anything to implement your programme, inadequate as it was, to lighten the misery and burden under which the people and youth were groaning. This is what Chandrashekhar, Mohan Dharia, Krishna Kant and their friends have been saying, for which they have been punished.

You have talked of 'drift' in the country. But was that due to opposition or to me? The drift was because of your lack of decision, direction and drive. You seem to act swiftly and dramatically only when your personal position is threatened. Once that is assured, the drift begins. Dear Indiraji, please do not identify yourself with the nation. You are not immortal, India is.

You have accused the Opposition and me of every kind of villainy. But let me assure you that if you do the right things—for instance, your 20 points, tackling corruption at ministerial levels, electoral reforms, etc., take the Opposition into confidence, heed its advice—you will receive the willing cooperation of every one of us. For that you need not destroy democracy. The ball is in your court. It is for you to decide.

With these parting words, let me bid you farewell. May God be with you.

Jayaprakash

Nayantara Sahgal

Acclaimed novelist Nayantara Sahgal, Indira Gandhi's cousin, vehemently opposed the Emergency rule and the quelling of dissent that came along with it. As a mark of protest, she resigned from the Sahitya Akademi's Advisory Board for English. The following is a copy of her resignation letter.

Letter to Dr R.S. Kelkar

10 Massey Hall
Jai Singh Road
New Delhi 110001
14 May 1976

Dr R.S. Kelkar
Secretary,
Sahitya Akademi
Rabindra Bhavan
New Delhi 110001

Dear Dr Kelkar,

Thank you for your letter of 20/21 April.

I wrote to you on 27 August 1975 on the matter of censorship, and you assured me in your reply of 29 August that you would place my letter before the president of the Akademi on 8 September. You now say that you have had no time to do so.

The question of free expression and the free circulation of ideas is crucial to a free society. I should have thought could be as important as this to the Sahitya Akademi, which is concerned with writers and their work. Your failure to bring this issue to the notice of the president convinces me that the Sahitya Akademi of India does not concern itself with free expression. Indeed it seems willing to be a servile body, an obedient servant of dictatorship. Let me assure you that had Jawaharlal Nehru, its founder, been alive today, he would not have tolerated such a situation. Indeed he would probably have been in jail, for he would not have kept quiet on any matter concerning human freedom.

I regret I cannot serve on any committee that is so lost to self-respect as to remain silent on the censorship that is strangulating India today. Kindly accept my resignation. I hope you will be good enough to convey the precise reason for it to the other members of the Advisory Board for English, and to place it on your records.

I am sending a copy of this letter to the president and the vice-president of the Sahitya Akademi.

Yours sincerely,
Nayantara Sahgal

NIRMAL VERMA

Nirmal Verma (1929–2005) was a noted Hindi writer. In July 1976, when the Emergency had gone on for a year, he contributed the following essay to Seminar.

For an Alternative Vision

India, until recently, enjoyed a unique place in the world of warring ideologies in so far as it bore the burden of poverty and democratic conscience at one and the same time, refusing to bargain one for the other. In this respect, it could easily be distinguished from the other countries of the third world, who adopted the 'values' of the colonial rulers, even after their liberation from colonial rule. No less a perceptive person than Fanon could evolve only a negative stance of anti-imperialism, without offering any alternative system of values based on the specific experience of a different mode of life. It is significant that in the absence of any alternative vision of society, many of the ex-colonies rapidly lapsed into petty tyrannies, using the same instruments of oppression which their colonial rulers had once wielded against them.

India was different. In her struggle against the British, what she was fighting *against* was as important as what she was fighting *for*. After Independence, the task before the Indians was not merely to eliminate the remnants of a colonial past, but to replace them with those values (non-violence and freedom being the most crucial among them) which were evolved precisely during the process of the anti-colonial struggle. No other country in the third world evolved such a sophisticated value-system, not in abstraction but as an integral part of our political movement; it shaped itself in the thick of the battle as it were. Satyagraha was nothing but the unique strategy of human conscience against injustice—an attempt to extend morality in the political field. Non-violence was another such value.

Since no readymade ideology to fight foreign rule existed, it took years of continuous, tortuous debates before these values were finally crystallized. Such debates and controversies were *openly* published in the Indian press without the British rulers resorting to censorship, a fact which may seem curious in the present circumstances. From Raja Ram Mohan Roy to Gandhiji, the entire concept of 'political change' underwent a revolutionary transformation; it was deeply imbued with a cultural content, which excluded nothing and embraced all facets of human action. Politics, like a work of art, was embedded in total experience. Struggle against foreign rule was waged on the plane of values—linked with the process of total self-rejuvenation.

The fact that this process was thwarted after Independence has become, perhaps, the most tragic moment in modern history, comparable only to the events in Czechoslovakia. In both cases, an 'experiment with truth' was aborted before it could flower in all its uniqueness.

In India's case, the failure was not the result of external intervention; it was primarily caused by the reversal of our attitude to the concept of freedom. During the period of their resistance to British rule, Indians had become deeply suspicious of the coercive power of the State. Gandhiji's scepticism of the centralized power of the State was merely a reflection of what people at large felt. It was firmly believed that State power was found to degenerate, unless it was constantly corrected by and related to the other areas of man's life. This intimate relation between power and experience determined the *content* of man's freedom. No institution could be truly democratic unless it continuously subjected State power to the changing content of man's consciousness. Freedom could never be frozen within the existing institutions; if it didn't expand beyond the institutions into the fabric of man's life, it had a tendency to shrink back into the hands of a few individuals. It could thrive only in perpetual tension between the coercive power of the State, on the one hand, and man's expanding consciousness on the other.

India's case was unique, because in spite of enormous pressures, it refused to 'resolve' the tension by falling back on a totalitarian solution, as many countries of the third world, including China, had done. On the other hand, it failed to expand the democratic content of its institutions to the extent where it would have become impossible for any individual or political party to usurp the power of the State.

We lived in a state of unresolved tension. It could be resolved *creatively* by reshaping and decentralizing State power to make freedom real, a solution suggested by Gandhiji. The other, a clearly *negative alternative*, was to subvert the democratic content of freedom and make State power real. One was to face the difficult and unique challenge of self-liberation. The other was to relapse into the conventional pattern of tyranny.

Let us not delude ourselves that the freedom of the press and expression in themselves could be a source of liberation. The problem in the Indian context was whether those who exercised the freedom of the word were in any real way concerned in embodying the experience and awareness of the Indian people—their hunger and suffering and sense of deprivation. In India, during the last two decades, those who had a predominant control over the media had no experience of human suffering; those who really suffered had no word to express it. Despite all the noises that we made in the press and the Parliament, India remained a continent of silence.

Thus, attachment to the right of full expression becomes merely formal and decorative unless it is transformed into the *moral concern* for the full articulation of man's total experience. That such a concern was singularly absent in our intelligentsia was revealed in the most cruel light when it so smoothly adjusted itself to the changed circumstances after the Emergency. It felt no real anguish for the loss of freedom of the word simply because the intelligentsia itself was largely responsible for denuding the word of its moral content.

But, to infer from this, as our present rulers and some Marxists would like to infer, that liberty of expression, freedom of the press and the basic right of a citizen to have free access to all the sources of information, are mere 'bourgeois values' which can be shelved for the sake of some mythical progress, is to fall a victim to another form of self-delusion. All projects of 'revolutionary-reform' may become instruments of oppression if the people for whom they are designed are deprived of the right to judge and comment upon them in the light of their experience. The conviction of the oppressed that they must fight for their liberation is not a gift bestowed by the ruling leadership, but the result of the consciousness of the oppressed themselves.

India may have a single political destiny, but it has to be defined and reflected in terms of diverse visions. The suppression of any vision which shows a path different from the one sanctified by State power, would lead not merely to the impoverishment of our present, but would also distort the nature of our destiny stored in the future. Hence the necessity of the freest possible dialogue. India needs this dialogue, the freedom of a nation to talk to itself, more than any other country of the world precisely because we have not yet made a final choice in favour of one future or the other. India, fortunately, still has many of its options open, which are not available to the western world; to suppress free debate over these options is to close them for ever.

It is obvious that for such a dialogue to become effective, it would be necessary to go beyond the mere liberty of press and expression, but unless these basic liberties are respected, unless *they are constitutionally acknowledged as inviolable,* any process of going 'beyond them' would be self-defeating. Herein lies the sacredness of constitutions, not because they are perfect—they are not. At best they are a compromise between the reality and the ideal. Rights do not become real merely because they are guaranteed by a document. And yet because they are guaranteed, it is *assumed* that human freedom is sacred and unassailable, it is *hoped* that some day it will become real.

The Constitution serves as a test case for all our actions, both in the area of the conscience and of the dream. For this reason, sometimes very embarrassing situations arise for those totalitarian regimes which still cling to their revolutionary constitution—if only on paper. We face the curious spectacle in the Soviet Union, where the dissident intellectuals actually appeal to the government to respect the integrity of their own constitution.

Thus, what we term the 'formal' aspect of freedom ensured in the Constitution is both real and unreal—unreal because it is still to be translated into the actual fact of freedom, but it is also real in so far as it is the *symbolic* expression of what people wish to realize; like a tip of the iceberg, it gives a glimpse of man's aspirations which lie buried in our past, beyond time and beyond articulation. It is rooted in the totality of Indian experience, which is diverse and pluralistic in its structure, drawing sustenance not from the coercive power of the State, but from the interplay and interaction of various visions and voices. This has been the central core of the Indian ethos, what I called earlier our cultural experience, which regards the 'other' not as a hostile element to be suppressed and destroyed, but as an integral part of the whole.

I would like to stress this point here, because in recent months it is often argued that those who 'deplore' the loss of human rights are 'westernized' intellectuals having no understanding of the Indian reality. The truth is quite the contrary. It is essentially in the context of the Indian tradition, which has flourished as a result of the free interaction of diverse streams of thought, that the present atmosphere of intolerance becomes incomprehensible. The moments of anguish in Indian history are precisely those where the ethos of tolerance is disturbed by a monolithic power, one voice seeking dominance over the others, thereby violating the sacredness of the whole. The voices of protest against such a violation are very much in the Indian tradition; one is however not sure whether the measures of violation themselves do not accord with some of the models of the West.

What is, however, common both to the affluent societies of the West as well as to the poor countries of the third world is the supreme value which is attached to man's awareness of himself as a human being. No act of State power can be legitimate which violates this reality of awareness, forcing man to live in the 'reality' of others, a censored reality, which is the other name for darkness. Force, which is the normal attribute of State power, degenerates into violence, when it deprives man of his own humanness. Beyond this point, all the socio-economic programmes, however benevolent and beneficent they may be, turn into mere acts to legitimatize the violence.

This fact is often overlooked or deliberately distorted in the poor countries of the third world where acts of tyranny and violence are often justified by radical economic reforms. A choice is posed between bread and freedom as if one would necessarily be the price of the other. Of course, such a choice is never clearly stated. It is implicitly assumed that freedom of speech and expression, a free and uncensored press, free access to sources of information all that is necessary for man's awareness of himself as a human being are a mere 'luxury' in a society of 'starving millions' and have to be sacrificed for their emancipation. It is queer logic but it is often supported even by radical western philosophers like Jean-Paul Sartre who, ironically enough, used to justify the tyrannical acts of the Stalinistic regime precisely for the same reasons.

Apart from the fact that freedom is an indivisible and absolute value—it cannot be regarded as necessary in the West and a luxury in Asia—such a method of rationalization for the abrogation of human rights is both sinister and self-contradictory. Sinister because it assumes that human beings living in poor societies are *less than human*; they may be fed and clothed *on the condition* that they cease to exercise their critical consciousness, cease to be human. Thus, when an Indian worker or a Chinese peasant are deprived the freedom to express the reality of their experience in their own language, it is not a mere deprivation of a useless luxury, it is a fundamental violation of his person as a human being. The choice between freedom and bread is a false choice because man *needs* both in order to explore the *meaning* of his existence on this earth. To force such a choice is humiliating in a double sense—it is to humiliate the human being for his poverty as it is to humiliate the poor man for his being human.

But, apart from being sinister, such an argument negates itself in so far as it destroys the very conditions in which any radical reforms could be implemented. If reforms are for the people, the people should have free access to all the instruments through which they could make their experience available to the government. Indeed, policies would be radical not because of what is professed in them, but because of the extent to which this experience is incorporated in their formulation. It is irrelevant to discuss here whether the various 'point programmes' are good or bad if the instruments by which the goodness or badness of a programme is judged are themselves absent. Policies which are going to determine the future of a people cannot morally and legitimately be pursued in a situation where the people are debarred to debate freely about them.

I have come back to the point from which I had begun—the

tremendous importance of a nationwide free debate on all issues which concern the Indian destiny at the present moment. Such a debate must necessarily go beyond the 'parliamentary debates' between government and opposition parties, which in recent years had degenerated into a pathetic struggle for power. Instead, it should be a dialogue which the nation should conduct with itself, without the interference of State power. It should be free and uninhibited for, like an individual, a nation cannot examine its conscience in a state of fear.

Indeed, in order to be meaningful, such a debate should concern itself with the choices that we made at the time of Independence. It would be useless to blame this or that party for the present crisis—for after all it is the logical culmination of the choices that we made in regard to our institutions at the time of Independence.

Such a debate, in a way, would be a continuation of the process of self-examination which Gandhiji had initiated even before Independence, and which was suddenly interrupted after his death. Perhaps no moment could be better than the present one to pick up the threads once again from where he had left.

UMA SHANKAR JOSHI

Uma Shankar Joshi (1911–88) was one of the most noted names in Indian literature. He was the vice chancellor of Gujarat University between 1966 and 1972 and later became the chancellor of Visva-Bharati University, Santiniketan. A member of the Rajya Sabha during the Emergency, Joshi was fiercely critical of the way democracy was being strangled.

In Opposition to the Emergency

Mr Deputy Chairman, Sir, this is the most agonizing moment in five years of my association with this august House. I came here as a poet and a Vice-Chancellor with what fond hopes and dreams. I thought it was possible for India—an ancient people, though a new nation—to achieve socialistic aims through democracy. One thought that India was cut out for this role, that it would achieve social justice through peaceful means. However, yesterday our Home Minister came forward with a plea in favour of emergency, giving up all hopes for democracy in this great land.

He was pleased to lay the blame at the doors of opposition parties and certain happenings in our country. I belong to no party and I would take this opportunity to refer to one detail, about Gujarat. He was not holding this charge when the Nav Nirman movement started in Gujarat. I would like to point out to him that in the beginning it was the Congress Party people themselves who saw the rebirth of Mahatma Gandhi in the Nav Nirman youth. The Communist Party also, as far as I remember, was with the Nav Nirman youth. It was a different story after the ouster of the Ministry. Why did this happen? My plea is for a little self-searching rather than laying the whole blame at the door of the opposition. I have been crying hoarse that the ruling party like the muskdeer runs in vain all around for the opposition, for it is within its own self. The learned friends from the ruling party, the younger people, say that the emergency should have been clamped down on the country two years before or so. It would have been good if something had been done to implement the economic programme two years—I would say many more years—before. But that was not done and a political style developed which only hankered after having a huge majority, unmindful of heterogeneous elements which were counterproductive and which would not allow forward-looking policies of the party to be implemented.

Sir, I do not want to enter into further details. But even if what the Home Minister said was right regarding opposition parties, does it behove of him to suggest that 'If they, the opposition parties, are running democracy in our country, why should not we ourselves deal a death blow to it?' That would be a tragic hour in the life of our country. George Bernard Shaw said that the English people did everything on principle. If they beheaded a king, they beheaded him on principle. Our learned Home Minister says that everything is within the framework of the Constitution. So today, he will be able, with the majority that his party commands, to stifle the Constitution constitutionally. What does it lead to?

A clamp down of pre-censorship has never happened in India, not even under a foreign regime. We are afraid of truth. Where does this fear emanate from, fear which has engulfed the length and breadth of this vast land? Wherefrom has emanated this dark cynical shadow of fear—I mean, terror—which shows its ugly face all around? How many walls have been created after the 26th of June? You want to see that the country is not disintegrated. By switching off all information, rumours run amuck and truth is stifled. This is the fear of truth in a country which has a reputation of being a seeker after truth. This has damaged the image of India all over the world more than anything else.

I should like to press this point and to convey this through this august House to the Prime Minister that when Nehru and Shastri were our Prime Ministers, India, though a developing country trying to pull herself out, almost by the boot-strap, from poverty, was a respected country. It held its head high. Nehru, before laying down his pen, before writing 'Tamam Shud' to his book *Glimpses of World History* quoted from Tagore—where the mind is devoid of fear, where the head is held high, into that heaven of freedom let my country awake.

As Nehru himself said, he was more in tune with Tagore than Gandhiji. So long as he was on the world stage, even though this colleagues, as some people observed, were just Tito, Nasser and Sukarno, he himself always stood taller by a head. He represented a country which held its head high. What will happen to our Prime Minister when she goes abroad? She thinks very much of foreigners' opinions and rightly so, but the image has been damaged.

... If some leaders were found hatching a conspiracy, they should have been brought before a court of law. He may be J.P. He may be Mr Morarji Desai. He may be Mr Atal Behari Vajpayee, whoever he may be... But why penalize the people, who the ruling party thinks are, by and large, with them?

I appeal to the Members of the ruling party because now there is only one party. Already there are signs of their heading towards one party rule, towards the destruction of the federal structure, replacing it by the unitary structure. Already there are signs that the Gujarat and the Tamil Nadu Governments may find themselves in trouble sooner rather than later.

Not being a politician I do not want to enter into a discussion with the Home Minister, but how many Governments have been toppled by the ruling party? How many people have migrated from the opposition parties even here in this House to the ruling party? We are Nominated Members. Independent Members not belonging to any party. The ruling party on that side sucks from this side and whatever is left of the opposition is perhaps the best of them. So put them behind the jail. Have a one-party rule.

... Younger men and women talk lightly of the freedom of the press. People like me who have fought as a young college student have other views in the matter. There are elderly people here. I find the Home Minister himself white-bearded, very revered writer of Punjabi, Shri Gurmukh Singh Musafir and others are here. What have you been doing all these years? What have you done for Indian democracy? We are here today at a crucial hour. Have you gone to the Prime Minister and said that you will be blown but you hold these ideas? Is the Prime Minister on talking terms with thinking people in this country?

... Sir, before I conclude I would like to say one word ... though words have lost their significance. I am a votary of words. I cannot live without the word. I am a poet. I am an artist first and last. By chance I happen to be here. But what can word do to-day? We have been brought to such a catastrophe. All around there is an unthinking conformism ... which does injustice to their own selves and ultimately, to the Prime Minister and more important, to the country.

My appeal to the ruling party in particular and through them to the leader is: Do not be in a hurry to ring down the curtain on the First Republic.

Khushwant Singh on Operation Blue Star

In June 1984, Indira Gandhi's government carried out Operation Blue Star, sending the Army into the Golden Temple to extricate the militant religious leader Jarnail Singh Bhindranwale who had hidden there. This led to the destruction of religious property and several civilian deaths. The incident deeply affected the noted writer and journalist Khushwant Singh (1915–2014), despite his being an agnostic, and he returned his Padma Bhushan. The following is the speech he delivered in the Rajya Sabha in July 1984.

Mr Deputy Chairman, I speak with my eye on the clock and will be grateful if you keep your hand off the bell. I promise that I will not take more time than scheduled for my party.

We have had six hours of debate during which we heard learned discourses on Punjab politics and Akali factionalism and there has also been much recrimination between parties, each trying to blame the other. I think most people will agree that in the entire debate there has been total lack of a sense of gravity of the situation which is facing our country today. We are virtually on the brink of an abyss. There has been total absence of any realization that the country is practically breaking up. And there has been total absence of any viable suggestion on what we are to do in this situation.

I hope the Members will bear with me when I speak because I may have some very unpalatable truths to tell. I am aware of the fact that I am a nominated Member who, as things go in this House, is the lowest of the lower castes. But since I relinquished my Padma Bhushan in a state of emotion—I admit it because I felt deeply hurt—I was suddenly pitchforked into the eye of the storm and whether I liked it or not, without my seeking or relishing it, I found myself made into a kind of spokesman for the Sikhs. It is very ironical that I, although an agnostic, should have suddenly become relevant to the Sikh community and my three Sikh colleagues on the other side who claim themselves to be pucca Sikhs should have become totally irrelevant when it comes to Sikh public opinion. Whether you like it or not, I now echo the sentiments of fourteen million people. So, take note of what I have to say.

My heart is very full. I shall try to be as unemotional as I can. I will say very little about the action that the Army has taken except that I maintain this was a tragic error of judgement, a grievous mistake and a gross miscalculation which will cover many black pages in the history of India, the history of Punjab and the history of the Sikhs. I will say more on what not to do to retrieve the situation. I think the best way of seeing this problem is to see backwards, to see what the situation is today and take it back to the army action and decide whether the action that the Government took was justified or not.

The situation today is this that the religious susceptibility of every single Sikh has been deeply wounded. 99 per cent of these Sikhs had nothing whatsoever to do either with Bhindranwale or with Akalis, or with the Government or with politics of any kind. That should be borne in mind. What this action has done is to humiliate the pride of a very proud people and you know that a proud people do not forget nor forgive very easily. It is a wounded community in a vengeful mood. We have to do something to prevent it from exploding. What is more, it has widened the gulf between the Hindus and the Sikhs. The wedge was undoubtedly driven in by the Akalis, it was widened by this evil man,

Bhindranwale. This army action has made it so wide as to make it appear to be unbridgeable. It is unfortunate that the Sikhs who prided themselves as the first-class citizens of this country are now regarded as something worse than third-class citizens. As my friend, Shri Mohunta, pointed out the other day, the discrimination has not stopped. You have to go to any airport or travel by road or rail in northern India to see how a Sikh is treated. You will know what the discrimination is. You are constantly questioned. Even at the Srinagar airport this morning only the Sikh passengers were photographed when they were coming. Search is carried out and their cars are checked at the entry points. This discrimination is undoubtedly restricted to the bearded Sikh. Is it not wrong of them now to ask, 'Do Indians still regarded us as fellow Indians?'

In this situation, I have only two questions to ask: Could any action that alienated 14 million citizens of this country, who are the backbone of its defence services, who provide more than half of the food for this country and who live on the most sensitive borders that divide us from Pakistan be justified?

Is it really true, as the White Paper maintains, that there was no other alternative? And as the Government and some Members of the Opposition have also said ad nauseam that there was no other way? My answer to both these questions is an absolute no. I will try to spell out my views with reference to what the White Paper says. It says that two years of negotiations with the Akalis were negated by their intransigence. They kept on shifting their stand, they kept on adding to their demands and they kept on resiling from their demands under pressure of extremists. The accusation was repeated yesterday by the Prime Minister herself. Is it true that the Government did not shift from its stand, did not change its stance, did not resile from its stand? If you want any evidence of it, read the record of my former colleague, Shri Harkishan Singh Surjeet's speeches here in the discussions. He mentioned many instances when a settlement had almost been arrived at and it was the Government that changed its mind. Every time the talks broke down, the one statement that the Prime Minister made in reply to that was that some demands of the Akalis had been granted, and with regard to those that affected the neighbouring states, the neighbouring states had to be consulted. For two years we have been told that the neighbouring states have to be consulted. What happened in those consultations? Does it take that long to contact them in Chandigarh or Shimla to find out what their reactions were? The White Paper also maintains that, it was the Akali agitation which led to terrorism in the country. The Prime Minister herself repeated, 'I know from experience that these civil disobedience movements often degenerate into some kind of a violence.' It so happens that this is chronologically inaccurate. Terrorism preceded the Akali morcha. You may recall that first violence took place between Bhindranwale and the Nirankaris as early as April 1978. Thereafter, there were fake encounters between the police under Sardar Darbara Singh who was the chief minister of Punjab and so-called extremists which gave further fillip to those terrorist activities. The murders of the Nirankari Baba and Lala Jagat Narain took place before the morcha was launched. So, this inference that the pacifist movement led to terrorism is historically and chronologically inaccurate. It has been repeated from both sides of the House that the Government had no choice but to move the army into the Golden Temple. I had sought assurances and been given the assurance—I from here and the then home minister from there—that the army would not be moved in because the results could be horrendous. Did the Government ever consider two alternative possibilities? Number one, a commando action by people in plain clothes who would have gone and tried to overpower Bhindranwale and his men? There would have been a certain amount of loss of life; I have no doubt. But hundreds of innocent lives, including those of women and children, would have been spared. Did you ever consider the possibility of putting a cordon round the Golden Temple and the city of Amritsar, occupying the Guru ka Langar, cutting off food and rations and starving those people to come out? The results would have been quite different. No. The White Paper does not mention these alternatives. All we know is that to face about 300 to 500 armed desperados and no more—you sent in six divisions led by three full Generals, tanks, armed earners [sic], mountain guns and all the weapons at your command to [smoke] these people out. And instead of taking [the] two hours that you anticipated it took you more than two days to do it.

Mr Home Minister—new Home Minister—and Mr Deputy Chairman, I visited Amritsar a month after the action took place. I interviewed many people who were there, who were eye witnesses to the sad episode. Let me tell you that the figure of the death toll is considerably higher than what the White Paper mentions. I know the Akalis are producing their own White Paper. Perhaps it will be vastly exaggerated. But it is quite evident that the death toll was considerably higher than what you are admitting. And women and children and innocent pilgrims were also there. Even more, the damage to property is also extensive. However much you try to patch up it will not be patched up. The Akal Takht is in total shambles, including all the relics that were inside. You have maintained that no damage was done to Harmandar. But I have seen it with my own eyes. There are over 200 fresh bullet marks in Harmandar... (Interruptions) You can still see this if you go there. (Interruptions) Please bear with me. You can contradict me (Interruptions!) One Amrik Singh was inside.... (Interruptions).

Shri P.N. Sukul (Uttar Pradesh): What do you mean by fresh bullet marks? Did you see?

Shri Khushwant Singh: Yes. There have been earlier actions and the bullet marks were seen by those people at that time. They are new—through windows, coming from one side, going to the other. The archives of the Golden Temple alongside the Prakrima, which housed over 1000 hand-written manuscript copies of the Granth, the Hukmnamas (Ordinances) bearing Gurus' signatures, have gone up in flames. And this was not during the action; it was after the action that this thing took place. (Interruptions)

...Mr Deputy Chairman, I wish these members would hold their patience. I am now treading on a very sensitive ground but I think it should be recorded. And that is the role of the Army. We have treated the Army as a sacred cow. What has been done in Amritsar should go on record. I first draw your attention to this report in the *Times of London* dated 14 June based on Associated Press account which mentions that a number of Sikhs who were taken prisoner with their hands tied behind and shot in the head in cold blood. I have not heard a single word of... (Interruptions) Let the Government contradict it. This is the most serious allegation made. There are other equally painful things from people living in Amritsar... (Interruptions).

...I have made a reference to the role of the Army. I would also like to make a request to the new Home Minister to look into the charges that are now being levelled by the SGPC or whatever remains of it and the Akali Dal of the extensive looting that has been done in the neighbouring places.

Finally, we have been told how well the Army behaved. But it is with my own eyes on a wall alongside the Akal Takht I saw a notice saying, 'No smoking, no drinking allowed here.' You can came to your own conclusions. These are two heinous offences in any place of worship to the Sikhs. Obviously, the troops have been doing that there and the notice was put up for them and was not taken off by the time I spotted it.

Now, I have said enough of the damage done. I think it is far more important to turn to what possibly can be the healing touch. We have been told what a healing touch should be on Punjab Agitation.

...Let me talk now of your concept of the healing touch. The 'place of honour'—and I put the words in inverted commas—goes to the Government-controlled media and the press subservient to the Government. I just give you a few instances where the same person holds the gun in one hand and the microphone in the other—total monopoly of the microphone this is the kind of 'news' we can expect. We were told first that no woman had been killed. Then we were told thirteen women had been killed. Then we were told that it was one of Bhindranwale's renegades that killed the thirteen women. We were told by the press, 'from reliable sources,' page 1, column 1, that Bhindranwale has been killed by his own colleagues. On the third day it was said, Bhindranwale died in his own hand—on page 5, and finally it was said, no, he died fighting. We had the same kind of story about the discovery of heroin, of loose women—all taken up by this subservient press, and then they suddenly vanished or contradictions were published on page 3, bottom of column 8. This is the result of censorship. And this is not the healing touch.

I give you one instance of a fraud committed on the Sikh people. We are told that Gurubani Kirtan has been resumed from the Golden Temple early morning. I am an early riser and switch on my radio at 4.30 a.m. Mr Home Minister, take it from me. Kirtan is not from the Golden Temple; they are the tapes from Jullundur station. I may tell you why. Morning service consists of Asa Di Var, within which Ragis put in Shabads of their choice. These Ragis are clever people. They put in Shabads which have double meaning, talking about the wickedness of others. Obviously they were found unpalatable, because the Sikhs get different message from Asa Di Var. But for the last four days, including this morning, Ardas which comes at the end of the service, came in the middle because the poor man handling the tape did not know which comes first and which in the middle. So, we had a very charming situation of the alleged Bani coming from Harmandir Sahib, with Ardas coming in the middle. Please look into it. I will give you the dates also on which it has been going on; it was certainly this morning as well. Another healing touch.

Another example now. We know of the wide scale desertions of Sikh troops at different points. Why did they take place? Because of censorship the poor fellows did not know what was going on. If you

know the custom of army—some of my retired friends would know—
it is that every Sikh soldier is first made to take an oath on the Granth
about being true to his oath, sticking to it and fighting for the honour
of his country. Every time Sikh soldiers go into battle, a Granthi goes
with them with Granth Sahib carried on his head. Now, he was told, by
gossip or rumour, that one of the Granth Sahib itself has been hit and
the Golden Temple enshrining the Granth has been burnt. What are his
reactions? It is one of anger, frustration. As a leaderless man, be walks
out and says: I am going to the Golden Temple to defend it myself. Now,
we are told by a senior Army officer that the most condign punishment
will be meted out to those people. It is up to you to give them condign
punishment and see the result of that healing touch.

Now, I come to Kar Seva. It is quite obvious, you failed totally to get
anyone with any credibility to take on this function and you hit up on
this, if I cannot choose any kinder words... (Interruptions).

Mr Deputy Chairman: It will not go on record. You need not name...
(Interruptions).

Shri Khushwant Singh: All right; cancel those words. (Interruptions).

A Hon. Memeber: He has withdrawn the word.

Shri Khushwant Singh: Now, let us forget it. I am concluding, if they
allow me to conclude.

... I think it is quite evident to everybody in this country that whatever
this gentleman, let me call him gentleman, Baba Santa Singh, is doing,
is against the wishes of the community. The community is not going
to honour what he is doing. It will further exacerbate the feelings of
the community. It is also evident now that despite what has happened,
despite what you have done, you have not broken the back of terrorism.
Terrorism continues. There is hijacking, breaching of canal banks,
looting of banks and so on. It is evident from the fact of the enormous
security precautions taken in this free country for our President and the
Prime Minister. Despite these draconian measures to put down violence
in the midst of fear. You also know that you cannot keep the Army in
Punjab forever. There is a limit to it. You cannot keep a people down
with bayonets for too long. You should realize what the consequence
will be, in regard to these people, inflamed as they are, if suddenly, this
power, this control is taken away from them. I would like to place curtain
positive suggestions. I am a man who proposes grand gestures. I proposed
at one time that the Prime Minister should go to the Golden Temple as
a pilgrim. It was not taken seriously. I proposed later that the President

should go to the Golden Temple. No notice was taken of either of my requests. They visited the Golden Temple after the damage has been done. (Interruptions) May I suggest now a grander gesture? Now, Sir, I would suggest that the leaders of this country, Jagatgurus, Shankaracharyas and others, leaders of the Hindu parties like Advaniji, Vajpayeeji and others... (Interruptions) should join us in this Kar Seva. This is one of the ways in which we can heal the wounds. Lastly, we have a great day coming, the 12th of August. Raksha Bandhan. Let every Hindu tie a rakhi on the hands of a Sikh, which we shall reciprocate. These are the only ways in which you can repair the damage which you have done. Thank you, Sir.

KAIFI AZMI

Kaifi Azmi (1918–2002) was a leading Urdu poet and social activist. He joined the Communist Party when he was nineteen and was also a member of the Progressive Writers' Association. Human struggle, in particular the plight of the marginalized, is a dominant theme in Azmi's poems. His poems are passionate and direct, often blunt, depicting his impatience with any kind of oppression.

Second Storm

And then came a night
When bars shut down
All fire temples shut down.
He, who opposed the bars and temples,
A writer, willing to fight
For life,
Who had always fought against the will of God,
For man
Had been willing to take on even God
One day, while fighting, fell silent,
Covering his face with one of his books slept.
But his pen,
Which has a hundred names
And does a hundred things,

Is fighting in the same way still
It moves on in the same pace
Sometimes in this hand
Sometimes in another
Moving on, some fingers bent,
While others busy spinning
New conspiracies everyday
New ropes everyday
Hanged him from a stake.
No messages came from the skies
The heavens did not call him up,
But from his broken bones
The blood flowed in such a way
The ropes burnt
The conspiracies rotted away.
This is not a tale from Noah's time
It is a story of today,
He held the ocean on the tip of his tongue
And swung it into the sphere,
Picked up the earth in his beak
And tossed it into the void.
Forests and towns trembled
The ignorant trembled
The learned trembled.
This is not the storm in which the earth drowns
In this storm, the drowned earth emerges again.

Translated by Pavan K. Varma

NAMDEO DHASAL

Namdeo Dhasal (1949–2014) was a revolutionary Marathi poet born into the Mahar caste. In 1972, he and his friends founded the Dalit Panthers, a radical political group. His first collection of poems, Golpitha, was published in 1972 and caused a sensation. He did not write in standard Marathi, but used the language as a tool to express rage at the unjust conditions in society.

New Delhi, 1985

The needle probes for the artery;
Enemies of poetry gather in your city.

Your town is cursed with power;
Roses flow in this stream of blood;
The waters of your Yamuna stand exposed.

India Gate:
Over there, the Rashtrapati Bhavan.
How ruthlessly has this city been combed and groomed!
White elephants sway at the gate of the past.
Goldsmiths mould replicas of peacocks.
Your well-carpentered glory.
Long Kashmiri carpets are rolled out in your streets.
Armed regiments on alert;
The showy itch of culture;
Wooing guests, dancing before them;
Parading cavalry;
Anti-aircraft guns;
Nuclear missiles to frighten off enemies;
The President accepting a salute from those hanging between the
    sky and the earth;
The Prime Minister shaking hands
With the glorified blemished.
Bravo!
What a spectacular festival.

Translated by Dilip Chitre

SIDDALINGAIAH

*Siddalingaiah is a leading Kannada poet and public intellectual. He founded the
Dalit Sangharsha Samiti and played a significant role in the Dalit movement
in Karnataka in the 1970s and '80s. Lyrics from his first collection of poems*
Holemaadigara Haadu *were often sung at public meetings and demonstrations.*

The Dalits Are Here

The dalits are coming, step aside—
Hand over the reins, let them rule.

Minds burning with countless dreams,
Slogans like thunder and lightning,
in the language of earthquakes,
here comes the dalit procession,
writing [history] with their feet.

Into the dump go gods and gurus,
down the drain go the lawmakers.

On a path they struck for themselves
March the dalits in procession,
burning torches in their hands,
sparks of revolution in their eyes
exploding like balls of fire.

For the thorn bushes of caste and religion,
they were as thorns in the side.
They became the sky that looked down at
the seven seas that swallowed them.

Since Rama's time and Krishna's time
unto the time of the Gandhis,
They had bowed low with folded hands.
Now they have risen in struggle.

It grows, it breaks out of its shell
the endless dalit procession.
Bullet for bullet, blood for blood,
shoulder to shoulder, lives bound together.

Under the flag of dalit India
stood the farmers and workers.
Flowers bloom in every forest,
thousands of birds take flight,
the eastern sky turned red,
morning broke for the poor.

The dalits are coming, step aside!
The dalits have come, give it up!

Translated by M. Madhava Prasad

GADDAR

Popularly known as Gaddar, Gummadi Vittal Rao is a revolutionary poet from Telangana. He was a bank clerk, then a Naxalite activist spreading his message through folk theatre and songs mostly in the Telengana region of Andhra Pradesh. He was often forced to go underground and live in the jungle. A cult figure, he gave up the gun and remains a champion of the underprivileged.

The Rebellious Fields

The paddy fields ask,
Where's the farmer who quenched our thirst?
The cotton fields ask,
Where's the farmer who sprinkled blood to protect us?
They hug each other and weep—don't understand why
They roll on the ground and weep—don't understand why
The basmati asks,
Where's the sweat-scented farmer?
The masoors ask,
Where's that large-hearted man?
They thump their chests and wail—don't understand why
They question the dawn—don't understand why
The palak asks,
Where's the farmer so dear to us?
The coriander asks,
Where's the farmer so full of goodness?
They sobbed and sobbed and withered up—don't understand
    why
They waited and waited and shrivelled up—don't understand why
Windless, the red gram and the horse gram fields

Nod listlessly
They look in all directions and ask,
Where's the farmer so full of love?
They sink into sorrow—don't understand why
They've fallen senseless in grief—don't understand why
The snake gourd and the bottle gourd
The ridge gourd and beans
The eggplant so tender
Blood red tomatoes
All ask—where's the farmer
Who kissed us before we started rotting?
They slap their heads and cry—don't understand why
They wail loudly and cry—don't understand why
The onion and garlic
Groundnuts and potatoes—
All of which nestle in the earth mother's womb
As they grow up, ask
Where's our father who would show us the world?
They wept uncontrollably—don't understand why
They rot and die—don't understand why
All the cotton fields together
Spread a new garment over him
The dried sticks assemble themselves
Into a cot
The paddy straw becomes a mattress
So that his ribs wouldn't hurt
The betel leaf presses her mouth
Over his and kisses him
They cook seven kinds of rice
In a new pot
The kumkum tree shines
As the crescent moon on his forehead
They all say
We will leave with the farmer who gave us birth
They hug each other and weep—don't understand why
They roll on the ground and weep—don't understand why
They cry, our existence has lost meaning
They burn and burn on the pyre
And rise as an inferno

They burn to ashes
The villain who poisons the farmer
The sugarcane fields dive into the water
Release the drawing bucket and return
The green fields become red—don't understand why
They took to the path of the angry rebels—don't understand why

Translated by Naren Bedide

HARISHANKAR PARSAI

Harishankar Parsai (1924–95) was an acclaimed satirist and humourist of modern Hindi literature. The following essay by Parsai, a stinging piece of satire on cow worship in India during election period, continues to be relevant today.

In Other Lands a Cow Is Prized for Its Milk, in Ours It Is Meant for Clashes

One evening I had the good fortune to meet a Swamiji at the railway station. He was a tall, fair and well-built sadhu. Ruddy faced. Attired in silken ochre, wearing wooden-soled sandals and holding a walking stick with a golden tip. He was accompanied by a pint-sized teenaged sanyasi carrying a transistor in his hand, which was tuned in to the songs of [Mohammad] Rafi for his guru's benefit.

I asked: Swamiji, where are you headed?

Swamiji replied: Bound for Delhi, child!

I said: Swamiji, I am getting on in years, why are you calling me child?

Swamiji laughed and said: Child, you worldly people address a sixty-year-old waiter at a hotel as lad, don't you? In the same way, we [the royal 'we'] address you worldly beings as child. This world is a vast eatery in which we are the ones who eat and you are the ones who serve. Therefore, I address you as child. Don't mind; it's merely a form of address.

The way Swamiji spoke seemed interesting. I sat down beside him. He too sat cross-legged on the bench, making himself comfortable, and told his apprentice to switch off the transistor.

He started talking: Child, a religious war has broken out. The cow-protection movement has gained momentum. We will perform a satyagraha outside the Parliament in Delhi.

I said: Swamiji, what is this movement for?

Swamiji replied: You seem to be totally ignorant, child! We have to protect the cow, don't you see? The cow is our mother. It is being slaughtered.

I asked: Who is slaughtering it?

He replied: Infidel butchers.

I asked: Who sends the cows to them for slaughter? Your co-religionist cow worshippers, right?

Swamiji said: That is so. But what can they do? For one, the cow eats but is of no use; moreover, selling it brings in some money.

I replied: You mean he who has the cow slaughtered for money is the true cow-worshipper!

Swamiji gave me a long look. He said, you reason well, child! But this is an issue based not on logic but on feeling. Of the thousands of cow devotees who have flung themselves into the movement, it is doubtful if any of them rears cows. It is an emotive issue.

The way had been cleared for a discussion with Swamiji. What followed was a no-holds barred debate to delve into all aspects of the issue. For the benefit of those who set much store by getting to the essence of the matter, I am reproducing the conversation.

Conversation between Swamiji and 'Child'

Swamiji, you must be having cow's milk and nothing else?

No child, we partake of buffalo milk. The cow gives less milk and that too watery. On the other hand, buffalo milk yields thick cream and makes for delicious rabri.

So, do all cow devotees drink buffalo milk?

Yes, child, almost everybody.

In that case, there should be a movement for the buffalo's protection. They drink buffalo milk but address the cow as mother. Shouldn't the animal whose milk is consumed be addressed as mother?

You mean, we should consider the buffalo.… No child, logic has its place but this has to do with feelings.

Swamiji, why is it that devotion to the cow gathers strength on the eve of every poll? Is there anything special about election season?

Child, every time an election approaches, gau mata visits our leaders in their dreams and says, son, an election is at hand. Now start a movement for my protection. The people of the country are foolish. Run a campaign for my protection and win your election. Child, gau mata ensures votes for some political parties just as oxen secure votes for another party. Which is why political leaders launch a campaign immediately and induct us sadhus into it. We too relish politics. Child, you are asking all the questions. For a change why don't you tell us where you are going?

Swamiji, I am going to join the human-protection movement.

What is that, child?

Swamiji, just as I am ignorant about cows, you are ignorant about humans.

But who is killing humans?

Drought, famine and inflation are killing the people of this land. The profiteer and black-marketeer are killing them. The corrupt ruling structure is killing them. Moreover, the government has no qualms about getting its police to shoot citizens in any part of this land. In Bihar the people are dying of starvation.

Bihar? Where is the city of Bihar located, child?

Bihar is a region, it is a state.

In our Jambudwipa, right?

Swamiji, in this very country—in India.

You mean Aryavarta?

Yes, you may say so. Swamiji, why don't you also join the human-protection movement?

No, child, we are righteous people—saints. This will not be possible for us. To begin with, humans are inferior beings in our eyes. They demand that the wealth of temples and maths should be taken away by the government. Child, you let humans die. Protect the cow instead. Any living being is superior to humans. You are not able to see that whenever a fight breaks out during a cow-protection procession, humans alone end up getting killed. One more thing, child! What I can make out from your talk is that protection of humans would involve opposing profiteers and black-marketeers. This we would not be able to do, for these are the very people who fund the cow-protection movement. The dictates of religion have rendered us silent. Religion has made us hold our tongue.

In that case, let's not talk about humans. Increase my knowledge about cow protection. Imagine that you have wheat drying on your veranda and gau mata ambles across and starts eating the grain. What will you do?

What is this, child? I will hit it with a stick and chase it away.

But Swamiji, isn't she gau mata? She is worthy of worship and has come to dine at her son's. Why won't you welcome her with folded hands and say, Mata, I am blessed. Please make a meal of all the grain.

Child, do you take us for a fool?

No, I took you for a cow worshipper.

That I am, but not so foolish as to let a cow eat the grain.

But Swamiji, what kind of cow worship is this where a cow with a skeletal frame wanders through the neighbourhood foraging paper and cloth, and is beaten in the bargain?

Child, there's nothing surprising about this. In our land those whom we worship, we reduce to a sorry state. That is true worship. We consider women too as worthy of worship and you know well the abject state we have reduced them to.

Swamiji, in other countries they may not worship cows, but they keep them well, and the animals give abundant milk.

Child, let's not discuss other countries. We are far superior to them. That is why the gods reincarnate only in our land. In other countries a cow's usefulness is in the milk it gives; here, its utility lies in stoking clashes and inciting movements. Our cow is very different from other cows.

Swamiji, ignoring all other issues why have you and your associates plunged only into this one campaign?

Everything will be accomplished by this, child. If a law on cow protection is passed, this country will become prosperous by itself. Clouds will bring rain like clockwork, the earth will yield an abundance of grain, and factories will produce goods without operating. You are not familiar with the power and glory of dharma. The sorry state of the country that you can see is the outcome of dishonouring the cow.

Swamiji, westerners don't worship the cow, but even so they are prosperous.

Their god is different, child. Their god is not bothered about issues like this.

[Erstwhile] socialist countries like Russia also do not worship cows. Even so, they are prosperous.

They don't have any god, child. Hence, no blame attaches to them.

In other words, having a god spells nothing but trouble. He doles out punishment for everything.

The logic is right, but the feeling is wrong.

Swamiji, as far as I know, at this moment what is uppermost in people's minds is not cow protection but inflation and economic exploitation. They are determined to protest against inflation. They are intent on striking work to demand a hike in wages and dearness allowance. The people are waging a struggle for economic justice and here you are making a song and dance about the cow-protection movement. Is there any logic to this reasoning?

Child, there is a logic to it. See, the moment people demand economic justice, their minds should be diverted to something else, or else they pose a grave danger. When the people demand an end to inflation and profiteering, a hike in wages and an end to exploitation, we tell them, no, your basic demand is for cow protection. Child, we waylay people marching for economic revolution and tether them to the cow's post. The purpose of this movement is to keep the people continually distracted.

Swamiji, at whose behest do you keep the people distracted?

At the behest of those who would be affected by the demands of the people. This is dharma. Let me narrate an instance—one day thousands of starving people started marching towards the trader's godown to loot all his grain. The trader came to us. Please do something, swamiji, he said. These people will loot all my savings. Only you can save me. Whatever sewa you want, I will oblige. That was it, child. We rose, picked up a bone and went and stood on the temple platform. When those thousands of starving people raising slogans about looting the godown came in sight, I showed them the bone and said, somebody has defiled this temple of god. Some sinner threw this bone inside the temple. Infidels are desecrating our temples, destroying our religion. We should be ashamed of ourselves. I am starting a fast this very instant. My fast will end only when the temple is painted anew and consecrated with a havan. The people started fighting among themselves, just like that. I had succeeded in changing their slogan. When they were done with fighting, I said—blessed are the godly people of this country! Blessed is the trader of food grain Akumji! He has promised to foot the entire expense of the temple's purification. Child, the starving masses began hailing the very man whose godowns they had earlier wanted to loot. Child, this is the power and glory of religion. If we do not yoke them to the cow-protection movement, they will launch movements for the nationalization of banks, increase in their wages, and they will mount a campaign against profiteers. To keep them tangled thus is dharma, child.

Swamiji, you have really increased my knowledge. Just one more thing—there are cow-protection laws in some states and other states will follow suit. Then this movement will also come to an end. On what issue will you launch a movement then?

Oh child! There are so many issues on which a movement can be built. For instance, the lion is goddess Durga's vehicle. The circus people keep the lion caged, make it perform tricks. This is adharma—sinful. We will launch a movement against all the circuses in the country and have them shut down. God has another avatar as well—matsyavatar. The fish is a symbol of god. We will launch a movement against the fisher-folk, force the government's fisheries department to shut down.

Swamiji, the owl is goddess Lakshmi's vehicle. Something should be done about that too.

We are doing all this for that only, child! In this country the owl has nothing to worry about. It's having a good time.

Just then the train arrived. Swamiji boarded the train and left. The child stayed where he was.

Translated by Chitra Padmanabhan

DEVAKI JAIN AND NIRMALA BANERJEE

Devaki Jain and Nirmala Banerjee are well-known scholars of economics and women's studies. In this essay, an introduction to their book of the same name, they make a case for studying economics along the lines of gender and age, as individuals of different groups experience economic phenomena and policy differently from each other.

Tyranny of the Household

A perception which arises out of the studies of family and household, from the point of gender, is the troubled question of the traditional hierarchies associated with these forms of organization. Family with father and mother or husband and wife, the rituals that have gone into marriage, the rules of behaviour, and the role allocations that have been spelt out, sometimes provide an impossible barrier to equality between the sexes. Thus it is a common phenomena all over the world and across history—that, as women begin to feel their way and wish to affirm some autonomy for themselves, some freedom to choose and fulfill their individuality, the first institution that begins to crack is the family. It is understandable that today, women, whether in the first world, the socialist world or the third world, often attack the institution of the family as one of the strongholds of female oppression and want to challenge this concept, and ask for space to create new families.

These new families would try to have the sense of bonding, of responsibility, of social security, of even continuity as the old families had, but they would also provide the individuals choices in coming together, and building a relationship on their own terms, and not on terms handed to them by antiquity, traditions, ideology—most of which stemmed from patriarchy or male attitudes to female capabilities and roles.

It is difficult to demarcate, but it is important to show that the household as a concept does not necessarily come under the same form of attack because it is associated with residence. Yet, since very often the two are taken as one and the same, and since household is the term used more frequently in economic and statistical analysis, a detailed examination of the dynamics of the household is important. It can help not only to examine the types of tyrannies as well as possibilities that exist in the household, but also to see how far the concept of household can be reorganized to provide the kind of organization that women may want to belong to, especially in the developing world.

Family and household are not the same entity either conceptually or in relation to statistical theory and method. Household is usually defined in terms of residence or habitat and family in terms of something more intimate in human terms of relationships. In some ways the word family is used for representing the most primary form of social organization by sociologists whereas the term household is used by economists and statisticians, but again with the same purpose, namely, as the ultimate or primary unit of organization.

We have concepts like household occupation, household enterprise, household type, which are similar but not the same as family occupation, family enterprise or family type. A household may be engaged predominantly in a certain occupation but that may not be the family occupation or the family enterprise. Family occupation and enterprise seem to suggest either ownership by the family or some traditional homogeneous type of skill or activity.

Yet, analytically, especially when we look at age- and sex-based inequalities within these two forms of social and economic organizations, we find that the two are not very different whether within the household or within the family. Both in terms of allocation of social powers and in the allocation of physical items, women are always lower in the hierarchy. Further, if sometimes they do have positions of social power within the family due to age of custom or what are called the rules of conduct, this is certainly not associated with economic power, namely control over resources, incomes and their distribution.

Thus, it could be said that it is more often the case that the household more than the family contains or conceals within it gender-based inequalities. It is often also suggested that this inequality strides across the usual barrier of stratification such as class, caste, race and religion. It is even suggested that while in a highly stratified society like India it is difficult to justify gender as a basis of social and political formation, as gender too is riven by class-, caste- and religion-based distances, if conceptually we move away from *inter-household* distances to *intra-household* analysis, it is possible to find the basis for such formations. In other words, whereas clustering by class or caste is done on the basis of *units of household* clusters; clusterings on the basis of gender could be derived from the intra-household characterization, *units of individuals*. By emphasizing individual autonomy, perhaps women would provide a strategy for all, that is women, men and children. In other words women's choices of alternative paths to progress would establish opportunities for all.

Thus, women from within households have the common experience of facing different forms of intra-household subordination whatever the class or caste, and this common experience within this world of the household could not only provide the basis of organization but also provide perspectives which could be called feminism, or the method and articulation of women.

Today, amongst the poor in rural areas, whether they are scheduled castes or not, poverty and unemployment are so acute that there is a great push towards various types of migration which has also diluted the family. Then there is the economic phenomenon of female-headed household where women are bread-winners and nurturers. Family, therefore, is not a crucial foundation for these classes and castes.

In the Indian context, where the tradition of family, its bonds, its interdependence, its burning loyalty to each other are worshipped, whether they are real or not, the way the scenario is usually painted is to suggest the family is a homogeneous unit. Individuals work towards the optimization of family well-being. In other words, the interest of all members of the family would naturally coincide, as each of them would be working not for himself, but for the benefit of all the interconnected units. A father would labour to bring home bread for the rest of the family, the women, the children, his parents, perhaps even his brothers and sisters. The women and children in turn would work to look after each other and the rest. If one person in a family is called to represent the family, or given access to development opportunities, the interest of all would be covered, and, further, if information is being gathered for a decision-making purpose, whether it is to design a programme of benefits, whether to collect an opinion on the wider polity, or on local crises, one person from the family, male or female, should be able to reflect that family's needs.

This is perhaps quite all right when the family does have a lifestyle where there is some sharing of information, even if not sharing of tasks, and when there is at least a basic minimum wherewithal which does not require difficult decisions of distribution within the family. In other words, this is a fair presumption in families like yours and mine.

But in a household with a crisis of survival, with insufficient resources, at the lowest levels of poverty, the patterns of family life are different. Man, woman and child are all endeavouring to keep themselves alive through some activity, whether it is to dig for roots, to examine garbage for waste, or to travel long distances for wage work. There is not much time to share each other's lives around a family hearth or sitting room. Lives, by necessity, get acutely segregated both in space and in tasks and to that extent perceptions are limited to personal experience.

Men may know that their women are working hard to fetch water and fuel, to tend children or cattle, but they may not know how hard and at what cost. Women may know that their men are labouring for a wage, that a job may be humiliating and enervating—but they may not know what the men know. Domains of experience become thickly demarcated and so ignorance gets petrified. Individual members of the family are unable to speak for the others and those who have less access to this tool of communication, such as women and children, remain neglected.

Little children do not know family as we know it. What do the little children of construction workers in Delhi know of family, or of any social institution such as a school? They know rubble, they know one parent—or perhaps not even a parent—a sibling. They grow up without a neighbourhood, seeing large numbers of men and women working around them. Similarly, what would a child from Ratnagiri or from Tehri Garhwal know of family? The father may be away in Delhi working as a cook or a driver, if from Tehri Garhwal, or in Bombay, if from Ratnagiri.

Much has been written about the sociological family—the customary formal, non-formal rules and procedures that operate within it. But the sociological family is different from the economic family—and the economic family, especially amongst the poor, has not been studied sufficiently. These households are not institutions with rules and regulations. Their autonomy is a fiction, and the usual argument that any interference with allocations within the household is an aggression on the household's autonomy is a convenient and cruel morality or moral blindness. Where there are no choices, what freedoms are we taking away?

The much studied sociological family is often described as the microcosm of the world—or larger society. It may not be sufficiently realized how true this is of the economic family—for this economic household contains in it the economic characteristics of the larger world: namely unequal distribution of economic power; benefits related to ownership, capital, access, responsibility and gender. The less the resources in a family, the greater the inequality within it.

Many societies have attempted to move away from family to new forms of collective organization. The communes of China and Vietnam, the Kibbutz of Israel, the ashrams of Gandhi, and even the new communities in Europe and North America are examples of this thrust.

But while most of them arose out of an interest in reorganizing production and distribution, Gandhi's effort arose out of a recognition of the tyranny of the family on women. He wrote:

> Marriage is probably the oldest social institution and the most abused... In this unequal struggle of women against social tyrannies imposed on them, nothing has played so crucial a part as marriage. It is in fact the base from which the continuous attacks on them are made. For men it is a cloak which covers a multitude of their failings, the betrayals of their social obligations.

He saw role allocation, whether between men and women, or between castes and classes, as the source of stigma and subordination. So he made an attempt to make manual work, night-soil lifting, kitchen work and sewing, tasks for all men and women who lived in an ashram. Today, when women find the family tyrannical—in the West or East— they demand an end to role stereotyping....

U.G. Krishnamurti

Uppaluri Gopala Krishnamurti (1918–2007), popularly known as U.G. Krishnamurti, was a radical Indian thinker. He claimed enlightenment does not exist and that there is nothing to be taught or understood. His aim, he said, was to negate everything that can be expressed.

God Is Irrelevant

Is there a beyond? Because you are not interested in the everyday things and the happenings around you, you have invented a thing called the 'beyond', or 'timelessness', or 'God', 'Truth', 'Reality', 'Brahman', 'enlightenment', or whatever, and you search for that. There may not be any beyond. You don't know a thing about that beyond; whatever you know is what you have been told, the knowledge you have about that. So you are projecting that knowledge. What you call 'beyond' is created by the knowledge you have about that beyond; and whatever knowledge you have about a beyond is exactly what you will experience. The knowledge creates the experience, and the experience then strengthens the knowledge. What you know can never be the beyond. Whatever you experience is not the beyond. If there is any beyond, this movement of 'you' is absent. The absence of this movement probably is the beyond, but the beyond can never be experienced by you; it is when the 'you' is not there. Why are you trying to experience a thing that cannot be experienced?

Man has to be saved from God—that is very essential because... I don't mean God in the sense in which you use the word 'God'; I mean all that 'God' stands for, not only God, but all that is associated with that concept of God—even karma, reincarnation, rebirth, life after death, the *whole* thing, the whole business of what you call the 'great heritage of India'—all that, you see. Man has to be saved from the heritage of India. Not only the people; the country has to be saved from that heritage.

(Not by revolution, not the way they have done it in the communist countries—that's not the way. I don't know why; you see, this is a very tricky subject.) Otherwise there is no hope for the individual and no hope for the country.

That messy thing called the mind has created many destructive things, and by far the most destructive of them all is God. To me the question of God is irrelevant and immaterial. We have no use for God. More people have been killed in the name of God than in the two world wars put together. In Japan, millions of people died in the name of the sacred Buddha. Christians and Muslims have done the same. Even in India, five thousand Jains were massacred in a single day. Yours is not a peaceful nation. Read your own history—it's full of violence from the beginning to the end. Man is merely a biological being. There is no spiritual side to his nature. There is no such thing... All the virtues, principles, beliefs, ideas and spiritual values are mere affectations. They haven't succeeded in changing anything in you. You're still the brute that you have always been.

When will you begin to see the truth that the philosophy of 'Love thy neighbour as thyself' is not what stops you from killing indiscriminately but it's the terror of the fact that if you kill your neighbour you too will be destroyed along with him that stops you from killing.

God is the ultimate pleasure, uninterrupted happiness—no such thing exists. Your wanting something that does not exist is the root of your problem. Transformation, moksha, liberation, and all that stuff are just variations on the same theme: permanent happiness.

Religion Is a Neurological Problem

Religion is not a contractual arrangement, either public or private. It has nothing to do with the social structure or its management. Religious authority wants to continue its hold on the people, but religion is entirely an individual affair. The saints and saviours have only succeeded in setting you adrift in life with pain and misery and the restless feeling that there must be something more meaningful or interesting to do with one's life. 'Religion', 'God', 'Soul', 'Beatitudes', 'moksha', are all just words, ideas used to keep your psychological continuity intact. When these thoughts are not there, what is left is the simple, harmonious physical functioning of the organism.

Love, compassion, ahimsa, understanding, bliss, all these things which religion and psychology have placed before man, are only adding to the strain of the body. *All* cultures, whether of the Orient or of the Occident, have created this lopsided situation for mankind and turned man into a neurotic individual.

Man has already messed up his life, and religion has made it worse. It is religion that really made a mess of man's life. You cannot exonerate the founders and leaders of religions. The teachings of all those teachers and saviours of mankind have resulted in only violence. Everybody talked of peace and love, while their followers practiced violence.

ROMILA THAPAR

Romila Thapar is a leading historian whose primary area of research is ancient India. In the following essay, first published in 1981, she establishes how Indian tradition has been full of dissent—the Charavak and the Ajivika philosophies; the Buddhist and Jain philosophies; the Vaishnavas and the Shaivas; and the Tantrics. Thapar demonstrates how each of these schools broke away from a dominant mode of thinking to establish their own school of thought, and how, many a times, there was inter-sectarian rivalry too.

Dissent and Protest in the Early Indian Tradition

For many decades now it has been maintained that Indian civilization has shown an absence of dissent and protest. This has become so axiomatic on the Indian past that those who have occasionally questioned it have been labelled as anti-Indian. Such a view stems from a nationalistic over-simplification of Indian society as a vision of harmonious social relations in a land of plenty. Superimposed on this were the preconceptions of idealist philosophy that dissent required materialistic underpinnings, and philosophical themes of materialism in Indian thought have generally received short shrift from contemporary commentators. It is only in recent years that some attempts are being made to suggest that neither materialist philosophy nor dissent were wholly marginal in Indian society.[1] It still remains fashionable in some circles to deny the opposition between forms of orthodoxy and heterodoxy in the ideological traditions of the past, arguing that Indian religions were not based on dogma.[2] Yet the history of groups identified as having a community of religious beliefs, rituals and behaviour, among Buddhists, Jainas, Vaisnavas, Śaivas and Tantrics, is strewn with sectarian dogmatism which found expression not only in inter-religious but also in inter-sectarian rivalries, sometimes of a violent kind.

It has also been argued that there are no words equivalent in meaning to dissent and protest in the early Indian tradition; however there is no shortage of terms connoting what is implicit in the concept. Words for dissent and non-conformity such as *vimati, asammati, viparittā, ananukūla,* are described by many commentators as negative constructions and therefore alien to the language. The same can be said for words such as *dissent* and *non-conformity* which are also derived from negative constructions. What is of historical significance is not so much the syntactical structure of these words but the particular period and the historical context in which they find expression. In any case these terms *are* new in their specific use in other civilizations as well. The secularization of the adaptation of terms such as dissent and protest is a relatively recent phenomenon, but this does not preclude the occurrence of actions of dissent and protest in earlier times. Dissenting actions whether symbolic or overt, may not be consciously described as dissent, yet the dissent may be implicit in the nature of the action.

Dissent can be limited to questioning established ideologies or belief-systems, or becoming the core of a new ideology. The expression of dissent can thus be relatively confined until such time as it mobilizes action. Protest, therefore, involves more than dissent; it requires ideology, mobilization and clearly defined action. The action has to be legitimate for the groups using it and is often regarded as illegitimate by those whose views are being questioned. The recognition of a protesting group is therefore a gradual process in history and occurs only when such a group has gathered social force and has become, as it were, politicized. This often coincided with the acquisition of property and the establishment of relations with political authority; which, incidentally, frequently became a point of departure in that it brought about opposition within its ranks to the new situation. Conflicting views over the acceptance of property and involvement in society could be a cause for friction. Among the well-endowed sects, there were rivalries over succession to office which entailed the management of property. Whatever the reasons, breakaway groups justified the schism by appeal to doctrine.

It would seem self-evident that any society which is complex and registers change, as has been the case with Indian society, must also register ideas of dissent, protest and non-conformity; otherwise the very fact of change would be nullified. Protest and dissent are not always expressed through violent action and there is normally a large spectrum ranging from a rather passive non-conformity to violence. Equally essential is the mechanism for containing dissent and protest, which tries to avoid the disruption of society.

During the first millennium BC when the early Indian tradition was being formulated, evidence of overt oppositions is limited. But the expression of dissent through the questioning or even flouting of social norms is conspicuous. Sometimes it took the form of opinion systematized in the views of religious and philosophical sects; but it was also expressed through symbol and action. This often occurred in the form of opting out of society as it were, through various types of renunciation. But not all of these can be seen as protest. Some were attempts at seeking individual salvation and had therefore an other-worldly orientation. Only those forms can be regarded as expression of dissent which satisfy certain criteria. Opposition to existing social norms had to be consciously maintained even if it was expressed at a symbolic level; the new forms could become alternate sources of power; and the attempt was not so much to disrupt the existing system as to set up a parallel or alternate system. These criteria are a necessary pre-condition. Not all renouncers were or are protesters, for there are many in the past and even today, who, rather than utilizing renunciation as a technique of dissent, exploited it for mundane ends.

One of the paradoxes of the Indian tradition is that the renouncer, in spite of migrating out of society, remains a symbol of authority within society. An explanation of this paradox may emerge from an analysis of the social role of the renouncer. Apart from those who through austerity and severe discipline, both mental and physical, sought extrasensory power, there were many others who renounced their social obligations, joined an order and far from propagating a life-negating principle, sought to establish an alternate or parallel society. They combined in themselves the charisma of the renouncer as well as the concerns of social, and occasionally political, dissent. They were neither revolutionaries nor radical reformers; they can perhaps best be described, as I have argued elsewhere, as the makers of a counter-culture.[3] Their migration is symbolic since they re-enter the social arena in a changed guise. Such forms of renunciation were open to all. It was generally assumed however that members of the higher castes and upper levels of society would use this as their form of dissent. For those lower down, migration was rarely symbolic for it carried the bitterness of necessity. Some who joined the renunciatory orders were attempting to overcome the inequities of caste status by joining non-caste groups. Others, such as the peasants, were sometimes forced to migrate to express their discontent. I would like to examine more closely the evidence for the two ends of the spectrum: the open renunciatory groups and their relations with society, taking the case of the Buddhist *sangha*, and at the other end the specific limited group of the peasantry who, when they migrated, were articulating a particular discontent.

The first millennium BC is characterized by changes of at least three kinds which had a bearing on the realm of ideas. These changes were the evolving of a recognized social stratification, the emergence of towns and urban centres and, lastly, adjustments to the increasing authority of the state. It is with reference to these that I would like to consider the question of dissent.

Social stratification assumes divergent forms in different systems. In the monarchies frequent reference is made to castes functioning in the framework of the fourfold *varna* system. Within the hierarchy of this system the elevation of the *brāhmanas* brought, as its counter-poise, the new category later referred to as untouchables. The hierarchy of the fourfold system was based on the distribution of power, authority and access to economic wealth (whether in heads of cattle or in land) and kinship networks. The fact of untouchability highlights an additional feature—the distinction being justified on the basis of ritual purity and pollution which converted the candālas and other such categories into excluded groups. The oligarchies or chiefships do not register a four-caste stratification to begin with, but here the emphasis separated the landowning khatriyas of the rājakula from other clan members[4] and these in turn from the slaves and labourers, dāsa-bhrtaka, who worked the land.[5]

With the extension of agriculture, the growth of centres of craft production leading to networks of trade and the increasing political authority of the state, urban centres became a recognizable feature of the cultural topography. Most of them combined the function of capitals of the newly emergent states, the earlier janapadas, as well as centres of trade. Although the rural-urban nexus remained strong, the urban ethos was different. Urban centres provide evidence of a stratification in which the *setthi*, the merchant and trader was regarded as important. Towns were looked upon with some suspicion by the *brāhmanas* who declared that the good *snātaka* should avoid living in such places.[6] Evidently social taboos were liable to be eroded in the flux of urban life. The bulk of urban society consisted of those who laboured either as artisans or as wage-earners in commodity production, constituents of the amorphous category described as *śūdras* in the texts.[7]

This was also the period which saw the establishment of the state as embodying the necessary authority for the maintenance of law and order and for the protection of the people. In theory, the state, whether it took the form of a monarchy or an oligarchy, is an alternative to an otherwise nightmarish chaos. The *Mahābhārata* compares the kingless state to the lawless condition of the desiccated tank in which the big fish devour the little fish.[8] The *Rāmāyana* paints a distressing picture of the afflictions which beset a land without a king.[9] Drought is almost by implication associated with bad government or no government. Buddhist texts are equally graphic in depicting civil strife in the absence of a state.[10] The state was seen as an enforced necessity rather than a naturally evolved institution and the element of contract is implicit to a lesser or greater degree in most of these explanations of the origin of the state, irrespective of whether the state came about through divine intervention or the choice of the people. Whatever its origins, the state as representing political authority was new to the earlier lineage identity now being gradually weakened. In the monarchies the concentration of political authority was strengthened by religious sanction through a range of rituals such as those linked to status and power as in the *rājasūya*, *vajapeya* and *aśvamedha* in particular.

These trends incorporating social stratification, the power of the state and the economic thrust of the extension of agrarian systems and trade, became the substratum of historical activity in subsequent centuries as well. States expanded outwards from geographically nuclear regions, tribes and occupational groups were converted into castes, waste land was cleared for cultivation, new routes were forged and markets for trade, and this process provided a continuing historical momentum in the subcontinent up until recent centuries. This is in part reflected in the constant emphasis on the fear of chaos in the texts of later centuries. The emphasis did not arise from a paranoia regarding disorder but rather reflects the repeated formation of states in new areas which had on each occasion to be justified. State formation is a recognizable feature of historical change in the Indian subcontinent during the millennia AD. This necessitated highlighting the difference between the conditions within a state and non-state societies. Contrasting of chaos with order was part of the required emphasis on the sanction of the state, its legal authority often equivalent to coercion, which was summed up in the word *danda*. The literal meaning of *danda*, 'the rod', was not limited in connotation to physical force alone but was symbolic of all authoritarian sanctions which the state could use and which were essential to the functioning of the state. Significantly, the legal codes included a comment on all the minutiae of social and political life because the *dharmaśāstras* were again the primary texts of state legitimation. The stress on consensus in matters relating to law was in part due to the continuing authority of customary law and in part the absence of a uniform code. The sanction of the state therefore was endorsed by the appeal to a multiplicity of laws arising out of the separation of *varnas, śrenīs, jātis, janas,* which were sought to be ordered within the *varna* framework. The emphasis was on the disparate but coherent functioning of these various identities rather than a universal law to cover all identities.

The earliest expression of at least minimal dissent comes to us from the *Upanisads* in the earlier part of the first millennium BC. The search for a way to ensure liberation from rebirth and a better comprehension of man in the universe led to a questioning of the efficacy of existing forms such as the sacrificial ritual and a discussion of alternative techniques such as *yoga, tapas, dhyāna.* These have generally been interpreted as procedures for attaining *moksa* or liberation. Yet embedded in this debate is a call away from social mores; a non-conformity which is expressed through renunciation and migration to the forest. That acquisition of knowledge required a distance from society is in itself a rejection of conformity. Those that concerned themselves with such ideas were a restricted group and their autonomy and isolation was respected.

The more apparent social tensions and differences were doubtless resolved more easily in a society which was characterized by a smaller hierarchy of stratification, with fewer economic disparities in a pastoral-cum-agrarian system and with the authority of the over-arching state still to come. The margin for non-conformity in such societies is limited. Migration to the forest was at one level symbolic but at the practical level the absence of a vast social surplus made it easier to live off nature than off the village. This perhaps partially explains why renunciation is by and large alien to the *Rg Veda* and becomes important only in the more complex society of the later Vedic period. In the earlier society there is one category of persons who had the licence at least to indirectly comment on conformity; these were the poet-bards. Their expression of dissent took the very subtle form of gentle mockery to which even the gods were not immune. But their power lay in their eulogy of those heroes who were munificent gift-givers and in this the heroic chiefs made every effort to appease them.[11] This relationship is seen even more clearly in the earliest Tamil literature, the Sangam.[12] But the increasing importance of renunciation weakened the freedom of the bards and the renouncer gradually became the key figure associated with dissent.

A concession to these ideas is evident in the theory of the four āśramas, the four stages of life, where the dichotomy of observing social norms as symbolized in the householders/*grhasthin* is in opposition to the opting out of society, that of the renouncer/*samnyāsin*. That the theory of the four āśramas functioned to some extent as a safety valve would seem evident from the placing of *samnyāsa* in old age, after the completion of social obligations. The symbols of the renouncer such as matted hair, nakedness or the wearing of an animal skin, the breaking of food taboos, celibacy and the discarding of all possessions ran counter to social obligations. The dissenter was thus symbolically placed outside society but was not regarded as an outcast since the act of opting out was believed to imbue him with power. The source of power was the claim to extraordinary bodily control, magical and extrasensory knowledge, heightened energy and philosophical perception. All these went toward creating a charisma around those who practised and claimed these powers and gave them an authority which was difficult to explain in mundane terms. In time, the dissent became muted or even in many cases disappeared, but the authority remained, giving strength to the parallel system. That the actions and views of some renouncers were looked upon as a critique of society is evident from one of the late *Upanisads*, the *Maitrāyaniya Upanisads*.[13] It carries a list of the impediments to knowledge which include mendicants, the pupils of the *śūdras*, those of knotted hair (*cāta-jata*), those who wear the red robe and those who falsely argue against the Vedas. Among the renouncers there were dissensions ranging over degrees of conformity. The mere fact of being a renouncer did however imbue the person with authority in the eyes of the others.

The same authority gave direction to the protest at the individual level in later times in the practice of *dharnā*. But behind the act of dissent by the individual lay the sanction of society and tradition. *Dharnā* carries the connotation of a technique of confrontation in which an attempt is made to pressure a person through sheer will, persistence and an appeal to ethics rather than violence. The participants and the desired aim become interlocked in a process of attrition in which the intangible force of the cause can be converted into an ethical issue, a conversion which becomes more successful if it takes on the character of ascetic austerity and practice. The act of *dharnā* carries the suggestion both of confrontation as well as the mobilization of an ethical appeal. *Dharnā* was used to considerable effect in the second millennium AD by the *cārans*, the bards of Rajasthan. In conformity with bardic tradition they were inviolate as were the *sutas* of earlier times.[14] A *dharnā* by a *cāran* therefore carried the risk for the king against whom the *dharnā* was directed, of his being held responsible for the *cāran's* death.[15]

Not all the early renouncers chose to remain in isolation. Some among them returned to the margins of society and became the familiar mendicant wanderers, the *parivrājakas*. However, the larger and settled communities of monks emerged in times of a more developed economy, when such communities could be supported by rich villages and urban centres through alms-giving. The earliest monasteries were generally located in the vicinity of towns since the monks lived on alms and donations;[16] some were located along trade routes where travellers and merchants could use them as staging points and donations were again welcome.[17] In still later times when endowments of land constituted the more substantial part of donations, large monastic institutions became common in rural areas initiating a 'monastic landlordism'.[18] It is significant that such institutions were absent in areas of primitive agriculture.

The towns produced their own kind of dissenters, not all of whom became renouncers or monks.[19] Some took to philosophical acrobatics in arguments ranging from the eternalism of the soul and the world, to the notion of a first cause being irrelevant to understanding the origin of the world; the annihilationists supported the destruction of the living being and the hedonists held that the doctrine of happiness brought complete salvation.

Others were recognized by their sharp critique of society and its norms, which on occasion takes on the form of a world view of either sceptical or material philosophy. This was evident in the schools included in the category of Cārvāka and Lokāyata.[20]

These sects drew their audience from the townspeople, not to mention debating opponents among sects similar to theirs. Some opposed not only the observance of social custom and law but the entire structure of explanation. It is this which earned them the disapprobation of those less daring in their views and less willing to give free rein to complete rationalism and unflinching materialist explanations. The teaching of such groups is largely reconstructed from quotations which are referred to as part of the refutation of incompatible views or false doctrines in the literature of the more established sects.[21] That their ideas did attract a following is evident from the vehemence with which they are attacked in this literature. In this the Indian experience was not dissimilar to that of some other early cultures. Despite the sarcasm, the theme of rationality comes through clearly.

To argue that all religious rituals and the existing rules of morality were pointless would attract the wrath of those who accepted the tangibility of these rituals and morals, even though they might have been opposed to the particular forms. Monastic orders were as governed by rites, rituals and laws as was secular society, although they took a different form and catered to different needs. The questioning of the worth of alms and offerings laid the monks as open to attack as any member of society since the monks were dependent on such forms of support. Hence the scathing criticism of such views.

There was also the fear that extreme ideas would disturb the existing order. The logic of rational explanation would have required far more than merely opting out into a parallel system, it would have required changing the very structure of society. Few of these groups established any distinct organization and the force of their dissent tended to be dissipated in individual enterprise.

Another unchanging feature of the attack on rationalism and materialism was to describe such views as advocating a contingent morality and extreme hedonism. The familiar phrases ring out from the earliest texts with the warning that materialists do not distinguish between actions conducive to merit and those not so, since they are devoid of moral values and argue that all action has material causes and there is no reckoning after death. In spite of these attacks materialist ideas survived. The need for contradicting such views even in the form of ridicule, from time to time, was not merely a literary exercise but reflected the continuity of what were looked upon as unpalatable views. Mahendravarman's play, *Mattavilāsaprahasana* carried clear attempts at ridiculing heretics. But the tradition of anti-religious philosophical texts survived as is evident from the eighth-century work of Jayārāśi, the *Tattvopaplavasimha*.[22]

Among the other sects and groups were the Ājīvikas, the Jainas and the Buddhists. These were groups of renouncers for whom the monastery was to become an organizational base. The degree of dissent is determined both by the distance from society and by the symbols of identification. Thus to take the case of the Buddhists, the monastery was a parallel society in that it was totally different from conventional society but was not cut off, being dependent on the lay followers in villages and towns. The natural dichotomy remained that of the householder and the renouncer, expressed much more strongly in the symbols of differentiation, but the interlocking of the two also became essential.[23] This reciprocity was expressed at the symbolic level in the exchange of *dāna* for *punya*—gift-giving for merit.[24] Buddhist teaching lays stress on the distinctive roles of the *monk/bhikkhu* and the householder/ *gahapati,* and the separate methods of each in the search for liberation from rebirth; but at the more mundane level of the rise of the *sangha,* the *bhikkhu* had to be supported by *the gahapati.* The more tangible lay support for the Buddhists came from elite groups such as royal families, landowning clans, merchants and members of the richer guilds.[25]

The negation of social obligations is clear from the encouragement given to enter the monastery as early as possible, some seers arguing that the householder's *stage/grhastha-āśramas* should be altogether avoided. The breaking of caste rules lay in recruitment to the monasteries indiscriminately from all castes. The monks were required to live together and eat together thus contradicting the laws of commensality. The requirement that alms must consist of cooked food was again, for the erstwhile upper-caste monk, a departure from food taboos where uncooked food was the more acceptable.[26] The taking on of a new name unconnected with caste, reiterated the attempt to negate a caste identity. The new sectarian identity was recognized outwardly by the uniformity of robes and appurtenances carried by the monks. The removal of hair was again in marked contrast to the householder and to the matted hair of the ascetic. These were symbols of an expression of dissent.

The ultimate source of power for such groups came through entry into the parallel society of the monastery. Some of the charisma of renunciation was conceded to the monks but their greater strength lay in the institutional basis of the monastery. Here an emphasis was placed on egalitarianism and the negation of hierarchy although the monasteries were by no means the ideal egalitarian sanctuaries. Ownership of property vested in the monastery and as long as this precluded the individual monk from such ownership, it encouraged a degree of equality. But even the administration of property required an administrative hierarchy which began to erode the egalitarian basis of the institution.[27] The monastery gradually acquired the dimensions of an agency which cut across caste and lineage ties. That this did not lead to confrontation and conflict with social and political authority was perhaps because of the diversion of dissent into a parallel system. But part of the answer also lies in the relationship between the monastery and political authority. Initially, Buddhist monasteries did not open their doors to officers of the state.[28] The Jaina *sangha* prohibited friendship between monks and the king and his officers.[29] Doubtless this was to ensure autonomy from political interference as well as to maintain the distance required for independent functioning. However the acceptance of royal patronage became the thin end of the wedge. When the endowments took the form of substantial economic largesse, the monastery was forced to accept a close relationship with political authority.

It is perhaps in this process that the term *pāsanda* becomes crucial to the question of dissent and undergoes a change of meaning. The term occurs frequently in the Aśokan edicts where it carries the connotation of a sect with no apparent associations whether orthodox or heterodox (*savve pāsamdā, nānā pāsamdesu,* etc.).[30] In one case there is an indirect indication of not merely differences of opinion, which would be expected among sects, but even hostility since there is a plea for tolerance in permitting diverse opinions. Aśoka also refers to *bāmhanā va samanā va aññe pāsamdā* (*brāhmanas* and *śramanas* and other sects).[31] The phrase, 'brāhmanas and śramanas,' as used in the edicts has generally been taken as a comprehensive reference to a variety of sects. However, another source underlines the implicit hostility of the two by providing the simile of the mongoose and the snake.[32] Megasthenes also divides the caste of philosophers, as he calls them, into two, the Brachmanes and the Sarmanes.[33] Within the Buddhist tradition the fact of sectarian belief and action and false doctrine is very powerful. Those who give false replies— *setakāni vatthāni datvā*—at the Council of Pātaliputra are expelled.[34] In the famous Schism Edict of Aśoka, dissident monks (*sanghe bhettave*) and those who disrupt the *sangha* (*sangham bhakkhati*) are made to wear white clothes and expelled.[35] The sectarian developments within Buddhism and Jainism are evident from the history of the two religions, with dissenting sects breaking away and seeking to legitimize the break by arguing that it was sanctioned through a religious council. Thus many of the early major sects trace their origin to a schism at a council, the Theravāda to the Council at Pātaliputra, the Śvetambara to the Council at Magadha, and so on.

The antagonism implicit between sects at the intellectual and cult level was doubtless aggravated by the fact of some becoming recipients of royal patronage. This may well have intensified the antagonism into sharp hostility where the brahmanical groups would see non-brahmanical sects as heretics and argue that by not conforming to social mores they were disrupting society and in any case they were identified as the preachers of false doctrines. Dissent declines when protesters become inheritors. Those excluded from the inheritance have to point to the inheritors either as having betrayed the original dissent or as being the perpetuators of false doctrines aimed at the destruction of society. The Puranic literature makes it evident that the term *pāsanda* had changed its meaning and in later periods it is used for heretics of all kinds. A late Purāna, the *Brhaddharma*, illustrates this when it states that the *Pāsandas* and *Yavanas* will destroy the *varnāśramadharma*, create their own gods, write their śāstras in Prakrit and teach their own religious ideas.[36] Ultimately in still later usage the word *pākhanda* came to refer to a fraud as well. It is curious that in the Greek versions of the Aśokan edicts, 'sect' is translated as DIATRIBE, literally a discourse.[37] In its later form this word was also associated with hostility when it meant a discourse directed against a person or an idea.

The developments traced so far, involving the change in a religious group from a small number of adherents to an expansive movement incorporating sectarian growth, property relations and connections with political authority, were not, restricted to the Buddhists alone. The same changes were noticeable with some variation at many times and in many areas among sects belonging to the other major religions of India, such as the Jainas, Vaisnavas, Śaivas, Tantrics and still later, Islam. The growth of the sectarian āśramas, and *matha* or the Sufi *khānqah*, many of which received grants of maintenance and land, became a normal pattern in the historical evolution of such religious sects. The changes which they underwent were, therefore, in many ways similar to those of the Buddhist monasteries of earlier times. Not all of these, however, were dissenting groups. Some attempted to consolidate what they took to be orthodoxy on the wane; but they all included the technique of building an institutional base and this inevitably required them to come to terms with political authority. Theoretically renunciation included the renouncing of material possessions, and therefore there was a necessity for those renouncers who wished to build an institutional base to have to rely on patronage; the most effective form of patronage came from royalty.

The advantage to political authority of such a relationship, quite apart from the theory that patronage bestowed merit on the patron, was that such religious institutions could become centres of loyalty and support in far flung areas. Here they acted as avenues of social acculturation and political legitimation. However, political authority had also to follow a policy of appeasement, since from the late first millennium AD onwards religious establishments also played the role of centres of secular activities[38] and this carried the danger of their becoming the nuclei of popular opposition. Not only were many religious establishments, in effect, landed intermediaries with many fingers in many economic and political pies, but in some areas they almost doubled for the political authority. The relationship between the Jagannath temple at Puri and its political counterparts in the medieval period is an excellent case in point.[39] The geographical distribution of such establishments could also encourage sectarian loyalties cutting across political loyalties. Many religious establishments served functions parallel to the state in their handling of what might be called public welfare. That the Sultans of Delhi were apprehensive of the power of Sufi *khānqah* was part of the same syndrome. It is also not surprising that the Mughal emperors, including Aurangzeb, made donations to *brāhmanas* and Hindu religious establishments in certain parts of the empire.[40]

Religious sects were often the symbolic or potential carriers of dissent. The mobilization of dissent into protest did on occasion take overt forms, and where it concerned specific issues did not require the legitimation of a belief-system. The right to revolt is central to this question.

The concentration of power in the monarchical states provided the possibility of the counter-weight of protest against such power. Recorded incidents of such protest are not too many, but the evidence does suggest that the notion was familiar. The texts tend to be contradictory on this point. Some negate the right to revolt altogether.[41] Others concede it, provided it is motivated by the desire to terminate the wickedness of the king. Wickedness is defined as acting against the laws of dharma and the right is therefore morally justified.[42] The *Mahābhārata* justifies the right to revolt if the king is oppressive, and even permits assassination;[43] but its incidence is such as to suggest that this action would be restricted to *brāhmanas,* as in the case of the wicked king Vena,[44] suggesting that they alone had the moral right to kill a king. Buddhist *Jātaka* literature has many more references to protest by subjects against oppressive kings (*adhamena*), some of whom are banished.[45] Where a king is put to death for a moral offence, the actual killing is at the intervention of the god Śakra.[46] The right to revolt in Buddhist texts is extended to all subjects of the kingdom, but the context indicates that frequently it was limited to the citizens of the capital.[47] The terms used are *mahājana*—a large crowd which could include the people of the countryside and the town (*janapada negama*), *nagaravāsino* (the inhabitants of the city), *ratthavāsino* (the subjects). Generally the *mahājana* gathers in the capital where the opposition to the king is expressed.

In contrast to the *Jātaka* literature, non-Buddhist sources do not concede the right to revolt to all subjects. Kautilya's perspective reflects the culmination of the state as an agency of control with monarchy as the norm. The citizens cannot revolt, but the king must ensure their welfare. Interestingly, the only revolts which are discussed are palace coups and revolts led by officers, tribal chiefs and vassals, and these inevitably have to be suppressed.[48] There are however two specific references from the Buddhist sources to the citizens of Taxila rebelling against the oppression of the officials of the Mauryan administration.[49] The source of power in this category of protests lay in the fear that the revolt of the subjects would destroy the sanction of the king to rule and would disrupt administration. There was little fear of citizens in revolt taking over the reins of government, and in the Mauryan case it is stated that the objection was to the officials and not to the king.

Peasants are said to have occasionally resorted to migrations to express protest. This would not only disrupt the existing economy because of the desertion of villages and fields but would permit of new settlements if conditions were optimum beyond the boundaries of the kingdom: thus providing an alternative to the existing system. Kings are advised not to oppress their subjects by over-taxing them lest the latter migrate and thereby erode the prosperity of the kingdom.[50] Nor was the migration to new lands a mere gesture. In a period when the population was relatively small and land easily available, the migrations of peasants could well create revenue problems in the smaller kingdoms. It is not surprising that Kautilya, jealously guarding the state's control over uncultivated land, prohibits the clearing and settling of forest land without the necessary permission.[51] The Mauryan state also took the precaution of keeping its peasants unarmed.[52]

The threat of peasant migration, consequent to a refusal to pay taxes, occurs in later periods as well. With the establishment of a hierarchy of intermediary landowners, the link between the peasant and the land became more inflexible. In such circumstances, peasant migration, although it did occur,[53] would obviously have been more difficult than in situations where landed intermediaries were absent. Not surprisingly, peasant revolts become an equally effective form of protest, as is evident from at least the sixteenth century. It has been argued that some peasant discontent was spearheaded by the smaller landowners.[54] The migration of the peasantry would have undermined the income of such landowners, while those who espoused the cause of a heavily taxed peasantry would attract discontented peasants. Where the revolt was more than just a local refusal to comply with tax demands, the mobilization often developed religious overtones. The more organized peasant revolts over larger areas identified themselves by caste—such as the Jāt revolts—or by religious sects, such as the Satnāmis. The latter categories carried obvious influences from the widespread *bhakti* movements in northern India such as those of Kabir, Dādu and Nānak, which were to inspire a variety of social action far beyond the vision of the original teachers. The *bhakti* movement was not a pan-Indian movement, but included various sectarian movements with a flexible range of opposition to Vedic exclusiveness and brahmanical orthodoxy. What gives these movements a pan-Indian character is the broad similarity of their origins, their ideological articulation and the social use to which they were put.

Little is said in the early sources about dissidence or protest among the socially excluded groups, the *dāsa-bhrtaka* and the *candālas*. Although some slaves are described as treated ill and others well,[55] there are, in contrast to classical Roman times, no records of large-scale slave revolts. Perhaps the reason was the absence of the employment of slaves on a substantial scale for production. The excluded groups tend to remain excluded in the ideologies of all dissenters, although some are permitted to escape into the parallel society of the monasteries. Even the rationalists, while they do not condemn the excluded groups, do not claim them as part of their audience or encourage opposition to authority among these groups.

Socially excluded groups sometimes express their protest through millenarian movements. Such movements which are common in the Judeo-Christian and Islamic religions particularly in periods of major change, are barely evident within the indigenous religious traditions of India. Two examples of seemingly millenarian ideas are to be found in the coming of Kalkin as the final *avatāra* of Visnu[56] and the Buddha Maitreya, the saviour Buddha yet to come.[57] The social inspiration for such movements is however very different on the Indian scene. The Kalkin *avatāra* is the hope not so much of the down-trodden but of those who believe that Visnu will come to the aid of the righteous to put down the upstart *śūdras* who have been daring to controvert the law of *varna*. Kalkin, therefore, is the hope of those who have lost their privileges and feel thwarted by the trauma of the Kaliyuga. The Buddha Maitreya receives a marginal mention in the early Buddhist texts but develops into the saviour figure of the northern Buddhism of Mahāyāna at a time when there is competition from other religions and when Buddhism itself has split into the two major schools of Hīnayāna and Mahāyāna. The coming of the saviour is essentially to re-establish the power and the authority of the Buddhist *sangha,* rather than to help any oppressed group. Perhaps it is not entirely coincidental that the two movements which do in fact come very close to being Chiliastic movements if not millenarian movements in the strictest sense, those of the Satnāmis and the Munda rising under Birsa, were both movements in the proximity of Islamic or Christian ideas. It could be argued that this was less due to the Islamic and Christian religions *per se* and more to the theoretical social egalitarianism claimed by both these religions, and which, at the level of religious sanction to ideas of social equality, was more explicit in these religions than in other earlier indigenous movements in India.

There has been a tendency to view the role of religion and religious sects in the Indian tradition from a limited perspective. Discussion has centred around philosophical intricacies, the 'eel-wriggling' of doctrinal laws and the universe of icons and symbols. Too little attention has been given to the men and women who were the creators, the audience and the continuators of religious cults, sects and organizations. If doctrines and tenets changed it was because human requirements changed, as also the forms of dominant interests.

Religious sects are not static; they change with events. By definition a sect draws upon certain social groups which give it a social sanction and it reflects the changing fortunes of such groups or the incorporation of new groups. Orthodoxy and heterodoxy are never static conditions. Thus Theravāda Buddhism which questioned brahmanical orthodoxy came to be regarded as the orthodox tradition within Buddhism and against which there arose a number of schismatic sects. Other religious traditions in India showed similar distinctions. To the extent that a religious sect articulates social dissent, it reflects the aspirations of the social strata from which it draws its support. Buddhist sects were anxious to win the support of elite groups after a certain point in the history of Buddhism. The degree of dissent was muted by protest taking the form of ethical opposition, and the parallel society became at times almost parasitical. The dissent was further subdued when in the course of time Buddhist institutions began to appropriate the functions of the elite; a pattern of change which was to be repeated frequently in the strategies of many other religious sects. The building of *mathas* and *āśramas*, the acquisition of property and status, the manoeuvring of relationships with political authority, and the appropriation of the role of landowners and commercial entrepreneurs, converted the religious sect into a recognizable social group often ending up as a caste. Such sects therefore could not have spearheaded a radical change; they remained at best conciliating alternatives.

It is of considerable interest that in the Indian tradition the effective questioning of or breaking away from caste obligations required the form of a religious sect. This may be explained as being substantially due to the logic of caste society in which the non-observance of caste norms would otherwise have resulted in ostracism and low status. Given this basic premise anything short of an overthrowing of the structure of caste society made it necessary to legitimize the breaking of rules by seeking the identity of a religious sect and if possible also by building an institutional base to counteract the charge of losing status. The former was by far the easier way out and was resorted to, times without number. The building of an institutional base required the patronage of the wealthy. This weakened the thrust of dissent and diverted it into the formation of a parallel society rather than strengthening confrontation with the existing system. The parallel society not only legitimized the breaking of caste rules but also provided a mechanism for caste orthodoxy to accommodate this dissent, since the parallel system impinged upon but did not disrupt society.

The weakness of the parallel society is self-evident. It does not provide an alternative system for the entire range of social groups but only for segments; it presupposes the continuation of the existing society which permits a small percentage to opt out. The dissenting group remains enclosed and minimal. This is further emphasized by the fact that the parallel society because of the rules of celibacy perpetuates itself by recruiting members from the existing society. In a caste society each dissident group would tend to be confined to its own social milieu. Even those sects which began by cutting across caste ties would, with the weakening of their dissent and in the process of building institutional bases, tend to work within the confines of caste contours. The dissent has to be viewed not merely in terms of attitudes toward those in power but also toward the socially excluded groups. In the competition for status, even among the parallel systems, the socially excluded groups were only marginally involved and were often left to their own resources for mobilizing dissent.

Such considerations were not so primary in situations where the dissenters were low-caste groups who by dissenting were not lowering their status any further. If together with this the aim of dissent was not to raise social status or demand the equalization of status, but to protest against oppression, then the protest could be direct. Hence the possibility of peasant protest not requiring the legitimacy of religious form, in cases where a caste identity or a religious identity was used, as for example in the Satnāmi movement, it was more in the nature of extending the movement rather than acquiring legitimacy or, it could be said, to reflect a movement where differing statuses of peasants were involved. Yet even in these protests, whether migrations or revolts, the aim of the movement was to remove the immediate injustice. To argue that such movements were not protest movements because they did not envisage changing the system is perhaps to demand more from them than what they themselves envisaged at the time. The demand for changing the system as an essential quality of protest movements is not only relatively recent but requires certain historical preconditions which did not prevail in earlier times in India.

That religious sects do often become castes would substantiate the idea that certain forms of religious expression were indicative of dissent. In such cases social discontent was more than merely a marginal factor. Celibate monks cannot constitute a caste; although sometimes, in the transition to becoming a caste, celibacy is dropped, at least among those who are involved in the right to succession in property and office. The lay followers, however, can take on a caste status commensurate with the origins and the ranking of the sect. In such cases the social requirements of building a caste would take primacy over other considerations. Or alternately recruitment to the sect would become restricted to certain castes, and the identity or the sect and those castes would become close where the sect would articulate the ideology of the caste. The effectiveness of dissent lay in bringing about some degree of change in as much as the lay followers were able to either assert their status even if it was low in the *varna* hierarchy or on occasion acquire a higher social status. Ivory carvers and corn dealers, ascribed to *śūdras* status, used Buddhism in their demand for respect from others. But Buddhist lay followers did not aspire to becoming a separate caste and with the decline of *sangha*, they tended to be absorbed without identification, each into his own caste. The Lingāyats on the other hand were ultimately successful in asserting a higher status through a judicious use of the religious sect, social dissent and economic potential. In the more remote past the attempt seems to have been to try and bypass the *varna* hierarchy. From the late first millennium AD there are more examples of attempts to assert a higher status.

The accommodating of those who opt out is not merely a matter of putting a premium on toleration. To a greater extent it is an indication of a mechanism for containing dissent. Hence the acceptance of *sadhus, fakirs, yogis* and many other 'opters out'. Nor can this be explained in a facile fashion by speaking of the great religiosity of Indian society, for religious expression in itself has to be analyzed from multiple perspectives since it performs many functions other than the solely religious.

This interplay of vertical and horizontal structures in Indian society lends it a different complexion and provides it with a logic which has to be understood in relation to its own social context.

Dissent and protest are present in all complex societies and are frequently motivated by attempts at rationalizing discontent. The forms which dissent and protest take would naturally vary from one society to another but would be logical within the terms of the structure of each society. Early Indian society was not characterized by absence of striving for material progress accompanied by a decline in ideological evolution. As was the case with many other societies of the ancient world, it neither visualized an ideology directed towards a total change in society nor could it organize such a change. Dissent was resorted to more frequently than protest. The extension of protest to encompass dissent with the aim of restructuring society had to await more recent times.

Notes and references

1. Such as the studies of D.P. Chattopadhyaya, as for example, *Lokāyata*, New Delhi, 1968.

2. Pratap Chandra, 'Study of Ideological Discord in Ancient India', in S.C. Malik (ed.), *Dissent, Protest and Reform in Indian Civilisation*, Simla, 1977, pp. 85ff.

3. Romila Thapar, 'Renunciation: the making of a counter-culture?', in *Ancient Indian Social History: Some Interpretations*, New Delhi, 1978, pp. 63 ff. See Chapter 40 in this volume.

4. *Pānini*, VI.2.34.

5. *Kunāla Jātaka*, London, 1970, pp. 1 ff.

6. Gautama Dharmasūtra, *XVI.43*, Āpastamba Dharmasūtra, *1.3.9.4*, Vasistha Dharmasūtra, *XIII. 1.*

7. Manu VIII.410, 418; IX.334–5.

8. Śānti Parvan, 67.7–24.

9. II.61.7ff.

10. *Dīgha Nikāya*, III.92–3 ff.

11. As in the *dānastuti* hymns of the *Rg Veda*, V.27; V.30.12–14; VI.63.9; VI.47; VIII.1.33; VIII.5.37; VIII.6.47.

12. K. Kailasapathy, *Tamil Heroic Poetry*, Oxford, 1968.

13. *Maitrāyanīya Upanisad*, VII. 8, S. Radhakrishnan, *The Principal Upanisads*, London, 1953.

14. *Taittirīya Samhitā* IV.5.2, *namo sūtāya ahantyāya.*

15. N. Zeigler, 'Marwari Historical Chronicles', *Indian Economic and Social History Review*, April–June 1976, XIII, no. 2, pp. 219 ff.

16. Such as those in the vicinity of Rājagriha, Śrāvastī, and Kauśāmbi. N. Dutt, *Early Monastic Buddhism*, Calcutta, 1973, pp. 147 ff, 167 ff.

17. D.D. Kosambi, *The Culture and Civilisation of Ancient India*, New York, 1965, pp. 183 ff.

18. The concept of 'monastic landlordism' was used by Max Weber to indicate the change in the function of the monastery: *The Religion of India*, New York, 1958. Of the monasteries endowed with land, Nālandā was among the richest with as many as a hundred or even two hundred villages. S. Beal, *Life of Hsuan Tsang*, London, 1911, p. 212; J. Takakusu (tr.), *Records of the Buddhist Religion*, Delhi, 1966 (reprint), p. 65.

19. Diodorus XVII, 86; Curtius VIII.12.

20. K.N. Jayatilleke, *Early Buddhist Theory of Knowledge*, London, 1963. D.P. Chattopadhyaya, op. cit.

21. *Dīgha Nikāya* I.27, I.55.

22. A.L. Basham, *The Wonder that was India*, London, 1954, p. 297.

23. J.C. Heestermann, 'Vrātya and Sacrifice', *Indo-Iranian Journal*, 1962, VI, pp. 1–37. L. Dumont, 'World Renunciation in Indian Religions', *Contributions to Indian Sociology*, 1960, IV, pp. 33–62.

24. Romila Thapar, '*Dāna* and *Daksinā* as forms of Exchange', op. cit., pp. 105 ff.

25. *Mahāvagga* I.15.1–20; I.9.1–4. *Cullavagga* VI.4.9.

26. Manu IV.205–25, 247–50; V.5–56; XI.153–62.
27. *Vinaya* II.160–75.
28. *Mahāvagga* I.61.1 ff.
29. S.B. Deo, *The History of Jaina Monachism*, Poona, 1965, pp. 60 ff, 239 ff.
30. Rock Edict VII, X, XIII, Pillar Edict VI.
31. Rock Edict XIII.
32. *Vyākarana Mahābhāsyam*, II.4.9. Patañjali explains that they are permanently opposed. 1.476: *Yeśām ca virodhah śāśvatikah.*
33. Strabo, XV.1.59.
34. *Mahāvamsa*, V.270.
35. Schism Edict. J. Bloch, *Les Inscriptions d'Asoka*, Paris, 1950, pp. 152–4.
36. *Brhaddharma Purāna* III. 19.
37. D. Schlumberger and E. Benveniste, 'A new Greek inscription of Aśoka at Kandahar', *Epigraphia Indica*, XXXVII, part V, no. 35, pp. 193–200. H.W. Bailey suggests a possible Iranian root for the word *pāsanda* which he argues might have been *fras* + *anda* meaning the one who asks. This would not be very close to the Greek translation of Diatribe. H.W. Bailey, 'Kusānica', *BSOAS*, 1952, XIV, part 3, pp. 420–34.
38. This is apparent from the enhancement of the power of the religious donees to include not merely the right to collecting a large number of taxes, but also to taking over judicial administration. R.S. Sharma, *Indian Feudalism*, Calcutta, 1965.
39. H. Kulke, 'Royal Temple Policy and the Structure of Medieval Hindu Kingdoms', in A. Eischmann, et al. *The Cult of Jagganath and the Regional Tradition of Orissa*, New Delhi, 1978, pp. 125 ff.
40. K.K. Dutta, *Some Firmans, Sanads and Parwans*, Calcutta, 1953.
41. *Nārada* XVIII.20–2, *Bhāgavata Purāna* IV.13.23, *Arthaśāstra* XI.22–9.
42. *Agni Purāna* CCXXV.12.
43. XIII.60. 19–20.
44. *Visnu Purāna* 1.13.
45. *Khandahāla Jātaka*, no. 542.
46. *Manicora Jātaka*, no. 194.
47. *Padakusalamānava Jātaka*, no. 432. In the *Gandatindu Jātaka*, no. 520, the peasants migrate and desert their villages.
48. *Arthaśāstra* IX.3.
49. *Divyāvadāna* C. 372, p. 234, C. 407, p. 262, P.L. Vaidya (ed.), B.S.T. No. 20, Darbhanga, 1959.
50. *Arthaśāstra* XIII. 1.20–1.
51. Ibid., II.17.
52. Arrian, *Indika*, XI.
53. R.S. Sharma, op. cit., p. 268.
54. Irfan Habib, *The Agrarian System of the Mughal Empire*, Bombay, 1961, pp.

303 ff. R. Kumar, 'The Transformation of Rural Protest in India', in S.C. Malik (ed.), op. cit., pp. 268 ff.

55. e.g. *Jātaka* 1.451; I, 402; II.428.
56. *Visnu Purāna*, IV.24.
57. *Dīgha Nikāya*, III.74–8; *Mahāvamsa* XXXII, 81 ff, *Milindapañho*, 159.

NARENDRA DABHOLKAR

A rationalist and an author from Maharashtra, Narendra Achyut Dabholkar (1945–2013) founded and became president of the Andhashraddha Nirmoolan Samiti (ANiS) in 1989. He vigorously campaigned against superstitions and self-styled god men and made several failed attempts to get an anti-superstition law passed in Maharashtra. A victim of several death threats and assaults, Dabholkar was murdered on 20 August 2013 while out on a morning walk.

Faith and Superstition

The whole movement of eradication of superstition, Andhashraddha Nirmulan Samiti (ANiS) revolves round this subject and all the brickbats and bouquets that are showered on us are related to it. Some consider our activities to be quite purposeful, beneficial and reasonable, while others take them to be just the opposite. Unless superstitions are eradicated we will not be successful in the twenty-first century, say some while others think that eradication of superstitions is actually a facade for destroying God, religion and traditions. What is superstition after all? They ask. It is much the same as blowing the ash that gathers on a burning piece of charcoal. Once blown the charcoal shines again. Therefore, it is necessary to blow away the ash i.e., superstition, occasionally but taking care at the same time, not to blow out the fire itself.

Relativity of Faith

Why are there so many opinions about eradication of superstitions? The reason is that one person's faith is a superstition for another and what a third person considers to be a superstition is a very strong faith, almost a question of life and death for a fourth one. It thus becomes necessary to clarify what is faith and what is superstition. However one faces a difficulty here, because as we have already seen before faiths vary with times and individuals. All of us know what happened in Deorala some years back, where one woman committed 'Sati' and the whole country was agitated because people with personal stake tried to glorify the act. In fact the law banning the act of Sati has been passed long ago. But now people are incensed when a woman is burnt alive on the pyre of her dead husband. They demand strict implementation of the law; not only are committing Sati and abetting the act cognizable offences but even being present at the occasion in order to ennoble it, is a grave crime. Today everyone admits that the tradition of Sati is an out and out superstition. But was it so in the 19th century? When Lord Bentinck bravely saved the life of a woman from committing Sati, people of Banaras marched in a huge procession to protest against him. Who is Lord Bentinck to stop the woman from committing Sati? they demanded. The pious act of a woman committing Sati after her husband's death is our religious faith and we have the right to follow it. Our wise Shastris and Pandits challenged Lord Bentinck in the Allahabad High Court when he passed a law banning Sati. East India Company, they maintained, had no right to interfere with our religious faith. This nineteenth-century view regarding Sati is completely reversed now. This is temporal relativity of superstition. Now let us see how superstitions change from individual to individual. Everyone has seen the photograph of Satya Saibaba. To his disciples he is a great Baba, guru, sage and even Lord. What is so peculiar about this Baba? He just moves his hand in the air and gives you holy ashes, gold chains, silver rings and what not. It is claimed in his books that he even gives his disciples gold lockets and necklaces studded with jewels. These miracles have won him the faith of innumerable men and women, including the prime ministers and presidents of this country. On the other hand there also exist a number of individuals who consider these miracles nothing but fraud perpetrated on gullible people to boost idolatry and superstition. This can be called idiosyncratic relativity of faith.

The Meaning of Faith

The word faith has diverse meanings. Consider the following statements: I have faith in my mother and father; I have faith in my guru or baba; I have faith in my family deity and religion; I have faith in miracles, supernatural powers as also the power of the mantras; I have faith in equality and the Constitution of this country. In each of these statements the word faith has a different connotation, but very few people are aware of it. We generally accept that meaning of a word as it is commonly used. Suppose you come across a person, while strolling with a friend, whom you tell that the person approaching you is a 'chamcha' of such and such leader. Now 'chamcha' literally means a spoon. But when used to describe a particular person, your friend has no difficulty in understanding what you mean. Similarly the word faith when used in every day affairs, generally means religious faith, faith in the other world or in the liberation of the soul from the cycle of birth and death. Thousands of preachers from millions of temples have been drilling into our minds that we ought to have faith and faith alone can help us navigate safely the hazardous sea of life on this earth. Do not reason, they preach, for reasoning leads one nowhere. Let your emotions guide you instead. Do not allow your conscience or reasoning intellect hamper your religious path. What they preach and demand from you is certainly superstition and not faith. Let us consider another pair of words, here, before we dive deep into the discussion on superstition and faith.

Trust and Faith

See these statements now: I have faith in the fan in my room that it will give us cool breeze; I have faith in my fountain pen that it will print letters on a paper; I have faith in this loudspeaker that it will reach my voice up to you. Are these statements true? Some say they are. Others say they are not because however strong your faith may be in your fan, your pen and your loudspeaker, and whatever prayers you offer them, the pen won't work when the ink in it is finished and the fan and the loudspeaker will stop if the power supply is disrupted. This cause and effect relationship is already established. Therefore, it is a matter of trust and not faith. Similarly the assertions such as two multiplied by two is four; polio can be prevented by proper vaccination; zero was invented in India; Shivaji was a great king are all a matter of trust. If you observe the biographies of other contemporary kings, we notice that no other king can match the virtues and abilities of Shivaji. That is why I trust he is great. I now give you a contrary example of distrust. It is a true story. A woman with three children lived in a village, while her husband worked in Mumbai. Someone prejudiced him about his wife's character. He was furious. He returned to the village and confronted his wife. 'If you have a spotless character,' he insisted, 'then prove it by putting your hand in the pot of boiling oil in the temple and taking out the coin at the bottom of it. If your hands remain unscathed and your fidelity is proved I will accept you as my wife.' The poor woman was aghast and did not know what to do. Her brother, who knew that ANiS workers know and perform this trick, approached us. We taught him the trick and the sister performed the miracle in front of the whole village and saved her marriage. The point here is not that of the fidelity or infidelity of the woman and whether boiling oil will burn her hands or not when put in it. The point is whether there is any relationship between these two occurrences. Of course there is no relation what so ever. So a notion as silly as this without any basis of cause and effect relation is superstition. But what then is faith? This we shall examine in detail a little later. However, one must keep in mind that every time it is not possible to arrive at such an indubitable conclusion as above. Yet we cannot afford to wait every time, till it strikes us and have to carry on our work, despite the uncertainty. When faced with uncertainty, most people turn to faith for support. So when one believes in the existence of a thing in spite of there being no evidence to prove it, and continues to perform activities pertaining to it, it is a matter of faith for him. But more about it later.

Faith in One's Physician

Throughout their daily affairs, people are aware of what they do. They even examine their faiths. We often say that we have faith in our physician. It means that whenever anybody falls sick in the house, you take him to your family physician. The medicine he gives cures the patient. As this happens frequently, we develop faith in the physician. However, some time later, he fails to cure a sick child. The child had to be taken to a child specialist.

A couple of months later, another patient of your family, after a week's treatment by this same physician, had to be removed to hospital as the illness aggravated; now if any of your family member's illness aggravates under this doctor's treatment will you still continue with this family doctor? No, you will not. Now whatever has happened to your faith in this physician of yours? You bank on your experience of the last several months and conclude that your physician is not as effective now as he used to be earlier and you approach another doctor. However the important things that have happened during this period are:

You examined your faith in your physician's proficiency and concluded that it would not be proper to take any more patients to him. If despite your experience of repeated failures on his part, you keep approaching him, what would it mean? Faith? Superstition? Everyone, I am sure, knows the answer. The important conclusion one can draw from this situation is: any existing situation that prevails even after being questioned on the basis of knowledge and/or experience can be called trust or faith. If it ceases to be, after being questioned by knowledge and experience, it is superstition. The situation here is that your child is sick. Your experience is that earlier your physician was able to cure the child. The knowledge is that the doctor recently had stopped to be effective. Now you come to the conclusion that it is high time that you change your physician. Here we have obtained a method. We face situations, we get experience from life, i.e., from facing situations, we obtain knowledge, we then examine the situation with the knowledge and experience obtained and then take a decision regarding our faith. Of course all this sounds very simple but is extremely difficult to follow. Taking decisions regarding one's faith i.e., deciding whether it is a faith or a superstition is extremely difficult as it hurts one's ego. So one tends to avoid it. That is why it is all the more necessary for ANiS to pursue this movement vigorously.

Difficulties in Sorting Out Faith and Superstition

The difficulties arise out of three main reasons. The first is the word testimony; second, the testimony of the book and the third, utter reluctance of individuals to critically examine one's own faith and object to others doing so. Testimony of the word means the sanctity of the word uttered by a particular individual. His word is the ultimate truth and therefore beyond any critical examination by anyone. This is the stand people often take that makes it impossible to examine a faith. This has happened even in the field of science. Galileo invented the telescope. He requested his colleagues to look at the sky through it, so that they will see for themselves that there are three more satellites revolving round the planet Jupiter. In those days, all the content that was taught at the universities was what Aristotle had said and no more. Because his was the last word. His disciples firmly believed that anything that Aristotle did not say, did not exist. 'He was a master of all he knows.' Being Aristotle's disciples, Galileo's colleagues refused to look through his telescope. 'What you see are not Jupiter's satellites,' they argued, 'they are but stains on the glass of your telescopes.' On this Galileo suggested that he could clean the glass. 'If after cleaning the glass, you still see the satellites, there must be some defect in your eyes,' they maintained.

Galileo then requested them, to use their own faultless sight instead of his. But they refused to oblige him. They had absolutely no need for them to use their own sight. They firmly believed that their preceptor had passed on to them all the knowledge that there was through his word. They told Galileo, 'If not in your eye sight, it must be your brain where the damage has occurred.' This is word testimony.

Now, what is the testimony of the book? Let us see. I had been to Jalna recently. An official of the sugar factory there came to meet with me. He had read many of my books and he told me that he fully agreed with my views. But my colleagues ask me, he complained, 'When Dnyaneshwar, the great sage claims in his Gatha that the recitation of his Gatha will not only help one in several ways but it will also help get rid of ghosts if one is possessed. Doesn't it prove the existence of ghosts? Now if your Dabholkar asserts that there are no ghosts, do you mean to say that he is greater than Dnyaneshwar himself?' It is obvious, I humbly submit, that Dnyaneshwar is much too great but this fact does not prove the existence of ghosts. The sage, undoubtedly was a great poet and philosopher but that does not mean that whatever he wrote in his books is true to the letter and therefore should be accepted as irrefutable truth. And mind you, this does not diminish his greatness even a wee bit. Let us see how. In a fair or a pilgrimage there are crowds of people roaming about. Somewhere there happens to be a snake charmer surrounded by a big crowd. Then comes along a man with his 3-4 years old son and stops near the crowd. He stretches his neck, raises his heels but can't see a thing. His son suggests, 'Father, put me on your shoulder.' The father obliges. Now the child is able to see all that is happening in the centre of the crowd. He goes on describing, 'The snake charmer is playing his pipe and a cobra is swinging his hood in front of the snake charmer, etc., etc.' After hearing all this, the father would not scold his son, 'You brat, you are just four and I am thirty four. Do you mean to say that you can see and understand what I don't?' The child here does see and understand what the father does not, for, sitting on the father's shoulder the son has really become taller. We all have climbed up a huge ladder of seven hundred years and can now see farther sitting on sage Dnyaneshwar's shoulders. In his time, concepts like mental health, mental illness or the phenomenon of 'being possessed' were not clearly understood. Now they are. And to understand them we need not depend on the testimony of Dnyaneshwar's Gatha.

On inventing the telescope, Galileo proceeded to tell others that he thinks that the sun does not revolve round the earth but it's the earth that revolves round the sun. At this, the whole of Europe was agog. The universities of Europe, all along, had been teaching on the testimony of the Bible that, 'Our loving and kind Father in the heaven has put the sun and the moon in the sky for giving us the appropriate light during the day and night.' The same question propped up here too. Who is greater? The Bible or Galileo? The rest is history that we all know. Galileo was ordered to appear before the church. He was told that his crime was so grave as to invite nothing less than death penalty. However if he begs for pardon, admitting his crime, his life would be spared and he would get only life imprisonment. Galileo knelt down and begged for pardon saying, 'I am wrong and I promise that I will not repeat my mistake. I accept what is said in the Bible and reiterate that the earth does not revolve round the sun.'

The third difficulty in separating faith from superstition is that people do not examine their own faith nor do they allow others to do so. A number of Christian missionaries crisscross our country. They have a number of religious kith and kin here. They claim that if you sincerely pray to our Lord Jesus, the blind will see, the lame walk and the dumb talk. They organize big congregations to preach this. During the prayer sessions they invite blind, dumb and lame individuals from amongst the audience to the stage. An illusion is created that these people are actually being cured of their handicap. ANiS challenged the missionaries to let ANiS verify whether such supernatural means can really cure people of their defects. Such prayer sessions were organized in Kudal some time ago, for three consecutive days. The Kudal branch of ANiS offered to send ten blind students from a blind school there, whom the missionaries would kindly grant sight through their prayers or alternatively wind up their fraudulent trade. To this the educated Christian community reacted vehemently. Not only did they oppose us but they also insisted that their prayers are effective and the blind, dumb and lame do see, speak and walk as a result of blessings by Jesus. But for this to happen one must firmly believe in Him. The blind boys you are sending to us are unlikely to be firm believers. It is, therefore not possible to verify the fact and no point in examining our faith. We shall not allow you to do so.

You are aware that in Islam, marriage is a contract, while amongst Hindus it is a sacred religious rite. Whatever it may be, our Constitution provides for maintenance to be given to a woman when her husband divorces or abandons her. However, the Muslim Mullas and Maulavis argue that marriage being a sacred rite for the Hindus, a Hindu woman accepts her man, be he a gentleman, a drunkard or a brute kicking her all along. On top of it she prays for being his wife in the next seven births to come. But for us, as per our book, marriage is simply a contract like the one between a landlord and his tenant, both parties being free to end it when necessary to do so. Such being the nature of their religion and marriage, Muslim men do not owe any maintenance to their divorced wives. This argument is nothing but humbug. But Rajiv Gandhi succumbed to it and changed the law to deprive Muslim women of the legitimate right granted to all women by our constitution. After this an argument ensued between ANiS workers and the Maulavis. We argued that this attitude of theirs will bring five crore Muslim women on to the streets to demonstrate and demand their right. They said they couldn't care less. As citizens of this country, we do care, we told them. 'Beware,' they warned us, 'we are not going to tolerate any meddling into our faith in our religious books!' Let us take one more example, this time, from the Hindu community. The annual conference of the eminent writers of Maharashtra (Sahitya Sammelan) is a well-known platform for cultural development and reform. In 1994, this conference was held in Kolhapur. It was inaugurated by lighting a lamp in front of a photograph of the Gajanan Maharaj of Shegaon. The biography of this Maharaj is available for anyone to know what kind of a man he was. It says that he had performed a number of miracles, no verification of which is now possible, since he is not alive anymore. His biography also reveals that if he was clothed in rich garments, he would throw them away and run around naked; he would kick a plateful of delicacies offered to him and pick up bits of food from a dump of rubbish; he would not bathe for days and constantly smoke a chillum. To any question from any person, he would answer, 'Ganagana ganat bote'—whatever it means! Now a person of such nature, who was not able to clean, feed and clothe himself like a normal human being, could not give any sermons because he could make only the unintelligible sounds mentioned above. How could such a person inspire the progressive platform of the eminent literary persons? And to add to it many Maharashtrians were angry that such a question was ever raised by anyone! They had firm belief in this Maharaj of Shegaon and would not tolerate it being questioned or even discussed by anyone and would never do so by themselves. This amply shows how difficult it is to distinguish between faith and superstition.

Why insist on criticism? People wonder why we insist on examining everything. Yes, ANiS does insist on examining everything, because such insistence alone can bring about human progress. Let us see how. Thousands of years ago, the primitive man lived in forests. He did not know why there was lightning in the sky; why did the skies grumble; why did it rain cats and dogs; why did fires break and burn whole forests; how did volcanoes prop up and who makes storms and earthquakes. Naturally, he thought that all these phenomena are caused by some powerful supernatural deities. He had to trust them, have faith in them. He considered the five elements—earth, water, fire, wind and sky— to be those superpowers and made them his deities. He then started propitiating them, worshipping them. Does the same situation continue to exist today? When you reach home and light your gas burner or stove with a matchstick, do you first salute the matchstick and the match box and pray, 'Oh fire God give me the power to cook my food?' Certainly not. What was a God once upon a time is now seen as a simple chemical reaction, a scientific rule.

The whole history of mankind is nothing but the history of examining faiths. Had the faiths remained unexamined, today's human culture could never have come into existence. During the whole human history, whenever any new thinking occurred, it shook the old faiths. But these shocks proved beneficial. The Copernican Revolution was one such shock. It revealed to us that our age-old notion that 'the earth is the centre of the universe and the whole universe revolves round it and in fact exists for the sake of our earth' is false. We realized that, in fact, our galaxy is one of the thousands of such galaxies, while our sun is just one of the two hundred billion suns and our earth is one of the nine planets revolving round the tiny sun that is ours. This knowledge changed the outlook of man completely. Now we do not accept the old notion, propagated by almost all religions, that some supernatural powerful being created human beings. We know that man came into being as a logical developmental stage in the course of evolution of life. This has added a new dimension to the life of man. It means that human beings examined their faiths and changed themselves thereby. This enabled them to gradually acquire control of the universe. Faiths that change with progress are not necessarily regarding science only. They could also be in the field of social structure. There was a time when the king used to be the God incarnate. 'You have nowhere to go when the king beats and the storm strikes', as the saying goes. It means that these phenomena are controlled by supernatural power and not by man. Today we are aware that most societies have discarded this concept regarding the king. He too is a citizen now and equal before the law like all other citizens. This new stance is the result of examining the old concept 'the king can do no wrong'. This progressive step brought about a change in our social structure. Democracy is certainly a step ahead of monarchy. Thus it is necessary to examine faiths in the field of social structure too. However, human societies tend to oppose any examination of their faiths, cling to their belief in the Book or the Word, tolerate no criticism and maintain status quo at great costs. This human tendency makes it difficult to distinguish faith from superstition.

Reasons Why Some Superstitions Fade Away

Despite the above tendency many superstitions just fade away. Certain conditions conducive to the fading of certain superstitions develop as time passes. The superstitions that are based on ignorance just disappear in the light of new knowledge. There was a time when man did not know why people develop fever and with it sores on their faces. After some days the fever would subside and the sores would heal but leaving scars and making the faces of the poor victims ugly. It was thought to be the wrath of a certain deity. Eventually vaccination against this disease of small pox was invented. The research revealed that the small pox germ is transmitted only from one human being to another. It became obvious that if the disease is checked till no single case of small pox could erupt, the disease could be eradicated completely. Adequate measures were taken to do so and now not a single case of small pox could be found even if a prize worth a lakh of rupees is announced. Even the need for vaccination has vanished as also the wrath of deity with it. Knowledge replaced ignorance, dispelling all superstitions about small pox.

Another category of superstitions is inhuman superstition. They are brutal in nature and are despised by society. People feel outraged and disgusted with them. For example, you are all aware of the devdasi custom in certain parts of our country. According to this custom, if a young girl develops a clotted lock of hair (called 'Jat') she is married to a deity. At times young girls are married to a deity because their parents take a vow to do so. Such a marriage is most unnatural and the young girls end up either being sold into the red-light area of Mumbai or in hands of the village hoodlums. All their dreams of happy marriage and family are thrown to the wind. This custom prevails even today. The ANiS movement has managed to arouse a sense of outrage and disgust about it in the society. Society's support is extremely important for the eradication of this atrocious superstition of devdasi. Horrifying methods are used in some superstitions of this type. Some people in order to fulfil their vow, incise the skin of their forehead with a knife; some others rush to the wall of a temple and bang their head against it. These strange ways are very dangerous and involve risk to life. No religion, saint or a deity has ever prescribed such bizarre ways of worship or appeasement of deities. So in the case of these practices, it is comparatively easy to convince people that they have nothing to do with religion and should be stopped forthwith.

In a society as life becomes fast, people find it very difficult to adhere to certain superstitions. These then, automatically pass into oblivion. Untouchability was strictly observed in the past in our society. It continues to some extent even today. Physical contact, eating together or intermarriage with members of lower casts was strictly prohibited. Prohibition of physical contact and eating together cannot exist anymore. Great reformers of the past have contributed to this change to some extent. But a bigger part is played by the increasingly fast life style of the society. Once you enter into a crowded bus or train, you are not likely to know who the person standing so close to you is. Prohibition of physical contact with lower caste in such a situation is meaningless. Similarly when you enter a hotel, you can never tell who had drunk from the cup before it is offered to you. Prohibition on eating together is thus impossible to practice. This does not mean that people have accepted that casteism is an atrocious and inhuman institution based on blind faith. For even today people religiously observe the third prohibition when it comes to finding a suitable match for their son or daughter, simply because it is quite easy to find out to which caste the match belongs. Even today a woman considers herself to be polluted during menstruation. But now she cannot abstain from all household work and restrict herself to a corner in the house. If she happens to be a working woman, which most likely she is, she certainly is not going to get three-four days leave every month. The changed circumstance has helped us get rid of the concept of pollution and avoiding contact with a menstruating woman.

The social reformers of the old have left us a good legacy that helps eradication of superstitions. At the beginning of the nineteenth century, especially in Pune, one would notice a number of women in dark-red sarees with their heads clean shaven. They were the hapless widows of those days when it was a matter of religious rite and faith that widows should shave their heads. This custom is not followed any more. However recently in Maharashtra, one woman expressed her wish to shave her head when her husband died. And one has to admit that if a man can shave his head at will, why not a woman? But is it all that simple? It is not. When does a man shave his head? He does it when he goes to Tirupati or as a funeral rite or to imitate a hero. The woman argued, 'I do not want to keep this long and luxurious hair of mine any longer after my husband's death and I have decided to shave it which I have every right to do.' Her hair was of course part of her personality and she had the liberty to do whatever she wanted to do with it. But others tried to convince her, 'See, shaving one's head means accepting the concept that a woman's life after her husband's death is worthless. She has no right to look good, so she should endeavour to remain unattractive. This concept is not just a superstition but a symbol of enslavement of women. When this ugly custom was abolished, it meant a step forward in women's freedom from superstition and enslavement. If you shave your head now in the name of your personal freedom it means starting this ugly practice all over again and doing away with the progress made through the last several decades. So we entreat you, please do not shave your head.' Fortunately, the woman did agree. Thus all those superstitions that are rooted in ignorance, or are inhuman and atrocious or out of step with the prevailing fast lifestyle or are opposed strongly by social reformers either vanish or are on their way out. Social atmosphere is becoming more and more conducive to their eradication. Yet a very big domain of superstitions has remained unaffected. We have to explore why and also acquire an insight into the nature of faith now.

Superstition—Support and Surrender

Let us discuss one more important point in Faith and Superstition— whether it is possible to eradicate superstitions completely in every individual. Here we must find out why people become superstitious. Once the well known writer Vijay Tendulkar while addressing an audience in one of our programmes said, 'Don't you think people become superstitious out of their need?' This needs deeper understanding. When a human being has to face a traumatic shock, in order to survive and not let the trauma destroy his personality, he resorts to some superstition for support, the shock may be due to the cancellation of his daughter's marriage at the eleventh hour or loss of his son's job or a serious accident in the family, etc. Let me illustrate. We say that a man's personality is good and a Bajaj scooter is good. The meaning of the first part of the sentence is that his hereditary characteristics and his upbringing influenced by the atmosphere he was brought up in, was good. The scooter is said to be good when its parts and their alignment are good. But even a good Bajaj scooter needs to be fitted by a shock absorber because the road on which you ride on it, may be full of potholes. The scooter and the rider should be protected as much as possible from these shocks. Our life too is full of such big and small potholes of disappointments. Man uses superstitions as shock absorbers to enable him to withstand the decimating disappointments. This of course is not good but understandable. Understanding human beings and their behaviour is the point here. That is why we always say in the ANiS movement, what we need is compassion, not anger and love instead of contempt. Human personality has many aspects and the ability to withstand stresses and strains varies from individual to individual. Sometimes people make fun of us. 'How long would you be able to boast of not being superstitious?' they ask us and offer the answer, 'Only as long as you are not face to face with any shockingly severe disappointment. You will know when you face one.' In a way they are right. It is not possible to find a vehicle that will not break even if it falls in a ditch. Similarly there could not be a human being who will not break down whatever be the shock and however severe it be. Of course this can be decided only when it occurs. But our point is different. Suppose a member of a family is seriously ill. Although he is being treated by a doctor, the situation is quite complex. Whether the treatment will work and the patient will recover is quite doubtful. At such times the doctor's treatment continues but in addition other means like sacred ashes of incense burnt in front of certain deities, sacred water given by a Baba, a talisman or amulet given by a witch doctor, etc., are also tried. This is understandable although irrational. However if you start using those ashes every time you cross a road or enter your boss's cabin because you are scared of crossing the road or facing your boss, it certainly means that you are enslaved by it. Here lies the distinction between using superstition and surrendering to it. When you surrender, you are no more a human being that reasons. Instead the need for support from superstition should gradually reduce as your personality gains strength.

Meaning of Faith—a Paradox

Now we turn to the most important point i.e., 'my faith' and what does my faith mean to me and also if my faith is superstition in your opinion and if so what does it mean to you. Since we respect individual freedom in this country, you are free to follow your faith. But at times two equally predominant faiths contradict each other as is the case in our country. Some feel that our country ought to be a Hindu nation while others think that this nation should not be allowed to become a religious state at any cost and remain a secular one. ANiS agrees with the latter. The problem here is how does one decide which of these is faith and which is superstition? Here we have to take into consideration an important aspect of the chemistry of faith. And that is, the fact that every faith is deeply coloured by emotion. A man cannot go by his intellect alone. Intellect as well as emotions form the basis of his decisions. So his decisions are coloured by his emotions and thereby create the problem of faith and superstition. Make a continuum with trust at one end and superstition at the other, placing faith in the middle. Now trust is where thought predominates while emotion has no place at all in it. If someone tells you very emphatically that two and two do not make four, you will take him to be a fool and just ignore him. Here he is not challenging your faith. But in case of those who sacrifice a human being in order to obtain a male child, it is sheer superstition that has no place for thought whatsoever. It is all entangled with just emotion. What is faith then? Faith is emotion that develops into thought founded in truth and translates into a motivating value. We have already seen that man has intellect as well as emotion and he needs both. A train cannot run with just an engine (i.e., intellect) but needs fuel as well (i.e., emotion). Many a time human beings instead of reasoning, let their emotions decide for them. One only needs to recollect the history of our independence. How many men and women leaped into the movement on the spur of emotion! It is human tendency to do so when emotionally charged. But that should not obliterate thinking altogether. This tendency of letting emotions rule over you with no place for thought becomes superstition. However if the decisions taken on the spur of emotion are put to test by reasoning it means developing it into a thought. There are two more criteria, in addition to the one just discussed, to distinguish faith from superstition, one is that faith is always motivational and the other that ennobles man's value system. Next we will discuss the four criteria that decide whether your belief can be called faith.

Four Criteria of Faith

What are these four criteria? The first is verifying the facts or the truth. The faith that does not allow to be questioned on the basis of facts or

truth is a superstition. What does this mean? Babasaheb Ambedkar gives
an apt illustration. Says he, 'If you find a yellow shining piece of metal, do
you burst with joy that you have found a precious piece of gold? No. You
argue with yourself that when put to the test of fire, the piece will shine
if it is gold and will not if it is only a piece of brass. You give so much
thought while deciding about a piece of metal. Why don't you take such
a considered decision regarding your values that guide and sustain your
life? You must take a decision about your values thoughtfully. It means
that you ought to put your faith to the test of the fire of truth.' The second
criterion of faith is non-violence. In any society people have diverse faiths.
They all should be allowed to preach and propagate their faiths as long
as they confine their activities within the bounds of propriety. To allow
people adhering to faiths other than ours to propagate, to consolidate
and to persuade others to accept that faith is akin to reverence for others'
faiths. It is tolerance and is rooted in non-violence, the fundamental rule
of life. And to insist that 'those who adhere to faiths other than ours
have no place here' is in itself an enormous superstition. Thus the first
criterion of faith is truth and the second non-violence. What is the third
criterion? It is being dynamic. It can be tested as below. Fear and lure
are two drives that weaken a human being's determination. For example,
you believe in your religion. Your faith is strong and deep. Now someone
asks you, 'Come on, I will give you twenty lakh rupees cash down, will
you change your faith?' It is likely that you first make sure that nobody is
around within a hearing distance and ask him, 'Will you really give me
that much money? Then maybe I need not fuss over my religion and do
as you ask me to do.' Similarly if someone puts a sword to your or your
child's throat and threatens, 'Either you change your religion or you (or
your child) are dead,' how will you react? You will certainly think, 'Let me
extricate my neck first, and then think what to do next. I can change my
hats any number of times only if my head remains intact on my shoulder.'
You will then tell him, 'My life is worth millions. I am prepared to change
my religion as you wish.' You also quietly contemplate, 'Eventually as the
situation improves I will be back into my fold again.' This you may call a
wise decision but you are certainly not faithful to your religion. In both
these cases it is not the faith but lure and fear that drive you to action
against your faith. Excepting such extreme situations, it should be the
other way round. The fourth criterion is that faith sublimates your value
judgement while, superstition on the contrary, debases it. Whenever I
accept something as part of my faith, I have to accept its value content

too. If Lord Ram occupies an important place in my faith, then the values—truth and constancy (to his wife despite the custom of the day of having several wives)—that he upheld should also be important to me. It would be quite interesting to find out whether those who extol Lord Ram so fervently accept and stick to these two values—Truth and Constancy—in their personal life.

About truth less said the better in this country. 'Truth alone triumphs' is our motto that is engraved on our national emblem. But our everyday experience tells us that untruth generally triumphs. And the reverence and the love of Ram does not cause any obstruction into our affairs. Let us now consider the other virtue of Ram, i.e., his constancy towards his wife Seeta, in that bygone era. Today bigamy is banned by law. It is a punishable crime. However while the whole country was being stirred to fight on the Ramajanmabhoomi issue, Maharashtra faced a stark reality. Six lakh of deserted and divorced wives with their children were thrown to the winds, for no fault of theirs. Is the life they are condemned to lead in agreement with Lord Ramachandra's ideals and values? (Cynics may say yes for Ram too had abandoned his pregnant wife.) If it is not, those who talk so passionately about their faith in Ram should equally be passionate about this issue of six lakh deserted and divorced women thrown out by their husbands. But all Rambhakts choose to keep mum. For them Ram is not important for the values he cherished. He is important for the votes they can get in his name. What we regard as faith, some of them call loyalty. Others describe it as sensible (or shrewd?) faith. The choice of the word aside, what is important is whether you examine your faith or not; whether you tolerate other faiths and do them no violence; whether your faith drives you to action. And lastly the most important factor is whether your faith makes you a sublime human being or a debased one. So, these are the criteria that help you examine your faith. Insistence on such examination alone brings about human progress. Discourse on faith and superstition therefore is an important matter in the ideological discussions of the ANiS movement.

MEDHA PATKAR

Medha Patkar is a social activist known chiefly for her work with people displaced by the Narmada Valley Development Project (NVDP), a large-scale plan to dam the Narmada River and its tributaries in the states of Madhya Pradesh, Gujarat and Maharashtra. The following is an extract from the speech she delivered during the Domkhedi Satyagraha in 1999, after breaking her eight-day fast. Today, the dam, which was pushed from one stage to another, has reached its final height, displacing thousands of villagers. Here, she says that one tapa (twelve years) of the struggle in the Narmada valley is over, but the struggle will continue.

One Tapa, One Vow

The struggle which started with the innocent, simple tribals dependent on nature was spread further on the fertile and flowering land of Nimad. It lived on the strength of the common people and fostered dialogue and active support from outside the valley. The depressed and toiling classes were integrated as a part of the struggle. They contributed their mite along with numerous activists in the valley, supporters and Baba Amte and Sadhanatai. I have been only incidental, but never distinct from the valley.

The Beginning of unity...

First and foremost, the struggle has demanded the right to information—about the cost-benefit of the dam and proof of its 'public purpose'. The people have also demanded explanations of how the trauma of displacement and environmental degradation is to be compensated. From 1985 to 1987, from the level of village patwari (record keeper) to the World Bank, we did not get the answers to our queries. If there are no answers, then the people give no clearance for the dam. The tribals of Vindhya & Satpuda ranges and people in Nimad declared opposition to the dam and showed that only the dam of their unity would be of any use to them (ekina baandhaja kamoma ava...).

The thought of opposing the dam itself has not evolved out of any alien dogma, philosophy or foreign finance. It has evolved through individual experience and experience of the people at each step. As a result, we have formulated our policy and opinion about large dams, tribal life, the means of livelihood and how these are being looted, the wide breach between agriculture and industry, village and city, the capitalist-market oriented objectives as well as a socially just and environmentally sustainable vision of development. We have also evolved an analysis of the objectives and process of planning, the foreign hand, its intervention, its effect and pressure, deception of the people affected by drought and flood, the conspiracies of today and the future scenario...and an alternative paradigm of development of water and energy resources with self-reliance in the direction of equality. We have explored every issue, tried to project these to the furthest extent possible, with more or less efficacy. We have extended the dialogue and tried to reach every forum. The commitment and efforts bore some fruits....

Not only for Narmada...

All this was not to save only one Narmada river and valley, or people affected by the Sardar Sarovar and all the big dams allied with it. We have to save the life and resources, the identity and dignity of the people, the farms, forests of every oppressed and depressed section of the population. That is why we will have to stop the Sardar Sarovar dam. We will have to stop it from going up to 139 meters despite the fact that it was taken up forcibly to 88 meters. We have to stop the game of the powerholders to cater to the interests of the few urban-industrial pockets while draining the natural resources and deceiving the people of Kutch and Saurashtra, in whose name the dam is being built.

The Struggle Ahead...

How all this will be possible? We will have to fight on. On a number of fronts, simultaneously, exploring and involving all possible avenues—just like the river, nay like the ocean. It will have to be a whirlwind of the people's movement; and it *will* be like that if the thousands and more thousands participate in it.

Some points of such a struggle have been envisaged by all the colleagues. Some of them I feel are necessary and inevitable. I want to appeal for the support and participation of all colleagues, supporters and people till the last moment. This is how the struggle can go ahead:

- We will be confronting the submergence, which is bound to come at any time, in the spirit of dedication and sacrifice. We shall stay put resolutely at the centres of Satyagraha, in every house, hoping that the water may not rise—yet ready to sacrifice life. We wish that Mother Narmada should remain free, flowing, even if we have to sacrifice [our lives]. We will see how many and who all would come and from where to be with us.

- The government shall not play the game of 'saving the lives' after it had fully prepared to submerge the entire valley. No false promises. If that happens, we will confront their design. We will decide the strategy and policy accordingly, and will not leave them scot-free this time.
- The time has come to raise questions about the judicial process through which the lives and resources of the people in the valley are being taken away. Why not question it? After all, the objective of such process is justice, and certainly not injustice. This is a part of the system created by human beings. It is not a matter of abstract theory, the questions are being raised out of actual reality.
- The impending submergence would violate the stipulations of the Narmada Water Disputes Tribunal (NWDT) and the orders of the Court itself. There is no land for resettlement. At this juncture we cannot but think of justice and injustice. How can it be otherwise? We are raising the issues, following the path of constitution and legal propriety, so that the judicial system would not be proved unjust due to the machinations of the power holders. May the dignity and position of the judiciary remain intact.

For a More Participatory Judicial Process...

- Is it not possible for the Court to examine all the issues raised by the tribals and peasants about the project?
- Is it not necessary for the judiciary to evolve new ways of independently finding out the truth in a dispute between the state power and the common, depressed classes and to do justice?
- Can't the court hold a 'Jan Sunwai' (Public Hearing) involving the victims, common people and people's organizations at their places about the issues affecting the hundreds and thousands of people? Why cannot the British legacy of judicial system be changed for the people?
- Is it not right that any judicial process in an issue like Narmada, with a large scale destruction of life and nature, be carried out only after suspending the project, without imposing this destruction?

We also must ponder:

- Whether it is just for the Court to give an order, involving the violation of the constitution, law and its own previous orders, which would strengthen the hands of the state power to suppress and intimidate the people's organizations, their feelings and thinking, allowing the state to become more oppressive?
- If the Court recognizes the violation of the Constitution, law and its own previous orders and after realizing the blatant injustice done due to its order, cannot the Court issue a new order to demolish the cause of injustice (as in case of SSP from 81.5 meters to 88 meters) or any other way out (for the construction above 81.5 meters) to stop the impacts of the earlier order?
- Why can't the apex court of this country challenge the administrative decision about any project in the name of 'Public Purpose', which would cater only to the political interests and consumption of the small section of the society, based on fraudulent cost-benefit analysis, and on the violation of constitutional, human rights?

Why cannot this happen in the democratic polity?

We would like to ask, and ask we will, to the nation.

We Will Stop Sardar Sarovar Project... if it only uproots and drowns people, without granting them their rights.

We are, beyond all these dimensions of the struggle, determined to question the Sardar Sarovar Project in the larger chain of the large dams on Narmada. Is it to benefit corporate, not communities?

The people's power has been challenging, on its own strength and on the basis of non-violent strategy, in Narmada and elsewhere, the alien, destructive and iniquitous policy. Now, the struggle in this monsoon in the valley will once again bring before the nation and the world our policy and strategy. The intellectuals would contribute their mite.

There will be an appeal in and outside the court, in keeping with all its dignity. The state and central governments will be told, as they already know, everything about the Satyagraha, about the fight between life and death.

Ultimate Non-violent Challenge... the Jal Samarpan

And yet, despite all this, if the work on the Sardar Sarovar Project is allowed to go ahead, then what? At the very least, without complete and just resettlement of all those who have already been displaced by the dam and dam-related works (canals, colony, sanctuary, etc.); without a review of the project through a new tribunal and people's hearings, if work on the dam proceeds, to such injustice we shall give the ultimate non-violent challenge though Jal Samarpan (Sacrifice in Water).

This would depend on the resumption of the work on the dam, in an appropriate situation and time.

This is not frustration, fear or helplessness, exhaustion or defeat. Nor is it escape from the struggle, rather it is taking the struggle to its height. This is the challenge. We embrace it for the sake of true development. This would serve as an appeal to the youth and people's power for the decades to come. This is not any Kargil war! This war will be fought with equanimity instead of hatred, peace instead of violence, on the path of change, until its culmination.

Our Vision Ahead

We hope that this situation does not come. We also want to live intensely and with all the joy and beauty of life. We have to bring in the people's rule in this country sans exploitation and oppression; to do away with casteism, communalism and war-mongering. We want to flourish with nature and nature to bloom with us; and to assert the rights of the dalits, toilers, tribals, peasants, women on that resource base. We have to bring in true development with the appropriate utilization of scientific knowledge and technology, new research for sustainable and just water and energy policy and development paradigm. We have to internalize the trinity of equality, modest lifestyle and self-reliance (samata, sadgi, svavalamban) at every level—individual, community to the nation-state....

GITHA HARIHARAN

*On discovering that she was not the natural guardian of her minor son,
acclaimed author Githa Hariharan decided to challenge the relevant sections
of the Hindu Minority and Guardianship Act, 1956 and the Guardian and
Wards Act, 1890 on the grounds that they violate the equality promised
by Articles 14 and 15 of the Indian constitution. In 1999, a judgment was
passed, stating that under Hindu law, the mother can also be the guardian of
her minor children. The following is her response to the judgement.*

Rehabilitating Mothers

On February 17, 1999, a Supreme Court bench, including the Chief
Justice of India, wrote a judgement about mothers and children. The apex
court ruled that 'it is an axiomatic truth that both the mother and father of
a minor child are duty bound to take due care of the person and property
of their child.' In a concurrent judgement, one of the members of the
same bench noted that 'the father by reason of a dominant personality
cannot be ascribed to have a preferential right over the mother in the
matter of guardianship since both fall within the same category.'

This was supposed to be a landmark judgement; a milestone in the
struggle for women's rights. I should have felt some sense of triumph. But
the truth that I could not fail to look in the eye was a simple question: are
we so blind that we need the law to tell us a mother has the right to be her
child's acknowledged guardian?

Five years ago, I discovered that though I am an adult citizen of India,
a working, taxpaying citizen, a wife and a mother—all things acceptable
and respectable—I am still not considered the 'natural guardian' of my
child. I had applied to the Reserve Bank of India (RBI) for its 9 per
cent relief bonds on behalf of my eleven-year-old son. I was told that
only the child's father could sign the application for either purchase or
repayment. My husband and I wrote to the RBI that for this purpose,
we were agreed that I would function as guardian. But the response was
unbending, and, we discovered, completely legal: if I wanted to sign as my
child's guardian, I would have to produce a certificate from a competent
authority to prove that my husband was 'unfit'; or that he was dead; or
that he had taken to vanaprastha.

Consider the ironies: like any other woman, I had been brought
up in a world that told you in a myriad ways that your raison d'être is

motherhood. Again, like most women, I had made my peace with biological and societal expectations. But to be told that I could be considered the natural guardian of 'illegitimate' children, not 'legitimate' ones! And that I was legally fit only to be a caregiver, not a recognized decision-maker on matters concerning my child's welfare! How is it that the law had no problems with my paying tax on my child's income, out of a mere mother's earnings?

With the help of the Women's Rights Initiative programme of the Lawyers Collective, my husband and I filed a writ petition in the Supreme Court challenging the constitutional validity of the Hindu Minority and Guardianship Act (1956). Section 6 of this Act states that the mother is the natural guardian of her legitimate minor child 'after' the father; section 19 of the Guardian and Wards Act (1890) debars the court from appointing the guardian of a minor whose father is living, and is not, in the court's opinion, unfit to be a guardian. Together, these sections have usually been interpreted by the courts to mean that the child's welfare 'rests' with the father. The result: the mother is stripped of her right to be an equal partner in parenthood. The crux of our writ petition was the question, what disqualifies a mother from making decisions about her child's welfare? There is no social, economic, scientific or biological basis to the assumption that a woman is not capable of guardianship. And if there is no rational basis to this law, what is the sole criterion at work? The mother's gender. Did this not violate the equality promised by Articles 14 and 15 of the Constitution?

We were not the first to ask for a rational approach to the question of guardianship. Not only had there been numerous such cases, usually coming up for consideration when there was a custody dispute between parents; but in its 135th Report in 1989, the Law Commission concluded that these two legal provisions are unconstitutional. It recommended that both the mother and father be declared natural guardians with equal rights over the child. The Commission also recommended that the mother retain custody till the child is twelve. The rationale is that the child's welfare determines questions of guardianship and custody; not rights based on gender alone.

Ten years after these recommendations, in 1999, in a country that is clearing its throat for futuristic talk about the millennium, the law has acknowledged, albeit in cautious terms, that the mother too can be the guardian of 'the person and property' of her child. The law in question— or the offending section—has not been struck down. But the Supreme

Court has reinterpreted the reading of the same law so that it alters the balance of power, which has always been tilted heavily in favour of the father in all family laws. This is particularly true for matters of custody, where the 'natural guardianship' of the father weighed heavily with the court while granting custody orders. The judgement will enable women, for centuries effectively marginalized in the family unit by customary laws, to come out of the closet and be legally rehabilitated.

What does all this mean in reality, shorn of legalese and rhetoric? It means that a woman trapped in an unhappy marriage, or a violent domestic situation, need not compromise her wellbeing and that of her child's simply out of fear of losing access to the child. It means that a mother's signature will count on application forms for school and college admissions for her child; on medical permission forms; on passport application forms. It means the mother can invest in her child's name or at least participate in decision-making about her child's financial welfare. Though conventional wisdom maintains that the father plays the primary role and the mother the supporting role in financial support of the child, certain facts about the growing financial role of mothers have now been 'officially' taken into account. An increasing number of women across social classes are contributing to household incomes. Since the priority of earning women is childcare, their income goes towards the children or the general good of the household—this is the rationale behind various government and non-government development programmes that aim at the mother so as to cover the entire family. Across classes, women are often functioning heads of households without the title.

This is a first step towards visibility. The legal experience of other countries indicates that the 'rights of parents and children' do not have to be in opposition to women's rights. In England, for example, so absolute were the father's rights that 'he could lawfully claim from the mother's possession even a child at her breast.' English law has made a journey worthy of imitation from a position not unfamiliar to us. In the 1980s the emphasis shifted from parental rights to responsibility. Neither parent is 'privileged' in the eyes of the law as the natural or legal guardian of the child. In this sense, both mother and father have equal rights to parenthood. In India, where we are so often smug about our dedication to 'family values', we are yet to ensure that the future we travel towards will see a more egalitarian family unit. High on our agenda for the new century has to be re-appropriating women's issues from communalists, or self-serving politicians, or the crumb-throwing paternalistic pillars of our society.

D.N. JHA

Dwijendra Narayan Jha is a leading Indian historian. In The Myth of the Holy Cow, *he argues that beef played an important part in the cuisine of ancient India, long before the birth of Islam. When the book was first published in 2001, the then ruling government and various fundamentalist groups called for it to be burned in public.*

From *The Myth of the Holy Cow*

> Mother cow is in many ways better than the mother who gave us birth. Our mother gives us milk for a couple of years and then expects us to serve her when we grow up. Mother cow expects from us nothing but grass and grain. Our mother often falls ill and expects service from us. Mother cow rarely falls ill. Our mother when she dies means expenses of burial or cremation. Mother cow is as useful dead as when alive.[1]

These are the words of Mahatma Gandhi explaining the importance of the cow. His explanation, devoid of religious rigmarole, is quite simple: the cow is important because of its resource value in an agrarian society whose members derive a substantial part of their sustenance from its milk and other dairy products. But Gandhi contradicts himself and says elsewhere, 'the central fact of Hinduism is cow protection... The cow protection ideal set up by Hinduism is essentially different from and transcends the dairy ideal of the West. The latter is based on economic values, the former... lays stress on the spiritual aspect, viz., the idea of penance and self-sacrifice for the martyred innocence which it embodies...'[2] This statement of Gandhi is significantly different from the former, in that it lays stress on his religious commitment to protect the cow.

Most Hindus today are guided by a religious concern for cow protection. Therefore an average Indian, rooted in what appears to him as his traditional Hindu religious heritage, carries the load of the misconception that his ancestors, especially the Vedic Aryans, attached great importance to the cow on account of its inherent sacredness. The 'sacred' cow has come to be considered a symbol of community identity of the Hindus whose cultural tradition is often imagined as threatened by Muslims, who are thought of as beef eaters. The sanctity of the cow has, therefore, been announced with the flourish of trumpets and has been wrongly traced back to the Vedas, which are supposedly of divine origin and the fountainhead of all knowledge and wisdom. In other words, some sections of Indian society trace the concept of sacred cow to the very period when it was sacrificed and its flesh was eaten.

More importantly, the cow has tended to become a political instrument in the hands of rulers over time. The Mughal emperors Babar, Akbar, Jahangir and Aurangzeb are said to have imposed a restricted ban on cow slaughter to accommodate Jaina or Brahmanical sensibilities and veneration of the cow.[3] Similarly Shivaji, sometimes viewed as an incarnation of God who descended on earth for the deliverance of the cow and the Brahmana, is said to have proclaimed: 'We are Hindus and the rightful lords of the realm. It is not proper for us to witness cow slaughter and the oppression of brahmans.'[4] But the cow became a tool of mass political mobilization when the organized Hindu cow-protection movement, beginning with the Sikh Kuka (or Namdhari) sect in the Punjab around 1870 and later strengthened by the foundation of the first Gorakshini Sabha in 1882 by Dayananda Sarasvati, made this animal a symbol of the unity of a wide ranging people, challenged the Muslim practice of its slaughter and provoked a series of serious communal riots in the 1880s and 1890s, although attitudes to cow killing had hardened even earlier,[5] there was undoubtedly a 'dramatic intensification' of the cow protection movement when in 1888 the North-Western Provinces High Court decreed that a cow was not a sacred object.[6] Not surprisingly, cow slaughter very often became the pretext of Hindu–Muslim riots, especially those in Azamgarh district in the year 1893 when more than a hundred people were killed in different parts of the country. Similarly in 1912–13 violence rocked Ayodhya and a few years later, in 1917, Shahabad witnessed a disastrous communal conflagaration.[7]

The killing of cattle seems to have emerged again and again as a troublesome issue on the Indian political scene even in independent India despite legislation by several states prohibiting cow slaughter and the Directive Principles of State Policy of the Constitution, which directs the Indian state to '…to take steps for…prohibiting the slaughter of cows and calves and other milch and draught cattle.' For instance, in 1966, nearly two decades after Independence, almost all communal political parties and organizations joined hands to mastermind a massive demonstration by several hundred thousand people in favour of a national ban on cow slaughter. This culminated in a violent rioting in front of the Indian Parliament and the death of at least eight persons and injury to many more. In April 1979, Acharya Vinoba Bhave, often called the spiritual heir to Mahatma Gandhi, went on a hunger strike to pressurize the central government to prohibit cow slaughter throughout the country and ended it after five days when he succeeded in getting the Prime Minister Morarji Desai's vague assurance that his government would expedite anti-slaughter legislation. After that the cow ceased to remain much of an issue in the Indian political arena for many years, though the management of cattle resources has been a matter of academic debate among sociologists, anthropologists, economists and different categories of policy farmers.[8]

The veneration of the cow has been converted into a symbol of communal identity of the Hindus and obscurantist and fundamentalist forces obdurately refuse to appreciate that the cow was not always all that sacred in the Vedic and subsequent Brahmanical and non-Brahmanical traditions—or that its flesh, along with other varieties of meat, was quite often a part of *haute cuisine* in early India. Although the Shin, Muslims of Dardistan in Pakistan, look on the cow as other Muslims do the pig, avoid direct contact with cows, refuse to drink cow's milk or use cowdung fuel and reject beef as food,[9] self-styled custodians of non-existent 'monolithic' Hinduism assert that the eating of beef was first introduced in India by the followers of Islam who came from outside and are foreigners in this country, little realizing that their Vedic ancestors were also foreigners who ate the flesh of the cow and various other animals. Fanaticism getting precedence over the fact, it is not surprising that the Rashtriya Swayamsevak Sangh, the Vishwa Hindu Parishad, the Bajrang Dal and their numerous outfits have a national ban on cow slaughter on their agenda. The Chief Minister of Gujarat (Keshubhai Patel) announced some time ago, as a pre-election gimmick, the setting up of a separate department to preserve cow breeds and manage Hindu temples,[10] and recently a Bajrang Dal leader has even threatened to enrol 30 lakh activists in the anti-cow slaughter movement during the Bakrid of 2002.[11] So high-geared has been the propaganda about abstention from beef eating as a characteristic trait of 'Hinduism' that when the RSS tried to claim that Sikhs were Hindus, there was vehement opposition from them and Sikh youth leader proposed, 'Why not slaughter a cow and serve beef in a gurdwara langar?'[12]

The communalists who have been raising a hullabaloo over the cow in the political arena do not realize that beef eating remained a fairly common practice for a long time in India and that the arguments for its prevalence are based on the evidence drawn from our own scriptures and religious texts. The response of historical scholarship to the communal perception of Indian food culture therefore, has been sober and scholars have drawn attention to the textual evidence on the subject which, in fact, begins to be available in the oldest Indian religious text, *Rgveda*, supposedly of divine origin. H.H. Wilson, writing in the first half of the nineteenth century, had asserted that the 'sacrifice of the horse or of the cow, the *gomedha* or *asvamedha*, appears to have been common in the earliest periods of the Hindu ritual'.

The view that the practice of cow sacrifice and eating beef prevailed among the Indo-Aryans was, however, put forth most convincingly by Rajendra Lal Mitra in an article which first appeared in the *Journal of the Asiatic Society of Bengal* and subsequently formed a chapter of his book *The Indo-Aryans* published in 1891. In 1894 William Crooke, a British civil servant, collected an impressive amount of ethnographic data on popular religious beliefs and practices and devoted an entire chapter to the respect shown to animals including the cow.[13] Later, in 1912, he published an informative piece on the sanctity of the cow in India, but he also drew attention to the old practice of eating beef, and its survival in his own times.[14] In 1927, L.L. Sundara Ram made a strong case for cow protection for which he sought justification from the scriptures of different religions including Hinduism. While he did not deny that the Vedic people ate beef,[15] he blamed the Muslims for cow slaughter.

In the early 1940s P.V. Kane in his monumental five-volume *History of Dharamasastra* referred to some Vedic and early Dharmasastric passages that speak of cow slaughter and beef eating. H.D. Sankalia drew attention to literary as well as archaeological evidence of eating cattle flesh in ancient India.[16] Similarly, Laxman Shastri Joshi, a Sanskritist of unquestionable scholarship, drew attention to the Dharmasastra works that unequivocally support the prevalence of meat eating, including beef eating, in early India.[17]

Needless to say, the scholarship of all authorities mentioned above was unimpeachable, and none of them seems to have anything to do with any anti-Hindu ideology. Nor can they be described as Marxists, whom the Sangh Parivar and the saffronized journalists and publicists have charged of distorting history. H.H. Wilson, for example, was the first occupant of the Chair of Sanskrit at Oxford in 1832 and was not as avowedly anti-Indian as many other imperialist scholars. Rajendra

Lal Mitra, a product of the Bengal renaissance and a close associate of Rabindranath's elder brother Jyotindranath Tagore, made significant contribution to India's intellectual life, and was described by Max Mueller as the 'best living Indologist' of his time and by Rabindranath Tagore as the 'most beloved child of the muse'.[18] William Crooke was a well-known colonial ethnographer who wrote extensively on peasant life and popular religion without any marked prejudice against Hinduism.[19] L.L. Sundara Ram, despite his somewhat anti-Muslim feeling, was inspired by humanitarian considerations. Mahamahopadhyaya P.V. Kane was a conservative Maharashtrian Brahmana and the only Sankritist to be honoured with the title of Bharatratna. H.D. Sankalia combined his unrivalled archaeological activity with a profound knowledge of Sanskrit. Besides these scholars several other Indian Sanskritists and Indologists, not to mention a number of western scholars, have repeatedly drawn our attention to the textual evidence of beef and other types of animal flesh in early Indian diet. Curious though it may seem, the Sangh Parivar, which carries a heavy burden of 'civilization illiteracy', has never turned its guns on them but against historians who have mostly relied on the research of the above-mentioned distinguished scholars.

Notes

1. *Harijan*, 15 September 1940. It was suggested by Marvin Harris that cow protection 'was a major weapon in Gandhi's campaign against both British and Moslems' ('The Cultural Ecology of India's Sacred Cattle', *Current Anthropology* 7 [1966], p. 58) but that was immediately contested by N.K. Bose who asserted that 'cow protection was as much a part of Gandhi's "constructive programme" as, say, the removal of untouchability' (ibid., p. 60).

2. M.K. Gandhi, *How to Serve the Cow*, Navajivan, Ahmedabad, 1954, pp. 85-6.

3. L.L. Sundara Ram, *Cow Protection in India*, The South Indian Humanitarian League, Madras, 1927, pp. 122-3, 179-90.

4. Śiva Digvijaya quoted in Sundara Ram, *Cow Protection*, p. 191.

5. This is evident from the facts that much before the inception of the cow protection movement, Raja Rammohun Roy (1772-1883), who denounced India's religious divisions and superstitions, wrote a tract in defence of beef eating. It was entitled 'Hindu Authorities in Favour of Slaying the Cow and Eating its Flesh'. See R.K. Dasgupta, 'Spirit of India-I', *Statesman*, 15 March 2001.

6. Sandria B. Freitag, 'Contesting in Public: Colonial Legacies and

Contemporary Communalism', in David Ludden, ed., *Making India Hindu,* Oxford University Press, Delhi, 1996, p. 217.

7. Sandria Freitag, *Collective Action and Community: Public Arena and the Emergence of Communalism in North India,* Oxford University Press, Delhi, 1990, Chap. 6; Gyan Pandey, 'Rallying round the Cow', in Ranajit Guha, ed., *Subaltern Studies,* vol. II, Oxford University Press, Delhi, 1983, pp. 60-129.

8. Several scholars have participated in the discussion on the sacred cow complex and the management of cattle in India. An idea of the nature of debate in the late 1960s and 1970s can be had from Marvin Harris, 'The Cultural Ecology of India's Sacred Cattle', *Current Anthropology* 7 (1966), pp. 51-66; Alan Heston, 'An Approach to the Sacred Cow of India', *Current Anthropology,* 12 (1971), pp. 191-209; John W. Bennett, 'Comment on: An Approach to the Sacred Cow of India by Alan Heston', ibid., p. 197; Corry Azzi, 'More on India's Sacred Cattle', *Current Anthropology,* 15 (1974), pp. 317-24; V.M. Dandekar, 'Cow Dung Models', *Economic and Political Weekly,* 4 (1969), pp. 1267-9, 1271; idem, 'India's Sacred Cattle and Cultural Ecology', ibid., pp. 1559-67; idem, 'Sacred Cattle and More Sacred Production Functions', ibid., 5 (1970), pp. 527, 529-31; K.N. Raj, 'India's Sacred Cattle: Theories and Empirical Findings', ibid., 6 (1971), pp. 717-22; *Seminar,* no. 93 (May 1967), issue on the cow.

9. Frederic Drew, *The Jummoo and Kashmir Territories: A Geographical Account,* Edward Stanford, London, 1875, p. 428; J. Biddulph, *Tribes of the Hindoo Koosh,* Calcutta, 1880, pp. 37, 1123-13; *Imperial Gazetteer of India, Provincial Series: Kashmir and Jammu,* Calcutta, 1909, p. 108. For a discussion and further references see Frederick J. Simoons, 'Questions in the Sacred Cow Controversy', *Current Anthropology,* 20 (1979), p. 468.

10. *The Times of India,* 28 May 1999, p. 12.

11. *Frontline,* 13 April 2001, p. 97.

12. Rajesh Ramachandran, 'A Crisis of Identity', *The Hindustan Times,* 7 May 2000.

13. W. Crooke, *The Popular Religion and Folklore of Northern India,* 2 vols., 4th rpt., *Munshiram Manoharlal, Delhi, 1978.*

14. W. Crooke, 'The Veneration of the Cow in India', *Folklore,* XXIIII (1912), pp. 275-306.

15. L.L. Sundara Ram, *Cow Protection in India,* The South Indian Humanitarian League, Madras, 1927, p. 8.

16. H.D. Sankalia, '(The Cow) In History', *Seminar,* 93 (1967).

17. 'Was the Cow Killed in Ancient India?' *Quest,* 75 (1972), pp. 83-7. This is a review article on a book entitled *Beef in Ancient India,* authored by one Mr. Dalmia and published by Gita Press, Gorakhpur. No date.

18. For details see *Rajendralal Mitra: 150th Anniversary Lectures,* The Asiatic Society, Calcutta, 1978.

19. For a brief note on the activities of William Crooke see Editor's Introduction in William Crooke, *A Glossary of North Indian Peasant Life*, ed. Shahid Amin, rpt., Oxford University Press, Delhi, 1989.

PRAKASH N. SHAH

Prakash N. Shah is a respected Gujarati intellectual and the editor of the journal Nirakshak. *The following is an article written by him after the 2002 Gujarat killings.*

N.M. and Kalinga? Impossible, Thrice Impossible, Brother Gill!

As I pick up my pen I realize it is exactly three months since Godhra. Our natural expectations of clean governance have been thwarted by the administration of N.M. Setting aside the exception of the anti-Sikh riots of 1984, the bloody shame of a pogrom has been thrust upon Gujarat for the first time since India became a Republic. But we reserve our comments on that for now. We also put aside the question of N.M.'s action-reaction theory in the context of the behaviour of the kar sevaks on the way to and from Ayodhya by rail. We certainly reiterate our feelings and our demand that every timely step, ranging from critique to punishment, be taken along specific guidelines as regards inhumanity of the Godhra episode. But at this moment, at the very start of this comment, we wish to remind you of the pain we had expressed in the very first week of March; namely, that whatever was done by the Sangh-recognized government and the Sangh family outside the government was such that Musharraf, of all people, could sit in judgement against you and me. A question of propriety does arise when the military dictator of a fundamentalist state starts advising a secular democratic nation about the standards it ought to maintain. But why have we come to such a pass that he can take such a liberty is also a question that arises.

Early in the morning we were reminded of Musharraf. The immediate cause, a couple of statements from K.P.S. Gill. I must confess I've always had nagging doubts about the authority of military and police chiefs to advise us on matters pertaining to democratic processes and civil society. My simple understanding is that minimizing the need for the military and the police defines a mature society. We did not find it a happy state of affairs when in 1985, during the rule of Madhav Singh Solanki, at the time of the anti-reservation riots and the communal twist given to the riots, we, as a non-party civic group, under the leadership of Umashankar Joshi, approached our governor B.K. Nehru with a request to hand over the city to the Army. But what other option is there when the government itself is a wicked partner in inciting anti-peace actions that lead to violence of anarchy? We remember Umashankar recalling the famous lines of Ramanbhai Neelkanth: 'He who awakens the evil inclinations of others / Sets in motion a dangerous game / Having broken the embankment of a full lake / Who has ever succeeded in controlling the torrent?' So, in these circumstances, it is not unnatural for Gujarat to accept, with some reservation, the arrival of the military and the appointment of Gill as security advisor to C.M. Narendra Modi—be it against his wish or according to Article 355.

Be that as it may, only last week, barely forty-eight hours after the departure of the army, disturbances in Godhra and Gomtipur-Rakhial (Ahmedabad) erupted; and reports of bomb blasts in Vadodara and elsewhere keep coming in. Given this situation, Gill's voice sounds a note of sanity and security. He has said, 'I can curb violence, but true peace is in the hands of the elected government and its administration as well as in the hands of the people.' But along with this, a significant thing that he mentions is the Kalinga episode. Gill reminds us that seeing the enormous cost—in bloodshed and destruction—of the victory of Kalinga, Emperor Ashoka undertook introspection and underwent transformation. A similar process of introspection on what happened or what has been done, Gill adds, usually takes place among people and the administration about ten days after any outbreak of violence. This has been his experience while combating violence. But here in Gujarat month after month, the time goes on and yet the Kalinga-touch of Ashoka still eludes us.

I find Gill extremely naïve indeed! Who will remind you, my dear chap, that there was a sage among us by the name of Kripalani. It was a time when Indira Gandhi had fielded her own candidate, V.V. Giri, against the official candidate of the Congress, N. Sanjeeva Reddy. She appealed to the very Congress M.P.s to vote according to their conscience (and not according to the whip.) The great Kripalani retorted immediately, saying, 'My dear lady, try to understand this much. Even if you're a thief, you have to have the stature of a Valia (a great bandit) for your conscience to be stirred. For petty thieves, where is the question of conscience?' Not that we have the authority of giants like Kripalani, but we can deifinetly say this much to Gill: for the Kalinga-touch, one needs the measure and stature of Ashoka.

Who is the person in this case? In a special issue of *Seminar* (May 2002) on Gujarat, Ashis Nandy has recalled his first impression of Narendra Modi whom he met more than a decade ago when he (Modi) was a little known Sangh pracharak or BJP official: 'It was a long, rambling interview, but it left me in no doubt that here was a classic, clinical case of a fascist ... Modi, it gives me no pleasure to tell the readers, met virtually all the criteria that psychiatrists, psychoanalysts and psychologists had set up after years of empirical work on the authoritarian personality... I still remember the cool, measured tone in which he elaborated a theory of cosmic conspiracy against India that painted every Muslim as a suspected traitor and potential terrorist. I came out of the interview shaken and told (Achyut) Yagnik that, for the first time, I had met a textbook case of a fascist and a prospective killer, perhaps even a future mass murderer' (p 18). If Ashis Nandy, sitting so far away, takes no delight in recalling this, you and I, as concerned citizens of Gujarat and as soldiers of social transformation do not like it either. But in the people's struggle to get out of the bloody encounters and the chain of dissension, we cannot afford to ignore the evidence of our eyes and ears and memory.

However, I intend to discuss, by the way of example, the appointment of the Justice K.G. Shah Commission and the addition of Justice G.T. Nanavati as head, for the judicial enquiry into the carnage at Godhra and the subsequent events. I am doing this in the hope some touch of the Kalinga episode may be felt if not by the so-called leader, at least by some of his followers and especially by the common people, willy-nilly regaining their senses after the initial madness. The appointment of Justice K.G. Shah (and him alone) was controversial from the beginning. You could even say that the question of the Commission's credibility was raised, either formally or informally, in different ways, by both the National Human Rights Commission and the National Minorities' Commission; the demand for the appointment of a sitting supreme court judge did not come only from our civic voices or from the leader of the opposition, Sonia Gandhi, but also from the Minorities' Commission itself, appointed by the present NDA government. Here too, those in the know of things recalled the Supreme Court's observation while overturning the ruling of this retired judge of Gujarat, which said, 'This judgement is not based on the understanding of any evidence but on imagination.'

Since Nanavati, a retired judge of the Supreme Court is sitting on this Commission, as the natural head, there is now some easing of tension. Nanavati is conducting a judicial enquiry into the anti-Sikh riots of 1984. The Gujarat BJP and its supporters keep raising the bogey of 1984 to escape the responsibility of the present. But if the NDA government, under the leadership of the BJP, feels the need of a new Commission for a truthful and full investigation into the events of 1984, it must accept the concept of honest investigation into the events of 2002. In a conversation with Manoj Mittal of the *Indian Express* Justice Nanavati has said, 'Accusations of well-planned violence, of the connivance and inaction of the government and the fact that most of the casualties were from the minority community are similarities between two carnages.' Some people defend 2002 by citing the example of 1984; they angrily demand a fresh examination to replace the 'farce' which was the old enquiry. But why do the same people soft pedal the application of the same demand to the events of 2002? The answer to this question is, in a way, clear—and that is, the finger points towards them.

But we want to draw the attention of the wider civil society of Gujarat to the official release of the government regarding the appointment of Justice Nanavati:

'The government had appointed a judicial Commission for an investigation into the Godhra Railway massacre and the subsequent violent events. But unfortunately, some vested interests tried to drag this noble, trustworthy and popularly acceptable institution of a judicial enquiry Commission with a retired judge, into controversy. They have taken advantage of the disturbed atmosphere to keep the enquiry Commission in a state of controversy. Now that peace has been restored, the government has taken an important decision to reconstitute the present judicial Commission. This has been done for the sake of maintaining the dignity of an institution like that of a judicial Commission, for the bright future of the state in the public interest, as well as with the noble aim of avoiding any doubts about the good intentions of the government.'

Widespread public opinion and pressure from the Centre have forced the Gujarat government to seek the services of Justice Nanavati. But instead of accepting them with grace, it gives in with contempt. You can see that the government had raised a contentious point by appointing the useless Justice K.G. Shah Commission. In fact, such a Commission should have been of high calibre, trustworthy and acceptable in the popular mind. When the government finally realized this, instead of accepting it with an open heart, it resorted to making half true statements about the reasons that led it to reconsider its decision; thus, while repairing the damage, it kept snapping and pampering its own ego. And to crown it all, it did not feel the need to announce that from now on, this Commission would work under the leadership of Justice Nanavati. The government's attitude was not that correcting a mistake, but that of being forced to recant and eat its own words.

There is quite a lot of anticipatory joy in certain circles of the Gujarat BJP with regard to the holding of elections before March 2003. Following on the heels of the Central observer for the state, Ramdas Agrawal, the national president Jana Krishnamurti is about to visit us to make a rough estimate. It remains to be seen to what extent the popular vote in Gujarat is ready to come forward with mature reflection to renew the license of a leadership that has not shown the least sign of the Kalinga touch. Putting ideologies aside, even on moral grounds, I have no doubt that N.M.'s license must be revoked. But that does not mean that civil society of Gujarat has to place its confidence in those who are opposing N.M. within the BJP. The frightening capacities of N.M. which were perceived by Ashis Nandy may be the individual achievements of this leadership, but they must have been fed by a specific ideology also. Besides, we must ask where were all those people now banding together against N.M., during the recent carnage? What were they doing and do they have an iota of regret or remorse? Not only this. The civil society of Gujarat is not likely to let them off without asking them what their ideological stand is, whether they have had the sense to see the dangers of fragmenting the nation on communal lines.

The main point is that without a strong fabric of civil society, popular struggle against internal and external terrorism will not be of much use. No doubt, military intervention and deployment are needed, but only occasionally. There is a definite role to be played by the government, the ruling party, the opposition; but its test, aim and ballast are one and the same—civil society.

Translated by Francis J. Parmar

Khadar Mohiuddin

Khadar Mohiuddin is a Telugu poet. His poem 'Birthmark' highlights the state of Muslims in India and the ways in which their place as citizens of the country remains always suspect, and how they are time and again forced to prove their loyalty.

Birthmark

A certain fiction bit me
    a distortion
        a slander

August 10, 1995
that's the day I was born

    in a small village
        in a remote corner of Krishna district

Long before I was born
    my name was listed among traitors

History depicted
    son as stepson
        divided brother from brother
and left me alone

Textbooks laughed at me
    in my childhood

I was just becoming a person
when this history drove strange fears
    deep into me
        tortured me, threw me
            to the howling winds

The present makes me responsible
    for things I've nothing to do with

The present casts around me
    shadows of suspicion

Shadows watching me
   over my head
      always, all ways

They squeeze my existence into numbers

They see 1947
   in the umbilical cord, freshly cut
      its end still wet with the blood
         of the baby born in my house

Hindu—Hindu—Hindustan
Muslim go to Pakistan

Another place to go as well
You will know its name as hell

Helpless in the theatre of slogans
   I'm imprisoned in the present

No constitution pats my back
The throne of three lions
   smiling behind their whiskers
      takes no notice of me

I have no human form
   except as an alien
      as some kind of memorial to 1947
         in the mind
            of the first-class citizen

Yes, I'm a conspirator
   aren't I?

It's no conspiracy to identify
   Islam with Islamabad
It's no conspiracy to dig up
   the earth under the feet
It's no conspiracy
   to make me a refugee
   in the very country of my birth
It's no conspiracy
   to poison the air I breathe
   and the space I live in

It's certainly no conspiracy
    to cut me to pieces
    and then imagine an uncut Bharat

My religion is a conspiracy
    my prayer meetings are a conspiracy
    my lying quiet is a conspiracy
    my attempt to wake up is a conspiracy
    my desire to have friends is a conspiracy
    my desire to live is a conspiracy
    my ignorance, my backwardness, a conspiracy

If I marry, it is a conspiracy
if I have kids, it is a conspiracy

I sell flowers on the sidewalk
    for a morsel of rice
I sell fruits, peanuts
Fix broken umbrellas, watches
Sew clothes on porches
Card cotton
    to live in peace
        in quiet

But suddenly
my blood flows in the streets
    like a river that purifies them

Before an election,
    before all sorts of events,
        my blood directs the future of this country

My blood
provides the magic touch
    that flies the candidates
        right into the Parliament hall

It paves the way
    for real estate

It's the armour
    of political power

It's the assuring hand
    that raises them to position

My blood becomes the auspicious dot
    on Mother India's forehead
        the red lotus to be worshipped

Every step I put forward
    turns into a pool of blood

My house fuels their fireworks
My house burns for their festivals
My house turns into the ashes of their demon on every Diwali

The dove's eggs
    the ancient man preserved for future generations
        in history's nest
            are crushed

I hear the echo
    of Mother Earth's breaking ribs
        for the last time

I dream no more in my mother tongue
My thoughts take form in the language of the masters
Cricket matches weigh and measure my patriotism
Never mind my love for my motherland
What's important
    is how much
        I hate the other land

My role as an evil-clown-antagonist
    entertains the audience
        on silver screen
            on the theatre stage
It leaves me handicapped

Forgive me, friends
I can't revere your great poet
    when he makes up new words
        to disfigure me

I am not moved by the
passion of the people's singer
   He sees no difference between
      the muslim tyrant
         and the muslim poor

When they talk of me
   as a synonym of violence
      and a symbol of intolerance
         I laugh it off

When they tell you
   cycles of demons stories
   to warn you of your future with me
      I laugh it off
When the rulers' watchdogs
   bark history into religion
   turn religion into history
      I laugh it off

But what I hear in response is slander

No, mine is not really a laugh
   It's a cry of pain
      that I swallow day after day
Article 370
   and the barbed wire of personal law:
      They strangle me
I am the victim

Secularism in words
   unconcerned with actions
      kills me
Again, I am the victim
I know you've said my birth was blemished
That's my birthmark

What's this affinity between the rulers' strategies
   and the rope that tightens around my neck?

Why does the stream of my blood flow
   between the two pieces of land

they secretly divided among themselves
like a boundary agreed upon?

I shouldn't ask

On the tips of the tridents
     on the bayonets of the police
         on the ballot boxes
my birthmark sheds blood.

I can't question why

Yes, my birthmark is me
     my existence, my citizenship

It's my ancestral property
     inherited from the earth
          the sky, the air
               the surroundings I live in

It's a wound that never heals.

Translated by V. Narayana Rao

RENUKA NARAYANAN

*Renuka Narayanan is a commentator and columnist on religion and culture.
This essay is an excerpt from her book,* Faith: Filling the God-sized Hole.

Celebrate 'Subversion'
(As the ancients once did)

We all have heard the counter-theories that 'conscience' is nothing but
a socio-political construct, a spiritual imposition meant to keep us in
check, that religious precepts are the injection needles. What we need
to question, though, is the operation of this conscience. There's a master
template for sure, which is universal: do not harm others by word
or deed.

It is when we get to the 'field operations' of the spin-doctors that we run into trouble. The spin-doctors of course are the sacerdotal class, the professionals of religion. In simple language, the priests or clergymen of every patriarchal faith (are there others, of influence?). While important social constructs like law and accountability have grown from religious belief, the petty dos and don'ts of 'religious practice' seem to have harmed more than helped. We would not have the caste system, the suppression of women or racism otherwise, would we?

In these days of dogma and bloc-thinking, it seems crucial that we remember the subversive elements who refused to toe the establishment line. Let's call it 'erupting humanity', the breed that refuses to meekly lie down and get arranged in priestly pigeonholes, but seeks to understand the 'laws of life' individually, using the human intellect as a tool and not as a vessel. A terrific example is the Mother of the Universe herself, Kamakshi Amman, who apparently appeared as an ugra avatar or fierce apparition, to rid the world of a demon. Brahma the über-patriarch 'advised' her to simmer down and marry Shiva in his aspect of Ekambareswar—but she refused! When pressured, she politely but firmly told the entire gang of gods that if 'He' needed a wife that badly, they should hold a yagna and summon forth a 'golden doll' (Bangaru Kamakshi) and park her besides Shiva. Are you surprised that almost no God-fearing Hindu is told this feisty ancient legend?

I really can't understand the priests. They themselves accommodated this splendidly 'disobedient' story in the living pravaha or flow of tradition; it was they who ensured that this story was kept alive from generation to generation. Why, then did they keep it low-key and let their own mothers and daughters be squashed? Censorship actually came later. Wheel north, flying across the land to Punjab. Here's a sixteenth-century Sufi verse: O God, do not mind my faults / There is nothing worthy in this unworthy one. Pity me / To the worldly, their worldly pride, to fakirs, the wrap of renunciation; / I am neither a recluse, nor worldly; / Let little people laugh at me! Says Husain, God's fakir, My friend is the Terrible One. Does it really bother you that it's by Madho Lal and his lover Husain whose verse were apparently not included in the Guru Granth Sahib because the authors were gay? And since the British days, only sanitized Hinduism seems acceptable!

MAHASWETA DEVI

Mahasweta Devi (1926–2016) was one of the biggest names in contemporary Indian literature, a Bengali writer and activist who worked extensively with the marginalized sections of society. The following is an excerpt from a speech she delivered at the Frankfurt Book Fair in October 2006.

The Republic of Dreams

... Nothing happens unless you know how to dream. The Establishment is out to destroy, by remote control, all the brain cells that induce dreams. But some dreams manage to escape. I am after the dreams that have escaped from jail. The right to dream is what allows mankind to survive. If you end the right to dream—which the entire world and everyone is doing—you destroy the world. The right to dream should be the first fundamental right.

... Since the 1980s, I have been vocal about the daily injustice and exploitation faced by the most marginalized and dispossessed of our people: tribals, the landless rural poor who then turn into itinerant labour or pavement dwellers in cities. Through reports in newspapers, through petitions, court cases, letters to the authorities, participation in activist organizations and advocacy, through the grassroots journal I edit, *Bortika*, in which the dispossessed tell their own truths, and finally through my fiction, I have sought to bring the harsh reality of this ignored segment of India's population to the notice of the nation, I have sought to include their forgotten and invisible history in the official history of the nation. I have said over and over, our Independence was false; there has been no Independence for these dispossessed peoples, still deprived of their most basic rights.

Let the people trace their hands over every alphabet until they can write for themselves: I know, I can, I will.

How to save and protect one's culture in these circumstances? Which culture do we protect? And what do we mean when we speak of Indian culture in the twenty-first century? What culture? Which India? Sixty years after our hard-won Independence, the khadi sari is India just as the mini skirt and the backless choli are. A bullock cart is India just as much as is the latest Toyota or Mercedes car. Illiteracy haunts us, yet the same India produces men and women at the forefront of medicine, science and technology. Eight-year-old children toil mercilessly, facing unimaginable working conditions and abuse as child labourers. That is India. On the other hand, there is another lot of eight-year-olds who spend their time in air-conditioned classrooms and call their mothers at lunch break using their personal mobile phones. That too is India. Satyam Shivam Sundaram is India. Choli ke peechchey kya hai is also India. The multiplex and the mega mall are India. The snake charmer and the maharishi—they too are India.

Indian culture is a tapestry of many weaves, many threads. The weaving is endless as are the shades of the pattern. Somewhere dark, somewhere light, somewhere saffron, somewhere as green as the fields of new paddy, somewhere flecked with blood, somewhere washed cool by the waters of a Himalayan spring. Somewhere the red of a watermelon slice. Somewhere the blue of an autumn sky in Bengal. Somewhere the purple of a musk deer's eye. Somewhere the red of a new bride's sindoor. Somewhere the threads form words in Urdu, somewhere in Bengali, somewhere in Kannada, somewhere in Assamese, yet elsewhere in Marathi. Somewhere the cloth frays. Somewhere the threads tear. But still it holds. Still. It holds.

The pattern shifts, flows, stutters, forms again and changes shape from one season to the other. I see one India in the pattern. You see another. Light and shadow play. History and modernity collide. Superstition and myth, Rabindrasangeet and rap, Sufi and Shia and Sunni, caste and computers, text and subplot, laughter and tears, governments and oppositions, reservations and quotas, struggles and captivity, success and achievement, hamburgers and Hari Om Hari, Sanskrit and SMS, the smell of rain and the sound of the sea. A seamless stitching. Many, many hands have stitched, are stitching and will continue to stitch India. My country. Torn, tattered, proud, beautiful, hot, humid, cold, sandy, bright, dull, educated, barbaric, savage, shining India. My country. And its myriad cultures. From time immemorial to now, the twenty-first century. From the Indus Valley to the Bluetooth handset, India has seen it all, contains it all within itself and its cultures. There is room in India for all faiths, all languages, all people. Despite the communal crises, despite the fundamentalism, the backwardness of rural life, the memories of underdevelopment which are no memory but reality for us, the threat of AIDS, tsunamis, earthquakes, floods and droughts, farmer suicides, police violence, environmental disasters wreaked by industries and farmland being bought over by multinational companies, despite the battering by history and circumstance, India still is. Its culture still is. Hence we all still are. India has learnt to survive, to adapt, to keep the old with the modern, to walk hand in hand with the new millennium whistling a tune from the dawn of time. This is truly the age when the joota is Japani, the patloon Englistani, the topi Roosi. But the dil—the dil is and always will remain Hindustani.

As we face the future, and as I stand here, invited to speak of my country's culture before such an eminent gathering and at such an honourable occasion, I wish to share my dream of where I would like to see my India go. I have spoken of the fundamental right to dream. I would now like to exercise that right.

I dream of an India where the mind is without fear and the head is held high. Where knowledge is free. Where the world has not been broken into fragments by narrow domestic walls. Where words come out of the depth of truth. Where tireless striving stretches its arms towards perfection. Where the clear stream of reason has not lost its way in the dreary sand of dead habit.

I dream of an India to which the word 'backward' does not and cannot ever apply. I wish to be Third World no more but First, the only world. I wish for children to be educated. I wish for women to step into the light. I wish for justice for the common man. Survival for the farmer. Homes for the poor. And hope for all. I wish for debts to cease. For poverty to vanish. For hunger to become a bad word that no one utters. I wish for the environment to be protected, to be loved and restored. I wish the land to be healed, the waters to be pure again. For the tiger to survive. I wish for self-reliance, for self-respect, for independence from the shackles of superstition. I wish for equal medical aid for all.

For light and water and a roof above every head. I wish for more and more books to be written, to be published, in every language there is in the country. Let the words pour out. Let the stories be told. Let the people read. Let them learn to read. To trace their fingers over every alphabet until they can spell their names. Their addresses. Until they can write for themselves: I know. I can. I will. Let us fight ignorance with knowledge. Let us battle hatred with logic. Let us slay evil with the sword of the pen.

I wish for no more satis, no more dowry deaths, no more honour killings, no more flesh being bought and sold. Let no more parents sell their children to survive. Let no more mothers drown their daughters in the dead of night. Let the downtrodden awake, let the forgotten faces and the muffled voices arise to claim their own. Let the pattern make room, let these new threads find place, let new colours set afire the tapestry. Set ablaze the future. Into that heaven of freedom, let my India awaken again and again. It is a big dream, I know. But not an impossible one.

When I speak of Indian culture, then, I speak of all this. Culture is what will take us into the future yet keep us in close contact with our roots, our history, our tradition, our heritage. Culture will let us take a quantum leap and land on the moon but first, before all that, it must help us take a few small steps towards understanding ourselves better, towards knowing each other better. Culture must once again remind us to be a tolerant and truly secular people.

I have tried in my own way to give you a picture of this culture. But how am I to even begin arriving at a definition that will be acceptable to all across an India that is so chaotic? So calm. So flexible. So rigid. So rich. So poor. So understanding. So easy to be misunderstood. After all, there are many Indias, as I say over and over again. Simultaneous. Even parallel.

And whose culture is it anyway? Yours? Mine? Theirs? There are so many 'theirs' in the land of my birth who have nothing but the harsh landscape of surviving from day to day. The dispossessed remain with us after six decades of becoming possessed of a freedom we all fought for. They all fought for.

I claim elsewhere to have always written about the 'culture of the downtrodden'. How tall or short or true or false is this claim? The more I think and write and think some more, the harder it gets to arrive at a definition. I hesitate. I falter. I cling to the belief that for any culture as old and ancient as ours to have survived over time and in time, there could only be one basic common and acceptable core thought: humaneness. To accept each other's right to be human with dignity.

This then is my fight. My dream. In my life and in my literature.

A. REVATHI

A. Revathi is a transgender activist and writer from Tamil Nadu. The following is a speech she delivered at the First Asia Pacific Court of Women on HIV and inheritance and property rights, Colombo, 18 August 2007.

Property as Selfhood: A Hijra Experience

My name is Revathi. I am from Tamil Nadu, India. Before I go into who I am, it is important to note the reality of my community and its status in India today and all the struggles that are part of our community. I will begin my speech with a small song.

> Mother didn't accept
> Father didn't accept
> Society didn't accept
> We have no property. No happiness.
> No home. No work.
> I want to be a mother,
> A daughter, a sister, a grandmother, a granddaughter.
> Our world is a separate one.
> We are struggling people.
> Our family is the hijra family.
> Rowdy's blackmail. Police violence. False cases. People's ridicule.
> We beg. We do sex work. We go through torture on a daily basis.
> We too love. We too feel.
> All we want to do is live like humans with dignity.
> We have entered the field of struggle.
> You should understand our feelings.
> Don't feel sympathetic. Just give us our rights.
> Our mother should accept.
> Our fathers should accept.
> The society should accept us.
> We should get property.
> We should get happiness.
> We should get a home.
> We should get a job.

Thank you for listening patiently to this song.

All those born as human beings, have to struggle in their everyday lives. This morning, we have heard different stories of different struggles. For us hijras, life itself is a struggle. From the song you would have got a sense of the state of our community. I was also a sex worker once like many others from my community. My family didn't accept me. Later they did.

When it came to the division of property, my brothers asked me why I
needed property as I had no wife or children. This was because I had had
a sex-change operation and become a woman. They refused to give me
my share of the property for this reason and instead they offered to give
me a small sum (compared to the property that is rightfully mine) that
I was to take and leave. My father then asked me to come to the lawyer's
office. The lawyer asked me not to come dressed up like a woman and
said that I should cut my hair, wear pants and a shirt and come. But this
is not dressing up. This is who I am. I told the lawyer this repeatedly. He
asked me to sit outside for a while. Then they called me back inside. The
lawyer asked me if I trusted my father completely. I said that I'd trust him
irrespective of what he does. He said we could fight for the property that
was duly mine in court. For that they would need a power of attorney. I
then gave my father the power of attorney.

One day, my brothers and my father called me and asked for Rs
40,000, claiming that to be the money spent on the official document-
writing for the property division. I had no money and when I told them
that it was impossible for me to get so much money, they said, 'Suck
someone's cock, mother fucker! You want the property but you won't
give money for the expenses? We will give you Rs 1 lakh. Just take that
and shut up. First of all we should not have allowed you inside the house
with that sari. If you go to court beyond this, we will tell the court that
we don't know who you are and that our brother is a man. Or we will cut
your hair when you're asleep. We will burn you alive.'

My family is important to me. My family's love is important to me.
So I just took the Rs 1 lakh they gave me and went away. But why did my
father ask for a power of attorney? Many families don't accept people like
us. Mine did. So I thought my father would stand by me. But I learned
my lesson.

All the siblings who inherited the property had to give Rs 10,000 to
my sister. She had received land and other property during her wedding
from my family but, beyond that, she was to get this Rs 10,000 from
every part of the property once divided. She had no individual property
rights. Women do not have those. It is by virtue of being a woman that
I was denied them as well, just like my sister was. They asked me to give
Rs 10,000 from the one lakh I got. I was eventually left with Rs 90,000.
I couldn't just deposit the money and live on the interest of Rs 900 that
would come from that. Irrespective of who it is—family or friends—I
realized that to be respected, you need to have money.

I then came to Bangalore. In Bangalore, I did sex work for five years in the midst of violence from police and goons. I wasn't even able to open a bank account. I didn't know how to. There were no NGOs then to help us. This was fifteen years ago. In this situation, as I didn't have a bank account, I would give chunks of Rs 10,000 or Rs 15,000 in cash to my father. When the property was divided, my father received the old house in which we all used to live. With the Rs 2 lakh that I had given my father, he renovated the old house. He wrote a will saying that although his son had become a woman after being born a man, and as I was the only one supporting them then, the house would be bequeathed to me when my parents died.

After he wrote the will, due to too much violence and torture from the police and goons, I stopped doing sex work and joined an NGO called Sangama. My starting salary was Rs 2,500, which was not enough to even pay my rent in a big city like Bangalore. Then, I couldn't give money to my father. I couldn't buy new clothes for my brothers or for my nieces and nephews. The way they treated me when I went home changed drastically. Earlier they used to prepare elaborate meals for me, but now they began to fight with me. Many small squabbles would come up. During those, my father would say, 'I have written this will. But I can write as many wills as I please.' Only the last written will would be valid and he said that he would bequeath the house to me. My brothers were jealous of me and because the big house was being renovated, they did not want me to own it at any cost. 'Why does this cunt need such a big house? He has no wife or children,' they would say. My father would then tell my brothers not to worry and that the house would not be transferred in my name but in the name of his grandchild; that too, to a male progeny. Only those who would take forward the family name (read male persons) were to be in that house. I, a woman, had no right over it. I then asked my father to register the house in my name. I was told that it can't be registered till my father's death. Then, when I then asked him about the Rs 2 lakh I had given him, he asked me what proof there was of me having given him money. My own father asked me for proof. I told him that every brick in that house was the proof. They would tell him about the torture I had to go through with the goons and the police and how I had to sleep with many men and end up half-dead at the end of the night to earn that money. The world calls me a whore. But what name will it call all of the people who live off the money of this whore? I told my father I was a sex worker. So far I had been lying to him about my profession. I had said that I was doing dance programmes and acting in cinema to earn the money. But that day, heartbroken, I told him I did sex work.

He said that he had no money. He told me he had taken Rs 2 lakh from my sister and registered the house in her name. I asked him how he could register it in her name when they could not do the same in mine. I cried my heart out while asking him this. My mother and sister sympathized with me. They told him that he should get the house transferred in my name. But my parents always feared that I would give it away to the aravani community or to the man I may marry, or drink and waste money and lose the house; or, because of what they had done to me, they were scared that I would throw them out of the house. After considering all this, I wrote out a legal document saying that until their death, my parents would not be thrown out of the house. They live in that house and I take care of them even today.

The reason why I am telling you all this is because if I had not stood up against the police when I was doing sex work, if I had not stood up against the goons, if I had allowed the ridicule of society to push me into a corner, had I been scared and not fought for the property that was rightfully mine, I wouldn't be in front of you today telling you this story.

I am changing the world around me. I have changed the norms in my family. I have fought for the property that is rightfully mine, irrespective of my gender. It is all based on the belief that there will be victory at the end of the struggle. It is for this reason that I am in this court for the second time. Today, I work with the NGO, Sangama. I am writing books. I am writing my biography. I am acting in films. How was all this possible? I have also had my share of being scared of the world and sleeping on the pavements on torn sacks. I have also struggled like many others. But today I go through life with the resolve that I can survive and that I can help others survive and live with dignity. Thank you for this opportunity. Fear and tears are our biggest weaknesses. I call upon all women to awaken and fight for their rights. Thank you.

Translated by Ponni Arasu

SIDDHARTH NARRAIN

In 2009, the Delhi High Court read down Section 377 of the Indian Penal Code, which criminalizes 'carnal intercourse against the order of nature' and is used to harass and intimidate LGBTQ people. The decision was challenged in the Supreme Court by Suresh Koushal et al, and the court reversed the judgement, with one of the reasons given that the LGBTQ population is a 'minuscule minority' in India. Siddharth Narrain, one of the lawyers involved in the petition to decriminalize Section 377, wrote this cheeky letter as a response to the judgement.

Size Does Matter Your Lordships: A Letter to the Supreme Court

Your Lordships have called us, LGBT Indians, a 'minuscule minority'. Never mind that statistically we constitute at least 4 per cent of the population, which comes to over forty million people. Your Lordships say that there are only 200 persons impacted by Section 377 over the last 150 years. Never mind that there are millions of LGBT persons who have been under the shadow of this law for the last 150 years, discriminated against, blackmailed, harassed, outed to their families, driven to suicide, forcibly married, diagnosed as mentally ill, raped, assaulted, and disinherited.

Your Lordships say we are a 'minuscule minority'. Since you are so fond of dictionaries, let's flip one open.

Minuscule: The adjective minuscule is etymologically related to minus, but associations with mini have produced the spelling variant minuscule.

French, from Latin: minisculus—rather small, diminutive.

Let's flip to a thesaurus for good measure.

Minuscule: Synonyms: atomic, bitty, infinitesimal, miniature, microminiature, microscopic, tiny, minute, wee, weeny, teensy weensy, itsy bitsy, teeny weeny.

Reminds me of the Brian Hyland song, 'Itsy Bitsy Teenie Weenie Yellow Polka Dot Bikini'. Your Lordships may be familiar with the lyrics. They are appropriate for the occasion. It goes:

> She was afraid to come out of the locker
> She was as nervous as she could be

She was afraid to come out of the locker
She was afraid that somebody would see ...

Your Lordships say we are a minuscule minority. We say your role, as a guardian of the Constitution is to protect the rights of minorities, however itsy bitsy, teeny weeny, itty-bitty they may be.

I've thought long and hard about how your Lordships reached the conclusion that 'minuscule minorities' don't deserve rights. The logic of your statement eluded me all these days. Then, finally, it dawned on me. Of course, that was what your judgment is all about. That's the crux of your ninety-eight-page decision.

And you know what, I can't disagree with you on this one.

Size Does Matter.

Archana Varma

In an interview that appeared in a special issue of Naya Gyanoday *(a Hindi literary magazine published by Bharatiya Jnanpith) on infidelity, in August 2010, Vibhuti Narain Rai, a Hindi writer, former IPS officer and founder-editor of the Hindi journal* Vartaman Sahitya, *remarked, 'Feminist discourse has been reduced to a grand celebration of infidelity,' and 'Hindi women writers are competing with each other to prove who among them is the greatest slut (chhinal).' He denounced a woman writer's autobiography, saying it could have been more aptly titled 'How many times in how many beds.' Numerous women (and some men) writers and politicians protested and demanded Rai's dismissal; however, websites show that many men agree with his views. This reflective essay on feminist discourse in the Hindi literary world by Archana Varma, a well-known writer and critic, appeared in* Kathadesh *in Hindi and in* Seminar *in English in 2010.*

A 'Grand Celebration' of Feminist Discourse

... *Faithful or Unfaithful?* Autobiography has emerged as the literary genre of the discourse of selfhood. This discourse can be called the intellectual prelude to and literary expression of the politics of selfhood. Writing an autobiography is a special type of political act, a kind of disclosure that does not allow secrets to remain secret. Secrets are kept in cellars; they are the truths of society's private parts, and are dangerous to reveal. Unfortunately, we tend to read autobiographies, especially women's autobiographies, not as the disclosure of society's hidden truths but as a dissection and evaluation of the writer's personal character.

Certain centuries-old ready-made touchstones for character evaluation which have disappeared in much of the world, along with the era of chastity-belts and other such medieval instruments, are still used in Hindi-speaking society to evaluate women's 'good character', a concept still synonymous with bodily purity, with the lessons of modesty and shame instilled in the cradle, with the vow of silence, and with keeping family matters within the family. These are the basic stipulations of the social contract that defines women's lives. It is a woman's responsibility to keep secret that which is secret. Her 'honour' is preserved therein and for honour her life is staked. This stake is her prison.

If it is a woman's honour that is at stake, why does masculinity feel threatened when a woman stops worrying about her 'honour' and steps out of prison? After all, it is her own story that she tells; it is she who risks everything and 'loses' her honour. Why then, even after unjustly punishing the woman, does the man become obsessed with saving his own honour? Taslima Nasrin's autobiography is an important example of the personal becoming the political, and the labelling of Hindi women writers' autobiographies as 'a grand celebration of infidelity' is an example of the same phenomenon, albeit on a minor scale.

Actually, a story is never one person's alone. Paradoxically, an autobiography is even less so: it is not just about the writer but about the writer's contemporaries. Only after a couple of generations does it become a mere story.

Let us examine the real meaning of fidelity. In personal relations, a one-sided contract of fidelity produces a relation of master and dog: a relationship in which the one who surrenders only has permission to wag her/his tail. It is not as though without autobiographies there would be only fidelity in the world. Nor is it that there was no infidelity before society 'provided more occasions for interaction among men and women because of urbanization, industrialization, increased access to education, and transforming values.'[2] After all, since men have been writing stories of their sexual conquests for centuries, they must have had participating female and male partners.

Infidelity must indeed have commenced the very day when the

spontaneous desire to couple was made permanent through the legal institution of marriage, and when an unreciprocal fidelity was demanded of women so as to guarantee the rights of progeny and property. Love and marriage and fidelity and infidelity—they all existed. Only women's autobiographies did not exist. The woman's perspective was missing.

The woman has now broken the social contract which ranged her against her own self in a conspiracy of silence forged in the name of modesty, propriety, and shame. So far, if that silence was broken, it was, on the one hand, through the unbridled amorous vitality of folk songs and, on the other, through the forbidden utterance of the names of her own body parts, of menstrual blood, of pregnancy and childbirth, of women's diseases, undergarments, not to mention the names of injustices such as abuse and rape committed against her. When, in the span of a single generation, women began to discuss love affairs and infidelities in their autobiographies, they broke the contract of silence. This signifies the liberation of a woman's consciousness, both from her own stranglehold and from male power.

The first step to empowerment is this liberation of consciousness—before even the liberation from social and familial security, economic dependence and other such fetters. This liberation means freeing oneself from man's ability to 'blackmail'. The one who reaches a decision to write her own story is not practising infidelity—she has, in fact, changed the recipient of her fidelity. The old definition of infidelity simply connotes an exchange between the lover and the husband. But now fidelity means fidelity to truth.

Man perhaps cannot even imagine the internal and external struggle a woman undergoes to achieve this courage to speak, this fearless expression not just of independent consciousness but also of commitment to truth. So I would say that however insufficient and weak our feminist discourse might be, and however few these autobiographies might be, the silences broken by them are certainly cause for our next grand celebration.

Slut—Not a Matter of One Word: There is no need to debate whether 'slut' means a prostitute or a debauched woman. It is clear that the word was used as an insult. The patriarchal mentality of Hindi-speaking society has only one measure for male-female relations: the bed. Though that is a fundamental material reality, the man-woman relation has now grown beyond the three by six, or even the six by six enclosure of the bed. Varied and multi-layered partnerships and rivalries—intellectual, academic, professional, creative—have now become part of these relations. The sole meaning of emotional attachment is no longer physical attraction, nor is its sole destination the bed. The past hundred years of women's liberation have brought about multifaceted developments in women's personalities. She now experiences the basic need for friendship, of multiple and diverse kinds. Professions are now as important for women as for men, not only for livelihood, but also for personal fulfilment. Writing is one such profession. In professional life, mutual dependence grows and camaraderie develops, ranging from the discussion of news and workplace headlines over cups of coffee, to 'non-veg' jokes, mutual teasing, laughter, even conversations about household problems.

Having spent two-thirds of my life as a teacher in a prominent women's educational institution in the capital, I have seen this new woman from up close. Feminist discourse is the discourse of this woman. She finds the monogamy of love and marriage suffocating and its routine—including the bed—tiresome and boring. In this desert, the challenges, provocative intellectual exchanges and intimate jokes of the workplace revive her soul. For her, relations are governed not by monogamous desire but by companionship and friendship. But male mentality is still so limited that even the most open-minded man, the poet and writer who loudly curses the deformed thinking of other writers, cannot actually see past these limits. At most, instead of calling his friend a slut, he will magnanimously call her a girlfriend, ignoring the fact that in the Hindi world, a girlfriend is nothing but a slut.

In the world of writing, many generations are simultaneously active, and the difference of a few decades in age need not become a generational difference. Krishna Sobti, Manu Bhandari, Usha Priyamvada, Raji Seth, Jyotsana Milan, Mrinal Pande, Sudha Arora, Maitreyi Pushpa, Chitra Mudgal, Anamika, Jaya Jadwani, Pankhuri Rai, Pratyaksha, Kavita, Soni Singh are all contemporaries in a peculiar way. They may not all be feminists, but because of their independent personalities they embody a sharp attack on the roots of patriarchy and thus help us to realize the goals of feminism. If literature is a first-alert system for society, then Krishna Sobti may be considered a first-alert for Soni Singh.

Let me cite an observation made forty-five years ago by an old and now departed member of my family: 'Only loose women have personalities.' The context that provoked this comment was the following: his daughter-in-law, meeting her educated and talented sister-in-law (husband's sister) some years after her marriage, sorrowfully remarked that the sister-in-law seemed to have lost her 'personality'. In defence of his daughter, my relative questioned the very basis of a woman's personality. We don't seem to have made much progress in forty-five years. It is still the case that the woman is idealized in her disempowerment. Adjectives such as 'loose' and 'sluttish' become a means of disempowerment.

When the Red Fort was evacuated during the revolt of 1857, several women of the royal Mughal family were forced to adopt the oldest profession in the lanes of Chandni Chowk. They were called randi because at the time the word meant an upper class woman.[3] The word that then signified class later came to signify a profession. It is not clear whether randi is identical with chhinal (slut) because randi definitely came to mean 'whore'.

In this context, it makes sense to understand 'slut' or 'whore' as insults and to view the uproar of protest as a grand celebration, since the speaker's aim was to insult. But let's pause to consider. It may not be easy for us to swallow this, but after all prostitution too is a profession like any other. The illegal status of the slut keeps her oppressed, insecure and demeaned. Hers is the first stake in feminist discourse and in the struggle against oppression, and we must begin by transforming her name from a term of abuse to one of respect.

We know that such insults are the easiest and most effective weapons man uses to restrict and disempower woman. Even when equipped with the resolve of self-empowerment, engaged in breaking silences and challenging prohibitions through writing, still, somewhere in the depths of our subconscious, we measure ourselves by the touchstone of patriarchal sensibility. As though, obscurely, even today, modesty, propriety, silence, fidelity constitute a foundational social contract for women, which men may invoke with a casual joke. There are times when it is essential to state that this is unbearable, especially when the speaker's status renders his words authoritative.

But on the path to self-empowerment it is necessary to make one's armour impermeable. Protest is essential. But even more essential is blunting such weapons. It is essential to restore to the whore, the slut, and the loose woman her dignity, because she is a courageous woman who has a right to respect. Also because we know that those who shake our inmost being by using such words against us may well tender an apology when it suits them, but they will not change. Even if they are silenced, they will continue in their way of thinking. Therefore, we ourselves must snatch from these abuses their abusive potential.

One day I will hear 'loose woman', 'slut', 'whore', or perhaps just 'girlfriend'. They are all synonyms. In anger, I will say, 'Are you thinking of your mother or of your sister?' Then I will recognize the remnants of my own patriarchal sensibility. His mother or sister is also a woman. Better, I will laugh. Even better, I will turn and say, 'Thanks for the compliment.' One day. We await that day, which will inaugurate the third grand celebration of feminism.

Translated by Ruth Vanita and Simona Sawhney

Notes

1. The first half up to 'This stake is her prison' is translated by Vanita and the second half by Sawhney. Ruth Vanita is Professor, Liberal Studies, University of Montana; Simona Sawhney teaches Asian literature, intellectual history, and feminist thought at the University of Minnesota.
2. Quoted from Vibhuti Narain Rai's interview.
3. Readers of late-eighteenth- and late-nineteenth-century Urdu/Hindi poetry are aware that randi was used in the sense of 'woman' at that time. Poets like Insha and Rangin use it to describe noblewomen who are friends of princesses. It acquired its modern meaning of 'whore' only in the later nineteenth century, when any woman who was not a wife and who interacted with men came to be viewed as a prostitute (Ruth Vanita).

JAGRUP SINGH JHUNIR

*Jagrup Singh Jhunnir is a revolutionary poet and left-wing activist from Punjab. The following poem has been selected and translated by **Nirupama Dutt** specially for this volume.*

A Pistol for My Dowry

Should I not speak the truth, Father?
For how long will I bear these lies,
Suppress even my breath?
Do not wander, Father,
We must reach our destination.
A pistol for my dowry, Father.

In our villages the cobwebs of ritual...
Mother,
My innocent mother,
Let not daughters be born in villages
Where their desires are sold with their dowries.
A pistol for my dowry, Father.

I will not be a shoe for any foot,
I will not bear torment inflicted by anyone's son;
Tell me, Father,
Am I not the Queen of Five Rivers?
A pistol for my dowry, Father.

Some crush me when I am but a bud,
When I blossom, they turn away;
When sons are born, sweets go around,
They dance the bhangra and sing songs
I feel I am born as good as dead;
There are no sweets, no drums.
A pistol for my dowry, Father.

Those who toss her into the fire,
The sinners who rape my soul,
I must burn them alive,
Pay them twice over for their sins;
For once, let the enemies lose heart.
A pistol for my dowry, Father.

MEENA KANDASAMY

Meena Kandasamy is a poet, writer, activist and translator. Her work is focused on caste annihilation, linguistic identity and feminism.

Ekalaivan

This note comes as a consolation:

You can do a lot of things
With your left hand.
Besides, fascist Dronacharyas warrant
Left-handed treatment.

Also,
You don't need your right thumb,
To pull a trigger or hurl a bomb.

HILAL MIR

Hilal Mir is the editor of the newspaper Kashmir Reader. *The following is an article written by him in August 2010 for* Hindustan Times, *where he worked as a journalist.*

How I Became a Stone-thrower for a Day

I left Kashmir a year ago to preserve my sanity, frayed during the past two decades by the internalizing of the conflict. Covering it as a reporter for seven years felt like wading—despairingly—through the five rivers of Hades. My emotions stabilized a bit by the speed and normalcy of life in Delhi, I thought I could maintain a safe distance from the happenings. With this frame of mind, I landed on 4 July at Srinagar airport on a vacation.

Policemen and paramilitary soldiers were everywhere along the way. Driving me home, my friend Showkat, *Outlook* magazine's Kashmir correspondent, prepared me for the situation by narrating the horror he and a bunch of journalists from the *Indian Express, Sahara Samay* and *Tehelka* had faced a day before. While covering a procession marching toward the north Kashmir flashpoint of Sopur, they had been fired at by a policeman on the Srinagar highway. Shouting aloud about their press credentials had only invited abuses. They had to take cover in the nearby paddy fields, surprised that the bullet missed them. Showkat's wife had since asked him to quit journalism and raise chickens. It was the only day I saw shops open and traffic plying normally. From the next day, it was a return to the realm of Hades.

In the morning, one and a half kilometres away from my home, I went to the funeral of a seventeen-year-old blue-eyed, fair-skinned student, as handsome as Omar Abdullah, and a thirty-five-year-old father of two. According to the protesters, the boy had been hit in the head and then thrown into a flood channel by the police. The man had been shot dead during the boy's funeral procession. Women wailed, pulled out their hair, beat their chests and faces, and men shouted freedom slogans while the duo were consigned to the graves. I had seen this countless times in the past, but the rage this time was volcanic, fuelled largely by official lies, apathy and the validation of the bullet-for-stone method. People wanted revenge—though, at the same time, they were aware that their acts of revenge, stone throwing at best, would result in more deaths. It seemed a rage directed more towards one's helplessness than towards an armed soldier. Otherwise why would such 'frenzied' mobs sponsored by Lashkar-e-Toiba' not kill a soldier they had cornered on a road, but instead just beat him up, strip him and let him go?

This strange mix of rage and helplessness was to strike me and several journalists I was moving around with in the curfewed, restricted and deserted city. A Central Reserve Police Force (CRPF) soldier stopped us in the old city. A young reporter of a local English daily showed him a curfew pass issued by the government. The soldier tore it up and asked, 'Where is your bloody curfew pass now?' I had no time to get a curfew pass. I just showed my *Hindustan Times* ID card. I presume the word 'Hindustan' did the trick.

The next few days were spent in exhausting discussions on politics, in parks and the Mughal Gardens, leaving us with an aftertaste of impotent rage. The calm instilled by Delhi was wearing thin. I had always loathed the term 'objectivity' when it really meant balancing truth with a healthy dose of falsehood—or, even worse, 'national interest'. Much of the media were doing that. The state and central government were in a state of denial, effectively blaming the people for the mess. For the first time I felt like an ordinary Kashmiri and wanted to react like them. I was with other journalists when we went to Kawdara in the old city, where separatist leader Mirwaiz Umar Farooq was leading a demonstration that soon morphed into a clash between youth and CRPF soldiers (camping in a bunker as old the insurgency itself).

I picked up a stone from the debris of the housing cluster burnt by CRPF soldiers in 1990 and threw it at the soldiers, a few of whom were filming the stone-throwers with mini-cams. Caught, I could have been booked under the Public Safety Act and jailed for two years without a trial. I would also have been jobless because no news organization would have a felon on its desk. But I threw more stones. I later realized it was an atavistic reaction, as if it was the only legitimate thing to do in that cursed place. I had thrown stones twenty-three years ago when three people were killed for demonstrating against a hike in power tariff, an event that would catalyze the uprising of 1989. My journalist friends restrained me. Disoriented, I walked to my birthplace, Nawab Bazaar, in the old city, a kilometre from Kawdara.

Nawab Bazaar was as furious as it was twenty years ago. Angry youths whom I had seen growing up were pelting the CRPF bunker there with stones. Back then, militants had attacked it with AK-47 rifles. For me, the bunker represents an occupation of memories. It was built on the spot where a man sold phirni and children would line up for the sighting of the crescent, a harbinger of Eid. A short distance away, the Dogra maharaja's soldiers had shot dead my great-grandfather in 1931. Twenty years ago, when the bunker was being constructed, my father's bosom friend, a fanatical Congress supporter, prophesied that 'your eyelashes will turn grey, but the bunker will still be there'. He died last year. His eyebrows had started to grey and all his hair was silver.

Old demons were stirring up inside me. During nights I would look out of the window of my room, holding a digital recorder in any hand to catch freedom songs blaring from mosque loudspeakers and wafting through the quiet air. Twenty years ago I had heard and sung the same songs. The bunker in Nawab Bazaar has grown bigger and uglier, with all those barbed-wire loops, fences, gaudy paint and slits, demonstrating that the state does not tire. But neither do the people.

MONA ZOTE

Mona Zote from Aizawl, Mizoram, writes in English and her poems have been published in various journals and anthologies. Her use of unsentimental and troubling imagery to describe everyday life in the conflict-ridden Northeast India is startling. The violence and neglect, the cultural genocide and the ravages of insurgency in the Northeast are some of the key themes in her poems.

Rez

A boy & his gun: that's an image will do
to sum up our times
to define the red lakes
and razor blade hills of our mind. Out here *this place never*
     changes, never will
we will keep choosing grey salt, bad roads,
some think yellow flowers to grieve, alcohol over friendship...
cash for peace, God's grin of despair. If you think I'm
starting to regret
sticking around and kicking at the tombstones
(if not pulling out the AK-47)
remember the water lilies will bind you back.

Trench coat todesengel bringing *meaning to life thru death,*
          thru
an intimate if facile study of pain
and those other *mental stuff* like drawing
pictures of war
people getting shot
houses pulled down
heads shorn
traditional law custom *kultur*
junkies runners bootleggers scum scum scum
We too have spent our brutal spring *exacerbated*
          by a long tradition of self-enforced isolation,
          continued into a cold-blooded summer (I feel nothing,
          I fear nothing)
          we said *it wasn't intentional*
          and the grasshopper susurrus of our blood tells us how
          you feel almost an ability to be worse than what you are
          (Perhaps this explains why today in the middle of my
          room a black hole suddenly spins.)

Look, kid, thank you for the demonstration
& don't forget to take your angel home
even if you don't *feel like going back to school*
& if they ask you about life on the reservation
          if they say they want to hear about stilt-houses
and the dry clack of rain on bamboo

and the preservation of tribal ways
        give them a slaughter.

II

Let's hear from you, Angel. *Incredibly,*
        He spake: 'Four a.m. I rose from
the silicon box, wings quivering triumphant
if bleary-eyed, knuckles cramped,
having gunned down Virtual Viktor the smiling Ruskie,
        my erstwhile
friend, piss-full of vodka as he went—like the young in
one another's arms
drowning among the waves. You remember
        Star Trek via Doordarshan?

Do you remember?—Those Sunday ceremonies of
        mantraps
and Armageddon now!, logic and adventure,
new worlds braver than the last, those Tin Pan ships
        from an
interstellar Nineveh: amok times, yes. Also aboriginal.
        My shoes are Japanese
Christ, I can't forget Yaqob, surefire bet in the pro-
        wrestling ring—
man's champ or scapegoat, who can tell? He got the better
of me in the end but I...
I nailed his dreams to the cold ground.
In the distance, the guitars of Byzantium wept.

No, don't go there!
There be whales, cap'n, and pearls and eyes.
Thus let us venture to the noodle bar—'
        The immortal game

'—Mister Nighttime, what say? Admit modernity in,
sepia anime! Who
mourns for Adonis or Umrao Jaan? D'you remember
what the children sang—

        Your warriors are gone with Billy Bowlegs
        and Billy Budd swings from the mast

O moments that have passed like tears in rain

Toke this: things have to be the way they are
because gods can't remember, we angels do. In this
we are as mortal as you
though fiery we fell.
Swaraj: acid anthem in our veins.
But heart is truly Hindoostani

So many have fallen…these cinnamon groves. I swear…
I swear by the Wumpus, by Alphaman,
—the world's become
one big reservation. I should know,

I'm the Angel. I'm
in charge. You feel
that tightening of the temples as at some
momentous corner-turn of history? This tale, I fear, has
            just
begun to unfurl. Don't be afraid. Have a tsing pao—else,
            coffee?
Stay with me, boss. Stay.'

Screw it, let's *dance*!
or do origami.

III

A mindless year of mindless action.

If the moon looks grey tonight, if you think she weeps,
            it is because
            you live on a reservation

If as you walked the houses rose on all sides threatening,
            it is because
            you live on a reservation

If the wind brings no news of love, if the villas are silent
            and empty, it is because
            you live on a reservation

The things you have to say, no one can say them for you
The places you have to go, no one can go there for you
The hills you have to burn, no one can burn them for you.

ROBIN S. NGANGOM

*Robin Singh Ngangom is an acclaimed poet and translator from Shillong.
His works have appeared in leading journals and anthologies. In his poems,
he confronts and responds to the challenges faced by the people of the
Northeast—from insurgency to state-sponsored terrorism and negligence;
from ethnic cleansing to corruption.*

Revolutionaries

Before they used terror when things were beginning to go out of control
and people showed aberrant behaviour, revolutionaries had asked poets
in their lower ranks to compose patriotic songs for a country which
cannot be found on any map. They would coerce nocturnal drivers of
interstate buses to play tapes of one-act plays which are designed to make
unsuspecting passengers weep with patriotic shame. I know this for real,
I grew up with revolutionaries. They had even asked me to translate a
press release over the phone.

Before he became a sharpshooter of a revolutionary band my
childhood friend smelled of straw and cattle, and then one day he bridled
a horse and rode it hard through a busy marketplace scattering customers
and traders alike like straw in a gale. I was told that he buried a pistol at
my cousin's backyard just before he went under the ground. Only after
he came over ground with the venerable title 'Teacher', because Chinese
masters trained him, did I meet him on the street and he smelled like
designer clothes. He now keeps himself occupied with work contracted
out by the public works department and once asked me if I were married.
He has two wives, one of them an actor.

Before the crackling fire of revolution which warms the hearts of
boys we sat in a circle and talked endlessly about oppressors and life
in the jungle. Friends brought stories of the ordained, who survived
on roots and eggshells. We looked at Che's hammock with longing and

even mixed his cocktail but had no idea when to dig a tank pit. When little books with a star and red skins appeared it was too late for me. I had fallen in love, and although it broke my heart, my father sent me to another land with gentle hills, so that I can read other books which will make me stand on my bourgeois feet.

II

When they are not around they become butts of fun. The roving story then was of a wastrel who went home after midnight because he had wasted all his time with his layabout friends around a fire one winter night. He had to cross a walled house guarded by fierce dogs to reach his home. When the owner of the house who was woken up by the dogs asked, 'Who goes there?' the wastrel found his wits and replied, 'In the service of the motherland' in a solemn voice as one would expect a revolutionary to reply.

When they became arbiters when someone's duck was stolen or two women were fighting over one man I stopped being furious with them.

You should write when you can still laugh at yourself and the world, before you give yourself up to despair.

PAUL LYNGDOH

Paul Lyngdoh is a bilingual poet from Meghalaya, and his poems have appeared in various journals, magazines and anthologies. His poems, stemming from lived experience of insurgency and militancy, are intensely political in nature.

For Sale

For sale
this battered autistic land with its lucre-laden earth,
our precious minerals, medicinal herbs, rare orchids
and trees and fields and waters,
all these, and all else.
For sale

our young, nubile girls, beautiful like the land itself:
we prefer men from the lowlands,
or even from across the seas,
with a modicum of integrity
(marital status, religion or caste no bar)
only those owning a potbelly now,
or in the near future, need apply.
For sale
our cumbersome anachronistic tribal roots
that have thrown a spanner in our wheels of progress,
in our march away from our own
and have become a constant source of embarrassment.
For sale
our pride, values, work culture,
our sense of shame, our collective conscience.
No contact number is needed.
Our agents are everywhere.
You can meet them in the streets.

M.B. MANOJ

M.B. Manoj is a Malayalam poet and thinker. He played a leading role in the Students' Federation of India and later worked extensively with the Maoist CPI (M-L) party. After 1991, with the decline of Maoist movements in India, he turned towards Ambedkarite-Buddhist thought.

The Children of the Forest Talk to Yesu

We are not the ones who whipped you;
we even gave our land to hang your pictures
and adorn your statues
that lean forward from the Cross.

Why, Yesu, instead of talking straight,
did you ever lead us along
this torturous path?

Tell us the truth:
aren't You really
our betrayer?

You might have lived for
your twelve disciples;
what is that to us?

Here, on this churchyard,
Your devotees screamed with the same tongue
that had offered you prayers:
'This man is a tribal.
Throw him to the police.'
Yesu,
for which side did you then pray?

Does he/she
have any way left to freely walk,
be clothed,
to fall asleep?

We kept moving away,
farther away, as they drove us,
to the very edges of the earth.
Yet you keep returning
as People's Man,
as newspapers,
as The Public and as old rag.

Today, watching the nakedness
of your fair body, yet unburied,
let us speak the unsullied words
of the confessors:
'We will not hand over this land
even if four hundred thousand dead
are laid to rest.
Praise be!'

Translated by K. Satchidanandan

Basudev Sunani

Basudev Sunani is one of the leading Dalit poets of Orissa. His poetry collections include Asprushya (Untouchable)*,* Karadi Haata *(Bamboo Shoots Market) and* Chhi *(Sneer). He is also the author of several critical essays and short stories. Through his brutal and direct poems he highlights the ignominious position of the Dalits without wallowing in self-pity.*

Body Purification

If you can, but once,
fix a bone in your tongue,
stand firm on the ground
and ask yourself:
Which Ganges can clean
my shit-smeared body?
How many stacks
of tulsi leaves
to sanctify me?
How many tons of sandalpaste
to deodorize my body?

How do I look
when I clean your sewer tank
taking out bucket loads
of faeces floating
on the water used
to clean your bottoms?

How do I look
when I swim breathless
in the water flowing
straight out of your latrines
to clean the sewer depths?

What do I look like when I pick up
the maggot-infested mangy dog
to clean the street
so that your car
can have a smooth drive?

Once,
just one time,
guide the pupils of your eyes
towards the sun
and look at me,
and then only can you measure
the strength you have
within you.

Wherever I am
reeks of bad odour.
Your nose curls;
your mouth retches;
your eyes squirm.
But when I'm sick for a day,
your streets stay unswept;
the latrines choke;
hospitals groan
as patients go on a rampage.

Ask your grey cells
just once to explain
what Smriti, Purana,
Intelligence, Education mean.
I'm the one who handles shit
and eats his rice
with the same fingers;
and I'm the one
who knows the difference
between shit and rice.
Yet, I don't know
what Smriti, Purana,
Intelligence and Education are.

I've seen it all—
worms excreted from your innards,
snot and drivel
expelled from your mouth,
blood congealing
on your deathbed.

You may scoff and sneer at me,
but when I'm not around,
I know you have
a mental breakdown.

Fix a bone in your tongue
and tell me for once—
how much Ganges, tulsi
and sandal are needed
to purify and sanctify
my shit-smeared body.

Translated by J.P. Das

JYOTI LANJEWAR

Jyoti Lanjewar (1950–2013) was a noted Marathi writer, critic, poet, feminist scholar and social activist. In her poems, she wrote about the atrocities and challenges the marginalized face in their struggle for survival.

Caves

Their inhuman atrocities have carved caves
in the rock of my heart
I must tread this forest with wary steps
Eyes fixed on the changing times
The tables have turned now
Protests spark
Now here
Now there.
I have been silent all these years
listening to the voice of right and wrong
But now I will fan the flames
of human rights
How did we ever reach to this place
this land which was never mother to us?
Which never gave us

even the life of cats and dogs?
I hold their unpardonable sins as witness
and turn, here and now.
a rebel.

Translated by Shanta Gokhale

KUSUM MEGHWAL

Kusum Meghwal is a prolific Dalit writer and activist from Rajasthan. Through her works, she has consistently challenged casteist society and promoted a feminist consciousness in the politics of caste.

The Curse of a Scavenger Woman

Choose each and every thakur,
give birth to their children
and then
send the fair-skinned children
with a broom
in each hand
to the houses of their fathers
to collect their excreta.

Translated by Akshaya Kumar

SHILPA PHADKE, SAMEERA KHAN AND SHILPA RANADE

Shilpa Phadke is assistant professor at the Centre for Media and Cultural Studies at the Tata Institute of Social Sciences, Mumbai. Sameera Khan is a Mumbai-based journalist and writer. Shilpa Ranade trained in architecture from CEPT, Ahmedabad and was associate editor of the South Asian volume in the series 'World Architecture 1900–2000: A Critical Mosaic'. The following is an excerpt from their book Why Loiter? *in which they argue that the act of loitering is an effective way for women to reclaim public spaces.*

Why Loiter? Radical Possibilities for Gendered Dissent

The Tyranny of Purpose: The Window-Shopper and the Street-Walker

'Whoever, in any public place or within sight of, and in such manner as to be seen or heard from, any public place...by words, gestures, wilful exposure of her person...tempts or endeavours to tempt, or attracts or endeavours to attract the attention of any person for the purpose of prostitution; or solicits or molests any person, or loiters or acts such manner as to cause obstruction or annoyance to persons residing nearby or passing by such public place or to offend against public decency, for the purpose of prostitution, shall be punishable on first conviction with imprisonment.'
—Immoral Traffic (Prevention) Act, (1988)
under the Indian Penal Code

The visible Mumbai woman accesses public space purposefully, she carries large bags, parcels and babies to illustrate her purpose, uses her cell phone as a barrier between herself and the world, and heads unerringly for the ladies compartment of the local train. Women's demeanour in public is almost always full of a sense of purpose; one rarely sees them sitting in a park, standing at a street corner smoking or simply watching the world go by as men might. Our research demonstrates that women's access to public space involves a complex series of strategies involving appropriate clothing, symbolic markers, bulky accessories, and contained body language designed to demonstrate that despite their apparent transgression into public space, they remain respectable women, essentially located in the private.

Manufacturing respectability primarily involves illustrating linkages to familial structures and masculine protection. Women often wear traditional markers and signifiers of matrimony, particularly Hindu matrimony, on their bodies to underscore their connection to private spaces.[1] In fact sometimes unmarried women also wear them in order to appear more respectable. Women are also required to reflect respectability in the contained way in which they hold their bodies such as occupying the least possible space in public transport.[2]

Since education and employment are legitimate reasons to be in public space, women in Mumbai often use their identity as students or workers in order to enhance access to public space. Women also legitimize their presence in public space by exploiting acceptable notions of femininity that connect them to motherhood and religion. In our mapping of a large public playground in the mill-district of Mumbai, for example, we found that the only time women were found 'hanging out' was around the time the school, flanking the playground, ends for the day. These are mothers, many of whom come much before school closes to spend some 'official' time in public space with friends.

Similarly, older Hindu women often form bhajan mandalis (groups that chant devotional songs) and gather in public parks. The celebration of festivals like Ganeshotsav, Navratri and the month of Ramzan/ Ramadan, as also visits to temples sometimes late in the night (such as to Mumbai's famous Siddhi Vinayak Temple), offer women opportunities to access the celebratory public outside of their everyday lives. Some of these women acknowledge meeting friends for dinner before heading out to join the temple queue. These occasions offer spaces for momentary subversion and pleasure in the public that might otherwise be denied to them. At the same time, these spaces continue to be circumscribed by the performance of normative femininity.

Woman's fundamental out-of-placeness in public space is maintained through the hegemonic discourse which sets up an opposition between the 'good' private woman and the 'bad' public woman.[3] This binary dominates the perception of all women in public space; being in public without a purpose—that is, loitering—would automatically mark a woman as belonging to the latter category.[4]

There are however two kinds of women in Mumbai who do appear in public space without an apparent purpose; the window-shopper and the street-walker. The former, as consumer, embodies the raison d'être of the global city. The latter is there for work, but is not just undesirable but also illegitimate. In reality, neither is there without purpose, for both shopping and sex-work are productive activities.[5] Despite this apparent similarity the two are perceived very differently.

In a consumption-driven economy, shopping is an act that is both respectable and respected. The buyer therefore occupies a very privileged position. In our research on Mumbai we found that the spaces where women, especially middle-class women, are visible are inevitably spaces of consumption: shopping malls, coffee shops, lounge bars, nightclubs and discos. While many women articulate pleasure in these spaces, nonetheless, access to spaces of consumption demands a demonstration of the capacity to buy, and obvious, if unspoken, codes of dress and conduct underwrite women's presence there. Moreover, while most of these spaces masquerade as public spaces, they are actually private spaces. Women's presence in these spaces thus remains circumscribed and fails to adequately challenge the hegemonic narrative of the public/private binary.

The tyranny of manufacturing purpose then regulates women's access to the public. In our research mapping the paths of women and men in Nariman Point (a business district) in Mumbai, we observed that during lunchtime, most women who come down from their offices to get lunch (relatively few compared to men) go straight to the vendor, pick up their food and head back inside. Men on the other hand will dawdle outside, not only eating at the stalls but often hanging around on the street, before and after eating (Ranade 2007).

Failing in an adequate demonstration of purpose might leave the woman open to conjecture and the assumption that she is soliciting. Ironically, under the provisions of Indian law, sex-work is not illegal, but soliciting in public is, clearly demonstrating the desire for neat public/private boundaries and a conservative morality that would like to keep all sexual activities indoors.[6]

Sex-workers are seen to be engaging in work that is inherently risky and non-respectable and are therefore seen to be outside the purview of protection available to other women. Consider the Abhishek Kasliwal case in March 2006, in Mumbai, when a woman accused Kasliwal, a wealthy businessman, of repeatedly raping her inside his car. The media showed great interest in the case until police investigations suggested that the woman was probably a sex-worker who had been sexually assaulted in the process of selling sex. The tone of the reportage and investigation then changed. Once the victim was cast as a sex-worker she was seen unworthy of protection from a violent sexual assault and merited little media and police attention.

The public woman is not so much directly a threat to 'good' women as much as a warning to them of the consequences of violating the rules, namely, if they break the rules, they are no longer deemed worthy of 'protection' from society. In fact, society is perceived to be in need of protection from the risk of the contamination that sex-workers present (Phadke 2005).

The main cause for the anxiety posed by the presence of sex-workers in public space is the potential for confusion in distinguishing the respectable women from the unrespectable. To offer an example of how this plays out, in May 2006, the local police in an upmarket suburb of north-western Mumbai alleged that they had received complaints that women sex-workers were conducting 'business' by fixing up clients in the open seating spaces outside some popular neighbourhood coffee shops. As a result, the police prohibited the coffee shops from serving customers in the open yards outside their restaurants. Women patrons, in particular, were discouraged from sitting out. The connotation was clear: we are not sure which women are soliciting in such spaces and defiling them, so we shall ban all women from using these spaces.

All women are compelled to carry the burden of this anxiety when accessing public space. In using the demonstration of respectability as a strategy to access public space, women are not only circumscribed by the discourse of the public/private binary but go on to reinscribe it. For all women to be able to access public space unconditionally, we first need to dismantle the discourse of respectability.

The right to public space (rather than conditional access) can only come when all women can walk the streets without being compelled to demonstrate purpose or respectability, without being categorized into public or private women.[7] What would change if women preferred to exercise a right to public space rather than demand provisional access, or demanded pleasure without rationale or access without boundaries, or chose to *loiter*?

Loitering: Pleasure without Purpose?

As we collectively produce our cities, so we collectively produce ourselves. ...[If] we accept that 'society is made and imagined', then we can also believe that it can be 'remade and reimagined'.

—Harvey (2000, p 159)

When one thinks of people loitering in Mumbai, the image it conjures up is of messy, difficult to navigate street corners, the smell of low-cost tobacco, the sight of paan (betel nut) stains, the sound of boiling tea and unmodulated male voices. Etched into our imaginations is the vision of the unwashed male masses huddled together, unmistakably lower-class in attire and demeanour. Underlying this image is deep class prejudice.

Like tapori, lukkha, lafanga, vella, bekaar are other Indian terms used to describe a kind of purposelessness akin to loitering. They are all uncomplimentary terms suggesting not just the lack of employment but also the unease that the loiterer is potentially up to no good. Loitering then, as suggested in our discussion of the Mumbai tapori, is read as a suspicious performance of non-productivity. Women are not even in the reckoning since the assumption is that 'even good men don't loiter'.

Our intention [...] is to rethink the meanings implicit in loitering and to recast it not as an act of loss of choice but in fact as the very opposite, as an act of agency and desire. When we say loitering we mean not doing anything that has an apparent purpose, or as the dictionary definition suggests, 'to linger aimlessly'. Loitering unlike flânerie or tapori-giri is not attached to an identity. Its engagement with the city is not voyeuristic but rather organic and visceral for, unlike voyeurism, loitering implicates the loiterer as actor rather than surveyor. Loitering is an act one can indulge in without professing allegiance to any particular group, morality or ideology. It is a process that is temporally present. You are a loiterer only while you are loitering.

Loitering is fundamentally a voluntary act undertaken for pure self-gratification; it's not forced and has no visible productivity. Loitering can have no purpose other than pleasure. Pleasure which is not linked to consumption has the power to challenge the unspoken notion that only those who can afford it are entitled to pleasure, thus ensuring that marginal citizens are kept in their place. The possibility of a pleasure that does not cost anything and at the same time brings the 'undesirables' out into the streets making them visible, threatens to undermine established notions of urban social order.

This idea of apparent urban anarchy might be threatening to the maintenance of the status quo but for women it represents the possibility of redefining the terms of their access to public space, not as clients seeking protection but as citizens claiming their rights.

Imagine varied street corners full of women sitting around talking, strolling, feeding children, exchanging recipes and books or planning the neighbourhood festival. Imagine street corners full of young women watching the world go by as they sip tea and discuss politics, soap operas and the latest financial budget. Imagine street corners full of older women contemplating the state of the world and reminiscing about their lives. Imagine street corners full of female domestic workers planning their next strike for a raise in minimum wage. *If one can imagine all of this, one can imagine a radically altered city.*

We articulate four propositions to suggest exactly how loitering might succeed where other strategies fail, in creating a more inclusive city.

1. *Loitering holds the possibilities of disrupting the everyday performances of normative respectable femininity in public space through which an oppressive gender-space formation is maintained.*

To fully recognize the extent of these possibilities, it is essential to view gendered space as a constant *process* of *becoming*; gender as something we *do* rather than something we *are* (Ainley 1998). In doing so, we draw on the conception of gender as being a 'regulatory fiction' in society (Butler 1990) and space as being a social practice (Lefebvre 1991); both, in effect, being discursive formations or 'practices that systematically form the objects of which they speak' (Foucault 1972). When we see hegemonic gender-space as something that is not just contested but also constantly being *brought into being* through the everyday actions of men and women in space, rather than something women are *subjected to* by external totalitarian forces, it allows us to imagine possibilities of interrupting and opening up gaps in the relentless replication of unequal gender formations; gaps within which we can re-imagine a rightful place for women in the city.

One might therefore propose loitering as an act that has the possibility to allow the subject to renegotiate sedimented roles, to contest societal and personal expectations, and to enable interventions that fulfil and subvert definitional 'practices' of being. In this context, then, the errant, arbitrary, circuitous routes of the loiterer mark out a kinetic map of pleasure.

In the dialectical relationship between social structure and space, it is the body that becomes the medium through which socio-spatial formations are not just experienced, but produced, reproduced, represented and transformed. Bodies that challenge hegemonic notions of masculinity and femininity, or transgress the boundaries of appropriateness, pose a threat to the 'normalized' social order. Many lesbian women in our discussions articulated that when they chose to dress in less feminine, more 'butch' attire, they encountered hostility—ranging from staring to loud comments and occasionally attempts to physically evict them—mostly in all-women spaces like the ladies compartments of trains and women's toilets.

In a relative sense the female body, located 'properly' in the private space of the home, has the greatest potential to disrupt the structures of power in public space. The bubble of private respectability that women are expected to cloak themselves in cannot withstand the act of loitering because the two are based on contradictory imperatives—the former, one of maintaining privacy even in the public and the latter, that of taking pleasure in the public for its own sake. The presence of the loitering female body can then challenge the hegemonic discourse of gendered public space by reconstructing the connotative chains of association that connect loitering, respectability and normative femininity. This has the capacity to create a new set of relationships within and with public space through the ensemble of practices associated with women; relationships, which have the power to not just disrupt the dominant order in public space but to have a more long-term impact on how space itself is visualized.

The subversive potential of a visceral and 'subjective' engagement with the city has been explored by social thinkers starting from the second half of the twentieth century, ostensibly in reaction to the totalitarian master narratives that characterized the early part of the century. The potential in loitering might be visualized as an extension of the power of walking itself so eloquently imagined by de Certeau (1984) whose vision of walking as being simultaneously an organic act of belonging and a subversive engagement with the city informs our idea of loitering. For de Certeau, as people walk they reinscribe the city again and again, often in defiance of established patterns of urban order, each time differently making new meanings. Walking, according to him, is fundamentally an act of 'enunciation' through which the city, and in effect, social order is personalized, and in the process, altered.[8] Similarly, Scalway (2001) suggests that walking, which is an act of negotiation when it incorporates regard for the 'other', creates the possibility of meaningful citizenship right there on the streets.

In a variety of languages the terms used for transgressive women in public space are related to the act of being on the streets without purpose—strolling, roaming, wandering, straying, rambling—all terms that Solnit (2000) points out suggest that women's travel is invariably sexual or that their sexuality is inevitably transgressive when it travels.[9] Since it is street-walking—and the need to draw boundaries, to banish the ambiguities between street-walkers and women walking the street—that is the greatest source of anxiety in relation to public space, loitering in public space, not as respectable virtuous women but as citizens, transforms the very nature of engagement making the case that both the woman in the street and the street-walker are making exactly the same claim to space.

It is precisely because loitering is an embodied practice that seeks to transform the everyday acts of walking and looking in the city from acts that are means to an end to acts that are meaningful in themselves, that loitering becomes a compelling tool for change, allowing us to re-imagine the gendered experience of city spaces.

2. *Loitering encompasses a politics of visibility that is different from the subterfuges that women engage in to access the city anonymously.*

Women have often sought to access the pleasures of public city spaces by slipping into the city, merging with the crowd and not drawing attention to themselves. Scholars such as Wilson (1991) and Young (1995) suggest that large cities offer women some access to public space through anonymity.[10] At the same time, this brings with it only temporary and invisibilized access. Wilson also points out that, within the heterosexual discourse, the male gaze is focused largely on young and therefore sexually desirable women. It is women who are old or eschew the 'masquerade of womanliness' who could potentially become invisible, an act that brings a 'kind of negative freedom; but also a kind of social extinction' (2001:93). Garber (2000) also underscores the limitations of the liberating potential of anonymity, arguing that even for women, whose sexed identity is often obviously visible, the capacity to claim space rests on political organization and the ability to make the transition from invisibility to identity. For although in the short term, anonymity may be the obvious choice for women to enhance access to public space, the potential longer term risk of seeking anonymity could well mean the loss of substantive freedom and eventually a kind of political death wherein women forever remain outsiders to public space (Phadke 2005).

Expanding access through anonymity is not the same as staking a claim as citizens and will not in any way change women's location in or relationship to public space. Loitering, on the other hand, might often be unobtrusive but it is far from invisible. This means that the loiterer might sometimes merge into a crowd and at other times stand out. The loiterer is often unidentified but not anonymous. In fact, by the very act of doing nothing in public space, the loiterer demands identification. Loitering then has the potential to challenge gendered restrictions of access to public space by its very visibility.

3. *Loitering has the capacity to challenge the new global order of the city by compelling an engagement with the idea that the right to public spaces is a core component of citizenship.*

Urban scholars studying cities across the industrial and developing world have argued that people's access to public space and its resources reflects various hierarchies and patterns of discrimination. Access to public space is often sacrificed at the altar of safeguarding 'law and order'. Safety and order are prized in the new global city, and both are presented as the antithesis of what is embodied, literally and metaphorically, by the poor: their slums are unsanitary, their homes makeshift, their bodies unhygienic, and their very existence a source of threat not just to the middle classes but to the city itself. However, as historical evidence shows, attempts to cleanse and sanitize cities have often had the opposite effect of making cities even more fraught, violent and unsafe (Appadurai 2000, Davis 1990, 1992, Mitchell 2003).

The global claims of Mumbai are still new and fragile and therefore to be guarded zealously. One of the ways these claims can be buttressed is by clear definition of spaces as being inside-outside; public-private; recreational-commercial.[11] Loitering disrupts this imagined order of the global city. The act of loitering, in its very lack of structure, renders a space simultaneously inside and outside; public and private; recreational and commercial, rendering it in a constant state of liminality or transition. We submit that it is precisely this ambiguity that makes loitering potentially liberating. The very power of the liminal state lies in its lack of definition, in its defiance of being named. Loitering mocks the authority of any one group of people to determine the future of the city by speaking with visceral bodies and through the indeterminate nature of the identity of the loiterer.

The presence of the loiterer acts to rupture the controlled socio-cultural order of the global city by refusing to conform to desired forms of movement and location, instead creating alternate maps of movement, and thus new kinds of everyday interaction. It thwarts the desire for clean lines and structured spaces by inserting the ostensibly private into the obviously public. The liminality of loitering is seen as an act of contamination, defiling space. Loitering is a reminder of what is perceived as the lowest common denominator of the local and thus is a threat to the desired image of a global city: sanitized, glamorous and homogenous. Loitering then as a subversive activity has the potential to raise questions not just of 'desirable image' but also of citizenship: Who owns the city? Who can access city public spaces as a right?

In a time when the performance of a consumerist hyper-productivity is becoming deeply significant in global-aspirational Mumbai, the *choice* to demonstrate non-productivity can be profoundly unsettling. Loitering is a threat to the global order of production in that people are visibly doing nothing. It disrupts the image of the desirable productive body—taut, vigorous, purposeful—moving precisely towards the 'greater global good'.

Loitering is also a threat to the desired visibility of capitalist consumption in that there is no recognizable product; if a beverage is being consumed it is likely to be unbranded roadside cutting chai (three-quarter-cup tea). Loitering, in its defiant demonstration of lack of purpose, immediately refutes the possibility of being co-opted within global practices of consumerist inclusion.

4. *Finally, loitering makes possible the dream of an inclusive citizenship by disrupting existent hierarchies and refusing to view the claims of one group against the claims of another.*

Young (1995) suggests that the ideal of city life is not communities, for communities by their very nature are exclusive, but a vision of social relations as affirming group difference which would allow for different groups to dwell together in the city without forming a community. She argues that reactions to city life that call for local, decentralized, autonomous communities reproduce the problems of exclusion. Instead, Young imagines a city life premised on difference that allows groups and individuals to overlap without becoming homogenous.

The kind of exclusion that Young suggests is seen clearly in the local citizens' groups in Mumbai which are often founded on a corporate vision for the city built around zoning, segregation and finally exclusion.[12]

Building on Young's ideas, we would like to propose that the act of loitering has the potential to make such a vision of diverse city life possible. Our understanding of loitering in public space is based on the right of each individual, irrespective of their group affiliations, to take pleasure in the city as an act of claim and belonging. This is, however, not a notion that is located in a crude understanding of capitalism where each individual maximizes her pleasure in the city leading to the greater pleasure of society. Loitering is an act that could be solitary or in groups. At no point do we perceive the individual as divorced from her multiple locations and identities.

When we ask to loiter then, the intent is to rehabilitate this act of hanging out without purpose not just for women, but for all marginal groups. The celebration of loitering envisages an inclusive city where people have a right to city public spaces, creating the possibility for all to stake a claim not just to the property they own, nor to use the ownership of property as grounds for being more equal citizens, but to claim undifferentiated rights to public space.

This is the potential we see when we seek to reclaim the act of loitering as an act of the most basic citizenship. Here, we not only see citizenship as being linked to cities rather than nations (Holston and Appadurai 1996) but also understand it, not as an *a priori* position sanctioned by the state or collective agreement, but as a space to be claimed through performance (Donald 1999).[13] So when we ask to loiter then, we see loitering as a performance with the capacity to enable a subjectivity that can claim the position of a 'legitimate citizen'. This enactment of citizenship through loitering is further premised on the quest for pleasure, which, as suggested earlier, has the potential of being both non-divisive and inclusive.

It is only when the city belongs to everyone that it can ever belong to all women. The unconditional claim to public space will only be possible when all women and all men can walk the streets without being compelled to demonstrate purpose or respectability, for women's access to public space is fundamentally linked to the access of all citizens. Equally crucially, we feel the litmus test of this right to public space is the right to loiter, especially for women across classes. Loiter without purpose and meaning. Loiter without being asked what time of the day it was, why we were there, what we were wearing and whom we were with.

Notes

1. These symbols of matrimony include the mangalsutra, sindhoor and chooda, all meant to be worn by Indian Hindu women with some regional variations across the country. Sindhoor is the red vermillion powder smeared in the parting of one's hair, mangalsutra is the necklace of black and gold beads, and chooda refers to the red and white bangles worn on the arms.

2. For a discussion on the containment of women's bodies, see Bartky 1990, Butler 1990, Young 1990.

3. For more on the public/private women debate see Mitchell 2000, Rose 1993, Walkowitz 1992, Wilson 1991, 2001.

4. The control of the presence of 'respectable' women in public space is written into the law through a time regulation in the Factories Act of 1948 in India, which made it illegal for women to be employed/work between 7 p.m. and 6 a.m. As recently as 2003, the government proposed an amendment to this Act which would provide flexibility in the employment of women during night-shifts. This was done largely in response to the needs of new globally linked businesses like the software industry and call-centres.

5. For a discussion of women and consumption, see Friedberg 1993, Domosh and Seager 2001, McRobbie 1997, Morris 2000, Wilson 2001, Wolff 1985. For a discussion of sex-work and its implications for public space, see Nord 1995, Walkowitz 1992, Wilson 1991.

6. This is visible even when couples in public space are booked for obscene behaviour and fined. There has been a visible increase in the policing of couples in parks and on promenades in Mumbai. Couples are often censured for holding hands, and ostensibly threatening the moral fibre of Indian society. Some years ago in the Five Gardens area of Dadar, all park benches were made into single-seaters by the local corporation [official] to discourage couples from engaging in what he termed as 'indecent behaviour'.

7. We are well aware of the limitations of using the discourse of rights when we make a case for loitering. The feminist critique of rights as being individualistic, reifying liberalism and often reflecting existing hierarchies of all kinds and thus limiting the terms of the debate, is both valid and valuable. At the same time, the language of rights is also a powerful tool to promote greater inclusion in quest of a more egalitarian citizenship. In this article, we use the terminology of rights largely because of the absence of another way of expressing the entitlement of people to loiter. The language of rights, because of its widespread acceptance, offers a space, however inadequate, to make this claim.

8. Besides de Certeau, ideas of the Situationist Internationale (SI) continue to influence attempts to repersonalize the practice of urbanism.

9. While conducting a pedagogic exercise on where women would 'wait' for a friend on the street we find that most women sought the legitimacy of bus-stops where they might pretend to be commuters, for waiting, particularly at street corners, was an act synonymous with soliciting.

10. When we say anonymity here we refer to spatial and social elements of large and populous cities that allow for people to remain strangers to each other. For instance, some women in Baiganwadi, a slum in north-east Mumbai, pointed out that their own street was both a familiar and safe space but they still had to behave themselves. The road outside the slum was an intermediate space where they might be recognized, a space many of them described as threatening. Further beyond in the city was the space where they were anonymous, where they often felt the greatest degree of freedom. While anonymity does allow them to be in public space it does little to address the fact that each time they or women elsewhere in the city go out, particularly at night, the masquerade has to begin anew. Furthermore, for women, being intimately part of a homogenous community group often results in greater surveillance and restriction of their movements (Khan 2007, Phadke 2007). Our research suggests that women living in neighbourhoods peopled by their own communities often felt the most restricted while those women who were individual migrants from other towns and cities felt the greatest degree of freedom. This is interesting considering that women living on their own in the city have the least access to support structures that would enable them to produce safety for themselves.

11. The lack of modernist planning in Mumbai, where residential and commercial spaces are mixed, has been an important factor in making public spaces in the city more accessible to women. Our mapping of spaces demonstrated clearly that the number of women in one of the city's few business districts, Nariman Point, drops substantially before and after work hours as compared to other mixed-use areas like Chembur and Kalachowki.

12. In an attempt to cleanse and beautify city neighbourhoods and control local open spaces, middle-class residents groups have sprung up all over Mumbai. In many cases these are known as Advanced Locality Management or ALMs, which is a concept of citizen's involvement with local governance. These often tend to focus on 'beautifying' their neighbourhoods by getting rid of hawkers or slum encroachments.

13. Donald (1999) argues that the question of personhood is central to the definition of citizenship, and this personhood being historically contingent, citizenship is in perennial deferral. Being a citizen, then is not the occupation of a universal or institutionalized position but is a performance.

References

Ainley, Rosa (1998) 'Introduction' in Rosa Ainley (ed.) *New Frontiers of Space Bodies and Gender*, Routledge, London, pp. xiii–xvii.

Appadurai, Arjun (2000) 'Spectral Housing and Urban Cleansing: Notes on Millennial Mumbai', *Public Culture*, Vol. 12, No. 3, pp. 627–651.

Butler, Judith (1990) *Gender Trouble: Feminism and the Subversion of Identity*, Routledge, London.

Davis, Mike (1990) *City of Quartz: Excavating the Future in Los Angeles*, Verso, New York.

——— (1992) 'Fortress Los Angeles: The Militarization of Urban Space', in Michael Sorokin (ed.), *Variations on a Theme Park: The New American City and the End of Public Space*, Hill and Wang, New York, pp. 154–180.

De Certeau, Michel (1984) *The Practice of Everyday Life*, University of California Press, Berkeley.

Donald, James (1999) *Imagining the Modern City*, University of Minnesota Press, Minneapolis.

Foucault, Michel (1972) *The Archaeology of Knowledge*, translated by A. M. Sheridan Smith. Tavistock, London.

Garber, Judith A. (2000) '"Not Named or Identified": Politics and the Search for Anonymity in the City' in Kristine B. Miranna and Alma H. Young (eds), *Gendering the City: Women, Boundaries and Visions of Urban Life*, Rowman and Littlefield, Lanham, pp. 19–40.

Harvey, David (2000) *Spaces of Hope*, University of Edinburgh Press, Edinburgh.

Holston, James and Arjun Appadurai (1996) 'Cities and Citizenship', *Public Culture*, Vol. 8, No. 2, pp. 187–204.

Khan, Sameera (2007) 'Negotiating the Mohalla: Exclusion, Identity and Muslim Women in Mumbai', Review of Women's Studies, *Economic and Political Weekly*, Vol. 42, No. 17, pp. 1527–1533.

Lefebvre, Henri (1991) *The Production of Space*, Blackwell, Oxford.

Mitchell, Don. (2000) *Cultural Geography: A Critical Introduction*, Blackwell, Oxford, pp. 201–223.

——— (2003) *The Right to the City: Social Justice and the Fight for Public Space*, Guilford, New York.

Phadke, Shilpa (2005) 'You Can Be Lonely in a Crowd: The Production of Safety in Mumbai', *Indian Journal of Gender Studies*, Vol. 12, No. 1, pp. 41–62.

——— (2007) 'Dangerous Liaisons: Women and Men; Risk and Reputation in Mumbai', Review of Women's Studies, *Economic and Political Weekly*, Vol. 42, No. 17, pp. 1510–1518.

Phadke, Shilpa, Sameera Khan and Shilpa Ranade (2006) *Women in Public: Safety in Mumbai*. Unpublished Report submitted to the Indo-Dutch Programme on Alternatives in Development (IDPAD).

Ranade, Shilpa (2007) 'The Way She Moves: Mapping the Everyday Production of Gender-Space', Review of Women's Studies, *Economic and Political Weekly*, Vol. 42, No. 17, pp. 1519–1526.

Scalway, Helen (2001) 'The Contemporary Flâneuse—Exploring Strategies for the Drifter in a Feminine Mode', *The Journal of Psychogeography and Urban Research*, Vol. 1, No. 1. http://www.psychogeography.co.uk/contemporary_flâneuse.html. (accessed in June 2003).

Solnit, Rebecca (2000) *Wanderlust: A History of Walking*, Penguin, New York.

Walkowitz, Judith (1992) *City of Dreadful Delight: Narratives of Sexual Danger in Late-Victorian London*, University of Chicago Press, Chicago.

Wilson, Elizabeth (1991) *The Sphinx in the City: Urban Life, the Control of Disorder and Women*, University of California Press, Berkeley.

——— (2001) 'The Invisible Flâneur' and 'The Invisible Flâneur: Afterword' *The Contradictions of Culture: Cities, Culture, Women*, Sage, London, pp. 72–94.

Young, Iris Marion (1990) 'Throwing Like a Girl: A Phenomenology of Feminine Body Comportment, Motility and Spatiality' in *Throwing Like a Girl and Other Essays in Feminist Philosophy and Social Theory*, Indiana Univ. Press, Bloomington, pp. 141–159.

——— (1995) 'City Life and Difference' in Philip Kasinitz (ed.), *Metropolis: Center and Symbol of Our Times*, New York University Press, New York, pp. 250–270.

NABANEETA DEV SEN

Nabaneeta Dev Sen is an eminent poet and writer in Bengali. She received the Sahitya Akademi Award in 1999 and the Padmashree 2000. Although she mainly writes about patriarchy and women's role in post-Independence India, she has also written on communalism and the Naxalite movement.

Festival

The moment one man comes out on the street,
    a stone in his hand
Two of us stand up to him with brickbats
The moment a man falls, bloodied,
Bright-eyed we lay down seven more, as bloody
The gentle souls who once rushed to take care of the wounded

Now stand at their balconies, clapping, cheering
Someone's wife has been taken away in the dead of night?
Come, let's drag all the women from their village,
    stripped naked, in broad daylight
Some bastard has gouged out a boy's eye?
We'll rip out the eyes of the whole nation.

Now we establish a new Rakhi festival
We've fixed up a wonderful programme for Brother's Day
With a heavy, spiked iron ball dangling from
    An invisible chain
We shall beat our breasts
And pierce the three worlds every waking moment
With the soundless cry of the soul
Ha bhai re, ho bhai re[1]...
Put your ear to the anthill[2] And you shall hear that cry...

Translated by Pratik Kanjilal

Notes

1. Allusion to Muharram
2. Reference to the penance of Valmiki, who composed *Ramayana*

DAYAMANI BARLA

Dayamani Barla is a journalist turned activist from Jharkhand. Barla is at the forefront of the Adivasi Mulvasi Astitva Raksha Manch, a people's movement that unites thousands of Adivasis, Dalits and farmers across Jharkhand. In the past decade, she has trekked from village to village, alerting those who stand to be displaced by a steel plant and protesting against dams on the Koel and Kari rivers.

Acceptance Speech for the Ellen L. Lutz Indigenous Rights Award, 2013

First of all I want to thank you—especially Cultural Survival—for honouring me with Ellen L. Lutz Indigenous Rights Award. In every nook and corner of this world—not just in India—global capitalism today is engaged in every possible effort to grab water, forests, land and rivers, which are actually a collective legacy of mankind. On the other hand, in order to protect our precious heritage of water, forests and land—we are involved in a struggle with a pledge from every single village of our land that we will not let go of even an inch of our ancestors' land.

... Following the path shown by our great hero Birsa Munda, another revolt is shaping today to defend Adivasi values, against displacement and to protect our water, forest, land, socio-linguistic and historical identity. I want to place Adivasi consciousness and culture within the periphery of these points:

- Collective lifestyle
- Communal ownership of natural resources
- Cooperative spirit
- Gender equality
- Collective decision and implementation in democracy

This is our core thinking. The place where I come from, Adivasis have struggled there for nearly 300 years and sacrificed their lives in thousands. Even today they are struggling and sacrificing their lives. I am also a humble part of this struggle and I am immensely happy for that.

Great revolutionaries such as Baba Tilka Manjhi, Binray-Sindray, Sidhu-Kanhu, Chand-Bhairav, Phula-Jhano, Birsa Munda, Gaya Munda became martyrs for these very values I described above. And in our times, inspired by these great revolutionaries, we are struggling again not only to save nature and its resources, our society, language and culture but also to create a new society.

The indigenous people of Jharkhand, Dalits and working masses have a father-son relationship with nature. Their social, linguistic, cultural, religious, economic and historical existence continues to live in water, forest and land. These communities will exist so long as they are linked with water, forest and land. When Adivasis and indigenous society get displaced from their land, forests and water, they not only get displaced from their dwellings and livelihood but also from their social values, language and culture, economy and history. If we look at the global history of indigenous people, it becomes clear that indigenous communities remain alive only in those places where there is water, forest and land, mountains and waterfalls. Indigenous society is a part and parcel of nature. By separating them, we can neither conceive of Adivasi-indigenous society nor of forests, rivers, waterfalls and mountains. Just as a fish cannot remain without water, likewise, indigenous society cannot live without its natural heritage.

Taking cognizance of this truth, after India's independence, when the authors of the Constitution were giving legal framework to the rights of its peoples, Adivasi-dominated areas were given a special status in the 5th and 6th Schedule of the Constitution. In the 5th Schedule, a legal right has been granted that every Village Council (Gram Sabha) in a village will control and utilize natural resources, forests, water and land falling within their jurisdiction according to their traditional communal rights. Whenever the government or any agency wants to acquire any land for developmental purposes, it cannot be acquired without the assent of the local Gram Sabha or Village Council.

Jharkhand is a tribal dominated state. History is a witness that this area was replete with pristine forests. Indigenous communities fought with tigers and bears, snakes and scorpions to make it habitable. It is for this reason that the indigenous tribal communities were given a special right related to land—forest protection for inhabiting this land under Chhota Nagpur Tenancy (CNT) Act 1908 and Santhal Pargana Tenancy Act. Under CNT Act, no outside agency can acquire indigenous communities' land. But today, the government, corporate entities, land mafias in collusion with government's anti-Adivasi and anti-farmer policies and police-bureaucratic nexus are violating this law and indigenous Adivasi farmers are being evicted and rendered landless.

The government has been acquiring land arbitrarily wherever it fancies under the Land Acquisition Act 1894. It does not respect even those provisions of the law which are in public interest. The provisions which were in the interest of indigenous tribal communities are being amended to benefit private companies. For this very reason, in the post-Independence period, more than 20 million indigenous tribals have been displaced from Jharkhand state. Where are these displaced persons? In what condition are they? The government or the political parties do not care two hoots. The displaced Adivasi communities have today lost their identity. Their social values and collective existence stands shattered. Today, neither do they have a language nor a culture.

Despite legal protections, such as the CNT Act 1908 and Santhal Pargana Tenancy Act, and the 5th Schedule and 6th Schedule provisions in the Constitution, the state government is violating them with impunity and illegally acquiring the lands, forests, rivers and mountains of indigenous tribal communities. At the same time, it is handing them over to corporate entities. The government is illegally snatching the forests, fertile agricultural lands and water sources of indigenous farmers after signing Memorandums of Understanding (MOU) with mining companies. Wherever the government is acquiring land in the name of development or for companies or factories or for mining, it is not seeking permission of either the owner or the villagers or the Village Councils. Neither is it seeking assent of the villagers. Wherever it feels like acquiring land, it is doing so using violence and terror using the police.

After the formation of the Jharkhand State, within twelve years, the state government has signed MOU's with 104 corporates. Out of these, 98 per cent are mining companies. Each and every company wants dam for water, land for plant, land for transportation, urbanization and market for their coal, iron ore, bauxite and mica mines.

If the government gives land for mining to all companies, Jharkhand will lose its environment and the land will become infertile. In ten years, four times more population will get displaced from its habitat and livelihood than the entire displaced populations since Independence.

Human rights are being attacked left, right and centre. In the entire Jharkhand state, mass movements are going on for protection of water, forests, land and environment. All through the country, farmers are today living under the shadow of terror of displacement. The welfare state is dubbing them as anti-social elements, extremists and Maoists and implicating them in dozens of false cases and packing them off to jails.

Our ancestors had always challenged the culture of domination since the indigenous people believe in cultural diversity and pluralism. We want a new society which respects all cultures. These days, in our country, a political campaign is going on for cultural supremacy at full speed. It has threatened religious and cultural minorities in the name of holistic unitary cultural nationalism. In past twenty years, Indian democracy has witnessed the participation of have-nots as much as attacks by cultural nationalists. In such an atmosphere, so as to save secular India, the importance of pluralistic Adivasi cultural viewpoint increases significantly. Our entire Indian subcontinent is waging a decisive battle between liberalism and fanaticism. Since this is the same era in which old feudal values are being made the basis for promoting neo-liberalism. This is a strange irony. In past two decades, we have witnessed big corporate control over our forests, land, water, rivers and seas. We are also witnessing how religious, communal passions are being abused to strengthen the new economic paradigm. But I am grateful to all those who are struggling incessantly against this phenomenon and giving a voice to the dreams sowed by indigenous ancestors and the freedom fighters. It is possible to create a society in harmony with these dreams—a society which has no place for anyone's domination.

The struggles for preservation of water, forests, land and collective ownership of communities over natural resources are inspired by these very dreams. In last twenty years, mass movements have not been weakened by the corporate loot and acts in their defence. On the contrary, the have-nots are coming together in strength on a common platform. When our state of Jharkhand came into existence after a hundred-year struggle, the forests danced in joy and the sound of the Mander (a musical instrument) reverberated in the air. But our happiness proved to be a momentary one. Barely within a few months of our state's formation, the peaceful movement which was struggling to keep the flow of Koel and Karo rivers for thirty years, was now riddled with bullets ordered by the official bureaucracy.

Koel and Karo are not just rivers—they are a cultural identity. They are also a fundamental basis of our livelihoods. When eight Adivasis and one indigenous person were martyred on 2 February 2001, we realized that the state whose foundation stone was laid on 15 November 2000 is not for us. And we saw how we were challenged while playing with our existence and for exploitation and loot of our natural resources. Let me say that the tribals and indigenous people of Jharkhand fully accepted the challenge put forth by the government and the corporates; and the slogan of 'We will not give an inch of our land' started reverberating across the 33,000 villages of Jharkhand. This voice was eloquently raised by various mass organizations and Adivasi indigenous organizations.

With the commissioning of Koel-Karo project, nearly 2,50,000 indigenous people and tribals would have got displaced. 55,000 acres of agricultural land would have got submerged. 27,000 acres of forests too would have submerged. A sacred religious site, Sarna Sasan Diri, worshipped by some eighty tribal communities would have gone under water.

In Kathikud block of Dumka district of Jharkhand, RPG Group started seizing land for coal mines. The villagers did not want to give land for coal mining. For years, the villagers have been on the path of struggle to save their lands and forests. Apart from coal mining, the company wanted to set up a plant for producing electricity. The villagers organized rallies against the forcible acquiring of their lands. The police fired on the rally—one comrade died on the spot and dozens were injured. Later another injured comrade died. Yet another became disabled and one comrade lost both his eyes permanently.

The government implicated the leader of this movement Muni Hansda and his comrades for being extremists. Muni Hansda and his comrades were thrown in jail for seven months.

In 2003–04, in Pachuwad block of Sahebganj district, Penam Coal Mines started clearing villages and forcibly acquiring farmer's lands. The villagers kept resisting. Later on, with the help of touts, land Mafiosi and police administration, the company forcibly evicted the villagers. Not just this, the leader of the movement, Sister Balas was killed.

In the Potka Block of eastern Singhbhum district, forcible eviction started for setting up Bhushan Steel Plant. The villagers have been resisting this from the beginning. Here also, false cases were lodged against dozens of men and women leading the movement. Several comrades remained in jail for three months.

All those areas where the government is preparing to give land to companies for iron ore mines, are being declared as Maoist-affected areas and innocent villagers are being thrown in jails, after having called extremists. In these areas, the government is launching Operation Greenhunt and flooding them with the Central Reserve Police Force. Women and young girls are becoming victims of rape. They are getting battered, sandwiched between the establishment and the extremist organizations.

Of the 20 million displaced in the name of development, nearly half are women. These displaced women have migrated to other states to earn their living. Or else they have become maid servants in metropolis. Some sell grass to find one meal in a day. Young girls and kids have absolutely no access to education. 98 per cent displaced young girls and kids are illiterate. 95 per cent are anaemic. 95 per cent women have no house. They are forced to spend their lives like animals living near dirty drains in slums in cities.

The government has abdicated all constitutional responsibilities it had towards its citizens. Now, in order to arrange land for corporates, the constitutionally stipulated Land Acquisition Act too has been thrown out of the window and attempts are being made to pave the way for direct sale of land to the companies. All the companies are being allowed to acquire land from the villagers by hook or by crook. The companies are sending their touts and looting the land wherever they like. If any villager or land-owner tries to resist, s/he is implicated in false cases and packed off to prison.

In Chandan Kyari Block of Bokaro district, Electro Steel Company bought land for setting up a steel plant by terrorizing the villagers. Some land-owners got some compensation, some got nothing. The company grabbed thousands of acres land for its coal mines. The company owners promised the touts that they will give the price of land as well as compensation money. In compensation, they will give jobs also. Land was acquired in 2005 for coal mines but till this date neither have the villagers been paid the full price nor given any jobs.

In Torpa, Kamdora, Karra and Rania blocks of Khoonti and Gumla districts, global steel giant Arcelor Mittal wanted to set up a 12-million-ton steel plant by razing to ground forty villages. The company wanted to acquire the village lands by hook or crook. In 2006 we started mobilizing the public against the forcible land acquisition under the banner of Adivasi Moolwasi Astitva Raksha Manch (Adivasi Indigenous People Existence Defence Forum). After a protracted struggle lasting days and nights since 2006, our organization was able to save the future of hundreds of thousands from displacement as well as the environment. Along with Mittal, Ispat Industry too was looking to acquire 8,000 acres of land for a steel plant. Apart from these, dozens of small industrial families too would have landed up to grab our land and forests.

There was a proposal to construct a dam near Rehadgada village on Karo river to make water available to companies and industrial magnates. Another dam was to be constructed at Karra block on Chhata river. Several dozen villages would have got displaced due to these dams. Similarly, half the population of indigenous Adivasi community would have got displaced in Khoonti district. At Nagdi, Kanke in Ranchi, the government prepared papers for fraudulently acquiring 227 acres of land. On the basis of such papers it claimed to acquire the land. However, I asked for information under the Right to Information Act from the Land Acquisition Department. Their reply clearly stated that in 1957–58, there were 153 owners of land in Nagdi. Of these 128 refused to take any money in exchange for land.

The government says that the said land has been acquired for Ranchi Birsa Agricultural University. When I asked the Birsa Agricultural University for information in this connection, they said that they had no information regarding land acquisition. On the other hand, indigenous land-owners have been cultivating the said land for ages—and are doing so even today. They have also been paying taxes to the government till 2012. Peasants have been resisting selling land since 1957–58. I want to tell you that we are not against educational institutions. We want institutions to come up—not on our fertile lands but on infertile wasteland.

These days, the government is snatching these lands forcibly. Villagers are resisting all this. Then dozens of false cases were foisted on us. Four comrades were imprisoned in July 2012. This includes two female comrades. Thereafter, I was imprisoned for two-and-a-half months under a false case. Dozens of village women have false police cases against them.

The government says that those getting displaced will be compensated. At the same time they will also be rehabilitated and given alternative housing. But the question is—what will the government and the companies compensate for? Can they re-establish and rehabilitate our pure air, pure food, rivers, waterfalls, our language and culture, our sacred religious site Saran Sasan Diri, our identity and our history? No, that is absolutely impossible. We indigenous communities believe that our history, language, culture, sacred religious sites like Saran Sasan Diri, our identity and history cannot ever be rehabilitated. Nor can it be ever compensated for.

We are not anti-development. We want development but not at our cost. We want development of our rivers and waterfalls. We want development of our forests, mountains, ecology and agriculture. We want development of social values, language and culture. We want development of our identity and our history. We want that every person should get equal education and healthy life. We want polluted rivers to be pollution free. We want wastelands to be turned green. We want that everyone should get pure air, water and food. This is our model of development.

The concept of Jharkhand that was being talked about in the past, was simply forgotten by our politicians in power. But the people's struggles have given it a new dimension. In thirteen years, the way all the steps were taken to attract the companies. In the same way, strong and expanding people's struggles have given a new perspective to the concept of Jharkhand.

This perspective is to make livelihood as the basis of indigenous people's culture. This is to sculpt a new model of development which has a scientific thinking like the indigenous lifestyle and the technology should work in harmony and cooperation with nature. The thinking should not be just to take away from nature. The greatest emphasis should be on selection and implementation of plans in tune with people's thinking. There should be such technological development which makes the eternal value of coexistence dynamic. Our tribal dance forms, notes, tunes and harmony of our songs and all the sounds are evidence enough that we have a strong relationship with the idea of coexistence. Even now whenever there is any celebration of a hunt from the forest, the material is shared not just between humans but also between humans and animals. We want to see alive the fundamental spirit of this celebration in our economic system. In other words, we want to change the ways and means of the current economic model with a model of humane development.

We know that this challenge is not a small one. Just by our wishful thinking, this desire will not get fulfilled. That's why we see the cultural movement as a socio-economic wave, as a global movement event. We strongly believe that the world of our dreams is not far off.

You have honoured me with this prize which I dedicate to the struggling Adivasi tribal and indigenous farming communities whose part I am proud to be. Their affection and conviction has showed me the right path at every difficult turning. I want to reiterate that I will try to get their affection and faith more and more and join hands with the poor, exploited, the marginalized working masses of cities and villages in their democratic struggles and keep marching forward in unison with them.

My Johar (traditional greeting) to all the struggling comrades all over the world.

ABHAY XAXA

Abhay Xaxa is a research activist from Jhansi. He joined the Adivasi movement at a very young age, and is the National Convenor of the National Campaign on Adivasi Rights.

I Am Not Your Data

I am not your data, nor am I your vote bank,
I am not your project, or any exotic museum object,
I am not the soul waiting to be harvested,

Nor am I the lab where your theories are tested,
I am not your cannon fodder, or the invisible worker,
or your entertainment at India Habitat Center,
I am not your field, your crowd, your history,
your help, your guilt, medallions of your victory,
I refuse, reject, resist your labels,
your judgments, documents, definitions,
your models, leaders and patrons,
because they deny me my existence, my vision, my space,
your words, maps, figures, indicators,
they all create illusions and put you on pedestal,
from where you look down upon me,
So I draw my own picture, and invent my own grammar,
I make my own tools to fight my own battle,
For me, my people, my world, and my Adivasi self!

KANJI PATEL

Kanji Patel is an award-winning poet-novelist from Gujarat and an Adivasi activist. He is currently Honorary Director of the Adivasi Academy, Tejgadh (Chota Udepur, Gujarat). His works revolve around folk and Adivasi communities, and are written in a dialect of Gujarati spoken in the Panchmahali Bhili region.

Victual

Eyes, head
Hands, fingers
In harrumph, clucking, clicking, war-cries
I speak
Munch jujubes
Poised on all fours drink from the rivulet
Live off the mowra tree

Allow me to live, will you?

Why is the forest and papers pact

Still unresolved?
With papers, a bund was built
On the waters
On mother earth
Resulting in a drought
Huts tied into bundles
Took to the path
Farming abandoned
Papers went berserk in revelry

In this hand came a plate:
   - King, King, give us food
   - You tell me, should I fill my belly or yours?

Translated by Rupalee Burke

IROM SHARMILA

Irom Sharmila is a civil rights activist from Manipur. In November 2000, she began a hunger strike to protest the Malom Massacre, during which ten civilians where shot and killed by members of an Indian paramilitary force while waiting at a bus stop. Her primary demand to the Indian government was to repeal the Armed Forces (Special Powers) Act, 1951. She was arrested by the police three days later on charges of 'attempting suicide', and was force-fed through a nasal feeding tube for the next sixteen years. The following is a letter she wrote to Prime Minister Narendra Modi two years before ending her fast on 9 August 2016.

An Open Letter to the Prime Minister

This letter was handed over through the President of the Manipur Pradesh BJP, Shri. Th. Chaoba.

To
The Honourable Prime Minister of India

From
Irom Sharmila Chanu,
Imphal Central Jail

Dated: 27th May, 2014

Honourable Prime Minister, Shri Narendra Modiji,

A hearty congratulation from a young woman demanding for Right to Life under the Constitution of India to the newly elected Prime Minister of India!

First of all, I seek your pardon for any lack of etiquette in addressing you as the Prime Minster of India. I, Irom Sharmila Chanu, the lone hunger striker for repeal of the AFSPA, 1958 from the whole of areas in the country that come under the purview of this act, would like to draw your kind attention to my humble appeal for getting the innocent people, numbering around 4 Crores, free from the injustice, meted out by the Parliament of India.

Why should the Indian Parliament treat us, the inhabitants of the North East Region of India differently from the rests of people in different states of India at large by declaring our region as disturbed areas, under which the Constitution provides, the Armed Forces, even to the rank of a Havildar, the power to kill with full impunity, torture and rape anyone on mere suspicion of being an insurgent in their eyes? Why should so many women be exposed helplessly to their sexual pleasures? Holding with such Licence to kill under the AFSPA, 1958, the Government of India has been committing thousands of the killings and enforced disappearance of innocent people over the last few decades. This has resulted into same number of surviving widows and thousands of lamenting parents for their love[d] ones, leaving behind thousands of women-headed families!

The Chiefs of the Indian Army remain strongly against the repealing of the AFSPA only because they are too scared and insecure in their movements without excess power provided by this Act. As the consequence of their barbaric acts towards the innocent people, who are considered inferior and wild stupid beings in their eyes, and are very likely to retaliate suddenly and stealthily against the inhumanness of the Indian Armies, out of rage amongst the masses.

With such mindset of the army chiefs' tactics of controlling the insurgency and upholding AFSPA in the north east states of India and the state of Jammu and Kashmir has only been helpful in begetting more and more insurgent parties in the long run. I consider, the only solution to the liberation or separation movements in the North East region of India will be none other than changing of the mindset of the mainstream masses and power holders in politics at large to stop discriminations and step-motherly treatments meted out at the looks of Mongoloid features.

Please, do provide us with the basic right of being a human so that we can live with self-respect and dignity. Under the disturbed areas status the State has exploited our tourism industry by restricting any tourist from abroad which should provide us large income in exchange of our traditional manual products with which we would also expand our knowledge and horizons from such interactions with advanced countries of the world.

Please don't see me as a supporter of any insurgent party by the only notion of the way I protest against. Instead, please do see me as conscientious human being who doesn't want to have a permanent home and food nor adopt any particular religion or citizenship like the birds in nature so that I am accessible, wherever and whenever needed. I want to wonder around in the world as long as my body and soul are in union. And, I want nothing from this mundane earth, except enjoying the feeling of Importance with my birth as a rational, social animal to the following generation after my departure from the world, In that case, the future generations who would be born after me and whose knowledge about my living past would also be from the history, only will surely be want to transform the bad side of my own being into good, owing to the glory of my good actions of which I had meted out during my living space in this world.

Do prevail over the nation with the practice of nonviolence under your leadership and ensure democracy takes roots in the country by repealing AFSPA from the whole areas inhabited by around 4 Crores of people in the North East and elsewhere. Crores of rupees which is allocated every year to eradicate insurgency can be utilized productively for the uplift of the poor peasants who feed the Crores of Indians by transforming all the armed recruiting centres and barracks in every nook and corner of our states into fertile paddy fields that once it were for the farmers so that we can live a contented and peaceful lives.

Now, that you are not only the head of the State but popularly elected leader by the whole of the nation for a change, holding with the greatest power to command in your hands. Like the enlightened emperor Asoka of KaiInga after witnessing the huge devastation with heaves of deaths and lamentations that prevailed over the whole land as a consequence of historic battles, do rule your nation with the weapon of Ahimsa so that you may reap only with peace and love of your peoples to allay the fears of Anti-Modi groups since the incidents of Godhra in 2002 and transform them into your beloved friends for a peaceful and vibrant society.

At my personal level, your historic victory over the recently concluded Parliamentary election and your becoming the Prime Minster of India was also envisioned in my dreams, nearly 5 years back in 2009, when I saw you standing few metres apart right in front of me with smile. I waited for this day to see you in that position, today. It has been dream fulfilling for me also.

In those very days, I knew nothing about you except with a notion of a violent leader. But, recently after hearing from the Newspapers of your pronouncement as the Prime ministerial candidate of BJP in the 16th Lok Sabha election, I did recollect myself of my past dream of your standing before me and sharing the dreams with my near and dear ones, here. So, we were hopeful and prayed for your victory. Now, it turns out that the dreams were a prophecy that came true in your assuming the highest post of the State.

I now count the days of my freedom with the repeal of AFSPA, 1958 with your efforts in the Parliament. So, do be the omnipotent leader who eventually breaks my fast of 14 years by repealing the Act. You'll be blessed by the souls of those innocent people who are no more and millions of young people like me and my intimate friends who wish to lead protected life by the law of the land with dignity or let us gain Nirvana from this crazy world of power abuse of the mundane world and liberate our souls from the body that enjoy No Right to Life guaranteed under the Constitution of the country. The choice is in your hands under your able leadership.

Thank you for your kind attention.

With utmost regards
Irom Sharmila Chanu.

U.R. ANANTHAMURTHY

U.R. Ananthamurthy (1932–2014) was an influential and multi-award-winning Kannada writer and critic. As is evident in his works, particularly Samskara, *he was a harsh critic of Hindu caste hierarchies and disliked extremism of any kind.* Hindutva or Hind Swaraj, *his last work, is a creative response to the rise of Hindutva nationalism in India.*

From *Hindutva* or *Hind Swaraj*

No matter how vehemently Indians declare that we are non-violent, in our movies and songs we applaud those who come to power through extreme violence. People may practise non-violence in their daily lives but the Indian psyche also admires acts of brutality. Even the names of many Hindu deities would suggest such a reading. Consider the name Murari[1]—one who has vanquished the demon Mura. We do not extol Shivaji for his acts of good governance, but for his skill with counter-offensive tactics. We forget Emperor Ashok in our political discourse.

It is the same in Europe; perpetrators of violence become rulers. If you go to the Tower of London, you will see several queens were put to death because they did not produce a male child. Up until now, human history has only recognized heroes who have emerged victorious in a battle. We thought that Gandhi's message of freedom through ahimsa heralded a change. Ironically, ahimsa was fraught with violence too. Streams of blood flowed during the Hindu-Muslim riots. With a staff taller than himself, Gandhi walked barefoot through Noakhali. India celebrated Independence in the absence of Gandhi.

How did Gujarat produce a pan-Indian hero? The Gujarat massacre took place when [Narendra Modi] was chief minister. To say that he tried to prevent it but failed would mean he was weak. Nobody can say that. One is reminded of an image used by the poet Adiga. When yajnas are conducted everyone present is involved in some task or the other. But a mantrajnya, an expert in the mantras, does not participate. He is known as the 'brahma', and is crucial to the ritual. The brahma does nothing.

Modi was the brahma. Whatever happened has happened. Raskolnikov was tormented by the thought that he should not have committed murder. A hapless prostitute teaches him love. Modi also feels remorse. But of another kind. A remorse that says if a pup gets run over by a car, what can be done? One could say, oh poor thing. If the car had stopped, would the puppy have lived?

Here I will dare to express a thought. Maybe this is why the people of India appreciated Modi; see how he silenced the minorities. On NDTV 24x7, Barkha Dutta invites a prominent Muslim and encourages him to praise Modi. We no longer see the harsh-sounding Modi. This is a Modi beloved of all. Who is this Modi created by everyone, including the media?

We are bombarded with images of Modi offering flowers, paying homage to a small photograph of Gandhi. All our apprehensions are dispelled, and what emerges is the image of a new-age leader with foresight, who works without sleep, wears attractive clothes, a turban, holds a mace in his hand—transformed from the outside but unchanged within. He has kept his wife away, he has liberated himself from his past and his caste, has become the new-age Shivaji and Patel. So what if the country is clouded with the smoke of forgetfulness? So what if we forget Gandhi? Why, we could even erect a statue of Gandhi in London's Westminster if a trade deal is struck.

In the first budget that the Modi government presented, crores of rupees were allocated for a statue of Sardar Patel. I will hazard a couple of guesses about why no one talks about this. First, to set up Nehru as the prime leader, his followers relegated the popular people's leader, Sardar Patel, to the background. Because of that, the Congress is not in a position to oppose the proposal. Second, Modi cannot openly install a statue of his real leader, Savarkar. Although Savarkar was acquitted of a murder charge, his name is sullied. There is a photograph of him in Parliament. That is sufficient for now. In any case, in the development agenda, there will be airports, universities, large buildings and textbooks. Whatever Nehru supporters have done, Modi can do too. Advani may also get a place of honour as a stone statue or a plaque.

It seems to me that the Gandhi era has come to an end; Savarkar has triumphed. Perhaps his victory is transient, but for now he has won. We do not want a Hindu religion with its superstitions, its caste system, its sacred rituals and the like. Let all Hindus unite because the Muslims are united. We will confront them. Let us create a strong Bharat. This is what Savarkar advocated. He didn't even believe in God. Like Gandhi, he condemned untouchability. Savarkar could interact with Jinnah as an equal. Jinnah was not fettered by religion. Nor was the rationalist Savarkar.

I call Savarkar a rationalist because, for him, what mattered were factors
that unified several states into a single nation. He knew that only if this
happened would Bharat gain pre-eminence in the world. We liberals are
cautious and view everything with suspicion. We lack the aggressiveness
to silence the differences. So some Muslims will keep picking quarrels.
As will some Dalits. And the Shudras. Also the cosmopolitan Brahmins.
Everyone is constantly engaged in some squabble or other in this great
chaos. The problem confronting us liberals is how to resolve these
internal quarrels without losing our individual morality and humanism.
A tentative, subtle sensibility is, some believe, an undesirable trait in the
ruler of a nation.

See how Modi was able to silence the Ambedkarites in Uttar Pradesh.
And then pay obeisance to Ambedkar's statue.

See how he put down the Lohiaite-turned-casteist Yadavs. In the
future, will the neo-Brahmins and the Manu followers in India's 24x7
media still invite the liberals who have been mouthing the old tiresome
clichés? That too when Modi, who can shut them up, is himself from the
'Mandal' caste and the prime minister of the country?

But there is another important fact we must pay heed to. The middle
classes, the Shudras, the Dalits and the Muslims have also been swayed
by Modi's oratory. They seem to have given up leftist politics in the sway
of Modi's honeymoon period. Perhaps it is only the Earth that will speak
the leftist language now, battered and infuriated as she is by Modi's
developmental agenda. Perhaps she will unleash her fury through the
weapons of storms, thunder, lightning, rain, floods and earthquakes.

The liberals, now sidelined, are afraid that the idea of nationhood—
if carried to an extreme—can become fascist. There is a good reason
for their fear—this was the story of the two world wars. The notion of
nationhood is raising its head once again in China too. Our neighbour
has given up Mao's policy of popular consensus, turning instead to global
capitalism, and has grown quickly and enormously. Stalin drew Soviet
Russia into one nation and eliminated all opposition. This is also how
the process of change that began with the French Revolution in Europe
ended with Napolean.

He who does not dream is not human. One dreams of the well-being
of mankind, a green earth and clear sky. A dream of Gandhi's ahimsa. A
dream where man works for a living, uses the benefits of science wisely
and makes sure the environment is not destroyed.

Gandhi's *Hind Swaraj* envisaged such an India. Modi's victory is in direct opposition to that dream. His triumph has moved closer to Savarkar's idea of Hindutva, without actually saying so.

Translated by Keerti Ramachandra with Vivek Shanbhag

Notes

1. Murari: After Krishna destroyed the fortified city of Pragjyotisha, slew Mura, a great demon, and burnt his 7,000 sons, he came to be known as Murari. (The word 'ari' means enemy.)

NAYANTARA SAHGAL'S SPEECH AT ALIGARH MUSLIM UNIVERSITY

A fierce guardian of the principles of democracy, Nayantara Sahgal was among the writers who returned their Sahitya Akademi Awards to protest the murder of the rationalist Dr M.M. Kalburgi. The following is the text of a speech she delivered at Aligarh Muslim University on 10 December 2015.

I never had the good fortune of meeting Professor K.P. Singh, but from what I have learned about him, he was a distinguished academic who headed the department of Hindi here and retired as Dean of the Faculty of Arts in 1997. It is interesting that this university has set up a memorial lecture for a scholar and professor of Hindi. He was also an innovator who founded a Lekhak Sangh as a common platform for Hindi and Urdu literature. In connection with this, I am reminded of a story about Jawaharlal Nehru which Professor K.P. Singh would have enjoyed. Soon after Independence, when it was being decided how many Indian languages should be recognized by the Constitution, about thirteen were put on the list. Nehru looked down the list and then said to the official concerned, 'Why is Urdu not on the list?' The official replied, 'Because it is nobody's mother tongue.' Nehru said very firmly, 'It is mine,' and he had Urdu added to the list. Professor Singh recognized the naturalness of Hindi and Urdu sharing a platform since these languages, like the people and cultures they represent, have met and mingled and influenced each other, and in fact, the 'ghar ki boli' that most of us speak in north India is

Hindustani, a mixture of the two. India showed another kind of wisdom in including English on that list and making one more Indian language of it, and it has been an asset to us in dealing with the world and with each other. It is also a recognition that we, as individuals and as nations, are the result of all the influences that have gone into the making of us. The past cannot be wiped out. It is an integral part of us. You can change the name of Aurangzeb Road but you cannot alter the fact that Aurangzeb is part of Indian history.

Apart from Dr Singh's academic distinction, I am sure this university honours him for the human being he was, a man who was committed to the values of our secular democratic republic, and one who played an active part in defence of these values whenever the need arose. I, who never met him, am missing him today, because these values are now in danger, and we are in need of people like him who will speak out against the prevailing policy to destroy them. The danger we are in today is from a mentality that wants to wipe out our celebrated diversity, and make us into a Hindu rashtra, which makes nonsense of the reality of our multi-religious, multi-cultural civilization. Hindutva—as this ideology calls itself—is a political invention that has nothing to do with true Hinduism, just as Muslim fundamentalism has nothing to do with true Islam. It is significant that neither Hindu nor Muslim extremists played any part in the fight for freedom from British rule led by Mahatma Gandhi. Both stayed out of it, and both, by staying out of it, gave their approval to Britain's divide-and-rule policy. Muslim extremists profited by it to create a Muslim state, Pakistan, and Hindu extremists, who are in effective power for the first time in India, are now trying to make a Hindu state out of India. This continuation of Britain's divide-and-rule policy divides the people of India into Hindus and 'others'. It ignores the fact that India rejected a religious identity at Independence because our founding fathers believed that a country has no religion. It is people who have religions, and in a democracy they have the right to practise their different religions and their different ways of life as equal citizens. Hindutva does not share this mindset, and now that it is in power, it has set out to abolish every trace of it.

The diversity, and the culture of pluralism, which have been part and parcel of our social fabric for centuries, and have enriched us in so many ways, is now under attack, and the campaign to undo our pluralism is what I have called the unmaking of India. I would like to take this opportunity to talk to you about how this 'unmaking of India' is proceeding, and how Indians like myself are dealing with the situation and the hostile atmosphere that we all now face, where it has been made clear to us that no disagreement to the Hindutva ideology will be tolerated. The first evidence we had of this was when the directors of our premier institutions were thrown out and replaced by unqualified appointees of the RSS [Rashtriya Swayamsevak Sangh]. Next, educational institutions are being brought under the Hindutva scanner, and textbooks and curriculums are being revised to promote its ideas. History, science, and other subjects will be re-written, using the Vedas as their reference point and as the fount of all knowledge. Already we have heard it said in all seriousness that Ganesha's elephant nose was grafted on by Vedic surgery and that India was nuclear in Vedic times. When I recall that our first education minister was the learned Maulana Abul Kalam Azad, and compare him with those who occupy the education and culture ministries today, I want to weep. This government's distortion of education is the most deadly and alarming aspect of the fundamentalist agenda, since it will produce an ignorant future generation if it is allowed to proceed. But this program is already underway. I can only describe it as an iron curtain coming down on the whole field of knowledge and on freedom of thought. It is for educational institutions to challenge this trend, and a group of academics have already issued a statement in this connection.

Along with this we have been seeing violent attacks on freedom of expression. The Tamil writer, Perumal Murugan, was hounded out of his home village by Hindu fanatics who objected to a novel he had written, and threatened him with death unless he stopped writing, so he has been forced to give up his great talent and the profession by which he made a living. And though it is known who his attackers were, no action has been taken against them. Two distinguished Maharashtrian writers, [Narendra] Dabholkar and [Govind] Pansare, both highly respected rationalists who questioned superstition have been murdered. Another rationalist, the famous Kannada writer, Professor Kalburgi, has likewise been murdered—all three writers were killed by gun-toting motorcyclists who, to this day, have not been named, arrested or delivered to justice. All this while, the authorities have remained silent. In particular, it has been deeply disturbing that the Sahitya Akademi, set up as an autonomous institution, and as the guardian and promoter of literature, did not speak up to condemn these murders, or to say a word in defence of freedom of speech. In protest against this terrible silence, I returned my Sahitya Akademi Award. Six Kannada writers, protesting against Kalburgi's murder, had already returned their awards to the Kannada Akademi, and the Hindi writer, Uday Prakash, had returned his to the national Sahitya Akademi. Up till now more than forty writers have returned their awards, and some have resigned from their positions in the Akademi.

The most remarkable thing about this development is that it has been spontaneous, not planned or organized. The accusation against us is that it has been a 'manufactured' revolt. It is obvious that these accusers don't know anything about writers. We live in different, far-flung parts of the country. We write in different languages. We do not know each other. We cannot read each other. Most of us have never met each other. The decisions we made to return our awards or resign our positions in the Akademi have been entirely personal decisions, coming at different times from north, south, east and west. No one consulted anyone else about what to do. We acted individually. Another accusation against us was that we all belonged to the Congress party or had received favours from the Congress. This is an equally absurd charge because I am sure that most, if not all, of the writers do not belong to any political party. Even I, who was born and brought up in a Congress family, do not belong to the Congress. And certainly I have received no favours from it. Quite the contrary, since I vigorously opposed the Emergency of 1975 and have written extensively condemning it. An even more ridiculous charge against us is that we were seeking publicity and looking for importance. I had to assure listeners when I was on an NDTV programme, that writers are not looking for importance, they are looking for publishers. While we were being attacked by our own government, you may have heard that writers from 150 countries have given us their backing in our fight for freedom of speech, and recently 200 British writers marched in support of us during Prime Minister Modi's visit to London, demanding that the British prime minister take up the question of human rights with Modi.

But what started as a wave of protest against the assault on freedom of speech has since become a much larger battle. When a poor blacksmith, Mohammed Akhlaq, was dragged out of his house and brutally lynched in Dadri village, on the supposed charge that he was a beef-eater, it became clear that ours had become a battle to fight for the very meaning of India as a plural society, and as a secular democratic republic whose Constitution guarantees every Indian the right to live, eat, and worship as he or she chooses. Because of this horrifying lynching of a poor and helpless man who had done no one any harm, the country was shocked into realizing the nature of the problem we are now facing. What had begun as a writers' protest against the campaign to silence us—if necessary, by murder—has been joined by artists, actors, film makers, historians, sociologists, and scientists—none of whom are willing to keep silent while all that India stands for is being systematically destroyed. Nothing like these spontaneous reactions, coming from so many different disciplines, against the unchecked tide of hatred and intolerance in this country, has ever happened in any other country. Historians are protesting against the substitution of mythology for history. Scientists are protesting against the destruction of the scientific temper, and the spirit of enquiry, without which no nation can call itself modern. Recently an eminent scientist, Dr P.M. Bhargava, who is the founder-director of the Centre for Cellular and Molecular Biology, has returned his Padma Bhushan to the president, saying he was deeply concerned that 'the government has deserted the road to democracy and is driving my beloved country on a path that will make the country a religious autocracy.' In his letter he also says, 'Steeped in superstition, unreason and irrationality, much of what the RSS and the BJP do goes against the grain of the scientific temper.' Dr Bhargava is, of course, a Hindu himself. A retired Admiral of the Indian Navy, who is also a Hindu, has registered his own passionate protest in a letter to the president and the prime minister, also rejecting the ideology of Hindutva, and asserting his faith in a plural and diverse India. The actor, Saif Ali Khan, son of the Nawab of Pataudi, has said, 'We are a blend, this great country of ours. It is our differences that make us who we are. I have prayed in church and attended Mass with my wife, Kareena, while she has bowed her head at dargahs and prayed in mosques. When we purified our home we had a havan and a Koran reading and a priest sprinkling holy water. The fabric of India is woven from many threads.' It is that fabric woven from many threads that our protesting voices are determined to preserve. The president and the vice president have both felt compelled to make public statements against intolerance and the crushing of dissent in the country. There is a general public demand that the doors to knowledge be kept open, that creativity—in art, in literature, in cinema, in research—be left free to flourish, and that India must remain a country where the fresh air of different ideas and approaches, different viewpoints and ways of life and thought, will continue to invigorate us as they have done for centuries.

We are a country of dissenters, and dissent has never been confined to an intellectual elite. It has come from the ground. It has come out of ground realities, and out of the desperate needs of ordinary people. It has covered a whole range of issues—justice for the victims of the Bhopal gas disaster, issues concerning environment, arbitrary land acquisition, the setting up of nuclear plants, the Narmada Dam Andolan, the Chipko movement in Uttarakhand to protect forests, and now voices are being raised in Dehradun where I live against the plan to set up a so-called 'smart city' which will be a satellite city set up to provide facilities and benefits to corporate houses. It is these acts of questioning whichever government rules the land, by ordinary citizens who insist on being heard, that have kept our tradition of criticism alive.

Recently the people of Bihar have shown that they do not accept Hindutva. Let us remember, too, that criticism is a long practiced and accepted tradition in India. Different interpretations led to different versions of the Ramayana—Valmiki's and Tulsidas's. Dissent within Hinduism led to a major reform, the Bhakti movement, which declared there were no priests, popes, or holy books between man and God, and that religion was a direct and intensely personal experience. Dissent within Hinduism has also focused on Hinduism's two great crimes, sati and untouchability. We look upon dissent as a democratic right, so long as it is non-violent. Unfortunately, those who cannot tolerate differences of opinion have not observed this rule, and are continuing to resort to intimidation, abuse, death threats and the murder of those who do not agree with them. Many Indians are now living in uncertainty and fear. All of this makes it more than ever necessary for us to speak out against attacks on our right to disagree, and on the values that are the foundation of modern India. The one thing we cannot afford to do is to keep silent. No one has called for the need to speak out so eloquently as Faiz Ahmed Faiz: 'Bol, ye thora waqt bahut hai / Jism o zaban ki maut se pahle / Bol, ke sach zinda hai ab tak / Bol, jo kucch kahna hai keh le.'

We need to speak out not only when our own rights are violated, but when those of others are attacked. Individual or community rights have no meaning, and cannot be safe from harm, if they do not apply universally to all human beings. Therefore, when Christian churches have been vandalized, and nuns have been raped, would it not have been a powerful statement of condemnation if Hindus, Muslims, and Sikhs and others had got together and joined forces to show that they would not stand for this kind of thuggish violence against any community? Should we not have raised our voices when Christmas Day, the holiest day in the Christian calendar, was re-named 'governance day'? Many of us felt a loathing that the day of Christ's birth was wiped off the calendar in this fashion but we did not join forces to say so. Equally we felt a loathing that Gandhi Jayanti was wiped off the calendar, but we let it pass and kept our disgust to ourselves. The reason why the writers' protest has become a much greater awakening and made a nation-wide impact is simply because it did not remain an isolated protest. Many different disciplines across the nation spoke out, not only in support of the freedom to write, but of freedom generally.

So far I have talked of Hindu fundamentalism and the damage it is doing to our country. But there are other religious fundamentalisms among us which every religion needs to disown. The worst victims of all fundamentalisms are always women. When Hitler's Nazi party came to power in Germany, German women were ordered to breed more Nazis to increase the numbers of the Nazi super race, and to confine themselves to children, church, and kitchen. We are hearing an echo of this in the opinion of a Hindutva leader that Hindu women must have ten children to increase Hindu numbers. Women are also being told how to behave, how to dress, and what time of day they must return home. The head of the RSS has himself announced that Hindu marriage is a contract according to which a woman is only a housewife and cannot work outside the home. In such outrageous statements, coming from people in authority, the gender equality that universal suffrage and Indian citizenship gave us nearly seventy years ago is being rubbed out of sight. One of the landmark legislations of the Nehru government during the 1950s was the Hindu Code Bill. Hindu women had had no rights until then. The Bill gave them divorce and inheritance and other rights for the first time in history. It did not go far enough, and it took several years to pass in Parliament, but it was a beginning—and even so it had to put up with a lot of opposition from the Hindu right wing, including those who stood and shouted outside the Parliament and threw stones at it. Reform takes courage, and our first government showed courage when it took this controversial step. It provided the legal framework for the women's rights it covered, though society still had, and still has, a long way to go to catch up with the law. Since then laws have been considerably enlarged and strengthened in the field of women's rights. But finally a workable equality can only come from a common civil code—which will ensure that all Indian citizens, which includes all Indian women, no matter what religion or community they belong to—will be entitled to the same rights. The time to bring about a major reform of this kind is when communities are ready for it. Jawaharlal Nehru had hoped that a common civil code would come about in time. Now, because Hindutva is trying to Hinduize India, there is suspicion of such a measure. Yet, enlightened leaders of all religions must in due course work out this problem. India has proved that a deeply religious country of many religions can be a secular republic. I have no doubt that it can evolve a common civil code.

It is often said that this or that reform cannot be accepted because it will hurt the sentiments of a community. The answer to that, surely, is that there are sentiments that have to be hurt. If we had been afraid of hurting sentiments, we would still be burning widows. If we had been afraid of hurting sentiments, women would never have come out of purdah.

I am hesitant to speak about educational reform since I am not in touch with this subject. But, should reform also not be considered in the field of education by our religion-run schools, especially at a time when education is being endangered by a narrow primitive mindset that does not belong in the twenty-first century? Religion-run schools—Hindu, Muslim and Christian—impart a particular religion-ruled outlook. They might, in reaction to the Hindutva bulldozer, cling more closely to their own orthodoxies. But this is a trap they should not fall into. They should in fact do the opposite. While teaching the values of their religion, they should open up to all available knowledge, to ensure that their young are not left behind, and that they can qualify for the best job and other opportunities that the country offers. Women must, of course, have the same educational, and later the same career opportunities, as men.

A country is a work in progress. It needs watchdogs to keep democracy working; to insist on explanations and accountability when things go wrong, from whichever government happens to be in power; and to raise questions and demand answers when these are required. This has always been important, but never more than it is today, with a government whose proclaimed intention is to blow up the very foundations on which we stand. Today we cannot afford the luxury of remaining silent. Speaking for myself, and I am sure for all those who have made their views public during this on-going crisis, we will continue to make ourselves heard.

Amartya Sen

This essay is the text of the Rajendra Mathur Memorial Lecture, organized by the Editors Guild of India in Delhi and delivered on 12 February 2016 by Amartya Sen, Nobel Prize-winning economist and philosopher.

Dissent and Freedom in India

I begin on a self-indulgent note. 'How is Amartya?' asked my uncle Shidhu (Jyotirmoy Sengupta)—cousin of my father—in a letter written from Burdwan Jail, on August 22 of 1934, before I was one. He complained about the name 'Amartya', given to me by Rabindranath Tagore, and argued that the great Tagore had 'completely lost his mind in his old age' to choose such a 'tooth-breaking name' for a tiny child. Jyotirmoy was in jail for his efforts to end the British Raj. He was moved from prison to prison—Dhaka Jail, Alipur Central Jail, Burdwan Jail, Midnapur Central Jail. There were other uncles and cousins of mine who were going through similar experiences in other British Indian prisons.

Jyotirmoy himself came to a sad end, dying of tuberculosis, related to undernourishment in the prisons. As a young boy I was lucky to have a few conversations with him, and felt very inspired by what he said and wrote. He was committed to help remove 'the unfreedoms heaped on us by our rulers'.

How happy would Jyotirmoy have been to be in today's India, with the Raj dead and gone, and with no unfreedoms imposed on us by the colonial masters? But—and here is the rub—have these unfreedoms really ended? The penal codes legislated by the imperial rulers still govern important parts of our life. Of these, Section 377 of the code, which criminalizes gay sex, is perhaps the most talked about, but happily a Constitution bench of the Supreme Court is re-examining it. It is, however, often overlooked that the putting on a pedestal of the sentiments of any religious group—often very loosely defined—is another remnant of British law, primarily Section 295(A) of the penal code introduced in 1927. A person can be threatened with jail sentence for hurting the religious sentiments of another, however personal—and however bizarrely delicate—that portrayed sentiment might be.

The Indian Constitution, despite claims to the contrary, does not have any such imposition. In a judgment on March 3, 2014, the Supreme

Court in fact gave priority to the fundamental right of the people to express themselves, as enshrined in the Constitution. The Constitution's insistence on 'public order, decency or morality' is a far cry from what the organized political activists try to impose by hard-hitting kick-boxing, allegedly guided by delicate sentiments. The Constitution does not have anything against anyone eating beef, or storing it in a refrigerator, even if some cow-venerators are offended by other people's food habits.

The realm of delicate sentiments seems to extend amazingly far. Murders have occurred on grounds of hurt sentiments from other people's private eating. Children have been denied the nourishment of eggs in school meals in parts of India for the priority of vegetarian sentiments of powerful groups. And seriously researched works of leading international scholars have been forced to be pulped by scared publishers, threatened to be imprisoned for the offence of allegedly hurting religious sentiments. Journalists often receive threats—or worse—for violating the imposed norms of vigilante groups. The Indian media has a good record of standing up against intimidation, but freedom of speech and reporting need more social support.

To see in all this the evidence of an 'intolerant India' is just as serious a mistake as taking the harassment of people for particular social behaviour to be a constitutional mandate. Most Indians, including most people who are classified as Hindu (including this writer), have no difficulty in accepting variations in food habits among different groups (and even among Hindus). And they are ready to give their children the nourishment of eggs if they so choose (and if they can afford them). And Hindus have been familiar with, and tolerant of, arguments about religious beliefs for more than 3,000 years ('Who knows then, whence it first came into being? ... Whose eye controls this world in highest heaven, he verily knows it, or perhaps he knows not,' Rigveda, Mandala X, Verse 129). It is a serious insult to Indians—and to Hindus in general—to attribute to them the strange claims of a small but well organized political group, who are ready to jump on others for violations of norms of behaviour that the group wants to propagate, armed with beliefs and sentiments that have to be protected from sunlight.

The silencing of dissent, and the generating of fear in the minds of people violate the demands of personal liberty, but also make it very much harder to have a dialogue-based democratic society. The problem is not that Indians have turned intolerant. In fact, quite the contrary. We have been too tolerant even of intolerance. When some people—often members of a minority (in religion or community or scholarship)—are attacked by organized detractors, they need our support. This is not happening adequately right now. And it did not happen adequately earlier as well. In fact, this phenomenon of intolerance of dissent and of heterodox behaviour did not start with the present government, though it has added substantially to the restrictions already there. M.F. Husain, one of the leading painters of India, was hounded out of his country by relentless persecution led by a small organized group, and he did not get the kind of thundering support that he could have justly expected. In that ghastly event at least the Indian government was not directly involved (though it certainly could—and should—have done much more to protect him). The government's complicity was, however, much more direct when India became the first country to ban Salman Rushdie's *Satanic Verses*.

So what should we do, as citizens of India who support freedom and liberty? First, we should move away from blaming the Indian Constitution for what it does not say. Second, we should not allow colonial penal codes that impose unfreedoms to remain unchallenged. Third, we should not tolerate the intolerance that undermines our democracy, that impoverishes the lives of many Indians, and that facilitates a culture of impunity of tormentors. Fourth, the courts, particularly the Supreme Court, have good reason to examine comprehensively whether India is not being led seriously astray by the continuation of the rules of the Raj, which we fought so hard to end. In particular, there is need for judicial scrutiny of the use that organized tormentors make of an imagined entitlement of 'not to be offended' (an alleged entitlement that does not seem to exist in this particular form in any other country). Fifth, if some states, under the influence of sectarian groups want to extend these unfreedoms through local legislation (for example, banning particular food), the courts surely have to examine the compatibility of these legislation with the fundamental rights of people, including the right to speech and to personal liberties.

As Indians, we have reason to be proud of our tradition of tolerance and plurality, but we have to work hard to preserve it. The courts have to do their duty (as they are doing—but more is needed), and we have to do ours (indeed much more is surely needed). Vigilance has been long recognized to be the price of freedom.

ROHITH VEMULA'S LAST LETTER

Rohith Vemula (1989–2016) was a doctoral scholar at Hyderabad University. His suicide note, in which he described the humiliation Dalits across India continue to endure, is one of the harshest indictments of inequality and injustice in Indian society.

Good morning,

I would not be around when you read this letter. Don't get angry on me. I know some of you truly cared for me, loved me and treated me very well. I have no complaints on anyone. It was always with myself I had problems. I feel a growing gap between my soul and my body. And I have become a monster. I always wanted to be a writer. A writer of science, like Carl Sagan. At last, this is the only letter I am getting to write.

I loved science, stars, nature, but then I loved people without knowing that people have long since divorced from nature. Our feelings are second handed. Our love is constructed. Our beliefs coloured. Our originality valid through artificial art. It has become truly difficult to love without getting hurt.

The value of a man was reduced to his immediate identity and nearest possibility. To a vote. To a number. To a thing. Never was a man treated as a mind. As a glorious thing made up of stardust. In [e]very field, in studies, in streets, in politics, and in dying and living.

I am writing this kind of letter for the first time. My first time of a final letter. Forgive me if I fail to make sense.

May be I was wrong, all the while, in understanding world. In understanding love, pain, life, death. There was no urgency. But I always was rushing. Desperate to start a life. All the while, some people, for them, life itself is curse. My birth is my fatal accident. I can never recover from my childhood loneliness. The unappreciated child from my past.

I am not hurt at this moment. I am not sad. I am just empty. Unconcerned about myself. That's pathetic. And that's why I am doing this.

People may dub me as a coward. And selfish, or stupid once I am gone. I am not bothered about what I am called. I don't believe in after-death stories, ghosts, or spirits. If there is anything at all I believe, I believe that I can travel to the stars. And know about the other worlds.

If you, who is reading this letter can do anything for me, I have to get seven months of my fellowship, one lakh and seventy five thousand rupees. Please see to it that my family is paid that. I have to give some 40 thousand to Ramji. He never asked them back. But please pay that to him from that.

Let my funeral be silent and smooth. Behave like I just appeared and gone. Do not shed tears for me. Know that I am happy dead than being alive.

'From shadows to the stars.'

Uma anna, sorry for using your room for this thing.

To ASA family, sorry for disappointing all of you. You loved me very much. I wish all the very best for the future.

For one last time,

Jai Bheem

I forgot to write the formalities. No one is responsible for my this act of killing myself.

No one has instigated me, whether by their acts or by their words to this act.

This is my decision and I am the only one responsible for this.

Do not trouble my friends and enemies on this after I am gone.

ANIRBAN BHATTACHARYA AND UMAR KHALID

Anirban Bhattacharya and Umar Khalid are students of Jawaharlal Nehru University. They are also members of Bhagat Singh Ambedkar Students Organization, JNU. In February 2016, students organized a peaceful protest on the JNU campus against the execution of Afzal Guru, an accused in the Indian Parliament attack case. This protest faced a severe backlash from the college administration as well as the government and sections of the media. The following is their response to the backlash.

JNU Protests: What Is at the Core of the Ongoing Movement?

'Perhaps you pronounce this sentence against me with greater fear, than I receive it,' exclaimed Giardono Bruno as the judges sentenced him to death in the year 1600. Bruno, amongst other things, by questioning the centrality of Earth in the universe, had committed the ultimate crime by questioning the existing Catholic beliefs—the 'official truth' of those times. Bruno was put on trial by the Roman Inquisition for seven years and burned at the stake as a heretic. Condemned for his views during his lifetime, Bruno, however, is remembered today as one of the torchbearers of free speech and inquiry—many of whose views were later proved correct. However, if one thought persecution of those holding views contrary to 'the official truths' of the times was a prerogative of feudal lords that came to end with the medieval times, one needs to just look around in our own country today.

Students of JNU are the latest addition to the list of uncomfortable voices that the government is attempting to silence. This list is long, and includes Kabir Kala Manch, a fiery group of young Dalit artistes, civil rights activist Binayak Sen, writer Arundhati Roy, Delhi University lecturer Dr G.N. Saibaba and many others. Many centuries later, it seems that the ghost of Bruno has come right back, this time not to haunt Rome, but the Indian state. As the 'official truths' behind nationalism, democracy and development become difficult to sustain, we see sentences being pronounced with ever greater frequency to declare citizens as heretics—anti-national is the new word for them. And the responsibility for these pronouncements has also been increasingly outsourced. Apart from the judges in the courts, the lynch-mob on the street, shrill anchors on television, are also the university administrations who have taken upon themselves the responsibility of becoming the judge, jury and the prosecutor, when the call of 'duty' comes.

As we write this piece, we hear the Delhi High Court putting on hold the punishments meted out to students by the university administration. Sending it back to the Vice Chancellor for reconsideration of students' appeals, the court also asked the students of JNU to call off the indefinite hunger strike that had entered its 16th day (Friday).

The punishments meted out to the students by the university administration through the farcical High Level Enquiry Committee set up to probe the now infamous 9 February events was Plan B of the government to witch-hunt some of the most vocal student activists of the university. Plan A, of creating a spectacle through media trials, prime-time national/anti-national debates, police raids in the university hostels and sedition cases had not just failed to intimidate students, but had instead backfired miserably. It led to an unprecedented solidarity across the country and made campus-level student activists national icons in the anti-fascist struggles.

So now, as per this Plan B, the onus has shifted to a pliant university administration under a newly appointed Vice Chancellor (with close affinities to the RSS) to operationalize the witch-hunt. In the face of a complete media blackout and in the midst of some of the most adverse weather conditions, students were on a hunger strike for over two weeks demanding the scrapping of the punishments—that includes rustications, hostel evictions, fines and debarment from entering campus. The same university administration that remained indifferent to the security of students when they were facing death threats, only to become very pro-active in imposing punishments, once again moved to an indifferent mode during the strike as student lives were once again at stake. The health of all striking students has taken a beating, many have collapsed, been hospitalized but the fall of one comrade has only seen many others take their place.

In appearance, the ongoing movement may be seen as being a protest against certain punishments. But at the core of this protest, at the essence of it, lies our resolve to protect free speech and our democratic space in this campus. Any acceptance of punishment on our part, even if in a modified form, would be an admission of guilt on our part. It would constitute a betrayal of the four decades of our students' movement that has built this space. It is this culture of democracy, questioning and interrogating 'official truths' that has inspired thousands of students to stand up and speak truth to power. It was here, that Indira Gandhi was stopped from entering after she came to visit the campus in the period after Emergency, for her role during that period. Or a decade back, Manmohan Singh was greeted by students with black flags for the erstwhile UPA government's sell-out of the country's education and resources. For the Sangh, this democratic space has always been an eyesore. Only last year the RSS mouthpiece had devoted one of their covers to JNU, branding the university 'a den of anti-nationals'.

Today, by punishing us, the real target is the democratic space and the students' movement of JNU.

Having and expressing a political opinion—even on Kashmir, the question of self-determination, Afzal Guru's execution or death penalty—is no crime. And even the Constitution safeguards this right. We, however, live in paradoxical times. The most fascist and authoritarian of all governments, who trample free speech every day, call themselves democratic and deeply committed to freedom of expression. We need to call this bluff, fight back and uncompromisingly defend our right to dissent by continuing to raise questions that discomfort those in power.

Just a few months back, before the witch-hunt of students started in JNU, a similar script had played out in the University of Hyderabad. By witch-hunting Rohith and his comrades, the government thought they were making an example out of them which will scare others into silence. Little did they realize, far from the example they wanted to create out of him, he became a different kind of an example for the students. Rohith's struggle in his life and in death, the connections he made of varied oppressions, the philosophical insights and the rebellion contained in his suicide letter—all of these became examples, or rather inspirations, for many to take on the same path as Rohith.

Today, the responsibility and the challenge lies on the shoulders of the JNU students' movement to pick up from where Rohith left.

It is said that speech is really free, only if it hurts. It is more than obvious that as we speak up against the anti-adivasi/pro-corporate 'development' model of the state, or against entrenched Brahmanism, or patriarchy or communalism—it will most certainly hurt the sentiments and interests of those in power. Our resolve therefore must be to go on hurting them.

BHAIRAV ACHARYA

Bhairav Acharya is a lawyer who specializes in the defence of free speech. In the following essay, a version of which first appeared on TheWire.in, he traces the questionable presence of the sedition law in the Indian Constitution and the perils of having such a law in a democratic society.

The Second Coming of Sedition

A plaque on the wall of Courtroom 46 in the Bombay High Court proclaims: 'There are higher powers that rule the destiny of men and nations and it may be the will of Providence that the cause which I represent may prosper more by my suffering than by my remaining free.'

The plaque remembers Bal Gangadhar Tilak's defiant speech to the court in 1909 after being convicted of sedition by a colonial jury. Tilak's cause was not restricted to political freedom; as the editor of the Kesari, at the time the highest circulating newspaper in the country, Tilak represented freedom of speech in India. 108 years later, what would Tilak have made of the republic that he helped to create?

The notion of sedition lingers on in India, refusing to go away, silencing students, doctors and writers today as it did nationalist leaders a century ago. Even as other advanced democracies have abolished sedition, it has enjoyed a resurgence in India. This is ironic because sedition had an uncertain birth.

'An Unaccountable Mistake'

Although present in Thomas Macaulay's draft penal law submitted to governor-general George Eden in 1837, the sedition provisions mysteriously vanished when the Indian Penal Code was enacted in 1860. It was an 'unaccountable mistake,' said James Stephen, the viceroy's law minister, which he remedied by re-introducing sedition into the law in 1870.

A mistake seems unlikely, although it is the most cited explanation for the disappearance. The Indian Penal Code was an important pillar of colonial rule in India, enacted only two years after the Great Revolt of 1857 ended. If the colonial authorities simply forgot to enact Macaulay's draft sedition offence, which would have enabled the silencing of other would-be critics of British rule, it was a lapse of incomparable negligence.

On the other hand, some commentators have argued that because speech was already heavily policed by the colonial government, the sedition offence was unnecessary and deliberately left out of the law. Its reappearance in 1870 is attributed to the failure of the 'Wahabee' trials in which the colonial government's evidence was too feeble for even a colonial court. A more catch-all law was needed to secure easy convictions.

The Golden Age

Enter the sedition offence. Enacted in 1870, it criminalized speech that 'excited feelings of disaffection to the Government.' This peculiar Victorian formulation remains the law in India today. In 1898, one year after Tilak's first sedition trial, the offence was widened to embrace the bringing of the government 'into hatred or contempt.' The language is significant—it protects the government, not the nation.

Doubly fortified by their expansive sedition law, the colonial authorities swung into action. Several regional newspapers across the country were harassed and their editors arrested. Sedition was not restricted to the press—it was used against theatre artistes, writers, folk singers, and ordinary citizens.

These measures were accompanied by a significant infrastructural build-up of censorship law. Magistrates were given the power to bind *potentially* seditious people to a bond—this had the effect of turning sedition into a prospective thought-crime. The state did not even have to meet a nominal burden of proof. The hitherto unknown offence of 'promoting inter-class enmity' was created. Vague laws were made to ban meetings and newspapers.

That was sedition's heyday. It shackled the speech and freedoms of Indians. In 1922, Mohandas Gandhi was convicted of sedition. He, too, remained defiant: 'I am here to submit to the highest penalty that can be inflicted upon me for what appears to me (sedition) to be the highest duty of a citizen,' he told the judge. 'The only course open to you, is either to resign your post or to inflict on me the severest penalty.'

A Bad Bequest

The British left India but left their laws behind. Free India inherited the sedition offence along with the rest of the colonial government's censorship apparatus. Why were these provisions not immediately repealed? Perhaps the nascent Indian state was insecure. Born amidst strife and volatility, it turned to the same laws that enabled colonial control.

The sedition offence was criticized by members of the Constituent Assembly, many of whom had suffered its arbitrariness. It was intended to be overridden by the constitutional right to free speech. But sedition was never removed from the Indian Penal Code. In 1951, Prime Minister Jawaharlal Nehru substantially weakened the right to free speech when he oversaw a constitutional amendment which made freedom of expression subservient to 'public order,' a nebulous concept that shelters vague offences like sedition.

Nehru claimed that sedition was an 'objectionable and obnoxious' offence, but his government did nothing to repeal it. For his part in preserving the legal architecture of colonial rule, Nehru must be harshly judged. Later, on the eve of the Bangladesh War in 1971, the Law Commission thumpingly endorsed the criminalization of sedition because its 'ultimate end is to destroy the bond between the Government and those whose obedience the Government is entitled to command.'

What would Gandhi have made of this claim that sees citizens as obedient subjects? 'Affection [to the government] cannot be manufactured or regulated by law,' he told the judge at his trial. '[Sedition] is the prince among the political sections of the [law] designed to suppress the liberty of the citizen.'

An Unwelcome Return

Tilak, Gandhi, and their compatriots are long gone, as has colonial rule over India, but sedition remains in the law. In 1950, the Punjab High Court (as it was then called) struck down the sedition offence because '[a] law of sedition thought necessary during a period of foreign rule has become inappropriate.' In 1958, the Allahabad high court struck down sedition for 'striking at the very root of the Constitution which is free speech.' Unfortunately, these decisions were overturned by the Supreme Court in 1962, amidst the war with China, leaving the colonial crime of sedition alive.

Many decades have passed since the creation of the republic. The existential anxiety that afflicted newly-created India has abated. But today's government appears no less insecure than its predecessors. In February 2016, sedition law was used against students at Jawaharlal Nehru University for speaking what many people believe are simple truths. For others who disagreed, the claims represented dissenting opinions. The law must protect dissent, it is the cornerstone of freedom in a democracy.

In recent years, governments across the political spectrum, at the centre and the states, have used sedition to silence dissent. Sedition has been used against anti-nuclear protestors, doctors, cartoonists, writers, editors, professors, and students. All of the victims were peaceful and non-violent—their views did not incite imminent violence. Their circumstances are quite similar to the previous century's victims of colonial rule, during the golden age of sedition.

The increasing use of sedition in the twenty-first century, no matter the government in power, has set India upon a dangerous, backwards-facing trajectory. This must be corrected. Sedition is an outdated offence, incompatible with modern India. It must be weeded out of the law.

HARSH MANDER

Harsh Mander, writer, human rights worker, columnist, researcher and teacher, works with survivors of mass violence and hunger as well as with homeless persons and street children. He quit the Indian Administrative Services following the Gujarat killings of 2002. In this essay (an earlier version of which appeared in Seminar*), he writes about the necessity of dissent for civil servants.*

Conscience, Not Obedience

A powerful permanent civil service, selected on merit, is one of the legacies of colonial rule that India's post-colonial political leadership consciously chose to preserve in free India. The higher bureaucracy retains even seventy years after Independence many of its colonial cultural legacies of the conspicuous trappings of power, including sprawling bungalows, liveried staff, flashing car beacons and peremptory sirens.

Despite these symbols, the transition of post-colonial India to a parliamentary democracy entailed the transformation of the permanent bureaucracy (at least theoretically) from masters to servants. The people were now sovereign, and exercised their sovereignty through public representatives elected by a process of universal adult franchise. The bureaucracy were now servants of the people, not their remote and unaccountable masters.

It is often believed that this metamorphosis in a democracy of the permanent executive from master to servant, entailed that the highest ethic of a civil servant was now one of obedience to the will of the people, as articulated in the will of the people's representatives. I will argue that on the contrary, precisely because the civil servant is a servant of the people and the Constitution, his or her highest duty is not of obedience but of conscience. I believe that a democracy guarantees to civil servants not only the right, but even enjoins on them the duty, to dissent in response to the call of their conscience.

I begin this investigation with a brief evaluation of the contributions of the civil service to the people and the country in independent India. What is most germane to such an assessment is the mettle with which the civil service stood up in times of national crisis. In the early, relatively idealistic decades after Independence, the civil service lived up better to the expectations of the people, especially in the way it organized relief camps for millions of refugees uprooted by the country's bloody Partition, and organized their rehabilitation. This remains to date arguably its greatest contribution to nation building. It also played its role in helping give shape, with scientists, engineers, farmers and workers, to Nehru's aspirations to build India's economic infrastructure and become self-sufficient in food.

The civil service in the first decade after Independence also succeeded in substantially abiding by and operationalizing the steely Nehruvian political resolve of restraining divisive and communal organizations and politics, as a result of which the troubled and deeply wounded country was remarkably free of communal riots after Gandhi's assassination at the hands of extremist Hindutva radicals. This era of communal peace endured for more than a decade, until the Jabalpur riots in early 1961. Fault lines had of course already begun to appear—such as when the District Magistrate K.K. Nair in Ayodhya opened the locks of the Babri Masjid for Hindu worship in 1949, laying the foundations for a communal dispute which was to tear the country apart three decades later—but these were relatively rare. The country could still rely on the higher civil service to act without communal partisanship in religious and ethnic disputes, despite its many other betrayals and failures— including growing corruption, and its complicity in the pervasive failure to implement land reforms across the country.

India witnessed a spectacular nation-wide mass betrayal by the civil service during the twenty-one-month state of Emergency imposed from 25 June 1975 to 21 March 1977, by President Fakhruddin Ali Ahmed, on the advice of Prime Minister Indira Gandhi under Article 352 of the Constitution of India. This enabled the Prime Minister to accomplish the large-scale suspension of the fundamental rights guaranteed by the Constitution, elections, a free press and civil liberties. Tens of thousands of political opponents were jailed. A judicial commission led by Justice Shah which later investigated these traumatic and shameful twenty-one months of suspended freedoms, observed that, 'The decision to arrest and release certain persons were entirely on political considerations which were intended to be favourable to the ruling party. Employing the police to the advantage of one party is a sure source of subverting the rule of law'.[1] The Commission was particularly scathing about the role of most Indian Administrative Service officers who, it found, obeyed orders even though these were unjust and politically motivated. It documented cases of IAS officers undertaking the 'forging of records, fabrication of ground[s] of detention, ante-dating detention orders, and callous disregard of the rights of detainees as regards revocation, parole, etc.' It said that civil servants displayed loyalty to government in power in order to advance their careers. It observed that 'Even the cream of the talent in the country in the administrative field often collapses at the slightest pressure'.[2] Justice Shah famously observed that during this phase, when the civil service was asked to bend, it crawled. In other words, its fault was that not that it failed to obey, but that it obeyed too uncritically and unresistingly the illegal and venal instructions of its political masters.

Four decades later, in 2016, when I observed Delhi's Police Commissioner obediently arresting left-leaning students critical of the central government on grave charges of sedition, based on flimsy and probably fabricated evidence, while allowing lawyers to thrash them in court, I wonder how little has changed in this culture of abject unprincipled obedience. Julio Ribeiro, a retired police officer respected for his integrity, declared in the *Indian Express*, 'I would never have agreed to take up cudgels against a bunch of idealistic students just to humour the party in power!'[3] He added, 'If shouting slogans against the injustices of the caste system or against the perceived inequalities suffered by the poor in our land is interpreted as being anti-national, I am afraid that many, many more students, activists and others crying out for justice are going to be branded in a similar manner. That is totally unacceptable... I disapprove vehemently of doctored and concocted videos designed to send leftist students to jail. To my mind, such concoction of evidence is worse than the crime the student is supposed to have committed and deserves a punishment equal to the one sought to be inflicted'.[4] Speaking of the deliberate inaction of the Delhi police when lawyers attacked student leader Kanhaiya Kumar in court in the same case, he stated: 'It frightens people like me when Delhi's lawyers ape their counterparts in Pakistan and go on a rampage in the hallowed precincts of our temples of justice, attempting to lynch prisoners in the custody of the police. It frightens people like me when the police force, of which I was once a proud member, stands and stares and does nothing when nationalists take the law into their own hands in the very presence of the upholders of the law. It frightens me even more when I suddenly realize that the man at the head of this force is studiedly selective in the enforcement of the law'.[5]

The same failure to resist illegal orders with devastating consequences has marked official behaviour in virtually every later hour of major national crisis. I will dwell more closely on the specific complicity of public officials in communal and caste massacres, because I regard the recurrent refusal of the large majority of civil servants to resist venal political directions to allow the targeted slaughter and rape of persons because of their religious or caste identity to be among the most profound betrayals of the civil services. But there are many other failures as well: the failure to end endemic hunger despite the massive stocks of rotting food grains in government warehouses; the flawed, infirm and corrupt implementation of numerous programmes to address poverty and provide social protection, laws for protecting Scheduled Castes and Tribes from discrimination and violence, and laws and programmes for gender equality; the failures of public education and health marked by not just low allocations (for which civil servants may escape some of the blame as these are primarily political decisions) but by abysmal standards of public service and accountability and the exit of not just the middle classes but civil servants from these public services; the active complicity of the permanent executive in the denial of human rights, the fake extra-judicial 'encounter' killings and suppression by brute force of militant Maoist Naxalite uprisings and separatist insurgencies in the North East and later in Punjab and Kashmir; failures to hold criminally accountable Union Carbide in the poisonous gas leak which killed thousands in Bhopal in 1984; a continued participation in spectacular levels of crony capitalism; and many, many others.

~

By way of illustration, I will elaborate on the nature and consequences of the failures of the higher civil services in just one area, and this is of their complicity, substantially through culpable inaction, in a series of communal massacres. Even during the 1960s and '70s, there was frequent evidence of partisan action by the civil services and police against minorities during recurring episodes of communal violence. But until the 1980s, there was still an unwritten agreement in our polity that even if politicians inflamed communal passions, the police and civil administration would be expected to act professionally and impartially to control the riots in the shortest possible time, and to protect innocent lives. There were several failures in performance, and minorities were targeted in many infamous riots, but the rules of the game were still acknowledged and in instances adhered to, which is why the higher civil and police services were regarded as the steel frame vital to preserve the unity and plurality of the country, although there were signs of this steel frame weakening and rusting.

The 1980s saw the breaking of this unwritten compact which has led to the corrosion and ultimate collapse of the steel frame. It became— and continues to be—a frequent practice for higher civil and police authorities to be instructed to actively connive in the systematic slaughter of one community, and to do this mainly by delaying, sometimes by several days, the use of force to control riots. Local state authorities have complied, and rioters were unrestrained by state power in their mass murder, arson and plunder.

The turning point was the brutal massacre of around 3,000 Bengali Muslim people, including many women and children, in Nellie in 1983, and the 1984 massacre of more than 3,000 Sikhs on the streets of the national capital in the wake of Mrs Gandhi's assassination at the hands of her Sikh bodyguards in 1984, when the ruling Congress party openly engineered the massacre for partisan political gains. This was followed by the slaughter of unarmed Muslim youth at Hashimpura by paramilitary soldiers in 1987; the brutal slaughter of entire populations of Muslims in many villages in Bhagalpur in 1989; the demolition of the Babri Masjid in 1992 and the runaway communal slaughter that followed in its wake in Mumbai and Bhopal; the state-sponsored massacre of enormous cruelty in Gujarat in 2002; the anti-Christian slaughter in Kandhamal in 2006; the Kokrajhar killings of both Bengali Muslims and Bodo tribal people in Assam in 2012 resulting in the displacement of an unprecedented half a million people; and the Muzaffarnagar carnage in 2013. There is a similar grim roll-call of brutal anti-Dalit violence, including in Tsundur, Laxmanpur-Bathe, Kilvenmani, Villupuram, Dharmapuri, Bathani Tola, Jhajjar, Khairlanji, and many others.

In the aftermath of the Gujarat carnage in 2002, when I chose to put in my papers and end my career in the Indian Administrative Service, I wrote for *Outlook*, 'Civil and police authorities today openly await the orders of their political supervisors before they apply force, so much so that it has become popular perception that indeed they cannot act without the permission of their administrative and political superiors, and ultimately the chief minister. The legal position is…unambiguous, in empowering local civil authorities to take all decisions independently about the use of force to control public disorders, including calling in the army… The law is clear that in the performance of this responsibility, civil and police authorities are their own masters, responsible above all to their own judgement and conscience'.[6]

The general failures of the higher civil services during communal massacres are to abet the slaughter of religious minorities and disadvantaged castes mainly by the enormous crime of deliberate and culpable *inaction* by public officials. The draft of the Communal and Targeted Violence Bill (prepared in the National Advisory Council but rejected even before its introduction in Parliament in 2013)[7] sought to make such deliberate inaction by public servants a crime (linking this with the principle of command responsibility). In simple words, this is the crime of public officials allowing organized and armed mobs to attack people—kill, rape and burn—only because of their religious or caste identity, simply by not acting to restrain them and failing when necessary to call in the army to control the rampaging crowds.

It is an increasingly rare experience to encounter exceptional women and men of strong moral character in the civil and police services who have defied political directions to allow communal and caste violence, and have resorted instead to the salutary application of force to control mass communal violence without recourse to political clearances. But the actions of such officers demonstrates that given administrative and political will, no riot can continue unchecked beyond a few hours.

I can give many examples. But one that is particularly heroic because such few officers stood tall at that time, was that of police officer Rahul Sharma, posted during the 2002 Gujarat carnage as the Superintendent of Police in Bhavnagar District. On 2 March 2002, a mob of several thousand people converged on a madrassa with 400 boys. But Sharma ordered police firing, saving the lives of all the children. Journalist Kingshuk Nag states that this angered the then-chief minister Modi who felt that Sharma was 'trying to seek cheap publicity and act like a hero.' The Home Minister was also reportedly enraged because this was a rare district during the carnage where more Hindus were killed in police firings than Muslims. Sharma was transferred abruptly as a punishment to the police control room. There he observed that ministers and senior political leaders were continuously directing the rampaging mobs, and realized that the mobile phone records of those fateful three weeks would be crucial evidence of their involvement. He collected these records, but his superior officers refused to act on these. Sharma bravely presented these records to the judicial commissions of Justice Bannerjee and Justices Nanavati and Shah, and later to the Supreme Court-appointed

Special Investigation Team. Manoj Mitta describes how this evidence was crucial in nailing Minister Maya Kodnani's role in leading the murderous crowds in Naroda Patiya, contributing to her eventual conviction. For these actions, Rahul Sharma faced a host of retributive actions from the Gujarat government, and his career was destroyed. Ultimately he took voluntary retirement at the age of fifty. But when I met him (after he also suffered the personal tragedy of his wife's untimely death by dengue), he affirmed to me that he had no regrets for any of his official actions, because they were to advance justice and truth. He is among the most courageous persons I have met, in the civil services or outside, but he wore his heroism lightly and with both dignity and humility.

The failures of public officials during targeted communal and caste violence do not end with the culpable inaction (or more rarely openly partisan actions) that enable mass violence to continue. These are frequently followed by communally partisan patterns in arrests, failing to register and investigate crimes, facilitating impunity for most of the rioters, and consistent failures to extend reparations to the survivors. The Centre for Equity Studies has carefully examined the official record of four major communal massacres—Nellie in 1983, Delhi in 1984, Bhagalpur in 1989 and Gujarat in 2002—and found that there are recurring patterns in which impunity for the perpetrators is built into the criminal justice system, largely by the ways police refuse to file first information reports from victims and instead deliberately file omnibus, ambiguous complaints that blank out the names of both the accused and the witnesses, deliberately slipshod investigations, 'cross-cases' in which the victims are charged with false violent crimes in order to force them to 'compromise', and so on. None of this would be possible without the active complicity of police officers, and their large participation in this active subversion of justice for survivors of mass hate crimes is very unfortunate. The report also looks at recurring and shameful failures in the relief and reparations to survivors of these mass crimes, the central blame of which must be attributed to senior officers of the higher civil services.

Once again, let me illustrate this with another shining exception, again from Gujarat, reported by the New York Times.[8] Police officer Neerja Gotru Rao was deputed to reinvestigate the slaughter, as well as rape in some cases, of sixty-eight persons in Kalol village, after the Supreme Court ordered the reopening and reinvestigation of around 2,000 cases that had been closed alleging that there was no evidence.

The report describes her as 'a policewoman of uncommon courage'[9] who compassionately listened to the survivors, investigated fairly, and found the burnt remains of several victims. Her investigations led to the arrest of police officer Patil for his complicity in the mass crimes, including the destruction of evidence by burning the bodies of those killed, and of twenty-seven other accused persons.

I concluded my article in 2002 explaining my profound disillusionment with the higher civil services, which I loved in many ways and within whose ranks I spent some of the best years of my life. The service had offered me every opportunity to pursue and advance many of my beliefs in social and economic justice: 'Today, when I stand witness to the massacre in Gujarat enabled by spectacular state abdication and connivance—or to the national disgrace of people living at the edge of starvation even when godowns overflow with food grains—I recognize the cold truth that the higher civil and police services are today in the throes of an unprecedented crisis. The absolute minimum that any state must ensure is the survival and security of its people, and elementary justice. If state authorities wantonly let violent mobs target innocents without restraint—or let people die unmourned of hunger when mountains of food rot in godowns—and they continue to do this with impunity and without remorse or shame, then basic questions need to be asked.'[10]

~

There are indeed many honourable persons in India's higher civil services, mostly unsung heroes like Rahul Sharma and Neerja Gotru Rao. Yet the numbers who are willing to resist and dissent against instructions to deny people their constitutional rights, including to life, liberty and democratic dissent, and willing to extend equal protection of the law to people because of their religious, caste or ethnic identities or economic powerlessness—are becoming rarer with the passing of the years. The people of the nation owe a great debt to often little-known— and sometimes enormously valiant—voices of courage, conscience and dissent from within the ranks of the bureaucracy. But the unsung and mostly unknown heroes from within the bureaucracy who swim bravely against the current, refusing to obey unjust and illegal orders, could never gather sufficient critical mass for the permanent bureaucracy to act as a decisive bulwark against divisive communal and anti-Dalit politics, failures of justice, crony capitalism, denial of labour protections, the pauperization of the tribal people, destruction of the environment and the crushing of democratic dissent. The bureaucracy must carry therefore a very high historical blame for failures of the state in these times to extend equal protection of the law to religious, caste, ethnic and tribal minorities, to women, to the working classes, and to impoverished people in general.

In the nineteen years that I worked within the civil service, I found that obedience was repeatedly upheld as the paramount virtue of a civil servant in a democracy. It was commonly advocated by official and political superiors that the duty of a civil servant is to obey the orders of political masters without questioning these dictates, and to find ways to most efficiently implement these. Officers who dissented were not just inconvenient, but were actually stepping outside the boundaries laid down for the permanent unelected executive in a parliamentary democracy.

I apologize for a brief autobiographical interlude at this point, but it is unavoidable if I am to develop my argument. Like other colleagues who sought to abide by their conscience, I found myself tossed around from posting to posting, often every few months, twenty-two times during my nineteen years in the civil service. This caused me unfailing heartbreak repeatedly, but it is a known hazard of the profession which I needed to learn to stoically accept. I was by no means the first to face this, and I will certainly not be the last.

In my early years of service, the Chief Secretary (who heads the civil service in the state government) would sometimes call me after an untimely transfer and say that he was proud of my stands, but regretted his inability to protect me. More often, there was no call and no apology. However, I reached a low watershed once, after I was posted out of a district following the action I had taken after a communal riot. The Chief Secretary called me to the secretariat office and sternly counselled me: 'I believe that the time has come when you need to decide about whether or not you wish to continue in the service. The terms on which you are trying to engage with service of the government are just not acceptable. If the government tells you to throw poor people into the ocean, you have only two choices. You either comply, by tossing them into the ocean. Or you quit. But you are adamant, saying that I refuse to obey and throw the people into the ocean, and at the same time I refuse to quit. That is simply not acceptable. In a democracy, your duty is only to faithfully obey.'

I found myself profoundly troubled by this interview. What my official superior communicated to me that afternoon in effect was that, by refusing to obey my political and official superiors, I was not only being foolhardy and unmindful of the interests of advancing my career, and I was not only causing problems to the establishment and annoying them, but I was failing to abide by the limitations that a civil servant must accept in a democracy, by wilfully disobeying my official and political superiors. My disquiet arose because I was told that I was acting in ways that were *ethically flawed*. In this instance, I had been summarily moved out of my district charge, after I defied instructions from 'above' and instead ensured that leaders of the Hindutva organizations who had dangerously inflamed passions around the Ayodhya Ram Janmbhoomi movement and led the killings and arson in communal rioting in several towns of my district were arrested and grave criminal charges, including of murder, were slammed on them. I could understand that this would anger the government of the day, more so because it was of the political party which had led the agitation for the building of a Ram Temple at Ayodhya at the site of the medieval Babri mosque. But I could not understand or accept that my actions were ethically wrong, because although I disobeyed political and administrative orders, I felt that I had tried in a small way to uphold the secular democratic Constitution and its pledge of equal protection of the law to people of all faiths.

My disquiet led me to try to unravel what I believed instinctively to be the flawed ethics of my official superior. In stark terms, the question was: what is the highest duty of a civil servant in a democracy? Is it obedience or conscience? Does a civil servant have the right to dissent and even refuse to comply with orders that violate what she believes to be lawful, just and humane? My hunch was that conscience and dissent must be the paramount value for any public servant. If obedience indeed was the highest ethic of a civil servant, then in the excesses of the Emergency, or indeed the violation of human rights in insurgencies, or majoritarian partisanship in communal violence, civil servants could honestly plead that they were just faithfully implementing orders from their 'political masters'. How could they be then held guilty of complicity in grave injustice against defenceless citizens? Yet I was not alone in regarding these as shameful, even criminal abdication of duties by civil servants, with catastrophic outcomes for the people and the country. Where then was the moral paradox?

~

I believe firstly that if there is indeed a duty of obedience, then it can only be to the lawful, officially stated and publicly espoused objectives of the government, not the unlawful, unstated directives of elected political or superior administrative actors in the executive. Let me illustrate. The official position of governments is that legislated land reform laws should be faithfully implemented. But the unstated orders of political superiors are almost invariably that powerful landowners should not be dispossessed of their land holdings. Whenever I tried to distribute ceiling surplus agricultural land to the landless, or restore land illegally expropriated from tribal land holders, the ministers and local elected representatives would react with horror as though I was a closet Maoist who had penetrated the ranks of the civil service. They would instruct me, sometimes even supported explicitly at the highest levels of the state government, to stop implementing these progressive land reform laws. I developed a standard answer to such demands from elected representatives: 'I did not make the law, but I have been given the duty to implement it. If you think the law is unjust, please go to the legislature and change it. But you cannot first pass laws in favour of the poor, and then order me not to implement them. I am not bound by these orders.'

The same chasm between the stated legal policies and the actual will of the executive can be found everywhere. The stated policies are for fair and non-partisan action in communal, caste and gender violence, but the unstated political or administrative directives often advocate biased action against vulnerable and oppressed castes, religious and ethnic minorities and women. The law enjoins respect for human fundamental rights, but there is often open and unapologetic political endorsement, even at the highest levels of the executive, for torture and encounter killings. The law makes corruption a criminal offence, but in practice this is endorsed as the grease that makes the giant sluggish state machinery function.

I can understand the claim that it is the duty of public officials to faithfully implement orders of the political executive and the administrative hierarchy when these are lawful orders, in conformity with the official stated policies of government. In fact, if officers are faithful to the stated policies and laws of government, the officer will then be bound to implement land reforms and other progressive legislation, to protect oppressed and dispossessed minorities, castes and women, fight corruption and respect human rights. But the reality is that in obeying and implementing in letter and spirit these stated lawful policies, the officer will frequently be *disobeying* the unstated, unlawful goals of the superior executive. The civil servant who chooses to obey these unlawful directives cannot claim ethical defence in the duty of obedience of civil servants in a democracy, because even if faithful obedience is the highest duty of the official, the obedience cannot be to unlawful orders. I found belatedly my answer to my Chief Secretary: it is unlikely that the stated lawful orders of the government would be to throw poor people into the ocean. These could be the illegal directives of my official superiors, but far from it being my duty to obey these, my only obligation is to resist and actually disobey these orders. Therefore I can legitimately disobey, dissent and still refuse to quit the civil service, if I choose to do so.

The problem, however, is not so easily fully resolved. Not all statutes or government policies are just and conforming to the interests of disadvantaged citizens. There are a whole body of laws and policies that I believe to be wholly unjust, such as those that vest security forces with special powers in troubled regions, laws that enable involuntary acquisition of land, laws that criminalize beggary and destitution, and policies to demolish urban slums, to name only a few. Does the civil servant have the right to dissent and refuse to implement laws and policies which contravene his or her conscience? I have always believed this to be the case. The civil servant does not surrender this inalienable right to individual conscience even after joining public service in a democracy, precisely because it is a democracy; and a civil servant does not cease to be a sovereign citizen even while accepting the responsibility of becoming the instrument to implement the will of the sovereign collective of people as reflected in the will of their public representatives.

I exercised what I saw to be my right to dissent with even lawful official instructions from my political and administrative superiors if I regarded these to be unjust. When in my career I refused to obey official directives from the highest political executive—for example, to use force to crush democratic dissent in the movement against the Sardar Sarovar Project in the Narmada Valley; or to displace farmers of twenty-two villages in Singrauli for a super-thermal power plant without even an elementary rehabilitation plan; or to open fire on an angry crowd of coal miners enraged at the collapse of the mine due to the carelessness of their managers; or to demolish urban slums; or to drive away or lock up the homeless and destitute—I feel that I disobeyed my superiors legitimately.

But I recognize that there can be reasonable unease about endorsing the ethical right of all civil servants to act in obedience to their conscience rather than the directions of the political executive, even when these conform to the law and the stated policies of the government. It can be argued that if every public official was free to disobey laws and policies which they regarded to be unjust, then this could be a prescription ultimately for anarchy. But I would counter that if every civil servant was bound to obey every official law and policy, even if this contravened her conscience, then this could lead ultimately to fascism. And if the ultimate choice for my country is between anarchy and fascism, my choice would be for anarchy! A story is told of the training of youth recruits by the Nazis. They were given puppies when they joined, and encouraged to develop bonds of affection with these little creatures. One day the commanding officer would order them to strangle the animal to death. Only if they complied, and that too without flinching, did they pass the test of being reliable Nazi workers. On the contrary, many of us would find reliable an officer who would not only flinch, but stoutly refuse to obey such an order. Only such an official would have had the strength of character to defy the Emergency of 1975–78 or the carnage in Gujarat in 2002.

The question then is whether this right to act by one's conscience is unlimited and unqualified for a civil servant. Clearly it is not. Suppose a civil servant believes, say, in the Maoist project of the violent overthrow of the state, or secession to form say Khalistan, and uses his or her offices to actually protect militants and promote insurgency, I would regard these actions as illegitimate. Likewise, if the official's conscience leads to active complicity in the demolition of the Babri Masjid, I believe the official has crossed dangerously, even criminally, the ethically permissible limits of dissent in public service.

There seems a paradox and a serious logical flaw here. If I suggest that the civil servant has the right to act by her conscience and disobey orders of her superiors, then is there not a contradiction in suggesting that these forms of dissent are impermissible for a civil servant? But I would argue that there is no real contradiction. The limits to dissent by public servants are laid down by the letter and spirit of the Constitution of India. The Constitution declares India to be a socialist, secular democracy. I believe that when one joins the civil service, one must subscribe fully to the Constitution, and its basic features and values, as well as to upholding the integrity of the nation. These basic features are lucidly—and luminously—spelt out in the Preamble of the Constitution: Justice,

Liberty, Equality and Fraternity. If one's conscience is in disagreement with the basic values of the Constitution itself, then there is no legitimate space for such dissent in one's duties as a civil servant. Civil servants cannot ethically act on their beliefs in the course of their duties if they dissent with secularism for instance—as interpreted as equal protection under the law and equal legal citizenship rights to all regardless of their faith, gender, caste, language, ethnicity and wealth. They cannot differ with other core features of our Constitution, such as the principle that the state must intervene to defend the rights of disadvantaged people including through affirmative action; or reject universal adult franchise as just a sham democracy. They are not morally permitted to uphold untouchability, or violence against women and discrimination because of gender, or communalism, or bonded labour, or the deployment of violence as a legitimate instrument of political aspirations.

The Constitution therefore sets out the non-negotiable limits of dissent of public servants. It defines for those to who accrue the powers of the state the frontiers of conscience and discretion. Civil servants must obey faithfully, defend and uphold the Constitution and all it stands for. But in the commodious spaces within the four walls of the Constitution, I believe the civil servant retains the rights of conscience and dissent, of course against illegal orders, but even against lawful orders, policies and programmes that the civil servant believes to be unjust.

Is dissent, in obedience to the call of one's conscience (within the limits laid down by the Constitution) just a right of the civil servant, or a duty? I believe that public officials are not servants of their administrative superiors, or of elected representatives, or even of the government that employs them. They are servants firstly of the people—especially of the disadvantaged and oppressed—and of the Constitution. In the service of these masters, they would do well to heed the example of Gandhi, who declared that he recognized only one dictator, and that was the still feeble inner voice of his conscience. If the voice of their conscience so compels civil servants, their highest duty is indeed to dissent. Only if they act consistently with their conscience and in conformity with the Constitution, would the people whom they serve be in safe and caring hands.

Howard Zinn in an interview with Sharon Basco in 2002 extended this counsel not specifically to civil servants but to citizens in general. However, civil servants are also citizens, and his words are something every civil servant would also do well to heed. He declared that 'obedience to government certainly is not a form of patriotism. Governments are the instruments to achieve certain ends. And if the government goes against those ends, if the government is not defending our liberties, but is diminishing our liberties... At that point...the most patriotic thing (is) to disobey the government'.[11]

Notes

1. Srivastava, Aparna (1999). *Role of Police in a Changing Society*. APH Publishing. Quoting Chapter XV of the 26 April 1978 Interim Report the Commission.
2. Mooij, Jos E. (2005). *The Politics of Economic Reforms in India*. SAGE.
3. Ribeiro, Julio. 11 March 2016. 'BJP's Handling of JNU Row will backfire like Shah Banoo case did on Congress'. *Indian Express*.
4. Ribeiro, Julio. 29 February 2016. 'Lament of an anti-national'. *Indian Express*.
5. Ibid.
6. Mander, Harsh. 22 April 2002. 'Call of Conscience, Cast of Character'. *Outlook*.
7. Full disclosure: I co-convened the working group in the NAC for drafting the Communal and Targeted Violence Bill, with Farah Naqvi
8. http://www.nytimes.com/2004/10/17/world/asia/indian-muslims-hope-is-one-good-policewoman.html
9. Ibid.
10. Mander, Harsh. 22 April 2002. 'Call of Conscience, Cast of Character'. *Outlook*.
11. Howard Zinn, Interview with Sharon Basco, 3 July 2002. [http://howardzinn.org/dissent-in-pursuit-of-equality-life-liberty-and-happiness/ Accessed 30.03.16]

KIRAN NAGARKAR

Playwright, critic, screenwriter and award-winning novelist, Kiran Nagarkar has written consistently, clear-sightedly and fearlessly on a range of issues confronting contemporary India. This open letter, written in March 2016, was first published in Scroll.in.

A Letter to Modi: Why Is There Such a Gap between Your Wonderful Words and Your Actions?

Dear Prime Minister Modiji,

On March 17, you outdid yourself on the first day of the World Sufi Forum hosted in Delhi. What could one say except 'What a speech, how moving.' You had done your homework and you obviously have total recall (it would also be interesting to find out who your speechwriters are) but the fact remains that you are able to reproduce their amalgam of fact and rhetoric into an extempore mix.

This is what you said:

'Welcome to a land that is a timeless fountain of peace, and an ancient source of traditions and faiths, which has received and nurtured religions from the world. Welcome to a people with an abiding belief in Vasudhaiva Kutumbakam, the world is one family.'

Let me not resent the liberties you took with our past, but pass it off as your version of Indian history. The list of the saints you name and quote is like a who's who in not just the Indian Sufi world but the whole international Sufi heritage—the Persian poet-philosopher Sadi, and Delhi's own Mehboob-eh-Ilahi, Hazarat Bakhtiyar Kaki and Hazrat Nizamuddin Aulia. You also referred to Khwaja Moinuddin Chishti, Bulleh Shah, Baba Farid, Amir Khusrau, Maulana Hussain Madani, Jalaluddin Rumi, Guru Nanak, Buddha, the Guru Granth Sahib, Mahavir, and Mahatma Gandhi. And you ended with the timeless prayer 'Om shanti, shanti, shanti.'

You had some genuinely wise things to say, like: 'We must reject any link between terrorism and religion. Those who spread terror in the name of religion are anti-religious.'

What noble sentiments. Now here's a prime minister that I felt we could all be proud of. And yet there was this low whisper telling me again and again something that the British Underground, along with the local train stations in Mumbai, have told us for years—mind the gap, mind the gap, mind the gap. That is the gap between the trains and the platforms where so many fall and are injured or die. In your case, Prime Minister it's the credibility gap—the chasm between your wonderful words and zero action.

Let me quote your very words:

'...It is through openness and enquiry, engagement and accommodation, and respect for diversity that humanity advances, nations progress and the world prospers.'

What sane words. You remind me of Bhishma Pitamah from the *Mahabharata* at such times. You speak as wisely as the noble son of Shantanu. And just like him, when it's time to take a stand and back your words with concrete action, you retreat into silence and let the other leaders do the dirty work and take the blame. Or even worse, you pretend what is happening has nothing to do with you. You will recall that just a day after you spoke at the World Sufi Forum, your Minister of State for Human Resource Development, Ram Shankar Katheria, addressed a crowd of 5,000 in Agra. *The Times of India* reported that Katheria had demanded the withdrawal of hate speech cases against BJP and VHP leaders in Agra. 'If these cases are not withdrawn within the assured time, then Agra would witness a different Holi,' Katheria was quoted as saying. If this is the minister for education, the good Lord may not be able to help the students of Jawaharlal Nehru University or any other university.

The minister was referring to arrests made after several Bharatiya Janata Party [BJP] and Vishwa Hindu Parishad [VHP] leaders, including Katheria, made inflammatory speeches at a condolence meeting of a Vishwa Hindu Parishad worker in Agra in February. The worker was murdered, allegedly by a Muslim. At the condolence meeting, the BJP and VHP leaders equated Muslims with demons. VHP's district secretary Ashok Lavania called for murder. 'Revenge for the killing of one brother, demands the killing of 10 rakshas,' he said. After protests following the hate speeches, FIRs were finally lodged against BJP leader and corporator Kundanika Sharma and three others. There was none against Katheria since, like his seniors, he claimed he never said anything against the Muslims. It is these cases that Katheria now wants withdrawn.

The American effect

Have you heard 'Strange Fruit', a song that Billie Holiday, perhaps the most famous black jazz singer from the United States, sang? And each time she did, she broke down. I must confess I had no idea what she was talking about for the longest time.

Here are the lyrics of 'Strange Fruit', Prime Minister:

Southern trees bear a strange fruit,
Blood on the leaves and blood at the root,
Black bodies swinging in the southern breeze,
Strange fruit hanging from the poplar trees.

Pastoral scene of the gallant south,
The bulging eyes and the twisted mouth,
Scent of magnolias, sweet and fresh,
Then the sudden smell of burning flesh.

Here is fruit for the crows to pluck,
For the rain to gather, for the wind to suck,
For the sun to rot, for the trees to drop,
Here is a strange and bitter crop.

She was of course singing a dirge for all those black victims of lynchings by white supremacists. Oddly enough, we who are so fond of emulating the American way of life—that country's fixation with free markets and the 1 per cent who earn far more than what at least 50 per cent of the population does—seem to have now decided to copy some of the worst American values when it comes to our minorities.

As you are well aware, earlier this month in Jharkhand, Mohammmad Majloom, 35, and Inayatullah Khan, 12, were gagged, their hands and legs tied and they were hung from a tree after being beaten with sticks and strangled.

Majloom was a trader escorting a few cattle to the market with the son of another cattle trader. The police think that the duo were murdered because the culprits wanted to steal their cattle. But they are also investigating the connection that one of the killers had with the Gau Raksha Samiti. If theft was the only reason, then one can—by a far-fetched stretch of the imagination—understand the murders. But the manner in which the man and boy were gagged, their bodies strapped and strung on the trees suggests a vile and violent hatred of the two.

Is it possible to talk to you, Modiji? After all you are not the Prime Minister of just the Rashtriya Swayamsevak Sangh, the Bharatiya Janata Party and its affiliates, but of all the people of India. These people elected your party to power. We may not see eye-to-eye on some matters, a few of them very sensitive and crucial, but that's all the more reason for us to sit down and have a conversation instead of a one-way *Mann ki baat*, or your preferred see-no-evil, hear-no-evil, speak-no-evil stance.

Where does this violence come from? Not just the bloodthirsty violence in Muzaffarnagar, Dadri and other places but the violence in speech? Why this insecurity when you won fair and square with an overwhelming majority? Why this continuous victim-syndrome as

Pratap Bhanu Mehta pointed out recently—whether it's the Finance Minister, Arun Jaitley, accusing Sahitya Akademi's award-winning authors of 'manufacturing protests' for returning their awards, or your Human Resources Development Minister, Smriti Irani, insisting that the Jawaharlal Nehru University [JNU] students were guilty of sedition even when she knew very well that the video footage had been doctored? What was the need for Rajnath Singh to retweet a fake Twitter handle that suggested that Pakistan-based Lashkar-e-Taiba chief Hafiz Saeed had supported the so-called seditious events at JNU in February?

Why this demand for every Indian to prove his or her loyalty to our country by saying 'Bharat Mata ki jai?' I'm sure, Prime Minister, you don't want to hear these words spoken by all those who have defrauded our country of thousands of crores, or have stabbed it in the back, and yet have the gall to swear their loyalty to Bharat Mata. Why fear the freedom of thought encouraged by the best universities? Why must those who don't fall in line with the tenets and theology of the ruling party be demonized? One thing that has bothered me for a long time (and let me clarify quickly that it has nothing to do with you) is a legacy of the previous government in Maharashtra. Perhaps you can help us in this matter. Here in Maharashtra, the national anthem is sung before every film shown in the theatres. Often, this happens before the audience is about to watch some dreadful Hollywood blockbluster like *Deadpool* or a mindless Bollywood song-and-dance extravaganza. If this is not a travesty of our anthem, I don't know what is. Along with the rest of the country I sang 'Jana Gana Mana' full-throated for the first time on the two most important days in our nation's history—on August 15, 1947, and on January 26, 1950. Let us honour our flag and our national anthem and not invoke them so meaninglessly as if we do not understand the significance and the history of our unique non-violent, freedom struggle.

Surely we can talk about these points without getting defensive or seeing some devious traitorous intent behind these questions.

But let me come to an issue that has been on my mind, and that I have wanted to share with you for several months. Let me repeat an old adage you may be familiar with: every action has a reaction. So far the Bharatiya Janata Party, the Vishwa Hindu Parishad, the Bajrang Dal, the Rashtriya Swayamsevak Sangh and many of its other incarnations have initiated various schemes to harass and victimize minority communities like the Muslims and Christians through their *love jihad, ghar wapsi, bahu lao, beti bachao* tactics.

It is these Hindutva groups that helped fan a frenzy around the slaughter of cows and eating beef, often in states where the slaughter of cows and consumption of beef had already been banned. Sometimes, this hysteria has tragic consequences. Last year, the farm labourer, Mohammad Akhlaq, in Dadri near Delhi, was falsely accused of having beef in his fridge. He and his youngest son were beaten with bricks by a Hindu mob. Akhlaq succumbed to the murderous attack while his son was critically injured. The Bharatiya Janata Party-led government in Maharashtra also banned the sale of old cattle with the result that the already beleaguered Indian farming community was driven further into penury and often to suicide.

How come, dear Prime Minister, you have not read the riot act to your Islamophobic ministers, legislators, parliamentarians or the rest of the Parivar even once since you came to power? Some folks believe that it is because of these tirades and hate-filled actions that the BJP did not win the Delhi and Bihar elections, and predict that the elections in the four or five states due in the coming months will not be a walkover. I am no oracle but I know one thing for sure, your voter base is very strong.

Modiji, you are an astute politician and statesman. Can you not see that actions as well as the lack of action have consequences especially in these dark times? Surely you are familiar with the proverb 'as you sow, so shall you reap'. As I said earlier, even silence has consequences. I cannot and will not believe that you want to alienate our Muslim brothers and sisters across the subcontinent and make the country one of the best recruiting centres for the Islamic State. So why have you not stopped this persecution of our own Muslim citizens?

I have heard many experts opine on television that our intelligence agencies are doing a fine job of keeping track of those Muslims who wish to join the Islamic State. I am glad to hear that but complacency would be a prescription for disaster. I have also heard them say authoritatively that our Muslim community will never really join the Islamic State in any substantial numbers. That is a marvellously myopic statement. As we have seen time and again, including the 26/11 attacks on Mumbai and the latest attack in Brussels, you don't need large numbers, you need just three to seven efficient and focused operatives to execute a deadly attack. Secondly, anyone with a little common sense will tell us that no community, however small, will have infinite patience and forbearance if continually provoked and prodded, and made to live in tension and fear. No, there will come a point when it will feel it has nothing to lose and strike back.

But here is the crux of the matter. Why in God's name and in the name of our Constitution are we so hell-bent on offending a huge chunk of India's own citizenry? The most important principle of secularism is to take everybody along. Muslims like Dalits, have had a rough deal long enough. We have to open the doors to state-of-the-art education for them and make sure that they find suitable employment. It is our responsibility to erase the ignorance and superstition that Kabir and the other bhakti saints saw as the root cause of all our ills. We must welcome an open wide-as-the-sky mindset so that no Indian is left behind.

Come, Prime Minister Modiji, live up to your own words and show us the way to be together whatever our different faiths, agnosticism or atheism.

Yours truly,
Kiran Nagarkar

KEKI N. DARUWALLA

A major Indian poet and short-story writer, Keki Daruwalla is also a former officer of the Indian Police Service. In this essay, he highlights the fundamentalism that has crept into society and the need to do away with laws that encourage intolerance.

Of Dissent and Laws

Free speech and dissent have become battlegrounds today. The battleground is not restricted to metaphor or hot air spouted through the media, but is getting physical, with a forensic smear to it. Voices are becoming shriller from both sides. It is hoped sanity will be restored. Free speech, even reasonably free speech is passing through odd times, mostly because it is being assiduously and mischievously distorted. When opposing parties and classes have their own agendas which they stridently support, such outcomes should be expected.

The tussle so far is within the ambit of our legal codes. But we Indians are good at sidestepping law, misusing law and sometimes, if goaded forcefully enough by politicians in power, distorting the spirit behind the law. That is worrisome. Our slow, grating legal system, bedevilled as it is with its stodgy focus on rusty procedures and slowed down by an intensely litigant public, is further hampered by some old outdated laws left behind by the British, laws that have become irrelevant today.

Is India (its legal framework and its civil and uncivil halves of society—we have both in good measure) the right place for the arts to flourish? Can the country make such a claim when we have laws like 295 (a) and 153 (a) of the Indian Penal Code (IPC)? Through these two laws, Rahu and Ketu of our legal system, any writer or artist could be jailed for hurting religious sentiments. Everything is grist to the religious mill, from Salman Rushdie to Sacha Sauda, and rumours of beef to plastic cows. In a lighter vein, we could take a hypothetical case. A doctor writes on the perils of diabetes, and next day the sugar lobby of Maharashtra or Uttar Pradesh could file a case against him for hurting its sugary sentiments. The doctor could wake up in the cooler.

Or to get down to reality—the Indian reality, it may be remembered, has a surreal smear to it—take the case of poor Shaheen Dhada, barely twenty-one years of age, whom self-righteous Maharashtra policemen arrested for questioning the total shutdown of Mumbai for Bal Thackeray's funeral, in a Facebook post in 2012. This had nothing to do with religious sentiments. A friend of hers, Renu Srinivasan, liked the post. She too was whisked away. No one of course has ever touched the Sena guys for diatribes against South Indians, Muslims and, lastly, people from U.P. and Bihar. Surely Mumbai would not have closed down but for the fear of what the Sena would do if it did not shut down.

In another such incident, the Catholic church filed a report against Sanal Edamaruku, and forced him out of India for challenging a report of water dripping from the toe of Christ at Our Lady of Vellankanni Church in Mumbai. He correctly attributed the drip to damp walls and defective plumbing in an overhead pipe and provided the proof in a televised debate, while a large crowd gathered to attack him. This miracle-buster is reported to be stuck in Finland since 2012. He had earlier successfully withstood the chanting of a stupid tantric who boasted he could kill people by chanting mantras. Edamaruku asked him to chant his 'murderous' mantras, and of course nothing happened to him. He was and is a rationalist.

To come to revered Ram Rahim, the head of what can be described as a cult-cum-ashram 'Sacha Sauda'. A year ago the entire Sikh peasantry was up in arms against him, as also against the Akal Takht for pardoning him, because he had dressed up as Guru Gobind Singh. We need to come to that later. Punjab had a tough job controlling Sikh mobs out for his blood. There are rumours that he has also dressed up as Lord Vishnu. Now who would know how Vishnu or Shiva dressed? Their 'attire' has come down to us from calendar art and the likes of Ravi Verma.

A harmless comedian, Kiku Sharda, (comedians are mostly harmless) mimicked Ram Rahim exquisitely. The district police of Kaithal flew their police inspectors to Bombay to arrest him for mimicking Rahim. He was brought to Haryana, and released on bail on orders of the court. But even as he was travelling on his way back to Delhi, the Fatehabad police (again in Haryana) got into the act and re-arrested him. The feelings of another disciple had been hurt in Fatehabad district. Hurt sentiments can pluck you out of cars and put you in the lock-up, even if you have a bail order in your hand. This judicial comedy or to appropriately term it, comic tragedy, must have cost the state a few lakhs. And incidentally while Haryana could spare police manpower for this kind of farcical appeasement of a cult, it couldn't spare enough police to control the rioting Jats in the recent stir for reservations in February 2016. Over twenty men died in the riots and property worth hundreds of crores was burnt.

You could write a slightly explicit love poem and some ascetic sanstha could file a case in Kashmir and another in Nagercoil against the poet. My name itself could hurt a votary of prohibition. If he was chummy with a police inspector, he could register a case against me. I could wake up and find that nomenclature has turned into an albatross around my neck—Coleridge please don't turn in your grave. I hope I could also register a case against the blighter for hurting my (alcoholic) sentiments. It would be fun if we were to stand before the same magistrate, as both complainant and accused.

When Siddhartha Kararwal's 'Divine Bovine'—a plastic cow floating in the air, tied to a balloon—was brought down by the Jaipur police on complaints by hurt-sentiment types, artists were asked by the law if the plastic cow was alive or dead. Is the police at the thana level equipped to sit in judgement over such cases? The policemen who seized the cow, according to press reports, were constables, not even sub-inspectors. The artist, it is reported, wanted to draw attention to the plastic bags which cows swallow as they rummage through rubbish dumps. Let us not forget that Jaipur has been a culprit twice—first when Salman Rushdie was invited to the Jaipur Literary Festival in 2012 (Muslim sentiments were hurt) and second when in 2013, Ashis Nandy had to face the brunt of hurt Dalit sentiments.

Seriously, we are aware of the genesis of section 295(a) IPC. Mahashe Rajpal, the author of *Rangila Rasul*, a scandalous book on Prophet Muhammad's wives and sexual habits was acquitted in April 1929. There was no existing law against insult to religion. Hence outraging religious feelings through 'deliberate and malicious intent' was brought into the law book through section 295(a). The author, Rajpal, was stabbed to death by one Ilm-ud-din, who was defended by Muhammad Ali Jinnah among others, but hanged within six months. Our system would take six years now. Jinnah's appearance, be it noted, was pro forma. It was something akin to Jawaharlal Nehru's appearance at the INA trial, where it was Bhulabhai Desai who argued.

Why must artistic freedom be subordinated to that fake penumbra of hurt sentiments? Why should hurt sentiments turn into a collective? Can't they be confined to liverish individuals? And why must a phone call from Mr Dinanath Batra lead to pulping a book? (Incidentally, now other publishers have rushed in and published the same book in enormous numbers.) I would go a step further. Why should hurt religious sentiments get priority over mere religion-less sentiments? Why are we giving so much importance to religions, leave alone religious sentiments, in a secular country? Witness the way protesting writers and later artists and scientists were reviled by right-wingers and pseudo right-wingers who merely wanted to curry favour with the powers that be. An actor went around with a procession protesting against the protestors. Ever heard such nonsense? And the gentleman was privileged to have an audience with the prime minister the same day.

The Supreme Court gave an excellent riposte to embarrassed Meerut lawyers wanting the film *Jolly LLB* to be banned. In the movie, Meerut lawyers were shown petitioning a court where they inadvertently referred to Director of Prosecution as 'Director of Prostitution'. (Delhi lawyers who beat up the JNU Students' Union President Kanhaiya as he entered the courts were never embarrassed, not even when their hooliganism was shown on T.V.)

The Hon'ble Court told the Meerut lawyers: if you don't like the film don't see it. Simplest answer. Why can't we carry this logic to its conclusion? You don't like *Satanic Verses* by Salman Rushdie, don't read it. Plastic cow hurts your eyes, (never mind all the plastic bags that hungry cows swallow) don't watch it. You don't like M.F. Husain's paintings, don't go to that art gallery. But don't drive him out of the country! I saw an exhibition of his at the National Gallery of Modern Art (Jaipur House, Delhi). There was one vast painting where he showed a bull (Papal Bull, kindly note) buggering Europa, the icon after whom Europe is named. The concept was brilliant, risqué humour and metaphor blended exquisitely. No one raised slogans, no one threw stones. How come? Nor did Europe protest.

I have a suggestion. Make these sections, the ones which deal with hurt sentiments, non-cognizable. A case can be registered, but not investigated, till a magistrate sanctions it. This way someone more educated and knowledgeable than a sub-inspector would apply his mind to the case. Don't invite the police into your bedrooms, into your kitchen (beef), art displays (remember M.F. Husain and the plastic cow). Restrict the police to ill-lit streets and dark alleys.

Matters don't end here. What if the laws, rather a particular law, is stretched to fix a specific individual group or institution? What if the implementers turn draconian, as happened in JNU where almost all the office bearers of the JNU Students' Union were put in prison and the Delhi police, obviously prodded by its masters in the North Block, applied sedition laws against youngsters. Sedition! As the cases are *sub judice* it may not be proper to comment. But the home minister and the BJP president have made quite a few statements about the meeting and the shouting of 'seditious', anti-national slogans at the meeting (read, Pakistan zindabad, azadi for Kashmir and speeches about Afzal Guru, the Kashmiri hanged during the UPA regime for involvement in the attack on Parliament). Audio tapes of the meeting brandished about, turned out to be doctored initially. The Delhi police commissioner under whose regime the sedition law was invoked was made a Member of the UPSC after his superannuation.

The Delhi police should have known the law or studied case law on the subject before applying the draconian 124 A IPC. (Sedition entered the British law in India in the 1870s and UK has deleted sedition from its own law book!) The Kedar Nath Singh vs Union of India case decided by a constitutional bench of the Supreme Court should have stopped the police from going overboard to please its political masters. The judgement laid down that allegedly seditious speeches were punishable only if they were an incitement to violence and public disorder. In another case, Shreya Singhal vs Union of India, the Hon'ble Court drew a distinction between 'advocacy' (not punishable) and 'incitement' (punishable). Police of all states should know that the Supreme Court overturned convictions under section 153 A IPC in Bulwant Singh vs State of Punjab where the charge was that the accused had shouted slogans like 'Khalistan zindabad' and 'Raj karega khalsa'.

What about 'doctored' tapes that later turn out to be 'genuine' on a second opinion? According to reports in early June 2016, five of the seven audio tapes have now been found 'genuine'. Similarly, meat found in Dadri, which had been certified as goat meat, has suddenly now been certified as belonging to 'cow and its progeny' by another lab. The murder of Mohammad Akhlaq in Dadri turned out to be the result of a false rumour that he had stored beef. The police, it is reported, was keener to take possession of the meat from his fridge rather than attend to the victim who had been beaten to death by the mob. These later twists may or may not inspire confidence, but it is the courts which have to decide.

What happens where the circumstances are similar, but different laws are applied? The Patidar agitation for reservation in Gujarat attracted the sedition law. In a similar agitation for reservation in Haryana, where over twenty people were killed and property worth crores was destroyed during the Jat reservation stir, no case of sedition was registered.

And what about laws that are patently retrograde? For instance the Muslim Women (Protection of Rights on Divorce) Act, 1986, passed by Rajiv Gandhi's government in order to nullify the Supreme Court judgement in the Shah Bano case, where maintenance of the divorced wife Shah Bano was ordered. Shah Bano's husband, advocate Mohd. Ahmed Khan of Indore had divorced his wife and driven her and her five children out when Shah Bano was sixty-two years old. He had married a second and younger wife. Be it known that when she applied for maintenance before a lower court, the magistrate had granted her and her five children a monthly allowance of Rs 25—generous magistrate. Shah Bano filed a revision before the High Court, which allowed her alimony. Her husband went in appeal to the Supreme Court. The Supreme Court, in a landmark judgement from a five-member bench, invoked Section 125 CrPC and awarded her Rs 500 a month, to be paid by the husband. The All India Muslim Personal Law Board and Jamiat Ulema-e-Hind had joined as intervenors on behalf of the husband. Rajiv Gandhi's government with its brute majority (the kind we have these days) passed the law mentioned above which gave a Muslim divorced wife Iddat—maintenance for ninety days after the divorce. Orthodoxy was pleased, mandir and Mandal politics got a boost, and the charge of 'pseudo-secularism' and needless appeasement of minorities against the Congress was proved in the eyes of many. (Incidentally, the Sangh Parivar which had opposed the Hindu Code Bill, now joined the battle for justice for divorced Muslim women).

Civil society needs to be on its guard with regard to bad laws like the Muslim Women (Protection of Rights on Divorce) Act (the title is searing in its irony), draconian laws like POTA, (now repealed) and a slew of anti-conversion laws passed by state legislatures. It is for the courts to decide if these laws go against the grain of the Indian Constitution which has put down a slew of articles granting religious freedom. Article 25 specifically gives one the right freely to profess, practice and propagate religion. We also need to be wary about harsh implementation of laws by pliant police forces. Lastly the government, the party in power and the RSS, need to be more understanding when dealing with dissent. They need to realize what a hash they made of it when writers, and later artists and scientists, started voicing their feelings and returning awards.

Mrinal Pande

Mrinal Pande is an acclaimed author and journalist. She writes in both Hindi and English and her work spans fiction, plays and essays on contemporary India and its women. Here, she examines the idea of nationalism as embodied in the figure of Bharat Mata.

Nationalism and the Cult of Bharat Mata

In 1950, when India became a secular Republic, I was four and my mother was twenty five. I grew up hearing how, if it were not for an unusually liberal grandfather who packed off Mother and her siblings to Tagore's Shantiniketan (where she spent the next twelve years and emerged a graduate), my mother would have been home educated and married off in her early teens, like most girls from upper-caste middle-class families. Also were it not for the subsidized university education and western science, my father, a humble village postmaster's son, would never have acquired a first-class Master's degree in Chemistry. My sisters and I were told repeatedly that our right to a wholesome education and a well-paid job afterwards, was absolute. But they never let on that both within most families and on the campuses of 1930s, the Indian bourgeoisie remained a very complex and deeply divided phenomena. We were never told about the ideological divide within Gandhi's Congress or even within our own larger family. Were they faced, as a writer and an educationist setting up a chain of state-run schools with local help in a far off Himalayan region, with inevitable clashes with their Brahminical tradition-bound families or the state government? Did they take them on? Or capitulated on various fronts? Was it worthwhile? As I watched the repeated suppression of writers, thinkers, intellectuals and students, and a string of lies spewed out by our rulers to justify it, I was so upset I could hardly speak. Peace protests, pacifist appeals and a global protest against the suppression of free speech, nothing seemed to work as the nation entered a long tunnel of fascism with a domestic face, that of lawyers and party activists who called themselves proud sons of Bharat Mata and beat up protesting citizens calling them traitors and seditionists.

At that point one began re-reading the literature and popular tracts from the 1920s. It is obvious that back when our parents were growing up, there were two opposing sets of views about the nationalist discourse and cultural identity of the Indian middle classes. On both sides national and traditionally embedded social values about class, caste and gender fed into each other. So while our Mother and her siblings were enjoying their school years in one of the most liberal co-educational campuses in the country under the benign gaze of Tagore, Nandlal Basu, Kshiti Mohan Sen and Hazari Prasad Dwivedi, most girls in their age group were married off before they reached puberty to live lives as laid down by Manu centuries ago, as wives and mothers dependent on men. In the Hindi belt, a forty-page monograph on women's duties (Stri Dharma Prashnottari) published by the Gita Press was doing the rounds as a bestseller among middle-class families. It recorded a conversation between an ideal woman, Savitri and her dumb acolyte, Sarala whom she lectured about how to be a little woman and a good wife-mother. Here was a carefully drawn out template for an ideal Hindu woman whose morality, purity and chastity were to be the bedrock for the ideal Sanatan Hindu family, which in turn was deemed the building block of a truly Hindu Rashtra for the Hindu Right wing, that strongly opposed Gandhi and Ambedkar's vision of an egalitarian, secular India with caste and communal considerations gradually evaporating. Savitri's clearly enunciated views in the tract published by the Gita Press, Gorakhpur firmly said that a liberal western education to girls posed a grave threat to the nation and must be opposed. As they matured, women's strong sexual urges posed a threat to all. So to contain and channelize their strong sexuality before it created mayhem, girls must be married off before attaining puberty. It was only as mothers of sons that women became venerable and important as an ideal crucible for raising obedient and devoted citizens to serve the nation state.

With a template in place, the figure of the traditional Hindu Mother goddess was soon invoked. And in 1936, from Bengal, the land of Durga worshippers, came *Anand Math*, a novel in Bengali by Bankim Chandra Chattopadhyaya. It laid a solid foundation for a cult of Bharat Mata. In the preface to an English translation in 1992, the translator B.K. Roy declares that Bankim's 'great achievement for India was that he made patriotism a religion and his writings have become a gospel of India's struggle for political independence.' He goes on to describe how 'Bande Mataram' (I bow to the Mother Nation), a song sung by a band of revolutionaries in the novel, became a nationalists' rallying call. The translator thanks Bankim richly for having created a lineage of revolutionaries that would always be kept alive by Bharat Mata's militant Hindu nationalist sons and daughters.

The above vision was evoked on a spectacular scale in 1983 by the Vishwa Hindu Parishad when it combined the traditional abstract concepts such as gender and religious identity and sought to give them a physical shape by weaving together legends about the Mother Goddess and national heroes and consecrating them through age-old Vedic rituals. The tapestry thus created became the basis of a Hindu nation state which, in turn, was based on a combination of European political concepts of the nation state, progress and order, and patriotism by Veer Savarkar in 1922. But invented traditions are not static. They need to be reinvented in specific contexts to produce and challenge newer class, religion and gender-based identities. Post 1950s, justifying the Hindu patriarchy's differentiation of social space into private and public, required a new vision of the motherhood of Bharat Mata. None of the three major Hindu Goddesses, Maha Kali, Maha Lakshmi, and Maha Saraswati, are biological mothers. So the state's apotheosis into a Mata goddess required that the image of the Mother Goddess be trimmed somewhat and she be presented primarily as a devoted, selfless and spiritually inclined mother of Hindu sons. She inspired her sons to shed the blood of all those who resisted her aura, and be ready to lay down their lives, if need be, to save her honour and punish the infidels. The latter we are being told repeatedly are non-Bharat Mata worshippers who are unpatriotic seditionists and need to be taught a swift lesson by being beaten up and jailed. To inculcate this philosophy there has been a repeated insistence that all citizens, from cinema halls to the campuses, show unequivocal respect for Bharat Mata's symbols: the national anthem, 'Vande Mataram' and the tricolour.

Even though a temple to Bharat Mata had come up in the 1920s in Varanasi, another Bharat Mata temple came up in the pilgrimage town of Haridwar in the mid-1980s. It was built by one Swami Satymitranand Giri: a VHP leader praised (in the handbooks available at the temple) for having raised substantial funds in India and abroad from non-resident children of Bharat Mata. The English guide book, *Bharat Mata Mandir: A Candid Appraisal*, traces the Swami's decision to build a temple to a vision. 'In all ancient cultures, the Divine mother is the cause off (sic) Creation,' says the booklet. 'It is hoped that the visit to this shrine…will inspire devotion and dedication to Mother-Land.'(pp 1–2). Six weeks after the area for the temple was consecrated, the VHP mounted an all India Ekatmata Yajna or Sacrifice for National Unity, a carefully planned six-week event during which trucks dressed as Raths were used as mobile Bharat Mata temples. These transported images of Bharat Mata with pots of Ganga-jal all over India for mass rituals of public worship by all her deemed children (read Hindu nationalists). This made Bharat Mata or the concept of the nation as a militant goddess, a distinct all-India phenomena. And with that it was a certainty that the cult of Bharat Mata, like the (yet to be built) Ram temple in Ayodhya, would be used by the political arm of the Sangh Parivar for whipping up support for a Hindu Rashtra and consolidating the Hindu votes in its favour.

The three floors above the Bharat Mata shrine contain shrines to Shoor (military heroes), Sants (Saints) and last but not the least, Satis, pious women who chose to burn themselves on a pyre after their husbands died. The floor dedicated to great spiritual teachers is dominated by statues of Ramakrishna and his disciple, Vivekanand. There is also a statue of Shri Aurobindo, but his French wife, the Mother of Pondichery Ashram, is missing. The only woman honoured with a statue is Sharada Ma, the wife and disciple of Ramakrishna.

Problem is, Democracy, like capitalism is ultimately a numbers game. And today this heady mix of religion and politics has of late been begun generating toxic side effects among the 69 per cent of the population that did not vote Right. This is an unforeseen headache for the BJP. In the aftermath of the JNU events we saw its hitherto cocky leadership betray a certain paranoid sense of embattlement, as first the intellectuals and then the students and Dalits raised their voices against the State. The lesser members of the Party immediately went public and delivered hate speeches against the dissidents. They called for an all-out war against the seculars, the intellectuals, the Left and all those suspected of being Left sympathizers. Soon it was hard to dismiss them as the lunatic fringe as responsible members of the Union cabinet and BJP members of state assemblies began to articulate a deep hatred for the secular principles, gender, justice and free speech.

Something other than a lapse of logic seemed to be at work here. First a Dalit student killed himself leaving behind a note that squarely blamed an anti-Dalit government that had cut off his meagre stipend on the grounds of his being deemed a Left sympathizer. Soon a mob of, 'Jai Bharat Mata' chanting bhakts in black coats were seen thrashing students, dissident lawyers and media men and women within court premises, baying for the blood of those they called desh drohi (anti-national) Pakistan (read Muslim) sympathizers. Channels who supported these self-appointed children of Bharat Mata, whipped up this hysteria further with doctored tapes and called for a state crackdown on all those that did not support their world view and theory of nationalism. Damage control failed. Dalit leaders, intellectuals and students refused to buy the argument first articulated by the Bharat Mata temple compendium, and later theatrically articulated by the Union Minister for HRD.

But no political power on earth has been able to muffle public dissent forever. It emerges first within homes and hostels, tea dhabas and office canteens, then spills over in public places till university campuses erupt like volcanoes. Prescribed normality then turns into a myth. At a point like this one finds, the only way to stay calm is to take each day as it comes, and to use what we know from history. Let them all come: the Right, the Left, the Socialists, the Dalit panthers and Tamil tigers, feminists and LGBT activists. Let our histories mix, anything, as long as they do not set about building a wall.

MALAVIKA RAJKOTIA

Malavika Rajkotia is a leading divorce lawyer in New Delhi. Her interpretation of the constitutional duty of the Supreme Court argues that it is one of the crucial checks and balances that keep a democratic government functioning as intended. Here, she writes about the importance of dissent within and from the judiciary in order to carry out this duty.

Dissent from and within the Supreme Court to Save the Constitution

Historically, power has evolved from the rule of the jungle to societies ruled by kings, as human as their subjects, but endowed with divine rights by the feudal social structures they presided over. One of the means of retaining feudal power was to kill dissent—and dissenters. The very idea of a democracy would have been seditious in such a context. Yet, political visionaries were beginning to think of building institutions that could transcend and survive the failings of the humans in power. These robust institutions would ideally protect individuals as they evolved and worked to realize their highest potentials.

The architecture of democratic constitutions is premised on separating the powers that were originally embodied in the monarch alone into the legislature, executive and the judiciary. The legislature consists of elected representatives in Parliament who enact law, the executive, which implements it, and the judiciary, which ensures that law-making and access to law are fair and equal to all. Each separate power centre should check the others from becoming the repository of all the power—essentially a reversion to the monarch's arbitrary rule, rendering the centres vulnerable to the vagaries of ordinary human limitations.

The structure envisioned is constantly dynamic. It may be prone to shift one way or another, depending on the personalities and ideologies of the elected individuals, bureaucrats or judges, but in a democratic state the three power centres constantly step in or away to maintain the ideal constitutional balance. This separation of powers prevents state machinery from collecting itself into one totalitarian entity against the individual.

The tension between the power centres is the muscle tone and it is maintained by the commitment of office bearers to maintain the highest standards of excellence, integrity and probity. If that commitment is compromised, the muscle tone atrophies, possibly leading to the collapse of the governing constitutional structure, which would render the officers guilty of abandoning their country to authoritarian rule. The oath that an office-bearer takes when entrusted with the management of a public institution is to uphold the integrity of that institution 'without fear or favour'. To maintain the highest integrity of any office thus must include, not just the ability, but the *duty* to dissent from any position taken by any other power centre that would degrade the constitutional ideal. It includes the duty to debate and dissent in order to arrive as close as possible to the constitutional ideal.

As institutions cannot be better than the humans that created them, processes to transcend human failings must be created, with the first step being to identify these failings. Even as long ago as Ancient Greece, philosophers realized the inherent nature of the state. The state after all consists of humans, and thus embodies their failings—with the original human failing being totalitarianism. The structure of the state is that of a Leviathan that feeds on individuals to perpetuate itself by swallowing dissent. Hence, debate is essential. As Pericles said: 'We decide and debate carefully and in person, all matters of policy, holding not that words and deeds go ill together but that acts are foredoomed to failure when undertaken undiscussed.'[1]

What is the spirit that informs this discussion and dialogue? Or, taken another way, what are the ethics that pervade institutions? The answer to this is that it is the same spirit that inhabits the majority of nations, constitutions and post-war international treaties—a spirit of idealism that cherished humanity and sought to create institutions to protect individual freedoms and rights.

~

In Britain, Parliament is supreme, with the judiciary having limited power to review parliamentary action. In India, however, following the US model, all government action is subject to judicial review.

The contrast between the two systems is reflected in the judicial approach in each country. Chief Justice Stone of the Supreme Court of the United States of America said in 1928: 'A dissent in a court of last resort is an appeal to the brooding spirit of the law, to the intelligence of a future day when a later decision may possibly correct the error on which the dissenting judge believes the court to have been betrayed.'

In contrast, the British judge Lord Kerr,[2] with characteristic English humour, said that he thought the brooding spirit of the law to be a 'bit much' and that his reasons for dissent were far more prosaic: he could not find himself in agreement with the majority.

Although India's Constitution envisaged the separation of power into three centres, practically speaking, there is a simpler, binary separation, as the executive branch merges into an arm of the legislature. Thus, the judiciary is required to compensate with a heavier presence and a wider reach.

It is practical to look to the judiciary to maintain constitutional supremacy, as judges are trained by the intellectual rigour of the law to strike balances of justice: they are free from the pressures of popular representatives who have (more often than not) tended to be dangerously populist, combining constitutional illiteracy with untrammelled personal ambition. That is not to say that judges are not capable of being self-serving, but at least they have the advantage of being trained for their role that many Parliamentarians and politically influential people do not.

By temperament and learning, an apex court is expected to stay a step ahead of the polity and to lead on the path of constitutional justice, rather than just reflect populist notions as elected representatives are prone to do. Further, the judges are expected to have no political commitment other than to the Constitution. While it would be naïve to expect judges to completely discard their own political leanings while interpreting the law, it is reasonable to expect that judicial training will minimize the effect of a judge reflecting his personal socialization in a judgment, as far as is possible without making the process of judging a mechanical exercise.

Thus, the judiciary has the task of exercising restraint on itself in keeping with the constitutional ideal, while also restraining governments. This is the spirit that informs the fine legal writings by the judges of our Supreme Court. Such a balance can only be arrived at in a judicious frame of mind—one that meditates on moderation. At this point, arises the often-asked question: who checks the judiciary? Law scholar Madhav Khosla quotes jurist M.C. Setalvad as saying that the Constitution checks the judiciary.

~

It is imperative that the judiciary should not be, or appear compliant with the government and Parliament. To maintain the independence of the judicial branch, judges must be willing to dissent even among themselves, in order to get as close as is possible to the Constitutional ideal.

An article on dissents in the Supreme Court of India[3] notes that dissenting judgments peaked in the first two decades, after which the rate has dropped. The authors of the article attribute the reduced rate of dissent to the heavy caseload of the judges.

Analyzing the work of the Supreme Court, Sudhanshu Ranjan notes that the judiciary has aggressively worked to guard its own jurisdiction, but on matters of civil liberties it has often agreed with the government position.[4] This is a matter of concern, since the entire exercise is, after all, about the rights and freedoms of the individual, and not for judges to retain power that a citizen has no assurance will be used to protect his/her own freedoms.

The judiciary also has to protect conscientious dissenters, who act as guardians of democracy by challenging state encroachments upon the constitutional rights of themselves and others, as when a great leader of the bar, Mr R.K. Garg, was asked by the bench in the Bhopal gas leak case: 'Whom do you appear for, Mr Garg?'

'My lords,' he replied, 'I appear for every citizen of this country.'

Lawyers, as officers of the court, must agitate and insist that judges discharge this very important constitutional duty.

There have been times when the tension of independence between the government and judiciary collapsed because the values of constitutional ethics and ideals had been eroded, and the country fell into a non-constitutional abyss. That was when the power centres collectively conspired to subvert the Constitution. We need to discuss what went wrong then to ensure that, not just the judiciary, but every citizen, is aware of the importance of keeping alive dissent and can understand why dissenters are essential for a vibrant nation. They must realize that their patriotic duty to a nation they are proud of is to dissent fairly and without fear.

~

The first notable case of the newly formed Supreme Court relating to civil liberties was that of A.K. Gopalan in 1950.[5] The majority favoured the government's position, ruling that as long as a person was deprived of his liberty by a process of law, it was not for the court to see whether that law was in consonance with the principles of natural justice.

Justices Fazl Ali and Mahajan dissented, holding that individual liberty cannot be curtailed without a full and fair hearing under any circumstance, including demands of 'public good'. The judgment as a whole can be read as an instance of the judiciary restraining itself from overstepping what it saw as its boundaries.

Successive governments began to grow more unchecked and began to subvert the judiciary. Over time, the Supreme Court realized that restraint is a virtue that no government can be accused of, and thus the boundaries of the judiciary have to widen to control the government from stepping on the rights of the individual. The process of this realization by the Supreme Court can be seen in the trajectory of its record on civil liberties.

~

During the 1950s and '60s, several land reform schemes were launched pursuant to the directive principles of state policy. As in the A.K. Gopalan case on civil liberties, the judiciary submitted to the legislative will by allowing a constitutional amendment permitting schemes which required the acquisition of land for 'public purpose,' i.e. redistribution of land.

In the cases of Shankari Prasad[6] and Sajjan Singh,[7] the Supreme Court upheld the Parliament's power to amend any part of the Constitution, endangering that institution and reducing it to the status of a paper that could be reprinted by any government. Renowned cartoonist R.K. Laxman encapsulated the problem of multiple amendments to the Constitution by successive governments: the famous Common Man enquires at a bookshop for a copy of the Constitution. 'Sorry sir,' says the bookseller. 'We do not stock periodicals.'

Fortunately, the court changed its mind in 1967, in the case of Golak Nath,[8] where it held that legislations seeking to appropriate private property violated the fundamental right to property, which could not be allowed in view of Article 13 of the Constitution, preventing the state from making laws that take away the fundamental rights of the citizen.

In 1962, through the fourteenth amendment, the government decided to place in the ninth schedule of the Constitution any enactment that it wanted to save from judicial review. This was challenged in the Kesavananda Bharti[9] case.

The court allowed this amendment by a 7:6 majority, with the cautionary caveat that no further amendment could alter the basic structure of the Constitution and, henceforth, the absolute protection of the ninth schedule would not be available to the government. The court could test every enactment and amendment to see whether it violated the Constitution's basic structure.

What exactly is this basic structure is a vexed question to this day. The cases we have discussed above relate to personal liberties and the right to property. Eventually, liberty was treated as part of the basic structure but the right to property was not.

~

After the Supreme Court reassured us that the basic structure of the Constitution was sacrosanct, the question of what happens to our rights when the Constitution itself stood suspended in a state of Emergency arose. That was the question at the heart of the A.D.M. Jabalpur case.[10] In this case, the majority ruled that the question of the basic structure did not arise when the structure itself did not exist in an Emergency. The A.D.M. Jabalpur case stripped all facades and exposed the judiciary at its nadir as completely and absolutely submissive and compliant to the government. Here is how it happened:

The 1970s were turbulent times. There were many popular uprisings in the country and Prime Minister Indira Gandhi claimed to be worried about civil unrest reaching boiling point. She announced that the nation was under internal threat, and thus in June 1975, the President was 'advised' to declare an Emergency. The immediate result was a seeming calm, when trains ran on time and roads were clear. (Incidentally, the obsession of authoritarian regimes with cleanliness at the cost of all else is noteworthy. It has a tendency to carry on, on its own momentum, beyond hygiene into cleansing places, spaces and identities: all churned to form a tidy line of 'one nation'.)

The call for Emergency met with robust opposition from intellectuals, students, activists and lawyers. Political protestors began being arrested under the dreaded Maintenance of Internal Security Act, 1971. Family and friends began moving various High Courts for writs of habeas corpus (literally: produce the body), seeking release of those detained. A set of state appeals from one such petition allowed by the Madhya Pradesh High Court became the lead case on the issue: Shiv Kant Shukla vs. A.D.M. Jabalpur. We have a fine drama played out, with the main actors being the government, Supreme Court and the bar that worked anxiously to protect their Constitution.[11]

The Chief Justice of India at the time was A.N. Ray. Fali Nariman, an additional solicitor general at the time, resigned in protest at the proclamation of Emergency. The Attorney General was Niren De, who did not resign. Chief Justice Ray was openly scornful of the basic structure doctrine laid out in the Kesavananda Bharti case, and there was some talk that he was setting up a bench to review it. Nanabhoy Palkhivala wrote to Prime Minister Indira Gandhi, beseeching her to refrain from pushing for the review of the basic structure doctrine, which was all that protected the country from dictatorship. Chief Justice Ray eventually dissolved the bench constituted for this review.

Now came the matter of who would constitute the bench to hear the habeas corpus appeals. Worried that Chief Justice Ray would select a pro-government bench, many leaders of the bar urged that a bench be selected according to seniority. They arranged for telegrams to this effect to be sent from around the country to the Chief Justice of India. The Chief Justice eventually constituted a bench of the five senior-most judges, including himself. Palkhivala argued that the hypothetical situation discussed in Keshavananda Bharti about the executive abuse of power had now become a reality.

The court then asked Attorney General Niren De whether there was any remedy if, during the Emergency, a police officer killed another man because of personal enmity. He replied that the answer to that question would have to be that there was no remedy.[12] Mr De is reported to have said that he had hoped his answer would shock the conscience of the judges into ruling against him. If that is true, he must have been horribly shocked at winning his case.

The judgment, given by Chief Justice Ray, is replete with platitudes that seem to be more to reassure himself than the country. The judge also referred to the government's care of the detenus as 'maternal'. Justices Bhagwati and Chandarachud, also on the bench, later publicly regretted their decisions. But for many it was salt to open wounds. It is unnerving that the highest court, that of last resort, leaves a margin for regret in a matter so vital, so basic, as life itself.

The lone dissenter was Justice H.R. Khanna. He held that even though the consequence of the textual approach was that fundamental rights could be suspended during an emergency, the *ethical* approach could not be discarded when interpreting matters of vital importance, such as personal liberty. Thus, the rule of law, with its concomitant rights of personal freedom, must be protected at all times and existed even outside and apart from the Constitution as a natural right. Justice Khanna was punished for his dissent by being superseded as Chief Justice.

~

After the Emergency, the Janata regime passed the 44th amendment in 1977, which is eulogized as having restored democracy. It made the basic structure of the Constitution immutable. But within the same amendment, is an insidious insertion that was never debated or challenged. The right to property ceased to be a fundamental right.

Lawyer Shanti Bhushan, a star due to his fearless opposition to the Emergency, explained to Parliament the reasons for this fundamental change in the Constitution. There have been too many past amendments about and around the fundamental right to property, he said.

According to Seervai,[13] this reason is neither true nor convincing. Several amendments in the past are no reason to do away with the right. It is an argument on precarious ground, since its logical conclusion is the danger that a hundred amendments to the Constitution over the sixty-six years of its existence are reason enough to do away with the Constitution itself.

This approach, made for short-term electoral gains, forgot that the fundamental right to property was placed by wise Constitution makers not necessarily to protect the landed rich, but also the medium and small land owners, and small property owners who do not have the cash to protect their property from encroachments by the state. The loss of this fundamental right needs to be analyzed, given the present impatience with rates of growth and untoward affection for systems that brook no dissent, in the name of 'efficiency'.

The recent controversy over the government land acquisition bill[14] propounded by the BJP would be less intense and fear-ridden if the repeal of the fundamental right to property had not created a vacuum that is now in danger of being filled by cronyism, allowing the influential to prey on small land owners and tribal rights in forest land.

There is no satisfactory explanation till date as to how this right, entrusted to the state by the people as fundamental, was dropped without rigorous debate and the chance to dissent.

An essay on this topic could have been seen as dated a few years ago, but the times that necessitate this book on dissent require the judiciary to be on alert more than ever before, because, as we know, history has a bad habit of repeating itself. Now, even more than before, dissent is an important expression of commitment to democracy and hence, to the nation.

Notes

1. Thucydides, *History of the Peloponnesian War*, Book II quoted in H.M. Seervai's *Constitutional Law of India*, New Delhi: Universal Law Publishers, 2015
2. Lord Kerr at the Birkenhead lecture in 2012
3. Yogesh Pratap Singh, Afroz Alam, Akash Chandra Jauhari, 'Dissenting Opinions of Judges in the Supreme Court', *Economic & Political Weekly*, January 30, 2016, Vol LI No. 5
4. Sudhanshu Ranjan, *Justice, Judocracy and Democracy in India: Boundaries and Breaches*, Routledge India, 2012
5. A.K. Gopalan v. State of Madras, AIR 1950 SC 27. A.K. Gopalan was detained under a preventive detention order, not a regular arrest warrant, and the case decided whether such an arrest was a violation of a citizen's fundamental rights.
6. Shankari Prasad vs Union of India, AIR 1951 SC 455 Article 13 of the Constitution said that the state shall not make any law that takes away or abridges the rights given to the citizens. In this case, it was argued that 'State' includes parliament and 'Law' includes Constitutional Amendments.
7. Sajjan Singh v. State of Rajasthan, AIR 1965 SC 845
8. Golaknath v. State of Punjab, AIR 1967 SC 1643
9. Kesavananda Bharati v. State of Kerala and Anr. (1973) 4 SCC 225 In 1970 Kesavananda Bharati, head of a Hindu Mutt, challenged the Kerala government's attempts, under two state land reform acts, to impose restrictions on the management of its property. This case concerned the right to manage religiously owned property without government interference.
10. A.D.M. Jabalpur v. S.S. Shukla, AIR 1976 SC 1207
11. Compared to those days of a robust bar, there may now be cause for anxiety about its present commitment to liberal ideas, which are also the basic structure of the Constitution—but that is another story.
12. Granville Austin, *Working a Democratic Constitution: The Indian Experience*, Oxford University Press, 2000
13. H.M. Seervai, *Constitutional Law of India: A Critical Commentary*, 4th Edition, Vol. 2, 1993, p. 1354
14. See: Land Acquisition, Rehabilitation and Resettlement (Amendment) Ordinance 2014, Land Acquisition, Rehabilitation and Resettlement (Amendment) Bill, 2015 See also http://www.prsindia.org/pages/land-acquisition-debate-139/

Dr Hafiz Ahmed

Dr Hafiz Ahmed was born in a Bengal-origin Assamese Muslim family in a remote village in Barpeta district of Assam. He has written fourteen books in Assamese including two poetry collections. Dr Ahmed is a well-known social activist in Assam. He was awarded the M. Elim Uddin Dewan Memorial Literary Award in 2015 for his contribution to Assamese literature and the Swahid Alif Uddin Memorial Award in 2017 for his struggle for the preservation of rights of the marginalized communities in Assam.

In early 2016, when Dr Hafiz Ahmed posted a poem 'Write Down, "I'm a Miyah"' on Facebook, it caused a sensation and several Assamese Muslims started sharing their experiences of discrimination. Soon, these poets got together to start a movement called Miyah Poetry, using the word 'Miyah' (Assamese slang for Bengali Muslims) subversively in order to assert their identities.

Write Down 'I Am a Miyah'

Write
Write down
I am a Miyah
My serial number in the NRC is 200543
I have two children
Another is coming
Next summer.
Will you hate him
As you hate me?

Write
I am a Miyah
I turn waste, marshy lands
To green paddy fields
To feed you.
I carry bricks
To build your buildings
Drive your car
For your comfort
Clean your drain
To keep you healthy.

I have always been
In your service
And yet
you are dissatisfied!
Write down
I am a Miyah,
A citizen of a democratic, secular, Republic
Without any rights
My mother a D voter,
Though her parents are Indian.

If you wish kill me, drive me from my village,
Snatch my green fields
hire bulldozers
To roll over me.
Your bullets
Can shatter my breast
for no crime.

Write
I am a Miyah
Of the Brahamaputra
Your torture
Has burnt my body black
Reddened my eyes with fire.
Beware!
I have nothing but anger in stock.
Keep away!
Or
Turn to ashes.

REZWAN HUSSAIN

Rezwan Hussain, also a Miyah poet, has a PhD in Biotechnology. He worked in the field of pharmacy for many years and is now an entrepreneur.

Our Revolution

Scold us
Kick us if you will
Patiently we will continue to build
Your mansions, roads, bridges
Patiently we will keep pulling your tired, fat,
Sweaty bodies in cycle rickshaws
We will polish your marble floors
Until they sparkle
Beat your dirty clothes
Until they are white
We will plump you up with fresh fruits and vegetables
And when you come visiting us in Tapajuli char,
We will offer you not just milk
But fresh cream

You continue to abuse us
Even today we are the thorn in your eye

But don't they say: Patience has its limits
Broken nails can cut through flesh
Even we can turn revolutionaries
Our revolution will not need guns
Our revolution will not need dynamite
Our revolution will not run on national television
Our revolution will not be published
On no walls will our revolution be painted
In red and blue clenched fists

Yet our revolution will singe, burn
Reduce your souls to ashes.

MANASH FIRAQ BHATTACHARJEE

Manash Firaq Bhattacharjee is a poet, writer, translator and political science scholar. His first collection of poems, Ghalib's Tomb and Other Poems *was published in 2013. He is currently Adjunct Professor in the School of Culture and Creative Expressions at Ambedkar University, New Delhi.*

The End of Tomorrow

Tomorrow someone will arrest you. And will say the evidence is that there was some problematic book in your house.

Tomorrow someone will arrest you. And your friends will see, on TV, the media calling you terrorist because the police do.

Tomorrow someone will arrest you. They'll scare all lawyers. The one who takes up your case will be arrested next week

Tomorrow someone will arrest you. Your friends will find you active on Facebook a day later. Police logged in as you.

Tomorrow someone will arrest you. Your friends will find that it'll take 4 days to find 1000 people to sign a petition.

Tomorrow someone will arrest you. Your little child will learn what UAPA stands for. Your friends will learn of Sec.13.

Tomorrow someone will arrest you. You'll be a 'leftist' to people. You will be ultra-left for the leftists. No one will speak.

Tomorrow someone will arrest you. The day after that, you will be considered a 'terrorist' for life.

Tomorrow someone will arrest you. The police will prepare a list of names. Anyone who'd protest will be named.

Tomorrow someone will arrest you. You'll be warned. You'll be a warning to everyone putting their hand into the corporate web.

Tomorrow someone will arrest you. Your home will be searched tonight. You will be taken for questioning now. Stop speaking.

Tomorrow someone will arrest you. The court, in a rare gesture, will give you the benefit of bail. The police will rearrest you in another case.

Tomorrow someone will arrest your children. You will be underground. Some measures are essential to keep a democracy alive.

Long Live Silence.

—Meena Kandasamy, 'Tomorrow Someone Will Arrest You'

Meena Kandasamy is an Indian poet, novelist and political activist who
has battled the country's monstrous caste system and culture of gender
discrimination since she was a teenager. But with her 2015 dystopic
poem 'Tomorrow Someone Will Arrest You', suddenly—and curiously
given her usual defiant attitude—she finds herself facing a force perhaps
too overwhelming to challenge. This monster's name is the acronym for
an Indian law: UAPA (Unlawful Activities Prevention Act, or Sua Act).
As she explains:

'Tomorrow Someone Will Arrest You' grew out of a series of Twitter/
Facebook posts following the arrests of two human rights activists,
Thushar Sarathy and Jaison Cooper, in Kerala on 29 January 2015. The
incriminating 'evidence' against them was the possession of a pamphlet
and books that criticized the development juggernaut. The Unlawful
Activities Prevention Act (UAPA) was clamped on the two activists—
it is an act that robs a citizen of his/her fundamental right to freedom
of expression, and allows the state to penalize people for their political
orientation.'

Kandasamy finds nothing concrete against which to raise the usual
battle cry, only fear:

> Tomorrow someone will arrest you. Your little child will learn
> what UAPA stands for. Your friends will learn of Sec.13.

> Tomorrow someone will arrest you. You'll be a 'leftist' to people.
> You will be ultra-left for the leftists. No one will speak.

The dark and totalizing nature of UAPA seems to baffle Kandasamy
as much as it scares her. After all, Sarathy and Cooper were well within
their democratic rights to protest the Kerala government's involvement
in land acquisition, forced eviction and the violation of labour rights of
migrant workers in the state. They also voiced strong opinions against
polluting industries through their blog posts.

There is of course extreme irony when she advises people to keep
silent and fear the law. Since her first collection, Kandasamy has written
extensively and candidly on caste and sexuality, including details of
her legal battle against her abusive ex-husband. She also added her
voice to those of women nationwide in the aftermath of a gang rape

in Delhi that received international attention in 2012. At that time, a cacophony of populist, middle-class demands for stricter laws (including capital punishment) overshadowed the movement to protect women's unrestricted movement in urban spaces. In a country reeling from extreme abuses of colonial laws, more laws were bad news. Kandasamy has also stood against laws that put restrictions on free speech and beef-eating in some parts of the country. Again and again, Kandasamy has defended her position with a trademark fiery disposition.

Kandasamy's father was a landless labourer from a lower-caste, nomadic community from Thanjavur, in Tamil Nadu, who moved to Chennai to escape poverty. One of the earliest political questions Kandasamy raised about her own life was: what forced her father to leave his birthplace? This question, which connects poverty and displacement, goes straight to the heart of twenty-first-century class conditions, and the limitations that class thrusts upon human lives. Her father's uprooted destiny leads to the heart of Kandasamy's writing.

At the age of seventeen, Kandasamy began to translate vernacular writings by Dalits—the most marginalized community in India—into English. Translating these writers gave her a larger perspective on violence, dispossession and human rights. And by translating Dalit authors, Kandasamy's literary and political identity was, in a sense, translated into the Dalit caste. Despite coming from a marginalized community himself, Kandasamy's father acted like a Hindu patriarch at home, making Kandasamy also acutely aware of her separate struggle as a woman. These combined marginalized identities find their way into her first two poetry collections, where she furiously asserts her rebellion against political violence and socio-religious/sexual mores. Her language is marked by a blunt, lyrical sensuality reminiscent of the Malayalam poet, Kamala Das. Critical debate around her work has focused on her poetry's raw style, which dissatisfied many readers looking for more nuance and complexity. Now, in 'Tomorrow Someone Will Arrest You,' irony gives Kandasamy's language poise and sparseness as she allows the law to speak through her.

The UAPA was passed in 1967. Initially intended to solve issues of communalization and caste violence, the law's enactment saw issues of 'sovereignty' and 'territorial integrity' take prominence. In the 2000s, in response to the Mumbai blasts of 2008, the UAPA was remade into an overarching law that would help the state control anti-state activities. Both substantive and procedural provisions from other draconian anti-

terrorist laws, like The Prevention of Terrorism Act (POTA) and the
Terrorism and Disruptive Activities (Prevention) Act (TADA), were
included within the UAPA. The amendment defined terrorism in an
imprecise manner, in terms of damage to property and disruption of
essential supplies, while it impinged upon the basic rights of citizens
to protest and peacefully demonstrate against the state. The UAPA was
authorized to detain suspects for almost 200 days without a proper
charge, and to declare organizations unlawful for two years, without
evidence. And now the law appears to allow police to arbitrarily blur the
lines between proof and suspicion: Sarathy and Cooper were arrested
in January of this year because 'pro-Maoist' materials were allegedly
found in their homes. They were eventually released on bail in March,
after petitions and protests were made by human rights activists and
others. But citizens involved in watchdog and legal protest activities
are in constant fear of similar harassment—especially in the regions of
Manipur and Kashmir, where yet another extraordinary, colonial law, the
AFSPA (Armed Forces Special Powers Act, promulgated by the British
in 1942) allows the army extra-constitutional powers.

In this context, Kandasamy's poetic Facebook posts are written in
a language reduced to an economy of fear, marked by repetition and
minimalism, with a precision that hesitates to move forward or say more
than what is necessary. The posts, joining together to form a sequence
of chilling aphorisms, also draw our attention to political structures
creating psychological traumas:

> Tomorrow someone will arrest you. And your friends will see,
> on TV, the media calling you terrorist because the police do.

> Tomorrow someone will arrest you. They'll scare all lawyers. The
> one who takes up your case will be arrested next week

> Tomorrow someone will arrest you. Your friends will find you
> active on Facebook a day later. Police logged in as you.

The 'you' under discussion here suffers not only a neurotic, Freudian
condition of alienation, but also radical abandonment, where the very
idea of belonging to the world comes into a crisis. 'You' end up not only
suspicious of the world but even yourself, as if no one can better betray
you but yourself. 'You' don't identify as your own self any longer; you
become a shadow-self.

Falling into the interrogative apparatus of the state is terrifying. The state, unlike a priest, doesn't work on the principle of redeeming you from sins, but on the principle of endlessly suspended suspicion. The state is not interested in 'you', but only in what you confess—and how that confession may work in its favour. The moral ties (and its constrictions) between 'you' and the priest are replaced by (extra) legality, where you become a mere confessing subject of law, being suspected of a crime you may not have committed. When the moral subject turns into a legal one, speech no longer remains a measure of truth but falsehood. You become the lying subject of a law that controls and transforms your language into that of someone you don't identify as your own any longer: you find yourself speaking as your own shadow.

And who is the 'someone' of Kandasamy's posts, who will 'arrest you'? The 'someone' is a no one, the figure of invisible, faceless power, another shadow. The indefinite 'arrest' of a 'you' by a 'someone' is precisely the Kafkaesque. It creates a dangerous interaction between two shadow-identities, where one plays an invisible game of control with the other. This situation recalls philosopher Gilles Deleuze's warnings in his famous essay 'Postscript on the Societies of Control'. Deleuze writes:

> In the societies of control [...] what is important is no longer either a signature or a number, but a code: the code is a password [...] The numerical language of control is made of codes that mark access to information, or reject it [...] the man of control is undulatory, in orbit, in a continuous network.

The essay argues that we are moving away from Michel Foucault's idea of the 'disciplinary society' (that aims at reforming deviant behaviour), to a more frightening network of a 'society of control', where spaces of individual freedom would increase along with means to control and regulate them whenever necessary. Deleuze envisioned a society of multiple surveillances, where you will have to live by the rules of a consensus, and where a mass-produced paranoia will be regulated by control. In addition to creating a schism within the lives of individuals accused of crimes, it will also seek out to regulate and coerce modes of resistance and protest against fabricated intimidations.

Deleuze's dystopian vision may be taking shape in India in response to the blanket term 'terror', under which the securitization of the state has become all-encompassing. Having declared this 'war on terror', democracy has turned against itself, against principles it held sacrosanct at least in rhetoric if not in practice. One of the most scandalous casualties has been the much avowed 'freedom of speech' itself, and the 'right to privacy'.

Jolly Chirayath, a human rights activist and a convener for a women's organization, suddenly came under police surveillance in March this year because of her alleged links with Maoists. In an interview she reiterated that belonging to a left ideology and reading books on Marxism doesn't make someone a Maoist. The repeated knocks at home by the police disturbed her. With succinct clarity, Jolly noted, 'The police are polite, but this is what I call civil violence. It is terrorizing those who question the supremacy of the State and its violence.' We have witnessed the famous case of Perumal Murugan, which saw the writer forced to announce giving up writing after he came under attack for blasphemy from caste outfits for his Tamil novel, *Madhurobhagan*. The lawyer who accompanied Perumal Murugan alleged that the writer was let down by officials and his exile was 'engineered by the police'. In 2012, two young women from the Thane district of Maharashtra, Shaheen Dada and Renu Srinivasan, were arrested and put under house arrest. Shaheen's crime was a post on Facebook that read 'Mumbai shuts down due to fear, not due to respect' a day after Shiv Sena leader Bal Thackeray died. Renu's crime was 'liking' the post. They were charged under all kinds of laws, for allegedly insulting and outraging religious feelings and creating hatred and ill-will. When democratic states usurp fundamental liberal rights in a belligerent and paranoid assault against terror, they expose the limits of democracy in our time.

Kandasamy's posts end with an ironic mimicking of passivity when faced with a real fear of coercion:

> Tomorrow someone will arrest you. Your home will be searched tonight. You will be taken for questioning now. Stop speaking.

> Tomorrow someone will arrest your children. You will be underground. Some measures are essential to keep a democracy alive.

> Long Live Silence.

This self-censorship is ironic, but conveys a fear of words that will be turned against 'you.' What 'you' speak may take an unintended life of its own, no longer in your control, but in the control of others who control you. Yet 'Tomorrow Someone Will Arrest You' offers a faint glimmer of hope, if only because Kandasamy manages to articulate and share her fear with the world.

The compulsion to repeat a trauma in anticipation of future traumas becomes a resistance in advance: the stubborn, persistent impulse of our irrational faculties to resist norms. Her posts mourn an evaporating freedom, while writing itself becomes an act of catharsis in the Freudian sense. Even the most helplessly stubborn of writings, exemplified in the last century by poets like Anna Akhmatova, Paul Celan, Yannis Ritsos and Nazim Hikmet, are also writings of immense grit and the refusal to submit. Kandasamy's writing against self-censorship, and the poem that results from it, is an irrational impulse against rationalist mechanisms of power.

Say It, While It's Time

What was not allowed to be said today will become unsayable tomorrow.

—Sneha Sharma, Facebook Post

Say it, while it's time,
What was not allowed to be said today will become unsayable
    tomorrow,
Say what is not allowed, what is unsayable in advance,
Say the blessed word, the abused word, the word that breathes,
Without pause, in the rising tide of your heartbeats,
Every word is a doorway, said a poet, every word is a reminder
Of another word, words are a night-sky of memory,
Say Azadi, without prepositions, without a name, a place,
Even a thing, Azadi means a lot, means everything,
Makes a tree catch fire, someone lose his way home, makes
Someone take the name of her lover without fear,
Say Azadi, for people who aren't free yet,
Say 'No' to the mothering of nations, there is no mothering
Without fathering, say no to a fatherly nation,
Say Rohith, say Najeeb, take the names of those who suffered the
    price
For not being Hindu, in a nation that isn't Hindu,
Say 'Pride' queerly, unfurl your colours like skins, nothing makes
    the sky

Bluer, streets more fragrant, than a mouth in another mouth,
Hands held by other hands, holding words of a love
Speaking its name, go hammer your lover's name in the air,
Say you are not afraid, name those who infect your silence, endanger
Your words, it is time you put those names on the banner
Of an hour under dispute, in danger,
Say 'Urdu', say it to those who partition languages,
Say it to them in Urdu, say it the way we drink in Urdu, we desire in Urdu,
In the Urdu of our complaints, our woes.

No Urdu in Dilli, Mian

In May 2016, two artists, a Christian and a Muslim, were drawing a couplet in Urdu on a wall in Delhi when they were attacked by members claiming to belong to the Hindu right and told to stop. This was an unprecedented episode of cultural policing in the capital of India, a place which reverberates with a history of brilliant poets during the Mughal era, who wrote in Persian and Urdu, and who were part of the common Indo-Islamic culture that thrived in these parts.

—For Akhlaq Ahmad and Swen Simon

You can't write Urdu
On Dilli's walls, Mian
There's a saffron lock
On your zubaan, Mian
Horsemen of all faith
Plundered Dilli's rūh,
They only blame it on
Your ancestors, Mian
From Bīdel to Ghalib
Run rosaries in Urdu,
They embalm history
With rare attar, Mian
You outlaw a tongue
By policing the wall?
The gardens, the air,

Breathe Urdu, Mian
In the heart of Dilli
Graves speak Urdu,
Even parrots, dusk,
And my jigar, Mian

JERRY PINTO

Acclaimed novelist and poet, Jerry Pinto, is also a teacher. In the following essay, he encourages students to question and protest so that they create a better future for not only themselves but also society.

'I Have an Old Faith in Youth'

With education as our weapon, said Martin Luther King Jr, we can change the world. You understand the true import, and power, of that statement when the government of the world's largest democracy sends its police into a university to arrest students for raising slogans.

Let us assume that education begins at school. Most schools are workshops. They give a student some tools and then they let her loose into the world and expect her to be able to find how to use these tools. They show her how to read and write, if she's lucky. They teach her how to multiply 212 by 3.24, and sometimes they teach her how to read a novel and sing a song with both head and heart.

After school, some of the lucky ones go to college. That should read, 'Some of the bright ones', but the world is not a perfect place and so many of those who end up in college do so because they are middle class, because their parents went to college, because they are expected to go to college in their demographic. Usually, this is not expensive; at the time of writing, most of the best institutions in the country are state-owned and state-run. But having put down even one rupee, we as a nation expect to see ten rupees' worth of value. In most cases, this is judged on the value of the job the child gets after the college education is over. It is never judged on what the student went in with and what the student came out as. If college education were to leave our children intact, with no changes in faith systems or thought processes, we would be quite happy.

This despite the fact that we know that we are supposed to be sending our children in to learn to think. To think about the problems of our society (Sociology) or of poverty (Economics) or of the way in which we have dealt with one half of humanity as if it were not human and we were not humane (Gender Studies) or of the way in which we think and don't think (Psychology) or the stories of our lives that we did not witness (History) or the stories of our lives that we are called on to witness (Media Studies). If we think about college this way, how could we possibly believe that a successful education can be anything but a complete change in the person who went in?

And here's another thought. A student goes into college to study history and economics and politics. What if she chooses to apply her learnings to her life? What if she turns those lenses on herself and her ambitions? What if she sees that silence has amounted to consent in so many places and so many ways? What if she reads the Constitution of India and sees that she has the duty to protect her own freedoms and the freedoms of others, or the country's forests and rivers, or its institutions of excellence? What if she then decides that she can do this by taking her protests to the streets? In Delhi recently, I watched as university students protested some scheme of marking that had been foisted upon them without warning. It had not been long since they had been brutally beaten by the police. And yet here they were. I watched them as they paraded past, shouting their slogans and chanting their rhymes. Some of the faces were intent, some of them were there because it was the place to be, some because it was a sunny day in winter. It wasn't very different from the reasons their parents go to political rallies.

They are human, these students, and their motives are mixed, but they are brave. They believe in justice still and they believe that they can change things. The system, they know, is stacked against them. But they will still throw themselves against it. And in doing so they will learn what the State is and who they are.

And that is what we expect of them. Or is it not?

~

The problem is that we don't know what we want from students. Centrally, of course, we want them to study. This is what they are supposed to be doing. But *what* is it that we want them to study? At the Social Communications

Media department of the Sophia Polytechnic where I teach journalism, we ask our students fairly regularly: What is the object of your study? The bright ones know the answer and say it with a hint of bubble-gum cynicism: We are here to get to know ourselves better. Whatever philosophic system we base our education on, this is eventually the object of the enterprise. The proper study of the human being is the human being. The unexamined life is not worth living. Neti, neti. Wherever you go, whatever you do, you circle back to yourself.

Now that we have set up this goal for our students, do we help them achieve it? The pressures on them are enormous. These pressures, we would like to imagine, come from that strange place: The Real World. 'You may be able to do this here,' we tell our students, 'but out in the real world...' and we shudder at the thought of what will happen to them there. This 'Real World' is also a fake construct. To the student, the world of college and university is a very real world and what happens there is also very real. Students kill themselves over their place in the percentile; this is because college is real for them even if their teachers think they are protected from reality. So when their teachers say, 'out in the real world', it just sounds like double-talk. More of the double-talk that will eventually transmute the philosopher's stone into base metal, more of the double-talk that will require them to think as their teachers think, write down what their teachers dictate, spit it out at the end of the year and move on. A student who steps out of line? Who thinks for herself? Who asks questions? Who challenges the status quo? She might be— again in that ideal world—the real student. Here and now, she is the one they are hauling off to a jail cell.

In that jail cell, she will have time to think—where do you think Pandit Nehru and Gandhiji got so much writing done?—and she will wonder at our lies. Education, we say repeatedly, is the only way out. Education, we say, is the leveller.

The Real World says: Education is the way to a big job, a big flat and a green card.

We say: There is no royal road to geometry.

The Real World says: There are royal tutors. Can you afford the classes?

Education, we say, is our one hope for the eradication of poverty, superstition, communalism, bigotry, inequality and gender insensitivity. Our young are the agents of change.

Then we think: Who is going to catalyze the agent of change? The teachers in the classroom?

When I look in the mirror, I don't see an agent of change. I just see someone who is trying to get his students to understand the meaning of the term 'deadline' and who is hoping that once they get that, the associated values—punctuality, reliability, professionalism—will follow.

This is what we want our students to become. We want to fit them into the Real World we have created. But what if they want to create a new world? What if they think our corrupt, polluted, sycophantic world is a monstrous construct of decadence and plain jobworthiness? What if they believe, as we ourselves believed not so long ago, that they could change the world and make it a better place simply by virtue of being different?

We've messed up—every morning we wake up to new evidence of how badly. Young people see this too. We didn't start the fire, we can sing; it was already burning. But what did we do to put it out? Or did we stand by and watch while others threw fuel on to the flames and danced around it?

Once, long ago, perhaps we were different, and if we were, it was for a brief moment. In our own lives we must see how tenuous a chance there is that the old, messy world we've created, or allowed, will be challenged, maybe changed. The thing about students' dissent is that it is time bound. Students have nothing to lose, but soon enough they stop being students. They become part of the system, they buy into it. And when they see how the system can benefit them, they become unconsciously status quo-ist. The firebrand has only to acquire his flat and car in order to find he's voting conservative and wondering if he should let his daughter go out late in the night as she seems to want to.

But as Vijay Tendulkar once said, 'I have an old faith in youth'. He was right. We can only hope our students will keep dissenting, will keep protesting. For all our good.

PURUSHOTTAM AGRAWAL

Purushottam Agrawal is an Indian writer, academic, novelist, literary critic, theologian, secularist, columnist and broadcaster. Here, he recounts the story of Nachiketa to illustrate the centuries-old tradition of debate and dissent in India and the necessity of protecting this tradition.

Let Us Strive for Fortitude … So That We May Ask Questions

ॐ सह नाववतु
सह नौ भुनक्तु
सह वीर्यं करवावहै
तेजस्विनावधीतमस्तु मा विद्विषावहै

Let both of us be protected together. Let both of us be nurtured together.
Let both of us together strive for fortitude. Let what we studied together be
glorious. Let none of us have any ill will.

The above invocation appears at the beginning of the *Kathopanishad*,
an ancient Sanskrit text that celebrates a young man's moral courage in
enquiring into the ultimate experience of death, and his guru's wisdom
in sharing knowledge with a deserving enquirer. It is a celebration of
togetherness in the adventure of asking, debating, exploring; togetherness
in the pursuit of knowledge, which, if genuine, is necessarily an act of
subversion.

The *Kathopanishad* is, at its heart, a dialogue between a disciple, or
student, and a guru. The student is a young boy, Nachiketa, whom some
would call audacious. A certain set of people today might even brand
him an 'intellectual terrorist', for he pestered his father endlessly with the
most inconvenient of questions.

And the guru is someone few of us want to meet: he is Yama; Death
itself.

Nachiketa had come to Yama without fear or rancour, and he waited
patiently for three nights to be heard. Pleased, Yama blessed the boy with
three boons. He also bestowed upon the youngster a unique honour,
naming one of the sacrificial fires after him: 'The fire named *Naachiketas*,
after you, shall be the most sacred and beneficial fire in sacrifice.' Though
thankful for this rare honour, Nachiketa was far from satisfied. He had a
query that only Yama could answer: what happens after death?

Incidentally, neither Nachiketa nor Yama is interested in super-
technological matters, things like spacecraft, genetic engineering or mini
nuclear bombs. Their concern, instead, is truly exotic—their concern is
with the meaning and purpose of existence. Some of their proud putative
descendants might term such preoccupation 'useless'. After all, haven't
the humanities been completely marginalized in our present university
system? Aren't there voices in the public domain today condemning
someone for doing research 'even at the age of 28' and accusing him of

indulging in 'parasitic intellectualism'? Hasn't there been widespread criticism of research in subjects which infect young minds with 'subversive ideas' and do not, apparently, contribute to the technological advancement and management of the nation?

Allow me at this point to recall a declaration by the spokesperson of the National Commission of Hurt Sentiments in my novel *NaCoHuS*: *'Technectual sab ka baap hai, intellectual hona paap hai...'* It is a sin to be an intellectual; the 'technectaul' is our Lord and Master.

In the *Kathopanishad*, however, neither the guru nor the disciple considers intellectual pursuit a sin or an act of terror. Nachiketa wants to know and Yama wants to ascertain his disciple's suitability as a recipient of knowledge. Both are convinced of the validity of the central question— one that remains till date abstract, abstruse and hence supposedly pointless: what happens after death?

'What happens after death?'

'How and by whom was all that is created? Was it at all *created* at some point of time or did it always exist?'

'What is the nature and function of time in existence?'

Such questions, which have been asked across civilizations and answered in many different ways, still remain urgent and relevant. And of course supremely disruptive.

And who knows the answers? May be the One who 'presides' over it all knows, as the 'Nasadiya Sukta' holds—but only momentarily, because it immediately inserts a caveat: 'Or maybe even He does not know...' And yet, these are the only questions worth asking, for without such enquiry life could not have progressed much; humans could not have moved from caves to metropolitan cities.

Yama was reluctant to answer Nachiketa's question. 'Not even the gods have found this question easy to handle,' he says in the *Kathopanishad*. 'Ask for something else instead; do not insist on the answer to this one.' He then tries to tempt Nachiketa with pleasures that the gods themselves enjoy: endless riches, great prestige and of course a very, very long life.

But Nachiketa, the enquirer, the disobedient child, remains unmoved. 'All these gifts are transient. A human being can never really be satisfied by riches, for how much can one consume? So what kind of enjoyment will such consumption bring to me?'

Nachiketa is echoing Maitreyee here, who on being tempted by her husband, the vedic sage Yajnavalkya, with similar boons, had asked, 'What should I do with that by which I do not become immortal?'

Yama does offer Nachiketa near immortality, but the boy is too clever for this. 'Long life?' he says to Yama. 'Having come to your abode, having become your disciple, having conversed with you, have I not already conquered the fear of life ending? Have I thus not already found eternal life?'

And so, having tested Nachiketa for commitment and competence, Yama has no choice but to satisfy the curiosity of his unique disciple. There is little point going into the details of the discourse Yama delivers on what happens to a human being after death. After all, the matter has to be explored by everyone in his or her own way. But it would be helpful to learn from both—from the student's courage and perseverance and the teacher's respect, despite his natural caution, for the questioner.

The point of this retelling of the Nachiketa-Yama story, of their shared intellectual adventure, is to understand the significance of the spirit of fearless inquiry, of complex arguments, of systematic and sustained engagement with fundamental questions of the human condition. The sound and fury generated in TV studios is no substitute for this. Debates cannot be resolved by the 'sentiment' of the crowd—nationalist, communist or of any other variety. It may be easy and tempting to brand intellectuals, scholars and students as 'anti-national', or 'enemies of the people', but such branding will at some point turn morons into murderers, who will ultimately not spare the 'nation' or the 'people', either. 'Technectuals' and managers have their own contribution to make, but wisdom and *science* are made possible by those who ask abstract and often unsettling questions and those who help them find the answers. These are the people I call intellectuals, and they thrive in societies where there is at least the implicit assurance that they will all be *protected together*.

Let us return to Nachiketa. How did he get the lifetime opportunity of having a dialogue with Death on the most fundamental questions of existence? Well, by questioning his father's intentions. By reminding the authority-figure of his deviation from the norms of proper conduct.

Nachiketa's father, Vajashrava, was a famed rishi. He was well aware of the rules of integrity and proper conduct, but he ignored them. He chose to reduce ethics and the notion of responsibility to a mere formality, exactly the way many powerful people today would love to have democracy serving merely as a convenient cover for their authoritarian fantasies. Vajashrava knew, but chose to ignore, that for any act, sacred or secular, there are norms. You must have the guts to question, debate or even discard these norms if you don't like them, but to swear by them in words and violate them in deeds is hypocrisy. Such hypocrisy is the way not of rishis and statesmen, but of the 'instruments of darkness' who 'oftentimes, to win us to our harm...tell us truths,/ Win us with honest trifles, to betray/ In deepest consequence.' And the consequences are suffered by the entire community—or nation, if you please. Nachiketa could see all this and chose to demand moral integrity. He chose to act as a genuine intellectual.

Vajashrava was performing a yajna, a sacrifice, that required the giving away of whatever he possessed, the underlying idea being that you do not treat the giving away as dispensing with household waste and useless objects; that you do not treat the receivers as beggars. Rather, you give away your best and dearest possessions. But Vajashrava was giving away aged, non-milch cows. He was violating the very spirit of the yajna and Nachiketa challenged him to honesty and rectitude by asking, 'To whom will you give me, Father?'

In a patriarchal society, what could be a more valuable 'possession' than a son, and a brilliant one, too? Therefore, Nachiketa's question—and indictment: 'To whom will you give me?'

Nachiketa pestered his father with the question, until, furious, the rishi snapped, 'To death, who else?'

This is the dramatic background to the real concern of the text: what happens after death? The enquirer is presented to the lord of death himself as a result of his moral confrontation with his father.

The story of Nachiketa the dissenter, and his guru, Yama, the lord of death, upholds the spirit of enquiry that will not be extinguished by fear or seduced by temptation. It is also unambiguous about the duty of the powers that be to make scholars and students feel safe and protected in their pursuit of knowledge, instead of persecuting them, putting them in jail or branding them as 'anti-nationals' and 'intellectual terrorists'.

Historically, the story also points to a troubling truth. Somewhere, in the centuries since the *Kathopanishad* was composed, something went wrong in India, so that we now have a tradition that glorifies Dronacharya—the guru who destroyed a student—and Shravankumar—the young man who personified unquestioning obedience—but that hardly ever enters into dialogue with the glorious adventure of Nachiketa.

To me, the message of the Nachiketa story is to guard and celebrate the desire to enquire, question and explore against all odds—even when threatened with an encounter with death. The hope is to create a society where debate and dissent are not criminalized. The aim is to earn fortitude. And the prayer is that glory should come not to us individually, but to the body and legacy of knowledge created *together* through debate and dialogue—तेजस्विनावधीतमस्तु

AMOL PALEKAR

Amol Palekar is a nationally and internationally acclaimed actor and director who has been active in the fields of performing and visual arts for the last five decades. Throughout his career, he has fought censorship and his commitment to the freedom of expression in art remains undiminished. Here, he looks at the history of film and theatre censorship in India and the legal and social structures that enable it, calling out the perils of giving in to the mob and the need for collective resistance.

Imprisoning Minds: On Censorship

August 29, 1970: The Maharashtra Theatrical Performances Examination Board (MTPEB) banned Vijay Tendulkar's play *Gidhade* (The Vultures), contending that its realistic portrayal of perverted socio-familial complications was unsuitable for a public performance. An extended battle led by the producer, Satyadev Dubey, and the director, Shriram Lagoo, resulted in the play being certified for release after a few token cuts. With a stroke of satirical genius, the play, on its release, began with the following deadpan announcement: 'In compliance with the objection from the censor board, the red stain on the rear of the sari of a particular female character who leaves the stage, back to the audience, will henceforth be blue in colour.' The show began to uproarious laughter and thundering applause, a landmark moment in the evolution of Marathi theatre.

August 19, 1974: The Maharashtra government decided to ban a production of Mahesh Elkunchwar's *Vasanakand* (The Inferno of Lust) that I directed. I appealed to the high court of Bombay for revocation of the ban. The MTPEB contended that 'The incestuous relationship between a brother and sister shown in the play is immoral, hence likely to offend audiences and may result in vandalism, triggering a law and order situation.' The court ruled unequivocally for the plaintiff, maintaining that 'If such situations arise, the government is administratively responsible for curbing the disorderly elements while protecting the artistes to complete their performance without any hindrance.' It was 5 p.m. when I got the order. Tearing my way through rush hour traffic from the high court to Ravindra Natyamandir, Prabhadevi, I was up on the stage at 7 p.m.

August 30, 1996: The Central Board of Film Certification (CBFC) objected to a scene from my film *Daayraa* (The Square Circle), and asked for some allegedly obscene dialogue and phrases to be deleted.

The narrative was of a romance between a man who turns into a transvestite after years of portraying female characters in folk plays and a woman forced to dress in male attire to ward off sexual predators.

The assiduous members of the board objected to a scene in which a 'madam', running a sex racket with her two henchmen, abducts a young girl.

Having sought an 'A' certificate in the first place, I fought endlessly.

Finally, with no deletion in any scene and minor changes in some dialogue, *Daayraa* went on to win the National Award and a Grand Prix in France.

2006: My film, *Thang/Quest*, a bilingual film in Marathi and English, dealt with the repressed homosexuality of its male protagonist who has a heterosexual marriage. A film that demanded deep introspection from the audience, it received, as expected, an 'A' certificate for the English version.

In a moment of perplexing and disheartening inconsistency, the same CBFC (with different board members though), decided to ban the Marathi version. This was certainly unacceptable to us. In the discussions that followed with the morality brigade on the CBFC, I drew attention to *Brokeback Mountain*, a prominent Hollywood film dealing with homosexuality, which had been certified for its release just a few months earlier. I asked if their implication was that the Marathi audience was less mature and tolerant than the English-speaking audience. Their retort was, 'These things may be okay in foreign films but they don't fit into our Maharashtrian culture.'

Even after I pointed out that great Marathi litterateurs such as S.N. Pendse, C.T. Khanolkar and Vidyadhar Pundalik had dealt with homosexuality in their fictional works, their nay was loud and clear. They backed off only when Sandhya Gokhale, my wife and writer and co-director of the film, demanded as a lawyer that they, 'must record their objections in writing so that a war may be waged in the court.' Without anything in writing, both versions of the film were released with 'A' certificates.

2010: When I read the script of Vivek Bele's play, *Maruti and Champagne*, I was excited by the prospect of a superb play in the offing. Anticipation soon curdled into despair when I learnt that the mention of Maruti 'offended the sentiments of a certain community' and was drawing shrill vituperation. I reached out to Mohan Agashe as a head of the production house of the play and offered him a hand to fight such extra-legal censorship. His prostration before the mob became evident when he said that the production was to be renamed 'Monkey Holding the Champagne'. I was disheartened, since such retractions boost the mobocracy. Moreover, he was an actor in Vijay Tendulkar's *Ghashiram Kotwal* which was similarly threatened, but which case had been successfully fought in the court.

January 2012: Symbiosis University, Pune, announced a private show of Sanjay Kak's short film on Kashmir, *Jashn-e-azadi*. Activists of the Akhil Bharatiya Vidyarthi Parishad demanded that the screening be cancelled as it was likely to hurt local sentiments. Obvious questions such as 'Has anyone who raises such objections actually seen the film?' or 'Can you identify specific objectionable material?' were given short shrift. Before spinelessly cancelling the show, the director should have spent a moment over the message his action sent to his students.

June 14, 2016: The CBFC raised an astonishing eighty-nine objections to *Udta Punjab* but refused to spell them out in writing. The source of panic was that the film might damage the reputation of the Punjab government.

In times past, Nargis Dutt, then addressing the Rajya Sabha as a nominated member, expressed anguish at the unflattering portrayals of Indian poverty seen through the lens of the legendary Satyajit Ray and his new-wave cinema contemporaries. She saw it as an affront to our national pride. How did the legend who immortalized the title *Mother India* descend to such inanity? Around the same time, the culture czar of the day, minister Vasant Sathe, placed a ban on my film *Akrit* from participation in international film festivals.

Senior artists, including Shombhu Mitra, P.L. Deshpande and Durga Bhagwat, addressed a joint letter to then prime minister Indira Gandhi, castigating this unreasonable fatwa. It was soon lifted.

Just for the record, Sathe had ordered a similar fatwa against foreign performances of *Ghashiram Kotwal* in 1980. Again, Indira Gandhi vetoed his decision.

Artistes have long been at the receiving end, often violently so, of the intolerant mob. Balbir Krishan, whose art echoes his homosexuality, faced a violent attack in Delhi; M.F. Hussain had to be in exile in his twilight years after facing death threats; Taslima Nasreen is still unable to find permanent sanctuary in India; Salman Rushdie's permission to speak at a literary festival in Jaipur was withdrawn at the penultimate moment; Mumbai University withdrew Rohinton Mistry's *Such a Long Journey* from its curriculum; a statue of Dadoji Konddev was spirited away overnight from its prominent location in Pune's Lal Mahal; Joseph Lelyveld's book *Great Soul: Mahatma Gandhi and His Struggle With India* was banned in quick succession by the Gujarat and Central governments. We have a long, ignominious history of abject prostration before intemperate, anti-intellectual mobs. I, for one, feel extremely agitated to see that despite these examples spread over five decades, nothing much has changed.

In Chapter 22 of his epic treatise on politics, Niccolò Machiavelli identifies three types of intelligence. 'One kind understands things for itself, the second appreciates what others can understand, [and] the third understands neither for itself nor through others.' He goes on to say, 'This first kind is excellent, the second good and the third kind useless.' It is sobering that it is the ubiquitous abundance of the last type that characterizes our society.

Katherine Mayo was an American historian whose polemical work *Mother India* drew opprobrium even from Mahatma Gandhi. In a stinging rebuke, he commented, 'It is the report of a drain inspector sent out with the one purpose of opening and examining the drains of the country to be reported upon, or to give a graphic description of the stench exuded by the opened drains.' Yet the Mahatma's open-mindedness became evident when in later years, he urged all Indians to read the book, if only to understand the calumny that the colonial masters poured on their subjects in a disingenuous defence of their occupation. It is to our country's eternal shame that the Mahatma's exhortation has been forgotten and, seven decades after Independence, the book continues to be banned in India.

I have been and, will remain, an untiring advocate against the mentality and mechanisms of censorship. Bans and censorships are abhorrent manifestations of denial of plurality of thought and voices of dissent. Anger at and, intolerance to dissent, makes fodder for an insidious form of anti-intellectual tyranny. It imposes the bigotry and narrow-mindedness of a bullying minority upon the largely apathetic majority. Whether this pressure is exerted through mechanisms of the state or otherwise, curbing and controlling artistic expression ultimately has a chilling impact on *all* expression, even the most anodyne sample.

Efforts at curbing expression share some characteristics:

- Censorship is cited as a tool to protect the nation's sovereignty and integrity. At the pinnacle of its imperial arrogance, the British Empire in India found no cause to curb overt challenges to its sovereignty. This is true for all manner of creative works of the times. There were no attempts to ban the Marathi play, *Kichak Vadh*, an allegory on the colonial despoilment of India, or a song like '*Door hato aye duniyavalon, ye Hindostan hamara hai*' on the grounds of sedition.
- 'Incitement to hostility between groups' or 'likelihood of grievously offending sentiments of a particular group/community/religion' is another weapon. One needs to look no further than the unambiguous decision of the Bombay high court in the matter of *Vasanakand* for a searing rebuttal of this argument.
- A perverse thesis is being introduced in social discourse on the arts. It runs along these disingenuous lines: 'The creative arts exist only to amuse and entertain. They have no business poking their noses in revealing a society's iniquities and injustices, its warts and blemishes.' The history of all creative expression readily reveals the hollowness and falsehood of this contention. Across the aeons, the artist has recorded, ridiculed and satirized her contemporary context.

The *Udta Punjab* controversy has abruptly brought this discourse out of the arcane realm of academic debate into the court of public opinion. It is not inconceivable that the current CBFC might be reconstituted. However, a fundamental reworking of the entire censorship structure needs legislative action. The Cinematograph Act, 1952 will need to be abrogated and fresh legislation drafted and adopted by the Parliament to replace it, keeping the changed circumstances of the twenty-first century in mind. It is anybody's guess how easily such a radical overhaul of the structure sits with an establishment that wishes to impose its will on what we will eat or drink, or what we may say or see!

There is a more fundamental issue that underlies the censorship structure. The constitutional validity of the Cinematograph Act needs to be challenged. Till this challenge is rigorously mounted, a few fatuous guardians of our minds and morals will continue to be entrusted with a crude pair of scissors to perform their hare-brained duty. It is a matter of *de facto* reality that the Act is patently discriminatory and falls foul of the overarching equality before the law guaranteed by Article 14 of the Constitution. What might the legal line of argument look like?

If

- literature, theatre (as an exception in Maharashtra), dance and other forms of creative expression are not subject to censorship; if speech, both written and oral, or articles, no matter how offensive, require no pre-screening nor attracts any censorship;
- television programming of any sort, news, current affairs, entertainment or whatever else, is free of censorship (except to the extent that it carries cinematic content);

Then

- What is the precise legal justification for encumbering the cinematic arts exclusively to the burden of censorship? Discriminating among the various forms of creative expression in this manner is irrational, unfair and untenable against the touchstone of the constitutional guarantee of equality before the law. What is the rationale behind and what is the object of such differentiation?

In our current situation, there are just two alternatives to put this discriminatory regime behind us. Either we dismantle the odious structures of cinematic censorship. Or we bring *all* creative forms of expression under censorship. Evidently, the latter option must be abhorrent in the extreme to any believer in India's democratic, progressive polity. An intelligent, culturally aware, literate, aesthetically evolved citizenry must take an uncompromising stance against illiberal forces of bigotry and thought control. All of us need to unite for such causes; else this will remain a solitary individual fight, making no dent.

Sandhya Gokhale sums it up well:

No nation-state accepts unbridled and unbounded freedom of opinion or expression. One person's freedom exists only with a deep commitment to the same freedom for his fellow citizens. In other words, one person's freedom does not come bundled with the right to trample upon those of his fellows. All freedoms are circumscribed within specific social and cultural contexts. As soon as we begin to accept this line of reasoning, we experience a sense of unease that something crucial and essential to freedom is slipping away. This is where we enter the amorphous terrain of individual or group specific constraints. In the scarcity or absence of ethics, values, respect, mutuality, it is easy to get mired in the quicksand of subjectivity. Perhaps it was precisely this sort of a world that Rushdie transported us to in his *Haroun and the Sea of Stories*. The Land of Chup is a land of oppressive silence where the sun would never rise. Right next door, the raucous, argumentative land of Gup, always enjoyed bright sunlight. It is for us to decide whether we want to be citizens of Chup or Gup. Freedom and rights are human artefacts. Do they deserve protection? Should we strive to protect those and to what extent and at what cost? We need to grapple with these and attempt to answer. Impotent finger-pointing at mobocratic armies of the intolerant and easily offended will only end in the pounding out of all freedoms and we would have brought this bleak consequence upon ourselves by our apathy. We will have to satisfy ourselves with little morsels of tightly circumscribed freedoms that the establishment tosses at us from time to time.

'Who controls the past controls the future; who controls the present controls the past.' Who can forget this memorable line from George Orwell's *1984*? If we want to have a sun rise every day as was shone over the land of Gup, the time to decide is high and that is a certainty.

Translated by Paritosh Joshi

SHANTA GOKHALE

Shanta Gokhale is a renowned writer, translator, cultural critic and theatre historian. In 'Asking Why, Saying No', she argues that artists must speak out against brutal regimes, and the politically and socially constructed divides in society in order to protect their intellectual and creative freedom.

Asking Why, Saying No

On 13 January 2015, Tamil writer Perumal Murugan posted the following message on his Facebook page: 'Perumal Murugan, the writer, is dead. As he is no God, he is not going to resurrect himself. He has no faith in rebirth. As an ordinary teacher, he will live as P. Murugan. Leave him alone.'

Murugan had been threatened and viciously pilloried by the right-wing nationalist organization, the Rashtriya Swayamsevak Sangh (RSS) for his 2010 novel *Madhorubhagan*. The novel told the story of a childless woman who takes recourse to an ancient ritual whereby women like her were permitted to have consensual sex with men other than their husbands to give themselves a chance to conceive. The permission was granted to them for one night—the night of the annual chariot festival of the Kailasanathar temple.

There had been no protests against *Madhorubhagan* when it first appeared; nor were there any in December 2013 when its English translation *One Part Woman* appeared. In May 2014, the political power at the Centre changed. The RSS became a dominant force. By 2015 right-wing groups had attacked the freedom of expression of several artists and cartoonists across the country. In December 2015, five years after *Madhorubhagan* had been published, the RSS burnt copies of it, accusing Murugan of showing the Kailasanathar temple and its women devotees in a bad light. On 12 January, Murugan was invited to a 'peace meeting' at the local Collectorate, ostensibly to create a space for an open dialogue between the two parties but in effect to humiliate him and force him to apologize for his writing. The meeting was presided over by the Collector herself. The following day, this professor of architecture, and author of six novels announced the death of Perumal Murugan, the writer, on Facebook.

Murugan had not thought to offend anybody. He had merely created an intensely human story using his community's history and culture as an active agent in his protagonist's fortunes. But those are precisely the fields where the political right meddles to engineer its dream society of uniform belief. Murugan had to be punished for daring to ignore their construction of history and culture, choosing instead to be faithful to the truth as he saw it.

Stepping back and away from his time and space, we come to a writer who took a conscious decision to use his art to oppose the kind of politics that drove Murugan to despair. George Orwell says in his essay *Why I Write*, '...looking back through my work, I see that it is invariably where I lacked a political purpose that I wrote lifeless books and was betrayed into purple passages, sentences without meaning, decorative adjectives and humbug generally.' It was the Spanish Civil War followed by World War II that told Orwell where he stood politically, and what he must do with that knowledge. He had to write directly, and when that was not possible, indirectly, against fascism and totalitarianism.

This was more easily decided than done. It was only in *Animal Farm* that Orwell realized fully his desire to fuse 'political purpose and artistic purpose into one whole'. It was because he managed to achieve this crucial balance that the novella has continued to speak to readers over the last seventy years, particularly loudly and relevantly to societies that have invested political power in single-ideology, single-culture regimes where sheep have been happy to chant 'Four legs good, two legs bad' to the dictates of pigs.

Being engaged, to use Sartre's term, does not severely challenge the principles of the novelist's art. A novel is, by definition, about people, places, events and history. The novelist orders these elements to create a world through which she can search for the truths of human life. Thus, even without an overt political purpose, her very assumption that truth is plural sets her apart and in opposition to the simpler world of singular truths propagated by religious and political orthodoxies. Consequently, her answer to the moralistically driven question, 'Who is right, Anna Karenina or Karenin, Emma Bovary or Charles?' can only be, 'I honestly don't know. Both perhaps; or neither.'

The same question may well be asked about Aravind Adiga's characters in *Last Man in Tower*. They, the residents of the fictional Vishram Society in Mumbai's suburb, Vakola, are initially right in refusing to fall for developer Dharmen Shah's monetary inducements to make them hand over their block of flats for redevelopment. But the temptation of

money, together with the fact that the building is falling to pieces, bring
all except one resident round to Shah's side. The exception is Masterji.
He begins as a man of principles; but soon appears to be driven more by
a stubborn refusal to change than by a watchful conscience. Meanwhile
the good people of Vishram Society turn into a blood-thirsty mob,
causing Masterji to wonder, 'Am I looking at good people or bad?' For
single-truth ideologies, such ambiguity is not merely unacceptable but
positively dangerous.

~

The word truth holds a vital place in this discussion. 'Truth in drama is
forever elusive,' said Harold Pinter in his Nobel Prize acceptance speech.
'You never quite find it but the search for it is compulsive. The search is
clearly what drives the endeavour. The search is your task.' However, while
fulfilling this task, the playwright, like the novelist, must find a way to
fuse her politics and her art into one whole. In a political play she cannot
give her characters the full freedom that she would otherwise give if she
were creating them purely out of observed life or her imagination and
even allowing them occasionally to lead her. Instead, she must now lead
her characters because a political play comes out of a place of knowledge,
not out of the ambiguities of not knowing. You are not searching for your
political position heuristically in the course of creating a work of art. You
already know where you stand, whether it is vis-à-vis totalitarianism or
brahminical Hinduism or caste hierarchies or gender discrimination or
exploitation of the poor and the weak or environmental degradation. If
you want to serve your politics and your art equally well, you must devise
strategies that will make your play an effective vehicle for both.

Some of the greatest political plays of our times have used subterfuge,
satire or allegory to achieve this purpose. In *Accidental Death of an
Anarchist*, Dario Fo creates a maniac protagonist who skilfully exposes
the truth—fudged by the police in their report—about the alleged
anarchist's death. He did not fall to his death accidentally. He was pushed
by the investigating police. Fo chose not to write the play as a drama
but as a grotesque satire, because the emotion that drama arouses in the
viewer leads to catharsis, depriving the play of its bite. 'When you laugh,'
Fo says, 'the sediment of anger stays inside you and can't get out. It is no
wonder that dictatorial governments always forbid laughter and satire
first, rather than drama.'

In 2003, Habib Tanvir and his troupe were attacked, by the Hindu right, in Madhya Pradesh for performing a seventy-year-old folk play, *Ponga Pandit*, which ridiculed the rituals prescribed by Brahmin priests to consolidate their power over people. In one incident in the play, a jamadarin, or sweeper, who is not allowed to enter a temple because she is supposedly untouchable, steals the temple gods to worship them at home. The brahminical Hindu right could not stomach the laughter that this provoked. They not only disrupted performances but physically assaulted the actors and Tanvir.

A similar response followed the first performances of Vijay Tendulkar's hard-hitting play *Ghashiram Kotwal*. An allegory tempered by irony and music, the play demonstrates the dangers involved in governments creating Frankensteins like Bhindranwale in Punjab and the Shiv Sena in Maharashtra, both during Congress rule. Casting around for a story and a form that would allow him to allegorize this contemporary situation, Tendulkar chose a small episode from Maharashtra's history as the narrative and a folk form from the Konkan called naman khele as its vehicle. Using the basic formations of naman khele allowed him the freedom he needed to move his characters around as he wished. Of his two equally unconscionable protagonists, one was Maharashtra's icon, the astute statesman Nana Phadnavis. The right-wing Brahmins of Pune (Phadnavis was a Brahmin) did not take too kindly to this portrayal. They demonstrated violently against the play and used all available means to stop it from going to Berlin where it had been invited to participate in a theatre festival. The play did go to Berlin, albeit after a cloak-and-dagger drama, and went on to become a hit on the Indian stage.

The final trigger for the form that G.P. Deshpande chose for his seminal political play *Uddhwasta Dharmashala* (Man in Dark Times), was the report of the House Committee of Un-American Activities which blacklisted 300 Hollywood artists as un-American. Amongst them was Charlie Chaplin who said, 'I don't want to make a revolution, only some good films.' Deshpande's play centres on an inquiry conducted by a panel of college administrators and lecturers who pretend to investigate a colleague's alleged ties with the Communist party, when they have already decided that he is 'guilty'.

The story is not much different when it comes to art. M.F. Husain was hounded out of the country by the Hindu right for painting religious and nationalist icons as nudes. His was not even an act of open dissent. But like laughter, an unclothed human body upsets the Hindu right.

~

When Iraq was invaded and bombs fell fast and furious, the Iraqi ceramist-sculptor Nuha al-Radi held an exhibition titled Embargo Art, to protest against the impossible sanctions that America had imposed on the country. The show comprised rows of figures made from recycled wood, painted and adorned with feathers. 'Hopefully we will recycle ourselves and survive,' she wrote. Dissent has always meant putting your head on the block. Not every artist has the courage to do so. Nor should she be asked to, thought Bertolt Brecht. In *Galileo*, after the astronomer has recanted, his student Andreas remarks bitterly, 'Unhappy is the land that breeds no hero.' To this Galileo quietly responds, 'Unhappy is the land that needs a hero.' Artists weren't meant to put their heads on the block. They were meant only to create.

The dissenting voice in fiction, theatre, cinema and art has been loud and varied. But even when the artist does not think of her work as a vehicle for dissent, one may confidently assume that something filters into it that announces her feelings about and towards her world. If even that does not happen, how will she answer the question, *koham*? Who am I?

The art that does not lend itself as easily to being political as the others is lyric poetry. The lyric poet's instinct is to write about trees, mountains, the changing seasons, memory and, most importantly, love in all its shades and moods. But if the poet lives fully in her time, with body, mind and soul engaged, and if her times are infected by man-made cankers that are destroying the values she deeply cherishes, she cannot allow her most impassioned form of expression—poetry—to remain unaffected. However, she must tread with great care on political ground, always watching out for the pitfall of poetry turning into a collection of propagandist platitudes and slogans. Also, she must take care at all times not to rise to the bait of the question, 'What is the purpose of poetry? If poetry has no demonstrable purpose but to be itself, what impact do you hope to make on the world with your dissent?'

W.H. Auden said in his poem 'In Memory of W.B. Yeats': 'Poetry makes nothing happen.' And so it does not. Expanding on the same idea, Habib Tanvir once told this writer in the course of an interview, 'The government launched a scheme for reviving our dying arts. A form had to be filled. It had three columns—survey, budget, result. I left the last column blank. Art is not like drought where you can count how many died; or an earthquake where you calculate the damage. Art never changes society. But art does something very precious. It paves the way for change, it affects opinions, it opens up minds.'

That, it would seem, is a good enough outcome. Not that outcomes have worried poets like the Chilean Nobel Laureate Pablo Neruda. He, once a writer of passionate, often erotic, love poetry, turned intensely political with the Spanish Civil War and its aftermath. Marking the shift from the personal to the political in his work, he wrote in 'Let Me Explain a Few Things', 'You will ask: and where are the lilacs / and the metaphysics petalled with poppies / and the rain repeatedly spattering its words... / Come and see the blood in the streets / Come and see the blood in the streets...'

The important point here is that this was as much good poetry as, 'I do not love you as if you were salt-rose, or topaz / or the arrow of carnations the fire shoots off / I love you as certain dark things are to be loved / in secret, between the shadow and the soul.'

In his well-known poem about dark times, Brecht posed the question, 'In the dark times / Will there also be singing?' To which the answer by all thinking, feeling artists of the last 100 years has been a resounding echo of his own: 'Yes, there will also be singing / About the dark times.'

Why is it so important that artists speak out against brutal regimes, against caste hierarchies, against second-class citizenship imposed on people for their gender or religion? It is important because all such socially and politically constructed divides take away from artists something that is the very life breath of their art: Freedom. Which poet would not like to be able to write of love all her life? Paint or sculpt when the trees are in leaf, birds are warbling and no bombs are falling on her head? Which music composer would not want to confide all the promptings of his soul freely to his score sheets without the shadow of Big Brother falling across them, making sure his music reflects the patriotism he is supposed to feel towards his country?

Defending freedom is an act of self-preservation for the artist. Standing up for it against hostile power structures is good for her and good for her art. Habib Tanvir was fond of telling a story about hilsa fish to illustrate how bad times could almost be seen as good times for art. 'The people of Dacca claim that their hilsa is better than Hooghly hilsa, because Hooghly hilsa swim with the current while theirs swim against it. That makes them tougher and sweeter.'

Besides self-preservation, there is another reason why artists must take a political position in their art. Personal integrity. If you do not do what every cell in your body urges you to do, you perpetrate the worst kind of falsehood upon yourself. You deny your own truth. For the seventeenth-century saint-poet of Maharashtra, Tukaram, the truth lay at the feet of his Lord Vitthal; and the only way he knew how to search for that truth was through poetry. His impassioned verses, full of doubt, love, devotion, humility and sharp observations about the hypocrisies of the priestly class and so-called men of God, were loved by the common people in whose sweet language they were written.

In one verse he says, 'The man who takes the name of Ram and Krishna in a simple, direct way / And contemplates within himself their dark-skinned forms / Although born a Mahar / Must be regarded as a Brahmin.'

In another he says, 'Oh how have these men turned into such humbugs? / They do terrible things yet call themselves sadhus / They smear ashes on their bodies / Close their eyes and commit sins. / They pretend to be ascetics / And celebrate festivals of sex / Says Tuka, words fail me in describing them / May fire come between me and them.'

Such outspoken criticism of their kind upset the powerful Brahmins of his village. Moreover, Tukaram, a non-Brahmin, had dared to do what only Brahmins were permitted to do—write religious verse. Raging against him, they ordered him to drown his manuscripts in the river Indrayani. Legend has it that they floated up intact at the end of the thirteen days he spent praying. We may interpret this as meaning that the objects were of little importance when the verses themselves had taken on an immortal life on the tongues of people. Tukaram's verses are remembered and sung even today. The status quo-ist poetry of his opponents, made flaccid through lack of friction, has been forgotten.

The third reason why it is imperative for artists to speak up is the obligation they owe to the future; to those not yet born who will still inherit the consequences of present times. Brecht writes, 'They won't say: the times were dark / Rather: why were their poets silent?'

Two days after the Brussels bombings of 22 March 2016, a woman standing with her child in the Place de la Bourse smiled into a television camera and said, 'Yes I'm happy. My happiness is their defeat.' Taking courage from her, I will say that, in the midst of the worst times, a simple lyric poem might also be a form of dissent. It would make people happy; and nothing rattles brute power more than the happiness of people in the midst of the sorrows that they have visited on them.

T.M. Krishna

T.M. Krishna is a renowned Carnatic musician and activist. He received the Ramon Magsayay Award (2016) for his forceful commitment as artist and advocate to art's power to heal India's deep social divisions by breaking barriers of caste, class and gender.

Myth and Reality

As one who is thought of as belonging to the 'world of culture', I would say that the first two years of the Narendra Modi government have been the most disturbing times that I can recall. It has been a period when the political context has forced me to ask difficult questions of what this nation really is as a cultural identity. An ideational collapse has occurred and you can see it even these paragraphs. I find I have used the word culture to describe what is essentially religious.

Would I have done this some years ago? I would not have. This too is a remarkable achievement by the present dispensation. It is not that Prime Minister Narendra Modi has stood up at the ramparts of the Red Fort and made a proclamation to the effect that India that is Bharat has one culture, in body, mind and soul, and its name is Hindutva. He has not done that. In fact he has, both in India and abroad, spoken of 'sabka saath', but his colleagues and political partners have blatantly espoused Hindutva. And he has not contradicted them.

Hindus have been told by Hindutva's spokespersons that for the last sixty plus years, this country has victimized and marginalized them. We have reached a point where this manifest untruth now carries the ring of historical truth. Hindus have been quite happily celebrating every festival with pomp; in fact the sizes of pandals during Ganpati utsav or Durga puja have only increased, the number of young people who visit temples has clearly been on the rise over the past decade or more and, let us not forget the proliferation of sadhus and gurus that dot our topography. If anything, the Hindu is far from being sunk or mass converted. But the fear of such a happening has been implanted in every Hindu mind.

Religious violence is not a creation of this government. The Congress can never atone enough for 1984. But there is a shift in the way society has taken to this new Hindutva political craftsmanship and that is for me the most worrisome trend. Today, violence of the religious/cultural kind is not just a tool of party politics and their attached lumpen outfits, today it is owned and worn on the sleeve with aplomb.

It is said with barely concealed anger that if a Hindu celebrates his religion, he is accused of being right-wing but a Muslim is never asked that question. Let us think about this, seriously. In this world's context, can we ever make this statement and actually believe it is true? If there is any community that has been globally vilified, it is the people of the Islamic faith, yet we are convinced that they have greater acceptance than the middle- and upper-class Hindu. There is enough data to prove that Muslims and Dalits are the most backward communities in this nation. There is no doubt that parties in and out of power, including the Congress and many Muslim leaders wearing various political hats, have only exploited the average Muslim voter, but should this make 'us' insensitive to 'their' real conditions? Worse is to think that Muslims are receiving benefits at Hindus' cost. This idea in itself entrenches an underlying cultural thought—that this is a Hindu land and that Muslims are guests. Not to forget the allied belief that Muslims are terrorists or possible terrorists, unless Hindu thought has touched them, and just in case you did not know, Sufism is quintessentially Hindu!

Another invented truism being spread around is that the education system has made people anti-Hindu and pro-religious minorities. Even more laughable is the assertion that leftist academicians with the connivance of western socialist scholars have wiped out Hindu goodness and achievements from our history. If we were to visit the innumerable religious studies, art and language departments around this country, we will find more PhDs that are seeped in Hindu religiosity than of the other kind. But from what the naysayers claim, India by now should have become a mini-Soviet Union, but we are not, and thank goodness for that.

For all the Hindu pride that is demanded of us, the last few years have witnessed a strong misogynist (let us remember that this is not just a male attitude) and pro-upper caste/class articulation of India. There is clearly a cultural strategy to linearize Hindu sanskriti and within it engulf all that has in the past and present questioned its organization. In the eulogization of Hindu history I also smell a strong whiff of appropriation combined with the establishment of a certain idea of the Hindu—one that emanates from the middle classes. There has been no attempt to address issues of gender, multiple genders or caste. If anything there is a suppression of such discourses. Suppression today is not enforced via a dictatorial ban, it is mobilized using fear.

The world of the arts, especially the classical and wannabe classical community (nobody cares about the rest) has heralded this government, for they believe that they are the true representatives of Bharatiya sanskriti. All of sudden many Hindutvas have emerged out of closet. There is clearly a streamlining of what is artistically Indian, where religious Hindu-inclined art forms are being pushed forward. Art and culture are going through a right-wing phase, even though at no point in India's independent history were the Hindu art forms targeted. Hasn't Bharatanatyam always been the 'number one' symbol of Indian antiquity?

We should not allow people to subsume culture into religious belief systems. But I now wonder whether the larger society really cares to engage with this thought. Sociologists, activists and cultural liberals vouch for India's syncretic identity providing us many living examples of wonderful people. But do these small pockets matter anymore? If anything they are being used to certify the real Indian—the one who accepts the Hindu as that mythic being.

As I end this piece, I feel another achievement of this government, at least in me—cultural pessimism.

Sagari R. Ramdas

Sagari R. Ramdas has a Masters in Animal Breeding and Genetics from the University of California, Davis, USA. She has worked with rural and Adivasi communities as a field veterinarian, trainer and researcher on livestock and peoples' livelihoods. This essay was written in September 2016.

Not for the Cow

As Bakrid approached, we witnessed a spurt in what have become regular attacks by cow vigilante groups against cattle traders, beef consumers and butcher communities across India. After Una, where gau rakshaks attacked Dalit cattle-carcass skinners, Dalits resisting this caste-imposed forced labour have cried out: 'Gai nu poonch nu tume rakho; ame amra zameen apo! Harka, chamra tame rakho; hume hamari zameen apo!' (You keep your cow's tail, skin, bones; give us our land!). They have faced increased attacks by gau rakshaks and the upper castes. Gau rakshaks have also begun to attack citizens on their use of leather goods.

Joining the monitoring and surveillance networks on cattle slaughter and beef is the Lala Lajpat Rai University of Veterinary and Animal Sciences, Haryana (my alma mater), with its as-yet-unpublished-in-the-public-domain lab report, 'confirming cow beef' in biryani in Mewat. In 2015, Haryana followed closely on the heels of Maharashtra, enacting the Gauvanshsanrakshan and Gausamvardhan Act, with stringent penalties for cattle slaughter, transportation of cattle for slaughter and possession of beef. Right from its earliest avatar—the Punjab Prohibition of Cow Slaughter Act, 1955—the burden of proof of innocence is placed on the accused.

Whilst the veracity of the tests and related procedures have to be interrogated, the state steadfastly asserts to having strictly implemented the law, using technologies to test for species differentiation in cooked meat.

Cut to Telangana: Pleas to prevent harassment of cattle traders, transporting bulls and bullocks during Bakrid, elicited a stony silence from the Telangana government, despite state slaughter laws permitting trade, transportation and slaughter of bulls and bullocks, certified 'fit for slaughter'. The same state, however, lent tacit support to gau rakshaks, with its public announcement on September 9, via the department of animal husbandry, requesting citizens to be alert to cow slaughter because of 'increased meat consumption' during Bakrid.

The debate here is not about whether meat samples tested positive or negative for cattle meat, or whether 'cow slaughter' is happening or not. It's about the state's intent to criminalize food cultures and livelihoods (in this case beef and its connected livelihoods), and by doing so criminalize entire communities, comprising 50 per cent of India's population. By stating that the law is aimed at protecting cows, their progeny, indigenous cattle breeds and the bovine economy, it camouflages the state's intent to use the law to defend a dominant notion of Indian culture.

As veterinarians and animal scientists, we know slaughter does not drive down animal numbers, but actually supports their reproduction, as evident in the case of India's buffaloes. We also have mounting evidence to show how slaughter bans actively depress cattle rearing.

It is farmers who sell their unproductive cow, bull or bullock, and not cattle traders who steal or forcibly purchase an owner's animal. Small and marginal farmers and landless labour, comprising 80 per cent of India's rural population, own 70 per cent of India's 190 million cattle and 108 million buffaloes. Farmers unable to feed, water, graze and manage their bovines, for reasons ranging from drought to collapsing milk markets, sell their animals. If not bought by another farmer, when purchased by traders for slaughter, they are spared from a slow death from starvation. The farmers' right to sell is critical to sustain livelihoods and nurture the livestock economy.

Far from protecting the cow, obstructing all post-farmer downstream economic activities via a slaughter ban spells the death knell for India's disappearing cattle economy. Cattle beef is a critical part of food cultures and a cheap source of protein; its skin is the basis of India's thriving leather industry valued at $11 billion generating 95 per cent of India's footwear needs; and its offals, used widely in the pharmaceutical and manufacturing industries, provides an 'unproductive' animal a robust market value, and the farmer an income.

Maharashtra farmers blame the slaughter ban on bulls and bullocks for massive declines in the resale value of bullocks. Prices fell by 40 to 60 per cent, forcing farmers to abandon their animals and forego money they relied upon in distress situations. Farmers purchasing drinking water through the drought of 2015 could not buy water for their animals and bemoaned their plight of being burdened with unproductive animals.

States with cattle slaughter bans propose increased public investments for gaushalas, and persuading farmers to rear unproductive animals for dung and urine. A farmer spends Rs 60,000 to maintain a cow/bullock, and she earns only Rs 20,000 annually from its dung and urine. Moreover, assuming one-third of India's cattle are unproductive, we are talking of a public outlay of Rs 6,363 billion annually or Rs 5,300 per citizen to shelter these cattle—all in the name of 'culture'. Enhanced public investment in safe, state-of-the-art slaughter procedures and stress-free transportation are priorities rather than slaughter and beef bans, and gaushalas, reported to be concentration camps of slow death.

Let's not forget, the same culture (and state) is silent on one of India's best-kept secrets: caste continues to inform the composition of India's workforce involved in the disposal of cows and their offspring. Excluding Dalits, Adivasis and Muslims, all other 'castes' refuse to dispose their dead bovines. Dalits and Muslims comprise 45 per cent and 55 per cent respectively of the 2.5 million workforce, engaged in downstream activities connected to dead bovines: flaying, curing and carcass removal/recovery, skinning, tanning and processing of hide, offals and production of leather goods. Paradoxically, in this flourishing industry, where caste hegemony forces Dalits to be engaged in 'removal and recovery of carcasses', which is the worst paid set of activities, upper castes control the vast earnings derived from India's expanding leather and beef industries.

Naresh Dadhich

Naresh Dadhich is former director of Inter-University Center for Astronomy and Astrophysics, Pune, and holds the M.A. Ansari Chair, Jamia Millia Islamia, New Delhi.

It's Time Indian Scientists Answered Their Call to Be Responsible Citizens

The Indian society is an excellent example of the actual realization of plurality, with its rich texture of flexibility and absorbing capacity. It has come about because the region has a long and scintillating history of interaction with the world outside—of diverse mores, languages and faiths through trade over land and sea routes for over 2,000 years. This was also accompanied with cultural and scholarly exchanges. Added to all that were external invasions and campaigns that brought in their own impact and influences. This is how the Indian society has come to be a diverse and plural system as it exists today. Its physical expanse, encompassing high snow-clad mountains to plains fed by rivers to desert descending down through the Western and Eastern Ghats and onto the peninsula. In fact, it is no surprise at all that such a human system could be anything else but plural. It also possesses a rich linguistic diversity, with a few hundred languages flowering together as well as an impressive spectrum of communities abiding by different faiths and religions.

People and their social systems over a period develop their own nature and existential identities. Without so much of an iota of doubt or hesitation, one can say that plurality is the nature of the Indian people and the Indian society. Henceforth, this should become the most abiding concern above anything else.

Civilization is essentially the measure of all that which is profound and sublime in human compassion, thought, creativity and imagination, and their actual realization in people's lives and living. One of the main concerns of civilization is the creation of new knowledge—of knowing the world around us, why all things are the way they are and their situation in the overall structure of the universe. And one of the most profound questions in this framework is who we are and how we came into being.

For creating and acquiring knowledge, we need a method that is reliable. Modern science has been and is that method. It is objective because it is logically consistent and independent of the observer and her location in spacetime. Above all, it demands observational and experimental verification of whatever is being propounded. This is why it is pertinent that it should be employed in everything we do. It is a truthful and reliable method of probing and realizing a truth. And the realization of truth in its various manifestations and flavours is, in turn, the main civilizational concern. The adoption of the scientific method therefore attains civilizational meaning and concern. It was just this realization that Jawaharlal Nehru was echoing when he pronounced the creation of a society with scientific temper. He was simply answering this call.

In the same vein, the adoption of the scientific method should be an integral part of an enlightened plurality.

Another aspect that is inherent in our investigation of nature is freedom. One should be free to give vent to one's thoughts, to speak out, if only to create new knowledge, beyond the primary freedoms of what to eat, wear and worship. This is freedom in all its encompassing expanse and meaning. Apart from the social and cultural aspects of freedom, it is also an integral part of knowledge creation. Freedom is oxygen for creativity, for inventing and discovering the new and the sublime as well as for sustaining and strengthening pluralistic ethos. It is the supreme and paramount value that is non-negotiable.

Now, a question: what is it that has agitated writers, scientists and intellectuals in general to raise their voices in protest?

A Space for Dissent

Any attack on the plural fibre of society that acts by constraining freedom and undermining the scientific method should in turn invite strong and effective protest from all stakeholders. This is exactly what one has been witnessing since the 2015 Science Congress at Mumbai University. There was a session in which the scientific method was undermined in the extreme at the altar of nationalism and jingoism. What was most surprising was that all this happened when the scientific programme had been scrutinized by a high-profile organizing committee comprising the country's top scientists heading various prestigious research and development organizations. The Science Congress is the largest gathering of its kind and is always inaugurated by the prime minister, a tradition founded by Nehru to indicate the government's commitment to science. At the same, there was no visible protest, nor voices of protest, from the attending scientists, save a few individual and scattered voices outside after the event.

A question follows as to how the offending sections of the Congress were allowed to happen, having until then been forums tasked with safeguarding the scientific method and ethos as so passionately spelled out by Nehru. Wasn't it a case of fear being in the air that top scientists could not resist the pressure building from different corners? They buckled and couldn't stand up to their grain and training. Or, it is possible that they might have been in resonance with what transpired at the Congress. However, either way is bad. If they had indeed buckled, it is concerning for their ability to register their protest. If the latter, it is a sign of how far we are yet to go before the scientific method becomes a benchmark, and our scientists stand by it, whatever the consequences may be.

Then, there were the cases of people being butchered on the suspicion of possessing beef, of slogans by the chief minister of Haryana and even a central minister one should 'go to Pakistan' if one wants to consume beef. The high and mighty of the establishment remained silent while their peers kept on dividing people and intimidating them. Ultimately, the Prime Minister spoke up—but not directly, only through the voice of the President. Is this not an attack on India's plural ethos, which is the true Indian identity?

Dissent is an integral part of a pluralistic and democratic society, so much so that its absence is a signal of incompletion. There must be a healthy and respectful space for dissent. When the Maharashtra government came up with an ordinance that made dissent a treasonable offence, good sense did prevail in time. However, the question is how the state could even have entertained such a thought. Should this not be a matter of concern for us?

Voices of protest against this environment are against the fear and anxiety causing the anguish and discomfort. And in this environment, neither is the government doing enough (at least visibly) to send a clear signal nor are the people, many of whom are complicit in having created this unhealthy and disturbing situation. We scientists stand against all this and not specifically to any action and event.

It is true that scientists have traditionally and generally remained aloof from broader social concerns and happenings. It would, however, be worth recalling the glorious tradition of socially concerned scientists like Bertrand Russell, Arthur Eddington and Martin Ryle, who were conscious objectors and refused to have any part in the World Wars. They were all very distinguished scientists of great repute and influence: Russell was the twentieth century's most influential scientist-philosopher; Eddington's expedition to study the total solar eclipse of 1919 found that gravity bends light, too, making Einstein a household name overnight; and Martin Ryle was a Nobel laureate and the father of radio astronomy, a new eye on the universe (at the time).

(On the matter of respect for dissent: the British government had supported Eddington's proposal for an eclipse expedition even in 1914 while he remained a conscious objector to the government's policies. Unfortunately, the expedition had to be aborted because clouds obscured the sky on the day of the observation.)

In India, it was Meghnad Saha who was perhaps the only distinguished scientist who participated in issues of wider social concern. He was a forceful critique of big dams and the Nehruvian development model. He fought the Lok Sabha elections as an independent and won. But apart from him, scientists of his calibre have have mostly remained silent.

Scientists and a Civilizational Morality

One of the reasons for this silence is that all scientific research is almost completely supported by government-funded institutions and laboratories. Experimental science needs a considerable amount of money. Another reason, possibly, is that our leading science and technology institutes recruit students right after school, and they largely host one or two perfunctory social science courses. Students, then, mostly remain oblivious to the general liberal intellectual discourse. This is a serious drawback in our higher education system. To be fair, administrators have recently become more aware of this and have introduced more liberal arts courses as well as helped organize off-course lectures and cultural activities.

But it remains that scientists, leaving aside some people in their individual capacities, have not joined any social protests as a group—except the one against the nuclear weapon. Following the protests by writers, some of us thought that scientists should also express themselves as concerned citizens, and so we put up a petition on Change.org for colleagues to sign on. While this picked up momentum, the ethics committee of the three science academies, perhaps suffering under the guilt of silence at the Science Congress, also came out in support, as did some very distinguished scientists. This was indeed very encouraging and gratifying: to see scientists join a wider, socially conscious and intellectual community for the first time.

Scientists should respond to their call as citizens. It is time for them—us—to be citizen-scientists and public intellectuals. It is the people at large who pay for our reasonable upkeep as well as for our equipments and experiments, and it is for us to be able to give full vent to our creative callings. In return, the people expect to receive guidance and advice on involved issues of science, as well as on anything else that has a bearing on the society, so that the people can make informed decisions. Even in a limited sense, scientists should contribute to raising the public understanding of science through outreach activities. This should become a part of the country's scientific culture. And when that happens, the question as to *why* scientists have joined in wouldn't arise. It would also be most liberating for us to be part of a wider community.

Dissent is not only to be tolerated but to be appreciated and encouraged as well for a healthier and enlightened society. In India, we have a rich tradition of dissent and debate; our mode of scholarly discourse makes it mandatory to present opposing viewpoints and then to establish the view in question, countering previous arguments and presenting new and clinching arguments in favour. This makes for a healthy and enriching intellectual interaction. This is a heritage we ought to be proud of, rather than machining it into a narrow-minded definition and using it to conflate a government's interest with the national interest. How deprived are they of this enlightened heritage who thought to sue dissenting people with treason?

Plurality is not just necessary for any society to be stable; in its enlightened form, it encompasses peace and harmony. It should therefore be *sought after*. This is one way in which we have been wealthier than those in the developed West, and we should all be aware and proud of it. And this wealth should be reared and preserved with much care and compassion. Adopting the scientific method should be taken as a new social value, like speaking the truth, because it is the only way to get a truthful, reliable view of something, as well as how we will eventually receive the knowledge of truth in its entirety. Plurality and the scientific method do have a civilizational context and they, therefore, must define a new civilizational morality. Anything that could even be construed to go against or be injurious to plurality and the scientific ethos should be taken as being civilizationally immoral. Civilizational morality, I believe, should override all other moralities that have contextual scope.

In raising a voice of dissent and protest against the spread of fear and anxiety among the people, I have simply answered my civilizational call. It is also a little offering to the glorious tradition of dissent set by our great predecessor scientists as conscious objectors.

It is an enlightened plurality that promotes and brings about peace and harmony and that is what we should all be seeking and working towards. When we don't know and don't understand each other, we fear each other. A lack of knowledge and understanding of others breeds fear. And the only antidote for fear is to know and learn about others through dialogue, discourse and investigations. It is therefore not enough to stop at tolerance—though it still is a prime and necessary condition; we have to strive towards engaging interactions and so create an enriched and enlightened society.

VIKRAM SONI

Vikram Soni is emeritus professor at Jawaharlal Nehru University, Delhi. He was among the first scientists to raise his voice against the murders of Dr Narendra Dabholkar and Dr M.M. Kalburgi.

A Wounded Civilization

There is a time in the affairs of people or nations when you have to speak out. We are living in such times; when a simple village person, of the Muslim faith, going about his daily routine is beaten to death in Dadri, in western U.P., for eating beef—something that has been going on for centuries. A hunk of meat found near his house, suspected to be the remains of a cow, provoked the local Hindu community to stone him to death. Such a reaction to such a normal activity is not normal and cannot have been spontaneous. We are then led to believe that the incident must have been provoked by an extremist fringe which presumed that such an inhuman act would go unpunished in the prevailing atmosphere of the present dispensation. And so it was that the act was not treated as a deliberate social killing. The governments did not take this act seriously and did not respond with a firm hand.

And out on a morning walk in August 2013, an enlightened senior citizen, Dr Narendra Dabholkar, was shot dead in Pune for campaigning against superstition. This was followed by a similar shooting of a senior author, Govind Pansare, who was taking a walk with his wife in Kolhapur, in February 2015. And another award-winning litterateur, Dr M.M. Kalburgi—who too opposed superstition and idolatry—did not even have to stir out into public space but was shot at home. And so have simple RTI activists been murdered for trying to expose graft. These are some of the prominent cases. There are definitely many, many more anonymous cases. They all point to the society and government becoming permissive to extreme, irrational, religious bigots—a trend that has put us in a civilizational crisis. The climate has changed.

Diversity and Civilization

Indian civilization is a truly plural one which unifies faiths and distils the wisdom of many streams of thought. There have been many practices and communities that have allowed space for each other and have lived together in peace and harmony for centuries. We celebrate the festivals and anniversaries of all faiths. This unifying weave of social and cultural threads defines our civilization's strength and stability. It is this which is being threatened by a rash of sectarian and bigoted acts that have recently escalated.

Diversity has an interesting history. To begin with, the hot earth was not very different from Mars and Venus with an atmosphere of over 95 per cent carbon dioxide (CO_2). Whereas Mars and Venus continue to be the same and without life, the diversity of plant and animal life on our planet has brought the CO_2 in the atmosphere down to 0.03 per cent. The diversity of living organisms has sustained life for over 2 billion years on our planet. It has kept the living planet in a roughly steady state by making networks between the species, by creating natural cycles for each element using its biodiversity.

So is the case with societies. Each strand of society is a strand of diversity with distinctive virtues, talents and inventions. When integrated together they can form an organic whole that is open to new ideas and evolution and progress. This has been particularly so for Indian civilization which has many strands.

It is interesting that the heirs of the famous Mongol, Genghis Khan, who came from the steppes of Siberia had, in a century, spread their dominance to all of Eurasia by imbibing and integrating into their ethos and governance the achievements and inventions of the Chinese civilization, the medicines and science and architecture of the Persians and the Abbasids, Indian philosophy and mathematics and the achievements of Roman Europe. It is said that the Mongols destroyed most of these cultures. But it is also said that the later Mongols ruled the whole of Eurasia by including the virtues and talents of the various cultures and not imposing theirs. Not just that, but they also adopted the different religions of different regions to identify with the residents. Kublai Khan in China became a Buddhist, his cousins in the Middle East adopted Islam and on the Western fringe yet other cousins adopted Christianity. They established the seafaring trade routes from China to Europe and the silk route from China and India through the Middle East to Europe ensuring security on these routes. They introduced paper money and shares. In a sense it was the precursor of a global market. It is said that it was the bubonic plague that wiped out this global integration by making people fearful, accusative and insular. The world may now be on course to repeat history even without the bubonic plague, simply by greed.

Finally, without diversity there can be no integration or network and without that there can be no steady state or progress. A United Nations is a genuine formation of many smaller nations. The plurality and diversity opens up a closed society to accept new ideas and move to progress. If we close down these pathways we become insular and frigid. In India we have maintained civilizational integration and a multi-religious society—an exemplary society for the torn and fragmented world we see today. Are we going to keep this value and safeguard it or fight and fragment? All present-day examples show us how intolerance and a lack of empathy for the others can cause fracture. Look at India and Pakistan, Israel and Palestine, the Shia and Sunni divide and the divisions between blacks and whites in the United States and South Africa and so many others. It is not easy and takes centuries to be inclusive and united but recent events have shown that it can be destroyed in a few years of greed, mutual hated and mistrust.

Values and Scientists

The literature fraternity was the first to act and return their awards in protest against the current events. The scientific community however seems to remain passive. But scientists are also part of society and it is times like these that call upon them to be conscientious citizens and to voice their concern. This is what roused my ire and my sentiment to write the first draft of the Scientists' Appeal and share it with some of my more concerned colleagues, Naresh Dadhich, Tabish Qureshi and T. Govindarajan who edited it and took this forward through Change.org and public statements in my absence. We also shared our statement with historians and authors, who thought it better that scientists do their own thing. This led to a campaign for scientists in India to wake up and make a statement—'Scientists for Ethical and Societal Values'—which began on October 18, 2015. These efforts gathered over 700 signatures and were sent to the President. We also suggested that this may be followed by stronger actions akin to the award winners of Sahitya Akademi and so it has. Remarkably, our science academies, which have never shown initiative or taste for such social action, also chimed in this time. You never know when the bell tolls! It is time that scientists get out of the straitjacket and move in to nurture their fellowship with all others. It is also time to understand that stand-alone science and technology are rather reductionist and must transform to holism to address the issues of our society and the planet.

In a fractured world we have to keep the plural faith that defines us as a civilization. To quote our Scientists' Appeal, 'As true adherents of science and its method, it is also our duty to help people at large to take informed and rational decisions, and particularly so in these volatile times.' Of course, this is an ethical issue of great concern and import—a 'dharma'—as enunciated by Buddha and Gandhi, who were both quintessential scientists and social reformers. On the 100th anniversary of Einstein's General Relativity, let's also pay tribute to the great man who stood for ethical and societal values and peace by speaking out for peace and harmony.

The State

It is indeed most remiss, vexing and worrisome that our governments do not act when innocent people are victimized for eating beef and sensible people are targeted for being against superstition. Instead, they delay action till they leave behind a poisonous legacy. This is an appeal to the government to act swiftly to stop this mayhem. It is not just victimizing innocent and enlightened people, but also killing them. Our Supreme Court though has shown much more wisdom and sagacity and courage by stating clearly that it will keep our ethical value system and the plurality and equality of all citizens intact.

Civilizational Crime and Punishment

The bigotry and inhuman conduct of extremists that has been allowed to take place of late is totally unacceptable. The time has come for us to say in a united voice that this must stop, the guilty must to be brought to book, victims must be duly compensated and rehabilitated. All this should not only be effective but must also be visible. Our civilization is much older than the country and must be zealously guarded. I suggest that strictest action be taken against any such anti-human, anti-civilizational assaults and that anyone provoking such actions must be criminally indicted with punishment beyond that reserved for anti-national activity, as this is even worse.

We condemn the atrocities and join the protest of litterateurs and other groups in awakening people and the central and state governments to the dangers of not acting.

LAILA TYABJI

Laila Tyabji is a social worker, designer, writer and craft activist. She is one of the founders of Dastkar, a Delhi-based NGO that works to revive the traditional crafts of India. This essay is the text of the speech she delivered at the Rohini Ghadiok Annual Oration, 2016.

A Matter of Identity

I never knew Rohini Ghadiok, but I have been thinking about her. Who was she, and how would she have liked to be remembered? What would she have put first—being Indian, being Hindu, being part of an uprooted North-West Frontier family, being a woman, a feminist, an activist, a liberal...? How would she have wanted to define her own image? I suspect, like most of us, she would prefer to be simply herself, without these labels that both straitjacket and stereotype one. Just six years after her death, she would find rather strange this business of tolerance/intolerance and the nationalist/anti-national controversy that has engulfed us today.

India's contradictions intrigue and exasperate. For example, we invest India with a female form, we worship women as goddesses, we castigate anyone who will not shout 'Bharat Mata ki Jai'; but, at the same time, we abuse women, negate them, deny them access to our masjids and mandirs, rape them with impunity—casting them always as inferior and willing victims.

Another anomaly is that despite being such a diverse multicultural country, we are increasingly trapped by these crude, simplistic labels; we are judged by those labels, and are also expected to behave like the label.

Take myself. I have no objection to saying 'Bharat Mata ki jai', but I do object to it being made a litmus test of my patriotism. Just as I would object to wearing a hijab as a test of my being Muslim.

I am ambivalent, therefore, about this business of identity—linked as it so often is to religion or ideological belief. Religion and identity can be powerful tools for transmitting cultural values, bonding and sharing. They can be equally powerful catalysts to creating division and distrust.

One of the most maddening things is trying to explain to the majority that the scary, stereotypical Muslim—fanatic, backward, dirty, violent, with multiple wives and multiple children—is not necessarily the norm, and that most of them are, quite literally, just like you and me!

Pat comes the answer, equally maddening: 'But then YOU are really not a Muslim...' That is, I do not wear a burkha, have not borne those multiple children, do not believe in reservations or 'appeasement', and support, like my parents before me, a Uniform Civil Code.

I am liberated, educated, happily unmarried—certainly not oppressed, reactionary or ghettoized. Nor is my difference from the stereotype entirely due to the social strata from which I come, or family. In fact, working and living as I have done with craftspeople all over India for the last four decades, many of them Muslim, I do not know a single one who fits that chilling profile.

Yes, some of the Muslims I know grow beards or wear burkhas, many are uneducated except in their professional skills, quite a number pray five times a day and observe the Ramzan fasts, but I have not yet encountered anyone with latent terrorist traits; and even on those intimate evenings round the village fire, where someone from one community will naturally tell jokes or bitch about the other, I have not heard even the most orthodox mullah support the kind of vicious violence now bracketed with Muslims all over the world. Possibly, I am a lucky exception—I like to think I am the rule. Statistics tell us that ISIS supporters form only 0.16 per cent of the world's Muslim population.

So, why these myths and bogeys? Mostly, it is ignorance. We think that in this globalized world of instant electronic communication, we all know everything there is to know about each other. Far from it— the increase of so many different forms of media and information, the mushrooming of local newspapers, magazines, TV channels, websites and blogs in multiple regional languages, each catering to particular interest groups, means that people are even more trapped in their own blinkered mindsets, receiving information and images that subscribe to their own world view. There are new social media fatwas—young school children sending chain WhatsApp messages urging their friends to boycott Shah Rukh Khan's films because he is a 'Bad Man', a reward to slap Aamir Khan, five lakhs to kill Kanhaiya.[1]

In the 1980s, I was conducting a design workshop on appliqué with a group of women in a resettlement colony outside Ahmedabad in Gujarat. Three days into the workshop, a communal riot broke out in the city. Arson and looting turned into mob warfare. The trouble spread into the slum suburbs. The patchwork women were Muslim; most of their husbands and fathers worked in the city. They drove bicycle rickshaws, sold vegetables and groceries on small handcarts, or were unskilled labour in factories. Now they were trapped, unable to go out for fear of reprisals. I spent a week there, trapped along with them.

Every day people were brought—burnt, wounded, maimed—into the community centre, where we sat matching colours and cutting patterns. A child's eyes had been gouged out; the brother of one of the women had been burnt alive in his cycle rickshaw. The reality was dreadful, but the rumours and counter-rumours made it worse. The local maulvi made a rabble-rousing speech, saying one Muslim was equal to ten kafirs. Horror stories abounded, spread and fed by pamphlets, cassettes and the local Urdu radio station.

Just across the road, separated by a line of police trucks, was a Hindu slum. I had worked with some of the women there, too, so on a relatively calm afternoon I nipped across. Over cups of tea I heard identical counter-horror stories, with the Muslims as the villains this time (as an educated NGO-lady from Delhi, my own Muslim status was temporarily forgotten!). When I told Vimlaben, one of the women, that Sakina's little son had been killed, her eyes flooded with tears, all animosity was forgotten, only shared experiences of working together remembered. She insisted on coming with me to condole. Others followed. That evening the women of both communities got together and swore not to let violence enter Juhapura again. Even after the horrifying pogroms of 2002 in Gujarat, the women stayed united, travelling together to bazaars, protecting one another.

It is not a coincidence that centres of India largely unaffected by communal violence are those where the different communities are economically interlinked and interdependent—Banaras for example, where the silk weavers are Muslim and the dalal wholesalers are Hindu; or Lucknow, where Hindu traders market the chikan embroidered by Muslim karigars. Nor is it a coincidence that Ahmedabad, routinely disrupted by communal tensions, is where Muslims and Hindus share similar professions, incomes, educational levels and aspirations; competitors for the same turf, rather than essential links in an economic value chain.

Kutch is a part of India where for centuries dozens of different tribal and other communities have lived together in extraordinary amity. Shared economies and differing, but compatible, skills helped mutual bonding and trust—the Muslim Khatris dyeing and block-printing for the Vankar weavers and Rabari and Jat embroiderers, the Mochi community supplying beautifully worked footwear and saddles. Isolation from mainstream politics helped, too. In 2001, a devastating earthquake put Kutch on everyone's front pages. I was there a few days after the event. The different agencies which came into the region for 'relief' work each had its own agenda. They attempted to create conflicts between different castes and communities. Rumours of fabricated 'incidents' were rife, and both the locals and the outside agencies were playing one off against the other, for everything from tents to spiritual solace. Relief was doled out according to religious denomination or political affiliation. The BJP, under the aegis of Sahib Singh Varma, was vying for 'adopting' the village of Dhamadka, and dividing it into Muslim, Harijan and upper-caste Hindu camps; World Vision was distributing Bibles; and RSS and Jamaat-e-Islami banners were everywhere. 'All we want is the means to stand on our feet again; we will rebuild our own lives ourselves,' said one exasperated ajrakh printer from Dhamadka. Nevertheless, it created fissures that still exist. Today there are two separate block-printing villages, one mainly Hindu, the other Muslim, competing instead of working together. And craftspeople tell us politicians are playing the same games again. This is frustrating and sad.

I come from a family which CHOSE multi-cultural India over monotheistic Pakistan. Despite our home being attacked and looted, and my father almost killed (a Hindu saved him by gunning down the man who was trying to shoot him), my parents and our large extended family of Tyabjis, Latifs, Alis and Hydaris, all decided to stay in India. We were proudly Indian, celebrating its syncretic culture, festivals, monuments, music, art, literature, even its gods and goddesses (I have a particular affection for Ganesh). It was inconceivable that we would exchange the eclectic vibrancy of India for the claustrophobia of an Islamic state. It never occurred to us that for some we were 'the other'. An occasional snide and ignorant remark by a stranger on a train, a vegetarian village hostess reacting apprehensively to a meat-eating 'Mohammedan', a chronic inability to pronounce or spell one's name correctly, were just funny anecdotes to counterpoise incredible acceptance, sharing and warmth, and an amazing, common, yet plural, culture. Its richness made every other country seem insipid and dreary.

Then came the attack on the Golden Temple and the 1984 Sikh killings, followed by the demolition of Babri Masjid—the unthinkable had happened. With these licensed assaults on religious places, the India of our aspirations and certainties also splintered and broke. Instead of a dream we seemed to be living a nightmare. Breaking the Masjid seemed to free unsuspected venom in the most unexpected people. Even in my sanitized upper-middle-class Delhi life, I received a stream of anonymous hate mail telling me to go back to my 'dunghill in Pakistan', and threatening everything from rape to extermination, culminating in a box of human excreta (disarmingly packed in a Kwality Sweets dabba!). It was easy to begin imagining oneself as a victim.

But in the days following 6 December 1992, my organization Dastkar and I received countless letters from craftspeople all over the country, deploring the demolition of the Masjid as an act against all faiths, and appealing for peace and the brotherhood of man. A typical one came from two Brahmin weavers in Karnataka, written for them by the village 'English speaking' scribe. 'God is all wheres [sic],' it said, ending, 'Do not weary [sic], we are praying.'

It is these voices, less strident, but mercifully still in a majority, to which we must listen lest we fall into the fatal mindset of 'persecuted minorities'—a ghettoization of the mind and the spirit that leads inevitably to further alienation and marginalization. It would make us truly the second-class citizens some want us to be.

The craftspeople I work with suffer similar forms of disenfranchisement, seen at best as picturesque exhibits of an exotic but irrelevant India, rather than the skilled professionals they are. There is a poignant story of craftspeople taken to a Festival of India in London. It was winter, and cold. They rushed off to Oxford Street, bought bright, striped sweaters and socks, and big, shiny watches to show their 'forrun-returned' status. At the Exhibition Gallery, Indian officials told them to take off their sweaters and watches, put on their turbans and pointy-toed juthis—otherwise they would ruin the photographs by not looking like 'craftspeople'!

Back in India, the reverse goes. When I ask the lambani craftswomen why they prefer wearing horrid nylon mill-printed saris rather than their own glorious mirrored and embroidered costumes, they say it is because as 'junglee' tribals they are not allowed into temples or even cafés. The veteran Shilpi, Parameshwar Acharya, indignantly spluttered that although he was a master sculptor in the tradition of Vishwakarma, he was lumped with jharu-makers and cobblers, rather than as an artist. Craft is a profession that neither gives economic returns nor social status.

When the National Master Craftsperson and Shilp Guru awards are given, the names and photographs of the President, ministers and secretaries to government are listed in the media announcements, the names of the shilp gurus and master craftspeople being honoured are not. Not a photograph, not a mention of the craftspeople's names and skills. The National Awards, meant to be a prestigious annual recognition of India's extraordinary masters, are lumped together every three to four years; the awardees are hustled onto the stage, told not to speak to the President, and robbed of a small moment of glory in their hard, underpaid lives. I feel stricken and ashamed when I think of the pomp, splendour and media coverage of the Padma awards, especially since I got mine on the back of the skills of these very people. No wonder young craftspeople are leaving the sector in droves. 'I have received many awards, but I still work on the footpath,' said one. 'It's the grave pit, not the loom pit,' says another, his grim words borne out by recurring headlines of starvation deaths of handloom weavers.

When we began our Dastkar Ranthambhore project twenty-five years ago to create livelihood options for the relocated villages around the tiger park, we encountered Gendi Lal, a leather craftsman in Kundera village. He had lost his living because of local herders and farmers opting for new plastic chappals instead of his sturdy but more expensive leather ones.

We helped him and a group of five to six other leather workers use their amazing punching, plaiting and cutwork skills to make sandals, chappals, bags, belts and accessories for the urban market. These proved immensely popular. Soon Gendi Lal and his group were travelling all over India, supplying to retail stores as well as selling directly through the Dastkar Bazaars. Gendi Lal was soon able to send his son Puran to a fee-paying school, and we next heard that he had got admission to college. Sadly, college taught the boy to look down on the very profession that had given him his education. When he completed his graduation he could not get a job, but he did not want to continue in the leather business. In vain, we told him that his education and literacy would give him that edge to take the family skill to the next entrepreneurial level. These days, Puran loiters around Sawai Madhopore town, occasionally getting a part-time job at the village school, generally unemployed—his aspirations far exceeding his abilities. He prefers being an out-of-work graduate to being a leather craftsperson. How can we re-establish the social acceptability of craft?

Both urban movers and shakers and rural craftspeople need to break out of the caste system of City vs Village, Literate vs Non-literate, new Western Technology vs Traditional Skill sets, and cherish the unique knowledge systems that are our heritage. If we can do it for Yoga, we can certainly do it for craft.

In 1985, I went to SEWA in Lucknow to work with 100 chikan-embroidery women. They were black burkha-ed, illiterate, earning about Rs 100-150 a month, housebound, and totally dependent on the local mahajan to fetch their work and pay them. Sitting together embroidering, teaching them new skills and designs, we naturally talked about everything under the sun. They were stunned that I, a well-brought-up, believing Muslim woman, could also be liberated, happily unmarried, earning my own living, travelling the world, untrammelled by purdah or convention.

Our first argument took place when I was furious with them for signing, unread, a petition about the Shah Bano judgement, just on the say-so and biased, retrograde interpretation of the Quran by local male chauvinist maulvis. They listened to all this chat, wide-eyed, slightly disbelieving, slightly envious, slightly shocked. They certainly did not relate it to the realities of their own lives. When six of them bravely agreed to come to Delhi for an exhibition, the men of the mohalla threatened to burn down the SEWA Lucknow office, accusing us of corrupting their women's morals.

Today, those hundred SEWA women have grown to over eight thousand. They travel all over India, happily doss down and sing bhajans in a dharmashala, or cook biryani at the Bombay YWCA. They interact with equal ease with male tribals from Madhya Pradesh and sophisticated buyers from Milan. They march in protest against dowry deaths as well as Islamic fundamentalism, demand financial credit and free spectacles from the government. They value their own skills, self-confidently refusing to give either Mulayam Singh or Mayawati a discount! They earn in thousands rather than in hundreds, have their own savings bank accounts, and have thrown away centuries of repression and social prejudice along with their burkhas.

It has changed their attitudes to society, religion, marriage. Once again, sharing with, and actually knowing 'the other', has broken down all the silly phobias. But at the same time, they realize that their own cultural identity—represented in their stitches and motifs—is also their strength.

We, too, need to examine and re-evaluate some of our social myths and misconceptions, both about ourselves, and others. To see ourselves clearly and stop our 'sentiments' being 'hurt' every time someone shows us the other side of the coin.

Cultural identity, too, often seems something WE feel proud of, but which others use to box us into stereotypes. Jokes about Sardarjis, Gujjubens and Bongs are legion. We love them, but feel outraged when they are levelled at ourselves. We Muslims talk proudly about our language, culture, tehzeeb and food—others think beards, burkhas, violence and multiple marriages. (Saleem Kidwai once told me that homosexuality was also attributed to Muslims!) And yet the extraordinary mix of different races, religions, geographies and cultures India encompasses is our greatest asset—an inheritance that we can shape into an incredible strength, or treat as a terrible liability.

I have always thought the ideal for India is a salad, with each ingredient distinct and differently delicious, blended together with a truly secular dressing. But all too often, we seem set on making it into a soup, all elements pulped into a homogeneous, boring, bland mush with a single dominating majority flavour. What a loss this would be!

I love India and intend to live and die here, but I also want to be able to freely question its imperfections. Just as I have the freedom to say that Islam has been hijacked by a gang of demonic and utterly vile hoodlums, and that the rest of us Muslims seem helpless to combat this evil. One's religion or political leanings should have absolutely nothing to do with freedom of speech. Nor should 'tolerance' play a part in this equation. Dialogue, dissent and debate are what fuel a working democracy. So do the different voices and identities in our society.

'Intolerance' is a dreadful word, even more horrifying in practice. But 'tolerance' is only marginally better. I don't want to be 'tolerated' in condescending, rather grudging acceptance—as if I (and other minorities) were something not very nice that will not go away! I want my being here to be taken for granted. I feel an integral part of this nation, and I want everyone else to think so too. 'Tolerance' implies you can just about exist as long as you do not step out of line. This is an attitude typified by the Haryana chief minister's comment that Muslims can stay in India as long as they do not eat beef,[2] or our minister of culture remarking that former President Abdul Kalam was a good man 'in spite of being a Muslim'![3] I think we need to do better for our minorities, be they Muslims, Christians, Dalits, transsexuals, tribals, women in miniskirts, people with same-sex partners, artists flying fanciful styrofoam cows in the sky... None of us want to be 'tolerated'. We want to be ourselves. It is not a favour—it is our constitutional right.

Sixty-eight years after Independence, it still seems difficult for many to understand that, Christian or tribal, Aamir Khan or Aam Admi, most of us are just thoroughly ordinary Indians, seeking happiness, sanity and security like everyone else. And wanting our own voice. Why cannot we all simply 'adjust' to each other and the cultural baggage we each carry—just as we do in our over-crowded trains and buses, amicably negotiating awkward tin trunks, crying babies and strangely wrapped parcels, miraculously bonding over our tiffins.

It is tedious that one's own patriotism needs constant justification, including a certificate that one does not eat beef or critique the nation. I am utterly amazed that Aamir Khan's confession of momentary vulnerability should be termed a 'moral offence'.[4] The poor man has just adopted two drought-affected villages in Maharashtra. But he remains the third most-hated man in Google's survey of Indian social media. If women say we feel unsafe on the roads of Delhi, will we suddenly be seen as 'anti-national'?

The savage killing in Dadri[5] evoked widespread and vocal outrage, but as incident has followed incident, the assault on freedom of speech in JNU and Osmania, and the subsequent war of words between self-named 'nationalists' and outraged 'liberals' have obscured the other equally horrific murders, rapes and assaults on Dalits and tribals, the ongoing civil liberty infringements and killings in Kashmir, Bastar and the North East, and the current callous indifference to terrible drought. I am still haunted by the murder of that ninety-year-old Dalit, hacked and burnt to death, his only crime being that he wandered into a temple.[6] It is difficult to have the bandwidth to react strongly each time. But every time we fail to rise up in outrage it becomes easier for saffron apologists to rationalize these as 'unfortunate accidents' stemming from 'hurt sentiments' or 'presstitute' misreporting.

There is so much discrimination in Indian society, with age-old prejudices of caste, religion and gender coexisting with newly coined ones born of education, wealth, power and privilege, even the colour of skin—all being expressed in openly aggressive new ways. Some attract more public attention than others. Our own subjective prejudices intervene. People feel strongly about Kashmir, but less so for Kashmiris. We need to speak out for all those under threat—be they tribals, women, minorities, Dalits, inter-caste lovers, the LGBT community, rationalist thinkers, activists, even our degraded environment. It is a heartbreakingly long list. But we cannot let outrage fatigue overtake us.

Equally urgent, we need to find new ways of expressing our dissent and distress at this rapidly fragmenting India. Sharing our pain with like-minded social media 'friends' is cathartic but ineffective. Violence and entitlement may end with a hatchet or bomb, but it all begins in the head. As our educational and cultural institutions increasingly lose independence and direction, and the media concentrate on sound and fury rather than content, we need the energy of sustained public pressure to kick-start the process of healing, thus renewing a sense of the joys and benefits of free speech and plurality, and a real understanding of India's past.

At a dinner party, a young America-returned IT executive vociferously rejoiced that 'that bloody invader' Aurangzeb had been displaced by Abdul Kalam on a major Delhi road. I said that I held no particular brief for Aurangzeb, whose repressive Puritan policies had damaged his co-religionists as much as everyone else, but to call him an invader was mistaken. He was (like me) a fifth-generation Indian, with more Rajput blood in his veins than Central Asian. The young man's jaw fell agape. He confessed that he had never realized this. He had ignored, too, that unlike the British, the wealth Aurangzeb and the other Mughals created remained in India, their chosen country of adoption. Aurangzeb imposed punitive taxes, but also actively promoted Indian industries, publicly pronouncing that his treasury belonged to the nation rather than himself. He was not a very nice man, who definitely went a bit off-balance at the end, but during his reign India became the world's richest country and its products were sought after everywhere.

Like many young Indians, my dinner companion was a victim of a one-dimensional version of Indian history. So much of the prejudiced polarization taking place today is because of incorrect and inadequate knowledge. The standard textbooks ignore the multiple strands that make up our extraordinary country—the knowledge systems, folklore and legends of tribals, the multiple interpretations of music, art, architecture, poetry, food, costume and dance that enrich us. There is no single stream of Indian cultural or social practice. When I asked the young man whether he really wanted an India sanitized of all alien un-Hindu influences—without cricket, qawwali, the Taj and the Bahai Temple, biryani, shabad gurbani, samosas, the choral Northeast music that hugely impressed President Obama, salwar kameez, Shah Rukh Khan, McDonalds, momos, blue jeans and the gentle messages of the Buddha—he looked a bit sheepish! We need to beware of catchy emotive generalizations, of stereotyping national identity.

Nehru is not much quoted today—for me he remains an ideal. Let us remember what he said: 'Culture is the ability to see the other's point of view.' We need to remember that 'the other' is just one more quite ordinary, sometimes tiresome, but potentially valuable person—part not just of the past, but also the fabric and future of this nation. The differences between 'us' and 'them'—of language, food, clothing, social practices—are what gives that fabric its colour, pattern and shape, and makes India so special—our truly incredible India.

When Dastkar started its project in Ranthambhore, I lived and worked out of a small one-room hut in Sherpur village. The women crowded around, fascinated by this Delhi 'behen ji', while I taught them craft skills as earning for themselves and their families. Initially, women of different castes and religions wanted separate timings to come to the room. The first time a Dalit woman came for work she crouched outside the door. It was she herself, not the upper-caste women, who explained—with shocked disbelief at my naiveté—that she could not enter. I had to literally pull her in. When a Muslim child urinated on the floor, the Hindu women fled in horror and wanted the whole place lippai-ed! Today, the 500-plus men and women in the project work, travel, cook, eat and drink together, marvelling at the folly that kept them separate for so long. At the annual picnic the men make the women sit, and serve them—Hindus and Muslims, Dalits and upper castes alike. Once again, sharing with and knowing each other has broken down previous taboos and fears.

I love India's multi-layered multiplicity, its synergies and paradoxes, its many diverging and converging cultural streams, its colour and chaos, the hit-and-miss jugaad (innovate fix) of past and present, malls and mandirs, East and West, its unexpected but inherent resilience. In any case, good or bad, it is our country. We need to remember it also belongs to so many others.

To quote from a poem by Khwajeh Hafiz Shirazi:

I once asked a bird, 'How is it that you fly in this gravity of darkness?'
She responded, 'Love lifts me.'

Notes

1. Kanhaiya Kumar, former President of the Jawaharlal Nehru University Students' Union, and leader of the All India Students' Federation.
2. In an interview with *The Indian Express* published on 17 October 2015.
3. In an interview with India Today TV on 18 September 2015.
4. Speaking at the Ramnath Goenka Excellence in Journalism Awards, 2015, Aamir Khan had expressed disquiet at the growing climate of intolerance in India, and said that for the first time he had felt unsafe living in the country. For this, he was widely vilified for being 'anti-national'.
5. On 28 September 2015, a mob assaulted and lynched Mohammed Akhlaq—and severely injured his son Danish—in his home in Dadri, Uttar Pradesh, on suspicion of storing and consuming beef.
6. In October 2015, Khimma Ahirwar, a ninety-year-old Dalit man in the Hamirpur district of Uttar Pradesh was hacked to death and then burnt. While the police initially said that Ahirwar had been killed for trying to enter a temple, it later changed its story and said that Ahirwar had been killed because he had refused to hand money over to his drunken assailant.

ZAKIA SOMAN AND NOORJEHAN SAFIA NIAZ

Zakia Soman and Noorjehan Safia Niaz are founding members of the Bharatiya Muslim Mahila Andolan, a self-help group for women. They appealed for a ban on triple talaq in India in November 2015.

Why We Are Seeking a Ban on Triple Talaq

Indian Muslims are the largest minority, comprising 17.2 crore of India's population, according to the 2011 Census. Large sections of Muslims live in poverty, socioeconomic and educational backwardness. Muslim women are a minority within this minority and their condition and well-being has never got the attention it deserves.

The leadership has always been orthodox, male-driven and not democratic. These so-called leaders, whose only identity is religious, have appointed themselves custodians of Indian Muslims. And it has only suited the political class to form a nexus with them for electoral purposes.

The persistent poverty and marginalization of Muslims speaks for the kind of leadership it has been. The question of justice and equality for Muslim women has been persistently evaded by these elements. As a result, triple talaq still takes place sixty-nine years after India's independence and, indeed, 1,400 years after the Quran gave equal rights to women.

There is a clear-cut case for the legal abolition of triple talaq; the biggest reason being that it is absolutely un-Quranic. In fact, there is no mention of triple talaq in the Quran. The Quran gives equal right to the wife and husband to obtain a divorce. A number of verses clearly lay down the procedure of divorce and none of these has any reference to the oral unilateral instant divorce or triple talaq as is common in our country.

In cases of marital discord, there are clear-cut verses calling for a dialogue between the couple lasting over a period of four months. There is an emphasis on attempts at reconciliation, failing which there should be mediation by relatives from both sides. This process must continue for the specified time period and the onus of conducting this process is on the husband. If there is no hope at the end of this process, only then can the talaq happen.

It is shocking that the incidence of triple talaq is unique to India. It is not legal in any of the Muslim countries anywhere in the world. It is not valid even in Egypt, Turkey, Syria, Pakistan and Bangladesh—where the majority of Muslims follow the Hanafi school of jurisprudence as in India. Even in India, the Shia sect does not recognize triple talaq as valid.

The Quran is the holiest source of guidance for Muslims. There is also great reliance on the *Sunnah* or the traditions of the Prophet. There is a well-known incident where the Prophet was displeased and clearly stated so when a man divorced his wife, unilaterally, in an instant.

Marriage is a serious affair in Islamic jurisprudence. Marriage is a social contract as per Islamic law. It is a contract between two parties to marry and live together as husband and wife based on certain agreements. It is rather admirable that 1,400 years ago, the idea of a social contract between two individuals of male and female gender with all provisions of a modern contract was in place.

The consent of the wife, the pre-agreed mehr or dower amount, the promise of a maintenance allowance, the promise of support in the form of a house and necessities—all these form part of the nikahnama or marriage contract between the bride and the groom. Not only this, there must be witnesses from both sides who must testify to the nikahnama. Certainly, the question of unilateral action such as the utterance of talaq, talaq, talaq as seen in our country is out of place.

Triple talaq takes place owing to the patriarchal mindset of the religious orthodoxy who not only allow it to continue but spread misinformation that it is valid in religion.

Our various studies indicate that the religious orthodoxy has successfully manufactured a case that legitimises triple talaq if you are a Muslim. We have documented evidence about qazis (clerics) all over the country putting their stamp of approval on oral unilateral talaq. The patriarchal orthodoxy has resisted any talk of abolition of this un-Quranic practice.

As a matter of fact, reform in the Muslim personal law is the need of the hour. The two colonial-era laws are highly inadequate to address issues such as the age of marriage, triple talaq, custody of children, halala, polygamy, inheritance, etc. The gender-just Quranic injunctions on all these matters cannot be translated into reality until a codified Muslim personal law is enacted in India. Pending that enactment, legal abolition of triple talaq is the immediate solution. Several ordinary Muslim women are suffering owing to this practice. They are rendered homeless and destitute overnight without any support for themselves and their children.

The Constitution promises gender justice as does the Quran. This injustice to Muslim women must stop; triple talaq should be abolished. The times are changing and so are people. The Muslim woman today is aware and vocal about her rights. She understands that injustice has continued for far too long. She is herself capable of reading and interpreting religious tenets. She knows that an inhuman practice like triple talaq cannot be sanctioned by religion. All over the country, young Muslim women are standing up to demand an end to this practice. Quite a few have gone to the Supreme Court for justice.

Globally, too, there is a movement for gender justice in Islam. Several scholars are interpreting the text in a humane and gender-just framework. Indian women draw tremendous inspiration and support from these scholars. The bogus argument about 'interference in our religion' whenever any mention of gender justice comes up must stop.

The simple truth is that those who are raising this bogey are instrumental in the worst interference in the Quranic rights of Muslim women. But this cannot continue any more. The Indian Muslim woman must get justice.

SONI SORI

Soni Sori is a human rights activist and an Adivasi school teacher from Chhattisgarh. She was arrested by the Delhi Police's Crime Branch for Chhattisgarh Police in 2011 on charges of acting as a conduit for Maoists. During her imprisonment, she was tortured and sexually assaulted by the police. After being acquitted in April 2013 due to lack of evidence, she began campaigning for the rights of those caught in the conflict between Maoist insurgents and the government, in particular criticizing police violence against tribespeople in the region. 'The State is Lawless' is an extract from a speech she delivered in Mumbai in 2016 at an event commemorating retired Justice Suresh Hosbet's contribution to the human rights struggle in India.

The State Is Lawless

...In Bastar, law has its own way of functioning. When a woman is raped anywhere in the country, the Supreme Court intervenes, asks for immediate action, an immediate FIR and investigation. But this is not the case in Bastar. There is no law, no system, and no sensitivity in handling women in this region. Let the Supreme Court say anything, let the High Court give any directions, the police here will do as they like. They do not care for law or for its people. If you take cases of sexual assault by the police in Bastar, you will find even after an FIR, the police do nothing. On the contrary, the victims live under constant terror here. And the police continue to unleash its terror on people here. If the state machinery continues to work like this and the government neglects lives here (Bastar), people will continue to die here. It appears that the system is built to harass people here and the police continue to operate with complete impunity.

Take the recent case of killing of two young school-going boys. One of them was sleeping in the house. When the armed force entered his house, he kept saying I am a school-going child. Look at my Aadhar card, look at my school I-card. I am not a Naxal. Even as he continued to beg, the policemen dragged him out of the house, thrashed him badly and took him far away from the house and gunned him down. Even in case of such a brutal, cold-blooded murder, there is no FIR against the police, no investigations. What law is this which allows the state to kill without any accountability, with such impunity? If there is a justice system in place, if there are courts to deliver justice, then they should have to function too. Then why doesn't it work in Bastar? His family is running from pillar to post seeking justice.

Another villager called Karma was killed by the police and declared to be a Naxalite. His family produced his citizenry documents to establish he was a law-abiding citizen and had no link with the arms movement. If a person has lived all his life in the village, and has been publicly present, how can police then declare him a Naxalite and that too after his death? We ask when did he go underground, when did he pick up arms, when did he become a Naxalite, when did the government declare reward on his name? Even when they brutally murder our people, we still hold on to bleak hopes that someday we will get justice. Instead, the same police officers unabashedly come and threaten us. They threaten women of dire consequences. They threaten to kill young boys of the family. What type of state is this which hates its own people?

It has become so easy for Chhattisgarh government to declare anyone and everyone a Naxal. Those assigned with the task of upholding democratic principles in this country are busy killing it. Murderers are secure in this democracy, but the victims are not.

Women particularly are easy targets here. Young mothers in Bastar mostly step out to nearby areas to work as agricultural labourers. They time their work in such a way that they are able to take periodic breaks to breastfeed their infants who are left back home. As these women take these breaks and head home, they invariably are apprehended by the police. The police interrogate them as if they were Naxals.

Even when these young mothers tell the police they are headed home to breastfeed their children, the police do not relent. To prove their innocence, the women are forced to bare their chests on gun point and squeeze out milk. Even after all the abuses, she is made to wait, she cannot go and feed her hungry child. Can her frail body regenerate the milk once again in such a short time span? These daily abuses leave her humiliated and her child hungry. These abuses are not even accounted for. As if Adivasi lives are so dispensable that anyone can come and do whatever they like. There is no accountability of any kind.

We are not asking for some special protection for our people. We are only saying if there is an established legal system in this country, then the state should function within the limits. If the government wants our land and our wealth, doesn't it have the responsibility of protecting our interests too? Should development be an inevitable agenda, then the government should first have a system in place ensuring that every Adivasi life is protected and their interests secured. If government wants to procure our land, there is a law in place. Whether good or bad, the law exists and the government should at least try to stick to its own laws. How can this government kill Adivasis and speak of development? How can this be even termed as development? You cannot vacate villages, displace every one and claim that you worked towards development. If the government is really serious about development, it must focus on making lives of villagers better. There is no electricity, potable water, schools in most villages. Shouldn't the state focus on providing these things to the villagers instead of killing them?

The state is killing Adivasis in the name of development. Madkam Hidme of Gompad village is one of the recent victims of the state brutality. She was picked up from her house while she was sleeping, brutalized, gang-raped by policemen and then shot dead. We still decided to opt for a legal battle. On August 15, I along with her mother and sister went to her village and addressed the villagers and urged them to understand the values of democracy, their legal rights and the need to assert our constitutional rights. As planned, we looked for a place to hoist a flag in the village. We looked around the entire village but could not find a single school or aanganwaadi there. We finally went to one open space and hoisted the flag there. This is state's development! They can send policemen to Adivasi houses, brand them as Naxals and brutalize them, but cannot set up a single school in the village.

When Adivasis speak of development, there is no one to hear their voice. If they approach a collector for setting up of a school, they are sent away. The collector doesn't even give Tribals an opportunity to make an appeal. They want forest-dwellers to remain in the forest forever. They are not interested in our development. But when they want our lands and forests, they unleash terror on us and kill us.

After the gang-rape incident of Delhi, entire nation joined hands seeking justice for her. I am not saying that the incident was not brutal and we should not have come together for her, but such incidents happen every day in Bastar. Adivasi girls are assaulted every day in Bastar. But there is no one to fight with us. They rape us and then brand us as Naxals. But no one comes ahead in support of us and speaks against the state atrocities. What happened in JNU with Kanhaiya and Umar Khalid was terrible. But when it happened to those two young boys of Bastar, there was no uproar. The boys were simply killed and not one protest was organized anywhere outside Chhattisgarh. They were school-going kids. Imagine if this were to happen to some students in your college, how the entire nation would have joined hands against the atate and demanded immediate justice. Why doesn't the youth of this country assert itself when children are killed in Bastar? Will the government not kneel, if a concerted effort is made? Our children don't deserve justice?

Just when I was leaving for Bombay, five Adivasi youth (from the same village where two school kids were killed) came to me seeking help. They are afraid the police will kill them. We have moved a petition before the High Court. I asked them why are they so afraid. They said, the thanedaar has threatened them that on the first opportunity, he will get rid of them. Of them, three men have already been to jail. Other two have even surrendered under police pressure. Still they are not spared. The police now want to have them killed. Engulfed in fear, those men spend every night in the forest. Since police mostly strike at night, these men stay away during the night time. They go deep in the forest, wait for rains to subside, find some dry space and sleep. Such is the terror of police here. One can't sleep in their house, can't visit the market, and can't lead a normal fearless life.

Worst affected are young girls of twelve-thirteen years of age. They are forced to tie a mangalsutra around their necks. Hoping to be let off by the police, almost all girls are forced to move around with those black beads around their necks. Even then girls are not spared. The police continue to attack them. They are publicly humiliated, spoken to inappropriately in highly sexual tone, and many are even sexually assaulted.

This state claims to be protecting its Adivasi population. Is this the way to protect its people? In the name of Naxalism, they are openly brutalizing us and will eventually wipe out our existence.

There is a dire need to have more and more participation of civil society from rest of the country. While people are actively working in other parts, it is essential that they pay more attention to what is happening in Bastar. Media has an important role to play here. You have seen how attempts were made to completely crush the media here. But that should not discourage us. If some journalist travels from Delhi or Bombay or Kolkata, our stories will definitely travel outside.

An entire drama has been staged in the name of surrender. Young boys and girls are randomly picked up from villages and are shown as surrendered Naxals. These youths are given only two ultimatums, either to die or sign those papers. What do these terrorized youths know? They think signing those papers is a wise decision to make. Only to realize later that those papers declare them as surrendered Naxals.

As news spreads, the Maoists punish them. If the police let them go, the Maoists kill them. Adivasis are stuck between the police and Maoists. Either ways they get killed.

Another case of a boy named Arjun recently came to light. He was sent to jail in 2015. He was released on bail after spending few days in jail. On every court hearing, he would diligently be present before the court. Not once did he miss the court hearing. Suddenly one day, the police went to his house and arrested him. They declared that a Naxal who carried three lakh rupees reward on his head has been arrested.

This boy Arjun, who was arrested in another petty case and was released on bail, was not even in hiding. If the police wanted, they could have arrested him much earlier. He was lawfully released on bail by the court. There was no mention of the reward amount until he was re-arrested. His sister, who tried to speak up against the police, is now taken into custody. It has been over fifteen days since her illegal arrest.

This is the condition of Bastar, of Chhattisgarh. No voice of dissent can be raised; no Adivasi can raise her voice for justice. This state is lawless. No law, no rule applies here. The law that applies and governs the middle class, the ruling class and the upper caste in the rest of the country, does not protect the Adivasis of Chhattisgarh.

I have personally suffered a lot in past few years. It is not possible to fight the might of this state. But I will continue. This is no more my individual fight. It is the fight of every Adivasi here. We are threatened every day, our voices crushed; but we will continue to fight.

Translated by Sukanya Shantha

VARUN GROVER

Varun Grover is a comedian, screenwriter and lyricist. 'Ours But to Tweet and Die' is a satirical response to the media frenzy that followed the attack on a military establishment in Uri, Jammu and Kashmir, on 18 September 2016, in which nineteen soldiers lost their lives.

Ours But to Tweet and Die

I have a big window in my house, and, in the last two weeks, I've stared out of it a lot. I am waiting to see a mushroom cloud, some deadly rays, a bright streak of toxic fire and a chance to serve my country. I had happily, willingly, in full hosh-o-hawaas voted in a Twitter poll run by a very senior, intelligent, warm-faced Indian IAS officer that I am more than happy to die in a nuclear counter-attack by Pakistan. The poll was depressingly tilting towards the option that said Indians are not willing to die in return for a complete nuclear annihilation of Pakistan. But, thankfully, post-midnight, once the youth of this overwhelmingly young country got done with watching their nightly quota of adult videos on Redtube, and came back to Twitter, the 'happy-to-die' option started getting traction. India had spoken.

But it's a tough fortnight for lovers of the nation like me. I have dutifully forwarded every angry WhatsApp message back to every relative from whom I got it in the first place. I even called an uncle, my first phone call to him in the last eight years, to say aloud the lovely chant—'Doodh maangoge toh kheer denge, Kashmir maango ge toh cheer denge'—as soon as he picked up the phone. He told me about his honeymoon in Kashmir in 1974, and, I told him, had Patel been alive today, even my honeymoon would have been in Kashmir. He told me Nehru was an alcoholic, a womanizer werewolf and I told him how Lord Macaulay planned to enslave all Indians by teaching us English. He asked, 'Who is Macaulay? Is he Chinese, because, this Diwali, if we don't use Chinese maal, Pakistan will suffer 'cos our phuljhadi-anaars are funding the Taliban.' I told him to forget the Taliban and bathe his grandchild in gau-mootra because a nuclear attack is round the corner and nuclear rays can't penetrate gau-mootra and they will protect the two-year-old who hasn't signed up on Twitter yet. Then we hung up after promising to stay in touch on WhatsApp by sending multiple good-morning Ganeshas till the holocaust comes.

But where's the promised holocaust?

~

I have always had a complicated relationship with Pakistan. I used to wish we also had fast bowlers with a mastery of reverse swing and shiny hair flowing supremely like the tricolour in a Central university on a windy day. In my naïve childhood, I once even made a World Cup fantasy team called India-Pakistan XI comprising Sachin and Inzy and Kumble and Waqar—a team that would have beaten Australia with its Steve Waugh and Ponting easily, any day. And not just cricket, I have played that alternative history game many times in my head—what if the Partition had never happened? Manto would have stayed here, in Bombay, protesting Prohibition by drinking himself to death. We would have had Nusrat Fateh Ali Khan and Mehdi Hassan and Noor Jehan and Ataullah Khan and would never have been forced to steal tunes from them. Heck, we'd have had a real good, original Coke Studio. But then, on the not-so-bright side, we'd have had no '65 or '71, and, hence, no military victories or World Cup victories or even those oddly satisfying fights in YouTube comments where I once shut up a Pakistani by calling him a Porkistani.

But here we are, sixty-nine years after Partition, failed by our respective cowardly political systems, hoping for news anchors on both sides to tear up their baniyaans, thump their chests, let out a howl, and announce a farmaayishi war ka kaaryakram.

Arnab, if you are reading this: I love you. You are not a person anymore, but an ideology. Tum kitne Arnab maarogey, har channel se Arnab niklega. A reliable source via a WhatsApp forward told me that COAS, DGMO, PMO and others keenly watch your show every night, walkie-talkies in their hands, waiting for your green signal to start the war. I know you will use this power with great responsibility. I know you will do it soon. I can see it in your eyes that you are ready. I am ready too.

I am so ready that I caught two pigeons fluttering about my balcony this morning and took them to a pathology lab for X-ray. The resident doctor refused my request at first, but then I asked him if he is an anti-national to doubt my doubts on the pigeons. We tortured them asking, 'Bol kisne bheja hai tujhe?' but they seemed well trained to keep their mouth shut. We then put them under an MRI scanner but they flew away before the results could be captured. But I will keep trying.

It's tough, sustaining so much hate over such a long period of time. As Pakistani poet Jaun Eliya wrote, 'Ye mujhe chain kyon nahin padta, ek hi shakhs tha jahaan mein kya? (Why don't I feel good ever? As if there was only one person to think of in the entire world)' But then, true hatred requires relentless determination. If surgical strikes didn't scare them, sending Fawad Khan back would definitely have. Who wants a grown-up son to sit nithalla (idle) at home in these times of global recession? And if that also didn't make a dent, our news channels parading that arrested badmaash pigeon in Pathankot would definitely have sent shivers down the spine of many shareefs in Pakistan.

Hope the planets have aligned well for the final countdown. Hope both countries launch the nukes during school-hour, so that the kids get to see science in action. Dedicated teachers can explain things while it happens. Distributing pamphlets to students describing uncontrolled nuclear fission beforehand would be a good idea. I look out of the window again. No mushroom clouds yet. The wait to die is killing me.

MADHAVI MENON

Madhavi Menon is professor of English at Ashoka University.

On Homosexuality and National Anthem, the Supreme Court Has Offered Contradictory Reasoning

On December 11, 2013, Justices G.S. Singhvi and S.J. Mukhopadhyay of the Supreme Court overturned a 2009 Delhi High Court verdict on Section 377 of the Indian Penal Code. The section criminalizes any form of so-called 'unnatural' sex. The High Court judgment had made it impossible for Section 377 to be used to target consensual homosexual acts. But the Supreme Court verdict allowed homosexuals in India to be targeted once again by police and law-enforcement agencies for having consensual sex.

The apex court based its judgment on several factors, prime among which were the following two. First, it said there was no need for Section 377 to be overturned since it targeted only a minority population. The bench held that there was, at most, a 'minuscule fraction' of homosexuals in India. And such a minority did not merit the attention of the court.

Second, the Supreme Court judgment said that *were* such a law to be overturned, then that act would have to be performed by the country's legislature, not the judiciary. Parliament would have to take up the matter of rewriting the law. At the time, several legal eminences were of the opinion that this judgment constituted a classic case of passing the buck. Because the Supreme Court did not want to alleviate the plight of a minority that it might also have considered to be morally reprehensible ('We do not know any homosexuals,' the judges said while hearing the arguments), it decided to pass on the responsibility to a Parliament that was soon to be populated by a Hindutva-leaning majority.

It is worth remembering that in 2009, the United Progressive Alliance-led Union government had neither challenged the Delhi High Court ruling that read down Section 377, nor had it filed an appeal along with the others that were heard by the Supreme Court in 2012. At that time, the Union government seemed keen, it would be fair to surmise, that the apex court uphold the Delhi High Court's judgment on Section 377, and declare it illegal to target people for private consensual sex acts.

In 2013, the Supreme Court ceded the right to change laws to Parliament. But such a ceding seems to happen only in relation to certain laws. With others, there is a greater urgency to spread change.

Exceeding Judicial Mandate?

For instance, on February 14, Attorney General Mukul Rohatgi asked a Supreme Court bench led by Justice Dipak Misra to make even more expansive the impact of an order that Justice Misra and Justice Amitava Roy had passed in November that directed all movie theatres in India to play the national anthem prior to the screening of any film. Equally, the order ruled that all people at the movie theatre will need to stand when the anthem is played. There were also a variety of directives attached to this order, stating the exact provisions to be made by theatre owners during the screening of the national anthem.

Justice Misra observed on February 14 that he did not want his order to be the cause of even more moral policing. This comment was in response to several reported cases of vigilante violence in cinema halls against people who did not stand up when the anthem was played. Nonetheless, the government-appointed attorney general pressed for more action. Rohatgi said that the 1986 Supreme Court order allowing three children belonging to Jehovah's Witnesses—a Christian-based religious movement—not to sing the national anthem should be revisited. He also wanted the court to make it mandatory for the national anthem to be sung in schools since 'it is extremely important to instil a sense of nationalism from childhood'.

In pressing for these orders, Rohatgi expects the Supreme Court to rewrite the law of the land, and renege on the Constitution's commitment to both minorities and freedom of expression. As several people have pointed out, the Constitution of India does not mandate that anyone stand for, or sing, the national anthem.

The Prevention of Insults to National Honour Act, 1971, which was amended in 2003 and 2005, states only and clearly in Section 3, under the title, Prevention of Singing of National Anthem, that:

> Whoever intentionally prevents the singing of the Indian National Anthem or causes disturbances to any assembly engaged in such singing shall be punished with imprisonment for a term, which may extend to three years, or fine, or with both.

The Constitution of India says that no one should be prevented from singing the national anthem should they choose to. There is nothing at all in that document to mandate that people should stand.

Thus, we need to be clear about this: the Supreme Court's order of 2016 rewrote what the Constitution has to say on the matter of respecting the national anthem.

Article 51A of the Constitution of India (1949) says:

> It shall be the duty of every citizen of India to abide by the Constitution and respect its ideals and institutions, the national Flag and the National Anthem.

Part E on the same list of fundamental duties enjoins us:

> to promote harmony and the spirit of common brotherhood [sic] amongst all the people of India transcending religious, linguistic and regional or sectional diversities; to renounce practices derogatory to the dignity of women

And Section F asks us 'to value and preserve the rich heritage of our composite culture.

The order that the national anthem be played in all movie theatres and that all people stand for it is an exercise in sentimentalized fetishism. It makes people focus their energies around what is seen as a 'good' that acquires the value of the good-above-all-others. So even as open defecation continues in India, even as women continue to be raped, even as communal fears are at an all-time high, not standing for the national anthem becomes *the* crime that the government is keen on prosecuting.

Age of Hetero-Nationalism

This valorization of the one thing that counts as patriotic allows us to ignore all the other violations of our rights and duties that are perpetrated on a daily basis. It allows us to forget that we have a rich heritage and composite culture that does not mandate a uniform code of behaviour for all. It also encourages us to forget that there are many ways in which one can be patriotic. Most of them do not involve standing for the national anthem in a movie theatre.

What is also noteworthy is the relation between the 2016 judgment on the national anthem and the 2013 verdict on Section 377. In 2013, the Supreme Court said that it cannot rewrite the law, only Parliament can. In 2016, the apex court has not only rewritten the Prevention of Insults to National Honour Act of 1971 but has also, in effect, tried to amend the Constitution, all on its own.

In 2013, the Supreme Court judgment stepped away from its duty of protecting minorities. In 2016, the Supreme Court directive has moved towards the government's goal of promoting majoritarianism. In 2013, homosexuals were once again opened up to vigilante policing and blackmail. In 2016, the reach of moral policing and vigilantism has been extended even further. Over the last three years, India seems to have entered into a phase that might best be termed, for its valorization of moral codes of sexuality and patriotism, hetero-nationalism.

PINJRA TOD

Pinjra Tod is a collective effort by women students and alumni across colleges and hostels in Delhi that seeks to discuss, debate, share, mobilize and collectivize struggles against restrictive and regressive hostel regulations and moral policing by hostel authorities. It also campaigns for access to safe and affordable hostel accommodation and pro-active functioning of Sexual Harassment Complaints Committee Cells.

Our 'Hormonal Outbursts' Will Be Your Nightmare!

On the eve of International Working Women's Day, Maneka Gandhi has given a deeply patriarchal, casteist and classist statement to a media channel saying that hostel curfews are necessary as 'laxman rekha' for controlling women's 'hormonal outbursts', that the question of women's safety in colleges cannot be solved with just two Bihari guards with dandas, that there should be separate days for men and women to go to the library at night.

It's clear to us that she has said this today in response to the fact that women students across the country from Benaras to Mumbai, Delhi to Patiala, Lucknow to Hyderabad, Chennai to Ludhiana, Roorkie to Cuttack have come out strongly to assert their presence in the university space and claim over public resources.

Maneka's allusion to hostel curfews as 'laxman rekhas' exposes wonderfully what we have been saying right from the beginning, that these rules are not mere archaic rules, that underlying them is an elaborate system of Brahminical control over women's lives and decisions. It only further proves the fact that what we are fighting against is a massive structure, from the family whose opinion is sought by the administration to legitimize these rules to the structures of state power that seek to build their manuwadi edifices through regulation of women's bodies and sexualities.

Our 'hormonal outbursts' disrupts their constructions of 'bharat mata'.

Our 'hormonal outbursts' rips apart their attempts to control our desires and dreams!

Our 'hormonal outbursts' will not be fooled by your jumlas of 'safety'!

Our 'hormonal outbursts' refuses to be reduced to anatomy and biology!

Our 'hormonal outbursts' will be your nightmare!

GAUHAR RAZA

Gauhar Raza is a poet, activist and documentary filmmaker. A scientist by training and profession, he works at the National Institute of Science, Technology and Development Studies. 'Naya Libaas', which has been translated as 'New Robes' for this volume by the author, ran into controversy in March 2016 when a popular news channel branded the poet 'anti-national' for having recited this poem at the Shankar-Shad Mushaira in Delhi.

New Robes

What makes you think that the new robes
Will make the blood stains go away?

Homes that you have burned for years,
Their ashes now smother your faces
The painful sighs of children, coming in the dark,
Would make your feet tap, make them dance

The tears, sobs and sadness from homes
Would provide succour to your heart until now

Religion was an alcohol; it was distributed, it also intoxicated
And, in that stupor, you destroyed much

You abhor every flower, each colour, too
Who knows how many inheritances you have destroyed?
Every garden you have sowed with the seeds of hatred
Now that the seeds have flowered, you have come to reap the
    harvest
Walking upon the crutches of lies and deception
But now that you have found your feet, one wonders

After burning every city you claim
This is love for the nation,
this is service for her grandeur

The sounds of your footsteps made hearts sink
Bestial still are your advancing strides
We forget all this and walk with you?
Those daggers you conceal in your hands, your tridents, too
Forget the shining spears and walk with you;
Forget the red embers of your hate and walk with you
Walk with you and give you a chance

That blood, fire and tears have not satiated you
The nation is yet to be torn to pieces

Indeed you are quite close to the seat of power
but the path of Hitler, ends in hell
that hell which consumes all young bodies
that hell where love cries at her own pyre

I walk with you,
and give you a chance
You'll do the same that those who worship hatred
You'll do the same that believe in racial purity
do in other countries

I walk with you,
and give you a chance
How do I betray all those children,

and flowers, and colours?
How do I betray all those stains of blood?

Yes, your new robes cover your body
But no robe will ever cover your mind, your soul, your manners

What makes you think that the new robes
Will make the blood stains go away?

APOORVANAND

Apoorvanand is a professor at Delhi University and a regular columnist, in both Hindi and English, on issues of education, culture, communalism, human rights and democracy.

Crisis of Hinduism

Will the ship of India be able to come out intact from the stormy waters it is caught in? This is a question all those who love India are asking and they are not all necessarily Indians. For them, India has been an experiment to find an idiom of sharing for a diverse people. The existence of numerous religions, sects, languages and customs was welcomed as a resource to build this commonality and never resented as a problem by the makers of the nation. They resisted the temptation of erasing differences to create oneness.

Indian secularism was not a mundane principle of statecraft. It was a bold attempt to negotiate the labyrinth of nationalism by rejecting the straight path of uniformity. The easiest thing for India's founding fathers, all of whom were Hindus for Jinnah, would have been to say that Hindus were to be the benevolent patrons of Muslims and Christians. And Hindus they were, most of them at least—even Nehru called himself a Hindu.

Indian leaders saw the country as a message for the world. This is what Gandhi had in mind when he was invited by Sardar Patel to douse the fire of anger and hatred devouring Delhi, and told a friend that he could not give up on Delhi, for if Delhi goes, then India goes, and then there remains no hope for the world.

The idea was not to integrate the small into the big but to create equal relationships. The scope and sweep of the imagination of India was broad, not just geographically but psychologically too. It was to be an open space. In its beginning, it was inadequate. It had yet to develop the ability to hear the long-repressed voices of the Dalits and understand the Adivasis. There were also quarrels along the way but it started off as an interesting hypothesis.

The biggest achievement of the Indian nation was its promise to the identities, smaller in many ways to the Hindu identity: they are not expected to follow Hinduism or be its vassals. Hinduism, be it a religion or a way of life—was not to be the defining feature of India. It was this solemn promise which convinced millions of Muslims that despite Pakistan—created in their name—they could find peace in India.

Why did this promise convince the Muslims, under suspicion and attack in those days? Because they witnessed the sublime act of the leaders of the nation—followers of Gandhi—defending this promise, body and soul. It was this conviction that made Gandhi reject the proposal by Rajendra Prasad that cow slaughter should be prohibited in India. Gandhi was unambiguous in his resolve not to let such a law be passed as it would mean imposition of a particular way of life and privileging it over other lifestyles. Gandhi, a sanatani, a vegetarian devotee of the cow, warned Hindus against falling in this trap.

Today, when the chief minister of the state he was born in declares his intention to make Gujarat a vegetarian state, the promise that India was to those who live differently from vegetarian Hindus stands broken. When mutton shops are forcibly closed in Gurgaon under the watch of the police, the constitutional principle of freedom is violated.

We do not have a Gandhi or Nehru or Patel now to chide communal Hindus and make them see their folly. The state itself has turned into a bully. What, then, is to act as the safeguard? It was thought that the institutions created by the constitution's mandate would act as bulwark against any attack on this fundamental idea of India. We see them sadly inadequate to the challenge facing them.

That Hindus take pleasure in the humiliation of Muslims and also relish the deception and duplicity with which all this is done—in the name of hygiene, legality, economy, etc.—reflects poorly on them. India is definitely in crisis, but Hinduism is facing a greater crisis.

Indian Muslims have often been lauded patronizingly for having rejected the call of the Islamic State. They have invested heavily in the idea of secular India and stood by it. Can the same be said about Hindus in 2017? By siding with a politics which marginalizes minorities and seeks to subjugate them, they are losing their soul.

Gandhi had warned Hindus in his last days that if destroyed in India or Pakistan, Islam has other lands to realize its spiritual potential but if Hinduism is destroyed in India, it has no hope. By destroying others, it first destroys itself. It can grow, not by competing with others, but with itself. Gandhi was silenced not only because he favoured Pakistan or Muslims but also because he was constantly challenging Hindus. He considered it a weakness and sin for religion to align with the state—this was a lazy path, outwardly strong but hollow of spiritual content.

After Gandhi, this critical tradition in Hinduism stopped. Hinduism is not a source of creativity for literature and the arts in India anymore. The references to religion we find in music and dance also demonstrate that there is no new imagination of Hinduism, it is largely nostalgia for an imagined past. We do see modern philosophers using Islamic or Christian resources to address the dilemmas of our times. Hinduism has only pop philosophers giving sermons and churning out popular literature who ultimately build large statues of gods or turn propagandists for political Hindutva. It is exclusionary, inward-looking and fears to engage with others.

The rise of the Hindu state of India is thus also the decline and impoverishment of the promise of Hinduism. The corrosion of the state's institutional structure would affect our worldly life but this unchallenged takeover by Hindutva would turn Hinduism soulless. The task of recovering the Hindu self will not be easy then.

RAHAT INDORI

An eminent Urdu poet, Rahat Indori enjoys immense popularity in mushairas across the world and has also written lyrics for Bollywood songs. Apart from love, he also writes on contemporary issues in both the ghazal and the azad nazm forms.

Creating a New Circle of Splendour

Trying to create a new circle of splendour,
The lamps are busy fixing the air with wonder.

That person is not even a man in my eyes,
Whom the world wants to turn into a god, that bounder.

Don't bother them for the sake of god,
The patients are busy making medicine, tender.

Those who sent me wandering all my life,
Are constructing my mausoleum to bury me under.

And they, who claimed they'd make a sun,
Are tired now having rent lamps asunder.

These chosen folks who are the best of the lot,
They made me evil, I am their plunder.

Translated by Maaz Bin Bilal

If They Are Against, Let Them Be

If they are against, let them be, it's not the end of life,
This is all smoke, not the sky—this night.

If there's fire, then other homes too shall burn,
The houses here are not all mine.

I know the enemy isn't lesser, but,
They don't wear their life easy like mine.

What comes out of our mouths has the power of truth.
The tongue in my mouth isn't thine.

Today's masters of the throne won't be here tomorrow,
They're tenants, it's not their right divine.

Everyone's blood is mixed in the soil here,
Hindustan's not your dad's, nor mine.

Translated by Maaz Bin Bilal

Selected Verses

If the messiah were to side with pain, what will happen?
If traditions of tolerance freeze up, what will happen?

These lakhs and crores who pray five times a day,
If they really turn vendors of terror, what will happen?

Translated by Maaz Bin Bilal

~

As fragrance from flowers, I fly
As smoke off mountains, I fly

These scissors cannot keep me from flight
For I fly not with wings but with courage

~

Is there tension at the borders?
Find out if it is election time.

In the cities it is time for cordite
Come away to the village,
    where the guavas are ripe.

~

It is this faith we write, it is this faith we read
Make us not read anything else, it is the Quran we read.

Here are all our vistas, here are all our seasons
They're blind, if in these eyes it is Pakistan they read.

Translated by Anurag Basnet

JERRY PINTO

This is the text of the speech delivered by Jerry Pinto, in absentia, upon receiving the Sahitya Akademi Award for his novel Em and the Big Hoom.

Acceptance Speech for the Sahitya Akademi Award, 2017

These are trying times for all of us, but perhaps for writers most of all.

We have become the keepers of the flame, a task for which not all of us might be suited. Some of us might argue quite rightly that the truth is not of much concern for the fiction writer. Others might say with as much justification that the truth is one of the many shades that hangs around the birth of each new novel and it is not always a pleasant spirit.

So what is it we are supposed to be doing here? Are we to hold up a mirror to society? Can we say our mirrors are without flaws, that we offer a true reflection or do our political beliefs bend the light just that much, so that what is offered is a refraction?

In *Baluta*, which I had the good fortune to translate, the late Marathi writer Daya Pawar says that the books he read did not reflect his life at all but he suggests that this might have been why he enjoyed them.

The new criticism tells us that every writer only writes about himself or herself. If this is true, we run the twin risks of solipsism and narcissism. There are other critics who warn against cultural appropriation: that we may not write about that which we have not lived. What then is the role of the imagination in this space?

Each time I open a file on my computer, or pick up my pen, I run the risk of offending someone.

Is this risk implicit in reflection or is the problem refraction? Is it because I cut too close to the bone or is it because I allow my imagination to run wild?

And what is the role of the state in my life? I might have some rights, as a citizen of India, to the protection of my freedom of speech but since this is a right limited and hedged about, the protection extends only so far as the law will allow it. I do not know what the law will allow and will not allow because I do not know what a reasonable man will think and this legal fiction, the reasonable man, must now try to understand the unreasonable man of letters.

When Jesus preached the Sermon on the Mount, he was not being reasonable for he demanded that we give up the notion of 'an eye for an eye and a tooth for a tooth' and to turn the other cheek. When Rabindranath Tagore wrote *Char Adhyay*, a novel that interrogated the notion of nationalism, he was being an unreasonable man. When Ismat Chugtai tore the veils of feudalism and child abuse in 'Lihaaf', she was being an unreasonable woman. When Gandhi wrote polemics against the British rule, he was not being a reasonable man.

I return often to these men and women as my guides and my preceptors.

I think of Jesus using deceptively simple stories to drive home complex messages about justice and forgiveness; I think of Tagore's 'Where the mind is without fear'; I relish the elegance of the image of Chugtai eating oranges in the British court, refusing to be cowed by the law and its demands; I think of Gandhi retreating every week into silence and reaching out, connecting, talking to his correspondents about everything from their dietary problems to their spiritual quests to their political opinions.

These are my gurus. They teach me reason and they urge me to the unreasonable space of creation; they teach me to dream but they remind me that the dream is paid for in work; they teach me to think but they ask of me that I leaven reason with intuition; they demand that I write from a place deep within, a place where I make no calculations about what is acceptable and what is offensive.

I have not always kept the faith. I am human, after all. Most writers are. That's why we surprise ourselves when we create beauty for we know what kind of place it is made in.

But somehow, we have been handed the flaming torch of truth and we have been told, it is now yours to protect.

I am terrified.

But I am going to try. My gurus did.

RAVISH KUMAR

Ravish Kumar is a journalist and writer, and has extensively covered Indian politics. He was awarded the first Kuldip Nayar Journalism Award in March 2017.

Acceptance Speech for the Inaugural Kuldip Nayar Journalism Award, 2017

I'm ageing, and I thought I should bring something that I've written down. However, the mood and occasion is for an extempore speech.

At a time when politics is breaking down all boundaries of propriety. When brand-new idioms of slander are being created. To be felicitated, at a time when one's ability to tolerate is being trampled underfoot, is to glance at that clock on the wall which is ticking away. We've run out of ticking clocks and we have stopped recognizing time from its footsteps. Which is why we do not know this dangerous time which has slinked in and taken a seat next to us. We've become careless, and our sensitivity is running out, too. For they keep poking us with needles and we keep enduring the pain.

We've all become consumers of storms. When news of a storm arrives; when Gurgaon, or Delhi, or Chennai drowns, we switch to the weather reports. The news anchor, with her calm, even voice, gradually converts us into consumers of storms and typhoons, and we merely wait for them to pass. The following morning we hear: A car was stranded in the flood, and the three people trapped inside it drowned.

To die is not only to be burned in a crematorium, or to be buried in a cemetery; to die is also that fear which terrorizes you, and prevents you from speaking, from writing, from listening. We're dying. We're transforming into that consumer which that weather-report news anchor wants us to be.

We've all been seated in an examination hall, one which is raided time and again by flying squads. They search your pockets, or ruffle your answer sheets to check. You know you don't cheat, yet the flying squads arrive every once in a while, spread terror, and leave. You believe that the very next moment you will be declared a cheat. You may think that such a thing will not come to pass—look around and see how many are being entrapped in legal cases. These are those very flying squads who come, search your pockets, but never catch the real thieves. Yet they instill the fear that you will be declared a thief. Legal cases, police officers, income tax officials have all become very active, their roles are much more dynamic than ever. And the chief police officer of our times is the news anchor. He transforms every evening into a lock-up in which he confines each one who raises a voice in protest, opposition or dissent, each one who has an alternative point of view, and gives each one a beating. So far, you've remained enmeshed in the issues of first-degree, third-degree, the fake degree. He applies third-degree torture each evening with great ease. That news anchor is the biggest goon of our times.

I am very happy that at this time—in this very society—when the news anchors of media channels have become goons, a new breed of strongmen, there exist people who are taking the risk of felicitating a news anchor. In the society that is yet to come, after these storms have passed, when the history of the news anchor, his goondaism, and the goondaism of his language is being written, you will be remembered for this evening, and that you had gathered to honour a news anchor. Your evening will not have been wasted.

Yes, you cannot change janaadesh—the 'People's Verdict'.[1] But *this* is also a verdict of our times. If *that* is a verdict of our times, so is this.

~

Thank you, Gandhi Peace Foundation. Imbued in this award is the sweat of journalists. When one receives anything from the seniors of one's profession, it is as if one's prayers have been answered.

We all revere Kuldip Nayar saheb. Crores of people have read your writings, sir. You've been to that border and lighted candles there, that border in whose name hatred is being spread everyday.[2] The name of that country is being used to malign people of this country. Perhaps the importance of the candles you lighted could not be fathomed when there was still time. If we had cradled that flame, that light, it would not have remained the passion of a few, but become the light of knowledge for a vast number of people. We made that mistake then, and we are still making that mistake now. How many people speak of love? I doubt people love at all today.

~

Sometimes I think this and fear: What if a member of an anti-Romeo squad was to fall in love?[3] In the throes of love, he would rip apart like an old kurta. I pray that such a man never falls in love and that he, at the very least, receives the strength to bear the romantic songs of Kishore Kumar. In Uttar Pradesh, the People's Verdict has been passed on Shakespeare's hero. We pray that Romeo's soul rests in peace. If you have ever loved someone in your life, pray for your own souls, too. I hope that, some day, in some election in America, the People's Verdict will be passed on the characters of Premchand's stories. It may already have been, who knows?

We will soon be seeing Anti-Cauliflower, Anti-Coriander squads…

~

We are not constructing possibilities, we are seeking them—where are they? within whom? who has kept them alive? At times I find craven, these possibilities which lie dormant within these people. 'For how long are we safe?'—we are forgetting the savour of living in the grip of this worry, and are losing the courage to keep those possibilities alive. We are merging our individual possibilities with that of others. We've had enough of the *Ramayan* recitations of self-contradiction. Everyone I meet seems to me a teacher of self-contradiction. If you want to seek an alternative in politics, learn to resolve self-contradictions.

Many are those whom compromises have left half-dead. They, too, have played a role in ushering in the times in which we live. They who had the responsibility to do something in the past let us down. In the past people joined institutions and kept hollowing them out. It is in their time—leaving out a few notable worthies—that the worm entered the bud. Those who spoke of alternatives, their dialogue with society ended. Society, too, recognizes just one agent of change: the political party. The other agents of change have also been captured by politics. There is thus no point in fleeing politics any longer. Of course, it is a different matter altogether if one wants to accomplish the work of one year in a century.

It is when the good fail that the citizen takes a risk with the bad. He loses every time but, each time, he bets on a major political party. The Gandhians, the Ambedkarites, the Socialists, the Leftists, and all of those others whom I've left out—why is it that whenever big storms blow it is they who are uprooted? Keep yourself from becoming a bonsai garden. It is because of you who quit political parties that these parties have deteriorated. Dynastic politics began to dominate some, corporate politics others. The power to combat communalism has never been in evidence, neither earlier, nor now. Why then should we mourn their passing? But if we have any remorse, we must accept the challenges that are before us.

I have never considered politics my calling but to those who are engaged in it, I say: Return to the political parties, don't keep running around. It is now time to emerge from seminars and meetings. They are spaces for academic discussions, necessary spaces, but they aren't political alternatives. It is time to wage a struggle, and re-enter political parties. Return to the parties and re-capture their organizations. The leaders occupying those spaces are incapable of leadership. Remove them. They are cowardly people, full of deceit. This is beyond them. Their cowardice, their compromises, are setting fire to society day and night. They are dry wood and, because of their compromises, even a small spark can drift in and burn everything down. We still have enough human resources left among us. The people who are gathered in this room are sufficient, too. We can better politics.

~

I am receiving an award for journalism and I want to say a few words about it.

I am extremely pleased to report that there is no crisis in journalism today. This is the Golden Age of Journalism. Editors of newspapers, from the country's capital to its districts, have been swept up and taken by the revolution from the fields to the rooftops. At long last they have fully realized the purpose of being journalists. Haven't we been seeing, for many decades, how hard journalism has been trying to become one with the establishment and with power...? The agents of political parties began to sidle into our newsrooms; now the newsrooms have themselves become political parties. When they were securing licenses to set up hotels and malls, to dig mines, this is what they had been preparing for. The media is very hungry. This is the age of merger journalism, dissolved journalism, a far cry from the age of alternative media. The ideology of the ruling party is a giant, in front of which the journalist finds himself a dwarf, and understands that he stands before the mouth of Lord Krishna.

The journalism of India, and its media organizations, are in the golden age of pleasure. If you aren't convinced, open any newspaper or turn on any news channel and you will find only excitement and joy. If you join them in their joy, your troubles will seem lesser. Never have suited-booted anchors seemed so handsome after having surrendered their freedom; women anchors have never seemed so beautiful flattering the government. The newsroom is empty of reporters, good journalists are waging war with each other to be recruited in *The New York Times* and *The Washington Post*. That *Washington Post* in which journalists compete to see who can most effectively raid the basements of the city to unearth news against the government. I know, too, of the mischiefs of *The New York Times* and *The Washington Post*. But, at the same time, we also hear that in India, journalists are being asked to quit newsrooms. The sources of information are dry. It is obvious that impressions and speculation are the chief information of our times. Anchors are cursed to become spokespersons for parties; they aren't journalists anymore, but salesmen for the government.

When a People's Verdict arrives, why do journalists feel that it has been passed upon them? Had they also been contesting elections? Is it necessary that the People's Verdict should affect journalism? Yet there are many journalists walking around Delhi, confused, wondering what they should do now that the UP elections have ended. What then were you doing after Bihar,[4] or after 1977[5], or before 1977; what were you doing before 1947 and what will you do after 2025?

What this means is that the journalist is no longer worried about the state of journalism; and you cannot fathom the joy of that reporter, now freed of the many problems of unemployment. It is beyond you. You are prejudiced. Go out and see how happy and pleased they are, how free they feel, having merged with an organization, a political party, or a cheap power conglomerate. You will be unable to measure the extent of their happiness. They've always been printing press releases; only, now they're singing them too. Only someone in Mumbai could have done such a thing but those of us in television are doing precisely this. Organize an *Indian Idol* competition for sycophancy, invite journalists to it, and see who can sing best about which political dispensation. The next time, honour them, too. It is important that we honour such sycophants while there's still time.

But if you want to fight, prepare to do battle with the newspaper, and with television. Quit your stubborn fight to save journalism. The journalist himself does not want to be saved. The few who still remain standing, it is not very necessary that they remain. It also isn't very difficult to oust them and there's no telling when they will be removed. When you are out and about on the streets tell people about the dangers—news channels and newspapers are the new shakhas of political parties; an anchor is more influential than even the general secretary of a political party. To create a political alternative, to *become* a political alternative, you must fight these new political parties. If you cannot fight, that is okay too. For the citizens have been trained well and they come around to enquire: Why do you ask questions?

Those who throw ink upon others are being made spokespersons and those who use ink to write are conducting propaganda [...] Yet, in such a situation, how can we forget those journalists who are working hard everywhere to preserve possibilities. I can understand their loneliness. I can also share their solitude. It could be that no space for them will remain but, in the coming times, these journalists will be doing others a great favour. From the districts to the capital I have seen many journalists struggle. Their stories may not be published, but they do have stories. If society does not support these reporters, then the loss will be that society's. If society deserts this journalist, then, one day, he will not be able to withstand his loneliness and his solitude. It is now time to look that society in the eye and say, 'You who desert us, you who abuse us, you do this not to remove us but to wipe out your own existence.' Ask them about their pain, those who still work in newsrooms. Television news anchors, even I, receive ten handwritten letters everyday. Ask about the pain they must feel when their stories remain unfeatured, and to whom they write desperate letters. They are a part of society too. This society, which heaps abuse on such reporters, is only compounding their pain. This society is conspiring to isolate the most restless, questioning parts of itself, and to kill it off along with its restlessness. In this way society itself becomes deadly.

In the meantime, I am grateful to all those journalists who still practise true journalism, how much ever of it they may be practising. The slumber of some journalists will be shattered, some will be fed up of sycophancy, some betrayed, and others used and cast aside. When they wake up, it is only the possibilities carefully tended to by those true journalists which will keep them from suicide. It is then they will understand: That which has been done, I should, too. It is that which will save me.

So keep alive the possibilities, to whichever extent is feasible. Do not view these times through either the lens of hope, or the lens of despair. We are standing on that track upon which an engine looms ahead. Hope will not save you, nor will despair. The hope is that the engine will not crush one, and the despair that it surely will. There is very little time, and it is travelling at great speed.

Translated by Anurag Basnet

Notes

1. A reference to the victory of the Bharatiya Janata Party in the Uttar Pradesh general elections of 2017. The party won 325 seats out of 403.
2. In 1992, Kuldip Nayar began the first of his many Independence Day trips to the border between India and Pakistan in Attari, which would culminate in the lighting of candles at midnight between 14–15 August. He would be joined by many people from all walks of life from both sides of the border in peacefully chanting: 'Hindustan-Pakistan dosti zindabad!'
3. Soon after the appointment of Yogi Adityanath as chief minister of Uttar Pradesh in 2017, posses of policemen called 'anti-Romeo squads' fanned out in the state, ostensibly to prevent the 'eve-teasing' of girls and women in public places. Given the powers granted to the police to summarily pick up and interrogate men and women, this was an excuse for harassment.
4. A reference to the Bihar Assembly elections of 2015. The elections were fought between, primarily, a coalition of parties called the Mahagathbandhan, the National Democratic Alliance led by the BJP, and the Left parties. The Mahagathbandhan won, and Nitish Kumar became chief minister.
5. The Emergency was unilaterally imposed by Indira Gandhi in 1975 and ended in 1977.

COPYRIGHT ACKNOWLEDGEMENTS

The publishers thank the following for their contributions to the volume: Radhavallabh Tripathi for translations of Dharmakirti, Rishabhdev, Bhartrihari, Sohnoka, Kshemendra, Bilhana and Kalhana; Reema Anand for the translation of Guru Nanak; Neelum Gill for translations of Sultan Bahu and Bulleh Shah; Shabnam Virmani and Vipul Rikhi for the translation of Shah Latif; T.P. Dhar for translations of Sauda Mohammad Rafi, Mir Taqi Mir and Mirza Asadullah Khan Ghalib; Shanta Gokhale for translations from *Kavya Phule* and 'Asking Why, Saying No'; Nirupama Dutt for translations of Sant Ram Udasi, Lal Singh Dil, Paash, Kumar Vikal and Jagrup Singh Jhunir; Harsh Mander for 'Conscience, Not Obedience: The Civil Service, the Right and the Duty to Dissent'; Keki Daruwalla for 'Of Dissent and Laws'; Malavika Rajkotia for 'Dissent from and within the Supreme Court to Save the Constitution'; Manash Firaq Bhattacharjee for the translation of Tulsidas, 'The End of Tomorrow', 'Say It While It's Time' and 'No Urdu in Dilli, Mian'; Jerry Pinto for "'I Have an Old Faith in the Youth'" and 'Acceptance Speech at the Sahitya Akademi Award, 2017'; Purushottam Agrawal for 'Let Us Strive for Fortitude... So That We May Ask Questions'; Naresh Dadhich for 'It's Time Indian Scientists Answered Their Call to Be Responsible Citizens'; and Vikram Soni for 'A Wounded Civilization'.

The publishers thank the following for permission to reprint copyright material:
Thanissaro Bhikku for translations of 'Assalayana Sutta' and *Terigatha* from *Access to Insight*, 2013; H.S. Shivaprakash for translations of Chennaiah, Basavanna, Allama Prabhu, Adaiah, Kalavve, Molige Mahadevi, Urilingadeva and Dhoolaiah from *I Keep Vigil of Rudra: The Vachanas*, Penguin Books India, 2010; Vijaya Ramaswamy for translations of Kalavve and Kadire Remmavve from *Divinity and Deviance: Women in Virasaivism*, Oxford University Press, 1996 and translations of

Sivavakkiyar and Uttiranallur Nangai from *Devotion and Dissent in Indian History*, edited by Vijaya Ramaswamy, Cambridge University Press, 2014; Basavaraj Naikar for translations of Sarvajna's vachanas from *The Vacanas of Sarvajna*, Authors Press, 2013; Columbia University Press for translations from *Puranaru* from *Poems of Love and War: From the Eight Anthologies and the Ten Long Poems of Classical Tamil*, edited and translated by A.K. Ramanujan, 2011; David Shulman for the translation of Sundarar from *Textual Sources for the Study of Hinduism*, edited by Wendy Doniger O'Flaherty, translated by Wendy Doniger O'Flaherty with Daniel Gold and David Shulman, University of Chicago Press, 1990; Vidya Dehejia for translations of Manikkavachakar and Andal from *Slaves of the Lord: Path of the Tamil Saints*, Munshirm Manoharlal Pub Pvt Ltd, 2002; Ranjit Hoskote for translations of Lal Ded from *I, Lalla: The Poems of Lal Ded*, Penguin Books India, 2011; Jerry Pinto and Neela Bhagwat for translations of Janabai and Soyarabai from *Eating God: A Book of Bhakti Poetry*, edited by Arundhathi Subramaniam, Penguin Books India, 2014; Mahesh Sharma for translations of Charpatnath from *Western Himalayan Temple Records: State, Pilgrimage, Ritual and Legality in Chamba*, Leiden/Boston: Brill, 2009; Linda Hess for translations of Kabir from *The Bijak of Kabir*, Linda Hess and Sukhdev Singh, Oxford University Publishers, 2002; Navtej Sarna for translations of Guru Nanak from *The Book of Nanak*, Penguin Books India, 2009 and of *Zafarnama* by Guru Gobind Singh, Penguin Books India, 2011; Rahul Soni for the translation of Meerabai from *Eating God: A Book of Bhakti Poetry*, edited by Arundhathi Subramaniam, Penguin Books India, 2014; V. Narayana Rao and David Shulman for translations of Annamacharya from *God on the Hill: Temple Poems from Tirupati: Annamayya*, Oxford University Press, 2005; V. Narayana Rao and David Shulman for translations of Kshetrayya from *When God Is a Customer: Telugu Courtesan Songs by Ksetrayya and Others*, University of California, 1994; Radhavallabh Tripathi for the translations from *Mahisasatakam* by Vanchanatha, New Bhartiya Book Corporation, 2010; Marxists Internet Archive for 'Those Iron Gates of Prison' and 'Communistic' by Kazi Nazrul Islam, translated by Sajed Kamal and 'Why I Am an Atheist' by Bhagat Singh, translated from Punjabi to Urdu/Persian by Maqsood Saqib, translated from Urdu to English by Hasan; V. Geetha and S.V. Rajadurai for translations of Periyar E.V. Ramasamy from *Words of Freedom: Ideas of a Nation*, Penguin Books India, 2010; Indian Renaissance Institute for 'Whither Congress? A Manifesto' by M.N.

Roy; Sukrita Paul Kumar and Katha for 'An Excerpt from *Kaghazi Hai Pairahan*', translated by M. Asaduddin and 'On Radha and Krishan', translated by Madhu Prasad and Sohail Hashmi from *Ismat: Her Life, Her Times*, edited by Sukrita Paul Kumar and Sadique, Katha, 2002; Tranquebar Press for 'Save India from Its Leaders' from *Why I Write: Essays by Saadat Hasan Manto*, edited and translated by Aakar Patel, 2014; Danish Hussain for the translation of Krishan Chander's 'New Primer for Hindi'; M. Asaduddin for the translation of Sa'dat Hasan Manto's 'Pundit Manto's First Letter to Pundit Nehru' from *Annual of Urdu Studies*, Vol. 11, 1996; *Seminar* for 'For an Alternative Vision' by Nirmal Verma and 'A "Grand Celebration" of Feminist Discourse' by Archana Varma, translated by Ruth Vanita and Simona Sawhney; Nayantara Sahgal for 'Letter to Dr R.S. Kelkar' from *The Political Imagination: A Personal Response to Life, Literature and Politics*, HarperCollins India, 2014 and 'Speech at Aligarh Muslim University'; Penguin Random House India for translations of Mirza Changezi and Firaq Gorakhpuri from *Celebrating the Best of Urdu Poetry*, translated by Khushwant Singh and Kamna Prasad, 2007, 'Second Storm' from *Selected Poems*, Kaifi Azmi, translated by Pavan K. Varma, 2001 and 'N.M. and Kalinga? Impossible, Thrice Impossible, Brother Gill!' by Prakash N. Shah, translated by Francis J. Paramar from *Gujarat: The Making of a Tragedy*, edited by Siddharth Vardarajan, 2002; Navayana for 'New Delhi, 1985' from *Namdeo Dhasal—Poet of the Underworld, Poems 1972-2006*, Namdeo Dhasal, translated by Dilip Chitre and 'Introduction' from *The Myth of the Holy Cow*, D.N. Jha, 2001; Siddalingaiah for 'The Dalits Are Here', translated by M. Madhava Prasad from *From Those Stubs, Steel Nibs Are Sprouting: New Dalit Writing from South India, Dossier 2: Kannada and Telugu*, edited by K. Satyanarayana and Susie Tharu, HarperCollins Publishers, India, 2013; Gaddar for 'The Rebellious Fields', translated by Naren Bedide, from The Shared Mirror, http://roundtableindia.co.in/lit-blogs/?p=2753; *TheWire.in* for 'In Other Lands a Cow Is Prized for Its Milk, in Ours It Is Meant for Clashes' by Harishankar Parsai, translated by Chitra Padmanabhan; Devaki Jain and Nirmala Banerjee for the excerpt from *Tyranny of the Household: Investigative Essays into Women's Works*, Shakti Books, 1985; Romila Thapar for 'Dissent and Protest in the Early Indian Tradition'; Sahmat for 'Faith and Superstition' by Narendra Dabholkar from *The Republic of Reason: Words They Could Not Kill: Selected Writings of Dabholkar, Pansare and Kalburgi*, 2015; Medha Patkar for 'One Tapa, One Vow'; Githa

Hariharan for 'Rehabilitating Mothers', https://www.githahariharan. com/downloads/write_up_on_case.pdf; Khadar Mohiuddin for 'Birthmark' from *Hibiscus on the Lake: Twentieth-Century Telugu Poetry from India*, edited and translated by V. Narayana Rao, The University of Wisconsin Press, 2003; Renuka Narayanan for 'Celebrate "Subversion"' from *Faith: Filling the God-sized Hole*, Penguin Books India, 2003; A. Revathi for 'Property as Selfhood: A Hijra Experience', translated by Ponni Arasu from *Law Like Love: Queer Perspectives on Law*, edited by Arvind Narrain and Alok Gupta, Yoda Press, 2011; Siddharth Narrain for 'Size Does Matter Your Lordships: A Letter to the Supreme Court' from Kafila, https://kafila.online/2013/12/16/size-does-matter-your-lordships-a-letter-to-the-supreme-court/; Meena Kandasamy for 'Ekalaivan'; Hilal Mir and *Hindustan Times* for 'How I Became a Stone-thrower for a Day' from *Until My Freedom Has Come: The New Intifada in Kashmir*, edited by Sanjay Kak, Penguin Books India, 2011; Mona Zote for 'Rez', Robin S. Ngangom for 'Revolutionaries' and Paul Lyndoh for 'For Sale'—all from *Dancing Earth: An Anthology of Poetry from North-East India*, edited by Robin S. Ngangom and Khynpham S. Nongkynrih, Penguin Books India, 2009; M.B. Manoj for 'The Children of the Forest Talk to Yesu', translated by K. Satchidanandan from *No Alphabet in Sight: New Dalit Writings from South India, Dossier 1: Tamil and Malayalam*, edited by K. Satyanarayana and Susie Tharu, Penguin Books India, 2011; Basudev Sunani for 'Body Purification' from *Cast Out: Poems of Anger and Angst*, translated by J.P. Das, Rupantara, 2009; Aparna Lanjewar for 'Caves' by Jyoti Lanjewar, translated by Shanta Gokhale from *Poisoned Bread: Translations from Modern Marathi Dalit Literature*, edited by Arjun Dangle, Orient Blackswan, 1992; Kusum Meghwal for 'The Curse of a Scavenger Woman', translated by Akshaya Kumar from *Poetics, Politics and Culture: Essays on Indian Texts and Contexts*, Akshaya Kumar, Routledge, 2009; Shilpa Phadke, Sameera Khan and Shilpa Ranade for 'Why Loiter? Radical Possibilities for Gendered Dissent'; Nabaneeta Dev Sen for 'Festival', translated by Pratik Kanjilal; Dayamani Barla for the speech she delivered upon receiving the Ellen L. Lutz Indigenous Rights Award; Abhay Xaxa for 'I Am Not Your Data' from *The Shared Mirror*, http://roundtableindia.co.in/lit-blogs/?p=1943; Kanji Patel for 'Victual', translated by Rupalee Burke from *Asymptote*, January 2017; Esther Ananthamurthy and HarperCollins Publishers for the excerpt from *Hindutva or Hind Swaraj*, U.R. Ananthamurthy, translated by Keerti Ramachandra with Vivek Shanbhag, Harper Perennial, 2016; Amartya

Sen for 'Dissent and Freedom in India', *The Indian Express*, 13 February 2016; Radhika Vemula for 'Rohith Vemula's Suicide Note'; Umar Khalid for 'JNU Protests: What Is at the Core of the Ongoing Movement?', by Anirban Bhattacharya and Umar Khalid, *The Indian Express*, 14 May 2016; Bhairav Acharya for 'The Second Coming of Sedition'; Kiran Nagarkar for 'A Letter to Modi: Why Is There Such a Gap between Your Wonderful Words and Your Actions?' from *Scroll.in*; Mrinal Pande for 'Nationalism and the Cult of Bharat Mata' from *Scroll.in*; Dr Hafiz Ahmed for 'Write Down I'm a Miyah'; Rezwan Hussain for 'Our Revolution'; Amol Palekar for 'Imprisoning Minds: On Censorship' from Indian Cultural Forum; T.M. Krishna for 'Myth and Reality', *The Indian Express*, 9 June 2016; Sagari R. Ramdas for 'Not for the Cow', *The Indian Express*, 17 September 2016; Laila Tyabji for 'A Matter of Identity'; Zakia Soman and Noorjehan Safia Niaz for 'Why We Are Seeking a Ban on Triple Talaq', *LiveMint*, 8 June 2016; Soni Sori for 'The State Is Lawless', translated by Sukanya Shanta from Round Table India, http://roundtableindia.co.in/index.php?option=com_content&view=article&id=8846:soni-sori-the-state-is-lawless-1&catid=119&Itemid=132; Varun Grover for 'Ours But to Tweet and Die', *The Indian Express*, 17 October 2016; Madhavi Menon for 'On Homosexuality and National Anthem, the Supreme Court Has Offered Contradictory Reasoning' from *Scroll.in*; Pinjra Tod collective for 'Our Hormonal Outbursts Will Be Your Nightmare!'; Gauhar Raza for 'New Robes'; Apoorvanand for 'Crisis of Hinduism', *The Indian Express*, 14 April 2017; Rahat Indori for his poems translated by Maaz Bin Bilal and Anurag Basnet; and Ravish Kumar for 'Acceptance Speech at the Inaugural Kuldip Nayar Journalism Award, 2017'.

www.ingramcontent.com/pod-product-compliance
Lightning Source LLC
Chambersburg PA
CBHW051946270326
41929CB00015B/2546